D1716495

CAPITAL MARKETS

K. Thomas Liaw

THOMSON

* ™

SOUTH-WESTERN

Australia · Canada · Mexico · Singapore · Spain · United Kingdom · United States

THOMSON

SOUTH-WESTERN

Vice President/Editorial Director:
Jack W. Calhoun

Vice President/Editor-in-Chief:
Michael P. Roche

Executive Editor:
Michael R. Reynolds

Developmental Editor:
Jennifer E. Baker

Sr. Marketing Manager:
Charlie Stutesman

Production Editor:
Daniel C. Plofchan

Manufacturing Coordinator:
Sandee Milewski

Senior Media Technology Editor:
Vicky True

Media Developmental Editor:
John Barans

Senior Media Production Editor:
Mark Sears

Compositor:
Buuji, Inc., St. Paul, MN

Printer:
Phoenix Color, Hagerstown, MD

Design Project Manager:
Rik Moore

Internal Designer:
Lisa Albonetti

Cover Designer:
John Robb, Robb & Assoc.

Cover Photographic Sources:
© PhotoDisc, Inc., Rik Moore, and
© Cartesia Software

Library of Congress Control Number:
2003105271

ISBN: 0-324-02420-7

To my family

BRIEF CONTENTS

CONTENTS

PART 4

International Financial Centers   383

PREFACE

Capital Markets is designed for undergraduate courses in capital markets or financial markets and institutions. *Capital Markets* is also suitable for introductory MBA classes. The book is written for those interested in global financial markets, investments, banking, and securities. It is well-suited for mainstream students who have already had an introductory finance course, providing a source of relevant knowledge in the increasingly integrated global marketplace. For practitioners, this book is a good reference for professional development.

Capital Markets provides a basic but comprehensive coverage of global financial markets and institutions, with a focus on globalization, deregulation and consolidation, and technology. The text is distinguished by its focused coverage of global markets, balanced coverage of securities markets, and emphasis on modern topics and market practices. Also unique is its inclusion of an entire section on global financial centers, including chapters on Euromarkets, the European Economic and Monetary Union, Japanese capital markets, Asian and Russian markets, and Latin American markets. In addition, the following chapter features have been developed with the aim of providing effective learning tools:

- *Chapter learning objectives* help the learner focus on concepts to be covered in each chapter.
- *Key terms* are highlighted in boldface to remind the reader of new and important terms for each chapter.
- *Internet links* direct learners to relevant Internet resources.
- *Markets in Action boxed features* take the reader into the real-world practice of finance or the most significant event in the relevant subject area.
- *Concluding Summaries* revisit main points covered in the chapter.
- *Review Questions* allows the reader to evaluate what he or she has learned with both quantitative and qualitative questions.

Capital Markets highlights the continuous and complex transformation of the financial services industry. A growing number of companies prefer to deal with one single financial advisor for all their capital needs. Select companies around the world have increasingly tapped international markets to enhance their global presence and to raise capital abroad. At the same time, investors have looked across national borders for new capital growth opportunities and diversification. Further intensifying the competitive environment is the emergence of nontraditional competitors and innovative information technology. Advances in technology have enabled clients to access financial services how, when, and where they choose. At the same time, many market participants believe there will also be boutique houses that specialize in specific market niches.

This book provides a comprehensive description of major players and activities in global capital markets. Specifically, the book first describes the trends in global capital markets and the essential role of central banking. Major institutions covered include commercial banks, investment banks, insurance companies, brokerage and clearing firms, and various types of investment management companies. The book also covers all major securities markets such as debt, equity, depositary receipts, mortgage- and asset-backed securities, repurchase agreements and securities lending, financial derivatives, and foreign exchange. Furthermore, particular attention is given to international financial centers such as Euromarkets, the euro, Japanese markets, and emerging markets. On each subject, global linkage and applications of technology are stressed. As such, the book has several unique features:

- ○ The book is comprehensive. Most books on the subject do not have such comprehensive coverage reflecting the new global financial service marketplace. The book covers many subjects that are essential but rarely mentioned in published capital markets books, including the new landscape of today's markets, financial insurance and reinsurance, brokerage and clearing, execution costs of transactions, American depositary receipts, the new euro, Japanese markets, and emerging markets.

- ○ The book offers balanced coverage on all major segments of global capital markets. The objective is to provide readers with an understanding of the overall marketplace. Many books with similar titles focus on specific segments such as fixed-income, commercial banking, or central banking.

- ○ Another advantage of the book is a real-world perspective. The book covers every subject and market with a thorough analysis of current trends and market practices, stressing applications of technology in the financial services industry. Information sources on the Internet are included as well.

- ○ The book integrates analytics into relevant subjects and chapters, instead of providing separate chapters or sections for theoretical modeling. Theoretical aspects such as yield curve analysis, spot rates, duration, risk measures, valuations of stocks and fixed-income securities, options adjusted spread, and mortgage prepayment are covered in appropriate chapters.

- ○ The text contains a *Markets in Action* boxed feature in every chapter following Chapter One. Examples include a day at the New York Fed trading desk, the tobacco bonds, the Orange County bankruptcy, and the initiatives taken by the New York Stock Exchange to restore investor confidence.

PRODUCT SUPPORT WEB SITE

The product support Web site for this text includes a variety of teaching and learning resources for instructors and students. Visit **http://liaw.swlearning .com** to download PowerPoint® slides, access ThomsonFN.com for free real-time quotes and unique signaling tools, and see the latest events in capital markets by accessing news items through NewsWire: Finance in the News. Instructors also may access the Instructor's Manual and Test Bank with a user-name and password, which may be obtained via the Web site.

PowerPoint to accompany Capital Markets

PowerPoint slides are available for download from **http://liaw.swlearn-ing.com** and include key figures and exhibits from the text. The PowerPoint slides are available to students as an aid to note-taking, and to instructors for enhancing their lectures.

INSTRUCTOR'S MANUAL

An Instructor's Manual with Test Bank (ISBN 0–324–27432–7) is also available to instructors. The Manual includes answers to end-of-chapter questions, as well as lecture outlines, and a bank of multiple-choice test questions.

ABOUT THE AUTHOR

K. Thomas Liaw is the department chair for Economics and Finance in the Peter J. Tobin College of Business at St. John's University. He has published books on investment banking, stocks, bonds, futures, and options. He coedited several books on emerging markets and has published articles in the areas of securitization, swaps, repurchase agreements, and market risks. His principal areas of teaching and research interests include capital markets, trading, risk management, and investment banking. Dr. Liaw has a consulting practice and serves as an adviser at several financial and technology companies. He also speaks on the subjects of investment banking and capital markets at corporate programs. Dr. Liaw holds his Ph.D. from Northwestern University.

ACKNOWLEDGMENTS

I want to thank many people who have helped me in numerous respects. Mike Mercier, who was the finance acquisitions editor, worked closely with me on this book until he moved on to become the publisher in economics. I very much appreciate his friendship, support, and help in structuring this book. Over the past several years, I have benefited from discussions on many relevant topics with the following executives:

Thomas Christman
Former Chairman and Chief Executive Officer, Carroll McEntee & McGinley

Christine Cumming
Director of Research, Federal Reserve Bank of New York

Dina Dublon
Chief Financial Officer, J.P. Morgan Chase

Herb Evers
President and Chief Executive Officer, HSBC Securities

Donald Layton
Vice Chairman, J.P. Morgan Chase

Robert Mello
Principal, R.L. Mello & Associates

Charles Menges
Principal, Sanford Bernstein

William Montgoris
Chief Operating Officer and Chief Financial Officer, Bear Stearns

Hans Morris
Managing Director, Salomon Smith Barney

Douglas Renfield-Miller
Managing Director, AMBAC

James Riley
Managing Director, Goldman Sachs

Author Soter
Managing Director, Morgan Stanley

Dirk Sturrop
Chairman, Global Financial Institutions (Merrill Lynch)

Kirk Wilson
Managing Director, Morgan Stanley

William Wolff
Managing Director, Lehman Brothers

Position and affiliation are as of time of our meeting.

This finished text has benefited from careful reviews by many finance professors and instructors. I would like to gratefully acknowledge their contribution to the final product.

Jeff Ankrom
Wittenberg University

M.E. Bond
University of Memphis

Samuel Bulmash
University of South Florida

Robert Cunningham
Alma College

David Fricke
University of North Carolina, Pembroke

Randal Gunden
Goshen College

John M. Halstead
Southern Connecticut State University

Jack Julian
College of Wooster

G. Wayne Kelly
Mississippi State University

Spencer Martin
Arizona State University

Cheryl A. McGaughey
Angelo State University

Ronald Moy
St. John's University

Rose Prasad
University of Central Michigan

Edward L. Prill
Colorado State University

Dennis Proffitt
Grand Canyon University

Bruce Rader
Temple University

William A. Reese
Tulane University

Patrick Rowland
University of Michigan, Ann Arbor

Atul Saxena
Mercer University

David P. Simon
Bentley College

Kuo C. Tseng
California State University, Fresno

X. Eleanor Xu
Saint Louis University

In addition, I want to thank Manuel Gonzalez, Craig Larrain, and Stephen Preziosi for their excellent research assistance. I would also like to thank the editorial staff at South-Western: Mike Reynolds, executive editor; Jennifer E. Baker, developmental editor; Charlie Stutesman, senior marketing manager; John Barans, media developmental editor; Mark Sears, media production editor; Dan Plofchan, production editor; and Sandee Milewski, manufacturing coordinator, for their continued enthusiasm and dedication to bring this project to fruition.

INTRODUCTION TO CAPITAL MARKETS

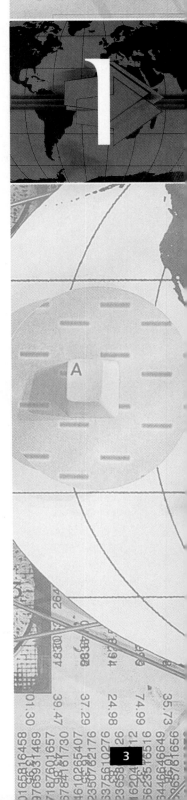

Global Capital Markets

In recent years, globalization, deregulation, and advances in technology have contributed to a dramatic reshaping of global capital markets. Companies around the world increasingly tap international markets to enhance their global presence and raise capital abroad. At the same time, investors look across national borders for new capital growth opportunities and diversification. Firms have expanded internationally as all major players look for new markets and new delivery channels. Additionally, financial deregulation in both developed and developing countries has accelerated the consolidation of the financial services industry. Clients increasingly prefer to deal with a single financial adviser for all their capital needs, and new types of financial entities offer a variety of services, often across international borders. Examples of this trend toward providing one-stop shopping include the formation of Citigroup from the merger of banking giant Citicorp and insurance giant Travelers Group, the acquisition of the U.S.-based Bankers Trust by German-based Deutsche Bank, and the formation of J.P. Morgan Chase from the merger of the commercial bank Chase Manhattan with the investment bank J.P. Morgan. Further intensifying the competitive environment is the emergence of nontraditional competitors and innovative information technology. Advances in technology enable clients to access financial services however, whenever, and wherever they choose.

The objectives of this chapter are to:
- Identify major trends in the global capital marketplace.
- Provide an overview of the book's contents.

TRENDS IN GLOBAL CAPITAL MARKETS

Deregulation, globalization, and technology have already transformed the global capital marketplace, and will continue to do so. The impact of these trends and other related factors will be evident throughout this book. This chapter provides an overview of the most important changes.

Deregulation

In recent years, the United States, the European Union, and Japan have all taken significant steps toward deregulation by lifting restrictions that limit the activities of financial services firms. Meanwhile, many developing countries attempt to stimulate growth by removing restrictions on their capital markets and on foreign investments.

In the United States, the recent financial market modernization legislation, the **Gramm–Leach–Bliley Act** of 1999 **(GLB)**, removed restrictions that had been imposed on the financial services industry during the Great Depression of the 1930s (the Glass–Steagall Act) and by subsequent legislation (see Table 1.1). These laws limited the ability of banks to engage in securities, commercial, and insurance activities. Perhaps most importantly, the GLB created a new regulatory playing field by permitting securities firms, banks, and insurance companies to affiliate with each other. As a result, financial services firms now have the essential flexibility to pursue whatever business strategy they want.

TABLE 1.1	*Key Provisions of the Gramm-Leach-Bliley Act*
Key provision	**Summary**
Affiliation	The act permits banks, securities firms, and insurance companies to affiliate within a new financial holding company structure.
Financial in nature	The act includes a broad definition of "financial in nature" and gives the Federal Reserve Board the authority to define additional activities as "financial in nature, or incidental or complementary to" financial activities.
Commercial basket	The act provides a grandfather provision that permits a securities firm that becomes a financial holding company to engage in commercial activities in an amount up to 15 percent of its consolidated annual gross revenues, excluding bank subsidiaries.
Privacy	The act requires all financial institutions to disclose to customers their policies and practices for protecting the privacy of nonpublic personal information.
Functional regulation	The act functionally regulates all insurance, banking, and securities activities.
Holding company regulation	The act limits the authority of the Federal Reserve Board to regulate, examine, and require reports ("Fed-lite" provisions) from functionally regulated subsidiaries of financial holding companies.
Operating subsidiaries	The act permits well-capitalized, well-managed national banks, with a satisfactory or better Community Reinvestment Act rating, to operate most financial activities through operating subsidiaries.
Unitary thrift holding companies	The act prohibits commercial companies from buying thrifts.

Source: *Gramm-Leach-Bliley*, Securities Industry Association (http://www.sia.com).

TABLE 1.2	*Recent Mergers and Acquisitions in the Financial Services Industry*		
Deal		Price ($ billions)	Year
American International Group acquired American General Corp.		24.6	2001
Citigroup acquired Grupo Financiero Banamex-Accival SA		12.5	2001
Citibank acquired European American Bank		2.0	2001
Wachovia merged with First Union		13.0	2001
GE Capital acquired Heller Financial		5.6	2001
J.P. Morgan merged with Chase Manhattan Bank		36.0	2000
Credit Suisse First Boston acquired Donaldson, Lufkin & Jenrette		13.5	2000
Alliance Capital acquired Sanford C. Bernstein		4.0	2000
Goldman Sachs acquired Spear, Leeds & Kellogg		6.3	2000
Charles Schwab acquired U.S. Trust		2.7	2000
UBS acquired PaineWebber		16.5	2000
Citicorp merged with Travelers		83.0	1998
NationsBank merged with BankAmerica		64.8	1998
Merrill Lynch acquired Mercury Asset Management (UK)		5.3	1998
BankBoston acquired Robertson Stephens		0.6	1998
Deutsche Bank acquired Bankers Trust		10.1	1998
Dean Witter merged with Morgan Stanley		10.2	1997
Fleet Financial acquired Quick & Reilly		1.6	1997
NationsBank acquired Montgomery Securities		1.2	1997

An immediate effect of the enactment of the GLB—an effect that began before 1999 in anticipation of the legislation—has been a trend toward consolidation within the financial services industry, as banks, securities firms, and insurance companies rush to merge with each other. Table 1.2 lists some examples of recent mergers and acquisitions between financial services firms.[1]

The GLB not only allows firms to consolidate and become larger, but also permits them to offer a wider selection of products and services. The convergence of financial services has permitted a financial services supermarket like Citigroup (http://www.citigroup.com) to offer a vast array of products and services including savings and checking accounts; credit cards; mortgages; stock and bond underwriting; homeowner, automobile, and life insurance; merger and acquisition advice; commercial loans; derivative securities; and foreign exchange trading. Similarly, other firms have explored new ways to develop the best mix of products and services that will enable them to compete in the new financial marketplace.

In Europe, the advent of the **European Monetary Union (EMU)** has had profound financial and political implications. As of 2002, twelve countries

[1]Some of these entities later underwent further mergers.

have joined the EMU and adopted a common currency, the **euro**. The newly created **European Central Bank (ECB; http://www.ecb.int)** now establishes and oversees a common monetary policy for these twelve countries.[2] The EMU has brought dramatic changes to the global capital markets and to the way Europeans do business with each other and with the rest of the world. In particular, the EMU contributes to a new and dynamic Europe. With only one common currency—the euro—businesses operating in the euro zone save on transaction costs and can plan without currency uncertainty. Travelers within the EMU no longer have to change money, thereby saving both time and expense. Another benefit is market transparency—the ability to compare prices of goods and services in different countries. This stimulates competition, which drives down prices. Having one common currency also simplifies record keeping. In addition, in time, the euro will be used as one of the primary accounting units in international trade and as a reserve currency (a foreign currency held by a central bank for the purpose of exchange intervention and the settlement of inter-governmental claims). Finally, the introduction of the euro has led to lower interest rates in the EMU countries than would have been the case without the EMU. To join the union, European governments had to reduce their deficits, and the ECB's goal of maintaining price stability has put downward pressure on interest rates.

In Japan, the financial reform plans, known as **Japan's Big Bang**, focused on four areas: deregulation of financial products, promotion of free competition, removal of trading restrictions, and establishment of a reliable framework and rules for fair and transparent transactions. Under deregulation, a variety of new financial products have become available, expanding the menu of choices for borrowers and investors. Trading of options on individual stocks began in July 1997, for example. In addition, banks now can sell securities investment trusts/mutual funds and insurance. The reforms also provide for a holding company structure that allows various types of financial institutions to enter each other's business. In 2000, Daiwa became the first Japanese financial institution to set up a holding company. The holding company, Daiwa Securities Group (**http://www.daiwa.co.jp**), oversees Daiwa's operations in retail, wholesale, research, trust banking, finance, and other areas. Measures to lift trading restrictions have been gradually introduced since 1997. When fully implemented, broker-dealers will be free to trade listed securities off the floor of the stock exchange. Finally, the establishment of a fair and transparent marketplace is crucial to the success of the reform plans. To this end, the government has taken steps beginning in 1998 to set up accounting standards for various types of financial instruments. In summary, the financial market reforms aim to lower barriers separating banking and securities operations,

---

[2]These twelve countries are Austria, Belgium, Finland, France, Germany, Greece, Ireland, Italy, Luxembourg, the Netherlands, Portugal, and Spain.

deregulating trading commissions, and promoting the entry of foreign money managers. With these reforms, Japan has begun a structural revolution that will lead to a more Western-style financial system. Table 1.3 provides a summary of the financial reforms.

Many developing countries have also instituted reforms, taking steps to establish sound marketplaces where companies can raise long-term equity capital. These governments have also introduced measures to enhance the liquidity of their bond markets. The foreign exchange or currency market is also in a process of deregulation. More and more countries have opened their economies to foreign investors by lifting the limits on foreign ownership of stocks and ensuring the convertibility of their currencies. These reforms could present difficulties in the transitional periods, however, as inevitably some sectors will benefit from these changes and some will have to adjust. Furthermore, in a deregulated foreign exchange market, a large and sudden capital outflow could cause a financial crisis.

TABLE 1.3	*Summary of Japan's Big Bang Financial Reforms*

A. Products

More diverse debt instruments permitted
More diverse derivatives products permitted
New investment trust products developed
Definition of securities reviewed and broadened

B. Markets

Transaction system in stock exchanges improved
OTC market system improved
Solicitation process for unlisted and unregistered stocks deregulated
Stock lending market improved
Clearing and settlement process for securities improved
Inspection, surveillance, and enforcement strengthened
Full and timely disclosure of material information required

C. Intermediaries

Brokerage commissions deregulated
Activities of intermediaries deregulated
Holding company structure permitted
Asset management services improved
Monitoring system enhanced
Entry into securities businessses deregulated
Measures for investor protection implemented

Source: Financial System Reform, Securities and Exchange Council (Japan).

Globalization

With rapid advances in information technology and greater cooperation among financial regulators, the international capital markets have linked more closely. Larger sums of money move across borders, and more countries have access to the global capital market. To serve clients better, major financial services companies have become global competitors. Top financial institutions such as Morgan Stanley (**http://www.morganstanley.com**), Merrill Lynch (**http://www.ml.com**), Goldman Sachs (**http://www.gs.com**), Citigroup (**http://www.citigroup.com**), and J.P. Morgan Chase (**http://www. jpmorganchase.com**) have operations in almost all countries with significant capital market activities. Many other financial services firms also pursue a globalization strategy. At the same time, foreign financial institutions have expanded their operations in the United States. Examples of foreign firms with extensive U.S. operations include Deutsche Bank (**http://www.db.com**), UBS (**http://www.ubs.com**), HSBC Holdings (**http://www.hsbc.com**), Credit Suisse First Boston (**http://www.csfb.com**), ABN AMRO (**http://www. abnamro.com**), Daiwa (**http://www.daiwa.com**), and Nomura (**http:// www.nomura.com**).

The increased linkage of capital markets, as a result of the globalization trend, can lead to spillover effects and financial contagion. As shown in later chapters, the 1997 Asian financial crisis and the 1998 Russia's default on its debt quickly spilled over to other parts of the world and caused a global financial crisis.

Technology

Technological advances have challenged many of the fundamental assumptions about how markets work and facilitated the creation of new competitive structures. The Internet has changed the way firms reach customers and the products they can put at their clients' fingertips. The Internet and computer networks have processed more and more financial transactions. Millions of customers conduct their banking and stock and bond trading online. By presenting bills and delivering account statements, research reports, and other materials online, companies cut operating costs and improve efficiency. Alternative trading systems (ATS) and electronic communications networks (ECNs) now offer significant competition to traditional securities exchanges. These trading systems offer a mechanism for matching buy and sell orders without an intermediary. In addition, new technology has transformed securities trading by shortening the settlement cycle, the amount of time required for payment of funds and delivery of securities, from trade day + 3 days (T+3) to trade day + 1 day (T+1); and permitting decimalization. Decimalization has allowed the U.S. securities industry to take the revolutionary step of trading equity and option securities in dollars and cents instead of fractional increments, such as eighths and sixteenths, of a dollar. On January 29, 2001, the New York Stock Exchange (**http://www.nyse.com**) completed the conversion and began trading all listed issues in decimals. The Nasdaq (**http://www.nasdaq.com**)

completed its conversion in April 2001. Investors also now trade stock options in decimals. Decimalization has reduced the **bid-asked spread**, the difference between a dealer's asking price to sell and his or her bidding price to buy.

Advances in technology have brought about those changes and benefits. However, the increasing use of technology has had certain unfortunate side effects, such as prospects of computer failures due to hackers or terrorists. Corporations have to allocate resources to continuously upgrade their technology and to establish proper backup facilities and business continuity plans.

BOOK OVERVIEW

This book will provide a comprehensive description of the major players and activities in global capital markets. The book has four parts. Part I describes the trends in global capital markets and the essential role of central banking. Part II discusses major financial institutions such as commercial banks, investment banks, investment companies, brokerage and clearing firms, and insurance companies. Part III examines major financial instruments such as debt, equity, depositary receipts, mortgage- and asset-backed securities, financial derivatives, and currency. Finally, Part IV covers Euromarkets, the European Monetary Union, Japanese markets, and emerging markets.

Part I: Introduction to Capital Markets
Part I consists of two chapters. Chapter 1 outlines the major trends in the global capital markets and provides a brief overview of the book. Chapter 2 provides an understanding of central banking activities; in particular, the operations of the Federal Reserve System (the Fed) and their impact on global capital markets. The chapter also describes central banks in other major developed countries, including the European Central Bank.

Part II: Major Financial Institutions
The five chapters in Part II examine major financial institutions. Chapter 3 focuses on commercial banks. This chapter describes the structure of the banking industry and its regulatory environment, examines risks that banks face and the techniques they use to manage those risks, and discusses the one-stop shopping trend. The chapter also includes a discussion of banks' securities subsidiaries and the new financial modernization legislation.

Chapter 4 looks at investment banks. As the chapter describes, the business of investment banking is intensely competitive and is also trending toward consolidation and globalization. The scope of investment banking has expanded to include all major capital market activities, including underwriting, mergers and acquisitions, financing and asset management, financial engineering, trading, and securities lending.

Chapter 5 describes the structure and organization of various types of investment companies. The chapter also provides a thorough description of mutual funds, which are growing rapidly, especially in the overseas markets.

One of the driving forces behind this growth is the trend toward **defined contribution plans**; with these plans, the employee and the employer make regular contributions to the employee's retirement account, and the performance of the investments in the account will determine the amount of benefits the employee will receive upon retirement. The coverage goes beyond traditional mutual funds, however, to include venture capital, buyout funds, and hedge funds. Hedge funds are exclusive private investment pools that have made headline news on several occasions in recent years.

Chapter 6 provides an overview of brokerage and clearing companies and the services they offer. These services are fundamental to the seamless functioning of the financial markets. Investors rely on the services of brokers to facilitate transactions, so brokering is essential to active and liquid capital markets. In addition, interdealer brokering provides fixed-income dealers with best bids and offers on a real-time basis. This is key to dealers' market-making activities in the secondary market for existing, outstanding securities, and these activities in turn are the foundation of an active primary market for newly issued securities. Finally, clearing services enable transactions to be completed by providing for the payment of funds and the delivery of securities. Technology has played an essential role in this area.

Chapter 7 examines insurance companies and describes how the insurance industry has redefined itself in the face of consolidation, globalization, and changing distribution channels. By accepting premium payments from policyholders, insurance companies assume the financial risk if certain events occur. The uncertainty of the events and the liabilities arising from such events pose a big challenge for insurance companies in meeting these obligations. Most capital markets books classify insurance companies as either life insurance or property and casualty insurance companies. This chapter goes beyond this classification to also include health insurance, reinsurance, and financial insurance companies.

Part III: Major Capital Markets

Part III consists of eight chapters (Chapters 8–15) and covers the major financial instruments. In Chapter 8, we discuss U.S. government securities and the importance of the Treasury market. This is the largest and most active fixed-income market, and interest rates on Treasury securities are often a benchmark in global capital markets. Annual issuance is in excess of $2 trillion, and daily trading volume averaged more than $360 billion in 2002. The chapter reviews the auction techniques for Treasury bills and coupon Treasury securities and also describes dealer bidding strategies and trading, which are an essential part of the markets.

Chapter 9 covers the $1.5 trillion municipal debt market where local governments and certain nonprofit organizations issue securities—between $200 billion and $350 billion in recent years—to fund projects for the public good. This chapter reviews the issuing process and presents evidence on competitive bidding and negotiated deals. In addition, the chapter discusses default rates and financial insurance of municipal securities, as well as the new Municipal Securities Rulemaking Board's rules and the increased transparency introduced by the Bond Market Association's initiatives to post daily transactions online.

Chapter 10 describes the corporate fixed-income market. The chapter begins by describing the various types of debt instruments and then discusses market conventions, credit ratings, valuation, and risks of debt securities. In addition, the chapter discusses the private placement market where a select group of investors, who meet certain requirements, buy new securities. Another important aspect of this market is the shelf registration rule (Rule 415) that permits certain issuers to file a single registration document to sell securities within the next two years.

Chapter 11 covers the stock markets. This chapter examines the issuing process, Securities and Exchange Commission's regulations, and exchange listing requirements. The chapter also describes the structure of the secondary markets, market practices, execution costs, and valuation techniques. For many institutional investors, measuring execution costs is one of the fundamental issues in stock trading. This issue has attracted much attention and should be covered in a capital markets book.

Chapter 12 covers foreign stocks traded in the United States (American depositary receipts or ADRs). Investors looking at international securities hope to take advantage of new opportunities for capital growth and to add geographic diversification to their portfolios. At the same time, foreign companies increasingly tap the U.S. capital market to enhance their presence in the United States and to raise capital. ADRs offer a convenient way to bridge these needs. This chapter describes the structure, benefits, and types of ADRs. The chapter also covers depositary receipts in other financial centers.

Chapter 13 discusses securities backed by mortgages and other assets (securitization). By providing businesses with access to new sources of capital at lower costs, asset securitization has revolutionized the financing of businesses. The market for securitized financing now measures in the trillions of dollars. The securitization process began with mortgage pass-throughs and then encompassed other types of assets, including credit card receivables, automobile loans, tax liens, junk bonds, and tobacco settlements. This chapter describes the process and basic elements of securitization and all major types of asset-backed securities.

Derivative securities are the focus of Chapter 14. The chapter examines the motivations behind the explosive growth in derivative securities and provides an overview of the major types of derivatives including forwards, futures, options, swaps, and credit derivatives. The chapter analyzes each type of derivatives, with emphasis on the risk management aspects.

Chapter 15 covers the foreign exchange or currency market, the largest of the global capital markets with average daily trading volume in excess of $1 trillion. This chapter begins by providing an overview of the market's structure and the conventions for quoting exchange rates; then it explains how fundamental, political, and financial factors affect exchange rates. The chapter also discusses dealer operations and how participants use the market. Finally, it examines the spot market, forward contracts, futures and options, and currency swaps.

Part IV: International Financial Centers

The chapters of Part IV focus on capital markets outside the United States. Chapter 16 describes the development of the Euromarket and the instruments traded there. The Euromarket is a global market that encompasses all major financial centers throughout the world. Securities in this market have denominations in a currency different from that of the country where the securities are issued. These securities include Eurocurrency, Eurobonds, floating rate notes, Eurocommercial paper, euro median term notes, and euro futures.

Chapter 17 examines the European Monetary Union. The twelve participating member states have formed a monetary union and have effectively merged their capital markets, dramatically changing the financial landscape. As the chapter explains, the euro's arrival has forced Europe's fixed-income investors to adopt new strategies and asset classes. The euro has also effectively ended currency risk within the euro zone, so the focus of equity investors shifts from country-based investments to sector analysis.

Chapter 18 discusses the capital markets in Japan and the ongoing financial reforms that dramatically reshape these markets. As the chapter describes, by promoting fair markets, free entry, and global competition, the Japanese hope to upgrade their markets so that they will rival New York and London. The Japanese government has more than $4 trillion in outstanding debt, and Japanese private savings amount to about $10 trillion. Hence, it is of vital importance for students and market professionals to understand the implications of these changes for Japan's capital markets, including the effects on Japanese government bonds, corporate debt, stock markets, mutual fund business, and credit ratings.

The last three chapters of the book, Chapters 19–21, explore emerging markets. Chapter 19 describes emerging markets in general and examines the four financial crises of the 1990s (Mexico in 1994–1995, Asia in 1997, Russia in 1998, and Brazil in 1999). Emerging markets have increasingly become an integral part of global capital markets, arousing great expectations despite the recent turmoil. Many emerging countries have taken steps to build more efficient capital markets. Nevertheless, as the chapter explains, several risk factors are unique to emerging markets. The chapter also discusses the issuance and trading of Brady bonds, which were created in the 1980s to resolve the emerging market debt crisis by converting loans into collateralized bonds with a reduced interest rate.

Chapter 20 provides a brief description of the financial markets in Russia and many countries in Asia, including China, Hong Kong, Indonesia, Malaysia, Singapore, South Korea, Taiwan, and Thailand. Recent events in Asia have posed a great challenge for global capital markets. The devaluation of the Thai baht on July 2, 1997, set off a financial crisis that quickly spilled over from Asia to financial centers in other parts of the world. In August 1998, Russia defaulted on its bond obligations, sparking another crisis in the global financial system. This chapter provides a chronology of the crisis and examines its causes and the global contagion. Finally, Chapter 21 provides an overview of the financial markets in the three largest countries in Latin America—Argentina, Brazil, and Mexico.

Key Terms

bid–asked spread 9
defined contribution plans 10
euro 6
European Central Bank (ECB) 6

European Monetary Union (EMU) 5
Gramm-Leach-Bliley Act (GLB) 4
Japan's Big Bang 6

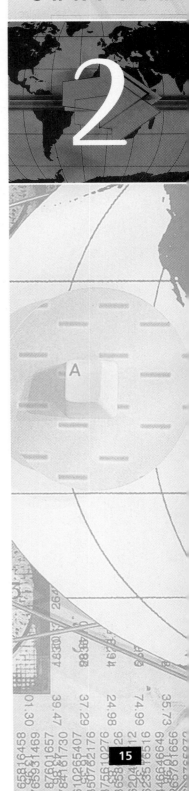

Central Banking and Capital Markets

Most countries have a central bank that serves as the bank of both the government and the banking system. Although each central bank has a slightly different range of activities, all central banks play a key role in determining the availability and cost of money and credit. As a result, they have tremendous influence on the capital markets.

This chapter looks first at the central bank of the United States—the Federal Reserve System, or the Fed. After describing the structure of the Fed, the chapter examines the tools that the Fed uses to conduct monetary policy, including repurchase agreements and matched sale-purchase agreements. These transactions affect the interest rate on bank reserves, known as the federal funds rate. As the chapter explains, changes in the federal funds rate transmit quickly to other short-term rates, but the transmission to rates on long-term securities is less straightforward. The central banks of other industrialized nations conduct similar types of operations to carry out their monetary policy objectives. The chapter concludes with an examination of the European Central Bank and the central banks of Great Britain and Japan.

The objectives of this chapter are to provide an understanding of:
- The U.S. Federal Reserve System.
- The mechanics of repurchase agreements.
- How open market operations affect market interest rates.
- Monetary policy tools of the European Central Bank.
- Monetary policy tools of the Bank of England and the Bank of Japan.

THE FEDERAL RESERVE SYSTEM

The **Federal Reserve System** (http://www.federalreserve.gov) serves as the U.S. central bank. It consists of the Board of Governors and twelve Federal Reserve Banks (FRBs). The Board resides in Washington, D.C., and the twelve FRBs are in major cities throughout the United States. A major component of the Fed is the **Federal Open Market Committee (FOMC)**, which consists of the seven members of the Board and five of the twelve FRB presidents.

The Fed conducts monetary policy, supervises and regulates banks, and provides payment services. Its goals are to achieve price stability, sustainable growth in economic activity, and stability in the financial system. In formulating its monetary policy—the actions taken to influence the amount of money and credit in the economy—the Fed has several tools at its disposal.

The basic link between monetary policy and the economy is the **federal funds market,** which is the market for bank reserves. **Reserves** are the funds that depository institutions hold against deposits. Reserves are kept either as vault cash at the institution or as non–interest-bearing deposits at an FRB. The federal funds market provides a mechanism for institutions with excess reserves to earn a yield by selling (lending) reserves to institutions running a reserve deficit, frequently on an overnight basis. Such transactions redistribute bank reserves but do not change the total amount of reserves. The interest rate on federal funds is the **federal funds rate**.

The Fed has three main tools that it can use to affect conditions in the reserves market: reserve requirements, the discount rate, and open market operations. Through its reserve requirements, the Fed requires banks to keep a percentage of their deposits on deposit at an FRB. The discount rate is the rate charged to financial institutions when they borrow reserves from an FRB. Although reserve requirements and the discount rate play a role in monetary policy, open market operations are the most powerful and flexible monetary tools that the Fed has available. Open market operations involve the buying and selling of government securities in the open market. As will be explained in detail later, these transactions have an immediate effect on the federal funds market by increasing or decreasing the amount of reserves. The resulting changes in the supply of or demand for federal funds will change the federal funds rate.

Economic conditions in the United States are the Fed's primary concern in formulating monetary policy, but as global financial markets have become more integrated and interdependent, the Fed must often consider financial events in other countries as well. In March 1998, for example, the Fed adopted a directive indicating that it leaned toward higher interest rates. However, after Russia's default on its debt and currency devaluation, which shook global financial markets in the third quarter of that year, the Fed actually ended up cutting rates.

The Board of Governors

The main governing body of the Fed is the seven-member Board of Governors, which has responsibility for the formulation of monetary policy. The Board carries out its responsibilities in conjunction with other components of the Fed. The Board sets reserve requirements, shares responsibility for discount rate policy with the FRBs, and, through the FOMC, determines open market operations. In addition, the Board has supervisory and regulatory responsibilities over member banks, bank holding companies, and foreign banks in the United States. The Board also sets margin requirements, which limit the amount investors can borrow from a broker for stock trading.[1]

The chair of the Board has formal responsibilities in the international arena as well. For example, the chair is a member of the Bank for International Settlements (BIS; **http://www.bis.org**), an international organization (a bank for central banks) established to foster cooperation towards monetary and financial stability. The chair is also regularly a member of U.S. delegations to key international finance and banking meetings. Alan Greenspan is currently the chairman of the Board.[2] Ronald Reagan originally appointed him in 1987, and Bill Clinton reappointed him to a fourth four-year term in 2000.

Federal Reserve Banks

There are twelve Federal Reserve districts; each has a Federal Reserve Bank (FRB). The twelve FRBs are in Boston, New York, Philadelphia, Cleveland, Richmond, Atlanta, Dallas, Chicago, St. Louis, Minneapolis, Kansas City, and San Francisco (see Figure 2.1). Each FRB acts as a depositary for the member banks in its own district.

The FRBs influence monetary policy in several ways. The twelve FRB presidents, together with the seven governors of the Board, are voting members of the FOMC. The president of the Federal Reserve Bank of New York (New York Fed) serves on the FOMC on a continuous basis, while other presidents serve one-year terms on a rotating basis. The trading desk at the New York Fed, known as the Open Market Desk, carries out the open market operations that implement the FOMC's policy objectives. In addition, eight times each year, the FRBs gather information on current economic conditions in their respective districts. FOMC and the Board use this information in formulating monetary policy.

The Board has delegated some of its supervisory responsibilities to the FRBs. These responsibilities include conducting field examinations and inspecting state-chartered member banks, bank holding companies, and foreign-bank offices in the United States.

---

[1]Currently, the initial margin requirement is 50 percent.

[2]His term ends in 2004.

FIGURE 2.1 | *Federal Reserve Bank District Map*

THE TWELVE FEDERAL RESERVE DISTRICTS

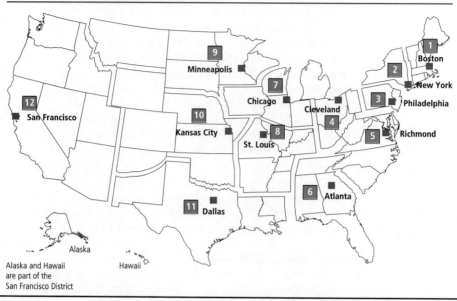

Source: Board of Governors of the Federal Reserve System (1994); *The Federal Reserve System, Purposes and Functions*, Eighth Edition, page 8.

Federal Open Market Committee

The Federal Open Market Committee (FOMC) is the most important policy-making body of the Fed. The FOMC meets eight times a year, at intervals of five to eight weeks, but a special meeting can be called if circumstances require immediate action. At each meeting, the FOMC develops its policy priorities and writes a directive that lays out guidelines for implementing its policy. At the February and July meetings, the FOMC also prepares materials to be covered in the chair's semiannual testimony before the House and Senate Banking Committees, known as the Humphrey-Hawkins testimony after the statute that mandated it.

Before each meeting, the committee members receive three documents known by the color of their covers:

- **Green book:** The green book contains two parts. The first part summarizes recent developments in the U.S. economy and in international markets; the second part provides detailed, sector-by-sector coverage of these developments, including a review of trade statistics, international financial transactions, and foreign exchange markets.

- **Blue book:** The blue book reviews recent and prospective developments related to interest rates, bank reserves, and the money supply. The February and July editions contain two additional sections. The first section presents simulations of economic conditions over the next five to seven years; the second offers forecasts of economic growth and monetary aggregates for the next two years based on the green book's baselines and alternative policy scenarios.

○ **Beige book:** The beige book reports on regional economic conditions in each of the twelve districts. The FOMC generally releases the beige book to the public about two weeks before each FOMC meeting. It can be downloaded at **http://www.federalreserve.gov/policy.htm**.

At each FOMC meeting, the committee considers what its policy will be for the next five to eight weeks until its next meeting. In particular, the FOMC decides whether to change the target federal funds rate and, if so, what the size of the change will be. The FOMC then addresses the wording of the directive that will guide open market operations at the New York Fed. If the FOMC decides to change its target for the federal funds rate, it releases a statement early in the afternoon. The minutes of each meeting become available a few days after the next regularly scheduled meeting. The following, for example, is an excerpt from the August 2002 meeting minutes:

> . . . In the committee's decision of policy for the inter-meeting period ahead, all the members were in favor of an unchanged policy stance consistent with maintaining a target rate of 1¾ percent for the federal funds rate.

Federal Reserve Financial Services

In addition to its role in monetary policy, the Fed provides a variety of services for depository institutions. These services include supplying currency, clearing checks, maintaining accounts, and operating an electronic funds transfer system. The Fed also provides various services for the U.S. government.

The Fed supplies many of the basic financial services upon which the nation's economy depends. The FRBs distribute currency and coins to depository institutions to meet the public's need for cash. The Fed also serves as a central check-clearing system; processing checks; routing them to the depository institutions on which they are drawn; and transferring funds through the accounts that depository institutions maintain with the FRBs. As for accounting services, the FRBs maintain and monitor accounts for depository institutions in their respective districts. The FRBs settle the payment transactions by debiting the accounts of the depository institutions making payments and crediting the accounts of the receiving institutions. The Fed also operates an electronic payment delivery system, called the Automated Clearinghouse, which processes electronically originated credit and debit transfers for participating institutions nationwide. These institutions often use this system for payroll direct deposit, corporate payments to vendors, Social Security payments, and utility payments.

In addition, the FRBs maintain securities accounts and effect transfers of book-entry securities for **Fedwire** participants. The Fedwire is a real-time, gross settlement system that processes and settles each transaction individually.

When a depository institution transfers funds, it irrevocably authorizes its district FRB to debit the amount from its deposit account at the FRB, and instructs the receiving depository institution's FRB to credit the same amount to the receiving institution. An important aspect of the Fedwire is its so-called **delivery-versus-payment (DVP)** feature. This means that the final transfer of securities happens if and only if the final transfer of funds occurs.

Besides the gross settlement Fedwire, the FRBs offer net settlement services to clearinghouses as well as other settlement arrangements. Instead of settling trade by trade, a net settlement system nets the credits and debits and settles the difference. The clearinghouse provides the FRB with a settlement sheet that lists the participant's net debits and credits, and they then post entries to the FRB accounts for immediate settlement.

Finally, as the fiscal agents and depositaries for the U.S. government, the FRBs perform a variety of services for the Department of the Treasury, other federal agencies, and government-sponsored enterprises. For example, the FRBs conduct the auction of Treasury securities. They assist in the auction by accepting and processing tenders and issuing securities to the successful bidders.

PRIMARY DEALERS AND REPURCHASE AGREEMENTS

When the New York Fed conducts open market operations to implement the FOMC's policy directive, it purchases or sells government securities in the open markets, most often in the form of a repurchase agreement or a matched sale-purchase. A **repurchase agreement (repo)** is a sale of securities with a commitment to repurchase the same securities at a specified price in a specified time period. When the Fed conducts repo transactions (called **system repos**), the Fed buys collateral, temporarily adding reserves to the banking system. This results in an increase in the money supply and hence a lower interest rate. When the repo matures, the Fed sells the collateral, which automatically drains the added reserves. A **matched sale-purchase** has the opposite effect: the Fed sells collateral and drains funds from the financial system with the objective of raising interest rates.

The counterparties of such transactions are the **primary dealers**, which are financial institutions designated by the New York Fed as its trading counterparties. It will help us to examine the primary dealers and the repo market before discussing open market operations in detail.

Primary Dealers

Primary dealers are either banks or securities broker-dealers. In either case, they must meet certain capital requirements to ensure that they can participate meaningfully in both the Fed's open market operations and its Treasury auctions. Table 2.1 lists the primary dealers designated as the Fed's trading counterparties. In addition to meeting the capital requirements, primary dealers must provide the New York Fed with information and analysis on their weekly trading activities, as well as their cash, futures, and financing market positions

TABLE 2.1	*Primary Dealers*
ABN Amro Bank, N.V., New York Branch	Goldman, Sachs & Co.
BNP Paribas Securities Corp.	Greenwich Capital Markets, Inc.
Banc of America Securities LLC	HSBC Securities (USA), Inc.
Banc One Capital Markets, Inc.	J.P. Morgan Securities, Inc.
Barclays Capital, Inc.	Lehman Brothers, Inc.
Bear, Stearns & Co., Inc.	Merrill Lynch Government Securities Inc.
CIBC World Markets Corp.	Mizuho Securities USA, Inc.
Credit Suisse First Boston Corp.	Morgan Stanley & Co. Inc.
Daiwa Securities America, Inc.	Nomura Securities International, Inc.
Deutsche Banc Alex. Brown, Inc.	Salomon Smith Barney, Inc.
Dresdner Kleinwort Wasserstein Securities LLC	UBS Warburg LLC

Note: This list is as of December 9, 2002

Source: Federal Reserve Bank of New York.

in Treasury and other securities. On an average day, primary dealers traded close to $370 billion in Treasury securities in 2002. Table 2.2 (see p. 22) lists their average daily trading volume from 1996 to 2002.

Repurchase Agreements

Government securities dealers borrow huge amounts of short-term funds to finance their positions every day, and often they find the least expensive way to do so is through the repurchase agreement (repo) market. In a typical repo transaction, a dealer puts up liquid securities as collateral against a cash loan while agreeing to repurchase the same securities at a future date at a higher price that reflects the financing costs. Figure 2.2 (see p. 22) depicts a typical transaction. The sale is the start leg, and the repurchase is the close leg. The party that lends securities in exchange for cash is the **collateral seller**. The counterparty that takes in securities and lends out funds is the **collateral buyer**. In practice, market participants often describe repos from the dealer's perspective. Thus, when a mutual fund lends money to a dealer by way of purchasing the collateral and agreeing to resell the same collateral back, the transaction is called a repo. Similarly, when the trading desk at the New York Fed temporarily supplies funds to the market by buying securities from dealers with a commitment to resell, the transaction is called a repo or a system repo. On the other hand, when an institution borrows funds from a dealer by selling the collateral and agreeing to repurchase the same, the transaction is called a reverse repo.

Primary dealers finance a significant portion of their securities inventory through repos. According to data published by the Bond Market Association (**http://www.bondmarkets.com**), the average daily amount outstanding of repos in recent years has been more than $3 trillion. Table 2.3 (see p. 23) lists the average daily outstanding volume of repos from 1996 to 2002.

TABLE 2.2 | *Primary Dealers' Average Daily Trading Volume of Treasury Securities*

Year	Volume ($ billions)
1996	203.7
1997	212.1
1998	226.6
1999	186.5
2000	206.6
2001	297.9
2002	366.4

PRIMARY DEALERS' AVERAGE DAILY TRADING VOLUME

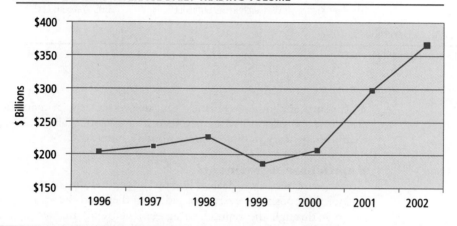

Source: Bond Market Association (http://www.bondmarkets.com).

FIGURE 2.2 | *Structure of a Typical Deliverable Repo*

START LEG

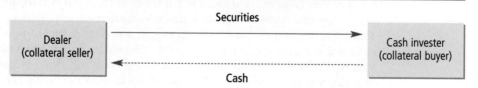

CLOSE LEG

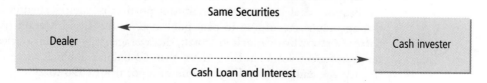

| TABLE 2.3 | *Average Daily Amount of Repurchase Agreements Outstanding* |

Year	Volume ($ billions)
1996	1,691
1997	2,042
1998	2,525
1999	2,431
2000	2,533
2001	3,098
2002	3,788

AVERAGE DAILY AMOUNT OF REPURCHASE AGREEMENTS OUTSTANDING

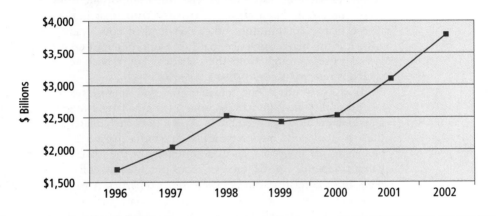

Source: Bond Market Association.

Dealers and other market participants often execute repos for a short period of time. One-day transactions are **overnight repos**, while longer maturities are **term repos**. Repos may be arranged on an open basis and terminated when either party chooses to do so. The interest rate the collateral buyer demands for such a loan is called a **repo rate**. Many factors go into the determination of the repo rate, such as the term of the repo, the type of collateral, the credit quality of the borrower, and market conditions. The overnight repo rate generally falls below the federal funds rate, reflecting the security the cash lender enjoys in a collateralized repo transaction. At times, some securities such as the most recently issued (called on-the-run) Treasury notes trade at a lower rate. Collateral that commands a lower repo rate is said to be on **special**.

Once the repo rate is determined, one can calculate the dollar amount of interest earned on the invested funds as follows:

2.1

$$I = F \times rr \times \frac{M}{360},$$

where I denotes the dollar amount of interest, F the amount of funds invested, rr the repo rate, and M the term of the repo transaction.[3] For example, a $50 million overnight repo investment at a rate of 4.70 percent would yield interest of $6,527.78:

2.2

$$\$6,527.78 = \$50,000,000 \times 4.70\% \times \frac{1}{360}.$$

Repo transactions also have several other important features. The collateral seller commonly has a **right of substitution**; that is, the right to take back the security and substitute other collateral of equal value and quality for it. Also, it is the market practice that the coupon interest coming due on the collateral passes through from the collateral buyer back to the collateral seller, which is referred to as **coupon pass-through**.

Both parties to a repo transaction expose themselves to credit risk due to the possibility that the market value of the collateral might change. To obtain an added cushion against a fall in the value of the collateral during the term of the repo, collateral buyers typically demand a margin or **haircut**, which is a percentage of the collateral value in excess of the loan. The percentage of the haircut depends on the type of securities used as collateral, the term of the repo, and the relationship between the two parties. A haircut of 1–2 percent is common when coupon Treasury securities are the collateral. The haircut is higher if the collateral seller uses mortgage-backed securities or other instruments with lower credit quality. For a term repo, when the collateral value changes, either the amount of the loan or the amount of collateral takes an adjustment.

Triparty Repos

Two types of arrangements affect the transaction for the underlying collateral in a repo. In a **deliverable repo**, the money borrower delivers the underlying securities against payment, with the collateral returned and the loan plus interest paid at maturity, as shown in Figure 2.2. The associated transaction costs include clearing fees, wire transfer charges, custodial fees, and account maintenance expenses. To avoid some of those costs and increase the cash investor's return, dealers offer alternatives that do not require the actual delivery of the collateral. The most popular choice is the **triparty repo** in which a custodial bank stands between the two repo counterparties. The custodial bank maintains accounts for both parties, so the actual delivery of the collateral and cash

---

[3]A repurchase agreement is a money market instrument, which explains the use of the 360-day year convention.

can be reduced to credit and debit transfers within the same bank, which eliminates the Fedwire charges. In a triparty setup, the entire burden of obtaining both the pricing and marking to market the collateral becomes the contractual obligation of the custodian.

Another factor that has contributed to the popularity of the triparty formula is the Fed's decision to impose a fee on **daylight overdraft**, the amount a financial institution has overdrawn on the Fedwire during the day. On April 14, 1994, when this regulation took effect, the Fed started charging fees on daylight overdrafts on an intraday basis. At the big clearing banks, bond dealers have much of the responsibility for the overdrafts every morning when they return cash borrowed through conventional deliverable repos. Thus, the overdraft charges give dealers strong incentives to abandon the deliverable format. The triparty agreements eliminate the need for cash transfers over the Fedwire and hence the daylight overdrafts.

During the term of a triparty repo, the custodian bank marks to market the collateral daily (that is, the market value of the collateral is recorded every day). Additional securities must be delivered to the collateral buyer's account when a deficit exists, with excess securities returned to the dealer's account when an excess exists. On the termination date, the custodian transfers the principal and repo interest from the dealer's cash account to the investor's designated account. Simultaneously, the custodian returns the collateral from the investor's collateral account to the dealer's collateral account. Figure 2.3 (see p. 26–27) depicts the mechanics of a triparty repo.

OPEN MARKET OPERATIONS AND CAPITAL MARKETS

The trading desk at the New York Fed carries out the FOMC's directive on **open market operations** by trading government securities with primary dealers. Though it sometimes purchases or sells government securities outright, repos are the most common approach.

Through these open market operations, the Fed changes the supply of reserves in the banking system and hence the level of the federal funds rate. Reserves are funds depository institutions must hold as vault cash or on deposit at an FRB as a percentage of deposits. When the Fed purchases government securities, through either an outright purchase or a system repo, it increases total bank reserves. Conversely, total reserves decrease when the Fed sells securities or engages in a matched sale-purchase. Changes in the federal funds rate are generally transmitted quickly to money market instruments such as Treasury bills and commercial paper. The impact on longer-term interest rates and the foreign exchange market is more complex and less predictable.

Open Market Operations
To implement the FOMC's policy instructions, the trading desk, or Open Market Desk (OMD), at the New York Fed seeks to adjust quantities of reserves of

FIGURE 2.3 | *Mechanics of a Triparty Repo*

START DATE

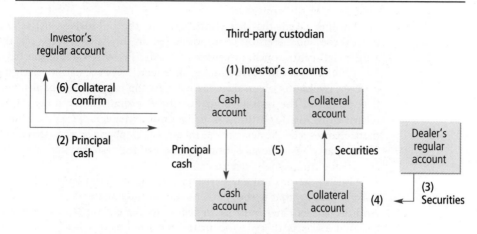

1. The investor is provided with two accounts at the custodian free of charge:
   - A cash account
   - A collateral account
2. The investor deposits funds into its cash account at the custodian.
3. The dealer delivers eligible securities to the custodian.
4. The custodian values the securities and verifies that they comply with the agreed-on collateral requirement.
5. The custodian simultaneously transfers the securities to the investor's collateral account and the funds to the dealer's cash account.
6. The custodian sends collateral confirmation to the investor.

DAILY SUBSTITUTION

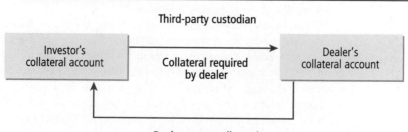

A. Substitution of collateral may take place, if needed, on a daily basis.
B. The dealer presents the custodian with a list of securities to be returned and a list of replacement securities for delivery to the investor's account.
C. The custodian values the new securities, verifies their eligibility, then moves the new securities to the investor's collateral account, and returns the requested securities to the dealer.

FIGURE 2.3 | *Mechanics of a Triparty Repo (continued)*

TRADE TERMINATION

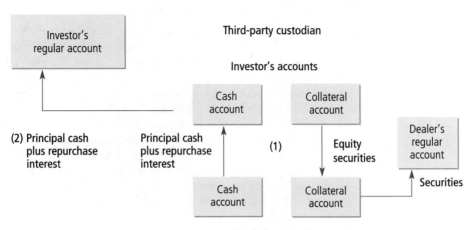

1. Upon termination of the transaction, the custodian transfers the principal and repo interest from the dealer's cash account to the investor's cash account. The custodian simultaneously returns the securities from the investor's collateral account to the dealer's account.
2. As instructed by the investor, the custodian will pay the principal and repo interest to a predesignated customer bank account.

depositary institutions in a way that will encourage the federal funds rate to trade around the target level established by the FOMC. To do this, the OMD first develops estimates of the banking system's demand for total reserves. It then estimates the volume of nonborrowed reserves (that is, reserves that institutions do not borrow from the discount window) that will be available to the banking system in the absence of any additional open market operations. If estimated supplies differ significantly from estimated demands, the OMD will add or drain reserves to balance supplies with demands.

Open market operations involve the buying and selling of government securities, either through outright purchases and sales or through temporary transactions.[4] When the OMD executes outright purchases to increase reserves in the market, it asks dealers to submit offers to sell securities to the Fed. The OMD selects from among the dealers' offers to achieve the lowest prices

---

[4]For repurchase and matched sale-purchase transactions, the OMD sends an electronic announcement to primary dealers and asks them to respond within ten to fifteen minutes. The OMD usually notifies all dealers whether they accepted or rejected their offers within five minutes of the closing time for the response.

(highest yields) for its purchase.[5] Conversely, when the OMD executes outright sales to drain reserves, it asks dealers to submit bids to buy securities from the Fed. The OMD selects from among the dealers' bids to achieve the highest prices (lowest yields) for its sale.

Frequently, the OMD uses short-term repos, for a period of up to fifteen days (usually one to seven days), with dealers to add reserves on a temporary basis. Repos are more convenient than outright purchases when the Fed wishes to inject large amounts of reserves temporarily. Repos have very low transactions costs and allow the OMD to respond quickly when reserves fall short of the desired levels. Occasionally, the OMD also arranges customer-related repos, known as **customer repos**, with dealers on behalf of foreign official accounts.

As mentioned earlier, the term repo refers to transactions from the perspective of the dealers. Under the repo arrangements, or system repos, the OMD buys securities from dealers who agree to repurchase them at a specified price on a specified date. When repurchasing the collateral, the dealer pays the original price plus an agreed-on amount of interest to the Fed as payment for the use of the funds. Hence, the added reserves extinguish automatically when the repo matures.

The changes in reserves affect the potential of the banking system to create transaction deposits. For example, assume the reserve requirement is 10 percent and the Fed conducts a $100 million system repo. The Fed's action will add $100 million in reserves to the banking system. Given a reserve requirement of 10 percent, the bank that receives the $100 million must hold $10 million in required reserves and may lend out $90 million. If the borrower then writes a check to someone who deposits the $90 million, the bank receiving the deposit can lend out $81 million. As the process continues, the banking system can expand the initial increase in reserves of $100 million into a maximum of $1 billion of money. The ratio of the money created by the banking system to the initial injection of $100 million in reserves is the **deposit multiplier**. In the real world, leakages from the banking system reduce the size of the deposit multiplier. Among the important leakages are the public's desire to hold cash and the presence of unutilized lending capacity.

The OMD awards the repos on a competitive basis. Each primary dealer submits the rates it is willing to pay for the repo. The OMD accepts the offers, beginning with the highest rates submitted; this process ends when the total accepted approximates the volume of reserves to be added to the banking system. The New York Fed pays for the collateral by directly crediting the reserve

---

[5]The Federal Reserve Act does not give the Fed the authority to purchase new Treasury securities for cash. In a refunding, the Fed cannot subscribe for a larger amount of the issues offered than the amount of the maturing securities it holds. In such a case, the Fed submits noncompetitive tenders at the auction. On the other hand, the Fed can reduce the system's portfolio by redeeming a part of the maturing holdings. See Chapter 8 for a detailed discussion of Treasury securities auction.

account of the commercial bank where the dealer has its account. As a result, the Fed has created new bank reserves.

Matched sale-purchases have the opposite effect on bank reserves. The start leg of the transaction drains reserves initially, and later the close leg returns them to the banking system. In arranging a matched sale-purchase, the OMD selects a Treasury bill in which the Fed has ample holdings and invites dealers to specify interest rates at which they want to purchase the bills for same-day delivery and to resell them back at a specified future date. Box 2.1 (see p. 30) describes a typical day at the OMD.

Open Market Operations and Yield Curves

Open market operations affect the federal funds rate and other short-term interest rates in a predictable way. When the market doesn't anticipate a change in policy, short-term interest rates typically adjust in line with the policy action. When the market widely anticipates an action, however, interest rates often complete most of the adjustment in advance of the action and show only slight additional movement as a result of the policy decision.

The transmission from short-term to long-term interest rates is less straightforward, as the shape of the yield curve is difficult to predict. As depicted in Figure 2.4 (see p. 32), a **yield curve** plots the yield to maturity against the term to maturity for Treasury securities. The **yield to maturity** is the annual return investors will earn if they hold the security until maturity. For example, the yield shown for a 5-year note in Figure 2.4 is 4.73 percent, and the yield shown for a 10-year note is 5.07 percent. Many market observers believe that the shape of the yield curve reflects both expectations of future short-term rates and preferences for liquidity. Because credit demand and inflationary expectations change over the course of the business cycle, so does the shape of the yield curve. Therefore, the impact of open market operations on longer-term interest rates often depends on how the policy action affects expectations of future short-term rates. For example, if market participants interpret a tightening move that decreases the money supply as a precursor of many more such steps, long-term rates may build with this expectation and move up in line with or even more than short-term rates. In contrast, if a tightening comes at the tail end of a series of anti-inflationary rate hikes, long-term rates may actually fall as market participants expect interest rates to move lower in the future.

Government Debt and Open Market Operations

The huge amount of marketable Treasury debt, in the form of Treasury securities, serves the financial markets and the Fed well. Trading activities provide the Fed with information about the market's expectations of future inflation. Without government borrowing, there would be no Treasury bond market, and the Fed would have to rely on other securities for its open market operations.

Furthermore, the financial markets would lose the Treasury benchmark for pricing other fixed-income securities at home and abroad (because yields on

MARKETS IN ACTION   A Day at the Open Market Desk

The morning is filled with information-gathering activities to prepare for the day's policy decisions. By the time of the morning conference call, when the plan of action is presented to an FOMC member and senior Board staff members, the market information will have been synthesized and pulled together to explain price movements and sentiments. The reserve forecasts are presented to explain the Open Market Desk's course of action. The afternoon is spent on more information gathering, telephone meetings with a couple of primary dealers, and market analysis. The day's activities include:

1. Early Morning Activity

At the OMD, a staff member talks with contacts in Europe beginning at around 7:00 A.M. eastern time. These conversations provide insights into how U.S. Treasury debt and other dollar-denominated debt have been trading in European markets. When speaking with the European contacts, the person also discusses trading activity in Asia. Trading in New York can begin at anytime, but it generally starts around 7:30 A.M.

Meanwhile, computer reports of factors affecting reserves arrive at the New York Fed from other Federal Reserve Banks. The projections staff begins compiling and evaluating the material. The information is used to update forecasts of nonborrowed and required reserves.

2. Other Preparatory Activities

As trading activity picks up through the morning in New York, trading room staff members speak about market developments with primary dealers and other active market participants.

Another trader talks with reserve position managers at most of the largest banks. These conversations give a sense of whether the federal funds market may tighten or ease over the day. The OMD's projections are updated as new information flows in.

3. The Treasury's Balance and Foreign Official Investments

A daily conversation with the Treasury takes place around midmorning. Prior to this call, a projections

staff member explains data revisions to the OMD staff member who will recommend the daily program of action to the Manager.

When both the Treasury and the New York Fed's staff suggest that the balance is likely to move away from desired levels, the Treasury will, if possible, take action to bring the balance back in line by transferring funds to or from depository institutions' Treasury Tax and Loan Note Options Account.

Another important item for completing the reserve forecast is the size of the foreign repurchase agreement pool. That forecast is prepared from information provided by the New York Fed's central bank services area.

4. Formulating the Day's Program

Staff members at the OMD develop a plan of action for the day. At the beginning of the maintenance period, a general plan is considered, with the recognition that forecast revisions may call for modifications.

If temporary operations are considered, the staff recommends the operation's timing and maturity. Often, the staff favors a series of shorter operations because of the prospect of revisions to the reserve forecasts.

Near the end of the reserve maintenance period, the OMD staff will look closely at the behavior of borrowed and excess reserves to date to see if the path assumptions are likely to hold.

As the discussion progresses toward a conclusion, a member of the money market staff will write a program indicating the action planned for the day. Once the program is drafted, the Manager or another officer will review it. Meanwhile, in the trading room, people who follow the various markets will prepare notes so that they can cover market developments that morning during the conference call.

5. The Conference Call

The next step in the process is the morning conference call. The call takes place at 10:20 A.M. The call links the OMD with the office of the Director of the Division on Monetary Affairs at the Board and with one of the four Reserve Bank presidents (outside of New York) serving on the FOMC. The call enables

MARKETS IN ACTION   A Day at the Open Market Desk

the OMD to consult with one of the committee members concerning the OMD's execution of FOMC instructions.

6. Executing the Daily Program
Any temporary transactions authorized in the program are carried out directly after the conference call, shortly after 10:30 A.M.

When arranging repos, the OMD sends out a standard message indicating the type of operation, its maturity date, and if it is a multiday operation. The message includes a deadline, generally ten to fifteen minutes after the announcement. The computer sorts the offerings, displaying the amount at each rate from the highest to the lowest rate. Once the officer decides the amount to accept, the designated trader will mark the stopout point on the computer screen and release the results.

If the day's action is a matched sale-purchase, the entry time and announcement procedures are the same as for a repo, but some aspects of the operation are slightly different. The OMD indicates the specific Treasury bill it is selling from the System's portfolio. The message to the dealers indicates the market rate at which the System will sell the bill. Dealers are instructed to enter the amount they are willing to buy and the rate at which they will reoffer the security. The rate of discount set by the Desk determines the price realized by the System on its sale, while the competitively set reoffering rate

determines the prices at which the System reacquires the same bill on the specified future day.

When the OMD executes an outright transaction, a message is sent to each primary dealer over the Fedline terminal indicating the maturity range and a deadline when the dealer's response must have been entered into the computer. The officers and senior staff choose the best propositions (based on maximizing yield to maturity), according to guidelines about the dollar volume to be chosen from each maturity range.

7. Daily Dealer Meetings
Each day, one or more OMD staff members who are involved in the daily process of implementing monetary policy hold two fifteen-minute telephone meetings with representatives of government securities dealer firms who have a trading relationship with the Federal Reserve. Over a four-week period, representatives from each of the primary dealers have the opportunity to speak with open market personnel. These discussions help the people from the OMD keep abreast of the forces at work in the financial markets.

Source: A. M. Meulendyke. *U.S. Monetary Policy and Financial Markets.* (New York: Federal Reserve Bank of New York, 1998). Excerpted with permission from Federal Reserve Bank of New York, 1999.

Treasury securities have been benchmarks in pricing other fixed-income securities).[6] Market participants would have to use other newly developed benchmarks.

Fed Watchers
Money and capital market participants watch the actions of the Fed closely. Financial firms employ economists, often called Fed watchers, to monitor the FOMC's decision-making process and to predict future tightening or easing through forecasting the variables they believe the Fed follows. Fed watchers

[6]The Treasury ceased issuing the 30-year bonds in 2001.

FIGURE 2.4 | *Yield Curve*

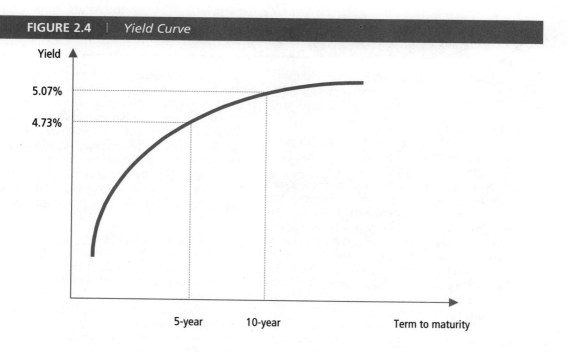

also follow speeches and public statements by FOMC members to get a sense of their concerns and priorities.

INTERNATIONAL ASPECTS OF MONETARY POLICIES

The United States is the largest economy in the world, and the dollar is a major currency held by foreign central banks for international settlement (called a reserve currency) and the medium of exchange for international transactions. Hence, the U.S. monetary policy has an important influence on the global capital marketplace. In recent years, however, this influence has begun to work both ways. As the global markets have integrated more and more, financial events in foreign markets influence U.S. monetary policy.

The widespread adoption of floating exchange rates and the lifting of restrictions on international capital flows has increased the interdependence of international capital markets. Under a floating exchange rate system, the market demand and supply determine the relative value of a currency. A floating exchange rate system leads to more independent domestic policymaking because policymakers feel less constrained by official balance of payments settlements. In addition, exchange rate changes tend to reinforce the effects of monetary policy. As an example, suppose that the Fed adopts a tightening stance, due to inflationary concerns, and conducts matched sale-purchases to raise short-term rates. Such tightening tends to restrain inflation and drive up the dollar's exchange rate. An appreciation of the dollar, in turn, increases imports and decreases exports, which contributes to slowing U.S. economic growth. At the same time, freer capital movements make the policy transmission mechanism more complex, because rapid and large financial adjustments have an immediate impact while more complicated real-sector adjustments in the industrial and service sectors of the economy may take months.

Continuing with the example, the tighter monetary policy raises nominal and real interest rates on short-term dollar investments relative to rates abroad. The higher rates encourage investors to shift from foreign currency to dollar assets, placing upward pressure on the exchange value of the dollar. While the U.S. tightening tends to raise the value of the dollar, the extent of this rise depends in part on foreign central banks' monetary policies. If foreign central banks take a similar tightening stance, the dollar's value may undergo little or no change. If foreign central banks maintain their interest rate levels, however, the value of the dollar may rise.

Another dimension of increasing international interdependence is that the Fed must take into account financial events in other countries as well as domestic economic conditions in formulating its policy. For example, as mentioned earlier, the Fed initially adopted a directive indicating that it leaned toward higher interest rates in March 1998. However, the Fed ended up cutting interest rates after Russia's default on its debt and currency devaluation triggered a global financial crisis in the third quarter of that year.

THE EUROPEAN CENTRAL BANK

In June 1988, Jacques Delors, then the president of the European Commission, chaired a committee to propose the steps for the introduction of the European Economic and Monetary Union (EMU).[7] On the basis of the Delors report, the European Council decided to create the union in three stages (Table 2.4, see p. 34). The first stage, which began in July 1990, aimed to lift all restrictions on the movement of capital between member states. On February 7, 1992, the members signed the Maastricht Treaty, which provided a framework for the second and third stages. Stage two lasted from 1994 to 1998. On January 1, 1994, the European Council established the European Monetary Institute (EMI) to strengthen central bank cooperation, coordinate monetary policy, and prepare for the establishment of the European System of Central Banks. The European Council also agreed to name the new common currency unit to be introduced at the start of stage three the euro (€). The establishment of the European Central Bank followed on June 1, 1998.

Stage three began on January 1, 1999, with the creation of the EMU. The twelve participating countries are Austria, Belgium, Finland, France, Germany,

---

[7]See Chapter 17 for a detailed coverage of the EMU.

TABLE 2.4 | Steps in the European Monetary Union

STAGE ONE	STAGE TWO		STAGE THREE		
July 1, 1990 Start of Stage One	Jan. 1, 1994 Start of Stage Two	Dec. 1995 Resolution of Madrid Meeting	Early 1998 Resolution of the European Council	Jan. 1, 1999 Start of Stage Three	Jan. 1, 2002 Conversion of Currency
Full liberalization of capital movements	Establishment of European Monetary Institute	Euro will be the new single currency	Confirmation of 1999 as starting date	Irrevocable fixing of exchange rates between member states	Euro becomes legal tender
Coordination of economic, fiscal, and monetary policies	Autonomy of national central banks	Preparation of legal framework by end of 1996	Group of participating countries	ECB assumes monetary policy responsibility	Exchange of notes and coins
			Establishment of European Central Bank	Start of currency changeover	Conversion of all monetary values not yet denominated in euros

Source: European Central Bank and Deutsche Bank.

Greece, Ireland, Italy, Luxembourg, the Netherlands, Portugal, and Spain.[8] The union fixed exchange rates between the participating countries, and set a single monetary policy for all member states. The euro became a currency in its own right and began to be used in the banking system in 1999, but euro notes and coins did not start circulating among the general population until 2002.

The European System of Central Banks

The European System of Central Banks (ESCB) includes the European Central Bank (ECB; http://www.ecb.int) and the national central banks of all fifteen European Union member states (Denmark, Great Britain, and Sweden are members of the European Union but have not joined the EMU). The term **Eurosystem** refers to the ECB and the national central banks of the member states that have adopted the euro. The Eurosystem has set maintaining price stability as its primary objective. Its basic tasks include the following:

° Defining and implementing EMU monetary policy
° Conducting foreign exchange operations
° Holding and managing foreign exchange reserves
° Promoting the smooth operation of payment systems

The ECB's capital is 5 billion euro. The national central banks are the subscribers and holders of the ECB's capital. The subscriptions are proportional to each member state's share in the gross domestic product and population of the

[8]Greece did not join until 2000.

European Union. Table 2.5 lists each member state's capital subscription to the ECB. In addition, the central banks of participating countries provide the ECB with foreign reserve assets up to an amount equivalent to 50 billion euro. The contribution of each central bank is in proportion to its share of the ECB's subscribed capital, and each central bank holds a claim on its contribution.

Monetary Policy

The Eurosystem's monetary policy tools include open market operations, standing facilities, and reserve requirements. Open market operations play a very important role in changing interest rates, managing market liquidity, and signaling the Eurosystem's stance on monetary policy. As in the United States, repurchase transactions are the most popular tool used in the Eurosystem's open market operations.

The Eurosystem engages in several types of open market operations:

1. The main refinancing operations are regular liquidity-providing repos with a term of two weeks. The national central banks execute these operations weekly.

TABLE 2.5 | *Capital Subscriptions to the European Central Bank*

National Central Bank	Subscribed Percentage (%)	Amount Subscribed (€)	Percentage to Be Paid	Amount Paid (€)
Germany	24.4096	1,220,480,000	100	1,220,480,000
France	16.8703	843,515,000	100	843,515,000
Italy	14.9616	748,080,000	100	748,080,000
Spain	8.8300	441,500,000	100	441,500,000
Netherlands	4.2796	213,980,000	100	213,980,000
Belgium	2.8885	144,425,000	100	144,425,000
Austria	2.3663	118,315,000	100	118,315,000
Greece	2.0585	102,925,000	100	102,925,000
Portugal	1.9250	96,250,000	100	96,250,000
Finland	1.3991	69,955,000	100	69,955,000
Ireland	0.8384	41,920,000	100	41,920,000
Luxembourg	0.1469	7,345,000	100	7,345,000
Subtotal	80.9738	4,048,690,000		4,048,690,000
Great Britain	14.7109	735,545,000	5	36,777,250
Sweden	2.6580	132,900,000	5	6,645,000
Denmark	1.6573	82,865,000	5	4,143,250
Subtotal	19.0262	951,310,000		47,565,500
Total	100.0000	5,000,000,000		4,096,255,500

Note: Greece joined the EMU in 2000. Great Britain, Sweden, and Denmark are not EMU member countries.

Source: European Central Bank.

2. Long-term refinancing operations are liquidity-providing repos with a maturity of three months, conducted monthly.
3. Fine-tuning operations happen on an ad hoc basis to manage market liquidity and steer interest rates. These operations are aimed at smoothing fluctuations in interest rates caused by unexpected changes in market liquidity.

The purpose of standing facilities is to provide and absorb overnight liquidity; signal the direction of monetary policy; and set boundaries, or limits, for overnight interest rates. The Eurosystem uses two standing facilities to affect its policy objectives. Through the **marginal lending facility**, participants gain overnight liquidity from national central banks against eligible assets. The interest rate charged on the marginal lending facility sets the ceiling for overnight market interest rates. In contrast, financial institutions can use the **deposit facility** to make overnight deposits with national central banks. The interest rate on this facility is the floor for the overnight market interest rate.

The Governing Council of the ECB sets reserve requirements on credit institutions in the euro area. The primary purpose of the requirements is to stabilize money market interest rates. Institutions holding required reserves receive payment at the rate of the Eurosystem's main refinancing operations.

Counterparties and Eligible Assets for Monetary Operations

The Eurosystem has established various criteria for the counterparties to its transactions. Credit institutions subject to minimum reserves may access the standing facilities and participate in open market operations. The Eurosystem has selected a limited number of counterparties to participate in fine-tuning operations.

The Eurosystem requires all of its counterparties in credit operations to have adequate collateral. There are two categories of eligible assets, tier one and tier two. Tier one consists of marketable debt instruments that satisfy eligibility criteria specified by the ECB. Tier two assets include additional assets that meet eligibility requirements specified by the national central banks.

CENTRAL BANKING IN GREAT BRITAIN AND JAPAN

Like the Fed, the Bank of England and Bank of Japan have significant influence on their domestic financial markets and the global financial system. The Bank of England's Monetary Policy Committee sets interest rates to meet its inflation target. In Japan, the Bank of Japan's Policy Board has that responsibility.

Great Britain

The Bank of England (BOE; http://www.bankofengland.co.uk) is responsible for setting interest rates. The BOE's monetary policy objective is to ensure price stability and, without prejudice to that priority, to support growth and employment. The BOE's Monetary Policy Committee (MPC) makes decisions on interest rates at its monthly meetings. The committee announces the decisions immediately following the meeting, and publishes the minutes of the meeting after the subsequent meeting.

The main instrument of the BOE's monetary policy is the short-term interest rate. Through its daily operations in the money market, the BOE supplies the funds that the banking system needs to achieve balance by the end of each settlement day. By setting the interest rate for these operations, the BOE affects the general level of interest rates in the marketplace. In the past, the BOE traded Treasury bills and other eligible local authority and bank bills. Since the introduction of the repo market for gilts (British government securities) in 1996, the BOE has focused on setting the **official dealing rate** (the repo rate) to affect its monetary policy. The BOE's purchase of gilt collateral adds funds to the system and hence lowers interest rates. When the BOE sells gilt collateral, market interest rates rise as funds are drained from the banking system. The counterparties for BOE operations include banks, building societies, securities firms, and discount houses.[9]

The BOE influences the exchange rate through direct market intervention. When the pound sterling is weak, the BOE can purchase sterling in an attempt to halt its decline. The BOE will sell sterling if perceived as too strong. As part of the changes required by the Bank of England Act of 1998, the BOE now manages its own pool of foreign exchange reserves, separate from those managed on behalf of the Treasury.

Prior to April 1998, the BOE also managed the government's debt. Since then, the responsibility for managing government debt and overseeing the gilt market has been assigned to a new Debt Management Office, an executive agency of the Treasury.

Japan

The missions of the Bank of Japan (BOJ; **http://www.boj.or.jp**) are similar to those of other central banks: to maintain price stability and to ensure an orderly financial system. Its monetary policy tools include reserve requirements, the official discount rate, and open market operations. The Policy Board meets once a month to determine the future direction of monetary policy. At the conclusion of each meeting, the BOJ issues a press release indicating whether or not there is a change in interest rate policy.

The official discount rate is the interest rate the BOJ charges when extending loans to financial institutions that have accounts at the BOJ. Loans by the BOJ take the form of a discount of bills or loans on bills. In a discount of bills, the BOJ rediscounts qualified commercial bills submitted by the financial institutions. In loans on bills, qualified bills or securities for the loans extended to

---

[9]Building societies are institutions that accept deposits and lend money to people buying houses. Discount houses are specialist money market dealers.

the financial institutions. Changes in the official discount rate signal the BOJ's stance on monetary policy.

The BOJ engages in open market operations in two areas. By supplying or withdrawing funds in the interbank market, the BOJ influences short-term interest rates. The BOJ also often purchases or sells bills or bonds to change interest rates. Because of the prolonged economic stagnation Japan has experienced in recent years, the BOJ has lowered the overnight rate to almost zero percent.

The BOJ operates a financial network system (BOJ-NET) to process settlements of funds and government securities. BOJ-NET offers services for the transfer of funds, foreign exchange, and Japanese government securities. Like the Fedwire, BOJ-NET is a delivery-versus-payment system in which delivery of government securities occurs simultaneously with the corresponding transfer of funds.

The BOJ engages in several international activities as well. The BOJ provides yen accounts to foreign central banks and governmental institutions. It makes capital subscriptions and extends loans to international organizations such as the International Monetary Fund (IMF) and the Bank for International Settlements (BIS). The BOJ also monitors exchange rate developments. It intervenes in the foreign exchange market as an agent of the Ministry of Finance.

CONCLUDING SUMMARY

Central banks play a pivotal role in financial markets by setting monetary policy and regulating financial institutions. This chapter examined several central bank operations that have a major impact on money and capital markets. The chapter began with a comprehensive look at the U.S. Federal Reserve System, including the Board of Governors, the Federal Reserve Banks, and the Federal Open Market Committee. The FOMC makes decisions that affect the federal funds rate. The Open Market Desk at the New York Fed implements the FOMC's directive usually by way of repurchase transactions with primary dealers. Primary dealers are banks and securities broker-dealers that trade in U.S. Treasury securities with the New York Fed. If the Fed intends to drain reserves from the banking system and thus raise the federal funds rate, the OMD will usually engage in a matched sale-purchase transaction in which it sells Treasury bills to primary dealers, while simultaneously agreeing to repurchase the same bills within a short period. In contrast, a system repo will add nonborrowed reserves to the banking system and hence lower the federal funds rate.

The advent of the European Economic and Monetary Union in 1999 has created a significant economic zone. Countries in the euro zone use a common currency and are subject to the monetary policy set by the Eurosystem. The Eurosystem has several tools available to affect its intended policy objectives. These tools include repurchase transactions, standing facilities, and reserve requirements.

The Bank of England and the Bank of Japan both gained their "independence" in 1998. Hence monetary policy is independent of fiscal policy, which remains the responsibility of the Treasury in England and the Ministry of Finance in Japan.

Key Terms

beige book 19	green book 18
blue book 18	haircut 24
collateral buyer 21	marginal lending facility 36
collateral seller 21	matched sale-purchase 20
coupon pass-through 24	official dealing rate 37
customer repo 28	open market operation 25
daylight overdraft 25	overnight repo 23
deliverable repo 24	primary dealer 20
delivery-versus-payment (DVP) 20	repo rate 23
deposit facility 36	repurchase agreement (repo) 20
deposit multiplier 28	reserves 16
Eurosystem 34	right of substitution 24
federal funds market 16	special 23
federal funds rate 16	system repo 20
Federal Open Market Committee (FOMC) 16	term repo 23
	triparty repo 24
Federal Reserve System 16	yield curve 29
Fedwire 19	yield to maturity 29

Review Questions

1. In the United States, the Fed has the responsibility of setting and implementing monetary policy to achieve the objectives of price stability and sustainable economic growth. What are the Fed's policy tools? Which tool is the most flexible and most frequently used by the Fed?

2. In addition to formulating monetary policy, the Fed provides several services to the financial marketplace. Briefly describe these services.

3. Delivery-versus-payment is an essential element of the Fedwire. What does delivery-versus-payment mean? Why is it important?

4. Explain why many market participants prefer the triparty repo structure to the deliverable repo format.

5. In the repo market, the term *special* means that the security commands a lower repo rate than the general collateral rate. Why do certain securities go on special?

6. The FOMC ends its meetings with a press release stating its policy, even if it has decided not to change the federal funds rate. Is such openness good or bad for the financial markets? Why?

7. Describe the mechanics of a system repo and explain how it affects the short-term interest rates.

8. What is a matched sale-purchase transaction?

9. The Open Market Desk at the New York Fed elects to do a system repo for $500 million. If other factors are held constant, what will happen to the supply of bank reserves? To deposits and loans? To the level of interest rates?

10. Is the overnight repo rate generally lower or higher than the federal funds rate? Why?

11. The Eurosystem sets the monetary policy for the euro zone countries. Standing facilities are one category of its open market operations. How does the Eurosystem use such facilities to set limits on overnight interest rates?

12. The Bank of Japan has lowered the overnight interest rate and the discount rate in recent years to stimulate economic activity. What are those rates now?

13. Compare central bank monetary policy operations in the United States, the European Monetary Union, Great Britain, and Japan. What are the overnight interest rates in these markets?

Select Bibliography

Beckner, S. K. *Back from the Brink: The Greenspan Years.* New York: John Wiley & Sons, 1997.

Blinder, A. S. *Central Banking in Theory and Practice.* Boston, Mass.: MIT Press, 1999.

Boivin, J., and M. Giannoni. *Has Monetary Policy Become Less Powerful?* Staff Report #144, Federal Reserve Bank of New York, March 2002.

Broz, J. L. *The International Origins of the Federal Reserve System.* Ithaca, New York: Cornell University Press, 1997.

Buraschi, A., and D. Menini. "Liquidity and specialness." *Journal of Financial Economics* 64, no. 2 (May 2002), pp. 243–284.

Drossos, E. S., and S. Hilton. "The Federal Reserve's contingency financing plan for the century date change." *Current Issues in Economics and Finance* 6, no. 15, Federal Reserve Bank of New York, (December 2000).

Fabozzi, F. J. *Securities Lending and Repurchase Agreements.* Burr Ridge, Ill.: Irwin Professional Publishing, 1996.

Feldstein, M., ed. *The Costs and Benefits of Price Stability.* Chicago: University of Chicago Press, 1999.

Goodhart, C. A. E. *The Central Bank and the Financial System.* Boston, Mass.: MIT Press, 1995.

Hunter, W. C., and S. D. Smith. "Risk management in the global economy: A review essay." *Journal of Banking and Finance* 26, issue 2 (March 2002), pp. 205–221.

Johnson, D. *Payment Systems, Monetary Policy and the Role of the Central Bank.* Washington, D.C.: International Monetary Fund, 1997.

Kuttner, K. N., and J. J. McAndrews. "Personal online payment." *Economic Policy Review* 7, no. 3, Federal Reserve Bank of New York, (December 2001), pp. 35–50.

Liaw, K. T., and T. E. Christman. "The markets for repurchase transactions." *Corporate Finance Review* 2, no. 1 (July/August 1997), pp. 22–30.

Meulendyke, A. M. *U.S. Monetary Policy and Financial Markets.* New York: Federal Reserve Bank of New York, 1998.

Stewart, J. B. Jr. "Changing technology and the payment system." *Current Issues in Economics and Finance* 6, no. 1, Federal Reserve Bank of New York, (October 2000).

MAJOR FINANCIAL INSTITUTIONS

PART

2

Commercial Banks

The banking environment has undergone a structural change. Financial innovations, advances in technology, deregulation, and globalization have broken down the boundaries between traditional industry sectors, and have contributed to increased inter- and intra-industry competition. Because of technological developments, banks have branched into distant regions via electronic media. Today, the large multinational banks compete with each other for business on every continent. At the same time, nonbank financial institutions now offer many traditional banking services. Deposit insurance, reserve requirements, and capital requirements are among the very few traditional characteristics still possessed by banks.

Facing this increasingly competitive and global market environment, banks have expanded and continue to expand the array of services they offer. Deregulation has spurred this proliferation of banking services, which has removed most of the restrictions—imposed during the Great Depression of the 1930s—that prevented banks from offering other financial services. As a result, commercial banks have entered new areas of business such as investment banking, insurance, and asset management. The formation of Citigroup from the investment banking firm Salomon Smith Barney, the insurance company Travelers Group, and the commercial banking giant Citicorp exemplifies this trend toward the creation of financial services supermarkets.

The objectives of this chapter are to provide an understanding of:
- The trends in the banking sector.
- The implications of the financial modernization legislation.
- Bank reserve requirements and capital requirements.
- The use of technology in banking.
- The main risks banks face and how they manage each type of risk.

MARKET OVERVIEW

Traditionally, banks have played several key roles in the economy. In their inter-mediation role, banks transform client savings into credit for businesses and individuals. As payors, banks make payments for goods and services on behalf of their customers. In their guarantor role, banks provide guarantees of customers' debt obligations. In addition, banks act as agents on behalf of their customers to manage and protect their property or to issue and redeem their securities. Furthermore, banks play an important policy role in that they serve as a conduit for the Fed's monetary policy actions to maintain price stability and sustainable economic growth.

Today, banks not only continue to perform these functions but have added a host of new ones as well. As other financial services firms, such as securities houses and mutual fund companies, have begun to offer services that compete with traditional banking services, banks have countered by offering new products and services and developing new methods of delivering them. Banks today do a lot more than just take deposits and make loans, as Table 3.1 shows. These functional changes have precipitated changes in organizational structure and a trend toward consolidation that continues to transform the banking industry.

Organizational Structures

Banks fall under two categories of organization: independent banks or bank holding companies. An independent bank is a bank that doesn't operate under the control of a multibank holding company. Although an independent bank is often part of a one-bank holding company and may operate branches, it typ-

TABLE 3.1	*Banking Services and Products*

Traditional Services and Products:

Deposits and loans (consumer and business)
Currency exchanges
Safekeeping of valuables
Supporting government activities with credit
Trust services
Financial advising

More Recent Services and Products:

Cash management
Equipment leasing
Venture capital
Insurance services
Retirement plans
Securities brokerage investment services
Mutual funds and annuities
Investment banking and merchant banking

ically conducts its business in its local or regional community. Most large bank-ing institutions are bank holding companies. A **bank holding company** owns and manages subsidiary firms. The holding company is the parent organization, and the operating entities are the subsidiaries.

By definition, a small bank holding company has total consolidated assets of less than $150 million, has no debt outstanding to the general public, and does not engage in nonbank activities involving financial leverage or in credit-extending activities. Large bank holding companies are either: (1) holding companies with total consolidated assets of $150 million or more, or (2) multi-bank holding companies, regardless of size, that have debt outstanding to the general public or engage in a nonbank activity involving financial leverage or in credit-extending activities. Table 3.2 lists the top fifteen bank holding com-panies in the United States. The largest banking concern, Citigroup, has total assets of more than $1 trillion. Thirteen bank holding companies have assets of at least $100 billion.

Geographic Expansion and Globalization

Such large bank holding companies have occurred in part by deregulation, which has removed restrictions on the ability of banks to expand geographically. In the past, bank branching across state lines was illegal unless the states involved expressly permitted interstate branching. The Riegle-Neal Interstate Banking and Branching Efficiency Act of 1994 (IBBEA) permitted interstate branch banking, thereby changing the landscape and structure of the banking industry throughout the United States. Under the IBBEA, beginning on September 29,

TABLE 3.2 | *Top 15 Bank Holding Companies by Total Assets*

Rank	Name	Headquartered State	Total Assets ($ billions)
1	Citigroup	NY	1,057
2	J.P. Morgan Chase	NY	712
3	Bank of America	NC	619
4	Wachovia	NC	319
5	Wells Fargo	CA	311
6	Banc One	IL	262
7	Taunus Corporation	NY	225
8	FleetBoston	MA	192
9	ABN Amro North America	IL	174
10	U.S. Bancorp	MN	164
11	HSBC North America	NY	110
12	SunTrust	GA	106
13	National City	OH	100
14	Keycorp	OH	80
15	Bank of New York	NY	76

Note: Data are from National Information Center (http://www.ffiec.gov/nic) and are as of March 31, 2002.

1995, a bank holding company can acquire a bank in any state. There are two important restrictions, though. First, the holding company's community re-investment record must pass a review by the Federal Reserve Board of Governors.[1] Second, limits on deposit concentrations apply; the total amount of insured deposits that any banking organization may obtain by mergers and acquisitions caps at 30 percent in a single state and 10 percent nationally.

Another aspect of this geographic expansion is that more large banks have gone global. Large U.S. banks such as Citibank, J.P. Morgan Chase, Bank of America, and Bank of New York provide banking services in many countries. Similarly, foreign banks such as Deutsche Bank, UBS, and Sumitomo have operations in the United States. These global banks compete with each other on almost every continent of the world.

Functional Expansion

A functional expansion has accompanied the geographic expansion of banks, which has enabled banks to go far beyond their traditional functions and become veritable financial services supermarkets. A series of deregulatory measures, which removed many restrictions that had been imposed on the banking industry during the Great Depression of the 1930s, has contributed to this functional expansion. The intent of this legislation had been to try to ensure the safety of the financial services industry by sharply segregating its three main components—banks, securities firms, and insurers.

One of the key pieces of this legislation was the **Glass–Steagall Act** of 1933. Section 20 of the act prohibits the affiliation of a member bank (a bank that is a member of the Federal Reserve System) with a company "engaged principally" in underwriting or dealing in securities. In 1987, the Federal Reserve Board of Governors interpreted that phrase to allow bank subsidiaries, so-called **section 20 subsidiaries** or **underwriting subsidiaries**, to under-write and deal in securities that a member bank itself could not underwrite or deal in. The Board approved applications by three bank holding companies to underwrite and deal in so-called tier 1 securities such as commercial paper, municipal revenue bonds, mortgage-backed securities, and securities related to consumer receivables. In 1988, the Board allowed five bank holding companies to underwrite and deal in tier 2 securities (all debt and equity securities).

The Board of Governors established a revenue test to determine whether a company "engages principally" in underwriting and dealing for the purpose of section 20. Initially, a section 20 subsidiary could not derive more than 5 percent of its total revenue from activities involving bank-ineligible securities. The Board increased the limit to 10 percent of total revenue in 1989 and raised it to 25 percent in 1997. Finally, with the passage of the Gramm-Leach-Bliley Act of 1999 (GLB), the limit was effectively eliminated. Under the act, a bank holding company that elects to become or be treated as a financial

---

[1]Congress enacted the Community Reinvestment Act in 1977 to encourage federally insured financial institutions to meet the credit needs of the entire community, including low- and moderate-income residents.

holding company may engage in securities underwriting, dealing, or market-making activities through its subsidiaries (called **securities subsidiaries**).

The GLB did far more than just eliminate the limits of the revenue test. The act has enabled a financial services firm, such as a commercial bank or a securities house, to become a one-stop shop that can supply all of its customers' financial needs. By allowing banks, insurance companies, and securities firms to affiliate with each other, the act has opened the way for financial services supermarkets that offer a vast array of products and services including savings and checking accounts, credit cards, mortgages, stock and bond underwriting, insurance (homeowners, auto, and life), mergers and acquisitions advice, commercial loans, and derivative securities and foreign exchange trading. Box 3.1 (see p. 48) describes the first and largest of these financial supermarkets in the United States.

The GLB has not only opened up new opportunities for banks but has also provided significant protection for investors and consumers, while striving to create a level playing field for all financial services firms. It established a new system of functional regulation whereby banking regulators oversee banking activities, state insurance regulators supervise insurance activity, and securities regulators supervise securities activities. In this new regulatory environment, investment-banking houses can offer a full menu of financial services to meet client demand. At the same time, commercial banks can engage in formerly forbidden activities such as stock underwriting and dealing.

Consolidation Trends

The wave of consolidation that accompanied those organizational and functional changes is reshaping the banking industry. Mergers and acquisitions (M&As) among banks and financial services companies occur at a torrid pace. Megamergers—M&As between banks with assets over $1 billion—have become common. Some of the marriages are reaching the scale of supermega-mergers, M&As between institutions with assets of over $100 billion each. Recent examples of supermegamergers include Citicorp-Travelers, BankAmerica-NationsBank, Banc One-First Chicago, Norwest-Wells Fargo, and Chase Manhattan-J.P. Morgan. Forces behind the consolidation trends include technological progress, improvements in financial condition, excess capacity, international consolidation of markets, and deregulation of geographic or product restrictions.[2] Table 3.3 (see p. 49) reports on trends in the number of banks and branches insured by the Federal Deposit Insurance Corporation (FDIC). As shown in Table 3.3, the number of banks has declined, but the number of branches has increased over the years.

Advances in information and computer technology have had tremendous impacts on banking, but larger financial institutions can use many of the new tools of financial engineering more efficiently. Some new delivery methods such as phone centers, automatic teller machines (ATMs), personal computer (PC) and Internet banking, and back-office operations may exhibit greater

---

[2]Berger, Demsetz, and Strahan (1998).

MARKETS IN ACTION   Citigroup

3.1

On April 6, 1998, Citicorp and Travelers Group announced that they had agreed to merge, forming Citigroup, Inc., the first true one-stop shop in financial services in the United States. On September 24, 1999, Citicorp and Travelers Group received approval from the Fed to merge. Following a mandatory fifteen-day waiting period, Citigroup officially opened for business on October 8, 1999. The company, comprised of Citibank, Travelers, Salomon Smith Barney, Commercial Credit, and Primerica Financial Services, delivers a full range of products and services to over 100 million customers in 100 countries. Citigroup offers traditional banking, consumer finance, credit cards, investment banking, securities brokerage, asset management, and property, casualty, and life insurance (Citigroup has spun off part of property and casualty insurance). In addition to Smith Barney, Citigroup consists of four groups: Consumer Group, Corporate and Investment Banking, Citigroup International, and Global Investment Management and Private Banking. The following chart depicts the organizational structure of these four groups:

Citigroup Organizational Chart

Citigroup

Consumer Group	Citigroup's Corporate and Investment Bank	Citigroup International	Global Investment Management and Private Banking Group
Citibanking	Global Securities Services	Citibank	The Citigroup Private Bank
Cards	Global Equities		Citigroup Asset Management
CitiFinancial	Global Fixed Income		Global Retirement Services
Primerica Financial Services	Global Investment Banking Global Relationship Banking		Travelers Life and Annuity
	Cash, Trade, and Treasury Services		Citigroup Alternative Investments

Source: *How Citigroup Is Organized*, Citigroup, Inc.

economies of scale than traditional branching networks. Through M&As, banks can take advantage of these economies of scale and enhance their efficiency.

Improvement in the financial condition of banks was another factor behind the recent rise in M&As among banks in the 1990s and 2000. With few exceptions, bank profitability has been on an upward trend during those years.[3] The

---

[3]One such exception occurred during the third and fourth quarters of 1998 in the wake of the global financial crisis.

TABLE 3.3		Number of FDIC-Insured Commercial Banks and Branches								
	1934	1942	1950	1958	1966	1974	1982	1990	1998	2000
Main offices	14,146	13,347	13,446	13,124	13,538	14,230	14,451	12,343	8,774	8,315
Branches	2,985	3,555	4,832	8,955	17,029	28,651	39,783	50,446	61,902	64,079
Total offices	**17,131**	**16,902**	**18,278**	**22,079**	**30,567**	**42,881**	**54,234**	**62,789**	**70,676**	**72,394**

Source: Federal Deposit Insurance Corporation (http://www.fdic.gov).

net income of FDIC–insured commercial banks increased from $15.99 billion in 1990 to $44.62 billion in 1994 and to $71.18 billion in 2000. Low interest rates and high stock prices also helped fuel the consolidation trend during the 1990s.

Savings Institutions

Another trend in the banking industry has been the gradual decline in the relative importance of savings institutions. Savings institutions include savings and loans (S&Ls) and savings banks. These depository institutions, which are regional in nature, have traditionally specialized in meeting the needs of individual and household consumers. The number of savings institutions has steadily declined from more than 3,600 in 1985 to 1,590 by the end of 2000. Table 3.4 (see p. 50) provides a summary of financial data for commercial banks and savings institutions. For commercial banks, net income rose from $18 billion in 1985 to $71 billion in 2000. Total assets increased more than twofold, from $2.7 trillion to $6.2 trillion. During the same time period, equity capital tripled. In contrast, assets at savings institutions remained flat. Equity capital more than doubled and net income increased from $5.5 billion in 1985 to $10.7 billion in 2000. In 1990, however, savings institutions lost over $4 billion.

Credit Unions

A credit union is a nonprofit depository institution established to provide banking services to its members. Because members own and control credit unions, they do not issue shares in the public market. Each institution decides whom it will serve. Most credit unions provide services to residents of a particular community, a group or groups of employees, or members of an organization or association. There are two special types of credit unions. Community development credit unions serve primarily low-income members in distressed and financially underserved areas. Corporate credit unions do not serve retail customers but act as a credit union for credit unions, providing investment, liquidity, and payment services for their member credit unions.

Credit unions are either state or federally chartered. A state regulatory agency supervises state-chartered unions, and the National Credit Union Administration (**http://www.ncua.gov**) supervises federally chartered credit unions. Credit union accounts are insured for up to $100,000 each by the National Credit Union Share Insurance Fund.

TABLE 3.4	Financial Data for Commercial Banks and Savings Institutions ($ Billions)

COMMERCIAL BANKS

	1985	1990	2000
Net income	$17.9	15.9	71.1
Total assets	2,730.6	3,389.4	6,238.7
Equity capital	169.1	218.6	529.5

SAVINGS INSTITUTIONS

	1985	1990	2000
Net income	5.5	-4.7	10.7
Total assets	1,262.6	1,259.1	1,221.8
Equity capital	44.7	67.5	103.2

Source: Federal Deposit Insurance Corporation.

Credit unions often offer very competitive rates on everything from savings accounts to automobile and home loans, in part because they are not-for-profit institutions and do not have to pay taxes. They also have lower marketing costs and overhead than commercial institutions. Thus, they can pay their members above-average rates on deposits and charge below-average rates on loans and credit cards.

Between 1960 and 1981, there were more than 20,000 credit unions in the United States.[4] Since 1981, the number has steadily declined, to 10,684 in 2000. Nevertheless, membership has increased from 12 million in 1960 to 45 million in 1981 and to almost 80 million in 2000. Thus, the average size of credit unions has increased. As membership increased, total savings in credit unions climbed from $5 billion in 1960 to $64 billion in 1981 and to $390 billion in 2000. Loans followed a similar trend, increasing from $4.4 billion in 1960 to $309.4 billion in 2000. Total assets crossed the $100 billion mark in 1984 and reached $450 billion in 2000. Note, however, that the total assets of $450 billion for the whole credit union industry was less than half of Citigroup's $1 trillion in assets.

REGULATORY ENVIRONMENT

Banks are the core of the financial system. Not only do banks hold a significant portion of household assets, but they also have the power to create money and play a key role in the Federal Reserve's ability to influence market interest rates. Consequently, ensuring the safety and soundness of the banking system is crucial for the U.S. economy. The safeguards established to protect the

[4]Data are from the Credit Union National Association (http://www.cuna.org).

banking system include reserve requirements, capital requirements, and deposit insurance. Box 3.2 (see p. 52) summarizes the most important legislation enacted to regulate (or deregulate) the U.S. banking industry. In addition, the Basel Committee on Banking Supervision of the Bank for International Settlements (http://www.bis.org) has established capital requirements for various risks. This institution regulates U.S. banks as well.

Reserve Requirements

Reserve requirements refer to the percentage of deposits that a bank must hold either as vault cash or on deposit at a Federal Reserve Bank. The Monetary Control Act of 1980 (MCA; part of the Depository Institutions Deregulation and Monetary Control Act) authorized the Board of Governors of the Federal Reserve System to impose a reserve requirement. Federal Reserve Regulation D sets uniform reserve requirements for all depository institutions that have transaction accounts or nonpersonal time deposits.

Transaction accounts include checking accounts, NOW accounts, savings accounts, and accounts that permit more than a limited number of telephone or preauthorized payments or transfers each month. Time deposits are deposits or certificates with an original maturity of at least seven days and savings accounts that allow the institution at least seven days' notice by the depositor before a withdrawal takes place.

To relieve small depository institutions of the burden of reserve requirements, each depository institution has a zero percent reserve requirement on the first $5.5 million of its reservable liabilities in 2001.[5] Transaction accounts over $5.5 million up to $42.8 million have a reserve requirement of 3 percent. Transaction accounts over $42.8 million have a 10 percent reserve requirement. Hence, for most banks the marginal reserve requirement is 10 percent. Table 3.5 (see p. 55) lists the reserve requirement schedule for depository institutions.

Under the regulation, a bank's average reserves over the period ending every other Wednesday must equal the required percentage of its average deposits in the two-week period ending Monday, two days earlier. Thus, the reserve computation period begins on a Tuesday and ends on a Monday fourteen days later. A bank's average reserves over the period ending every other Wednesday must equal the required reserves. The key goal of reserve management is to keep legal reserves at the required level with neither excess reserves nor a reserve deficit. If a bank has temporary excess reserves, it will generally lend out the funds, called federal funds, to other banks that have reserve deficits. If the excess reserves are long lasting, the bank could purchase securities or make new loans. If a bank runs a reserve deficit, it will usually borrow federal funds from other institutions. The interest rate in the federal funds market is the federal funds rate.

---

[5]The exempt amount receives an annual adjustment by a factor equal to 80 percent of the percentage change in total transaction accounts in the United States. This is the reservable liabilities exemption adjustment.

MARKETS IN ACTION   Important Banking Legislation

3.2

National Bank Act of 1864
Established a national banking system and the chartering of national banks.

Federal Reserve Act of 1913 Established the Federal Reserve System as the central banking system of the United States.

The McFadden Act of 1927 Prohibited interstate banking.

Banking Act of 1933 (Glass-Steagall Act) Established the FDIC as a temporary agency. Separated commercial banking from investment banking, establishing them as separate lines of commerce.

Banking Act of 1935 Established the FDIC as a permanent agency of the government.

Federal Deposit Insurance Act of 1950 Revised and consolidated earlier FDIC legislation into one act. Embodied the basic authority for the operation of the FDIC.

Bank Holding Company Act of 1956 Required Federal Reserve Board approval for the establishment of a bank holding company. Prohibited bank holding companies headquartered in one state from acquiring a bank in another state.

International Banking Act of 1978 Brought foreign banks within the federal regulatory framework. Required deposit insurance for branches of foreign banks engaged in retail deposit taking in the United States.

Financial Institutions Regulatory and Interest Rate Control Act of 1978 (FIRIRCA) Created the Federal Financial Institutions Examination Council. Established limits and reporting requirements for bank insider transactions. Included major statutory provisions regarding electronic fund transfers.

Depository Institutions Deregulation and Monetary Control Act of 1980 (DIDMCA) Established "NOW accounts." Began the phase-out of interest rate ceilings on deposits. Established the Depository Institutions Deregulation Committee.

Granted new powers to thrift institutions. Raised the deposit insurance ceiling to $100,000.

Depository Institutions Act of 1982
(Garn-St. Germain Act) Expanded the FDIC's powers to assist troubled banks. Established the Net Worth Certificate program. Expanded the powers of thrift institutions.

Competitive Equality Banking Act of 1987
(CEBA) Established new standards for availability of expedited funds. Recapitalized the Federal Savings & Loan Insurance Company (FSLIC). Expanded the FDIC's authority for open bank assistance transactions, including bridge banks.

Financial Institutions Reform, Recovery, and Enforcement Act of 1989 (FIRREA) FIRREA's purpose was to restore the public's confidence in the savings and loan industry. Abolished the FSLIC and gave the FDIC the responsibility of insuring the deposits of thrift institutions in its place. The FDIC insurance fund created to cover thrifts was named the Savings Association Insurance Fund (SAIF); the fund covering banks was called the Bank Insurance Fund (BIF).

Abolished the Federal Home Loan Bank Board and created two new agencies, the Federal Housing Finance Board (FHFB) and the Office of Thrift Supervision (OTS), to replace it.

Created the Resolution Trust Corporation (RTC) as a temporary agency of the government with the responsibility of managing and disposing of the assets of failed institutions. Created an Oversight Board to supervise the RTC and the Resolution Funding Corporation (RFC) to provide funding for RTC operations.

Title XXV of the Crime Control Act of 1990
(Comprehensive Thrift and Bank Fraud Prosecution and Taxpayer Recovery Act of 1990) Greatly expanded the authority of federal regulators to combat financial fraud. Prohibited undercapitalized banks from making golden parachute and other indemnification payments to institution-affiliated parties. Increased penalties and prison time for those convicted of bank crimes, increased the powers and

MARKETS IN ACTION   Important Banking Legislation (continued)

authority of the FDIC to take enforcement actions against institutions operating in an unsafe or unsound manner, and gave regulators new procedural powers to recover assets improperly diverted from financial institutions.

Federal Deposit Insurance Corporation Improvement Act of 1991 (FDICIA) Greatly increased the powers and authority of the FDIC. Recapitalized the Bank Insurance Fund and allowed the FDIC to strengthen the fund by borrowing from the Treasury.

Mandated a least-cost resolution method and prompt resolution approach to problem and failing banks and ordered the creation of a risk-based deposit insurance assessment scheme. Restricted brokered deposits, the solicitation of deposits, and nonbank activities of insured state banks. Created new supervisory and regulatory examination standards and put forth new capital requirements for banks.

Housing and Community Development Act of 1992 Established regulatory structure for government-sponsored enterprises (GSEs), combated money laundering, and provided regulatory relief to financial institutions.

RTC Completion Act Required the RTC to adopt a series of management reforms and to implement provisions designed to improve the agency's record in providing business opportunities to minorities and women when issuing RTC contracts or selling assets. Expanded the existing affordable housing programs of the RTC and the FDIC by broadening the potential affordable housing stock of the two agencies.

Increased the statute of limitations on RTC civil lawsuits from three years to five, or to the period provided in state law, whichever is longer. Also provided that in cases in which the statute of limitations had expired, claims could be revived for fraud and intentional misconduct resulting in unjust enrichment or substantial loss to the thrift. Provided final funding for the RTC and established a transition plan for transfer of RTC resources to the FDIC. Set December 31, 1995 as the RTC's sunset date when

the FDIC would assume its conservatorship and receivership functions.

Riegle Community Development and Regulatory Improvement Act of 1994 Established a Community Development Financial Institutions Fund, a wholly owned government corporation that would provide financial and technical assistance to CDFIs.

Contained several provisions aimed at curbing the practice of "reverse redlining" in which nonbank lenders target low- and moderate-income homeowners, minorities, and the elderly for home equity loans on abusive terms. Relaxed capital requirements and other regulations to encourage the private-sector secondary market for small business loans.

Contained more than fifty provisions to reduce bank regulatory burden and paperwork requirements. Required the Treasury Department to develop ways to substantially reduce the number of currency transactions filed by financial institutions. Contained provisions aimed at shoring up the National Flood Insurance Program.

Riegle-Neal Interstate Banking and Branching Efficiency Act of 1994 (IBBEA) Permitted adequately capitalized and managed bank holding companies to acquire banks in any state one year after enactment. Provided that concentration limits apply and required Community Reinvestment Act (CRA) evaluations by the Federal Reserve before acquisitions are approved. Beginning June 1, 1997, allowed interstate mergers between adequately capitalized and managed banks, subject to concentration limits, state laws, and CRA evaluations. Extended the statute of limitations to permit the FDIC and RTC to revive lawsuits that had expired under state statutes of limitations.

Economic Growth and Regulatory Paperwork Reduction Act of 1996 (EGRPR) Modified financial institution regulations, including regulations impeding the flow of credit from lending institutions to businesses and consumers. Amended the Truth in Lending Act and the Real Estate Settlement Procedures Act of 1974 to streamline the mortgage lending process.

MARKETS IN ACTION Important Banking Legislation (continued)

Amended the Federal Deposit Insurance Act (FDIA) to eliminate or revise various application, notice, and record-keeping requirements to reduce the regulatory burden and the cost of credit. Amended the Fair Credit Reporting Act to strengthen consumer protections.

Established consumer protections for potential clients of consumer repair services. Clarified lender liability and federal agency liability issues under the Comprehensive Environmental Response, Compensation, and Liability Act (CERCLA). Directed the FDIC to impose a special assessment on depository institutions to recapitalize the SAIF, aligned SAIF assessment rates with BIF assessment rates, and merged the SAIF and BIF into a new Deposit Insurance Fund.

Gramm-Leach-Bliley Act of 1999 Repealed the Glass-Steagall Act of 1933. Modified portions of the Bank Holding Company Act (BHCA) to allow affiliations between banks and insurance underwriters. While preserving the states' authority to regulate insurance, prohibited state actions that have the effect of preventing bank-affiliated firms from selling insurance on an equal basis with other insurance agents. Created a new financial holding company, under section 4 of the BHCA, authorized to engage in underwriting and selling insurance and securities, conducting both commercial and merchant banking, investing in and developing real estate, and other "complimentary activities." Also put limits on the kinds of nonfinancial activities these new entities may engage in.

Allowed national banks to underwrite municipal bonds. Restricted the disclosure of nonpublic customer information by financial institutions. Required all financial institutions to provide customers the opportunity to "opt out" of the sharing of the customers' nonpublic information with unaffiliated third parties. Imposed criminal penalties on anyone who obtains customer information from a financial institution under false pretenses.

Amended the CRA to provide that financial holding companies cannot be formed before their insured depository institutions receive and maintain a satisfactory CRA rating. Also required public disclosure of bank-community CRA-related agreements. Granted some regulatory relief to small institutions by reducing the frequency of their CRA examinations if they have received outstanding or satisfactory ratings. Prohibited affiliations and acquisitions between commercial firms and unitary thrift institutions.

Made significant changes in the operation of the Federal Home Loan Bank (FHLB) system, easing membership requirements and loosening restrictions on the use of FHLB funds.

Source: Federal Deposit Insurance Corporation (http://www.fdic.gov). Reprinted with permission from the Federal Deposit Insurance Corporation.

For example, suppose that a bank has a reserve deficit of $30 million and purchases that amount of federal funds at a rate of 4.82 percent to meet its reserve requirement for seven days. The cost to the bank will be

$$\boxed{3.1} \qquad \$30,000,000 \times \left(\frac{0.0482}{360} \right) \times 7 = \$28,116.67.$$

Note that a 360-day year is used in the denominator because the federal funds market is a money market.

TABLE 3.5	*Reserve Requirement Schedule*
TYPE OF DEPOSIT	**RESERVE REQUIREMENTS**
Net Transaction Accounts	
$0 to $5.5 million	0%
$5.5 million to $42.8 million	3%
More than $42.8 million	$1.119 million plus 10% of amount over $42.8 million
Nonpersonal time deposits	0%

Note: The Monetary Control Act of 1980 requires that the amount of transaction accounts against which the 3 percent reserve requirement applies be modified annually by 80 percent of the percentage change in transaction accounts held by all depository institutions. The schedule listed in the table became effective in September 2001.

Source: *Reserve Requirements*, the Federal Reserve System, 2001.

Capital Requirements for Credit Risk

Banks also have to meet risk-based capital standards that protect against **credit risk**, or the risk that a bank will sustain a loss as a result of the default of a borrower or a counterparty. Banks also base the guidelines used to evaluate capital adequacy on the perceived credit risk associated with balance-sheet assets, as well as certain off-balance-sheet items such as unused loan commitments and letters of credit. The most important element is the linkage between a bank's minimum capital requirement and the credit risk of its assets through a risk-weighted system. A leverage ratio requirement supplements the risk-based capital guidelines.

For the purpose of risk-based capital, a bank's total capital consists of two major components: core capital elements (included in tier 1 capital) and supplemental capital elements (included in tier 2 capital).

○ **Tier 1 capital** is the sum of core capital elements (common equity, qualifying noncumulative perpetual preferred stock, and minority interest in the equity accounts of consolidated subsidiaries) less goodwill, unrealized holding losses in the available-for-sale equity portfolio, and other intangible assets that do not qualify within capital.

○ **Tier 2 capital** consists of a limited amount of the allowance for loan and lease losses, perpetual preferred stock that does not qualify for inclusion in tier 1 capital, mandatory convertible securities and other hybrid capital instruments, long-term preferred stock with an original term of twenty years or more, and limited amounts of term subordinated debt, intermediate-term preferred stock, and unrealized holding gains on qualifying equity securities.

The sum of tier 1 and tier 2 capital, less any deductions, makes up the total capital.

Each balance-sheet asset and off-balance-sheet item falls under one of four broad risk categories based on the perceived credit risk of the obligor, guarantor, or type of collateral. These risk categories have assigned risk weights of 0 percent, 20 percent, 50 percent, and 100 percent. Table 3.6 displays the risk weights and asset categories. One multiplies the appropriate dollar value of the assets in each category by the risk weight associated with that category, and then adds together the resulting risk-weighted values for all of the risk categories. The resulting sum is the bank's total risk-weighted assets.

Off-balance-sheet items integrate into the risk-weighted assets through a two-step process. First, one calculates an on-balance-sheet credit-equivalent amount by multiplying the face amount of the off-balance-sheet item by a credit-conversion factor (see Table 3.7). One can then categorize the credit-equivalent amount in the same manner as on-balance-sheet items.

For a derivative contract; that is, a contract that derives its value from the underlying assets or from an index such as an index of interest rates or exchange rates, the credit-equivalent amount is equal to the sum of the current exposure of the contract and the estimated potential future credit exposure. The marked-to-market value of the contract determines the current exposure. If the marked-to-market value is positive, then the current exposure is equal to that value. If the marked-to-market value is zero or negative, the current exposure is zero. One can estimate the potential future credit exposure of a contract by multiplying the notional principal amount of the contract by a credit-conversion factor. Table 3.8 displays the conversion factors.

The calculation of capital and risk-weighted assets determines whether the bank meets the minimum capital standards. First, one calculates the risk-based capital ratio, defined as $TC/TRWA$, where TC is the total capital and $TRWA$ is the total risk-weighted assets. Bank examiners compare a bank's capital ratios to regulatory minimums and with peer-group averages. Banks must have a minimum capital ratio of 8 percent, with at least 4 percent taking the form of tier 1 capital. Risk-based capital does not take explicit account of other types

TABLE 3.6 | *Risk Weights and Asset Categories*

Risk Weight (%)	Credit Risk Exposure	Example of Assets in Category
0	Zero	Direct obligations of the federal government. (Examples: cash, U.S. Treasury securities, mortgage-backed securities issued by the Government National Mortgage Association)
20	Low	Indirect obligations of the federal government, full faith and credit municipal securities, and domestic depository institutions. (Examples: federal agency securities, municipal general obligation bonds)
50	Moderate	Loans secured by one- to four-family properties and municipal securities secured by revenues for a specific project (Examples: residential mortgages, municipal revenue bonds)
100	High	Other claims on private borrowers (Examples: commercial loans, corporate bonds, loans to less developed countries)

Source: *Commercial Bank Examination Menu*, Board of Governors of the Federal Reserve System, Washington, D.C., 1999.

TABLE 3.7	Conversion Factors for Off-Balance-Sheet Items
Conversion Factor (%)	Examples of Off-Balance-Sheet Items
100	Standby letters of credit issued to back repayment of commercial paper
50	Standby letters of credit that guarantee a customer's future performance and unused bank loan commitments covering periods longer than one year
20	Standby letters of credit backing the issue of state and local government general obligation bonds Trade-based commercial letters of credit and bankers' acceptances
0	Loan commitments with less than one year in remaining maturity, guarantees of federal or central government borrowings

TABLE 3.8 | Conversion Factors for Derivative Contracts (in Percent)

TYPES OF DERIVATIVE CONTRACT

Remaining Maturity of Contract	Interest Rates	Foreign Exchange Rate and Gold	Equity	Precious Metals (excluding gold)	Other Commodities (excluding precious metals)
One year or less	0.0	1.0	6.0	7.0	10.0
One to five years	0.5	5.0	8.0	7.0	12.0
Over five years	1.5	7.5	10.0	8.0	15.0

of risks such as interest rate, liquidity, market, or operational risks, however, so examiners generally expect banks to operate with capital positions above the minimum ratios. Banks that do not meet the minimum have to develop and implement plans for achieving adequate levels of capital.

Another requirement is that a bank must have a tier 1 leverage ratio of at least 3 percent; the **tier 1 leverage ratio** is the ratio of tier 1 capital to total average assets. An institution operating at or near this level ought to have well-diversified risk, including no undue interest rate risk exposure, excellent asset quality, high liquidity, and good earnings. Table 3.9 (see p. 58) shows an example of capital and leverage ratios.

In addition to looking at those ratios, bank examiners also use the CAMELS system to rate the quality of a bank's operations. **CAMELS** is a numerical rating system based on the examiner's judgment of the bank's **C**apital adequacy, **A**sset quality, **M**anagement quality, **E**arnings record, **L**iquidity position, and **S**ensitivity to market risk.[6] The rating scale ranges from 1 to 5, with 1 indicating strong performance and 5 unsatisfactory performance. Banks with a composite CAMELS rating of 4 or 5 receive examinations more frequently than banks with a rating of 1 or 2.

[6]The original CAMEL rating system was adopted in 1979. It is maintained by the Federal Financial Institutions Examination Council. Starting on January 1, 1997, a sixth rating component was added to address sensitivity to market risk; hence, the CAMELS system.

TABLE 3.9 | *Example of Capital and Leverage Ratios*

Assets	Amount ($ millions)	Risk Weighting (%)	Risk-Weighted Amount ($ millions)
Cash	15	0	0
Treasury securities	300	0	0
Balances at domestic banks	15	20	3
Municipal general obligation bonds	20	20	4
Residential mortgages	100	50	50
Commercial loans	300	100	300
Credit-equivalent amount of off-balance-sheet items	150	100	150
Total	900		507
Tier 1 capital	30.42		
Total capital	45.63		

$$\text{Tier 1 capital ratio} = \frac{\$30.42}{\$507} = 6\%$$

$$\text{Total capital ratio} = \frac{\$45.63}{\$507} = 9\%$$

$$\text{Tier 1 leverage ratio} = \frac{\$30.42}{\$900} = 3.38\%$$

Capital Requirements for Market Risk

The risk–based capital standards primarily address bank exposure to credit risk. With the increased prominence of trading activities at many large banking institutions, regulators have imposed a new requirement, known as the **market risk rule**, that sets minimum capital standards for market risk exposure. **Market risk** is the risk of loss from adverse movements in interest rates, exchange rates, equity prices, and commodity prices. Because the market risk rule principally addresses the market risk arising from trading activities (in fixed–income securities, foreign exchange, equity, and commodity contracts), only large banks with significant amounts of trading activity have to meet market risk requirements. In particular, the standards require any bank or bank holding company, with trading account positions exceeding either $1 billion or 10 percent of its total assets, to measure market risk with its own internal value–at–risk (VaR) model and to hold a commensurate amount of capital. The market risk rule became effective as of January 1998.

The requirements distinguish between general market risk and specific risk. General market risk is the risk that arises from movements in the general level of underlying market factors such as interest rates, foreign exchange rates, equity prices, and commodity prices. **Specific risk** is the risk of an adverse movement in the price of an individual security resulting from factors related to the security issuer. Thus, debt and equity securities in bank trading portfolios have specific risks.

As mentioned previously, the output of a bank's internal value-at-risk model determines the capital requirements for general market risk. A **value-at-risk (VaR)** model produces an estimate of the maximum amount that the bank can lose on a particular portfolio over a given holding period with a given degree of statistical confidence. VaR estimates, calibrated to a 10-day, 99th percentile standard, determine the general market risk capital requirement. For example, if the 10-day, 99th percentile VaR estimate is $10 million, then the bank expects to lose more than $10 million in only 1 out of 100 10-day periods. The capital requirement for general market risk equals the average VaR estimate over the previous 60 trading days multiplied by a scaling factor, which generally equals to three.

Capital requirements for specific risk cover the risk of adverse price movements resulting from factors related to the issuer of a security. A scaling factor of four determines the specific risk related capital requirements. The scaling factor could be adjusted when market practice evolves and banks can demonstrate that their specific risk modeling adequately addresses both idiosyncratic risks and event risks that a VaR model might not have captured.

New Capital Accord

We have just discussed that, under the Basel Capital Accord of 1988 (also known as Basel I), banks must set aside capital to meet requirements for credit risk. Starting in 1996, banks must meet trading-book requirements (market risk rule) as well. In 2001, the Basel Committee on Banking Supervision released a consultation package setting out details for the **New Capital Accord**, or **Basel II**, to promote the safety and soundness of the global banking system. Basel II introduces a more comprehensive approach to addressing risk, placing more emphasis on banks' internal risk methodologies, supervisory review, and market discipline. Basel II will take effect in 2006. Bank for International Settlements publishes detailed information on Basel II on its Web site (**http://www.bis.org**).

Basel II has three pillars:

○ Pillar 1 covers minimum capital requirements for market, credit, and operational risks.

○ Pillar 2 covers supervisory review.

○ Pillar 3 covers market discipline.

Under Pillar 1, minimum capital requirements for market risk are similar to those under Basel I. Pillar 1 sets new capital requirements for credit risk (more risk sensitive) and operational risk. The new credit risk requirements will be much more closely tied to the riskiness of particular exposures. Basel II aims at establishing a system that is more risk sensitive than Basel I. Thus, banks have incentive to pursue more sophisticated and effective risk-management techniques. Many banks in the developed nations have begun to develop their own

Internal Ratings Based (IRB) approach to assess the credit risk in their port-folios, under which banks have to estimate the probability of default associated with each borrower and the amount of losses if default occurs. Another new component for minimum capital requirements is operational risk, the risk of loss resulting from inadequate or failed internal processes, people and systems or from external events. Banks must establish a system to effectively manage operational risk and quantify the risk exposure. The total minimum capital requirement will be the sum of the requirements for credit risk, operational risk, and the current trading-book charge.

Pillar 2 aims at ensuring that financial institutions have adequate capital. Regulators will require banks to operate with capital above a Pillar 1 mini-mum. Pillar 2 also gives local regulators considerable discretion. It is therefore possible that different regulators take different approaches. Also, some countries may introduce Pillar 2 gradually.

Pillar 3 focuses on market discipline via disclosure requirements. Basel II distinguishes between required and recommended disclosures. Banks must dis-close required disclosure to qualify for a particular regulatory capital treatment; for example, to use the IRB approach. Recommended disclosures are disclo-sures that Basel II wants institutions to make in the interest of transparency. Financial institutions need to indicate in the disclosure information whether a reasonable investor would consider the matter important. In addition, under Pillar 3, banks that use internal methods for setting the Pillar 1 capital require-ments must disclose information on the nature of the procedures covered by the approach. Another area of quantitative disclosure covers the performance of the bank's rating process.

Deposit Insurance

The Federal Deposit Insurance Corporation (FDIC; **http://www.fdic.gov**) insures bank deposits up to $100,000 per account. The FDIC uses a risk-based system to assess deposit insurance premiums for the deposit insurance funds— the Bank Insurance Fund (BIF) and the Savings Association Insurance Fund (SAIF). The FDIC assigns each institution to one of nine risk categories based on its capital ratios (the capital group assignment) and other relevant informa-tion (supervisory subgroup assignment).

There are three capital groups, defined as follows:

○ Group 1 (well capitalized): The institution's total risk-based capital ratio is at least 10 percent, its tier 1 risk-based capital ratio equals or exceeds 6 per-cent, and its tier 1 leverage ratio equals or exceeds 5 percent.

○ Group 2 (adequately capitalized): The institution is below the well-capitalized level; its total risk-based capital ratio equals or exceeds 8 percent, its tier 1 capital ratio equals or exceeds 4 percent, and its tier 1 leverage ratio equals or exceeds 4 percent.

○ Group 3 (undercapitalized): The institution is worse than adequately capitalized.

After an examination and a review of pertinent information, the FDIC also assigns each BIF or SAIF institution to a supervisory subgroup based on its CAMELS rating:

○ Subgroup A: Financially sound institutions with a primary federal regulator's composite rating of 1 or 2.

○ Subgroup B: Weaker institutions with problems that, if not corrected, could result in significant deterioration. This group generally corresponds to the primary federal regulator's composite rating of 3.

○ Subgroup C: Institutions that pose a substantial probability of loss to the BIF or the SAIF unless those institutions take effective corrective actions. This group generally corresponds to the primary federal regulator's composite rating of 4 or 5.

The deposit insurance rate schedule for BIF and SAIF insured institutions is between 0 and 27 cents per $100 in assessable deposits, as shown in Table 3.10.

TECHNOLOGY IN BANKING

Technological advances including automatic teller machines (ATMs), telephone banking, personal computer (PC) banking, check imaging, and Internet banking have fundamentally changed the way banks conduct business. Consumers show strong preferences for transacting certain types of business electronically, such as paying bills, booking airline tickets, trading securities, and purchasing consumer products.

Telephone and PC Banking

Telephone banking enables customers to bank from home: they can pay bills by phone, transfer funds from one account to another, or just check an account balance anytime. PC banking provides an easy and convenient way for customers to access their accounts using a popular financial software package such as the bank's own proprietary software, Microsoft® Money®, or Quicken®. With PC banking, clients can check balances; confirm which checks, deposits, withdrawals, and ATM activities have cleared the account; keep track of credit

| TABLE 3.10 | *Deposit Insurance Rate Schedule (in basis points)* | | | |

SUPERVISORY SUBGROUP ASSIGNMENT

Capital Ratio Assignment	A	B	C
Well capitalized	0	3	17
Adequately capitalized	3	10	24
Undercapitalized	10	24	27

Source: *Risk-based assessment system—Current assessment rate schedule*, Federal Deposit Insurance Corporation.

card transactions; transfer funds between accounts; and communicate with the bank through electronic messages.

Check Imaging

Check processing is one of the most costly divisions of any bank. Through check imaging, banks use technology to help reduce costs. Special cameras, installed on the check-sorting devices, are used to create digital images of the checks to be processed. The banks next use images rather than paper in processing, which facilitates the rapid distribution of check information. Customers receive check images with their statements and an image archive replaces microfilm storage of checks with electronic storage. Thus, imaging technology streamlines the processing environment and provides banks with new capabilities that can be leveraged into new products and services.

Internet Banking

Banking on the Internet means a home computer can access a virtual 24-hour bank branch. With **Internet banking**, customers can dash off checks to anyone, anytime. The Internet also enables financial institutions to offer 24-hour lending services with immediate lending approval. Applicants can apply over the Internet while talking live with agents to obtain answers to questions or assistance in completing loan applications.

Many banks—including such major banks as Citibank, J.P. Morgan Chase, Wells Fargo, and Bank of America—offer their customers Internet banking as well as branches. On the other hand, a few Internet-based banks do not offer branch services to customers. Examples include NetBank (**http://www.net-bank.com**) and E*Trade Bank (**http://www.etradebank.com**).

CREDIT RISK AND LIQUIDITY RISK MANAGEMENT

Banks face credit, market, liquidity, and operation risks. As we have seen, credit risk arises from the possibility of default by counterparties, whereas market risk is the potential that the value of financial assets may decline due to a change in market prices or interest rates. **Liquidity risk** refers to the possibility that a bank will not have sufficient funds to meet its payout obligations. **Operation risk** is the possibility that employee error or system failure will occur.

This section covers credit and liquidity risk management, and the next two sections focus on the management of market risk and operation risk. Banks seek opportunities to take credit risk prudently and manage it effectively in order to create value for their shareholders. Efficient liquidity management enables banks to meet their cash needs and make new investments.

Credit Risk Management

Traditionally, the primary risk of banks has been credit risk that arises from the possibility that a borrower or counterparty will fail to meet its contractual obligations. It is important to realize that credit losses per se are not risky. A bank can factor predictable losses into its prices and covers them as a normal cost of doing business. The volatility of losses presents the most risk and is therefore the primary concern of credit risk management.

Credit risk management begins by measuring the default risk associated with all credit exposures, including loans, receivables, lending commitments, derivative contracts, and foreign exchange contracts. Management of consumer credit risk begins with an internal model that projects credit quality and establishes credit-underwriting standards. Ideally, the development phase of a consumer product establishes risk parameters. The cost of credit risk then integrates into the product's profit dynamics. For commercial credit risk, most banks manage to diversify exposures by obligator, risk grade, industry, product, and geographic location. Some banks also securitize some of their loans and sell off pieces to other investors.[7] But securitization requires homogeneous assets; assets with widely different characteristics and terms are difficult to securitize. Credit default swaps allow banks to isolate, price, and trade firm-specific credit risk by unbundling a basket of loans and transferring each component risk to those best suited or most interested in managing it. A **credit default swap** is a privately negotiated contract with payoffs linked to a credit-related event, such as a default or a credit rating downgrade. For example, in June 1997, an international bank that already had a basket of 20 loans, totaling more than $500 million to mostly investment-grade companies, wanted to lend more money to the same companies. J.P. Morgan sold the bank the right to require J.P. Morgan to pay off any of the loans if a borrower goes bankrupt. J.P. Morgan could retain the default risks in its portfolio and collect the premium, or sell them to institutional investors such as insurance companies, hedge funds, or other banks. Meanwhile, J.P. Morgan's client retains the actual loans and the customer relationship.

For risk management purposes, off-balance-sheet exposures are converted to loan-equivalent amounts. With respect to derivatives and foreign exchange contracts, banks utilize those instruments during the normal course of business. Although derivative and foreign exchange markets most frequently use **notional principal**, the nominal value used to calculate payments of financial contracts, as a volume measure, it is not a useful measure of credit risk. The notional principal typically does not change hands, but is simply a quantity for the calculation of interest and other payments. Commonly, the value of a derivative or a foreign exchange contract is marked-to-market. A positive marked-to-market value indicates that the counterparty owes the bank money, so the bank faces a repayment risk. When the marked-to-market value is negative, the bank owes the counterparty and thus does not have repayment risk. When a bank has more than one transaction with a particular counterparty, and there is a legally enforceable master netting agreement, the net marked-to-market exposure represents the netting of the positive and negative exposures with the same counterparty. Net marked-to-market exposure is a good

---

[7]Chapter 13 provides detailed coverage of the subject.

measure of credit risk under such circumstances. Major banks generally disclose their net marked-to-market exposures by customer type and credit rating in their annual reports.

Liquidity Risk Management

One of the most important tasks facing the management of any bank is to ensure adequate liquidity. Liquidity risk is the risk that the bank may be unable to meet a financial commitment to a customer, creditor, or investor when due. Lack of adequate liquidity is one of the first signs that a bank is in financial difficulties. The troubled bank begins to lose deposits, which erodes its supply of cash and forces the institution to dispose of its liquid assets. Other banks become reluctant to lend to the troubled bank. Eventually, the bank teeters on the brink of failure.

Liquidity management provides the proper mix of core and noncore deposits and capital to ensure sufficient funding for anticipated obligations and planned asset generation. **Core deposits**—stable deposits that are not highly rate sensitive—are a major source of liquidity for banking operations. Core deposits include savings accounts, checking accounts, money market accounts, and time deposits of less than $100,000. Liquidity can also be obtained through the issuance of commercial paper, medium-term notes, long-term debt, and preferred and common stock.

Marketable securities and other short-term investments can be readily converted to cash, if needed. In addition, loan syndication networks and securitization programs facilitate the timely disposition of assets and the obtaining of necessary liquidity.

MARKET RISK MANAGEMENT

The increasing importance of market risk has prompted the Federal Financial Institutions Examination Council to revise the financial institutions rating system. As explained earlier, in January 1997, a sixth component called "sensitivity to market risk" was added by the Federal Financial Institutions Examination Council to the original CAMEL rating system. Market risk is the exposure to an adverse change in the value of financial instruments as a result of changes in market factors such as interest rates, foreign exchange rates, securities prices, and commodity prices. For most banks without active foreign exchange or trading transactions, interest rate risk is the most significant type of market risk exposure arising from their asset-liabilities activities. **Interest rate risk** is the exposure to adverse changes in rates that affect revenues such as net interest income, securities gains/losses, and other rate-sensitive income/expense items. A variety of sources contribute to interest rate risk, including differences in timing between the maturities or the repricing of assets, liabilities, and derivatives. For example, changes in market interest rates affect a bank's net interest income, because the repricing characteristics of loans and other interest-earning assets do not necessarily match those of deposits or borrowings. Banks expose themselves to **basis risk**, which is the difference in the pricing characteristics of two instruments. For example, a bank faces basis risk when the prime rate determines its lending interest rate, but the interest rate it pays for funds changes with the LIBOR.[8] This section reviews several measures used in risk management, including gap analysis, duration gap analysis, and the value-at-risk approach.

Gap Analysis

Gap analysis is the simplest way of representing the interest rate risk component of market risk. Assets and liabilities are placed in gap intervals based on their repricing dates. The Fed requires commercial banks to report the repricing gaps for assets and liabilities with the following maturities:

1. One day.
2. More than one day to three months.
3. More than three months to six months.
4. More than six months to twelve months.
5. More than one year to five years.
6. More than five years.

One can calculate the net gap for each time period by subtracting the repriced liabilities in that interval from the repriced assets. A positive gap, with more assets repricing than liabilities, will benefit earnings in a rising interest rate environment because assets will earn more interest income. At the same time, interest expense will not rise as much. A positive gap will depress earnings in a declining interest rate environment because interest income will decrease by a larger amount than interest expense. Conversely, a negative gap will benefit earnings when interest rates fall and have the potential to depress earnings when interest rates rise. Here is a summary of these relationships:

Net Gap	Change in Interest Rates	Change in Net Interest Income
Positive	Increase	Increase
Positive	Decrease	Decrease
Negative	Increase	Decrease
Negative	Decrease	Increase
Zero	Increase	None
Zero	Decrease	None

Because this model bases the gap on a specific time point, there are actually two gaps: a periodic and a cumulative gap. The periodic gap compares rate-sensitive assets with rate-sensitive liabilities across a single point in time. The cumulative gap compares rate-sensitive assets with rate-sensitive liabilities over the time horizon from the present up to the designated time point.

---

[8]The prime rate is the base rate for loans to a bank's financially strong borrowers. LIBOR is the London InterBank Offered Rate, which is the interest rate major banks in London charge each other for borrowings.

TABLE 3.11	Repricing Gaps ($ millions)		
	Assets	Liabilities	Gaps
1 day	60	90	−30
1 day–3 months	90	120	−30
3 months–6 months	210	255	−45
6 months–12 months	270	210	60
1 year–5 years	120	90	30
Over 5 years	30	15	15

Table 3.11 shows an example of repricing gaps. The one-day gap indicates a negative $30 million difference between assets and liabilities being repriced in one day. The bank has borrowed more one-day funds than it has lent. If the overnight interest rate increases by 5 basis points, the annualized interest income will increase by $30,000. However, the annualized interest expense will increase by $45,000, resulting in a decrease in net interest income of $15,000.[9]

Duration Gap Analysis

Gap analysis is a useful tool for protecting against interest rate changes, but it does not fully account for the bank's equity value. Hence, management uses **duration gap analysis** to examine how the market value of shareholder equity will change when interest rates change. Duration gap analysis compares the price sensitivity of a bank's total assets with that of its total liabilities. The differential impact between these two is the resulting change in the market value of equity.

One can calculate duration as a weighted average of the time until the receipt of the cash flows. Chapter 10 covers the technical aspect of duration. In this chapter, we will use the duration concept to analyze the changes in bank equity value as a result of interest rate changes. Suppose D denotes duration, y the interest rate, and P the initial price. For any given change in interest rate, the change in value of the instrument equals approximately

$$\boxed{3.2} \qquad - D \times [\Delta y/(1 + y)] \times P,$$

where Δy is the change in interest rate; Δy is positive if the rate increases and negative if the rate declines.

Applying this formula to duration gap analysis, the change in the bank's net worth for any given change in interest rate is

$$\boxed{3.3} \qquad \left(- D_A \times \frac{\Delta y}{(1 + y)} \times A \right) - \left(- D_L \times \frac{\Delta y}{(1 + y)} \times L \right),$$

[9]One basis point is one-hundredth of 1 percent.

where A denotes assets, L denotes liabilities, and D_A and D_L indicate the duration of assets and liabilities, respectively. The first term in Equation 3.3 denotes the change in asset value, and the second term denotes the change in the value of liabilities. The formula can be simplified to

3.4
$$\frac{-\Delta y}{(1+y)} \times A \times \left(D_A - D_L \times \frac{L}{A} \right).$$

As shown in the above expression, a bank's interest rate risk relates to the size of the interest rate change, the size of the bank, and the leverage-adjusted duration gap. The duration gap provides information about how the market value of shareholder equity will change when interest rates change. A positive duration gap, in which the duration of assets (D_A) exceeds the duration of liabilities (D_L) adjusted for the ratio of liabilities to assets, will increase shareholder value in a declining interest rate environment and will depress shareholder value in a rising interest rate environment. Conversely, a negative duration gap will benefit equity value in a rising interest rate environment but will depress value in a declining interest rate environment. These relationships are:

Net Duration Gap	Change in Interest Rates	Change in Shareholder Equity
Positive	Increase	Decrease
Positive	Decrease	Increase
Negative	Increase	Increase
Negative	Decrease	Decrease
Zero	Increase	None
Zero	Decrease	None

As an example, a bank manager has calculated that the duration of assets is 5 years and the duration of liabilities is 4 years. The manager learns from the bank's economic forecast that interest rates should go up by 30 basis points, from 8.00 percent to 8.30 percent. The bank has total assets of $500 million, liabilities of $400 million, and shareholder equity of $100 million. The increase in interest rates will result in a decline in bank value of $2.5 million:

3.5
$$\frac{-\Delta y}{(1+y)} \times A \times \left(D_A - D_L \times \frac{L}{A} \right)$$

$$= \frac{-0.003}{(1+0.08)} \times \$500m \times \left(5 - 4 \times \frac{\$400m}{\$500m} \right) = -\$2.5m.$$

However, gap analysis cannot reveal the impact of such factors as new pricing strategies for consumer and business deposits, changes in balance-sheet mix, or the effects of various options embedded in balance-sheet instruments. Therefore, a bank usually supplements a gap analysis with simulations under a variety of interest rate scenarios.

Market Risk Management

As we have seen, gap analysis captures interest rate risk, but market risk also arises from adverse changes in foreign exchange rates, commodity prices, and equities prices. The common representation of market risk is the value-at-risk (VaR) measure. Banks, in their annual reports, disclose their interest rate VaR, foreign exchange VaR, commodities VaR, and equities VaR for each market factor. Since prices do not move in the same direction and by the same proportion, typically a portfolio benefits from a diversification effect that will lower the VaR of the whole portfolio. That is, the portfolio VaR is less than the sum of the component VaRs.

The VaR can be estimated using several methods, including historical simulation, the parametric approach, and Monte Carlo simulation. Under the historical simulation approach, one can construct the distribution of profits and losses by using the observed past changes in the market factors during each of the last 250 trading days to calculate the values of the current portfolio.[10] This results in the building of 250 sets of hypothetical market factors using their current values and the changes that occurred during the time period. One can use these hypothetical values to compute 250 hypothetical marked-to-market portfolio values. Comparing those 250 hypothetical portfolio values with the current value of the portfolio produces 250 profits and losses on the portfolio. Once the calculation of hypothetical marked-to-market profit or loss for each of the last 250 trading days occurs, the distribution of profits and losses and the VaR can then be calculated.

The parametric approach assumes that the underlying market factors have a multivariate normal distribution. Therefore, the distribution of marked-to-market portfolio profits and losses is also normal. A key step in this approach is risk mapping, which entails taking the actual instruments and mapping them into a set of simpler, standardized positions or instruments. Each of these standardized positions connects with a single market factor. In essence, for any actual portfolio, risk mapping finds a portfolio of standardized positions that is equivalent to the original portfolio. This portfolio of standardized positions has the same sensitivities to changes in the values of the market factors. The VaR of that equivalent portfolio can then be calculated.

In many respects, the Monte Carlo simulation approach is similar to historical simulation. The main difference is that, rather than using the observed past changes in the market factors over the last N trading days, the Monte Carlo simulation relies on a chosen statistical distribution that its proponents believe adequately captures or approximates the possible changes in the market factors. Then, a random number generator creates thousands or tens of thousands of hypothetical changes in the market factors. These changes help to calculate thousands of hypothetical profits or losses on the current portfolio and to construct the distribution of possible portfolio profit or loss. Finally, this distribution determines the VaR.

---

[10]The time period used is generally one year, so the number of days used is often about 250.

Although VaR estimates a bank's exposure to market risk factors in normal markets, it does not capture the risk of unlikely, but still plausible, events in abnormal markets. Hence, many institutions include stress tests in their market risk management process. Effective stress tests involve changes in market rates and prices that result from prespecified financial scenarios, including both historical and hypothetical market events. Continuous review and updating of stress scenarios are key to the success of stress testing.

OPERATION RISK MANAGEMENT

Banks, like all large corporations, face various types of operating risks. Examples include fraud by employees, unauthorized transactions by employees and customers, and errors related to computer or communications systems. The experience of the Bank of New York in 1985 demonstrates the significance of operation risk. During a computer malfunction, the Bank of New York could accept deliveries of securities, but it could not make them. The Bank had to pay out funds when accepting deliveries of securities on behalf of its clients, but it could not take in any money because it could not deliver the securities out to counterparties. The bank had to borrow $22.5 billion from the New York Fed to cover the deficit created by the snafu. In recent years, the advent of the euro and Y2K issues raised the possibility of even more costly problems.

European Economic and Monetary Union

On January 1, 1999, the European Economic and Monetary Union (EMU) took effect (Chapter 17 provides a detailed discussion of the EMU), and introduced the new common currency, the euro (€). The exchange rates of the currencies of the 12 participating countries (Austria, Belgium, Finland, France, Germany, Greece, Ireland, Italy, Luxembourg, the Netherlands, Portugal, and Spain; Greece joined in 2000) were fixed irrevocably. Until 2002, the national currencies and the new euro coexisted. During the three-year transition period from 1999 to 2002, banks that had exposure to the euro, whether through foreign exchange business, custodial services, cash management, or funds transfer services, had to have the capability to service clients in both national currency units and in euros. The costs for a large bank ran into the tens of millions of dollars.

Year 2000

The year 2000 problem (Y2K) involved the ability of time-sensitive computer systems to recognize the date change from December 31, 1999, to January 1, 2000, and the worldwide challenge that ensued. Banks, the core of the financial system, not only had to assess and modify their own computer systems and business processes to ensure that they would continue to function but also had to assess the readiness of third parties with which they interfaced.

In addition to internal upgrading and testing, banks and securities firms participated in many tests with customers and in industry-wide (street) testing.

Street testing covered agencies such as the New York Fed, Depositary Trust Company, Automated Clearing House, Clearing House Interbank Payments System, Government Securities Clearing Corporation, National Securities Clearing Corporation, Mortgage Backed Securities Clearing Corporations, Society for Worldwide Interbank Financial Telecommunication (SWIFT), Clearstream, Euroclear, and others. Such testing was crucial since a failure of external interface could have a material adverse effect on a bank's operations. Banks also carried out major customer and business partner due diligence. Most large banks incorporated Y2K customer risks into their credit risk analysis and their credit and liquidity planning.

The banking industry prepared itself well for Y2K problems because of the close monitoring by many regulatory agencies. Nevertheless, central banks engaged in additional concrete actions, as well as public relations gestures. The Federal Reserve took several measures to prevent Y2K disasters:

- Making up to $200 billion in extra currency available.

- Setting up a special Y2K credit window for banks to borrow extra reserves. Extending the maturity of some repurchase agreements with primary dealers and expanding the collateral used in repos to include mortgage-backed securities such as Ginnie Maes and Freddie Macs.

- Selling liquidity call options that give primary dealers the right to borrow substantial funds from the Federal Reserve if the federal funds rate rose above 7 percent.

Most major central banks took similar steps. All the preparations and efforts paid off. The dire predictions of technological chaos resulting from the Y2K problem proved almost empty.

CONCLUDING SUMMARY

Citigroup offers services in traditional banking; consumer finance; credit cards; investment banking; securities brokerage and asset management; and property, casualty, and life insurance to over 100 million customers in 100 countries around the world. This financial supermarket exemplifies the trend toward one-stop shopping in financial services.

Technology has received a great deal of attention and has revolutionized the way banks operate. The challenge for banks is to have a well thought out strategic plan for their online banking activities. The challenge for regulators is to ensure that customers have full security and privacy.

In another important development, banks have gained new powers. Bank holding companies can now establish securities subsidiaries to underwrite and deal in corporate debt and equity securities. As banks expand the menu of products and services they offer, credit risk has become only one of their significant risk exposures. Banks' exposure to market risk arises from changes in interest rates, foreign exchange rates, securities prices, and commodity prices. To protect against credit risk, bank regulators impose risk-based capital standards. Each balance-sheet asset and off-balance-sheet item falls into one of four broad risk categories based on the perceived credit risk. For market risk, banks use the value-at-risk approach. Banks must calculate the amount of value at risk arising from each of the market factors. In addition, liquidity risk management and operation risk management are essential to successful banking operations.

Key Terms

bank holding company 45
basis risk 64
Basel II 59
CAMELS 57
core deposit 64
credit default swap 63
credit risk 55
duration gap analysis 66
gap analysis 65
Glass–Steagall Act 46
interest rate risk 64
Internet banking 62
liquidity risk 62
market risk 58

market risk rule 58
New Capital Accord 59
notional principal 63
operation risk 62
reserve requirements 51
section 20 subsidiaries 46
securities subsidiaries 47
specific risk 58
tier 1 capital 55
tier 2 capital 55
tier 1 leverage ratio 57
underwriting subsidiaries 46
value at risk (VaR) 59

Review Questions

1. What major roles do banks play in the financial system? Compare and contrast the traditional roles with the newer ones.

2. Bank holding companies have obtained new powers to underwrite and deal in securities. At the same time, regulators have imposed certain firewalls. What are the purposes of the firewalls?

3. Bank CBA has assets and capital as follows:

Assets	Amount ($ millions)
Cash	$ 12
Treasury securities	50
Balances due from domestic banks	22
Residential mortgages	100
Corporate loans	88
Off-balance-sheet credit-equivalent amount	38
Tier 1 capital	5
Tier 2 capital	8

   Does Bank CBA meet regulatory capital requirements?

4. Explain the CAMELS rating system.

5. A bank discloses that its total portfolio VaR is $26 million on December 31, 2002. This is based on a 1-day, 99th percentile standard. What does this mean?

6. How do CAMELS ratings integrate into the risk-based insurance premium system?

7. Asset securitization involves packaging bank assets and then selling them in the form of securities. Explain how securitization helps in the management of credit risk. Does it provide any benefits?

8. What is market risk? Does the market risk rule apply to every bank and thrift? Why or why not?

9. Discuss the major implications of the Gramm-Leach-Bliley Act of 1999.

10. What are the VaRs of the three largest U.S. banks? Compare their component VaRs and portfolio VaRs. Explain the differences between banks.

Select Bibliography

Berger, N. A., R. S. Demsetz, and P. E. Strahan. "The consolidation of the financial services industry: Causes, consequences, and implication for the future." *Staff Reports,* Federal Reserve Bank of New York, December 1998.

Cumming, C. M., and B. J. Hirtle. "The challenges of risk management in diversified financial companies." *Economic Policy Review* 7:1, Federal Reserve Bank of New York, 2001, pp. 1–17.

Federal Deposit Insurance Corporation. *History of the Eighties—Lessons for the Future.* Washington, D.C., 1997.

Galai, D., D. Ruthenberg, M. Sarnat, and B. Z. Schreber. *Risk Management and Regulation in Banking.* Hingham, Mass.: Kluwer, 1999.

Koch, T. W., and S. S. MacDonald. *Bank Management.* Fort Worth, Tex.: The Dryden Press, 2000.

Linsmeier, T. J., and N. D. Pearson. "Risk management: an introduction to value at risk." working paper, University of Illinois at Champaign-Urbana, 1996.

McLaughlin, S. "The impact of interstate banking and branching reform: Evidence from the states." *Current Issues in Economics and Finance* 1, no. 2, Federal Reserve Bank of New York (May 1995), pp. 1–6.

Radecki, L. J., and J. Wenninger. "Paying electronic bills electronically." *Current Issues in Economics and Finance* 5, no. 1, Federal Reserve Bank of New York (January 1999), pp. 1–6.

Rose, P. S. *Commercial Bank Management.* New York: McGraw-Hill, 1999.

Saunders, A. *Credit Risk Measurement: New Approaches to Value at Risk and Other Paradigms.* New York: John Wiley & Sons, 1999.

Terrile, J. G. *Y2K: Ready or Not?* Merrill Lynch Global Securities Research and Economics Group, July 1999.

Weinstein, S., N. E. Stroker, and R. W. Merritt. "Securitization and its impact on bank ratings." *Financial Services Special Report,* Fitch IBCA, March 1999.

Investment Banks

Traditionally, investment banks underwrote new securities and served as financial advisers for mergers and acquisitions. Today, investment banks face an intensely competitive environment, fostered by deregulation, particularly the Gramm–Leach–Bliley Act of 1999; by globalization, which has forced firms to maintain a presence in all of the world's major markets; and by technological advances, which create new products and new ways of delivering both new and old products. As a result, the scope of investment banking has expanded to comprise all major capital market activities, including underwriting, private placement, mergers and acquisitions, merchant banking, market making, proprietary trading, financial engineering, capital management, and securities services. In this chapter, we will examine all of these activities beginning with the traditional activities of underwriting and mergers and acquisitions. Of course, the investment banking business is inherently risky, so the chapter concludes with a discussion of how investment banks manage risk.

The objectives of this chapter are to provide an understanding of:
- The new market environment for investment banking.
- How investment banks underwrite a new security offering.
- The services investment bankers offer in mergers and acquisitions.
- The contributing factors behind the growth in financial engineering.
- The importance of research, sales, and trading to investment banking operations.
- Merchant banking and how it contributes to other areas of investment banking.
- The risks investment banks face and how they manage them.

MARKET OVERVIEW

Investment banks provide a variety of services such as helping corporations raise capital, advising on mergers and acquisitions, and trading with customers. As we have pointed out in earlier chapters, the financial services industry has undergone a dramatic restructuring. Investment banks, like other types of financial services firms, have pushed themselves to change and meet new challenges. The chairman of a major financial services firm—David Komansky of Merrill Lynch—has identified five qualities that a firm must have to achieve and maintain a leadership position in this uncertain and changing environment:[1]

1. A strong product line, because clients are increasingly demanding a full-service provider.
2. The ability to provide clients with an integrated solution to their financial needs.
3. A strong global presence.
4. Financial strength, which is necessary to retain the confidence of clients and maintain long-term relationships.
5. Integrity and teamwork, which are essential to creating trust and providing superior service.

Box 4.1 describes three investment banks that exemplify these qualities and have used them to succeed in the new environment.

Deregulation

Until 1999, the United States was the only developed country in the world that maintained legal barriers separating the various types of financial services. The Glass–Steagall Act of 1933 prohibited banks, insurance companies, and securities firms from merging with each other or from offering products and services provided by the other types of firms. Although deregulation in the late 1980s and early 1990s had chipped away some of the Glass–Steagall barriers, many restrictions still remained. By 1999, the three main segments of the financial services industry—banks, securities firms, and insurers—agreed that the barriers needed to be removed if U.S. firms were to compete effectively in the global arena. In 1999, Congress passed the Gramm-Leach-Bliley Act, which eliminated the Glass–Steagall restrictions.[2]

The new regulatory environment created by the 1999 statute has enabled investment banking houses to expand their activities and to offer a full menu of financial services to meet client demand. At the same time, however, investment banks face increased competition from other types of financial firms, including commercial banks, insurance companies, mutual fund groups, and

---

[1]David H. Komansky, "Building value in the securities industry," paper delivered at the Merrill Lynch Banking and Financial Services Investor Conference, New York, September 14, 1998.

[2]President Clinton signed the act into law in March 2000.

MARKETS IN ACTION   The Big Three U.S. Investment Banks

Morgan Stanley, Merrill Lynch, and Goldman Sachs are the three largest investment banks in the United States. They are also the preeminent investment banking firms in global financial markets. They hold the top ranks in most areas of the investment banking business.

Morgan Stanley formed as a result of the 1997 merger of Dean Witter, Discover & Co., and Morgan Stanley Group, Inc. This combination brought together world-class origination and distribution skills and a unique balance of institutional and retail capabilities. Morgan Stanley, which operates in twenty-three countries, maintains leadership positions in many of its businesses, including securities, asset management, and credit and transaction services. It is also a top-ranked firm in mergers and acquisitions, underwriting, and equity research. It has the highest market capitalization in the industry. It issues the Discover Card, which was started in 1985 and was marketed as the first value card, with no annual fees and a cash-back bonus. Discover Brokerage Direct is the firm's Internet brokerage unit.

Merrill Lynch provides investment, financing, advisory, insurance, and related services on a global basis. It became a public company in 1971. Its clients include individuals, small businesses, corporations, and governments. It is the largest securities firm in the United States, with 14,000 financial consultants. It is also the most global of all U.S. investment banks, operating in more than forty countries.

In 1995, Merrill acquired Smith New Court PLC to strengthen its equity sales, trading, and research capabilities around the world. In 1997, it purchased Mercury Asset Management, a firm based in the United Kingdom. The acquisition broadened its client base, investment capabilities, and asset management distribution system. In 1999, Merrill introduced a discount online brokerage unit. Clients have a wide range of options, including an Internet channel, for accessing information, financial planning, cash management, investment advice, asset and liability management, and e-commerce services.

Goldman Sachs is one of the best-run global investment banking and securities firms, providing a full range of investing, advising, and financing services worldwide. After more than a century as a private partnership, the firm became a public company in 1999. It has three principal business lines: investment banking, trading and principal investments, and asset management and securities services. The firm maintains a substantial and diversified client base, which includes corporations, financial institutions, governments, and wealthy individuals. Goldman Sachs does not operate a retail brokerage. It has made strategic investments in alternative trading systems to gain experience and participate in the development of this market. Goldman also provides online capabilities to its clients.

Source: Goldman Sachs, Merrill Lynch, and Morgan Stanley.

online service providers, which now can also offer a wider selection of services. Such competition affects investment banks' ability to attract and retain highly skilled individuals. It also puts pressure on the banks' ability to attract and retain clients and assets.

One-Stop Shopping and Consolidation

Investment banks meet the challenges of the new environment in several ways including expanding the services they offer and consolidating with other firms. We have already seen that commercial banks have united with insurers and securities firms to create financial supermarkets that offer one-stop shopping for all financial services needs. Investment banks have undergone a similar trend, driven both by the competition from other firms and by their corporate clients' desire to have financial advisers that can address all their needs, regardless of what types of instruments might be required.

Thus, investment banks have aggressively expanded the menu of services they provide, adding money lending, retail and institutional fund management, and trust services. Indeed, Wall Street firms now derive the majority of their revenues from sources other than the traditional investment banking activities. These other sources include trading and principal transactions, commissions, asset management, and securities services. In recent years, for example, at Goldman Sachs, Merrill Lynch, and Morgan Stanley, investment banking has accounted for no more than a third of total **net revenues** (total revenues minus interest expenses).

In addition, many investment banks look beyond their traditional client base of corporations and wealthy individuals. These banks have joined forces with retail brokerages to sell stock to small investors. As individuals have assumed more and more responsibility for their retirement savings, mutual fund sales have boomed. Hence, investment banks try to gain access to this growing market. The 1997 merger of the premier investment bank Morgan Stanley with Dean Witter Discover, the third largest retail brokerage firm, as described in Box 4.1, exemplifies this trend.

Globalization

In addition to expanding the products and services they offer at home, investment banks have also expanded geographically to become financial supermarkets to the world. With rapid advances in information technology and greater cooperation among financial regulators, the international capital markets have linked more closely. Larger sums of money move across national borders, and more countries have access to international finance. By going global, investment banks not only can serve their clients better but also can benefit greatly from the high growth potential of international markets. Regulatory frameworks in Japan, Europe, and developing countries have changed to accommodate and encourage private pension programs, more investments in securities, and greater participation by nonlocal firms.

Big Wall Street houses such as Goldman Sachs, Morgan Stanley, and Merrill Lynch all have a strong global presence and established leadership positions in core products. Although they are among a select few that have the ability to execute large, complex cross-border transactions, many other Wall Street firms also pursue a globalization strategy. As a result, U.S. firms have significantly increased their international securities activities, and U.S. investment banks have dominated global investment banking. Major U.S. houses earn between one-quarter and one-half of their revenues overseas. At the same time, foreign financial institutions have expanded their investment banking capabilities in the United States. Major foreign firms with operations in the United States include Deutsche Bank, Union Bank of Switzerland, HSBC, Credit Suisse First Boston, NatWest Markets, Nikko, Daiwa, and Nomura.

The Internet and Information Technology

The advent of the Internet and advances in information technology have aided all of the trends in investment banking discussed so far. As David Komansky, the chairman of Merrill Lynch, observed that, together, globalization and technology "have collapsed time and distance and opened a floodgate of opportunities for those who embrace them."[3]

The Internet and e-commerce have already changed—and will continue to change—the trading and distribution of securities. Many firms now use the Internet for extended trading in markets around the world. Communication with clients has also improved. Clients now have online access to research, mutual fund data, and valuation models twenty-four hours a day (see Box 4.2 on p. 78, for the Web sites of some major investment banks). Many firms now distribute security offerings online. In recent years, for example, online brokers such as Charles Schwab, E*Trade, and Wit SoundView have distributed security offerings online to retail customers, and Goldman Sachs has used its GS-Online system to distribute offerings via the Internet and other electronic means. Some have gone one step further to allocate shares of initial public offerings through online auctions. To increase their Internet capabilities, several investment banks have acquired or invested in e-commerce firms. For example, Goldman Sachs has invested in Bridge Information Systems, TradeWeb LLC, and Wit SoundView Group, and Merrill Lynch purchased D. E. Shaw's online trading division in 1999.

In addition to using the Internet, investment banks have developed software and information technology systems that enable them to enhance their service to clients, manage risk better, and improve overall efficiency and control. New software enables firms to tailor their research and services to each client's particular needs. By using the software, clients can gain immediate electronic access to all of a firm's products and services that might be of use. For example, at Goldman Sachs, clients and employees can use GS Financial Workbench to download research reports, access earnings and valuation models, submit trades, monitor accounts, build and view presentations, calculate prices for derivatives, and view market data. Most major investment banks provide similar services.

Technological advances have also enabled firms to design and price complex contracts and derivatives and to analyze their underlying risks. Every firm has software that enables it to monitor and analyze market and credit risks. Risk management software can not only analyze market risk at the firm, division, and trading desk levels, but can also break down the firm's risk into its underlying exposures. This permits management to evaluate the firm's exposure in the event of changes in interest rates, foreign exchange rates, equity

[3]David H. Komansky, "Merrill Lynch: At the threshold of a new world," paper delivered at the Goldman Sachs Financial Services Conference, New York, May 12, 1999.

MARKETS IN ACTION Major Investment Banks and Web Site Addresses

4.2

Investment Bank	Web Site Address
Bear Stearns	http://www.bearstearns.com
Credit Suisse First Boston	http://www.csfb.com
Deutsche Bank	http://www.db.com
E*Trade	http://www.etrade.com
Goldman Sachs	http://www.gs.com
J.P. Morgan	http://www.jpmorgan.com
Lehman Brothers	http://www.lehman.com
Merrill Lynch	http://www.ml.com
Morgan Stanley	http://www.morganstanley.com
Citigroup	http://www.citigroupgcib.com
SoundView	http://www.soundview.com
UBS Warburg	http://www.ubswarburg.com

prices, or commodity prices. Without such software, ventures into international markets and complex trading would be far riskier.

Finally, information technology has been a significant factor in improving the overall efficiency of investment banks (and many other businesses as well). Computerized and electronic trading is both more efficient and more accurate. Management now has real-time information on the firm's operations worldwide. This not only has made globalization possible but also provides for better decision-making and improves the firm's competitive edge.

UNDERWRITING

In a security offering, an investment bank plays three roles: adviser, underwriter, and salesperson. An investment banker advises an issuer as to the best timing for the offering, the size of the offering, and the optimal price of the transaction.[4] The investment banker also plays a major role in drafting the registration statement, which they file with the Securities and Exchange Commission. Beyond an advisory role, as an underwriter, the banker purchases the new issue and conducts a marketing program to sell and distribute the security to investors. Subsequent to the offering, the investment bank provides

---

[4]An investment banker who has established close relationships with corporate clients and brings in business is known as a rainmaker.

research and trading support for the company's security. This section describes the process for a typical new stock offering.

Preparing a Company to Go Public

Once a company has decided to float a security, the investment banker will advise the company on developing an organizational and capital structure that is relatively simple and can be understood by investors. The banker may also recommend a stock split or reverse split to bring the number of shares outstanding to a desirable level for a public offering. The company's needs determine the size of the offering, but it must be large enough to create sufficient interest within the investment community. An offering that is too small will be too illiquid to appeal to many investors. The offering price must also be tailored to the potential investors. Most consider the optimal range for most retail investors to be from $10 to $30 per share. Finally, proper timing is very important. Good market conditions should prevail at the time of the offering. During a down market, a company might have to sell the stock at a lower price, sell less stock than intended, or even postpone the offering.

Underwriting Syndicate

The company's investment bank also organizes the **underwriting syndicate**, which is a group of securities firms that purchases the entire block of the new security and redistributes the shares to investors. The lead or managing underwriter, the leading firm in the underwriting group, will head up this syndicate. Other members of the syndicate include the underwriting dealers and the selling group. Underwriting dealers commit their capital in the offering, while firms in the selling group simply act as brokers or simply help to sell the security and earn a commission. In a **firm commitment underwriting**, the underwriters purchase all of the new shares and resell them to investors. In contrast, in a **best-efforts underwriting**, the underwriters agree only to use their best efforts to sell the security on the issuer's behalf without any guarantee. In a firm commitment, the syndicate buys the total number of shares offered for an amount equal to the stated offering price, minus a percentage known as the **underwriting discount**. In addition, the underwriters usually have the right to exercise the **green shoe option**, also called overallotment, which enables them to purchase additional shares at an agreed-on price if there is strong demand for the new issue.

The managing underwriter often underwrites the largest percentage of the offering. The other syndicate members underwrite the balance. Each syndicate member receives an underwriting position based on its standing in the investment community and its ability to place securities. In this way, and through experience with other similar offerings, the managing underwriter can determine which syndicate member's orders are strongest and most likely to be placed with long-term investors. Hence, the managing underwriter can control the distribution of the stock and create a more orderly aftermarket. The **aftermarket** is the period after the new security begins trading during which members of the underwriting syndicate may not sell the security for less than the offering price.

Why does an investment bank organize a syndicate rather than underwrite the entire issue itself? By using a syndicate, the bank can ensure a broader distribution for the offering and potentially provide the impetus for other brokerage firms to initiate trading and research coverage for the new public company. The principal goals are to achieve broad recognition for the company and to create a strong aftermarket. In many cases, institutional interest and ownership set the tone for the valuation and trading of a company's stock and can contribute to the retail interest in an offering. The broader the retail and institutional support, the more stable the market for a company's stock, particularly in an initial public offering (IPO).

Filing the Registration Statement

Any new issue of securities must be registered with the Securities and Exchange Commission (SEC; **http://www.sec.gov**).[5] To do so, the company files a registration statement that discloses various kinds of important information about the company and the security for investors to consider when deciding whether to invest in the company.

The **registration statement** contains information about the company's business, its principal shareholders, its officers and directors, and their compensation. The company must also disclose the size of the offering, the intended use of the funds, and the risk factors. Audited financial statements must be included. Additional disclosures include the selling shareholders (if any), underwriting syndicate, type of underwriting, dividend policy, dilution, related-party transactions, and certain legal opinions. In a key portion of the filing, management discusses the company's financial condition, results of its operations, and its business plan.

Once the registration statement has been filed, SEC staff specialists review the statement to determine if it has made full and fair disclosure; in particular, they look for any misstatements or omissions of material facts that might prevent investors from making a fully informed investment decision. The SEC does not pass judgment on a proposed offering or evaluate its quality, however.

After reviewing the registration statement, the SEC typically sends the company a letter of comments concerning deficiencies and suggestions. Each comment must be addressed and resolved. If the SEC is satisfied with the amendments, it will declare the registration statement **effective**, meaning that the statement has been approved. Only then can the security be sold to investors.

The period of review of the registration statement is the waiting, or cooling-off, period. During the waiting period, the company or the underwriter has limits as to the activities it may undertake. Although the underwriting syndicate uses this time to try to arouse interest in the offering by distributing the preliminary prospectus and holding road shows, as described next, no actual sales can be made until the registration statement becomes effective.

---

[5]Most U.S. companies use Form S-1 to register with the SEC. Appendix B provides SEC Form S-1.

The Preliminary Prospectus

After the filing of the registration statement, the underwriting syndicate distributes a **preliminary prospectus** to brokers and prospective purchasers in an effort to arouse their interest in the offering. The preliminary prospectus is the main document the syndicate uses to sell the stock. As required by the SEC, however, the cover page must bear the caption "Preliminary Prospectus" in red ink (hence, a "Red Herring") and must state that the security may not be sold and that offers to buy may not be accepted prior to the time the registration statement becomes effective.

Under SEC rules, the preliminary prospectus may omit the offering price, the underwriting discount, and other details that depend on the offering price. Once the effective date arrives, the company adds the offering price and effective date to the prospectus. At that time, they issue the **final prospectus**. Table 4.1 lists the main items included in the final prospectus of Goldman Sachs, the last major investment bank to go public. They offered a total of 69 million shares, with the issue priced at $53.00, and the underwriting discount at $2.25 per share.

Road Shows

In addition to issuing the preliminary prospectus, the underwriting syndicate uses the waiting period to hold a series of road shows. A **road show** is a key marketing event in which representatives from the company's management meet with financial analysts and brokers to explain the company's market position, discuss how the company will execute its business plan, and show off the quality of the management team. Many analysts consider top management to be among the most important aspects of any company, and investors frequently base their purchasing decision on their perception of management.

TABLE 4.1	*Main Items Included in the Final Prospectus for Goldman Sachs*

1. Initial public offering of shares totaled 69 million shares
2. Initial public price per share: $53.00; underwriting discount: $2.25; proceeds to Goldman Sachs: $50.75 per share
3. List of representatives of the underwriting syndicate on the front and back cover pages
4. Prospectus summary
5. Risk factors
6. Use of proceeds
7. Audited financial reports
8. Management's discussion and analysis of financial condition and results of operations
9. Business and industry description
10. Management
11. Principal and selling holders
12. Related transactions
13. List of underwriters

The underwriters hope that the more potential purchasers learn about the company, the more likely they will be to purchase its shares—and thus improve its price performance in the aftermarket. The road show is also a kind of public opinion trial for the issuer's business plan. By the end of the road show, the managing underwriter should have a good idea of investors' interest and can use that information in determining the final price and size of the issue. An effective road show is crucial to the success of the offering.

Due Diligence and Effective Date

Before the registration statement becomes effective, the underwriter holds a due diligence meeting. The purpose of this meeting is to reduce the risk of liability associated with filing by ensuring that all material matters have been fully and fairly disclosed in the registration statement. Among other things, the participants list, gather, and authenticate such documents as the articles of incorporation, bylaws, and patents; check the completeness and accuracy of minutes; and verify the corporate existence.

In addition to holding the due diligence meeting, the underwriter must attend to several other matters in the period immediately before the registration statement becomes effective. There is no final determination of the size and price of the offering until this time. In establishing the size and price, the underwriter considers not only the indications of interest expressed by prospective investors but also such factors as the financial performance of the company, stock market conditions, prices of comparable companies, and the anticipated aftermarket demand. With the size and price set, the signing of the underwriting agreement, as well as the filing of the final amendment to the registration, ensues. This amendment includes the agreed-on price, the underwriting discount, and the net proceeds to the company. The underwriter typically requests that the offering be declared effective immediately upon the filing of the final amendment if the staff of the SEC's Division of Corporate Finance has no important reservations. The underwriter may then proceed with the sale of the security.

Aftermarket Support and Research

Immediately following an IPO, an aftermarket develops for the shares of the company's stock. Once the shares are in public hands, their price may go up or down on the basis of many factors, including ongoing demand for the stock, general market conditions, and most importantly, the company's performance. But in general, the offering price is lower than the aftermarket value. Such underpricing is a means of soliciting investor interest. Many institutional investors now expect such a discount in a new offering. Underpricing helps the underwriter as well. It reduces the risk of underwriting and gains the underwriter the gratitude of investors who purchase the IPO shares. It also reduces the possibility of shareholder lawsuits, which may be filed if there is a sharp decline in price.

Though an investment bank cannot make a stock price go up or down, it can write and disseminate research reports and sponsor timely investor meetings to help publicize the company's positive achievements. Such research can have a major impact on the stock price. It is common to see a strong demand when research coverage on a stock is initiated. Consequently, research capability is one of the key factors companies consider when selecting an underwriter.

Recently, however, many questioned Wall Street analysts' credibility. For example, New York State attorney general Eliot L. Spitzer's investigation revealed that even as Merrill Lynch's analysts advised investors to buy shares of certain companies, the analysts privately called these same companies' prospects doubtful. Many observers have pointed out that the fundamental problem is that many securities firms compensated their investment research analysts based on a formulaic percentage of investment banking revenues. To assure the independence and integrity of investment research, the Securities and Exchange Commission approved new ethics rules in May 2002. The rules require the securities firms to provide more detailed disclosure of conflicts and give lawyers and ethics officers at the firm a leading role in acting as gatekeepers between analysts and investment bankers. The rules also require analysts to disclose whether they or their firms hold stock in the companies under review and to list the percentage of all ratings that they have assigned to buy, hold, and sell categories. In addition, they must provide a chart that plots the historical price movements of a security and indicates the points at which the analyst began and changed ratings and price targets. Finally, the rules impose blackout periods that prohibit analysts from trading in the companies that they cover for thirty days before and five days after the publication of their research report.

The choice of exchange listing is part of the IPO process. The main securities trading markets are the New York Stock Exchange (NYSE; **http://www.nyse.com**), the American Stock Exchange (**http://www.amex.com**), the Nasdaq (**http://www.nasdaq.com**), and the regional exchanges such as the Boston, Cincinnati, and Pacific stock exchanges. The listing requirements vary from exchange to exchange. Each exchange publishes detailed requirements for listing on its Web site.

Underwriting Risks

When investment bankers underwrite an offering by firm commitment, they "sell" risk services to the issuers by assuming at least part of the risk associated with the offering, known as floating risk. A firm commitment becomes absolutely firm only after the signing of the underwriting agreement. The signing typically occurs just before the issue becomes effective. By then, all the marketing has been done, the road shows have been conducted, and the underwriter knows the degree of investor interests. The risk arises because the market may shift after a firm commitment on price has been made.

Floating risk consists of waiting risk, pricing risk, and marketing risk. During the waiting period, changes in the market environment often affect the

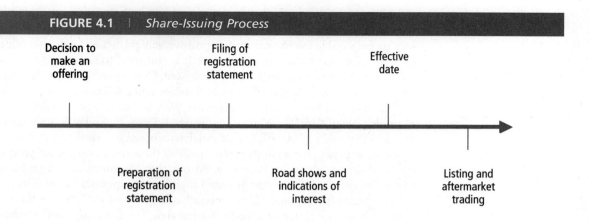

FIGURE 4.1 | *Share-Issuing Process*

offering price. The issuer mainly bears such waiting risk, but the introduction of **Rule 415 (Shelf Registration)** minimized this risk. This rule allows an issuer to file a single registration document indicating that it intends to sell a certain amount of securities at one or more times within the next two years.[6] In contrast, the underwriter bears the pricing risk and marketing risk exclusively. Pricing risk is the possibility that the market will decline after the signing of the underwriting agreement. Marketing risk is the possibility that the offering will not sell as anticipated. Marketing risk can be reduced by building a book of interests before the effective date and by aftermarket trading. Forming a syndicate in which each member takes only a portion of the offering also lessens the risk. Institutional sales are extremely important because they help investment bankers place large blocks of new issues.

Issuing Process Recapitulation

As this discussion has shown, the share–issuing process is complex and requires team effort. The process begins when the issuer decides to make an offering. The company then selects an underwriter to lead the offering. Next, they assemble a team consisting of the company's management, the company's counsel, the underwriter, its legal counsel, and independent accountants. The team then prepares the registration statement. During the waiting period, the underwriter schedules a series of road shows, and syndicate members solicit indications of interest from prospective investors. After the declaration of the registration as effective, investors buy shares, and aftermarket trading begins. Immediately after the issuance of a new stock, the company places a tombstone advertisement in financial newspapers such as the *Wall Street Journal* and the *Financial Times* that announces the particulars of the issue, including the amount of stock offered, its price, and the underwriters and dealers charged with its sale. Figure 4.1 illustrates the entire process.

---

[6]Shelf registration occurs primarily in debt issuance, and only rarely in stock flotation.

MERGERS AND ACQUISITIONS

Merger and acquisition (M&A) advice, like underwriting of equities and high-yield debt, is a high-margin business. For example, the $24 billion merger between Banc One and First Chicago in 1998 paid the advisers $53 million in merger fees. First Chicago's advisers, Lazard Freres and Goldman Sachs, each took in $16.5 million. Banc One's advisers, Merrill Lynch and Morgan Stanley, each received $10 million. Olivetti SpA's (Italy) hostile $65 billion bid for Telecom Italia SpA in 1999 produced as much as $200 million in fees for four investment banks. Mediobanca SpA, Lehman Brothers, Chase Manhattan, and DLJ shared the rewards from advising Olivetti, arranging loans, and selling bonds and stocks to finance the transaction.[7]

Investment banks frequently act as finders and/or financial advisers in M&As. Bankers are knowledgeable about potential sellers or buyers and are familiar with the terms of recent transactions; they are also adept at creating financing structures, arranging or providing bridge loans, offering fairness opinions, and conducting divestiture auctions. Clearly, M&As are a good business, because win, lose, or draw, they produce fees: fees for advising, fees for lending money, and fees for divesting unwanted assets.

Merger and Acquisition Fees

Fees are usually negotiable and contingent upon the success of the deal. In the past, the common fee schedule was the **Lehman 5-4-3-2-1** formula. Under this formula, 5 percent is paid on the first $1 million of sale price, 4 percent on the next $1 million, 3 percent on the next $1 million, 2 percent on the next $1 million, and 1 percent on the amount in excess of $4 million. For a large transaction, the fees are less than 1 percent of the deal's value. Currently, the fee is about 50 basis points for a $1 billion deal. For a $10 billion transaction, the fee might drop to 20–30 basis points. But there is no fixed rule; instead, the negotiation of fees takes place deal by deal.

Valuation Techniques

Valuation is an integral part of M&A advising. Many techniques exist to estimate the value of a business. They include discounted cash flow, comparable transactions, comparable company, breakup valuation, target stock price history, leveraged buyout analysis, multiple of revenues, book value, multiple of earnings, and liquidation analysis.

Many use the discounted cash flow (DCF) technique in evaluating internal growth investments and external acquisitions. It is a future-oriented approach that begins with a projection of the target's sales and operating profits. The determination of value occurs by evaluating the target company's cash flow projections and discounting those projections to the present value. Obviously, the usefulness of this technique depends on several assumptions,

---

[7]Chase Manhattan merged with J.P. Morgan, and DLJ merged with Credit Suisse First Boston in 2000.

including the impact on the company's other areas of business, length of the projection period, additional working or fixed capital requirement, discount rate, and residual value. The value of the DCF should be estimated under different scenarios.

Comparable transactions analysis focuses on recent transactions involving companies in the target company's industry or similar industries. The universe of comparable transactions provides a base for calculating acquisition multiples (of sales, earnings, cash flow, or other financial measures). These multiples are then applied to the target's financial results to estimate the value at which the target would likely trade. This technique is most effective when the availability of data on truly comparable transactions is not an issue.

The comparable company approach compares the value of the potential acquisition candidate with the market prices of publicly traded companies with similar characteristics. This method is similar to the comparable transactions approach in that it identifies a pricing relationship and applies it to the candidate's earnings or cash flow or book value. A change of control premium, combined with the value identified by this method, delivers the estimated valuation range for the target. One weakness of this technique is that it works well only when there are good comparables for the target. Another weakness is that accounting policies can differ substantially from one company to another, which could result in material differences in reported measures.

The breakup valuation technique involves analyzing each of the target's business lines and summing these individual values to arrive at a value for the entire company. One compares the total value to the acquisition cost, and then calculates the rate of return if value exceeds cost. This technique provides the required guidance under a hostile bid.

Target stock price history analysis examines the trading range of the target's stock over some time frame. The target stock price performance is analyzed against a broad market index and comparable company stock performances. The offering price comes from the price index plus some premium. If the transaction is a stock-for-stock exchange, a similar analysis happens in regards to the acquiring firm to determine the exchange ratio. Although this approach fails to account for future prospects of the company, it does provide information many find useful in framing valuations.

Leveraged buyout (LBO) analysis takes place when the target is a potential candidate for an LBO, which is a transaction used to acquire a company financed through debt. The objective is to determine the highest price an LBO group (a fund that specializes in LBOs) would pay. This is often the floor price for the target. On the other hand, it may set the upper value for the target if a corporate buyer cannot be located. The LBO analysis typically includes cash flow projections, tax effects, and rates of returns to capital providers. The analysis also incorporates financing for the LBO. The availability of financing depends on the timing of cash flows, particularly in the first few years after the completion of the deal. Thus, the value derived by the LBO approach can be materially affected by temporary changes in financing conditions.

Multiple of revenues is the so-called price-to-sales ratio. The basic concept is that the value is some multiple of the sales the target generates. This method implicitly assumes that there is some relatively consistent relationship between the business's sales and its profits. Obviously, the usefulness of the technique depends on the revenue-profit relationship. In practice, this method may be quite useful when acquiring a private company where gross sales are the only reliable data available.

The book value approach is an accounting-based concept and may not represent the company's earnings power. Generally accepted accounting principles permit the use of alternative depreciation and inventory methods. Also, the value of intangible assets may not be reflected in the balance sheet. Nevertheless, this approach does provide an initial estimate of goodwill in a transaction.

The multiple of earnings method involves taking the past or future income per share and multiplying that figure by earnings multiple, derived from publicly traded companies in the same industry. One difficulty is that the known multiple does not reflect control premiums. Another problem is that income does not necessarily represent cash flow from operations.

Finally, liquidation analysis can be used to establish a floor for valuation. This approach is valid if a business is a target for acquisition for its underlying assets rather than for its going-concern value.

FINANCIAL ENGINEERING

Financial engineering, or the development of new financial instruments such as derivative contracts using sophisticated mathematical and statistical models and computer technology, has become an integral part of investment banking. For example, the investment banking division at Goldman Sachs includes a New Products group that focuses on creating new financial products. As Table 4.2 (see p. 88) shows, the notional principal of swaps and related derivatives grew eighteen times in the 1990s—from $3.5 trillion in 1990 to $63.0 trillion in 2000.[8] The volume continued to increase to almost $100 trillion in 2002.

The explosive growth has occurred on several fronts and for several reasons. Credit derivatives, financial contracts whose payoffs depend on a reference credit, are relatively new and have widespread applications in managing risks. The development of high-yield bonds and asset-backed securities has provided borrowers with additional funding sources at lower costs. Transactions in repurchase agreements offer borrowers lower funding costs while giving lenders legal title to the collateral. Through swap contracting, borrowers and investors obtain a high degree of flexibility in asset-liability management at better terms. Advances in technology and the application of increasingly sophisticated models have provided the infrastructure that has made all of these examples of

---

[8]Chapter 14 provides a detailed coverage of various types of derivative securities.

TABLE 4.2	*Summary of Derivative Market Data*
Year	Total Outstanding ($ trillions)
1990	3.5
1991	4.4
1992	5.3
1993	8.5
1994	11.3
1995	17.7
1996	25.5
1997	29.0
1998	51.0
1999	58.3
2000	63.0
2001	69.2
2002	99.8

Note: Derivative market data include interest rate swaps, currency swaps, and interest rate options.

Source: *Survey and Market Statistics*, International Swaps and Derivatives Association, Inc. (http://www.isda.org).

financial engineering possible. The following discussion examines the factors that have contributed to the development of financial engineering.

Risk Management

Many derivatives transfer risks away from issuers or investors to others better able or more willing to bear them. For example, credit derivatives can help banks, financial companies, and investors manage the credit risk of their investments by insuring against adverse movements in the credit quality of the issuer. Companies can use currency swaps to manage foreign exchange risk and interest rate swaps to hedge against interest rate volatility.[9]

New Funding Sources

Financial engineering has led to a number of new funding sources. High-yield bonds (bonds with a credit rating below investment grade) provide smaller and less established companies with access to the corporate debt market. Without the high-yield market, those companies would be shut out of this funding source. Through asset securitization, illiquid individual loans and other debt instruments are repackaged into securities to further their sales prospects in the marketplace. In this way, asset securitization has created a new source of funding for the ultimate borrowers. For example, a mutual fund that purchases

---

[9]In a currency swap, two parties agree to exchange certain amounts of currencies on scheduled dates. An interest rate swap is a contract between two parties in which each party agrees to make a series of interest payments to the other on scheduled dates.

mortgage-backed securities supplies funds in the mortgage market. A debt issue structured with currency swaps broadens the investor base from national to global and frequently carries a lower rate of interest. In addition, a borrower can design a structured note with interest payments that rise and fall with certain indices or spreads; such an instrument may attract a new group of lenders that otherwise would be prohibited from investing in the indices or spread derivatives directly. Furthermore, fixed-income repurchase agreements broaden the funding sources to include those that will not or cannot make a collateralized loan, because repos are treated as securities transactions. Equity repos, or repos using equity securities as collateral, allow broker-dealers to finance their equity inventory from firms other than commercial banks.

Lower Funding Costs

Asset-backed securities (securities collateralized by mortgages or receivables) transform individual loans into marketable securities. Liquidity increases because mortgages and receivables can be sold in the liquid secondary market, even though the underlying assets individually are highly illiquid. The pricing transparency resulting from secondary market trading provides an objective valuation standard. The securitization process also broadens the market from local to national or even global. Naturally, the enhanced liquidity, pricing transparency, and higher demand lead to a lower yield and thus a reduction in funding costs.

Reduction in Transactions Costs

Asset-backed securities also benefit investors by providing them with a less expensive way to achieve diversification. For issuers, securities such as extendable notes and renewable notes reduce flotation expenses and transactions costs by giving either the issuer or the investor the option to extend the maturity without incurring additional expenses for registration and underwriting. Similarly, an interest rate swap agreement provides a corporate borrower the flexibility to change the nature of its interest rate obligation. For example, a company has already issued $100 million of 10-year fixed-rate bond, but wishes to pay floating interest rate. The company can enter an interest rate contract with a dealer in which the company will pay the dealer a floating rate of interest and receive a fixed interest rate from the dealer. By doing so, the company has converted its interest rate liability from fixed to floating. Without interest rate swaps, to accomplish the same objective, the company might have to retire outstanding bonds and float another security at significantly higher costs.

Tax and Regulatory Issues

Financial engineering also develops products that will enable clients to save on taxes. A typical pattern occurs when an investment banker develops a tax-advantaged product and convinces companies to issue it, only to have the government take actions to stop it. For example, prior to the passage of the Tax Equity and Fiscal Responsibility Act of 1982, zero-coupon bonds produced tax savings for corporate issuers because the tax code allowed an issuer of zero-coupon bonds to amortize interest expenses on a straight-line basis. Adjustable-rate convertible notes, typically issued at par and convertible into common stock, could be redeemed at just half the issue price. They were certain to be converted.[10] A 1983 IRS ruling treated them as equity from the start. More recently, Congress eliminated interest deductions on debt that is either more than forty years in maturity or payable as stock.

Advances in Computer Technology and Quantitative Finance

Technical advances and the development of financial theory are basic to the design, pricing, and trading of any new security. High-power computers and applications of quantitative methods in finance have contributed a great deal to financial engineering. High-speed processors and sophisticated software programs allow for sophisticated models that track complex mathematical relationships in global financial markets. Pricing and arbitrage in derivatives require such advanced computer technology. During the past two decades, a flood of people trained in quantitative methods has joined the securities industry. They have impacted trading a great deal, especially convergence trading, which exploits the out-of-line relationships among various securities under differing market conditions. They have played an even more important role in financial engineering.

RESEARCH, SALES, AND TRADING

As we have seen, investment banks perform the primary market function of underwriting new issues of securities. They subsequently distribute the securities to investors; the banks themselves do not hold much securities inventory. Investors' demand for the new securities will in part depend on the research coverage and the liquidity in the secondary market where outstanding securities are traded. Therefore, a reputable research team, an effective sales force, and the ability to make deep and liquid markets are essential to a successful underwriting business. In addition to their market-making role, many Wall Street firms engage in proprietary trading, or trading for the firm's own account.

Research

Behind every successful investment bank is a good team of research analysts. Investment research is a significant factor in a firm's ability to hold a competitive position in debt and equity underwriting and to generate commission revenues. Together with market making and proprietary activities, research can enhance the firm's understanding of markets and its ability to serve clients. *Institutional Investor* (**http://www.iimagazine.com**) and *Euromoney* (**http://www.euromoney.com**) regularly publish research rankings of the securities industry.

---

[10]Adjustable-rate convertible notes are a type of fixed-income security with interest rate reset periodically and are convertible into common stock.

Analysts spend their day poring over financial reports, scrutinizing corporate balance sheets, and crunching numbers, all in an effort to make proper recommendations on which investments to buy and which to sell. There are several kinds of analysts. Fundamentalists base their recommendations on what's happening at the particular company; they look at the company's financial condition, sales, management, and competition. Analysts who take a quantitative approach use computer programs and mathematical equations to study securities, markets, countries, and regions to identify trading opportunities. Technical analysts study past patterns in prices and volume to predict future price movements.

In addition to investment recommendations, securities houses also provide economic research, including macroeconomic forecasts of economic activity, foreign exchange movements, and interest rates. The Portfolio Strategy group forecasts equity market returns and provides recommendations on asset allocation. Many investment banks also have a commodity research group that provides research on the global commodity market.

Sales

The investment bank's sales team provides clients with a complete range of financial products tailored to suit specific needs. Sales people must ensure that products distributed by the firm match the needs of clients. The sales team also has the task of ensuring that clients receive their confirmations and settlements on time. Finally, sales professionals provide clients with a constant stream of market information to ensure that they are fully informed of market developments. Such information is vital to the success of the firm's trading desk as well.

Sales generate commission revenues from transactions in listed, over-the-counter securities, mutual funds, futures, and options. During a time of market uncertainty, trading in certain securities tends to decline, as occurred during the late third and fourth quarters of 1998 when Russia defaulted on its bond obligations, causing a global financial crisis. Commissions on derivative products usually increase at such times, as clients seek to hedge against the high levels of market volatility.

Trading and Market Making

The trading desk serves as a backstop to the investment bank's efforts by ensuring an orderly market for the firm's financial products. The trading team works closely with the sales team to provide clients with the necessary access to the market for transactions. The sales team also provides information on market flows to the trading desk so that traders can better position themselves.

Market making is an integral part of a dealer's business. Dealers stand ready to buy at bid and sell at offer. The dealer's perception of risks, such as price uncertainty and carry, largely determines the bid-offer spread.[11] During volatile periods, market makers widen the bid-asked spread to protect themselves. If a

---

[11]Carry is the difference between interest income and interest expense.

market maker feels that the market is going against her, she will hedge with other highly correlated securities. For example, a dealer that buys top-quality 5-year corporate bonds might borrow and sell (sell short) 5-year Treasury notes to hedge in a volatile market environment. Market making ensures that clients have access to the products at the current market price when they want them. Likewise, should the need arise for clients to sell back securities, the trading desk can bid at the prevailing market price.

Many investment banks also have a proprietary trading team, which trades on the firm's capital. Successful traders buy low and sell high, or short high and cover low. This seems simple, but it is not. To succeed, a trader has to understand that he competes with the sharpest minds. In addition, trading is a negative-sum game. Brokerage, exchanges, and advisory services constantly drain money away from the market. A trader has to be right more than half of the time just to break even.

The first step to successful trading is to ensure survival. Traders do this by making risk management a top priority. Most losers are washed out when trying to trade their way out of a hole. Many have difficulty taking a loss and continue to hang on to losing positions. It is important to understand that a 10 percent loss requires a gain of more than 11 percent just to get even, and that a 50 percent loss will require a gain of 100 percent to get back in the game. Typically, traders limit losses by placing a stop order, an order to sell the position when its price falls to a particular point to limit losses, as soon as they take a position. They usually set the stop at a level that limits the loss from any single position to a small percentage of the account.

Taking a profit can also be difficult, as traders sometimes become emotionally attached to their winners. When the market moves in the anticipated direction, a trader needs to decide whether to stay put, take profits, or add to the position. Successful traders set a certain objective for each position. Once they have accomplished the objective, they know when to take profits. Some might decide to let the position run, but in that case the stop must be adjusted in the same direction.

There are three basic approaches to trading: fundamental analysis, relative value or convergence trading, and technical analysis. Like the fundamentalists on the research team, trading fundamentalists focus on corporate and economic fundamentals. For equity and fixed-income securities, they analyze the economy, industry, and company. In commodities, fundamentalists study factors that affect market demand and supply. Economic fundamentals such as production and inflation, as well as political factors, affect currencies. In futures, expectations of interest rates and cash market conditions are important. Volatility and the expected direction of price movements play a large part in determining option valuations.

Traders who use relative value or convergence trading take a long position in one asset and a short position in another, with the expectation of earning revenues based on convergence in the relative values of the two assets. Temporary out-of-line relationships and eventual convergence can appear between different bonds of the same maturity, a cash bond and its futures contract, different maturities on the same yield curve, or bonds in different countries.[12] The opportunities may also appear in emerging market equities and equity indices.

Technical analysis rests on the assumption that securities prices tend to move in trends and that such trends can be predicted. Thus, technical analysts attempt to use information on past prices and volume to predict future price movements. They also attempt to time the markets.

ASSET MANAGEMENT AND MERCHANT BANKING

Many investment banks have also become increasingly active in asset management and merchant banking. Asset management includes two types of services: fund management and private client services. As investment banks have expanded into the mutual fund and alternative investment business, asset management fees account for a larger portion of their revenues. Goldman Sachs, Merrill Lynch, and Morgan Stanley, for example, all have at least several hundred billion dollars of clients' money under management. Because Chapter 5, "Investment Companies," covers investment management in detail, we will focus here on the private client services and merchant banking activities of investment banks.

Private Client Services

An investment bank's private client services target wealthy individuals and institutions. A private client financial consultant allocates a client's assets to different classes of assets based on the client's objectives and risk tolerance. Periodically, the financial consultant sits down with the client to review investment performance and change the allocation mix as needed. The consultant also recommends individual stocks or bonds to the client, often based on research reports from in-house analysts. For these services, the firm charges a fee of approximately 1–2 percent of the client's assets.

In today's competitive marketplace, private client services divisions are no longer merely selling stocks, bonds, and mutual funds; now they also pay attention to every aspect of the client's financial well being. For example, the private client group at Merrill Lynch uses what they call an asset-liability-transition strategy. They offer a client a total plan that includes asset management, liability management, and estate and trust planning. Clients can seek advice and guidance from a skilled financial consultant or engage in convenient, self-directed Internet investing, or some combination. Through such programs, investment banks provide clients with customized services that fit their unique and changing personal preferences and needs, with the added convenience of unified account access and reporting.

---

[12]A futures contract is an agreement to buy or sell an asset in a designated future month at a price agreed upon today by the buyer and the seller.

Merchant Banking

Many investment banks run **merchant banking** funds, which invest in corporate and real estate assets by committing capital to long-term equity investment opportunities. The investment bank typically commits a significant portion of its own capital to a fund. The remaining capital comes from clients such as pension plans, endowments, charitable organizations, and wealthy individuals. Some of these investment funds pursue long-term investments in equity and debt securities in privately negotiated transactions, leveraged buyouts, and acquisitions on a global basis. Most investment banks leverage their relationships with companies, investors, and financial intermediaries around the world to locate profitable investment opportunities. Each merchant-banking fund usually diversifies by industry, product type, geographic region, and transaction structure.

Merchant banking generates three revenue streams. First, the management fee is generally a percentage of a fund's capital. These annual management fees are relatively secure and stable. Second, the investment bank operating the fund receives incentive fees, usually 20 percent of the fund's capital appreciation and gains from its investments. Third, the investment bank typically commits a significant amount of its own capital, and hence receives its proportionate share of the fund's capital appreciation. In addition, merchant banking funds and their portfolio companies—companies the fund has invested in—often generate business for other divisions of the firm, including equity underwriting, leveraged financing, and M&A advisory. Merchant banking and proprietary positions (principal transactions) generate a significant portion of an investment bank's net revenues.

SECURITIES SERVICES

As part of their securities services, investment banks provide prime brokerage, financing services, and securities lending to clients such as hedge funds, pension funds, and wealthy individuals. Many investment banks, particularly those with primary dealership operations, also offer matched book business, which involves transactions in repurchase agreements and reverse repurchase agreements.

Prime Brokerage

Prime brokerage offers clients the capability of trading with many brokers through a single firm. Rapid technology advances have significantly altered the prime brokerage business. In addition to the basic custodial and securities lending services of a few years ago, leading prime brokers now offer online trade entry, Internet-based accounting and reporting, and real-time portfolio tracking systems that enable clients to manage their portfolios more efficiently. Today's prime brokerage services include access to a broad range of research and advanced risk evaluation tools. Some prime brokers offer centralized office facilities to lure clients. Examples of investment banks that provide prime brokerage include Merrill Lynch, Goldman Sachs, Morgan Stanley, Citigroup,

Lehman Brothers, Credit Suisse First Boston, Bear Stearns, Barclays Capital, and ABN-Amro.

Securities Lending

Many investment banks and securities houses actively participate in the securities lending business, which involves lending securities to borrowers who may sell them short or use them to satisfy an obligation to deliver those particular securities to another party. In return for lending its securities, the lender receives a fee that may amount to a few basis points a year. Collateralization usually happens with loaned securities. This reduces the lender's credit exposure to the borrower. The lender bears the market risk of the loaned securities, however, because the borrower has an obligation to ultimately return the securities, not the original market value of the securities, to the lender.

Lenders of securities include pension plan sponsors, mutual funds, insurance companies, investment advisers, endowments, bank trust departments, and individuals. Many investment banks have established relationships with lenders to gain access to large pools of securities. The demand for this service has grown rapidly because of the rapid increase in complex trading strategies that involve the buying and selling of various types of securities simultaneously.

Matched Book

As we explained in Chapter 2, a repurchase agreement is a transaction in which a money market participant acquires immediately available funds by "selling" securities and simultaneously agreeing to "repurchase" the same securities after a specified time at a given price. When described from the point of view of the cash lender, the transaction is called a reverse repo. As we emphasized, repo transactions between a dealer and a retail customer, or between a dealer and the Federal Reserve, are usually described from the dealer's perspective. Thus, a retail investor's purchase of the collateral and commitment to resell to a dealer is termed a repo, not a reverse repo. Similarly, when the Federal Reserve supplies funds to the market by buying collateral from dealers with a commitment to resell, the transaction is called a system repo.

Major dealers commonly use reverse repos to establish or cover short positions and to obtain specific issues for delivery to customers. Although reverse repos are similar to securities borrowing, reverses are typically cheaper and provide greater flexibility in the use of collateral.

Many dealers also act as intermediaries in the repo market between ultimate borrowers and suppliers of funds. A dealer acts as a principal on each side of the transaction, borrowing funds from one client and relending the money to another. This combination of repos and reverse repos is called a **repo book**. A repo book in which a repo and a reverse in the same security have the same terms to maturity is a **matched book**.

Dealers profit from matched book transactions because they earn the bid-ask spreads in the repo and reverse repo rates. At times, a dealer may choose not to match the maturities of the repos and reverses in an effort to increase profits. If the dealer expects short-term rates to rise in the near future, the dealer might arrange a repo with a longer term than the reverse. The longer term repo enables the dealer to lock in the prevailing lower financing rate, while the shorter term in reverse repo earns the dealer higher and higher rates as short-term rates rise. In contrast, in a declining interest rate environment, a longer-term reverse might be financed through a series of shorter-term repos transacted at successively lower rates.

RISK MANAGEMENT

At several points thus far, our discussion has alluded to risks that investment banks face. Indeed, risk is inherent in the investment banking business. Major types of risks include market risk, credit risk, operating and reputation risk, legal risk, and funding risk. The extent to which an investment bank properly and effectively identifies, assesses, monitors, and manages each type of risk is critical to its financial soundness and profitability. A broad-based portfolio of business activities helps reduce the impact that volatility in any particular area may have on profits. At every firm, the senior management takes an active role in the risk management process. In the changing and complex environment of global financial services, an investment bank's risk management policies and procedures are evolutionary in nature and are subject to ongoing review and modification.

Market Risk

Market risk refers to the risk that a change in the level of market prices, rates, indices, volatility, correlation, or other market factors, such as liquidity, will result in losses for a specified position or portfolio. Interest rate exposure results from maintaining market making and proprietary positions and trading in interest rate-sensitive instruments. An investment bank exposes itself to equity price risk by making markets in equity securities and equity derivatives and maintaining proprietary positions. The risk exposure to foreign exchange arises from making markets in foreign currencies and foreign currency options and by maintaining foreign exchange positions.[13] Furthermore, a modern investment bank exposes itself to commodity price risk in connection with trading in commodity-related derivatives and physical commodities.

Investment banks seek to manage these market risks by diversifying exposures, controlling position sizes, and establishing hedges in related securities or derivatives. For example, a firm may hedge a portfolio of common stock by taking an offsetting position in a related equity index futures contract. Adverse changes in the liquidity of the market, as well as the correlation of price

---

[13]There are two types of option contracts. A call (put) contract entitles the buyer the right to buy (sell) the underlying asset at the preagreed on price, called the strike price, anytime up to the contract expiration date.

movements between the security and the related hedge, limit the ability to hedge.

In addition to hedges, investment banks use a number of quantitative tools to manage market risk. Firms set risk limits based on selected business units and country exposures. They also carry out scenario analyses that measure the potential effect on net revenues of abnormal market movements.

Many investment houses use value-at-risk (VaR) models to estimate exposure to market risk. A VaR is the potential loss in value of a firm's positions due to adverse movements in markets over a defined time horizon with a specified confidence interval. For example, Goldman Sachs reported a firmwide VaR of $25 million, with a one-day time horizon and a 95 percent confidence interval, in its 2000 annual report. There is a 5 percent chance that the actual loss in one day will be higher than the reported number—possibly much higher. Goldman Sachs also reported separate VaRs of $11 million, $11 million, $17 million, and $7 million for interest rate, currency, equity, and commodity products, respectively. The sum of these component VaRs was $46 million. Hence, there was a diversification effect of $21 million. This effect arose because the four market risk categories were not perfectly correlated.

An inherent limitation of VaR is that past changes in market risk factors may not produce accurate predictions of future market risk. For example, the unprecedented volatility experienced in the third and fourth quarters of 1998 demonstrated the limitations of the VaR model. Prior to that period, the largest credit spread ever in emerging markets—that is, the yield of emerging market debt over that of a comparable U.S. Treasury security—over a one-month period was approximately 200 basis points. Unexpectedly, emerging market spreads widened by approximately 900 basis points in the third quarter of 1998. The VaR model would have considered only a widening of 200 basis points. Moreover, one-day VaR does not fully capture the market risk of positions that cannot be liquidated or offset with hedges within one day. Therefore, financial firms typically run stress tests to estimate the potential loss under extreme market conditions.

Credit Risk

Credit risk represents the loss that could occur if a counterparty or an issuer of securities or other instruments the firm holds fails to meet its contractual obligations. Annual reports also disclose the exposure of credit risk. For example, Goldman Sachs reported a total of $28 billion credit exposure in over-the-counter derivatives in 2000. To reduce credit risk, an investment bank often establishes limits for credit exposures and seeks to enter into netting agreements with counterparties that would permit the bank to offset receivables and payables with such counterparties. Other safeguards include maintaining collateral and continually assessing the creditworthiness of counterparties and issuers.

Most securities companies have established credit management systems that monitor current and potential credit exposure to individual counterparties and, on an aggregate basis, to counterparties and their affiliates. Such systems also provide management with information regarding overall credit risk by product, industry sector, country, and region.

Operating and Reputation Risk

A firm may face financial loss, regulatory risk, or damage to its reputation in the event of an operational failure or error. Failure to properly enter a trade into records may result in a delay in settlement or a breach of regulatory requirements. Settlement errors or delays may cause losses due to damages owed to counterparties or movements in prices. For example, if a firm fails to deliver a fixed-income security to a customer on a timely basis, the firm doesn't receive payment for the security but must instead credit the accrued interest to the customer starting on the settlement date. Most firms manage operating risk by maintaining backup facilities, using technology, employing experienced personnel, and maintaining internal controls. To maintain a solid reputation, most investment banks stress integrity and professionalism; as an example, see the business principles of a major investment bank in Box 4.3.

The Year 2000 problem presented an important operating risk. All financial firms allocated significant amounts of resources to monitoring or replacing portions of information technology systems and other systems to ensure that they would properly recognize and utilize dates beyond December 31, 1999. Failure to be Y2K compliant could cost a firm dearly, as it would have faced financial losses resulting from system malfunctions and lawsuits. All the upgrades and efforts paid off. The industry did not experience any major disruptions.

Legal Risk

Legal risk includes the risk that a firm will fail to comply with applicable legal and regulatory requirements and the risk that counterparty's obligations may be unenforceable. To guard against these risks, an investment bank will establish procedures addressing regulatory capital requirements, sales and trading practices, new products, use and safekeeping of customer securities, credit granting, collection activities, money laundering, and record keeping. Before dealing with a customer, the firm's legal counsel will examine the counterparty's legal authority and capacity, the adequacy of the legal documentation, and the permissibility of a transaction under applicable law. Counsel will also check to see whether applicable bankruptcy or insolvency laws limit or alter contractual remedies. In addition, the firm will have policies in place to ensure that its fiduciary obligations to clients are met.

Funding Risk

Ready access to funds is crucial to the business of investment banking. To reduce funding risk, securities firms maintain a cash position, borrow large sums in the debt markets, and secure access to the repo and securities lending markets; in some cases, they may sell securities and other assets.

MARKETS IN ACTION   Goldman Sachs Business Principles

4.3

The business principles of Goldman Sachs are:

1. Our clients' interests always come first. Our experience shows that if we serve our clients well, our own success will follow.
2. Our assets are our people, capital, and reputation. If any of these is ever diminished, the last is the most difficult to restore. We are dedicated to complying fully with the letter and spirit of the laws, rules, and ethical principles that govern us. Our continued success depends upon unswerving adherence to this standard.
3. We take great pride in the professional quality of our work. We have an uncompromising determination to achieve excellence in everything we undertake. Though we may be involved in a wide variety and heavy volume of activity, we would, if it came to a choice, rather be best than biggest.
4. We stress creativity and imagination in everything we do. While recognizing that the old way may still be the best way, we constantly strive to find a better solution to a client's problems. We pride ourselves on having pioneered many of the practices and techniques that have become standard in the industry.
5. We make an unusual effort to identify and recruit the very best person for every job. Although our activities are measured in billions of dollars, we select our people one by one. In a service business, we know that without the best people, we cannot be the best firm.
6. We offer our people the opportunity to move ahead more rapidly than is possible at most other places. We have yet to find the limits to the responsibility that our best people are able to assume. Advancement depends solely on ability, performance, and contribution to the firm's success, without regard to race, color, religion, sex, age, national origin, disability, sexual orientation, or any other impermissible criterion or circumstance.
7. We stress teamwork in everything we do. While individual creativity is always encouraged, we have found that team effort often produces the best results. We have no room for those who put their personal interests ahead of the interests of the firm and its clients.
8. The dedication of our people to the firm and the intense effort they give their jobs are greater than one finds in most other organizations. We think that this is an important part of our success.
9. Our profits are a key to our success. They replenish our capital and attract and keep our best people. It is our practice to share our profits generously with all who helped create them. Profitability is crucial to our future.
10. We consider our size an asset that we try hard to preserve. We want to be big enough to undertake the largest project that any of our clients could contemplate, yet small enough to maintain the loyalty, the intimacy and the esprit de corps that we all treasure and that contribute greatly to our success.
11. We constantly strive to anticipate the rapidly changing needs of our clients and to develop new services to meet those needs. We know that the world of finance will not stand still and that complacency can lead to extinction.
12. We regularly receive confidential information as part of our normal client relationships. To breach a confidence or to use confidential information improperly or carelessly would be unthinkable.
13. Our business is highly competitive, and we aggressively seek to expand our client relationships. However, we must always be fair competitors and must never denigrate other firms.
14. Integrity and honesty are at the heart of our business. We expect our people to maintain high ethical standards in everything they do, both in their work for the firm and in their personal lives.

Source: Goldman Sachs (http://www.gs.com). Reprinted with permission from Goldman Sachs.

Investment banks and securities firms depend on continuous access to the debt capital markets to finance their day-to-day operations. This access could be impaired by factors that affect the firm or the industry in general. For example, lenders may turn away from a firm that incurs large trading losses or discovers that one of its employees engaged in serious unauthorized or illegal activity.

If the firm cannot borrow in the debt market, it might have to liquidate assets in order to meet maturing liabilities. In an uncertain or volatile market environment, however, overall market liquidity may decline. For example, the spread for certain mortgage-backed securities widened to as large as 4–5 percent when rising interest rates dried up market liquidity in 1994; during that year the Fed raised the federal funds rate seven times. In such an event, the firm may be unable to sell some of its assets or may have to sell assets at depressed prices. Moreover, selling assets may be difficult if other market participants seek to sell similar assets in the market at the same time. During the Russian financial crisis in 1998, for example, many institutions simultaneously attempted to sell similar assets, which adversely affected the markets for some assets.

CONCLUDING SUMMARY

Investment banks derive revenues from a variety of sources, including underwriting, M&A advisory services, trading, merchant banking, asset management, and securities services. Some also engage in retail brokerage, which will be covered in Chapter 6, "Brokerage and Clearing Companies." Clients demand that banks provide this wide range of services on a global basis. Advances in technology have made it possible for large investment banks to become worldwide one-stop shops. Smaller investment banks have found this approach too expensive, so they focus on niche strategies.

Investment banking traditionally includes underwriting and M&A advisory services. Underwriting is a primary market service, in which investment banks buy the entire block of a newly issued security from the issuer and distribute the security to institutional and retail investors. For the service, underwriters receive, as compensation, the underwriting discount and the green shoe option to buy additional shares if there is a strong demand for the new security. Many corporate issuers select an underwriter that has a wide network for security distribution, aftermarket support, good research coverage, and the ability to satisfy future financing needs.

Merger and acquisition advice is a high-margin business. M&A bankers give advice on the deal, and sometimes the investment bank also provides bridge loans to enable the deal to be completed and enable the bank to receive the advisory fees. In complex deals, the bank's financial engineering team may devise an innovative financing structure that makes sense for both the buyer and the seller. With the continuing trend toward consolidation and globalization in many industries, the M&A market is an important revenue source for investment banking operations.

Research is essential to a successful investment banking business. Reputable research brings in underwriting business. Sales people have an easier time selling securities that the analysts recommend, and the trading desk relies on their recommendations when deciding how to trade. In addition, the asset management and private client services divisions rely on high-quality research. Investment recommendations also help the merchant banking division because merchant banking is a type of principal transaction; that is, the firm's capital is at risk.

As part of their service package, investment banks and securities firms also offer securities services. In prime brokerage, the service covers clearing and settlement, financing, securities lending, accounts reports, research, and office facilities. Many securities firms, especially those with primary dealership operations, also run a repo book. The repo desk finds securities the firm needs to cover shorts, obtains financing for the firm's security inventory, provides funding to facilitate customer purchases of securities, and engages in arbitrage strategies.

The expansion of investment banking services has been made possible in part by deregulation; in particular, by the Gramm-Leach-Bliley Act of 1999. The act has not only provided the necessary legal infrastructure for U.S. firms to effectively compete in the global capital markets, but also saves Americans an estimated $15 billion a year. Globalization and technology have collapsed both distance and time and presented challenges and opportunities for financial services firms.

Key Terms

aftermarket 79	matched book 95
best-efforts underwriting 79	merchant banking 94
effective 80	net revenues 76
final prospectus 81	preliminary prospectus 81
financial engineering 87	registration statement 80
firm commitment underwriting 79	repo book 95
floating risk 83	road show 81
green shoe option 79	Rule 415 (shelf registration) 84
legal risk 98	underwriting discount 79
Lehman 5-4-3-2-1 85	underwriting syndicate 79

Review Questions

1. What are the major trends in investment banking? What are the driving forces behind these trends?

2. Why is there a need for investment banks and securities firms to provide one-stop shopping?

3. Technology has changed and will continue to change the ways we do business. Discuss the impact of technology on the securities business.

4. What types of information are disclosed in the registration statement that a company issuing a new security must file with the SEC?

5. Underwriting is a profitable but risky business. What risks does the underwriter face? How has shelf registration shifted some of the security floating risks from the issuer to the underwriter?

6. The cover page of the prospectus for Goldman Sachs (May 4, 1999) indicated that the initial public offering price was $53.00 per share and the underwriting discount was $2.25 a share. Goldman Sachs was offering 51 million shares, and two institutional shareholders were each offering 9 million shares. What were the total proceeds, before expenses, to Goldman Sachs? What was the total amount of the underwriting spread?

7. TCB Corporation needs to raise $40 million to finance its research and development. The company has decided to sell new shares of common stock to raise the needed funds. If the offering price is $18 per share and the underwriter charges a 7 percent spread, how many shares need to be sold?

8. Financial engineering has become an integral part of the investment banking business. How does financial engineering help clients manage financial risks? Lower funding costs?

9. Merger and acquisition advice is a high-margin business. Describe how it also contributes to other businesses of an investment bank.

10. Why is research important to an investment bank?

11. Merchant banking generates several sources of revenues and brings in business to the firm as well. Discuss those revenue sources and explain how merchant banking contributes to other areas of an investment bank's business.

12. What is a repo book? What is a matched book? Why would an investment bank operate a repo book?

13. What are the main risks inherent in investment banking?

14. Obtain annual reports from three investment banks and compare their credit risk exposures. How do they manage these risks?

15. Consider the following information for two companies, TCCB and TCII.

	TCCB	TCII
Shares outstanding	54,000	3,200
Price per share	$45	$10

TCCB is acquiring TCII by exchanging 1,000 of its shares for all the shares in TCII. What is the cost of the acquisition if the combined firm is worth $2.64 million?

Select Bibliography

Beiss, J. *Risk Management in Banking.* New York: John Wiley & Sons, Inc., 2002.

Braddock, J. C. *Derivatives Demystified: Using Structured Financial Products.* New York: John Wiley & Sons, 1997.

Cecchetti, S. G. "The future of financial intermediation and regulation: An overview." *Current Issues in Economics and Finance* 5, no. 8, Federal Reserve Bank of New York, May 1999, pp. 1–6.

Das, S. "Credit risk derivatives." *Journal of Derivatives,* Spring 1995, pp. 7–23.

Gaugham, P. A. *Mergers, Acquisitions, and Corporate Restructurings.* New York: John Wiley & Sons, 1996.

Irvine, P., and J. Rosenfeld. "Raising capital using monthly income preferred stock: market reaction and implications for capital structure theory." *Financial Management* 29, no. 2, Summer 2000, pp. 5–20.

RiskMetrics Group. *CreditMetrics–Technical Document,* 1997.

Kanatas, G., and J. Qi. "Underwriting by commercial banks: Incentive conflicts, scope economies, and project quality." *Journal of Money, Credit and Banking* 30, no. 1, February 1998, pp. 119–133.

Krigman, L., W. H. Shaw, and K. L. Womack. "The persistence of IPO mispricing and the predictive power of flipping." *Journal of Finance* 54, no. 3, June 1999, pp. 1015–1044.

Liaw, K. T. "Book review—*The Day Trader's Manual: Theory, Art, and Science of Profitable Short-Term Trading.*" *Journal of Finance* 50, June 1995, pp. 758–761.

Liaw, K. T. *The Business of Investment Banking.* New York: John Wiley & Sons, 1999.

Neal, R. S. "Credit derivatives: New financial instruments for controlling credit risk." *Economic Review* Second Quarter, Federal Reserve Bank of Kansas City, 1996, pp. 15–27.

Prior, C., and T. Lott. *Vault Career Guide to Investment Banking.* New York: Vault Reports, Inc., 2002.

Schwartz, R. J., and C. W. Smith, eds. *Derivatives Handbook: Risk Management and Control.* New York: John Wiley & Sons, 1997.

Sherman, A. E. "Underwriter certification and the effect of shelf registration on due diligence." *Financial Management* 28, no. 1, Spring 1999, pp. 5–19.

Investment Companies

Investment management is an important segment of the capital markets. The industry has experienced tremendous growth in recent years, both in the United States and in foreign markets. Technology has been one of the key forces behind such strong growth. It has enabled the industry to provide better services, enhance information flows, cope with exploding volumes of transactions, and introduce a broad array of new products. As investment management has become one of the most attractive segments of the financial services industry, many firms have enhanced their existing asset management operations or added new ones. Well-capitalized international financial firms have been strengthening their asset management business with a global range of products and distribution capabilities. Many securities firms and commercial banks also offer money management services.

The objectives of this chapter are to provide an understanding of:
- ° The market for investment management.
- ° Mutual fund operations.
- ° The structure and strategies of hedge funds.
- ° The features and strategies of venture capital funds.
- ° The market for buyout funds.
- ° Opportunities in real estate investment trusts.

MARKET OVERVIEW

We invest for various reasons, such as saving for retirement, children's college education, or accumulating wealth. Investing through an investment management company is one of the many ways that can be used to meet these investment objectives. Investment management companies pool money from investors and invest in a portfolio of financial assets. This is indirect investing, in contrast to direct investing where investors invest directly in individual securities. Indirect investing has advantages over direct investing in terms of managerial expertise, diversification, administrative costs, and convenience. Investment management operations include unit investment trusts, closed-end investment companies, mutual funds, hedge funds, venture capital funds, buyout funds, and real estate investment trusts.

Investment management, especially of mutual funds, has been one of the fastest growing segments of the financial services industry in recent years. The increased popularity of defined contribution plans has partially fueled this growth.[1] As employers have substituted defined contribution plans for defined benefit programs or initiated new defined contribution plans, employees have assumed more responsibility for providing their own retirement income. Consequently, many people with relatively little investment experience have made important investment decisions. Mutual funds, with their professional managers and diversification possibilities, are an attractive choice. In addition, concerns about the future of Social Security and the need to save to meet the rising costs of their children's college education have spurred many households to invest their savings in mutual funds. As funds have proliferated to meet this demand and fulfill a variety of investor objectives, from conservative to aggressive, the demand for investment management services has also grown.

The emergence of new distribution channels has also stimulated the expansion of mutual funds. In addition to broker-dealers, banks, and insurance companies, financial planners play a significant role in fund distribution. Furthermore, many brokerage houses now offer a broad variety of funds through a single brokerage account, called a mutual fund supermarket. The rapid growth of Internet-based commerce will certainly have an impact on the evolving fund management business in the years to come. Almost every major fund company already has a Web site with extensive information, and the percentage of fund shareholders using the Internet has risen rapidly.

Investment management services are also in demand overseas, as many other countries experience a similar trend of transferring responsibility for providing retirement income from the employer or the public sector to the indi-

---

[1]Defined contribution plans and defined benefit plans are two types of widely used pension plans. In a defined contribution plan, the plan sponsor makes specified contribution into the plan on behalf of the participant. The amount contributed is generally a percentage of the employee's salary. The plan sponsor does not guarantee that the employee will receive any certain amount upon retirement. In contrast, under a defined benefit plan, the plan sponsor agrees to make specified payments to qualifying employees at retirement.

vidual. In Europe, there are expectations that private pension schemes like defined contribution plans will grow in coming years as a way of reducing reliance on state pension provisions. Many developing countries have also taken steps to shift from defined benefit to defined contribution plans in an effort to cut deficits and to reduce the financial burden of government. In Japan, the investment management business has benefited from financial market reforms.

The sustained growth in investment management and the trend toward one-stop shopping in financial services have led to consolidation in the industry. Table 5.1 lists examples of major transactions in recent years. As Table 5.1 clearly shows, various types of financial services companies have bought into the fund management business. For insurance companies, asset management is an integral part of the business. For commercial banks and securities firms, investment management expands the menu of products and services they can offer their clients. Furthermore, the income stream is less volatile than income from trading, underwriting, or merger and acquisition activities. The affiliated funds can also provide synergy to the bank's underwriting business. Table 5.1 also shows that investment management is increasingly a global business, not just in terms of global investing, but also in terms of having a global presence. For example, Merrill Lynch purchased Mercury Asset Management to tap into the markets in Europe, while Zurich Group acquired Scudder to pursue its global strategy.

TABLE 5.1	*Major Acquisitions of Fund Companies, 1997–2001*		
Date	**Target**	**Assets ($ millions)**	**Acquirer**
September 2001	Zurich Scudder	300,000	Deutsche Bank
April 2001	TCW Group	78,000	Societe Generale SA
January 2001	Mackenzie Financial	24,900	Investors Group
September 2000	Phoenix Investment Partners	60,832	Phoenix Home Life Mutual Insurance
June 2000	Nvest Companies	134,000	Caisse des Depots
June 2000	United Asset Management	188,000	Old Mutual
January 2000	U.S. Trust	86,100	Charles Schwab
September 1999	Allegis Realty Investors	5,900	UBS Brison
April 1999	Nicholas Applegate Fixed-Income	9,100	Westdeutsche Landesbank Girzoentrale
February 1999	Warburg Pincus Asset Management	22,000	Credit Suisse Asset Management
August 1998	Hilliard-Lyons	22,500	PNC Bank Corp.
August 1998	Frank Russell Co.	41,000	Northwestern Mutual Life
November 1997	Mercury Asset Management	180,000	Merrill Lynch
November 1997	Oppenheimer Capital	60,000	Pimco Advisors (67%)
October 1997	ANB Investment Management	28,000	Northern Trust
August 1997	Columbia Management	22,000	Fleet Financial Group
July 1997	American Century	60,000	J.P. Morgan (45%)
June 1997	Scudder, Stevens & Clark	120,000	Zurich Group/Kemper

Sources: Mutual Fund Cafe and *Wall Street Journal*, various issues.

TYPES OF INVESTMENT MANAGEMENT OPERATIONS

Before examining the various types of investment management operations in detail, it is helpful to have an overview of their distinctive characteristics.

A **unit investment trust (UIT)** is an investment company that purchases and holds a relatively fixed portfolio of securities. Investors who buy units in the trust will receive a pro rata share of principal and interest or dividends. UITs generally have a stated date for termination. After the dissolution of the trusts, the unit-holders receive all proceeds. Many types of UITs are available to meet various investment objectives and levels of risk tolerance. They include corporate bond UITs, equity UITs, international bond UITs, mortgage-backed UITs, municipal bond UITs, and government securities UITs. UIT investors generally pay a sales charge; discounts may be available for large purchases. UIT annual expenses are very low, and usually there are no annual management fees.

A **closed-end investment company** is a type of investment company that issues a fixed number of shares listed on a stock exchange or traded over the counter. After the issuance of the shares, investors buying or selling these shares do not deal with the fund company, but instead, trade with other investors. There are four main types of closed-end funds: international and global bond funds, international and global equity funds, domestic bond funds, and domestic equity funds. Demand and supply in the marketplace determine the price of a closed-end fund. The market price could be, and frequently is, different from the value per share. Many funds consistently trade at or around a particular level of discount or premium. Such a deviation from share value can occur for many reasons. For example, a closed-end fund that consistently outperforms others or offers a unique opportunity tends to trade at a premium. On the other hand, investor demand will be weak if a fund offers inferior returns or holds securities that are risky and difficult to evaluate.

A **mutual fund** is an investment management company that pools money from a number of investors who share similar investment objectives, such as obtaining current income, maximizing long-term capital growth, or a combination of the two. A professional manager manages the fund to achieve its objective. Each share represents a proportional ownership in all of the fund's invested assets. The **net asset value (NAV)** of a mutual fund determines its price. The NAV equals the value of the fund's assets, less its liabilities, divided by the number of outstanding shares. The mutual fund distributes its earnings to investors in proportion to the number of shares an investor owns as of a record dividend date.

A **hedge fund** is an unregistered, private investment pool bound by the investment agreement investors have signed with the sponsors of the fund. With the exception of anti-fraud standards, hedge funds are exempt from Securities and Exchange Commission (SEC) regulations, because they are private investment pools limited to investors who satisfy certain requirements. A hedge fund generally is not subject to any limitations in portfolio selection. It is also not required to disclose information about its holdings and performance. Under the typical fee structure, the hedge fund manager takes a fee of 1–2 percent of net assets, plus 20 percent of the gains, called incentive fees. Some funds have front-end charges as well. Most hedge funds require a high minimum investment; $250,000 or $500,000 is typical, though some have lower or higher minimum requirements. Under the National Securities Markets Improvement Act of 1996, hedge funds can accept investments from individuals who hold at least $5 million in investments or institutions with $25 million in investments. This rule intends to limit participation in hedge funds and other types of high-risk and high-leverage pools to highly sophisticated investors.

Venture capital (VC) funds make equity investments in entrepreneurial companies. The financiers recoup their investments when the company they have invested in (called the portfolio company) either goes public or sells out to another corporation. The VC market includes the merchant banking subsidiaries of large institutions such as investment banks, bank holding companies, technology companies, and insurance companies. The VC industry also has many specialized investment entities formed principally to make private equity investments. A private VC fund typically raises its capital from a limited number of sophisticated investors in a private placement and has a life of about ten to twelve years. The investor base consists of wealthy individuals, pension plans, endowments, insurance companies, bank holding companies, and foreign investors. VC firms earn income from two sources: the annual management fee and the profit allocation of the fund. The general partner (venture capitalist) typically receives 20 percent of the fund's investment profits, and the limited partners (investors) receive 80 percent.

Buyout funds are investment firms that invest in leveraged buyouts (LBOs), which involve the purchase of companies through the use of borrowed money to cover a substantial portion of the purchase price. Three factors generally are essential in conducting a successful LBO: the ability to borrow significant sums against the company's assets, the ability to retain or attract a strong management team, and the potential for the investment to increase substantially in value. The ability of a company to support significant leverage depends upon whether it can service the debt obligations. This in turn requires a selling company capable of generating large sums of cash on a regular basis or has substantial assets that can be sold to pay off the debt.

The last type of investment company covered in this chapter is the **real estate investment trust (REIT)**, a trust that pools capital from investors to acquire or to provide financing for real estate. It is like a closed-end fund for real estate in that retail investors can trade shares on a stock exchange. Investing in REITs gives an investor a practical and efficient way to include professionally managed real estate in an investment portfolio.

MUTUAL FUNDS

A mutual fund is an investment company that makes investments on behalf of fund shareholders who share common investment objectives. Through the pooling of investor money, a mutual fund offers investors a simple, convenient method of investing in a portfolio of securities. The invested securities and cash balance make up the assets of the fund. The value of a mutual fund portfolio fluctuates as investors invest or redeem money and as the value of the securities held by the fund rises or falls. An investor in a mutual fund purchases shares of the fund, with each share representing ownership in all of the securities the fund has purchased. Thus, each mutual fund investor owns an undivided interest in the portfolio and shares mutually with other investors in the fund's gains and distributions derived from the fund investment. Capital gains and dividends or interest income from these securities are paid out in proportion to the number of shares owned. Therefore, an investor who invests $5,000 will get the same investment return per dollar invested as a fund shareholder investing $500,000.

Mutual fund investing has many advantages. First, as mentioned earlier, an investor buying shares of a mutual fund buys an ownership interest in all of the securities the fund owns. Fund managers generally invest in a variety of securities, affording portfolio diversification. A diversified portfolio helps reduce risk because losses from some securities will be offset by gains in others. Thus, investors can blunt the effect of a decline in value of any particular security. The average investor would find it expensive and difficult to construct a portfolio as diversified as a mutual fund.

The second advantage is professional management. Professional money managers select securities that best match the fund's objectives as described in the prospectus. These managers have experience in interpreting the complexities of the financial markets and have talented analysts behind them who conduct extensive research on individual companies as well as the entire industry. Mutual funds provide an economical way for the individual investor to obtain the same kind of professional money management and diversification available to large institutions and wealthy investors.

The third advantage is that a variety of mutual funds are available. There are several thousand mutual funds representing a wide variety of investment objectives, from conservative to aggressive. Table 5.2 lists various fund objectives as classified by the Investment Company Institute.[2] Investors need to analyze their investment time horizon and risk tolerance level to determine what type of funds to choose. Additionally, it is easy to invest in mutual funds. Most mutual funds, whether managed by Fidelity or Vanguard, can be purchased at many brokerage firms such as Schwab, Quick & Reilly, and Merrill Lynch.

---

[2]The classifications vary from company to company. For example, Lipper has changed its classifications for general equity funds. The new classifications are aggressive equity, growth equity, general equity, value equity, and income equity.

TABLE 5.2	*Types of Mutual Funds*

Equity Funds

Aggressive growth
Growth
Sector
Growth and income
Income equity
Emerging markets
Global equity
International equity
Regional equity

Hybrid Funds

Asset allocation
Balanced
Flexible portfolio
Income-mixed

Taxable Bond Funds

Corporate bond
High yield
Global bond
Government bond
Mortgage-backed
Strategic income

Tax-free Bond Funds

State municipal bond
National municipal bond

Money Market Funds

Taxable money market
Tax-exempt money market-national
Tax-exempt money market-state

Source: *Mutual Fund Fact Book 2001*, Investment Company Institute (http://www.ici.org), Washington, D.C., May 2001.

Another benefit of mutual fund investing is that mutual funds issue both full and fractional shares. This allows investors to purchase shares based on an even dollar investment. Each full or fractional share represents ownership of the fund and does not imply a specific interest in any one investment in a portfolio. Additionally, mutual funds, unless closed to new investments, continuously issue new shares to or buy back shares from investors.

Finally, mutual funds are liquid. Investors can redeem shares any business day, unlike certificates of deposits, which cannot be sold without penalty until a predetermined date. Many mutual funds also offer check-writing and online payment privileges.

Mutual Fund Share Pricing and Performance

Mutual funds determine the price of their shares each business day. A fund's net asset value (NAV) is the value of all the fund's assets, minus liabilities, divided by the total number of shares outstanding. A fund's offering price is its NAV plus (if any) the applicable sales charge. The redemption price is its NAV minus (if any) the applicable redemption fee, or back-end load.

The Investment Company Act of 1940 requires each fund to price its assets based on their current value each business day. Specifically, the price must reflect the current market value of the fund's securities. Mutual funds generally value exchange-traded securities using the most recent closing prices. Other assets should be priced at fair value, determined in good faith by the fund's board of directors or trustees.[3]

Generally, a fund's pricing process begins at the close of the New York Stock Exchange at 4:00 P.M. eastern time. The fund's accounting agent typically has responsibility for calculating the NAV. For example, suppose a mutual fund owns a portfolio of stocks worth $10 million at the end of the business day; its liabilities are $1 million; and it has 800,000 shares of the fund outstanding. One can calculate the NAV as

$$\boxed{5.1} \qquad NAV = \frac{\$10,000,000 - \$1,000,000}{800,000} = \$11.25.$$

In addition to the NAV, mutual fund quotes typically include performance data such as returns year-to-date, 3-year, 5-year, 10-year, and since inception. Morningstar (**http://www.morningstar.com**) provides rich information about mutual funds that allows investors to learn, plan, research, and monitor. Mutual Fund Investor's Center (**http://www.mfea.com**) is a comprehensive mutual fund resource, with educational tools, news, and links to funds. Lipper, Inc. (**http://www.lipperweb.com**) provides similar services. Other valuable information sources on the Internet include Value Line Mutual Fund Survey (**http://www.valueline.com**), Mutual Fund Investor Guide (**http://www. investorguide.com**), and Brill's Mutual Funds Interactive (**http://www. brill.com**). Most brokerage houses offer similar services to account holders.

Mutual Fund Taxation

Mutual fund shareholders pay taxes on the dividends and capital gains the fund distributes. Investors who purchase shares at the wrong time (right before the ex-dividend date) will be taxed on dividends or capital gains that they have paid for. This occurs because a fund's NAV reflects the price of the securities

---

[3]A board of directors governs a mutual fund when the fund is established as a corporation. A board of trustees governs the fund if it is structured as a business trust.

it holds and any undistributed dividends and capital gains. When an investor purchases shares of the fund after the ex-dividend date, he pays a lower price per share because he will not receive distributions of dividends or capital gains. To illustrate this point, let's consider the following example. Suppose an investor wishes to purchase 1,000 shares of a mutual fund that currently sells for $10 per share on December 9. The fund will be distributing $2 per share in dividends, with an ex-dividend date of December 10. Therefore, the $10 price per share can be broken up into two parts: the $2 distribution of dividends and a value for the fund's NAV of $8. Suppose that the value of the fund's securities do not change between December 9 and 10. An investor who purchased this fund after December 10 would not be entitled to the dividend, and hence would pay $8 for a share of the fund. If the shareholder purchases the shares on December 9, however, she pays $10 and receives a $2 dividend distribution. This distribution is taxable and leaves the shareholder with a tax liability that would not have incurred if she had purchased the fund one day later.

Mutual Fund Fees and Expenses

Mutual fund investors may encounter several types of fees and expenses, which vary depending on the fund and how they purchase it. Investors may purchase mutual fund shares directly from the fund or through a broker, a bank representative, an insurance agent, or a financial planner. Financial planners offer various services, which include analyzing the investor's financial needs and objectives and recommending appropriate funds. They generally receive compensation through sales commissions or through 12b-1 fees. The 12b-1 fees are deducted from fund assets to pay for marketing and advertising expenses or to compensate sales professionals. By law, 12b-1 fees cannot exceed 1 percent of the fund's average NAV per year. In addition to 12b-1 fees, a fund's annual operating expenses include management fees, which are ongoing fees charged by the fund's investment adviser for managing the fund and selecting its portfolio of securities. These fees typically range from 0.50 to 1.5 percent. Funds specialized in small capitalization or certain niche areas charge a higher percentage of fees. Index funds buy and hold securities selected to represent a target index or benchmark such as the S&P 500 Index. Their management fees could be as low as 20 basis points.[4] In the long run, the impact of fee differentials on returns is significant. For example, suppose that two funds produce the same annual rate of returns before management fees (10 percent) to investors during a 30-year investment horizon. One fund charges 0.20 percent in management fees, while the other charges 1.20 percent. For an initial investment of $1,000, the fund with a lower fee will return investors $16,522. The higher fees charged by the other fund will decrease the terminal value of the same amount of initial investment to $12,556. The additional 1-percent fee has

---

[4]One basis point is one one-hundredth of 1 percent.

lowered the terminal value by $3,966; almost four times the amount of initial investments.[5]

Additionally, a shareholder may incur transaction expenses such as purchase, redemption, or exchange fees. Load funds charge a front-end load, a back-end load, or both. A front-end load, or sales charge, may be charged for the purchase of mutual fund shares. By law, this charge may not exceed 8.5 percent of the investment, although most fund families charge less than the maximum. A back-end load, sometimes referred to as a redemption or exit fee, is charged at the time of redemption. This fee typically applies for the first few years on a declining schedule and then disappears. A no-load fund does not have any front-end or back-end charge. An exchange fee may be charged when the shareholder transfers money from one fund to another within the same fund family. Finally, some funds charge an account maintenance fee to maintain low-balance accounts.

Growth of Mutual Funds

The mutual fund industry traces its roots back to nineteenth-century Great Britain. Most of the early British investment companies and their later American counterparts sold a fixed number of shares whose price was determined by supply and demand, similar to today's closed-end funds. The first open-end mutual fund (the Massachusetts Investors Trust) started in 1924.

Mutual fund investing began to grow in popularity in the 1940s and 1950s, but the explosive growth did not occur until the 1980s. In 1960, there were 160 funds with $17 billion in assets. Ten years later, there were 361 funds with total assets of $47.6 billion. By 1980, the number of funds had reached 564, and the total assets under management had crossed the $100 billion mark to $134.8 billion. Another milestone occurred in 1990 when the 3,105 funds managed more than $1 trillion in assets. By the end of 1996, total industry assets had increased to $3.5 trillion. Total net assets increased by about $1 trillion in each of the subsequent two years, 1997 and 1998. By the end of 2001, mutual funds had investments of almost $7 trillion. Table 5.3 shows how the number of funds and the components of total industry assets (money market, bond and income, and equity funds) have grown.

The enormous growth and diversity of the fund industry have led to the development of new fund categories with various investment objectives. Today's mutual fund menu runs the gamut from aggressive growth to global bond to niche funds that specialize in one segment of the securities markets (see Table 5.2). Nevertheless, funds can still be grouped into three general types: money market funds, bond funds, and stock funds. Money market funds invest in short-term securities that are highly liquid and low risk. These funds seek to maintain a stable NAV of $1, while providing a current level of income to shareholders. Bond mutual funds invest in fixed-income securities such as

---

[5]This example assumes annual compounding.

TABLE 5.3		Number of Mutual Funds and Components of Total Industry Net Assets			
Year	Number of Mutual Fund Complexes	Number of Mutual Funds	Money Market Fund Assets ($ billions)	Bond and Income Fund Assets ($ billions)	Equity Fund Assets ($ billions)	Total Industry Net Assets ($ billions)
1970		361				47.6
1980	123	564				134.8
1981	134	665				241.4
1982	150	857				296.7
1983	164	1,026				292.9
1984	189	1,241	233.6	54.0	83.1	370.7
1985	217	1,528	243.8	134.8	116.9	495.5
1986	261	1,840	292.2	262.6	161.5	716.3
1987	314	2,317	316.1	273.2	180.7	770.0
1988	349	2,715	338.0	277.5	194.8	810.3
1989	357	2,917	428.1	304.8	249.0	981.9
1990	361	3,105	498.4	322.7	245.8	1,066.9
1991	361	3,427	542.4	441.4	411.6	1,395.4
1992	364	3,850	546.2	577.3	522.8	1,646.3
1993	375	4,558	565.3	761.1	749.0	2,075.4
1994	398	5,357	611.0	684.0	866.4	2,161.4
1995	401	5,761	753.0	798.3	1,269.0	2,820.3
1996	417	6,293	901.8	886.5	1,750.9	3,539.2
1997	424	6,778	1,058.9	1,031.5	2,399.3	4,489.7
1998	419	7,314	1,351.7	1,195.3	2,978.2	5,525.2
1999	433	7,791	1,612.4	1,192.0	4,039.1	6,846.3
2000	431	8,155	1,845.3	1,160.7	3,963.1	6,964.7
2001	NA	8,307	2,285.3	1,271.4	3,418.2	6,975.0

Note: A fund complex is a group of funds, including one or more families of funds, under substantially common management.

Source: *Mutual Fund Fact Book 1996*, *Mutual Fund Fact Book 1999*, and *Mutual Fund Fact Book 2002*, Investment Company Institute (http://www.ici.org), Washington, D.C., 2002.

Treasury, agency, corporate, and municipal securities. Stock mutual funds primarily invest in common stocks.

Just as there are many types of funds, there are many management styles, but they generally follow one of two: active management or indexing. An **active management strategy** seeks to outperform the market by applying informed, independent investment management. Most managers employ this strategy. Major active management firms include Fidelity, Putnam, Scudder, Oppenheimer, INVESCO, Alliance Capital, Morgan Stanley, Merrill Lynch, and John Hancock, among others. The opposite is passive management, or **indexing**, in which the fund buys securities to replicate the performance of the overall market. The best-known index fund company is Vanguard.

Exchange-Traded Funds

An **exchange-traded fund** (ETF) is an index fund or trust listed on an exchange and can be traded like a listed stock during trading hours. Investors can trade shares in ETFs as a single security. These ETFs cover a wide variety of broad stock market, industry sector, international stock, and U.S. bond indexes. These ETFs add the ease and liquidity of trading to the benefits of traditional index investing. Examples of ETFs include Nasdaq-100 Index Tracking Stock (symbol: QQQ), S&P 500 Index (SPY), and iShares MSCI-Canada (EWC). The American Stock Exchange expects the amount of assets in ETFs to grow from $100 billion in 2002 to more than $500 billion by 2007.

Technology and Mutual Funds

Technological advances are some of the key forces behind the strong growth of the mutual fund industry. Technology has enabled the industry to provide better customer service and introduce a broad array of new products at a reasonable cost. In the 1960s and 1970s, mainframe computers and online transaction processing made it possible for mutual fund companies to manage the records of their shareholders. Advances in telecommunications enabled the companies to install 800 numbers and route incoming calls twenty-four hours a day, so that service agents could provide information and take orders over the phone.

In the 1980s, real-time data feeds and intraday fund pricing became a reality. The high-speed mainframes easily handled the increased trading volumes and the growth of 401(k) plans. Toward the end of the decade, personal computers (PCs) began to take over some traditional mainframe functions. Local area networks and nationwide networks integrated customer service functions.

During the 1990s, home PCs proliferated and Internet use exploded. The Internet has made it possible for users to gain electronic access to Wall Street research and real-time data. Many investment companies now offer extensive Web sites with rich information. Increasingly, customers are obtaining information and conducting their business online.

International Dimension

With continued technological advances, deregulation, and rapid growth in international money flows, the global economies and financial markets have become more integrated. Despite recent setbacks, many still expect Europe, Asia, and Latin America to present great investment opportunities. Trade agreements like the North American Free Trade Agreement (NAFTA) and the European Economic and Monetary Union (EMU) foster greater market access and investment opportunity. The World Trade Organization (WTO) has worked to lift tariffs and foreign exchange restrictions, spawning greater trade activity and opportunity for growth. In addition, the movements of many foreign markets do not correlate well with the U.S. market. Consequently, adding foreign securities to a portfolio can help manage investment risk by providing greater diversification. Such international investment can be accomplished conveniently through the purchase of international and global mutual funds.

International stock funds invest exclusively outside the United States, while global funds invest throughout the world including the United States. International/global funds can take advantage of investment opportunities around the world and the potential for higher returns. It is important to note, however, that these funds are subject to their own kinds of risks, including currency fluctuations and country risk. The recent financial crises in Asia, Russia, and Latin America—and their contagion effects on other markets—temporarily slowed the growth in exposure to emerging markets.

Not only Americans purchase foreign securities through international/ global funds, but investors in many other countries around the world buy shares in mutual funds. As mentioned earlier, Merrill Lynch's purchase of British-based Mercury Asset Management signifies the importance of the global asset management market. Worldwide assets in mutual funds grew from $2.853 trillion in 1991 to $11.920 trillion by 2000. The number of open-end investment companies also increased from 12,586 in 1991 to 52,735 in September 2001.[6] The growth in mutual fund assets worldwide can be attributed to several factors. The securities markets of many developed countries have benefited from favorable economic conditions in recent years. Second, mutual fund investing is popular because it provides a way of achieving a comfortable retirement and improved living standard. Third, as described earlier, many countries face the prospect of aging populations and the pressure to reduce government deficits, so they encourage private savings such as defined contribution retirement plans. Finally, the continued growth of the middle class worldwide has led to increased mutual fund investing.

Mutual Fund Selection and Asset Allocation

The type of mutual funds appropriate for a given investor depends on the individual's tolerance for risk and his investment horizon (or the time until the investor needs the money). Table 5.4 (see p. 118) provides a sample matrix of investment strategies. A capital preservation strategy is appropriate for investors who want income, a fair amount of stability, and some increase in the value of the investment. A strategy focused on moderate growth is for investors who primarily want a balance of moderate growth and moderate income with a fair amount of stability. For investors who want the potential for growth and capital appreciation, but also want some protection from stock market volatility, a wealth-building strategy is suitable. Aggressive growth is for investors who want the potential for substantial growth and capital appreciation.

In selecting a portfolio of mutual funds, an investor may also want to engage in asset allocation. Asset allocation is the process of strategically diversifying investments between stock, bond, and cash in order to achieve a return

---

[6]Data are for thirty-four countries, reported by the Investment Company Institute (http://www.ici.org).

TABLE 5.4	*Mutual Fund Investment Strategy Matrix*		
Tolerance for Risk	**Investment Horizon of 0 to 3 Years**	**Investment Horizon of 4 to 6 Years**	**Investment Horizon of 7+ Years**
High	Moderate growth strategy	Wealth-building strategy	Aggressive growth strategy
Moderate	Moderate growth strategy	Moderate growth strategy	Wealth-building strategy
Low	Capital preservation strategy	Capital preservation strategy	Moderate growth strategy

Source: *Fidelity Focus*, Fidelity Investments, Boston.

consistent with the investor's financial goals, investment horizon, and risk tolerance. A **strategic asset allocation** is a value-oriented technique that seeks to increase exposure to the market when recent market performance is poor, and to reduce exposure when recent market performance is good. In contrast, a dynamic asset allocation strategy uses a strategy to ensure that the value of the portfolio does not fall below a certain level (portfolio insurance) to avoid large losses and secure any favorable market move.

The benefit of risk reduction from diversification is well documented and understood. In addition, allocating money into various asset classes can improve overall returns. For example, suppose an investor has a two-year investment horizon and faces two types of funds in two different asset classes. Fund A provides a return of 40 percent in the first year and 0 percent in the second year. Fund B returns investors 0 percent and 40 percent during the same two-year period. Thus, investing in either Fund A or Fund B gives a total return of 40 percent. If the investor allocates funds into these two classes 50/50, the total return is 44 percent. An allocation mix of Fund A and Fund B results in an additional return of 4 percent.[7] Note that if the investor has perfect timing and invests in Fund A in the first year and switches to Fund B in the second year, the total return will be 96 percent. Most investors do not have a crystal ball, however, so they are better off diversifying their investments.

Asset allocation has a profound effect on the performance investors can expect from their investment portfolios over time.[8] Market timing and selection of individual securities account for less than 10 percent of a portfolio's performance. To develop an asset allocation program, investors should first determine their financial goals and investment horizon. They should also evaluate their level of risk tolerance, which depends on each individual's investment horizon, psychological ability to withstand market downswings, and financial situation. The next step is to develop a detailed asset allocation strategy using assets that complement each other. After the formulation of the blueprint for asset allocation, it is time to implement the strategy. The investor

---

[7]Note that, in order to maintain a 50/50 allocation mix, some funds will be shifted from Fund A to Fund B at the beginning of the second year.

[8]A study found that more than 90 percent of a portfolio's total rate of return can be attributed to its asset allocation policy.

reviews the performance of the portfolio periodically and compares it to his objectives. By periodically rebalancing the portfolio, the investor sells those assets that have appreciated and purchases those investments that have gone down in value. Such rebalancing helps maintain a constant portfolio risk level and prevents the asset allocation percentages from deviating from the plan.

STRUCTURE AND REGULATION OF MUTUAL FUNDS

Mutual funds are highly regulated financial firms that must comply with securities laws and regulations. This section reviews the basic structure of mutual funds and the regulatory environment in which they operate.

Basic Structure of Mutual Funds

The elements of a typical mutual fund structure include directors, investment adviser, principal underwriter, custodian, independent public accountants, and transfer agent. The directors or trustees of an investment company must perform their responsibilities with the care expected of a prudent person. They must evaluate the performance of the investment adviser, principal underwriter, and other parties that provide services to the fund. Independent directors, unaffiliated with the mutual fund, serve as watchdogs for shareholder interests. Investment advisory and distribution contracts must be approved by a majority of a fund's independent directors. The Investment Company Act of 1940 requires that at least 40 percent of the fund's board of directors be independent directors.

The investment adviser is responsible for making portfolio selections in accordance with the objectives and policies set forth in the prospectus. As noted earlier, most advisory contracts provide for an annual fee based on a percentage of the fund's average net assets during the year, generally between 0.5 and 1.5 percent (lower for index funds and higher for specialized funds). The principal underwriter markets and distributes mutual fund shares to the investing public, and independent accountants must certify the financial statements in a fund's annual report.

Most funds use bank custodians. The SEC requires mutual fund custodians to protect the funds by segregating their portfolio securities from the rest of the bank's assets. Fund transfer agents maintain records of shareholder accounts. Transfer agents typically serve as dividend disbursing agents as well. They prepare and mail account statements, tax information, and other notices to shareholders. Some transfer agents also prepare and mail statements confirming shareholder transactions and maintain customer service departments to respond to shareholder inquiries.

Mutual fund shareholders may purchase or redeem shares based on the NAV on the request date. Shareholders also have certain voting rights. Although most mutual funds no longer have annual shareholder meetings, certain matters such as changes in investment objectives or policies deemed fundamental require shareholder approval.

Regulation of Mutual Funds

The mutual fund industry is under a high degree of regulation. Congress enacted most of the federal securities laws that govern the industry in the wake of the stock market crash of 1929 and the Great Depression. These laws, intended to protect investors, include the Investment Company Act of 1940, the Investment Advisors Act of 1940, the Securities Act of 1933, and the Securities Exchange Act of 1934. Other important regulations include the Internal Revenue Code of 1986, state notice filing requirements, and antifraud statutes.

Under the **Investment Company Act** of 1940 **(ICA)**, a mutual fund's investment in each security is generally limited to an amount not greater than 5 percent of the fund's assets and not more than 10 percent of the outstanding voting securities of such issuer. The act also regulates the ability of mutual funds to employ certain investment techniques such as futures, options, and swaps. The act specifically prohibits certain transactions between a fund and its principal underwriter, investment adviser, or other affiliated persons.

The ICA requires all funds to safeguard their assets by placing them in the hands of a custodian and by providing fidelity bonding of officers and employees of the fund. Under the act, a mutual fund must determine its NAV each business day. Each mutual fund must maintain detailed books and records regarding the securities it owns and its outstanding shares, file semiannual reports with the SEC, and send such reports to shareholders.

The **Investment Advisers Act** of 1940 **(IAA)** regulates the activities of investment advisers, including advisers to investment companies and private money managers. The IAA regulation generally covers people who engage in the business of providing advice or issuing reports about securities to clients for compensation. Under the Investment Advisers Supervision Coordination Act of 1997 (IASCA), investment advisers must register with the SEC if they have more than $25 million in client assets under management or advise registered investment companies. Investment advisers who do not advise a registered investment company may rely on an existing exemption from SEC registration. This exemption applies to investment advisers who had fewer than fifteen clients during the past twelve months, do not hold themselves out to the public as investment adviser, and do not advise any registered investment company. Because the assets under management for some advisers may fluctuate above and below $25 million, causing needless SEC and state registrations and withdrawals, the SEC has raised the threshold for mandatory registration to $30 million. When assets under management dip below $25 million, withdrawal from SEC registration is required.

Even when investment advisers do not register under the IAA because they manage less than $25 million and do not advise a registered investment company, they may still be required to register under state law. State-registered investment advisers whose assets under management grow to $30 million must register with the SEC. All states have the authorization to enforce actions against SEC-registered investment advisers and associated persons under their antifraud laws. States also retain the authority to receive copies of documents filed with the SEC for notice purposes or to impose fees on investment advisers.

The **Securities Act** of 1933 requires that all prospective mutual fund investors receive a current prospectus describing the fund and that the fund provide, upon request, a Statement of Additional Information. Mutual funds are subject to special SEC registration rules because they continuously offer new shares to the public. To facilitate the continuous offering of shares, the act permits a mutual fund to update its prospectus at regular intervals, whenever material changes occur, and to register an indefinite number of shares. After the end of each fiscal year, mutual funds pay a registration fee to the SEC based on the shares actually sold. Mutual funds are permitted to net redemptions against sales when calculating their SEC registration fees.

The **Securities Exchange Act** of 1934 regulates broker-dealers, including principal underwriters and others who sell mutual fund shares, and requires them to register with the SEC. In addition, all sales and research personnel must demonstrate their qualifications by passing an examination administered by the National Association of Securities Dealers (NASD). A mutual fund's principal underwriter must have a Registered Principal. This officer must take special qualification examinations administered by the NASD.

The Internal Revenue Code of 1986 provides a mutual fund entity-level tax exemption if the fund distributes substantially all of its income to its shareholders. The mutual fund shareholders report the dividends received from the fund on their individual tax returns. Several types of income retain their character when they flow through a mutual fund to its shareholders. These include long-term capital gains (paid out as a capital gain dividend) and municipal bond income exempt from federal taxes (the exempt-interest dividend). In addition, all local governments recognize that the character of federal obligation interest, which is exempt from state and local taxation, can flow through a mutual fund to its shareholders.

State registration of mutual fund shares is optional. A state in which a fund intends to sell its shares, however, may require a notice filing. Once a mutual fund satisfies the notice filing requirements, it may sell its shares in a state. Mutual funds must also comply with state antifraud provisions.

HEDGE FUNDS

A hedge fund is a private investment fund that employs investment strategies involving various types of securities in various markets. The defining characteristic of a hedge fund is that it can take both long and short positions, and use leverage and derivatives. The fund is usually organized as a limited partnership. Investors in a hedge fund make their investment by contributing capital and gain admittance as limited partners. The general partner (GP) has discretion over investment strategies. The GP usually receives a fixed management fee of 1–2 percent of the assets under management as well as an incentive fee. The incentive fee is usually 20 percent of profits in excess of a chosen benchmark, although there are variations. The GP typically has a large investment in the fund.

The first hedge fund, managed by Alfred W. Jones, started in New York in 1949. Jones used a private partnership structure for operational flexibility, took long and short positions, and used leverage. His success led to a continuing growth of hedge funds. The activities of such funds have expanded in the past several decades. Many Wall Street firms have entered into the business. Additionally, many of the brightest stars on Wall Street and academics have started their own shops. By some estimates, there are currently more than 3,000 hedge funds managing hundreds of billions of dollars. Although the number and size of hedge funds are small relative to mutual funds, their growth reflects the importance of this alternative investment category for institutional and wealthy individual investors. Investment banks and institutional money managers target the hedge fund business as a fee-rich growth area that can help retain promising talent. The easing of the restrictions on the number of limited partners a hedge fund can have without having to register with the SEC also stimulated hedge fund growth.

Hedge funds now operate in currency, government securities, derivatives, and commodities transactions as well as merger and acquisition activities. Some use complex computer models to place huge bets on movements in financial markets. Recently, hedge funds have received significant attention from the news media and government regulators. The Long Term Capital Management (LTCM) crisis in 1998 raised concern that greater regulatory oversight in the hedge fund industry might be needed. Box 5.1 provides a detailed description of LTCM, its main trading strategies, and its near-collapse that threatened the stability of the global financial system.

Hedge Fund Structure

Hedge funds avoid regulation by limiting their clientele to a small number of institutions and very wealthy individuals.[9] Hedge funds seek high rates of return by investing and trading in a variety of financial instruments. The majority of U.S. hedge funds charge the standard "one-and-twenty," 1 percent management fee and 20 percent of the profits (called incentive fees). There are variations, of course. Most funds observe a **high-water mark**: if a fund loses money in a given performance fee period, investors will not be charged in later periods until the losses have been recovered. Another variation is the preferred return threshold: a fund will not collect an incentive fee until a specified rate of return has been achieved. Furthermore, most funds require that investments remain in the fund for a minimum duration, known as the **lockup period**. The common lockup period is one year, but a three-year lockup is not unknown.

Prime brokerage is an essential part of a hedge fund operation. It is a suite of services providing the fund with centralized custody, clearance, competitive

---

[9]Offshore hedge funds appear in locations outside the United States and offer their investment opportunities to non–U.S. residents.

MARKETS IN ACTION Long Term Capital Management

5.1

Sixteen partners established Long Term Capital Management (LTCM) in February 1994. Called the Rolls-Royce of hedge funds, it had a collection of the best minds and had high-flying success in its first three years of operations. The sixteen LTCM partners include several high-profile members such as John W. Meriwether, former vice chairman of Salomon Brothers; Myron S. Scholes, 1997 Nobel Laureate in Economics; Robert C. Merton, 1997 Nobel Laureate in Economics; and David W. Mullins, Jr., former vice chairman of the Federal Reserve Board.

The idea presented by the "dream team," as many called it, was good enough to lure eighty investors (with a minimum investment of $10 million), including some of the most respected names in the financial world. Bear Stearns President James E. Cayne and his deputy, Warren J. Spector, each chipped in. Merrill Lynch bought a huge chunk and marketed pieces of it to some of its wealthiest clients, including the company's chairman, David H. Komansky.

The core of LTCM's trading strategies was so-called convergence trading, which sought to profit from anomalies in prices among different segments of financial markets around the globe. As long as the relationships in returns mimicked their long-term historical patterns, LTCM would profit from the convergence on interest rate spreads and the volatility of market prices.

Certainly, the strategy was initially successful. In its first three years, LTCM produced incredible returns. In the first year, LTCM produced a return of more than 19 percent to investors. The fund returned 42.8 percent, after fees, in 1995 and 40.8 percent in 1996, before slipping to 17.1 percent in 1997. An individual or institution that had invested $10 million in 1994 would have received $18.2 million profits at the end of 1997.

The very efficiencies that LTCM and other funds brought to the global financial system, however, gradually reduced opportunities for above-normal profits. To sustain the substantial profits, LTCM returned $2.75 billion of capital to investors at the end of 1997. At its peak, LTCM had $160 billion worth of securities, more than thirty times its capital, and more than $1 trillion in notional principal amount of derivatives on its books. The firm took huge, highly leveraged positions, betting that interest rate spreads would narrow in the United States, Japanese, and larger European bond markets. But the opposite happened in the global flight to quality that followed financial turmoil in Russia. The fund also ventured into takeover investing (style drifting) and got hurt by declines in takeover stocks. On September 2, 1998, John Meriwether sent investors a letter, informing them that the fund was down 44 percent in August and 52 percent for the year. By the end of August, LTCM's capital was down to $2.3 billion, from $4.8 billion at the start of 1998. To make matters worse, the markets continued to move against LTCM in September.

In response to fears that LTCM's collapse could lead to global market turmoil and global recession, the Federal Reserve Bank of New York orchestrated a coordinated rescue in September 1998. A consortium of Wall Street firms agreed to pony up more than $3.5 billion to shore up LTCM, in exchange for a 90 percent stake in the hedge fund. Five of the firms also formed a new committee to oversee LTCM's overall strategy, procedures, controls, and even compensation. LTCM then gradually liquidated its positions and terminated its operations.

Sources: Liaw (1999), Perold (1999), and *Wall Street Journal* (various issues).

financing rates, securities lending, and office facilities in selected markets. A prime broker acts as the back office for the fund by providing the operational services necessary for the hedge fund manager to manage the business effectively. This enables the GP to focus on investment strategies rather than on operational issues.

Management Style

Hedge fund managers use many different management styles and pursue various trading strategies (Table 5.5). The risk to investors depends on the specific strategy pursued by the fund. As indicated in Table 5.5, a market-neutral strategy has low risk while emerging markets and macro styles post very high risks. Very few funds use only one strategy, and some change their investment styles over time. Even with the same investment style, the risks sometimes vary considerably. This can be largely explained by the differing liquidity of the fund's assets. For example, David Askin's funds (Granite Partners, Granite Corp, and Quartz Hedge Fund) were classified by market professionals as market neutral. Nevertheless, Askin's investments proved to be extremely risky, as the market for mortgage-backed securities became very thin and eventually caused the collapse of his highly leveraged hedge funds in 1994. Another good example is Long Term Capital Management, which was also classified as market neutral. In search of superior returns, LTCM leveraged its capital through repurchase agreements and derivatives transactions, relying on sophisticated mathematical models to guide its relative-value transactions. As Box 5.1 describes, LTCM initially generated superior returns but eventually increased its risk exposure in an effort to continue its outstanding performance. When Russia's default on its debt obligations in 1998 triggered a flight-to-quality and a flight-to-liquidity (investors rushed to buy top-quality securities with high liquidity such as the most recently issued Treasury securities), liquidity in the global financial system dried up, and LTCM nearly collapsed.

Hedge Fund Performance

Hedge funds have great flexibility in their investment options because they use financial instruments that are generally beyond the reach of mutual funds. This flexibility, which includes the use of hedging strategies to protect downside risk, gives hedge funds the ability to better manage investment risks. Studies have shown that hedge funds usually provide excellent returns to investors. Sources of such information include Van Hedge Fund Advisors (**http://hedge fund.com**) and the Hedge Fund Association (**http://www.thehfa.com**).

The strong performance results of hedge funds can be linked to their performance incentives, in addition to their investment flexibility. Unlike mutual funds, the hedge fund GP usually invests heavily in a significant portion of the fund and shares the rewards as well as the risks. The incentive fee remunerates the hedge fund managers in accordance with their performance. In contrast, mutual funds generally pay managers a fixed percentage of the amount of money attracted, regardless of performance. This incentive fee structure tends to attract many of Wall Street's best practitioners to the hedge fund industry.

Nevertheless, the collapse of LTCM and the failures of several other hedge funds in 1998 suggested that the hedge fund industry became the victim of its own success. First of all, the star managers attracted too much money so it was difficult to find similar investment opportunities to get top returns. This brought about a dilution of talent at the same time, meaning that some man-

TABLE 5.5	*Hedge Fund Investment Styles*		
Style	**Definition**	**Holding Period**	**Expected Volatility**
Emerging markets	Invest in emerging markets; shorting is not permitted in some markets, so managers must resort to other alternatives to hedge	Short/medium term	Very high
Short only	Go only short on securities	Medium	Very high
Macro	Strategies designed to profit from major currency or interest rate shifts	Medium	Very high
Sector play	Invest in a specific sector of the market	Medium	High
Distressed	Invest primarily in securities of companies in bankruptcy or reorganization	Medium/long	Moderate
Growth	Dominant theme involves high-growth firms	Medium/long	Moderate
Risk arbitrage	Simultaneously long the target and short the acquirer	Medium	Moderate
Convertible arbitrage	Long the convertible securities and short the underlying equities	Medium	Low
High yield	Invest mainly in non–investment-grade securities	Medium	Moderate
Event driven	Play on anticipated event	Medium	Moderate
Value	Dominant theme is intrinsic value: asset, cash flow, book value, and out-of-favor stock	Long	Low/moderate
Opportunistic	Momentum trading with short-term horizon	Short	Low/moderate
Market neutral	Combine positions to create a zero-beta portfolio	Short/medium	Low
Convergence	Exploit temporary out-of-line relationships; take profits when relationships among various securities return to historical norm	Short/medium	Low

Sources: *All About Hedge Funds,* Van Hedge Fund Advisors, 2001.

agers lacked the necessary skills to succeed. And with more and more funds pursuing similar trading strategies, the markets became more efficient and less profitable. Under pressure to produce, some funds use more leverage or change management styles, or both. Furthermore, many star traders did not do as well on their own. Once independent, they lost the support a big firm provides in risk monitoring, advanced technology, and multiple levels of management and governance.

VENTURE CAPITAL FUNDS

A VC firm often operates several VC funds; each pools funds from investors and invests in entrepreneurial companies. A VC fund passes through four stages in its life. The first stage, which usually lasts six to twelve months, involves fundraising to obtain capital commitments from investors. The second stage is the actual investment. The invested company becomes a portfolio company of the fund. This phase typically lasts for about three to seven years. During the next stage, which lasts from the time the fund makes the investment until the closing of the fund, the fund helps the portfolio company grow. The final stage in the life of a VC fund is its closing. The VC fund should have liquidated its position in all of its portfolio companies by the expiration date of the fund.

Liquidation takes one of three forms: an initial public offering, a sale of the company, or bankruptcy.

Compared with other types of investing, VC investing has several unique features. First, venture capitalists actively involve themselves in searching for candidates, negotiating, and structuring the transaction, and monitoring the portfolio company. Once they have selected a company for investment, VC professionals do not merely supply capital; they are active investors who also offer advice on strategic and financial planning and provide management oversight in order to enhance value. Frequently, VC professionals and the management of the portfolio company work in partnership. The venture capitalists' judgment and contacts can be helpful as the portfolio company expands and grows. In addition to serving as advisers, venture capitalists frequently serve as members of the board of directors of the portfolio company. Whether the VC fund will demand a majority of the board seats usually depends on how mature the business is and the fraction of the business the fund owns.

Second, VC investing generally intends to last for several years, typically three to seven, with the expectation of high returns when the portfolio company is successful and its securities soar in value. Venture funds often invest in common stock, stock plus debt unit, convertible debt, stock warrants, and preferred stock. Venture capitalists typically expect a high rate of return, commensurate with the high risk. Empirically, the overall stock market performance influences annual returns on VC investments, which are quite volatile.

The third difference is that the securities purchased by VC funds are usually privately held. When a venture capitalist finances a new business startup or a growth company, the company generally is privately held. If the VC fund invests in a buyout of a public company, the company is typically privately held after the buyout. Even in the rare cases when venture capitalists invest in public companies, they generally hold nonpublic securities.

Investment Strategies

Venture capital is high-risk, high-return investing. Before engaging in the costly and time-consuming evaluation process, venture capitalists need to define their goals and do research on the myriad of prospects in order to find a good match with the best financial and strategic edge. After the completion of this phase, most VC firms evaluate potential investments based on four fundamental criteria: management, marketing, products, and financial opportunity.

Management experience is a major consideration in evaluating financing prospects. Venture capitalists generally will not take an interest in a company unless it has superior management. An "A team" with a "B product" is more likely to get VC financing than a "B team" with an "A product."

The ideal target for VC funding is a company that has rapid growth and the potential to become enormous. The ideal product should have many proprietary features that differentiate it from others offered by competing companies. A commodity product that has no unique features can easily be manufactured by new entrants and hence is not attractive. In addition, the product should achieve above-average gross margins and offer repeat sales opportunities.

Once the VC fund managers identify a company that has superior management, an attractive market opportunity, and an excellent product, they seek to acquire a stake at as low a price as possible. The entrepreneur, on the other hand, wants the price to be as high as possible. Consequently, the price of the deal is the outcome of a complex negotiation process. Liquidity is the final goal. Thus, an assessment of likely exit opportunities happens before the investment of the money.

Venture Capital Transactions

Venture capital investing covers a wide range of the investment spectrum. Seed money provided to the entrepreneur establishes the feasibility of an innovative concept or product. Venture funds providing such first-round financing for risky investments are often called **VC angels**.

The next step is startup financing, which involves financing for product development and the initial phase of marketing. Then comes first-stage financing. At this stage of corporate development, the firm has developed a prototype that appears marketable. The firm begins its growth through second-stage financing. During the growth stage, VC funds provide working capital to finance goods in process, inventories, shipping, and the like. Gradually, this development process leads directly to third-stage financing. In this phase, funds finance major expansion when sales begin to take off. At a certain point in the process of corporate development, the company will be ready to go public or become a target for an acquisition. This stage marks the end of the VC financing cycle.

Exit Strategies

Venture capitalists plan their exit strategies when they make the front-end investments. Exit strategies include taking the portfolio company public or selling the portfolio company to another business. If the VC fund's exit is through a public offering, it can utilize several methods to resell its **restricted securities**, which are securities acquired directly or indirectly in a transaction not involving any public offering. Restricted securities can be sold via a subsequent private sale or a public offering registered with the SEC. Once the portfolio company has completed its initial public offering, the venture capitalists and other shareholders can sell their restricted securities without filing a SEC registration statement if it meets all SEC Rule 144 requirements, such as volume limitation, holding period, and SEC notification. The holding period required for the resale of a limited amount of restricted securities is one year. In addition, under amended Rule 144(k), nonaffiliates of an issuer may sell an unlimited number of restricted securities if at least two years have elapsed since the acquisition of such securities from the issuer or an affiliate of the issuer.[10]

Alternatively, the portfolio company could be acquired by, or merge with, another firm for the acquirer's stock, notes, or cash, or all three. If the venture

---

[10]The term *affiliate* includes the chief executive officer, insider directors, and major shareholders.

capitalist and other holders receive the acquirer's stock as principal consideration, the transaction can be regarded as a tax-free reorganization.

Information Sources for Venture Capital

The best sources of VC funding are the established boutiques and venture arms
of most major investment or commercial banks. *Platt's Guide to Venture Capital
Sources* is a comprehensive directory that lists the addresses and telephone numbers of VC companies. The National Venture Capital Association is another
source. The Directory of Venture Capital Clubs is an excellent information
source for first-stage venture capital. Other sources include Investors Network
(**http://www.investornet.com**), VentureOne (**http://www.ventureone
.com**), Vcapital (**http://www.vcapital.com**), and Vfinance (**http://www.
vfinance.com**).

BUYOUT FUNDS

Buyout funds are investment firms that invest in leveraged buyouts (LBOs).
LBOs use borrowed money for a substantial portion of the purchase price of
the buyout company. If the purchasers are management, the acquisition is
sometimes called a management buyout. An LBO firm has several basic characteristics. The first is that it uses other people's money, meaning that the LBO
firm often acquires companies with as little of its own money as possible. The
firm borrows the bulk of the purchase price from banks and other lenders. The
assets and future cash flows of the selling company typically secure the debt.
Consequently, LBOs generally involve low-tech businesses with a history of
consistent profitability and lots of tangible assets. To support acquisition debt,
the selling company needs to have low leverage in the first place. By using a
large amount of leverage, the buyout firm enhances its investment returns
because the lenders share little or none of the upside. Second, LBO firms generally look for distressed companies in out-of-fashion industries to avoid paying top dollar. After acquiring the company, the buyout firm seeks to enhance
its operating performance. Managers receive equity participation to achieve
this objective.

A Typical Buyout Financing Structure

Virtually all LBOs receive financing through a combination of senior debt,
subordinated debt, and equity. In part, the amount of debt that can be borrowed determines the amount of equity required in a transaction. The following describes the various components of financing in a typical LBO.

First, and probably the most important component of financing, is senior
debt. Typically 50 to 70 percent of an LBO's funding takes the form of senior
financing. A senior loan is collateralized by a first lien on the assets of the company. Banks generally provide senior financing, although privately placed notes
to institutional investors are also possible. Occasionally, a public issue of bonds
may be the source of senior debt.

The senior debt almost always includes a revolving line of credit, based on a certain percentage of the appraised liquidation value of the eligible accounts receivables and inventory. A revolving line of credit is bank line of credit on which the company pays a commitment fee and can take and repay the loan at will.

Another component of senior debt is a senior term loan. A certain percentage of the appraised fair market value of the land and buildings, as well as the liquidation value of the machinery and equipment, determines this loan. The predictability of cash flows to service senior debt also affects such loans. The term for senior term debt is usually five to eight years and, in the event of bankruptcy, holders will be paid before subordinated debt receives any payment.

Typically, 15 to 30 percent of an LBO is in the form of subordinated financing, generally raised from insurance companies or subordinated debt funds. Alternatively, a public offering of high-yield or non–investment-grade bonds to insurance companies, pension funds, and other institutional investors provides the financing. In many LBOs, the seller receives subordinated debt, which comprises a portion of the purchase price. The term of such financing is typically six to ten years, and there is commonly a deferral of principal payments until after the retiring of senior debt.

Equity financing accounts for the remaining 10 to 20 percent of the financing of an LBO. These funds make up the difference between the financing required and the financing available in the form of debt. Management usually invests in the equity of an LBO company together with an LBO fund, a corporate investor, or a group of institutional investors. The seller and subordinated lenders sometimes receive equity in the new company.

Leveraged Buyout Firms

The best-known buyout firm is Kohlberg Kravis Roberts & Co. (KKR). Other well-known firms include Clayton, Dubillier, & Rice; the Carlyle Group; Hicks, Muse, Tate & Furst; Advent International; Brera Capital Partners; Welsh, Carson, Anderson & Stowe; Apollo Advisors; Hellman & Friedman; Leonard Green & Partners; Fenway Partners; Thomas H. Lee Co.; Forstmann Little & Co.; and the Blackstone Group.

The buyout industry is global. Many U.S. shops have established or expanded operations overseas. For example, KKR; Clayton, Dubillier & Rice; and Hicks, Muse, Tate & Furst began setting up buyout funds for continental Europe before the advent of the European Monetary Union in 1999. Examples of funds targeted at buyout opportunities in Asia include Unison Capital, Patricof & Co. Ventures, and the Carlyle Group. At the same time, foreign firms have targeted the U.S. markets for potential acquisitions. London-based Doughty Hanson & Co. is one such example.

Leveraged Buyouts and Economic Benefits

Leveraged buyouts have been blamed for many things, from the federal budget deficit to unemployment. It is true that many LBOs have resulted in corporate restructuring and massive layoffs. The high leverage gives corporations huge tax savings, which reduce the government's tax revenues. Some commentators have also criticized the huge premium paid in LBOs and the large profits and fees earned by those who engineer the transactions.

In reality, LBOs are merely tools of economic organization. Most U.S. corporations fared poorly in the 1970s; many lost market share and profits to Japanese, German, and other overseas rivals. Management's mindset at that time was simply to hang on and not to take risks. But risk taking is as important to economic growth as technology, globalization, and productivity. Without risk taking, even the most promising technology would gather dust in the university laboratory. Michael Milken's junk bond finance and KKR's LBOs gave ambitious risk-takers the opportunity to establish a new entrepreneurial economy. In addition, with every LBO, more corporate senior managers got the message: take actions to improve performance or lose your job. Thus, the LBOs and hostile takeovers of the 1980s contributed to the emergence of the incredible economy of the 1990s.

REAL ESTATE INVESTMENT TRUSTS

A real estate investment trust (REIT) is an investment company that pools funds from investors and invests in income-producing residential and commercial properties. REITs differ from stocks only in that they are engaged exclusively in the real estate business. Otherwise, they pay dividends and may be listed on an exchange. As large blocks of real estate become equitized, investment opportunities in REITs will expand.

The REIT market has grown from 75 REITs with a market capitalization of $2.3 billion in 1980 to 182 REITs with a capitalization of $154.9 billion by the end of 2001.[11] Several factors have contributed to this growth. First, REITs are liquid investments. Many REITs, like closed-end funds, are listed and traded on exchanges. Thus, investors can buy and sell interests in diversified portfolios of properties easily. Second, REITs have a unique corporate structure that requires them to distribute at least 95 percent of their income to shareholders. Hence, they pay high dividends to investors. They are also free from taxation at the corporate level. Third, returns on REITs are competitive. During the period 1981–2000, the average annual return for equity REITs was 12.43 percent. During that time, the average returns for U.S. small stocks and the S&P 500 Index were 13.33 percent and 15.68 percent, respectively. Furthermore, REITs represent a good source of diversification for investment portfolios. During the period 1993–2000, the correlation of REIT returns with that of small stocks was 0.26; with the S&P 500, it was 0.25; and with long-term bonds, it was 0.16.[12]

---

[11]Data are from National Association of Real Estate Investment Trusts (http://www.nareit.org).

[12]Data are based on research conducted by Ibbotson Associates that was included in a May 29, 2001 news release.

There are three types of REITs. An equity REIT is a corporation that purchases, owns, and manages real estate properties. The revenues come from rent. A mortgage REIT is a corporation that purchases, owns, and manages real estate loans. Its revenues come from interest from the mortgage loans. The third type is a hybrid REIT that combines the investment strategies of both equity REITs and mortgage REITs. Among these three types, equity REITs account for the biggest share of the total market by far. In 2001, for example, equity REITs accounted for $147 billion of the $155 billion total market capitalization of REITs.

CONCLUDING SUMMARY

Investment management is increasingly an integral part of capital markets. It provides professional money management expertise to institutions and individuals. The industry is also an important funding source for corporations, providing private equity for new startups, buyout funds for corporate restructures, and mutual funds for public companies.

A mutual fund is an investment company that pools money from investors who share similar investment objectives and invests in various types of securities. Through the pooling of investor money, a mutual fund offers investors a simple, convenient way to invest in a diversified portfolio of securities. Furthermore, there are many types of funds available to meet different investment objectives. Many funds offer other services such as brokerages, online bill payment, and ATM/debit cards as well.

Hedge funds are private investment trusts that can only accept investments from investors who meet certain qualifications. Hedge funds operate in foreign currency, government securities, corporate securities, derivatives, and merger and acquisition activities. The majority of U.S. hedge funds charge the standard "one-and-twenty," 1 percent management fee and 20 percent incentive fees. Most funds observe a high-water mark. If a fund loses money in a given performance fee period, the investors will not be charged in later periods until the recovery of losses.

Venture capital firms make equity investments in entrepreneurial companies. A private VC fund raises its capital from a limited number of sophisticated investors and passes through four stages in its life. The first stage is fundraising. During the second stage, the actual investment is made. After the identification of a prospective target, satisfactory due diligence leads to an investment. The invested company then becomes a portfolio company. During the next stage, which lasts until the closing of the fund, the VC professionals help the portfolio company grow. The final stage is the closing of the fund.

Buyout funds are investment firms that invest in leveraged buyouts, in which they purchase companies using borrowed money for a substantial portion of the purchase price. If the purchasers are management, some call the acquisition a management buyout. There are three factors generally considered essential to conducting a successful LBO: the ability to borrow significant sums against the company's assets; the ability to retain or attract a strong management team; and the potential for the investment to increase substantially in value. Because of the high leverage, LBO lenders generally look for low-tech businesses with sufficient cash flows and many tangible assets.

Finally, a real estate investment trust is a type of investment company that differentiates itself by investing primarily in real estate. REIT shares trade on stock exchanges. Thus, they offer retail investors investment opportunities otherwise available only to those with larger resources.

Key Terms

active management strategy 115
buyout fund 128
closed-end investment company 108
exchange-traded fund (ETF) 116
hedge fund 108
high-water mark 122
indexing 115
Investment Advisors Act (IAA) 120
Investment Company Act (ICA) 120
lockup period 122

mutual fund 108
net asset value (NAV) 108
real estate investment trust (REIT) 109
restricted securities 127
Securities Act 121
Securities Exchange Act 121
strategic asset allocation 118
unit investment trust (UIT) 108
VC angel 127
venture capital (VC) 109

Review Questions

1. What are the main differences between a closed-end investment fund and a unit investment trust?

2. What are the main advantages of mutual fund investing?

3. The character of a mutual fund's income flows through to its shareholders. What does this mean?

4. A no-load mutual fund returns 12 percent to investors per year. A load fund charges a 5 percent front-end load and posts an annual return of 17 percent. For a one-year investment horizon, which is the better selection for investors?

5. A mutual fund owns three securities, as listed in this question. The fund owes ABC Bank $520,000, which it borrowed to cover earlier redemptions. The fund has issued 800,000 shares to date. What is the net asset value per share?

Security	Number of Shares	Price
A	25,000	$15.25
B	10,000	$22.375
C	30,000	$72.00

6. Discuss the main differences between hedge funds and mutual funds, covering management fees, incentive fees, investment strategies, the use of leverage, and trading strategies.

7. Many believe that hedge funds provide superior returns to select wealthy investors. Discuss the reasons for such superior performance.

8. Venture capital investing is different from other types of investments. Describe the unique features of VC investing.

9. Venture capitalists plan their exit strategies when they make the investments. Why is it important for venture capitalists to plan ahead? What are the exit strategies?

10. Find out the annual returns for VC investing, small stocks, and the S&P 500 Index in the past five years. Calculate the correlation matrix of these returns and discuss the implications of your findings.

11. What is a management buyout? What are the key factors a buyout specialist considers before making a buyout offer?

12. Search for a recent management buyout case and provide a summary of the characteristics of the target company. Are those characteristics similar to the ones discussed in the chapter? Explain.

Select Bibliography

Ackermann, C., R. McEnally, and D. Ravenscraft. "The performance of hedge funds: Risk, return, and incentives." *Journal of Finance* 54, no. 3, June 1999, pp. 833–874.

Baker, C. P., and G. D. Smith. *The New Financial Capitalists: Kohlberg Kravis Roberts and the Creation of Corporate Value*. Cambridge: Cambridge University Press, 1998.

Bogle, J. C., and P. L. Bernstein. *Common Sense on Mutual Funds*. New York: John Wiley & Sons, 2000.

Camp, J. J. *Venture Capital Due Diligence: A Guide to Making Smart Investment Choices and Increasing Your Portfolio Returns*. New York: John Wiley & Sons, 2002.

Chandler, B. *Investing With the Hedge Fund Giants* (2nd ed.). Englewood Cliffs, N.J.: Prentice Hall, 2002.

Crerend, W., and R. Jaeger. *Fundamentals of Hedge Fund Investing: A Professional Investor's Guide*. New York: McGraw-Hill, 1998.

Curtis, C. "Are banks making it in the fund business?" *ABA Banking Journal,* October 1997, pp. 57–64.

Gompers, P. A., and Lerner, J. *The Venture Capital Cycle*. Cambridge, Mass.: MIT Press, 1999.

Harman, D. K. *How to Run Your Own Money Management Business*. Burr Ridge, Ill.: Irwin Professional Publishing, 1995.

Journal of Private Equity. Various issues.

Liaw, K. T. *The Business of Investment Banking*. New York: John Wiley & Sons, 1999.

McCrary, S. A. *How to Create and Manage a Hedge Fund: A Professional's Guide*. New York: John Wiley & Sons, 2002.

Nicholas, J. G. *Investing in Hedge Funds: Strategies for the New Marketplace*. New York: Bloomberg, 1999.

Nicholas, J. G. *Market Neutral Investing: Long/Short Hedge Fund Strategies*. New York: Bloomberg, 2000.

Perold, A. F., "Long-Term Capital Management, L.P. (A)." Boston, Mass.: Havard Business School Publishing, 1999.

Perold, A. F., "Long-Term Capital Management, L.P. (C)." Boston, Mass.: Havard Business School Publishing, 1999.

Pozen, R. C. *The Mutual Fund Business*. Cambridge, Mass.: MIT Press, 1998.

Wall Street Journal, various issues.

Brokerage and Clearing Companies

On an average day, more than 1 billion shares change hands on the New York Stock Exchange, another 1.8 billion shares trade on the Nasdaq, and $300 billion worth of Treasury securities are traded. For each of these trades to take place, a buyer must be matched with a seller, and some means must be provided for the payment of funds and the transfer of securities. Also, the trading does not only occur in the United States; investors in other countries purchase U.S. securities, and U.S. investors increasingly look to foreign markets for diversification and higher yields. Similarly, U.S. companies often look abroad for funds when they need to raise capital.

The brokerage and clearing industries make all of these transactions possible. Investors and dealers rely on the services of brokers to facilitate their securities transactions. In the fixed-income market, interdealer brokers provide dealers with best bids and offers on a real-time basis. After brokers match buyers and sellers, settlement and clearing services provide for the payment of funds and the delivery of securities so that the transactions, international as well as domestic, can be completed.

Advances in technology have made possible the enormous increases in daily trading volume—up from only 157 million shares on the New York Stock Exchange and 132 million on the Nasdaq in 1990. Technology has also shortened the time to complete a trade and reduced the occurrences of the seller's failure to deliver securities or the buyer's failure to pay, which contributes to the markets' efficiency.

The objectives of this chapter are to provide an understanding of:
- The various types of brokerage services securities firms offer.
- Interdealer brokers' functions for non–exchange-traded securities.
- The trading mechanism in electronic communications networks.
- The importance of clearing and settlement.
- The services provided by various clearing firms.

MARKET OVERVIEW

The brokerage industry enables both the secondary and the primary markets for securities to function. By facilitating secondary market transactions, the industry contributes to the liquidity of securities traded in the secondary markets. Without that liquidity, the primary markets for securities would be much smaller, and businesses would have far more difficulty raising the capital they need to expand. Between 1990 and 2002, corporations and other institutions raised more than $24 trillion in the primary markets. Table 6.1 shows the amount raised each year.

The brokerage industry benefited from growth in both the primary and the secondary markets during the past decade. Commissions amounted to $33.7 billion in 2000, more than double their level of $16 billion in 1995.[1] The amount of funds lent to margin accounts surged from $6.2 billion in 1995 to $22.3 billion in 2000. The industry's profits reached an all-time high $16.3 billion in 1999, although profitability subsequently declined in 2000 and 2001.

Types of Brokers

Brokers can generally be divided into three types: full-service brokers, discount brokers, and electronic brokers (ebrokers). Full-service brokers provide a complete menu of financial services, including trade execution, research reports, financial advice, and financial planning. Discount brokers execute trades for customers for lower commissions but do not provide research or advice. Electronic brokers only offer their services online; some ebrokers charge as little as $7 for a trade of up to 5,000 shares. As most full-service and discount brokers now make their services available online, the distinction between ebrokers and other types of brokers has diminished.

Types of Accounts

The most basic account is the cash account. With a cash account, the customer pays the brokerage house the full transaction value for any securities purchased and does not borrow any funds from the brokerage firm. Alternatively, investors may open a margin account that allows them to borrow money from the brokerage firm to purchase securities. Margin accounts are subject to various rules and regulations. Before engaging in margin transactions, the investor has to deposit cash or eligible securities, known as **initial margin**, with the broker. The Fed currently requires investors to deposit an initial margin of 50 percent of the trade value before purchasing eligible stocks or convertible bonds. For example, assume an investor purchased 500 shares of Goldman Sachs at $72.30 a share on margin. The broker charged a commission of $15 for the trade. The investor had to deposit at least half of the value of the purchase plus commission. The amount of the trade was $36,150. The initial margin requirements

---

[1]Data are from the Securities Industry Association.

TABLE 6.1	*Capital Raised by the Securities Industry for U.S. Business and Governments*

Year	Amount ($ billions)
1990	536
1991	839
1992	1,129
1993	1,437
1994	1,043
1995	1,187
1996	1,381
1997	1,930
1998	2,600
1999	2,732
2000	2,570
2001	3,190
2002	3,500

Source: Securities Industry Association (http://www.sia.com).

would be $18,075. Thus the investor had to have at least $18,090 in the account to complete the transaction.

After the completion of the transaction, the individual exchanges and the brokerage firm will require that the investor maintain a certain equity level in the margin account, called **maintenance margin**. The New York Stock Exchange (NYSE; **http://www.nyse.com**) and the National Association of Securities Dealers (NASD; **http://www.nasd.org**) require customers to keep a maintenance margin of 25 percent of the market value of the securities in their margin accounts. Brokerage firms often require a higher percentage, as firms rate their customers and require a lower margin from their best customers and a higher margin from riskier customers. In addition, the Federal Reserve Board's Regulation T regulates credit extended by brokers and dealers. Regulation T requires that $2,000 in cash or securities must be deposited with a brokerage house before any credit can be extended.

Asset management accounts require a minimum balance to open and they charge an annual fee. All offer automatic reinvestment of the account's cash balances in money market funds. Typically, account holders receive a credit card and can also write checks against the account's assets. In addition, loans based on the marginable securities in the account can be obtained anytime.

In recent years, brokerage firms have begun to offer so-called wrapped accounts, in which the customer pays the brokerage firm a flat annual fee to cover all services and trading commissions. Many large full-service brokerage houses such as Merrill Lynch and Smith Barney offer these accounts.

Most customers allow their brokerage firms to keep their securities in a street name, the name of the brokerage firm. The customer receives a monthly statement showing all positions held in the account.

Types of Orders

Customers can place three basic types of orders: market orders, limit orders, and stop orders. A **market order** instructs the broker to buy or sell the securities immediately at the best price available at that time. A market order ensures that the transaction will be completed, but the price of the trade is unknown until it is executed.

A **limit order** specifies a particular price for the trade. In the case of a buy order, the customer specifies the maximum price that he is willing to pay; usually this price is lower than the current market price. In the case of a sell order, the customer specifies a minimum price that he is willing to accept to sell the security. A limit order can be effective for one day or good until canceled, which means that the order will remain in effect for six months unless it is canceled or renewed. There is no guarantee that the order will be filled. Limit orders can be specified as all or none (fill the whole order or nothing), immediate or cancel (fill any part of the order immediately or cancel the order), or fill or kill (fill the entire order or kill it).

A **stop order** can be used to purchase or sell a security after its price reaches a certain level. A buy stop order is placed above the current market price, and a sell stop order is placed below the current market price. A stop limit order becomes a limit order once the limit price is reached. For example, a buy stop order of 500 shares of Cisco Systems at $11 per share means that the order will be executed at the best market price once Cisco reaches $11 per share. A stop limit order for the same amount means that once Cisco reaches $11, the order becomes a limit order to sell at a limit price of $11.

FULL-SERVICE BROKERAGE

The securities brokerage industry encompasses a variety of financial institutions that offer investment services and financial products. Investors who want to have access to all the financial services available will often turn to a full-service brokerage firm. A global, **full-service firm** provides brokerage, investment banking, and asset management services to corporations, governments, and individuals around the world. A full-service brokerage firm will offer individual investors a full range of investment products, including stocks, bonds, mutual funds, certificates of deposits, insurance, and annuities. They also offer services such as advice on retirement planning, asset allocation, portfolio management, college funding, estate planning, and trust services. Some of the bigger full-service brokerage firms include Smith Barney, Merrill Lynch, Prudential, Morgan Stanley, and UBS PaineWebber.

Investors go to a full-service brokerage firm mainly because they want financial advice. Financial advisors spend time learning and understanding their clients' financial concerns and investment objectives and work to develop customized investment programs. As these relationships build over time, the advisor can anticipate the clients' changing needs and help adjust their investment strategies for milestones such as funding the children's education or retirement. As many full-service brokers now place more emphasis on providing a full range of financial advice, they derive a much smaller percentage of their revenues from commissions than in the past. Consequently, many full-service brokerage houses encourage their brokers to become more like fee-based professionals and less like salespeople.

Increased competition from low-cost discount brokerages and ebrokers has forced the full-service brokerage firms to ensure that they provide value for the higher fees that they charge. Superior service is now a basic requirement for all full-service firms. Customers expect access to investment and account information 24 hours a day, 365 days a year, across a variety of channels. Full-service firms have had to enhance their direct channels to offer this level of service. In addition, customers now demand more efficient execution of trades, fewer problems, and a faster resolution of problems when they occur.

For these reasons, full-service firms will have to aggressively focus and manage their business to remain competitive in the coming years. As investor sophistication and expectations grow, customers will demand more from their investment service providers. The key for full-service firms will be to respond to those investors who can benefit and derive value from the firms' core strengths, leading to profitable and sustainable customer relationships.

DISCOUNT BROKERAGE

With the deregulation of the brokerage industry in 1975, negotiated commissions became available to individual investors. Firms such as Charles Schwab (**http://www.schwab.com**) and Quick & Reilly (**http://www.quick-reilly.com**) first started to offer lower and lower commissions for executing transactions, later to become known as **discount brokerage.** Discount brokers do not offer investment advice to their clients, and they provide only limited services. Basically, they execute trades for independent investors who call on the telephone or use a personal computer to request a trade.

Discount brokerage firms have grown in popularity and have consistently increased their share of industry-wide retail commission revenues since 1975. This growth can be attributed in part to individual investors' increased willingness to make their own investment decisions. Individual investors today are more sophisticated than investors twenty years ago and have access to much more financial data. In addition to traditional resources such as *The Wall Street Journal*, investors now can turn to the Internet and cable television for investment information. As a result, many do not see any need to pay for professional advice and prefer to do their own research. Recognizing the potential of this market, discount brokers have been aggressive marketers; they have advertised heavily, opened up offices in well-traveled areas, and installed sophisticated telecommunications equipment to improve customer service. Their efforts to publicize low fees have been highly successful. Most clients of discount brokers say the lower commissions attracted them.

In the past few years, discount brokers such as Charles Schwab, Quick & Reilly, and Fidelity have taken their business online offering better service and even lower costs. Online trading, or buying and selling securities over the Internet, has become the new direction for discount brokerage. Together, the Internet and discount brokerages have in many ways transformed how our capital markets operate. These changes offer clear benefits, including lower costs and faster access to the market for investors. Investors need to remember the investment basics, however, and not allow the ease and speed with which they can trade to lull them into a false sense of security, or encourage them to trade too quickly or too often.

ELECTRONIC BROKERAGE

Just as the advent of the discount brokerage changed the brokerage industry in the late 1970s and 1980s, the electronic brokerage has transformed it in the 1990s and early 2000s. According to the Securities Industry Association, there were eighteen online brokerages, or ebrokers, holding 1.5 million accounts with $111 billion in assets in 1996. By 2000, ebrokers held 20 million accounts with $968 billion in assets. In 2001–2002, however, the growth in online accounts slowed, and the value of assets in these accounts, hurt by falling equity prices, declined.

The initial growth in online accounts occurred because discount broker-ages allowed their existing customers to trade online. When Charles Schwab began offering online brokerage, for example, the number of these accounts soared—without adding one new customer. Additional growth came from early-adopter types (those who like to try any new technology) who switched their accounts from traditional brokers or opened additional accounts to gain Internet access. Soon online-only brokerages, such as E*Trade (http://www.etrade.com) and Ameritrade (http://www.ameritrade.com) had growing account bases of their own. Today, online brokerages don't just convert discount brokerage customers and early adopters. They now sign up first-time, self-directed individual investors. These online brokerage houses offer one-stop shopping where investors can trade, research, track stocks, and customize their online portfolio accounts for a cost ranging from $7.00 to $29.95 a trade.

Leading ebrokers make online trading a virtual freedom. At one point, online trading meant trading only on desktop computers. Now with cell phones, PDAs, and laptops, investors can trade anywhere via these wireless devices. Such capabilities mean that, as long as investors are in an area of wire-less coverage, they can keep in touch with and respond to major moves in the market. They can trade, receive alerts, and check news from the car, from the golf course, or even from the beach.

Initially, the larger, more established brokers, especially the full-service firms, shied away from the online revolution, leaving the market open to upstart companies. Their concerns seemed to stem from the belief that electronic business would erode the role of traditional registered representatives (stockbrokers). Recently, however, the larger brokerage houses have realized that it is better for a firm to cannibalize its own business than to let a competitor do it for them. Brokerage houses have realized that they must expand their channels in order to remain competitive.

Another new development in recent years has been Internet brokerage houses including Schwab, E*Trade, and SoundView. These houses have expanded beyond stock brokering and now help to distribute shares of initial public offerings to retail customers. In the past, online securities firms and other discount brokerage firms did not participate in underwriting syndicates because they did not have armies of brokers to place stock with the right customers and research analysts and traders to follow the issue after it went public. Now the Internet and the exploding number of online investors have helped ebrokers join the club.

INTERDEALER BROKERAGE

Certain markets, such as the markets for Treasury and municipal securities, are not organized by a single entity like the NYSE or the Nasdaq system. Instead, they are informally organized around **interdealer brokers** who display bids and offers of other dealers anonymously.[2] Interdealer brokers enhance liquidity by providing a central mechanism to display the bids and offers of multiple dealers, and by allowing dealers and investors to trade large volumes of securities anonymously and efficiently. In the government securities market, for example, interdealer brokers compile the anonymous bids and offers of other government securities dealers and traders and display the quotations on screens located in the dealers' offices.

Dealers and other customers have direct telephone lines to the various individual brokers working at an interdealer broker. When a customer wants to buy or sell a security through an interdealer broker, she calls the assigned individual broker at that interdealer brokerage. Through the assigned broker, the customer can hit a bid (accept the bidding price to sell), lift an offer (accept the offering price to buy) shown on the screen, or tell the broker to post a new bid or offer on the screen. When the customer wants to hit a quote on the screen or enter a new quote, the broker announces the hit or new bid/offer to other brokers and enters the information so that it displays on internal and customer screens. Operating in this manner, interdealer brokers centralize the trading interest and provide a mechanism for customers to agree to the terms of a trade in much the same way as the registered exchanges and alternative trading systems do.

---

[2]The term *interdealer brokers* includes entities that certain markets refer to as brokers' brokers and blind brokers.

Major interdealer brokers in the U.S. Treasury securities market include Cantor Fitzgerald, Tullet & Tokyo Liberty, RMJ, Garban, and Hilliard & Farber. These brokers engage in trading other securities as well. Prebon Yamane, another interdealer broker, is a leading global intermediary in trading over-the-counter financial and energy products.

ELECTRONIC COMMUNICATIONS NETWORKS

Electronic communications networks (ECNs) are computerized trading systems that match buyers and sellers of securities. Instead of people executing trades over the computer, which is how the Nasdaq works, or through a specialist on an exchange floor, ECNs basically operate like giant eBays for securities. ECNs let buyers and sellers of stock meet without the use of intermediaries such as market makers and specialists.

The oldest and largest ECN is Instinet. Officially registered as a broker-dealer, Instinet enables its big institutional clients to trade millions of shares a day in many of the world's markets. Over the past several years, several new ECNs have sprung up (see Table 6.2). Nearly all of the major Wall Street banks, including Goldman Sachs, Merrill Lynch, and Morgan Stanley, have supported some alternative trading system. Some have invested in several systems.

Rise to Prominence

Since 1997, ECNs have stolen market share from the established exchanges. Both regulatory forces and technology contributed to the emergence of ECNs as a force on Wall Street. In January 1997, as part of its settlement of a 1996 antitrust investigation into collusion among market makers, the NASD issued new rules to govern how market makers handle customers' limit orders. Box 6.1 explains how these rules phased in. Under the rules, a market maker must post limit orders on the Nasdaq or send them to an ECN that will post them where everyone can see. Before the guidelines went into effect, market makers could ignore a limit order they did not like. In 1997, the only ECN of any con-

TABLE 6.2	*Electronic Communications Networks*
ECN	**Web Site Address**
Instinet	http://www.instinet.com
Island	http://www.island.com
Archipelago	http://www.tradearca.com
Attain	http://www.dom-sec.com
BRUT	http://www.ebrut.com
B-Trade	http://www.bloombergtradebook.com
NextTrade	http://www.nextrade.com

Sources: *Wall Street Journal*, various issues; and CNN Financial News.

sequence was Instinet, which maintained a network where institutional investors could trade in secret with each other and with market makers. Suspicious of this private party, the SEC effectively forced ECNs to post their quotes on Nasdaq's comprehensive trading bulletin board, known as a Level II screen. The screen displays the best prices and quantities of all market makers' and ECNs'. Buyers line up on the left and sellers on the right, with the best prices at the top. In an instant, these networks can match buy orders with any corresponding sell orders.

Allowing ECNs onto this system was a crucial change. Previously, an ECN could stay in business only if it could attract both buyers and sellers. Once ECNs could advertise trades on Nasdaq, however, they needed to supply only one party. The other side could come from anywhere else in the Nasdaq system. By forcing Instinet into the public marketplace, the SEC had inadvertently flung the marketplace open to ECNs.

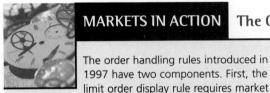

MARKETS IN ACTION   The Order-Handling Rules
6.1

The order handling rules introduced in 1997 have two components. First, the limit order display rule requires market makers holding customers' limit orders to reflect those orders in their quotes in the Best Bid and Offer (BBO) disseminated by the market. There are exceptions, such as when the order exceeds 10,000 shares, is less than 100 shares, or is an all-or-none order. Second, market makers may not post one quote on Nasdaq and a different quote on an alternative quote system such as an ECN. If the ECN upon which a dealer has posted a quote transmits its best market maker orders to the Nasdaq, which displays these quotes in accessible fashion, then the dealer can post different quotes on the Nasdaq and the ECN. If there is disruption of the communication link between the ECN and the Nasdaq, market makers receive an alert to the fact that the ECN alternative is unavailable.

With the SEC approval, the order-handling rules were implemented in a sequence of 22 waves, from January 20, 1997 to October 13, 1997. The universe for the initial waves was the set of top 1,000 Nasdaq securities, ranked by dollar trading volumes. The top 1,000 were subdivided into ten deciles. Waves 1 through 13 were drawn from all ten deciles. Wave 14 was the first wave in which stocks were drawn from the entire universe of Nasdaq stocks. The entire schedule was:

Wave	Date	Number of Stocks
1	Jan. 20	50
2	Feb. 10	50
3	Feb. 24	50
4	Apr. 21	50
5	Apr. 28	50
6	May 5	50
7	May 12	50
8	May 19	50
9	May 27	50
10	June 2	50
11	June 9	50
12	June 23	50
13	June 30	49
14	July 7	61
15	Aug. 4	250
16	Aug. 11	250
17	Sept. 8	850
18	Sept. 15	820
19	Sept. 22	850
20	Sept. 29	850
21	Oct. 6	850
22	Oct. 13	867

Source: NASD.

Advantages of ECNs

ECNs offer investors several advantages; most notably, extended trading hours and lower costs. Many ECNs offer extended trading hours. For example, Instinet and NexTrade provide electronic order execution services twenty-four hours a day. These innovations have forced the traditional markets to adapt. Both the NYSE and Nasdaq announced plans to extend their trading hours and to go public (Nasdaq went public in July 2002)—changes that are attributable to competitive pressures from ECNs.

Investors also like ECNs for other reasons. By executing trades electronically instead of by people, ECNs cut down on errors. The faster speed of execution also reduces the chance of **slippage**—a price change between the placement and execution of a trade. Also, trades executed through ECNs are inexpensive. When a customer goes to a market maker, and the spread is 5 cents, the customer technically pays an additional 5 cents per share. On an ECN, the brokerage firm places its own bid and ask, rather than relying on a market maker's best quotes. This increased competition has forced market makers to narrow their spreads. If a market maker does not offer a competitive price, it risks losing the trade because a brokerage firm can turn to an ECN. Another important benefit is anonymity. ECNs display the number of shares and the price, but they do not show the brokerage house or the investor that placed the order. On the Nasdaq, orders are identified only by the ECN's name. Anonymity is vital to big institutional investors, which are otherwise subject to front running. **Front running** is an illegal practice in which a broker affects a transaction on the basis of an impending order or trade. For example, employees of a brokerage firm, prior to executing a large customer order, place the same order for their personal accounts, thus front running the client. Though prohibited, front running nevertheless sometimes occurs.

Disadvantages of ECNs

Currently, one of the biggest challenges ECNs face is their lack of liquidity, particularly during extended-hours trading. ECNs are basically pools of limit-order trades that sit separate from each other. During the day, if ECNs cannot execute orders internally, they rely on the Nasdaq's SelectNet system to link up and pool their trading to improve liquidity. However, that option is unavailable during extended hours. Furthermore, ECN services are not widely available. Only select brokerage firms offer the ability to use ECNs to their retail customers.

Another problem is maintaining the necessary volume. Since ECNs charge a fraction of a penny per share traded, they have to have massive volume to make any money. The market downturn that began in the second quarter of 2000 presented difficulties for several ECNs. In September 2000, OptiMark suspended trading. Other struggling ECNs merged in order to survive (Tradescape.com with MarketXT, and Brass Utility with Strike Technologies). Many market observers believe that to survive, an ECN will have to differentiate itself and become more than just a machine matching buy and sell orders.

For example, Instinet has a strong hold on the institutional market, and Island has cornered a big slice of day trading (establishing and closing out the same positions during the same day).[3]

CLEARING AND SETTLEMENT

After a buyer and a seller have been matched, whether by a traditional exchange, by the Nasdaq system, or by an ECN, the "back office operations" of clearing and settlement take place. Clearing involves processing the trade and establishing what the counterparties to the transaction owe each other. **Settlement** is the transfer of money and securities between the parties to complete the transaction. Most Wall Street firms hire a clearing bank to receive and deliver money and securities as instructed by the firm's back office. A firm's money and securities accounts at its clearing bank together comprise the firm's **clearing account.**

In general, the clearing and settlement process involves three steps:

1. *Completing the trade ticket and conveying its details to the back office.* Whenever a trade occurs, the trader at the trading desk enters certain basic information on a trade ticket: whether the order is to buy or to sell, the quantity of the transaction, a description of the security traded, the account or the name of the counterparty and the trader, and the price. The time of the transaction is stamped on the ticket as well. In addition, the ticket is often assigned a code that designates the details of the trade.

2. *Matching the terms and configuration.* After the back office receives the trade tickets, it compares the details of each transaction against the records of the opposing firm to ensure that the purchaser and the seller agree on what is to be transacted and on the terms of the transaction. After the details match up, the back office prepares a confirmation; typically, this happens the night the trade is processed so that the confirmation can be sent out the next morning.

   In addition, each trade must undergo a series of computations, known as figuration, to calculate how much the selling firm will receive and how much the buying firm will pay. In fixed-income transactions, figuration includes **accrued interest**, the interest due on a fixed-income security since the last interest payment. The buyer of a bond pays the accrued interest in addition to the quoted price.

3. *Settlement and booking.* After the processing of the trade, the transaction is completed by delivering the promised securities and making the payments owed on the settlement date (the date on which the exchange of money and securities occurs). In addition, the trade must be booked, or entered on the firm's records. Part of the booking process is the recording of fees and commissions due to the firm.

---

[3]Instinet acquired Island in 2002.

This description has provided only a general overview of the clearing and settlement process. As the next sections describe, transactions involving different types of securities are cleared and settled in somewhat different ways and by different institutions.

U.S. Treasury Securities

The Treasury offers securities only in book-entry form (or in computer records rather than by traditional engraved certificates). These securities are settled through the Fedwire, which is an electronic transfer system used to transfer funds and book-entry securities. The Fedwire connects Federal Reserve Banks (FRBs) and branches, the Treasury and other government agencies, and depository institutions. All Fedwire transfers are completed on the day they are initiated and are done automatically on the Fedwire. An important feature of Fedwire transfers is that transactions are settled on a bilateral, trade-for-trade basis (gross settlement).

The Fedwire works in the following manner. Suppose a customer asks a bank to transfer funds. If the bank of the sender and that of the receiver are in different Federal Reserve districts, the sending bank debits the sender's account and asks its local FRB to send a transfer order to the FRB serving the receiver's bank. The two FRBs settle with each other through the Inter-district Settlement Fund, a bookkeeping system that records Federal Reserve inter-district transactions. Finally, the receiving bank notifies the recipient of the transfer and credits its account. The funds are available immediately. Once the transfer is received, it is final and cannot be reversed. If the sending and receiving banks are in the same Federal Reserve district, the transaction is similar, but one FRB does all of the processing and accounting.

A securities transaction is processed similarly. Suppose that GS Securities purchases $50 million of Treasury bills from BA Securities, and GS uses J.P. Morgan Chase as its clearing bank and BA uses the Bank of New York (BONY). J.P. Morgan Chase increases GS's securities account by $50 million and decreases its funds account by the same amount for the payment. At the other end, BONY decreases BA's securities account by $50 million and increases its funds account by $50 million. On the Fedwire, the securities move from BONY to J.P. Morgan Chase by book entry, and the payment moves in the opposite direction. Because funds and securities are transferred at the same time on the Fedwire, it is called a delivery-versus-payment (DVP) system.

In the government securities market, the Government Securities Division of the Fixed Income Clearing Corporation (http://www.ficc.com) provides clearance and settlement services to ensure orderly settlement. Its comparison and netting systems compare transactions, and then net them into one position per issue. The Government Securities Division also serves as the counterparty for settlement purposes for each transaction.

Corporate Securities

The National Securities Clearing Corporation (NSCC; **http://www.nscc .com**) clears and settles virtually all corporate stock and bond and municipal bond transactions in the United States. It is also a leading processor of mutual fund transactions and orders for insurance products.

The clearing and settlement takes place over a three-day cycle (T+3 or trade day + three) that begins on the trade date, T. On the trade date, firms record and transmit all of their trade details to the NSCC via computer. The NSCC then compares and matches the transactions. Once a transaction is entered into the NSCC's system as having been compared, the NSCC guarantees settlement. The guarantee begins at midnight on the day the trade is reported back to the participants as compared. From this point on, firms deal with the NSCC rather than with the counterparty.

After comparison, transactions enter one of the NSCC's three settlement systems: the Continuous Net Settlement (CNS) system, the Balance Order system, and Trade-For-Trade Settlement. The vast majority of trades settle in CNS, which nets transactions and utilizes automatic book-entry movement in a centralized and full-automated environment. In the netting process, the total amounts received and delivered for a given security are combined into one net position for each firm. For example:

- Firm A sells 1,000 shares of Z Corporation stock to Firm B.
- Firm B sells 1,000 shares of Z Corporation stock to Firm C.
- Firm C sells 1,000 shares of Z Corporation stock to Firm D.

The CNS system will net out Firm B and Firm C and instruct Firm A to deliver 1,000 shares of Z Corporation to Firm D.

Using the NSCC in the clearing and settlement process offers three advantages. First, the NSCC ensures that there is adequate system capacity to handle average trading volume and the unpredictable spikes as well. Second, because the NSCC guarantees a trade once the transaction enters its system as compared, parties no longer face the risk that a counterparty to a transaction will become insolvent. Net sellers have the obligation to deliver the securities to the NSCC, and net buyers receive securities from the NSCC rather than from the counterparty. Third, by netting the transactions, the CNS can reduce the total number of financial obligations requiring settlement by as much as 95 percent.

Mortgage-Backed Securities

The clearing and settlement process in the market for mortgage-backed securities (MBS) differs from the process in other securities markets in several ways. First, the settlement cycle is much longer in this market than in other securities markets. This lengthy settlement period increases the risk of price fluctuations and necessitates quick and accurate trade comparison and clearing processes. Second, the value of each transaction tends to be larger, typically $10 million or more. Another unique characteristic is that the seller of the MBS can deliver securities that vary by a certain percentage from the originally agreed-on face value (called the **BMA variance**).[4] The delivery variance permits an under- or over-delivery tolerance of 0.01 percent per million traded.

Like the NSCC, the Mortgage Backed Securities Division of the Fixed Income Clearing Corporation provides automated trade comparison/confirmation and net settlement services. In addition, it offers a real-time Electronic Pool Notification (EPN) system that enables market participants to transmit pool information quickly, efficiently, and reliably.[5] Before the introduction of the EPN in the early 1990s, market participants relied on phone and fax to exchange this information. Now successful delivery of pool information is denoted by an EPN time stamp and is independent of the recipient's retrieval of the message. The Mortgage Backed Securities Division has indicated that **fail** costs have been dramatically reduced as a result.[6]

The division operates two settlement systems: Trade-for-Trade and Settlement Balance Order (SBO). Users may choose SBO participation that includes Trade-for-Trade services, or have the option to be Trade-for-Trade members exclusively. The majority of trades are entered into the SBO system. Trades that are SBO-ineligible, or for which SBO is not desirable, are entered into Mortgage Backed Security Division's Trade-for-Trade system for individual settlement.

International Transactions

Every day a huge volume of international transactions take place as investors around the world seek diversification and higher yields and companies look for new sources of funds. Since the early 1990s, we have observed a dramatic increase in cross-border investing and the global integration of securities markets. These trends have happened because of a reliable clearance and settlement system for international transactions. The key institutions in this process are Euroclear, Clearstream, and the Emerging Market Clearing Corporation.

Euroclear (**http://www.euroclear.com**) is the world's largest clearance and settlement system for internationally traded securities. It is a delivery-versus-payment system with settlement in book-entry form. An overnight batch-processing cycle settles most trades. A daylight processing cycle also assists in the completion of settlement of unsettled transactions from the previous overnight process. Euroclear also offers a Securities Lending and

[4]The Bond Market Association publishes the variance.

[5]Every mortgage-backed security is based on a specific pool of mortgages, used to back the security.

[6]A fail is a trade that does not clear on the settlement date.

Borrowing Program, which enables participants to avoid costly fails by borrowing securities automatically during the settlement process. This program has resulted in a high settlement efficiency of 97 percent, meaning that only 3 percent of the trades do not settle on the settlement date. Through this program, lenders of securities can supplement their portfolio returns by lending securities for a fee to other participants that seek to avoid fails. In this way, lenders can earn competitive lending returns with no administrative burdens. They also retain most benefits of ownership when they lend their securities. In addition, Morgan Guaranty guarantees the return of lent securities (or cash equivalent).

In addition to these core services, Euroclear provides several other services such as wholesale custody, money transfer, and collateral management.

Clearstream (**http://www.clearstream.com**) is another major clearing and settlement system for international securities transactions. It offers settlement services for various internationally traded securities.[7] Supporting services include automatic securities lending, flexible financing, custody, and cash management. Clearstream uses delivery-versus-payment to minimize risk. On occasions when a customer cannot deliver securities at the designated time, Clearstream borrows securities on the user's behalf to fulfill the settlement commitments. Likewise Clearstream lends cash to ensure smooth settlement.

Clearstream offers a New Issues Acceptance service to lead managers, issuing and paying agents, and their advisers. The lead manager or issuing and paying agent must advise Clearstream on how to distribute the new issue. Securities may be delivered after the closing ceremony or prereleased, and distribution may be against payment or free of payment from the lead manager or issuing and paying agent's syndication account.[8] This service facilitates new issues of securities in the international markets.

Finally, the Emerging Market Clearing Corporation (EMCC; **http://www.e-m-c-c.com**) is a central resource for the clearance, multilateral netting, and risk management of transactions involving emerging-market debt instruments such as Brady bonds and other sovereign debt. A designated trade-matching system compares emerging-market debt trades executed by major securities firms that are EMCC members, and transmits them to the EMCC. Trades are then evaluated for eligibility. The clearing corporation guarantees accepted transactions and reports to members on an accepted trade report. The EMCC then calculates appropriate margin requirements daily, issues margin calls as appropriate, and manages the resulting collateral. At the final phase, the EMCC also transmits settlement instructions to Euroclear or Clearstream to complete the process on behalf of all EMCC member firms.

---

[7]Clearstream is the result of the merger between Cedel and Deutsche Borse Clearing in 2000. In February 2002, Deutsche Borse acquired 100 percent of Clearstream for 3.2 billion euro.

[8]A lead manager is the underwriter that has the primary responsibility for organizing the new issue. The lead manager recruits additional investment banks, negotiates terms of the issue with the issuer, and assesses market conditions.

CONCLUDING SUMMARY

The foundation of a capitalist economy is a liquid and transparent capital marketplace where corporations can raise capital to fund investment projects. Brokerage and clearing are the necessary building blocks for the efficient operation of the capital markets. All advanced capital markets have efficient brokerage and clearing services.

Brokerage services have evolved from full service to discount brokerage and ebrokerage. Investors can use either a cash account or a margin account to trade. They can place several types of orders to give instructions to brokers as to how the trades should be executed. With technological advances and deregulation, investors today have additional venues for trading. They can trade through intermediaries, such as specialists for NYSE-listed stocks or market makers for Nasdaq stocks. Electronic communications networks let buyers and sellers transact without the intermediaries.

After the execution of trades, the clearing and settlement process ensures the delivery of securities for the sale and the payment of money for the purchase. Several clearing companies provide these vital back office functions. Fedwire and the Fixed Income Clearing Corporation provide clearing and settlement for Treasury securities. In the corporate sector, the National Securities Clearing Corporation handles most transactions. Finally, Euroclear and Clearstream provide clearing and settlement services for internationally traded securities.

Key Terms

accrued interest 145
BMA variance 148
clearing account 145
discount brokerage 139
electronic communications networks
     (ECNs) 142
fail 148
front running 144
full-service firm 138

initial margin 136
interdealer broker 141
limit order 138
maintenance margin 137
market order 138
settlement 145
slippage 144
stop order 138

Review Questions

1. Use a numerical example to explain how you could use a stop order to lock in profits for a stock you purchased that has appreciated in price.

2. Online brokerages charge very small commissions. How do they make money? Describe several sources of their profits.

3. Interdealer brokers provide important services in the fixed-income markets. Why are their services important?

4. Do interdealer brokers function like an exchange? Explain.

5. What are the similarities and differences between an ECN and an exchange or the Nasdaq?

6. Describe how an ECN trade is completed. How much does the seller receive (per share)? How much does the buyer pay?

7. As a large institutional investor, would you prefer to trade over the ECN? Why or why not?

8. Netting is important in securities settlement. Provide an example to explain how netting reduces the settlement volume and costs.

9. What is the BMA variance in the mortgage-backed securities market?

Select References

Clearstream International. *Services and Products.* 2002.

Euroclear. *Services and Products.* 2002.

Government Securities Clearing Corporation. *Services.* 2002.

International Securities Clearing Corporation. *Services and Products.* 2002.

Mingle, D. L. "Behind the money market: Clearing and settling money market instruments." *Readings on Financial Institutions and Markets,* Peter Rose (Ed.). Burr Ridge, Ill.: Irwin Professional Publishing, 1994.

National Securities Clearing Corporation. *Annual Reports.* NSCC, 2001.

Securities Industry Association. *Securities Industry Briefing Book.* 2001.

Smith, J. W. "The effects of order handling rules and 16ths on Nasdaq: A cross-sectional analysis." NASD working paper 98–102, 1998.

Stigum, M. *After the Trade.* Burr Ridge, Ill.: Irwin Professional Publishing, 1988.

Tinic, S. M., and R. R. West. "The security industry under negotiated brokerage commissions: Changes in the structure and performance of New York Stock Exchange member firms." *Bell Journal of Economics,* Spring 1980, pp. 29–41.

Weiss, D. M. *After the Trade Is Made.* New York: New York Institute of Finance, 1993.

Insurance Companies

Insurance works as a kind of safety net for individuals and corporations. Insurance minimizes the possibility of financial loss by transferring risk from one individual entity to a group, or larger pool of entities. To help minimize the economic impact of personal, property, or liability risk, individuals and corporations transfer the risk of a loss to an insurance company in exchange for a predictable expense called a premium. An insurance company cannot accept every risk of a loss, however. An insurable risk generally has five characteristics. The risk of a loss must be important, accidental, calculable, definite, and not excessively catastrophic. The risk of losing a $1.50 pen is not insurable, for example, because such small losses tend to occur frequently and are very expensive to insure. Similarly, an insurance company would not insure a key employee who suffers from an incurable disease that will cause death within a given time, because there is little uncertainty concerning the payment of loss. Theoretically, the insurer could issue a policy, but the cost of such a policy would probably be too high for the prospective insured. The risk of damage to an automobile as a result of collision would be insurable, however. Once an insurance company assumes a risk, it sometimes spreads that risk through reinsurance or insurance securitization.

The objectives of this chapter are to provide an understanding of:
- Why individuals buy insurance.
- The regulatory issues affecting insurance and the accounting system insurance companies use.
- The various types of property and casualty insurance.
- The various types of life and health insurance plans.
- Bond insurance.
- How insurance companies lay off some of the risks they underwrite.

153

MARKET OVERVIEW

Insurance is an economic device whereby an individual or a business transfers the risk of uncertain financial loss by payment of a premium. Insurance does not eliminate or decrease the uncertainty as to whether an event will occur, but it does reduce the financial loss that would be incurred if the event does take place. From the viewpoint of a society, insurance spreads the losses that do occur. By providing a mechanism through which losses can be shared and uncertainty reduced, insurance brings peace of mind to society's members and makes costs more certain.

Incentives to Purchase Insurance

Despite its benefits, not everyone purchases insurance or attempts to insure against every risk. A brief discussion of marginal utility will help to explain who purchases insurance and why they do.

In standard microeconomics theory, most economists assume that more wealth is preferable to less. As one's wealth level increases, so does the satisfaction or utility attached to it. Figure 7.1 illustrates three wealth-preference

FIGURE 7.1 | *Marginal Utility Curves*

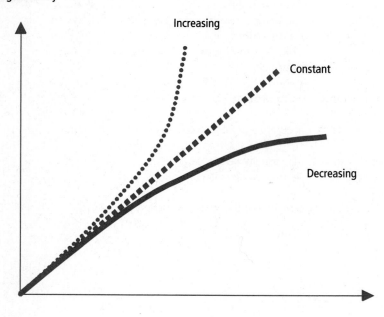

orderings, all of which show that utility increases with wealth. The linear dashed line represents a constant relationship between wealth and marginal utility. That is, for each unit change in wealth, the change in utility remains constant. This depicts the case of constant marginal utility of wealth. The dotted curve illustrates the case of increasing marginal utility. An incremental $100 provides more utility than the previous increment of $100. Finally, the solid curve illustrates decreasing marginal utility. Here again utility increases with wealth, but the rate of increase is decreasing.

Marginal utility has important implications concerning insurance. People who can be categorized as having constant marginal utility curves are indifferent to risk. People with increasing marginal utility curves are risk seekers and will not purchase insurance. On the other hand, people with decreasing marginal utility curves are risk-averse. By purchasing insurance, they can eliminate financial uncertainty and hence improve their welfare.

Figure 7.2 plots the utility of wealth curve for a representative person who has decreasing marginal utility. Suppose that a person has $100,000 in assets consisting of $70,000 in bank deposits and a $30,000 automobile. His total utility level is 900 utils. Assume that there is a 10 percent chance that his automobile will be demolished. If he does not buy insurance and the car gets totaled, he will be left with $70,000. At this point his utility level will be 600 utils. Hence, the expected level of utility without insurance is $(0.9 \times 900) + (0.1 \times 600) = 870$ utils.

FIGURE 7.2 | *Insurance and Utility Theory*

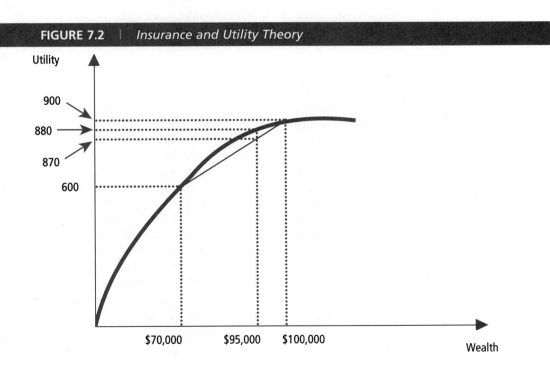

Now suppose that he can purchase insurance for $5,000. Thus, he has a guarantee of a net wealth of $95,000. If he purchases insurance that provides him with a certain position of $95,000, his utility level is 880 utils, which is greater than the expected level of 870 utils of uncertain outcome, as Figure 7.2 shows.

Types of Private Insurers

Private insurance companies can be divided into five basic types: life insurers, property and liability insurers, health insurers, reinsurers, and financial insurers. Life insurers sell life insurance and annuities on both an individual and a group basis. Property and liability insurers sell all types of insurance designed to indemnify for damage to property and for legal liability. Health insurers sell accident and health insurance, which, like life insurance, they provide on both an individual and a group basis. Reinsurers assume underwriting risks from other insurance companies in exchange for premiums. Finally, financial insurers provide guarantees for financial obligations such as municipal bonds and asset-backed securities (securities backed by pools of underlying assets).

Government Insurers

In addition to private insurers, the federal government and some state governments also offer insurance for various purposes. Government insurance programs have developed for diverse reasons. In some cases, governments have established them because the risks involved did not lend themselves to private insurance. In other instances, they originated because private insurers were unable or reluctant to meet society's needs for some form of voluntary insurance. Also, the government sometimes designs its programs to subsidize particular segments of society.

Over the years, the federal government has engaged in a number of voluntary insurance programs. The most notable is the Social Security program, which the federal government created in 1935 to help meet the risks of age and unemployment.[1] Under the program, the employer withholds Social Security and Medicare taxes from the employee's paycheck, matches that amount, and sends those taxes to the Internal Revenue Service. The employer also reports the employee's earnings to Social Security. Social Security payments begin in full at retirement age or with reduced benefits available at age 62 for those with at least 10 years of work. In the past, as another example of government insurance, the government offered war risk insurance for the U.S. merchant marine and other property owners and nuclear energy liability insurance. Private insurance programs currently operated by the federal government include veterans' life insurance, federal crop insurance, mortgage loan insurance, and the National Flood Insurance Program.

---

[1]The Social Security Administration Web site, http://www.ssa.gov, provides comprehensive information about social security.

A number of individual states offer private or voluntary insurance. About half of the states sell workers' compensation insurance. Some states offer health insurance for children whose parents cannot afford to pay for coverage from private insurers.

Globalization

Both economic growth and deregulation contribute to a trend toward globalization in the insurance industry. As suggested earlier, the demand for insurance correlates positively with growth in wealth. As wealth increases in most countries, the demand for various types of insurance increases as well. Hence, many insurance companies have attempted to expand their business abroad. The World Trade Organization (WTO) has aided their efforts, by working to open international markets for insurance and financial services. One of the WTO's goals is to reduce or eliminate government barriers that restrict foreign companies from offering services across national borders.

U.S. insurers have already established a significant presence abroad. American International Group (AIG), for example, receives half of its operating income from foreign sources. Other U.S. insurers with a significant presence overseas include CIGNA, Chubb, Reliance National Insurance, and Travelers. Many foreign insurers from the United Kingdom, France, Germany, and Japan have also entered the U.S. market. Such globalization of insurance will continue as the financial services industry continues to change and governments continue to lift restrictions on cross-border insurance sales.

Internet for Insurance Transactions

Like other industries, the insurance industry has gone online. Commercial insurers have moved aggressively to sell and service their policies over the Internet. Many insurers have moved their proprietary systems for dealing with agents to the Internet. The Internet enables insurers and their agents to do business together more efficiently.

REGULATIONS

For the most part, the states regulate the insurance industry through their legislative, judicial, and executive branches. State legislatures enact laws that govern the conduct of the insurance industry within a state's boundaries. State courts exercise control over the industry through their decisions interpreting the laws. The state's executive branch generally carries out the actual regulation through the commissioner of insurance. The National Association of Insurance Commissioners (NAIC; **http://www.naic.org**) has been an active force formulating regulatory guidelines for the insurance industry. Through this body, the state commissioners exchange information and ideas and coordinate regulatory activities. The NAIC has also established the Financial Regulation

Standards Accreditation Program to assist state legislatures and insurance departments in developing an effective system of solvency regulation.

Licensing and Examination

One of the very significant powers possessed by each state commissioner of insurance is the power to license insurance companies or to revoke those licenses. By licensing a company, the commissioner certifies its financial stability and soundness of operations. Once licensed, an insurance company must submit an annual report containing information about its assets and liabilities to the insurance commissioner. The commissioner's office also periodically inspects each company conducting business in the state. The insurance code normally requires that domestic companies be examined at least once every three years. Foreign companies are audited through a **zone examination system**; each state accepts the examination that has been conducted by another included in the zone.

Detecting potential failures before they occur is essential to protecting policyholders from insurer insolvency. Insurance regulators employ two mechanisms to detect financial problems: the NAIC Insurance Regulatory Information System (IRIS) and risk-based capital. Regulators adopted the NAIC IRIS in 1974. It signals financially troubled insurers by computerized analysis of selected audit ratios, covering overall operating tests, profitability, liquidity, and reserves. Under the risk-based capital standards, the amount of capital required for an insurer will vary, depending on the specific risks facing the insurer. The standards require a comparison between the insurer's risk-adjusted capital and actual capital. If there is a deficiency, the risk-based capital regulations require specific action, ranging from corrective action by the insurer to seizure of the company by the state insurance department.

Statutory Accounting Requirements

Insurance companies are subject to the **statutory accounting system**, which differs from generally accepted accounting principles (GAAP) in a number of ways. The first difference involves the criteria for inclusion of assets on the balance sheet. Although most noninsurance companies recognize all assets, insurance companies recognize only those that can readily convert into cash. Called **admitted assets**, they are the only assets included on the balance sheet of an insurance company. Assets such as office equipment, machinery, and furniture are nonadmitted assets, so they do not appear on the balance sheet.

A second major difference involves the valuation of assets. Under GAAP, companies must classify securities as held-to-maturity, trading, or available-for-sale. Companies value securities in the held-to-maturity category, such as bonds and mortgages, at amortized costs. Companies book assets in the other two categories at their market value. Under the statutory accounting, stocks are recorded at market value. Bonds not in default carry their amortized value, and those in default carry market value. Thus, changes in the market value of stocks held by insurance companies directly influence the equity section of the balance sheet, while changes in the market value of bonds that are not in default do not.

Statutory accounting and GAAP also differ in the way they match revenues and expenses. Under GAAP, revenues and expenses match up, with prepaid expenses deferred and charged to operations when the income produced is recognized. Under statutory accounting, all expenses related to acquiring a premium, once incurred, are charged against revenue when they are incurred, rather than being treated as capitalized and amortized prepaid expenses. The related premium revenue is treated as income only with the passing of time. In other words, revenue is deferred until earned. Thus, insurance companies account for their expenses on a cash basis and for their revenue on an accrual basis.

Regulation of Reserves

Because insurance companies collect in advance for a product to be delivered at some time in the future, insurance laws require specific recognition of the insurer's fiduciary obligations. This is accomplished by maintaining two types of reserve accounts: the unearned premium reserve and loss or claim reserve. The unearned premium reserve represents the premiums that the insured have paid in advance for the unexpired terms of their outstanding policies. As policyholders pay premiums, insurance companies enter the prepaid premiums as liabilities on their books. For each policy, the unearned premium reserve at the inception of the policy period is equal to the entire gross premium that the insured has paid. During the policy period, the unearned premium reserve for the policy declines to zero by a mathematical formula.

Because there may be delays between the time when a loss occurs and the time when the payment of a claim occurs, statutory accounting distinguishes between incurred losses and paid losses. **Incurred losses** are the losses that take place during the particular period under consideration. **Paid losses** refer to losses paid during a particular period regardless of the time when the loss occurred. The difference between paid and incurred losses is recognized through liability accounts called loss or claim reserves.

Investments

The insurance code of each state spells out the particular investments permitted to each type of insurance company in the state. In general, property and liability insurers have greater latitude in their investments than life insurers. Life insurance companies generally invest only a small percentage of their assets in stocks. For example, State Farm Mutual Automobile Insurance Company invested 43.9 percent of its assets in common and preferred stocks in 2001. In contrast, New York Life Insurance Company invested only 6.6 percent of its assets in common and preferred stocks.[2]

---

[2]Data are obtained from company reports.

Regulation of Rates

Almost all states regulate insurance rates, requiring that the rates be adequate, not excessive, and not unfairly discriminatory. Adequacy is the primary requirement. The rates, together with the insurer's income from investments, must be sufficient to pay all losses and expenses. In addition, the insurance rates must not be excessive. This means that insurers may not charge excessive rates to realize unreasonable profits. For example, an insurer may not charge a homeowner twice the premium for a similar policy paid by another home-owner whose house is in the same vicinity with the same market value. Finally, insurance rates must not discriminate unfairly, meaning that an insurance company may not charge a significantly different rate for two clients with approximately the same degree of risk.

Most states do not exercise any form of direct control over the level of life insurance rates. Property and liability rates represent a different case. Some states control these rates directly; the commissioner must specifically approve rates before they can be charged. Other states regulate the rates indirectly.

The Gramm-Leach-Bliley Act of 1999

As described in earlier chapters, the Gramm-Leach-Bliley Act changed the financial services industry by allowing affiliations between banks, securities firms, and insurers. The act did not significantly change the regulatory structure, however. Bank regulators continue to regulate banks, the Securities and Exchange Commission regulates securities firms, and state insurance regulators regulate insurance companies. The Federal Reserve serves as the umbrella regulator of bank holding companies and financial holding companies. However, in general the Federal Reserve cannot examine functionally regulated subsidiaries of these institutions.

PROPERTY AND CASUALTY INSURANCE

Property and casualty insurance is a mature industry in the United States. Almost every segment of the economy has exposure to it. **Property and casualty insurance** companies sell insurance policies designed to indemnify for damage to property and for legal liability. These companies provide a broad range of insurance protection against loss of or damage to property, loss or impairment of income-producing ability, damages caused by third party negligence, and loss resulting from injury or death due to occupational accidents.

Property and casualty insurance products can be classified as either personal lines or business insurance. The main items in personal lines are automobile insurance and homeowners insurance. Business insurance covers a wide range of items including property, liability, and professional malpractice insurance. Table 7.1 lists some of the major insurance companies engaged in these lines.

TABLE 7.1 | *Major Insurance Companies and Their Web Sites*

A. PROPERTY AND CASUALTY INSURANCE COMPANIES

Company	Web Site Address
State Farm Group	http://www.statefarm.com
Allstate Group	http://www.allstate.com
American International Group	http://www.aig.com
Farmers Insurance Group	http://www.farmersinsurance.com
Nationwide Group	http://www.nationwide.com
Berkshire Hathaway	http://www.berkshirehathaway.com
Liberty Mutual Insurance	http://www.libertymutual.com
Hartford Insurance Group	http://www.thehartford.com

B. LIFE AND HEALTH INSURANCE COMPANIES

Company	Web Site Address
Prudential Insurance	http://www.prudential.com
Metropolitan Insurance	http://www.metlife.com
Hartford Insurance Group	http://www.thehartford.com
TIAA CREF	http://www.tiaa-cref.org
New York Life	http://www.newyorklife.com
American General Group	http://www.agg.com
Equitable Group	http://www.equitable.com
Aetna, Inc.	http://www.aetna.com
Northwestern Mutual Group	http://www.northwesternmutual.com
Nationwide Group	http://www.nationwide.com
John Hancock Group	http://www.johnhancock.com

C. REINSURANCE COMPANIES

Company	Web Site Address
American Re-Insurance Company	http://www.amre.com
Arch Reinsurance Company	http://www.riskcapre.com
AXA Reinsurance Company	http://www.axa.com
Chubb Re	http://chubbre.com
CNA Re	http://www.cnare.com
GeneralCologne Re	http://www.gcr.com
PMA Reinsurance Corporation	http://www.pmare.com
PXRE Reinsurance Company	http://www.pxregroup.com
SCOR Reinsurance Company	http://www.scor.fr/us/index.asp
St. Paul Re	http://www.stpaul.com
Swiss Reinsurance	http://www.swissre.com
Toa Re Insurance Company of America	http://www.toare.com
Trenwick America Reinsurance Corporation	http://www.trenwick.com

Automobile Insurance

An **automobile insurance** policy is a contract wherein the owner pays a premium, and in exchange the insurance company promises to pay for specific car-related financial losses during the term of the policy. Auto insurance is often a legal requirement; state laws typically mandate that drivers must either have insurance or be able to provide evidence of sufficient financial resources to pay a judgment if they cause injury or damage to another person.

A policy usually covers the driver, spouse, other relatives who live in the household, and others who have permission to drive the covered vehicle. The liability coverage pays damages that an insured becomes legally liable to pay because of bodily injury to others and damage to property caused by an accident resulting from the ownership, maintenance, or use of the car. Most state laws require that motorists carry a minimum amount of liability insurance. The medical payments coverage assures that passengers in the car will receive necessary medical and dental services resulting from an auto accident, regardless of who caused the accident.

Some states also require uninsured motorist coverage. This coverage will pay for injury expenses incurred should the driver, family members, or passengers be involved in an accident with an uninsured motorist. It also provides protection in the event of a hit-and-run accident. Underinsured motorist coverage comes into play when the other driver is legally responsible for an accident and has coverage, but not enough to pay for all the expenses.

Another common loss is the physical damage that results from an accident. Insurers provide two types of physical damage coverage: collision and comprehensive. Collision coverage pays for any damage to the car caused by accidental impact with a vehicle or object. The actual cash value of the vehicle less the deductible (the amount of the loss that the policyholder must pay) is the maximum amount that can be paid. Comprehensive coverage pays for most types of damage to the car resulting from a situation other than a collision. Finally, policyholders may obtain additional optional coverage for such items as towing and labor and rental reimbursement.

Homeowners/Renters Insurance

Homeowners/renters insurance provides a range of coverage with choices on limits and deductibles. Most homeowner's policies cover the primary dwelling, other structures, personal property, family liability, and injuries to guests. In addition, optional coverage may be obtained for losses due to loss assessment, earthquakes, and floods.

Business Insurance

Business insurance protects against many types of business risks. Insurance may be obtained to cover losses to commercial automobiles, business property, cargo in transit or in storage, and tools and equipment, as well as losses caused by business interruption and crime. Business insurance also includes general liability coverage and umbrella excess liability insurance. Some corporations also purchase protection against political turmoil. After the World Trade Center attacks on September 11, 2001 (Box 7.1 shows the estimated amount of insured losses from the event), many U.S. multinational companies with overseas operations purchased special insurance to protect themselves not only against terrorism, riots, civil war, and coups, but also against nationalization and government interference with the flow of profits back home.

Nature of Liabilities

The liabilities of property and casualty insurance companies are shorter term than those of life insurance companies. Although the exact timing and amount of any liability are unknown, the coverage specified in the policy caps the maximum amount of claims. The most significant risk faced by property and casualty insurance companies is that a catastrophic event such as a hurricane or an earthquake will occur in a certain geographic area. Such risk can be managed through reinsurance or securitization, to be discussed in later sections.

LIFE INSURANCE

Life insurance provides families with protection against the loss of income that would occur as a result of the death of a family member. Companies also obtain life insurance to protect against the losses they would incur as a result of the death of a key employee. Life insurance companies offer two basic types of life insurance—term life and permanent life insurance, although there are also many variations on each type. Term policies provide life insurance for a

---

MARKETS IN ACTION   WTC Insured Loss Estimate

7.1

The terrorist attack of September 11, 2001, was the most expensive loss in the history of the insurance industry. The losses will impact the premium and availability of insurance coverage for years to come. Over 100 insurers around the world are expected to pay an estimated $40 billion in the course of settling tens of thousands of claims, according to the Insurance Information Institute (http://www.iii.org) estimate. The total amount of insured losses from the destruction of the World Trade Center was $40.2 billion, more than twice the insured losses from Hurricane Andrew that devastated south Florida. The breakdown of claims is as follows:

Business interruption: $11 billion.
Liability: $10 billion.
Property other than WTC buildings One and Two: $6 billion.
WTC One and Two: $3.5 billion.
Aviation liability: $3.5 billion.
Life insurance: $2.7 billion.
Workers compensation: $2 billion.
Event cancellation: $1 billion.
Loss of four commercial airplanes: $500 million.

Source: Insurance Information Institute (http://www.iii.org).

specified period of time. These policies provide benefits in the event of death, but they do not generate cash value. Permanent life insurance covers a longer period of time than term life and may extend for the entire life of the insured. This type of life insurance combines death benefits with a savings component. Part of the premium goes to cover the insurance benefits; the insurance company invests the remainder to build up a cash value that the policyholder may use in a variety of ways. Permanent life insurance includes whole life, universal life, variable universal life, and survivorship universal life.

With all types of life insurance, the insurance company charges a premium based on the predictable level of mortality of the insured. To calculate the mortality level, life insurance companies use mortality tables to estimate the number of deaths that are likely to occur in a given period for a large number of insured. Table 7.2 shows a condensed version of a mortality table.

Term Life

Term life insurance is an insurance policy that is in effect for a specific period of time. If the insured dies within that time frame, the beneficiary receives the death payment. If the insured survives that period of time, however, the beneficiary receives nothing and the coverage is terminated. The premium on a term policy is low compared to other types of life insurance policies due to the fact that it carries no cash value. Because the risk of death increases as people get older, term life insurance premiums increase with age. Some term premiums may rise every year, or every 5 to 10 years.

Whole Life

Whole life insurance has guaranteed premiums and death benefits and a minimum interest rate that will be credited to the funds accumulated in the policy. Under the whole life policy, the purchaser agrees to pay regular premiums to the insurance company in exchange for a death benefit and a cash value account where cash can accumulate on a tax-deferred basis. The policy remains in force during the purchaser's entire lifetime and provides permanent protection for beneficiaries while building the cash value account. The insurance company determines the earnings on the whole life policy based on the overall return on its investments. Earnings above and beyond those required to cover the death benefit can go to the policy's cash value account. The policyholder can borrow against this account, use it to pay premiums, or allow it to accumulate for retirement.

Universal Life

Universal life insurance is a variation on whole life. It differs from whole life insurance in that it allows the policy owner to vary, with limitations, the amount and timing of premium payments and the death benefit. For example, policyholders might choose a lower premium when they are younger and higher premium in their peak earning years. The insurance part of the policy is separate from the investment, or accumulation, portion. Insurance companies generally invest the money on behalf of the policyholders in money market

TABLE 7.2	*Condensed Mortality Table*			
	MALE		**FEMALE**	
Age	Deaths Per 1,000	Average Future Lifetime	Deaths Per 1,000	Average Future Lifetime
0	4.18	70.83	2.89	75.83
1	1.07	70.13	0.87	75.04
2	0.99	69.20	0.81	74.11
10	0.73	61.66	0.68	66.53
11	0.77	60.71	0.69	65.58
12	0.85	59.75	0.72	64.62
20	1.90	52.37	1.05	57.04
21	1.91	51.47	1.07	56.10
22	1.89	50.57	1.09	55.16
30	1.73	43.24	1.35	47.65
31	1.78	42.31	1.40	46.71
32	1.83	41.38	1.45	45.78
40	3.02	34.05	2.42	38.36
41	3.29	33.16	2.64	37.46
42	3.56	32.26	2.87	36.55
50	6.71	25.36	4.96	29.53
51	7.30	24.52	5.31	28.67
52	7.96	23.70	5.70	27.82
60	16.08	17.51	9.47	21.25
61	17.54	16.79	10.13	20.44
62	19.19	16.08	10.96	19.65
70	39.51	10.96	22.11	13.67
71	43.30	10.39	24.23	12.97
72	47.65	9.84	26.87	12.28
80	98.84	6.18	65.99	7.48
81	107.48	5.80	73.60	6.98
82	117.25	5.44	82.40	6.49
90	221.77	3.18	190.75	3.45
91	236.98	2.94	208.87	3.15
92	253.45	2.70	228.81	2.85
98	657.98	0.84	655.85	0.84
99	1000.00	0.50	1000.00	0.50

Soure: National Association of Insurance Commissioners.

funds. Sometimes, the policy contains provisions that allow the policyholder to choose the fund to invest the money. The accumulation fund receives the investment income. The interest rate usually is guaranteed for one year. At the end of that time, the policy owner receives notice of the rate for the next twelve-month period.

Variable Life

Variable life insurance is an investment-oriented whole life policy that provides a return based on an underlying portfolio of mutual funds including common stock funds, bond funds, and money market funds. This type of life insurance offers fixed premiums and a minimum death benefit. The return of the portfolio determines the amount of the death benefit or the value of the variable life policy.

The principal difference between whole life and variable life is the investment factor. Variable life invests in an assortment of mutual funds, rather than in long-term bonds and mortgages, as would be typical of a whole life policy. Variable life provides downside protection by guaranteeing that the face amount of the policy will never be less than the originally issued face amount no matter what the investment results are, as long as the policy owner pays scheduled premiums. This guarantee is unavailable in universal life.

Variable Universal Life

Variable universal life insurance combines the flexibility of universal life insurance with the investment account features of variable life insurance. As with variable life, the death benefit that variable universal life pays the beneficiary depends on the success of the investment. If the investment fails, there is a guaranteed minimum death benefit.

Survivorship Universal Life

Survivorship universal life insurance covers two people with one policy. The death benefit is paid to the specified beneficiary upon the second death. The premiums for this type of insurance are significantly lower than for a regular policy.

Term Life Insurance versus Permanent Life Insurance

Term life insurance provides maximum coverage at the lowest premium. The disadvantage, however, is that this type of insurance provides a death benefit only for a specified period of time. When the policy expires, so does the protection. Also, premiums tend to increase with each renewal, so the policy can become very costly.

For many people, permanent life insurance can be a better long-term choice. Cash value life insurance provides lifelong insurance protection. As long as the premiums are paid, the policy will not expire. Most permanent policies also pay dividends, which can be applied toward the next payment. Therefore, premium payments may end after a number of years, but coverage will continue for life. This kind of policy also allows the policyholder to obtain loans by borrowing against the established cash value.

Annuities

An **annuity** is a financial product in which policyholders pay premiums in exchange for an income for a specified period of time. During the accumulation period of an annuity, the insurance companies generally invest the money on behalf of the policyholders in a fixed account known as a guaranteed account. The company guarantees the principal and the interest rate. Interest rates are usually guaranteed for one year. During retirement, the owner has several options for withdrawing funds.

There are two basic classifications of annuities: immediate annuities and deferred annuities. An immediate annuity provides a secure and guaranteed way to turn the money set aside for retirement into retirement income. The annuity contract holder pays the insurance company a lump sum of money (called a premium) and, in return, has a guarantee of a steady stream of income payments for life or for a period of time that the contract specifies.

A deferred annuity helps customers set aside funds today for future retirement with tax-deferred growth on the principal. A deferred annuity is more flexible than an immediate annuity because it may be funded either with a single lump sum of money and/or with several smaller sums over a period of time. Thus, customers can tailor their savings rate to their unique situation. While they set aside money in the deferred annuity, the funds build, compounding over time at a tax-deferred rate. When owners retire, they withdraw the accumulated funds in the form of guaranteed regular income payments either for a period of time or over their lifetime. The payment of a deferred annuity can be fixed, variable, or indexed.

Guaranteed Investment Contracts

A **guaranteed investment contract (GIC)** is an investment product issued by an insurance company in return for a payment by an investor. The terms of GICs vary greatly, but they offer a relatively high initial return guarantee and impose restrictions on the investor's ability to withdraw funds. The failure of several insurers that were active issuers of GICs led investors to look for products with lower risks. One such product is synthetic GIC, a guaranteed account secured by a pool of assets owned by the investor. That is, the assets are segregated to protect investors from claims by the insurance company's general creditors.

The advantage of a GIC is that the interest rate is guaranteed. In recent years, however, investors have looked for better returns than those traditional GICs offered. At the same time they didn't want to risk their principal. Consequently, insurance companies introduced market-growth GICs. With these GICs, the return is calculated using a percentage of the increase in the underlying indices, or mutual funds, over the term of the investment. The percentage used to calculate the return is the market participation rate, which is set at the time of purchase. The original principal receives protection no matter how the market performs. If the market increases over the term of the investment, the investor benefits from the increase. Even if the market declines, the original investment has full protection.

Nature of Liabilities

Life insurance companies face two types of liabilities. For pure life insurance, the total amount of the claim is known when the insurer underwrites the policy, but the timing of the payment is unknown. For investment-oriented policies such as GICs and annuities, the risk is that the insurer's investment returns may not be sufficient to make the guaranteed payments to policyholders.

HEALTH INSURANCE

Private health insurance can be grouped into two broad categories: traditional and managed care. Under the **traditional indemnity insurance**, also known as fee-for-service insurance, the policyholder pays a certain amount of medical expenses up front, and afterward the insurance company pays the majority of the bill. With **managed care** plans, the insurer makes arrangements with a selected network of health-care providers to treat policyholders, who are offered significant financial incentives to use the providers in the network. There are three basic types of managed care plans: preferred provider organizations, point-of-service plans, and health maintenance organizations.

Traditional Indemnity Insurance

Traditional indemnity, or fee-for-service insurance, gives policyholders a high degree of autonomy to choose doctors, hospitals, and other health-care providers. These plans usually involve more out-of-pocket expenses, however. Often the policyholder must pay a deductible. Upon meeting the deductible, the insurance company will generally pay 80 percent of any covered doctor bills.

Preferred Provider Organizations

Preferred provider organizations (PPOs) are a type of managed care. PPOs make arrangements for lower fees with a network of health-care providers and then give policyholders a strong financial incentive to stay within the network. For example, a visit to an in-network doctor might require only a copayment of $10. Policyholders may refer themselves to in-network specialists without getting approval and enjoy the same low copayment. A policyholder who visits an out-of-network doctor, however, might have to pay the entire cost and then be reimbursed by the PPO for only 80 percent. Exclusive PPOs do not pay for any outside network costs.

Point-of-Service Plans

Point-of-service (POS) plans are similar to PPOs, except that they have a gatekeeper, called the primary care physician. The policyholder has to choose a primary care physician from the plan's network of doctors. This physician will refer the insured to a specialist if necessary. The policyholder does not have the freedom of going to a specialist directly.

Health Maintenance Organizations

Health maintenance organizations (HMOs) are the least expensive, but also the least flexible, type of health plan. HMOs generally gear their services toward members of group plans. HMOs typically have low copayments, and sometimes no copayments at all. An HMO requires the policyholder to see only its doctors and obtain a referral before seeing a specialist. An HMO may have central medical offices or clinics, or it may consist of individual practices.

Nature of Liabilities
Liabilities facing health insurance companies are mainly the claims for covered expenses. There is uncertainty as to when a covered illness will occur and how much it will cost.

FINANCIAL INSURANCE

Financial insurance, which covers municipal bonds, structured products, and bank obligations, provides protection against default risk.[3] Financial insurers guarantee that in the event that the issuer defaults, the interest and principal on the insured obligation will still be paid as scheduled. Each guarantee is unconditional and irrevocable, and covers the full amount of interest and principal for the full term of the issue.

Municipal bonds may be insured in the primary or the secondary market. In the primary market, financial insurance companies insure municipal financings in almost every new issue sector. In the secondary market, municipal insurance improves the quality and marketability of municipal bonds, thereby benefiting traders, bond dealers, and institutional investors.

In structured finance, financial insurance provides credit enhancements to securitizations backed by commercial or consumer assets. Financial insurance is also available for guaranteed investment contracts, letters of credit, and other financial obligations. The discussions in this section focus on the insurance of municipal bonds and asset-backed securities.

Benefits of Bond Insurance
Insurance adds several benefits to insured bonds. First, and most important, is enhanced security. Because the insurer will immediately step in and make the scheduled payments if an insured bond defaults, insured bonds receive the same credit rating, generally triple-A, as the insurer. Adding to the safety is the fact that the insurer has a strong incentive to monitor the performance of every insured issue to maturity. Insurers make on-site visits to issuers and require a variety of financial reports, which they carefully analyze for any sign of credit deterioration. Furthermore, rating agencies monitor the insurer on a regular basis. A second major benefit is enhanced liquidity. The trading of large volumes of insured securities happens every day in the secondary markets. Investors who wish to sell insured bonds before maturity often find a ready market for such highly rated bonds.

---

[3]Structured products are debt instruments that have been customized for the buyer, often by incorporating options.

It is important to know, however, that the presence of bond insurance alone does not guarantee a bond's price in the secondary market. The market conditions at the time of trading will determine the actual price. It is possible that a bond will be worth more or less than its original cost if sold before maturity.

Bond Insurance Criteria

To safeguard the ratings of the insured obligations and to protect the interests of the insured bond investors, insurers generally focus on insuring securities with a low risk of default. More than 95 percent of the obligations insured by triple-A insurers have a rating of investment grade before the guarantee is provided. By providing insurance only to bonds with a low risk of default, the triple-A insurers can minimize their claims-paying liabilities. This practice is known as remote loss, or zero loss underwriting.

Though specific underwriting criteria will vary by firm and by the type of bonds, several common factors can be identified. Municipal bond insurers will look at revenue and financial history, demographics, and quality of management. Insurers of asset-backed securities will examine the quality and amount of collateral. In addition, insurers will always conduct a thorough legal review of the securities to preserve the integrity of the deal and the rights of bond investors.

Bond Insurance Companies

Most bond insurers are monocline, meaning that they are in only one type of insurance business. Thus, a monocline insurance company is not exposed to risks from other lines of business. The four largest bond insurers are MBIA (**http://www.mbia.com**), AMBAC (**http://www.ambac.com**), Financial Security Assurance (**http://www.fsa.com**), and Financial Guaranty Insurance Company (**http://www.fgic.com**). All those insurers carry a rating of Aaa by Moody's (**http://www.moodys.com**), AAA by Standard and Poor's (**http://www.standardandpoors.com**), and AAA by FitchRatings (**http://www.fitchratings.com**). Bonds insured by these organizations receive the same triple-A rating.

Financial insurance companies must meet the requirements of insurance regulators in every state where they do business. They are also subject to intense scrutiny from rating agencies that evaluate and assign a rating to every transaction they insure. To test the adequacy of a company's capital resources, rating agencies apply a computer-simulated stress test that measures the firm's ability to pay claims at a level comparable to those experienced during the Great Depression.

In addition, rating agencies continually evaluate each bond insurer's claims-paying ability through detailed analyses of the company's financial resources, operations, and exposures, and they publish regular reports on each insurer. Among the key factors that rating agencies look at before assigning a triple-A credit rating are the quality of the insured portfolio, capital adequacy, financial performance, operating efficiency, risk management, liquidity of assets, reinsurance, and experience of management.

Nature of Liabilities

The liabilities facing bond insurers are the obligations to make timely payments of interest and principal, should the insured default. The contract specifies the maximum amount of such obligations. The uncertainty lies in the default rate and the timing of the default.

REINSURANCE

In a **reinsurance** contract, one insurance company (the reinsurer) charges a premium to indemnify another insurance company (called the ceding insurer or primary company) against all or part of the loss it may sustain under the issued policies. As such, reinsurance is a form of insurance for the primary insurer. Reinsurance should be considered as "insurance for insurance companies," a way for a primary insurer to protect against unforeseen or extraordinary losses. Reinsurance serves several functions: it limits liability on specific risks, increases individual insurers' capacity, enables primary insurers to share the liability when losses overwhelm their resources, and helps insurers stabilize their business in the face of the wide swings in profit and loss margins inherent in the insurance business. Table 7.1 lists some of the leading reinsurance companies.

Reasons for Reinsurance

The ceding companies purchase reinsurance for a variety of reasons. One reason is that reinsurance protects the ceding company against a single, catastrophic loss or multiple large losses, and thus allows the company to write larger amounts of insurance. Stabilization is another benefit, meaning that reinsurance helps smooth the ceding company's overall operating results from year to year. Reinsurance can also help a company that wants to exit an old line of business or enter a new one. Thus, reinsurance can provide a means for the reinsured to withdraw from a line of business or a geographic area or, alternatively, to spread the risk on new lines of business until premium volume reaches a certain point of maturity. Finally, reinsurance provides the ceding company with a source of underwriting information when entering a new line of insurance or a new market.

Types of Reinsurance

There are essentially two types of reinsurance arrangements: facultative reinsurance and treaty reinsurance. Under a **facultative reinsurance** arrangement, transactions with reinsurance occur on an individual risk basis, the ceding company has the option to offer an individual risk to the reinsurer, and the reinsurer has the right to accept or reject this risk. In contrast, under **treaty reinsurance**, the transaction encompasses a block of the ceding company's book of business. The reinsurer must accept all business included within the terms of the reinsurance contract.

Both types of reinsurance can be written on either a pro rata or an excess-of-loss basis. Under the pro rata approach, also called a proportional agreement, the reinsurer shares the same proportion of the premium and losses with the ceding company. When reinsurance is purchased on an excess-of-loss basis, the reinsurer indemnifies the ceding company against the amount of loss in excess of a specified retention.

As an example of facultative reinsurance on a pro rata basis, suppose that the ceding company reinsures a commercial umbrella policy with the following limit and premium:

Policy limit	$10,000,000
Annual premium	$100,000

The ceding company retains 30 percent net and obtains 70 percent facultative reinsurance on a pro rata basis. Reinsurance participation is expressed as:

$$\$10,000,000 \ (70\%) = \$7,000,000/\text{total reinsurance obligation.}$$

The premium due the reinsurer is $70,000 less the ceding commission to the ceding company. If a covered loss of $4,000,000 occurs, the ceding company would pay $1,200,000 (30 percent of the loss), and the reinsurer would pay $2,800,000 (70 percent of the loss).

INSURANCE SECURITIZATION

Hurricane Hugo (1989), Hurricanes Andrew and Iniki (1992), and the Northridge earthquake (1994) cost the property/casualty industry tens of billions of dollars. Losses from such catastrophic events could severely affect insurers and their policyholders. Thus, insurers have been looking at ways of financing their catastrophe risk. Reinsurance is not a reliable solution, because it experiences boom-and-bust cycles, which makes managing catastrophe risk a nightmare for primary insurers. In periods of few disasters, coverage is cheap enough. But after a string of losses, prices for reinsurance policy renewals can skyrocket. A capital market solution has emerged in the form of catastrophe **risk securitization**, in which insurers package their catastrophe risk as securities and sell to investors. Instead of transferring its underwriting risk to a reinsurer within the insurance industry, insurance company transfers the risk to the broader capital markets.

To decide whether to use risk securitization, an insurer uses its internal projections to determine its potential catastrophe losses and the amount of capital it would need to finance that risk on its own. The insurer then compares the cost of reinsurance and the cost of catastrophe risk securitization. Industry observers believe that access to the capital markets could one day play a significant role in strategies for financing catastrophe risk. For investors, risk securitization offers both potential returns from investing in investments for securitizing risk and an opportunity to reduce portfolio risk through diversification. The principal forms of securitization include contingent surplus notes, catastrophe bonds, catastrophe equity puts, and exchange-traded catastrophe options.

Contingent Surplus Notes

Contingent surplus notes (CSNs) are surplus notes that an insurer has the right to issue in the future to investors in exchange for cash. The right to issue the surplus notes hinges upon the occurrence of specific events. For example, suppose that an insurer wants to use CSNs to access additional capital in the event of a catastrophe. The insurer will arrange for a financial intermediary to set up an investment trust. The trust then invests in government securities or other liquid securities, and the intermediary sells shares of the trust to investors. This gives the insurer the right to issue surplus notes to the financial intermediary in exchange for cash or liquid assets, thereby increasing the insurer's surplus and enhancing its ability to pay claims. The intermediary in turn has the right to substitute the surplus notes for the securities held by the trust. The insurer pays fees to the financial intermediary in exchange for its commitment to purchase the insurer's surplus notes. After issuance of the notes, the insurer will pay interest and principal on the notes to the trust, and the trust in turn will pay the investors.

Nationwide Mutual Insurance issued the first CSNs in 1995. In this transaction, Nationwide set up a trust that borrowed $400 million in the capital market. The trust's sole purpose was to stand by to purchase a surplus note from Nationwide that would be issued if Nationwide incurred a catastrophe loss or certain other events. In the meantime, the trust invested its assets in triple-A-rated securities and incurred a small spread loss (interest expense exceeded interest income), which Nationwide covered.

Catastrophe Bonds

A **catastrophe (CAT) bond**, or "Act of God" bond, has special provisions that require investors to forgive some or all principal or interest in the event that catastrophe losses exceed the trigger specified in the bond. The trigger can be based on the catastrophe losses of a particular insurer or the industry overall, the level of a particular catastrophe index, or parameters of particular events. The triggers can also specify particular geographic areas and particular lines of insurance. The bond pays interest and returns principal the way other debt securities do, as long as the issuer does not experience a catastrophe in which it loses more than the agreed-on limit. When that happens, the insurer can pay claims with the funds that would otherwise have gone to the bondholders. For example, USAA floated a $477 million CAT bond issue in June 1997 to provide reinsurance protection. The loss threshold was $1 billion.

The issuing insurer generally establishes a special purpose reinsurer (SPR) to issue catastrophe bonds and then to sell reinsurance to a particular primary insurer. The use of an SPR eliminates the need for the insurer to carry debt on its balance sheet. An SPR can also protect investors from other credit risk inherent in the operations of the insurer. If the insurer were to become insolvent, the SPR would still have an obligation to repay the catastrophe bonds it sold to investors.

Catastrophe Equity Puts

Put options are securities that grant the buyer the right, but not the obligation, to sell a certain amount of a specified asset to the seller of the contract for a predetermined price during a specified period. **Catastrophe equity puts (CatEPuts)** are put options that insurers can buy from investors. Those options give an insurer the right to sell a specified amount of its stock to investors at a predetermined price if catastrophe losses surpass a specified trigger. Thus, the CatEPuts can provide insurers with additional equity capital when they need funds to cover catastrophe losses. In 1997, for example, LaSalle Re and Horace Mann Educators Corporation bought CatEPuts that provided each company with $100 million in contingent financing.

Exchange-Traded Catastrophe Options

Insurers wanting protection against catastrophe losses can also buy exchange-traded catastrophe options. These are standardized contracts based on catastrophe indexes. The indexes reflect the catastrophe experience of a large pool of insurers or the entire property/casualty industry. The contract entitles the insurer to a cash payment from the seller if a catastrophe causes the index to rise above a strike price specified in the contract. Such cash payments can help an insurer bolster its surplus and pay claims. As standardized instruments, catastrophe options offer added protection for a relatively low cost. However, using such options exposes the insurer to basis risk—the risk that the catastrophe index used in the contract is not perfectly correlated with losses experienced by the insurer.

CONCLUDING SUMMARY

In life or business, insurance is a fact of life. All forms of insurance, including life, health, property and casualty, and financial insurance, are based on the fundamental concept of risk sharing. Insurance cannot eliminate or reduce the probability of the underlying risk that an individual or a business faces, but it does alleviate the burden on any one individual or business when unfortunate events do occur. By providing a degree of certainty in an uncertain world, insurance improves the welfare of society.

Regulation of the insurance industry rests with the states. State insurance commissions license and examine insurers, set rates, and regulate insurers' investments and accounting practices. Governments, both federal and local, involve themselves in certain insurance business as well. For example, Social Security is a form of insurance. Employed people, together with their employers, pay Social Security taxes in exchange for benefits after retirement. Flood insurance is another example of the government's sponsorship of insurance.

Insurance companies, like their customers, spread risks by purchasing reinsurance. Two types of reinsurance are facultative reinsurance and treaty reinsurance. Transactions based on individual risk are facultative reinsurance. Under treaty reinsurance, the reinsurance bases the transactions on the primary insurer's book of business, not on individual risk. Purchasing reinsurance from reinsurers does not increase the capacity within the insurance industry, however. In contrast, insurance securitization expands the capacity to the global capital market. The primary forms of insurance securitization are contingent surplus notes, catastrophe bonds, catastrophe equity puts, and exchange-traded catastrophe options.

Key Terms

admitted assets 158
annuity 166
automobile insurance 162
catastrophe (CAT) bond 173
catastrophe equity put (CatEPut) 174
contingent surplus note (CSN) 173
facultative reinsurance 171
financial insurance 169
guaranteed investment
   contract (GIC) 167
incurred losses 159
insurance 154
managed care 168
paid losses 159

property and casualty insurance 160
reinsurance 171
risk securitization 172
statutory accounting system 158
survivorship universal life insurance 166
term life insurance 164
traditional indemnity insurance 168
treaty reinsurance 171
universal life insurance 164
variable life insurance 166
variable universal life insurance 166
whole life insurance 164
zone examination system 158

Review Questions

1. Briefly explain the main differences between the accounting practices used by insurance companies and those used by other companies.

2. Why are the liabilities and cash outlays of a property and casualty insurance company more difficult to predict than those of a life insurance company?

3. Are there restrictions on the assets in which an insurance company can invest? Explain.

4. What does "permanent life insurance" mean?

5. Obtain the annual reports of a life insurance company and a property and casualty insurer and compare the differences in their distribution of invested assets.

6. Compare reinsurance and insurance securitization.

7. What are the key differences between a mutual fund, a GIC, and an annuity?

8. Can a company insure its earnings? How does that work?

9. Explain how financial modernization legislation has affected the insurance industry.

10. "Increasing life expectancy implies more profits for life insurance companies." Do you agree with this statement?

11. What is zero-loss underwriting? Explain how it differs from the actuarial approach used by multiline insurance companies.

12. Describe the potential risks facing an insurer that has issued CatEPuts.

SELECT BIBLIOGRAPHY

Barth, M. M., and W. R. Felhaus. "Does rate regulation alter underwriting risk?" *Journal of Insurance Issues* 22, No. 1, 1999, pp. 26–50.

Briys, E., and F. D. Varenne. *Insurance: From Underwriting to Derivatives.* Boston, Mass.: Addison-Wesley, 2001.

Cummins, J. D., N. Doherty, and A. Lo. "Can insurers pay for the big one? Measuring the capacity of the insurance market to respond to catastrophic losses." *Journal of Banking and Finance* 26, issue 2, March 2002, pp. 557–583.

Evans, B. D. "Learning more about reinsurance." *Journal of Insurance Issues* 22, No. 2, 1999, pp. 17–183.

Gorvett, R. W. "Insurance securitization: The development of a new asset class." Working paper, College of Insurance (New York), 1999.

Graham, J. R., and C. W. Smith, Jr. "Tax incentive to hedge." *Journal of Finance* 54, no. 6, 1999, pp. 2241–2262.

Louberge, H., E. Kellezi, and M. Gilli. "Using catastrophe-linked securities to diversify insurance risk: a financial analysis." *Journal of Insurance Issues* 22, No. 2, 1999, pp. 125–146.

Lowe, T. C. *Business of Insurance.* Health Insurance Association of America, 1998.

Myers, G., and J. Kollar. "Catastrophe risk securitization: Insurer and investor perspectives." Jersey City, N.J.: Insurance Services Office, Inc., 1999.

Rejda, G. E. *Principles of Risk Management and Insurance.* Boston, Mass.: Addison-Wesley Publishing, 2000.

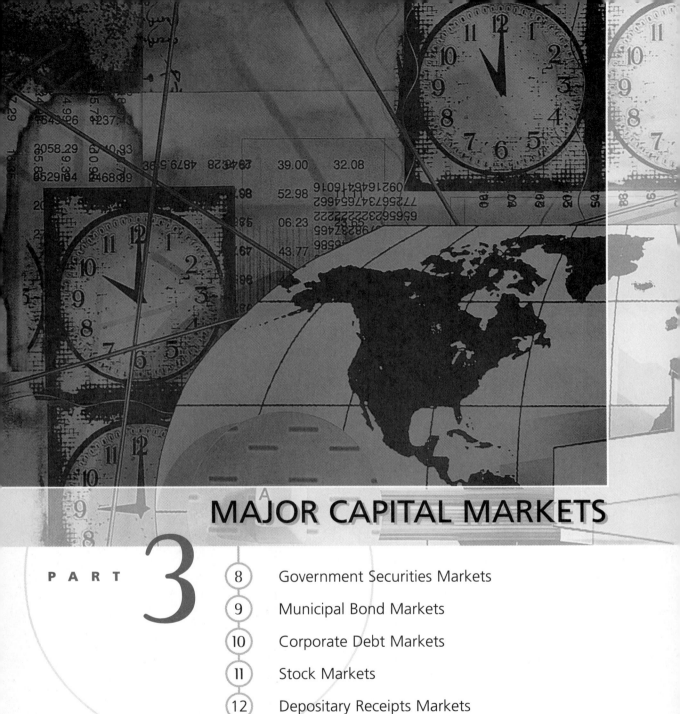

MAJOR CAPITAL MARKETS

Government Securities Markets

Over the past four decades, the U.S. government has experienced a budget deficit almost every year, except for a few years in the 1960s and the late 1990s. To finance these deficits, the government borrows by issuing Treasury securities. The government must sell securities not only to pay its current expenses but also to pay interest on the accumulated debt from past deficits and to pay off maturing debt. These sales take place in the U.S. Treasury market—the largest and most liquid fixed-income market in the world.

The objectives of this chapter are to provide an understanding of:
- The various types of Treasury securities.
- Market conventions and trends.
- Yields and spot rates.
- The valuation of Treasury securities.
- The Treasury security auction process.
- The process of trading Treasury securities before their issuance.

MARKET OVERVIEW

The sheer size of the government securities market is impressive. As of June 2002, the U.S. government's total debt amounted to more than $6 trillion.[1] Approximately $3 trillion of that debt is in the form of marketable government securities. Since 1997 the government has issued approximately $2 trillion in securities each year. The amount of issuance surged to $2.7 trillion in 2001. On an average day, the secondary markets traded approximately $300 billion worth of securities in 2001.[2] The average daily volume increased to more than $360 billion in December 2002.

Four types of government securities trade in the securities markets:

- **Treasury bills** are short-term securities with a maturity period of up to one year. Currently, the Treasury Department issues 4-week, 13-week, and 26-week bills.[3] These bills are discount instruments; they do not pay coupon interest. Holders of the bills receive the face amount at maturity.

- **Treasury notes** are medium-term securities that have a maturity of more than one year but not more than ten years. Currently, the Treasury issues notes with a maturity period of 2, 5, or 10 years. The 10-year note is the current interest rate benchmark.

- **Treasury bonds** are long-term securities with a maturity period of thirty years. The Treasury suspended issuance of the 30-year bond in October 2001. Notes and bonds pay coupons every six months; hence people also call them coupon Treasury securities (or coupon treasuries).

- **Treasury Inflation-Protection Securities (TIPS)** are inflation-indexed notes and bonds; the interest rate is fixed but the principal is adjusted for inflation. At maturity, holders will receive the greater of the par amount at original issue or the inflation-adjusted principal.

The introduction of TIPS was one of two major innovations in Treasury securities since the mid-1980s. The other was the introduction of a coupon-stripping program that allows coupons to trade separately from their underlying principal. The next two sections examine these developments in more detail.

Coupon Stripping

In February 1985, the Treasury introduced a coupon-stripping program called STRIPS (Separate Trading of Registered Interest and Principal of Securities). **Coupon stripping** strips interest payment coupons from a coupon treasury and treats the component coupons and the principal as separate securities. Market participants refer to these strips as Treasury zeros or Treasury zero

---

[1]Information about the public debt and Treasury security auctions is available at the U.S. Treasury's Web site (http://www.publicdebt.treas.gov).

[2]The Bond Market Association publishes the data at its Web site (http://www.bondmarkets.com).

[3]Previously, the Treasury issued a 52-week bill but discontinued it in 2001.

coupons. Each coupon strip entitles the owner to a specified amount of cash (coupon) on a specific date (coupon date), while the owner of the principal strip receives the principal amount at maturity. For example, suppose that a 10-year note with a face value of $1 million and a 5 percent coupon rate is stripped into its principal and 20 semiannual interest payments. The end result is 21 Treasury zeros, with each coupon strip paying $25,000 and the principal strip paying $1 million. Each of the 21 strips becomes a security, and each can be traded separately. As such, the program provides investors an additional option to buy just one of the coupon components or the principal component that were previously unavailable.

Since May 1987, the Treasury has also allowed the reconstitution of stripped securities. To reconstitute a stripped security, a financial institution or a government securities broker-dealer must obtain the appropriate principal component and all related coupon strips for the security. The principal and interest components must be in the appropriate minimum or multiple amounts for the particular security. Upon acquiring these components, the institution forwards them to a Federal Reserve Bank and requests that they be reassembled into a fully constituted Treasury security. The ability to reconstitute a stripped security improves market efficiency, because there are arbitrage opportunities if the price of the security is different from the value of all the components.

Treasury Inflation-Indexed Securities

Another important development in the U.S. government securities market was the introduction of Treasury Inflation-Protection Securities (TIPS) in 1997. With this type of securities, the Treasury calculates the semiannual interest payments and maturity payment based on the inflation-adjusted principal value of the security. Therefore, TIPS provide investors with protection against inflation.

The Treasury held the first auction of TIPS, a 10-year note, in January 1997. Since then, the Treasury has also issued TIPS with maturities of 5, 10, and 30 years. Once the TIPS are issued, the coupon rate set at auction remains fixed throughout the term of the security. The principal amount adjusts for inflation, but the inflation-adjusted principal will not be paid until maturity. The principal amount will not drop below the par at which the securities were originally issued, even though deflation could cause the principal to decline. The index for measuring the inflation rate is the nonseasonally adjusted U.S. City Average All Items Consumer Price Index for All Urban Consumers (CPI-U).

Interest on TIPS is based on a fixed coupon rate applied to the inflation-adjusted principal, so investors receive a guarantee of a real rate of return above inflation. The real yield is typically lower than the nominal yield. For example, at the close of February 1, 2002, the yield on the 30-year TIPS was 3.44 percent, while that on the 30-year fixed-principal bond was 5.40 percent. The yield differential of 1.96 percent reflected inflation expectations.

Advantages of Treasury Securities

Treasury securities offer several advantages to investors, the most important of which is safety. Essentially, the U.S. government's ability to raise taxes and print money backs Treasury securities. Hence, most consider these securities the safest of all investments in terms of credit risk. The certainty of interest and principal payments attracts people who rely on a dependable income stream. In addition, a wide range of maturities is available, from the very short-term Treasury bills to medium-term Treasury notes. U.S. investors also benefit because interest payments are free of state and local taxation. Yet another advantage is the high level of liquidity in the Treasury securities, which makes it easy to trade Treasury securities at the prevailing market price. Dealers, fund managers, and other institutions often trade in large volume. Large volume reduces bid-asked spread, the difference between what a dealer bids to buy and what a dealer offers to sell.

Because of the safety of Treasury securities and the political stability of the United States, foreigners often purchase U.S. Treasury securities whenever there is a financial or political crisis overseas. This phenomenon is a **flight to quality**. As we will discuss later, the demand for the newest Treasury security in any maturity segment is generally higher than for older securities. The higher level of liquidity means that it is easy to trade large volumes. Consequently, the foreign money that flows into the United States as a result of a flight to quality is often used to purchase the most recently auctioned Treasury securities. This phenomenon is a **flight to liquidity**.

A Note on Market Quotations

The *Wall Street Journal* and the business sections of most newspapers publish closing quotes (the last bid and offer prices at the close of the previous trading session) on all Treasuries, under the heading "Treasury Bonds, Notes & Bills." Data vendors such as Bloomberg (**http://www.bloomberg.com**) and GovPX (**http://www.govpx.com**) publish real-time quotes on their proprietary networks and Web sites. For Treasury bills, quotes include the maturity date, the number of days to maturity, bid rate, asked rate, changes, and asked yield. The bid and asked are quoted in terms of a rate discount. The bid rate is generally lower than the asked rate, because the price and interest rate have an inverse relationship. The asked yield is the investment yield or bond equivalent yield based on the asked discount rate quoted.

Quotes on notes and bonds include the coupon rate, maturity, bid price, asked price, change in price, and asked yield. The price quotes are based on the percentage of par value. For example, a bid of 100:04 means that the dealer bids a price of $100\frac{4}{32}$, or 100.125 percent of the face value. An asked of 100:06 means that the dealer offers to sell at $100\frac{6}{32}$, or 100.1875 percent of the par amount. The difference of $\frac{2}{32}$ between the bid and asked is the bid-asked spread. Changes are in 32nds. For example, a change of "+8" means that the asked price went up $\frac{8}{32}$ over the prior day. The asked yield represents the yield to maturity based on the asked price plus accrued interest. Yield to maturity is the rate that discounts all future periodic coupons and principal at maturity to the asked price. When one plots the yield to maturity against term to maturity, the result is a yield curve. Figure 8.1 displays a typical yield curve. If yields

FIGURE 8.1 | *A Typical Yield Curve*

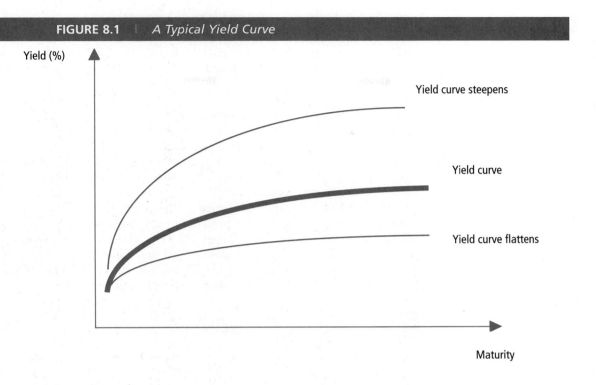

change by the same amount for all terms of Treasury securities, the yield curve has had a parallel shift. But this almost never happens. Under the normal yield curve environment, when the difference between the short-term and long-term yields increases, the yield curve steepens. In contrast, when the difference between the short-term and long-term yields decreases, the yield curve flattens. If short-term yields are higher than long-term yields, the yield curve is inverted.

Treasury strips are also quoted in terms of price. Abbreviations indicate the type of strip: "ci" indicates a coupon strip, "np" represents a note principal strip, and "bp" denotes a bond principal strip. TIPS are quoted on a price basis as well, but the yield is the real yield. It represents the yield investors receive in excess of and above inflation.

YIELD TO MATURITY AND SPOT RATES

An investor who purchases a Treasury security has to know how the security's yield is quoted as well as how it is valued. The yield quoted in the newspaper on a Treasury security is the yield to maturity; it is the discount rate that equates the present value of a security's future cash flows to its current market price. The Treasury yield curve can be used to estimate the theoretical spot rate curve, which is the graphic depiction of the term structure of interest rates. As explained later, fixed-income analysts often use the spot rates, instead of the yield to maturity, to value fixed-income securities. Furthermore, the spot rate curve can be used to compute forward rates to gauge the market's expectation of future interest rates.

Yield to Maturity and Valuation

A real-world example will help to illustrate the concept of yield to maturity. On March 24, 1999, the Treasury announced the auction results of a 2-year note (the auction process is covered in a later section). The coupon rate was 4.875 percent, and the Treasury awarded the notes to bidders at a yield of 4.995 percent. The issue was dated March 31, 1999; that is the coupon interest began to accrue on March 31, 1999. The price of a security is the present value of all future cash flows. In this case, for a face value of $100, the holder of the notes could receive half of the annual coupon ($2.4375) every six months plus $100 on March 31, 2001. The rate commonly used to discount those coupons and the final principal would have been 2.4975 percent, or half of the annual yield, because the note paid interest semiannually. Thus, the price was

8.1
$$p = \frac{\$2.4375}{(1 + 2.4975\%)^1} + \frac{\$2.4375}{(1 + 2.4975\%)^2} +$$

$$\frac{\$2.4375}{(1 + 2.4975\%)^3} + \frac{\$2.4375}{(1 + 2.4975\%)^4} + \frac{\$100}{(1 + 2.4975\%)^4} = \$99.774.$$

This is the formula for a 2-year note. In general, the following valuation formula can be used to calculate the price of a coupon Treasury security:

8.2
$$p = \frac{\dfrac{C}{2}}{\left(1 + \dfrac{y}{2}\right)} + \frac{\dfrac{C}{2}}{\left(1 + \dfrac{y}{2}\right)^2} + \frac{\dfrac{C}{2}}{\left(1 + \dfrac{y}{2}\right)^3} +$$

$$\cdots + \frac{\dfrac{C}{2}}{\left(1 + \dfrac{y}{2}\right)^N} + \frac{100}{\left(1 + \dfrac{y}{2}\right)^N},$$

where C denotes the annual coupon, N denotes the number of remaining coupons, and y represents the yield to maturity. This can be simplified to

8.3
$$p = \sum_{t=1}^{N} \frac{\dfrac{C}{2}}{\left(1 + \dfrac{y}{2}\right)^t} + \frac{100}{\left(1 + \dfrac{y}{2}\right)^N}.$$

The first term on the right is the discounted value of all of the N future semiannual coupons, and the second term is the present value of the final principal payment. As these equations show, the yield to maturity considers the timing of the cash flows. The yield to maturity also takes into account coupons as well as any capital gain or loss the investor will realize by holding the security to maturity, assuming interest rates remain the same.

Spot Rates

The valuation formula we just presented is actually incorrect. For simplicity, the formula discounted every cash flow, regardless of the timing of the receipt, at the same yield. In reality, each cash flow must be discounted at a rate corresponding to the timing of that particular cash flow. A coupon fixed-income security is a package of zero-coupon instruments; each component has a maturity determined by its coupon date or, in the case of the face value, the final redemption date. The value of the security should equal the value of all component zero-coupon instruments. Based on this concept, analysts use the following formula to price fixed-income securities:

8.4
$$p = \frac{\dfrac{C}{2}}{\left(1 + \dfrac{y_1}{2}\right)} + \frac{\dfrac{C}{2}}{\left(1 + \dfrac{y_2}{2}\right)^2} + \frac{\dfrac{C}{2}}{\left(1 + \dfrac{y_3}{2}\right)^3} +$$

$$\cdots + \frac{\dfrac{C}{2}}{\left(1 + \dfrac{y_N}{2}\right)^N} + \frac{100}{\left(1 + \dfrac{y_N}{2}\right)^N}.$$

Here, C denotes the annual cash flow and y_i denotes the discount rate for period i ($i = 1, 2, 3, \ldots N$). The appropriate discount rate, called the **spot rate**, now discounts each cash flow.[4] If the price of a coupon Treasury security with N coupon periods to maturity is p, the spot rate can be determined by solving for y_N:

8.5
$$\frac{y_N}{2} = \left[\frac{\dfrac{C}{2} + 100}{p - \dfrac{C}{2} \displaystyle\sum_{t=1}^{N-1} \dfrac{1}{\left(1 + \dfrac{y_t}{2}\right)^t}} \right]^{\frac{1}{N}} - 1.$$

[4] The term *spot rate* also refers to the yield on each component of Treasury strips. In this case, a spot rate curve is a graphic plot of the spot rate against the term to maturity of the strips.

The equation can also be used to determine theoretical spot rates and to derive a theoretical spot rate curve. The first spot rate (y_1) is the yield on 6-month Treasury bills, and the second spot rate (y_2) is the yield on 1-year bills. The 1.5-year spot rate (y_3) can be obtained by plugging the price of a 1.5-year Treasury coupon security, the coupon, and the 6-month and 1-year spot rates into the equation. Then the theoretical 1.5-year spot rate and the 2-year Treasury note price can be used to compute the 2-year spot rate. Thus, in general, formula (8.5) can be used to compute the theoretical spot rate for the Nth 6-month period. Plotting the theoretical spot rates against term to maturity produces the theoretical spot rate curve, which is the term structure of interest rates.

As an example, assume that the 6-month Treasury bill yield is 4.00 percent and the 1-year bill yield is 4.40 percent. The 1.5-year Treasury with a 4.50 percent coupon trades at 98:00, and the 2-year 5.00 percent Treasury trades at 99:00, with coupons paid semiannually. The 6-month spot rate is 4.00 percent and the 1-year spot rate is 4.40 percent. Using equation (8.5), the 1.5-year and 2-year spot rates are

$$\boxed{8.6} \quad \frac{y_3}{2} = \left[\frac{2.25 + 100}{98 - 2.25 \times \left(\frac{1}{(1 + 2.00\%)} + \frac{1}{(1 + 2.20\%)^2} \right)} \right]^{\frac{1}{3}} - 1 = 2.98\%.$$

$$\boxed{8.7} \quad \frac{y_4}{2} = \left[\frac{2.50 + 100}{99 - 2.50 \times \left(\frac{1}{(1 + 2.00\%)} + \frac{1}{(1 + 2.20\%)^2} + \frac{1}{(1 + 2.98\%)^3} \right)} \right]^{\frac{1}{4}} - 1 = 2.78\%.$$

On an annualized basis, the 1.5-year and the 2-year spot rates are 5.96 percent and 5.56 percent, respectively. The same process and equation (8.5) can be applied to relevant Treasury notes and bonds to obtain the theoretical spot rate curve.

Forward Rates

After the derivation of the theoretical spot rate curve, one can use it to infer the market's expectations of future interest rates, called implied **forward rates**. As an example, suppose that an investor has a one-year investment horizon and considers two alternatives:

° Alternative 1: Buy a 1-year Treasury bill.

° Alternative 2: Buy a 6-month Treasury bill, and when it matures, buy another 6-month Treasury bill.

The investor will be indifferent between those two alternatives if both produce the same returns over the one-year investment horizon. The investor knows that the 6-month bills yield 4.00 percent and the 1-year bills yield 4.40

percent, but he does not know what the rate on 6-month bills will be six months from now. The yield on a 6-month Treasury bill six months from now is the so-called forward rate. Given the observed spot rates, the investor can determine the forward rate on a 6-month Treasury bill that will produce a one-year return equal to the return from purchasing a 1-year Treasury bill.

By purchasing the 1-year Treasury bill, the investor will receive the face value ($100) at the end of one year. The price the investor pays is

8.8
$$p = \frac{\$100}{\left(1 + \dfrac{4.40\%}{2}\right)^2} = \$95.74.$$

If instead, the investor invests $95.74 in a 6-month Treasury bill that yields 4.00 percent, he will have $95.74 \times (1 + 2.00\%) = \$97.65$ after six months. At that point the investor will purchase another 6-month Treasury bill. Suppose that f is the forward rate on a 6-month Treasury bill available in six months when the first 6-month Treasury bill matures. The total dollar amount the investor receives at the end of the one-year investment horizon must be $100 if he or she is indifferent between the two investment alternatives,

8.9
$$\$95.74 \times (1 + 2.00\%) \times \left(1 + \frac{f}{2}\right) = \$97.65 \times \left(1 + \frac{f}{2}\right) = \$100.$$

Solving for f, the forward rate is 4.80 percent.

Here is how we use this rate of 4.80 percent. If the 6-month interest rate six months from now is more than 4.80 percent, then the total dollars at the end of one year would be more than $100 by investing in 6-month instrument and reinvesting the proceeds six months from now at the 6-month rate at the time. On the other hand, if the 6-month interest rate six months from now is less than 4.80 percent, then the total amount at the end of one year would be higher by investing in the 1-year instrument that earns 4.40 percent. If the 6-month interest rate six months from now is 4.80 percent, then the two investment alternatives will give the same result.

Generalizing from Equation 8.9, we can put the process for deriving the forward rate on a 6-month Treasury bill six months from now into a formula:

8.10
$$\frac{f}{2} = \frac{\left(1 + \dfrac{y_2}{2}\right)^2}{\left(1 + \dfrac{y_1}{2}\right)} - 1.$$

In the expression, y_1 is the 6-month spot rate, and y_2 is the 1-year spot rate since every six months is one time period.

In general, the formula for the implied forward rate is

$$
\boxed{8.11} \qquad \frac{f_{n,m}}{2} = \left[\frac{\left(1 + \dfrac{y_{n+m}}{2}\right)^{n+m}}{\left(1 + \dfrac{y_n}{2}\right)^{n}} \right]^{\frac{1}{m}} - 1.
$$

where $f_{n,m}$ is the m-period forward rate n periods from now, y_n is the n-period spot rate, and y_{n+m} is the $(n+m)$-period spot rate. To illustrate the application of the general formula, let us return to our example. Recall that the 6-month spot rate is 4.00 percent and the 1-year spot rate is 4.40 percent. Then the forward rate on a 6-month Treasury bill six months from now, $f_{1,1}$, is

$$
\boxed{8.12} \qquad \frac{f_{1,1}}{2} = \left[\frac{\left(1 + \dfrac{4.40\%}{2}\right)^{2}}{\left(1 + \dfrac{4.00\%}{2}\right)} \right]^{\frac{1}{1}} - 1 = 2.40\%.
$$

Thus, the forward rate is 4.80 percent, as we demonstrated earlier.

ISSUING PROCESS AND AUCTION

The U.S. government sells its securities at regularly scheduled auctions conducted by the Treasury Department. Table 8.1 shows the current pattern of auctions for marketable securities. Primary dealers buy most treasuries offered at auction (see Table 8.2). Primary dealers are financial institutions that actively trade government securities and have established business relationships with the Federal Reserve Bank of New York. Individual investors purchase on a much smaller scale. The minimum amount that may be purchased at an auction is $1,000, and any bid in excess of $1,000 must be in multiples of $1,000.

The auction process begins with a public announcement by the Treasury. The announcement typically includes the following information:

° The offering amount.

° A description of the offering, including the term and type of security, CUSIP number, auction date, issue date, dated date, maturity date, and interest payment dates.[5]

---

[5]The issue date is the date the new security is released to the market. The dated date is the date on which interest begins to accrue for coupon treasuries. If the dated date is earlier than the issue date, the purchasers also have to pay for the amount of accrued interest from the dated date to the issue date.

TABLE 8.1 | *Current Auction Pattern for Marketable Treasury Securities*

Security	Auction Schedule
4-week bills	Weekly
13-week bills	Weekly
26-week bills	Weekly
2-year notes	Monthly
5-year notes	Monthly
10-year notes	February, May, August, November

Source: Federal Reserve Bank of New York and Department of Treasury, 2002.

TABLE 8.2 | *Primary Dealers*

ABN AMRO Bank, N.V. New York Branch
Banc of America Securities LLC
Banc One Capital Markets, Inc.
Barclays Capital, Inc.
Bear, Stearns & Co., Inc.
BNP Paribas Securities Corp.
CIBC World Markets Corp.
Credit Suisse First Boston Corp.
Daiwa Securities America, Inc.
Deutsche Banc Alex. Brown, Inc.
Dresdner Kleinwort Wasserstein Securities LLC
Goldman, Sachs & Co.
Greenwich Capital Markets, Inc.
HSBC Securities (USA), Inc.
J.P. Morgan Securities, Inc.
Lehman Brothers, Inc.
Merrill Lynch Government Securities, Inc.
Mizuho Securities USA, Inc.
Morgan Stanley & Co., Inc.
Nomura Securities International, Inc.
Salomon Smith Barney, Inc.
UBS Warburg LLC

Note: The list is as of December 9, 2002.

Source: Federal Reserve Bank of New York (http://www.ny.frb.org).

- ○ Whether the security is eligible for stripping.
- ○ Procedures for submitting of bids, the maximum bid amount, and payment terms.

The Auction Process

After the Treasury announces an auction, bids are accepted up to thirty days before the auction and may be submitted electronically via the Treasury Automated Auction Processing System (TAAPS), Treasury Direct Web site (**http://www.publicdebt.treas.gov/sec/sectdes.htm**), by mail, or in person. Two types of bids can be submitted: noncompetitive and competitive. Small investors and individuals generally submit **noncompetitive bids**, in which the investor indicates the amount he or she wants to purchase without specifying a purchase price. The investor will receive the dollar amount submitted in the bid. In a noncompetitive tender, a bidder may not bid for more than $1 million in a bill auction or more than $5 million in a note or bond auction. The price is unknown until the announcement of the auction results. Primary dealers acting for their own accounts or on behalf of clients usually submit sealed **competitive bids** specifying both the amount and the price they are willing to pay. The bid is accepted if the bid yield is not higher than the highest yield the Treasury accepts at the auction. Otherwise, the Treasury rejects the bid.

A dealer cannot bid both competitively and noncompetitively for its own account in the same auction. They submit bids in terms of discount rate for bills, stated in three decimal places in 0.005 percent increments. The Treasury requires that competitive bids in note and bond auctions be expressed in yields using three decimals in 0.001 percent increments. The Treasury will accept these bids until 1:00 P.M. EST on the day of the auction. Ordinarily, primary dealers submit their competitive bids through TAAPS at the last possible moment, sometimes literally seconds before the deadline. The deadline for noncompetitive tenders is 12:00 noon EST on the auction date.

Competitive bidders may submit more than one bid. But no bidder may bid more than 35 percent of the total amount of the security being sold. Specifically, under the 35 percent rule, the bidder's net long position in the auction may not exceed 35 percent of the amount of the security in the auction.

The Federal Reserve Banks in New York, Chicago, and San Francisco consolidate the bids submitted through TAAPS. Immediately after 1:00 P.M. EST, the FRBs review and process these bids to assure compliance under the Treasury's Uniform Offering Circular. The Treasury in Washington, D.C. then sorts and reviews these bids electronically. The Treasury nets out the total amount of noncompetitive tenders and allocates the balance to competitive bidders with bids at or below the **high yield** (the highest yield accepted at an auction),[6] also known as the **stop yield**. The auction is a **single-price** (or **Dutch**) **auction**, meaning that both competitive and noncompetitive bidders are awarded securities at the price that results from the high yield (or high dis-

---

[6]The Treasury also awards full amounts of the security to Federal Reserve and foreign official bids.

count rate, for bills). All tenders at lower yields are accepted in full. All competitive bids at higher yields are rejected. The coupon rate is the high yield rounded down to the nearest one-eighth.

An Example of a Treasury Auction

As an example, suppose that the Treasury has received $1 billion in noncompetitive tenders in an $11 billion auction for 5-year notes. In that case, $10 billion in securities will be awarded to competitive bidders. For this auction, there are six competitive bidders, A, B, C, D, E, and F. Table 8.3 (see p. 192) shows the yield and the amount by each bidder, ranked from the lowest yield to the highest. The highest yield at which the $10 billion of securities can be sold is 4.250 percent. Under the Dutch auction system, all accepted bidders (A, B, C, D, and E) will pay a price that reflects a yield of 4.250 percent. In this example, D and E each bid $2 billion at 4.250 percent. After the security is awarded to A, B, and C, the remaining amount is $2 billion, so bidders D and E will each receive a $1 billion allocation.

The ratio of the bids received to the amount awarded is the **bid-to-cover ratio**. A high bid-to-cover ratio implies strength in the auction. Another measure known as the **tail** of the auction is the difference between the average yield of all accepted bids and the high yield. When traders form trading strategies after the auction, they use the tail as a measure of the auction's success.[7] The interpretation of a tail is more art than science, however. Generally, a short tail signals strength, so traders will trade more aggressively. A long tail indicates weakness in market demand, and hence traders will be cautious on the downside. At times, however, a long tail has a different implication. In an uncertain market environment, some bidders who need to have a specific security will be extremely aggressive. This will likely lead to a long tail. A short tail indicates a lack of such aggressiveness.

The Treasury announces the auction results within two hours of the auction, frequently by 1:30 or 2:00 P.M. EST. The announcement includes the amount of bids received, the total accepted, and the bid-to-cover ratio, as well as the high, low, and median bid, and the issuing price. For a coupon Treasury, the announcement includes a coupon rate as well. Table 8.4 (see p. 192) provides an example of the information included in a Treasury announcement of auction results of 2-year notes on January 23, 2002.

WHEN-ISSUED TRADING AND DEALER BIDDING STRATEGIES

A major feature of Treasury auctions is the "when, as, and if issued" trading, known as when-issued trading. The **when-issued (WI)** trading begins immediately after the Treasury announcement and lasts until the settlement date, the

---

[7]The marginal probability of losing an auction by lowering the bid price by a given amount increases as the level of competition increases. Therefore, auction theory generally predicts that lower dispersion of opinion will result in higher bids.

TABLE 8.3 | *Yield and Quantity of Competitive Bids*

Bidder	Bid Yield (%)	Bid Amount ($ billions)
A	4.245	2
B	4.246	3
C	4.248	3
D	4.250	2
E	4.250	2
F	4.252	1

TABLE 8.4 | *Main Items Included in the Announcement of the Results of a Treasury Security Auction of 2-Year Notes*

1. Information on the Issue

Issue date: January 31, 2002
Dated date: January 31, 2002
Maturity date: January 31, 2004
Interest rate: 3%

2. Yield and Price

High yield: 3.039%
Median yield: 2.980%
Low yield: 2.920%
Price: 99.925

3. Auction Allocation (amount in thousands)

Competitive tender: $37,307,340; accepted: $23,828,265
Noncompetitive tender: $1,071,788; accepted: $1,071,788
Foreign and International Monetary Authority tender: 100,000; accepted: 100,000
Subtotal tender: $38,479,128; accepted: $25,000,053
Federal Reserve tender: $5,766,370; accepted: $5,766,370
Bid-to-cover ratio = $38,479,128/$25,000,053 = 1.54

Source: "Public Debt News: Treasury Security Auction Results," Department of the Treasury, Bureau of the Public Debt (http://www.public debt.treas.gov/of/ofaucrt.htm), January 23, 2002.

date on which payment is made to settle a trade. Prior to the auction date, dealers and investors actively participate in the WI market. They may take either a long position or a short position in the security for a future settlement on the issue date. Thus WI trades are forward contracts to be settled on the new issue settlement date.

Before the auction, WI trading is in terms of yields. Following the auction, the Treasury announces the coupon and subsequently, WI trading is on a price basis rather than a yield basis. Generally, the issuance of securities occurs several days after the auction. WI trading ends when the new security settles. Prior to the settlement of the note, the buyer does not have to pay for the purchase. The interest starts to accrue after the settlement date on January 31, 2002. For example, as shown in Table 8.4, the 2-year note was auctioned on January 23, 2002 and settled on January 31, 2002. The when–issued trading ended on January 31, 2002. Figure 8.2 depicts the process of issuance.

WI trading affects the strategies bidders use in the auction because it affects their positions going into the auction. Bidders who buy a security in the WI market before the auction go into the auction with long positions, and those who have sold go into the auction with short positions. The WI market also serves a price discovery role; trading in this market provides vital information on the strength of demand for the security and on the disparity of bidders' views about the market. Such information helps in preparing bids. On the other hand, dealers who believe they have very valuable private information such as future interest rates may refrain from WI trading so that they can use the information in their bids.

TREASURY COUPON ROLLS

Treasury coupon rolls play an important part in the process of distributing new Treasury coupon securities. In a **coupon roll** trade, a dealer purchases an on-the-run, or most recently issued, Treasury security from a customer for next-day settlement and simultaneously sells to that customer the same amount of the recently announced new security for forward settlement. In a reverse roll, a dealer sells an outstanding issue and buys a new security. The forward in a roll trade, a WI sale, settles on the new issue settlement date. The roll is the spread between the yield on the new security and that on the outstanding issue in the same maturity segment. A "give" in rolls indicates that the WI security provides a higher yield than the outstanding issue. A "take" in rolls implies the opposite—the new issue has a lower yield.

Dealers use rolls to accommodate customers who have a preference for liquidity and tend to trade rolls to maintain positions in the current issues. Dealers also use rolls to position themselves for bidding at upcoming auctions. A dealer

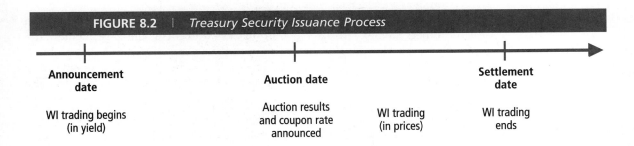

FIGURE 8.2 | *Treasury Security Issuance Process*

Announcement date — WI trading begins (in yield)

Auction date — Auction results and coupon rate announced

WI trading (in prices)

Settlement date — WI trading ends

will seek to execute a roll if he or she is short the outstanding issue because he or she anticipates a market decline or has to accommodate customers. By executing a roll, a dealer closes the short position on the outstanding issue and creates a short position on the new security. Hence the dealer has an incentive to bid more aggressively at the upcoming auction.

As an example, on March 17, 1999, the Treasury announced that a 2-year notes auction would be held on March 24, 1999. The issue settled on March 31, 1999. Trading of the 2-year roll began right after the announcement. The 2-year notes are issued monthly. A give (take) of 5 basis points in the 2-year roll means the dealer proposes to purchase the outstanding issue at the market yield against selling the new issue at a yield of 5 basis points higher (lower).

By executing a 2-year roll, the dealer acquires the outstanding 2-year notes for next day settlement against selling to the same customer the same par amount of the new note for forward delivery and payment on March 31, 1999. The customer is in effect "rolling" over the investment from the outstanding 2-year notes to the new 2-year issue, with a one-month extension in maturity. The customer can invest the funds received until the new issue settles. On the other hand, she gives up the accrued interest by selling the outstanding 2-year notes.

SHORT SQUEEZES

Dealers typically enter the auction with significant short positions, because they have sold before the auction the security to clients who prefer to own the new issue. This presents significant risks, however. A dealer who is short and cannot obtain a sufficient quantity of the security at the auction either must cover the short position before the issue date by buying in the WI market after the auction or must borrow the security on the issue date to make good on delivery. The most common mechanism used to borrow Treasury securities is the reverse repurchase agreement, in which the dealer lends money to the security holder in exchange for use of the security.[8] In such a reverse repurchase transaction, however, the dealer is still short in the security and is exposed to the possibility of being unable to purchase it at the anticipated price. In other words, the dealer is caught in a short squeeze. Put differently, a **short squeeze** occurs when an auction participant, or a group of participants, gains control of a majority of a certain security and withholds the supply from the cash or repurchase agreement markets.

A famous short squeeze occurred in 1991. The securities firm Salomon Brothers admitted to having controlled 94 percent of the 2-year notes auctioned on May 22, 1991, in violation of the Treasury regulation that prohibits a bidder's long position from exceeding 35 percent of the issue in any single auction.[9] Salomon acquired 44 percent of the notes at the auction and also

---

[8]See Chapter 2 for a detailed description of the repurchase agreement market.

[9]Salomon subsequently merged with Smith Barney to form Salomon Smith Barney, which is now a unit of Citigroup. In 2003, Citigroup renamed this unit Smith Barney.

allegedly prearranged significant trades with big investors to give the firm a dominant position in the security. Box 8.1 (see p. 197) provides a more detailed description of the violation and other scandals.

The 2-year notes are generally in high demand because they have the shortest maturity of coupon Treasury securities. Many investors around the world buy them at auction and hold them to maturity, but the price sometimes declines modestly immediately after the auction, when interest in the note fades. Consequently, a common trading strategy is for traders and arbitrageurs to short ahead of the auction and cover the short after the price declines. Contrary to expectations, the price of this particular 2-year note jumped sharply after the auction. The 2-year notes became so scarce that the collateral-specific repurchase agreement rates were about 75 to 200 basis points special. That is, holders of this particular note could borrow in the repo market at a favorable rate substantially below the market rate.

The scandal cost Salomon its top management, and it was fined nearly $300 million. The firm lost its credibility in the marketplace and might not have survived had not Warren Buffett, a major shareholder, provided a capital infusion and astute management to restore credibility. More importantly, in response to these problems, the Treasury introduced major changes in the Treasury market, including the right to reopen an issue. It also experimented for the first time with a Dutch auction for the 2-year and 5-year notes. As noted previously, the Treasury has now adopted the Dutch auction for all Treasury securities. Note that at the time of the Salomon scandal, the Treasury used multiple-price auctions to sell Treasury securities. Each accepted bid would pay a price that reflected the yield in the bid submitted. Thus, different dealers would pay different prices for the same security.

TRADING AND CLEARING

Once a Treasury security is issued, trading mainly occurs over-the-counter, with dealers, brokers, and other investors making trades by phone. In recent years, some dealers have set up electronic trading systems. The most active trading is generally in the on-the-run issues.

Treasury bills trade on a basis of discount rate and typically settle the same day.[10] The discount, the difference between the security's purchase price and its face value, is the investor's return.[11] The following formula is used to determine the purchase price for short-term bills:

---

[10]Settlement means payment for and delivery of a security so that the transaction is complete.

[11]The discount yield generally converts to investment yield when comparing returns. On bills having a current maturity of 182 days or less, the investment yield (y) is: $y = \dfrac{365 \times d}{360 - d \times M}$, or $y = \dfrac{FV - p}{p} \times \dfrac{365}{M}$. For bills having a current maturity of more than six months, one can calculate the investment yield by the

8.13
$$p = FV - d \times \left(\frac{M}{360}\right) \times FV,$$

where p is the purchase price, FV is the face value, d is the discount rate, and M is the number of days from settlement to maturity. As an example, suppose a bill with a current maturity of 175 days is quoted at a bid of 4.12 percent and an offer of 4.11 percent. The purchase price per $1 million for the bill is

8.14
$$p = \$1,000,000 - \$1,000,000 \times 4.11\%\left(\frac{175}{360}\right) = \$980,020.83.$$

Coupon treasuries trade on a price basis. The typical transaction size is $1 million to $100 million for institutions. Trades on coupon Treasuries generally settle on the next market day (called T+1 where T is the trade day), but cash or corporate settlements (T+3) can be arranged. The **invoice price** (also called the dirty price) of a coupon security consists of the quoted price (also called the clean price) plus the accrued interest. The accrued interest is calculated based on the actual number of days since the last coupon payment and the actual number of days in the coupon period or an actual/actual basis. For example, suppose that a 5 percent, 10-year note is quoted at a bid of 98:20 and an offer of 98:22. Assume that the number of days between the last coupon date and settlement is 136 days and the number of days in the coupon period is 183. If an investor purchases $1 million par, the total invoice price is

8.15
$$p = \left(\$1,000,000 \times \left(98 + \frac{22}{32}\right)\%\right) +$$
$$\left(1,000,000 \times \frac{5.00\%}{2} \times \frac{136}{183}\right) = \$1,005,454.23.$$

The total invoice price reflects the quoted price ($986,875, the first term on the right side of the equation) plus the accrued interest ($18,579.23, the second term on the right). The buyer has to pay the offer price plus the accrued interest to the dealer, because whoever has title to the security on the coupon date receives payment of the full semiannual coupon. Note that the Treasury pays interest every six months. Hence, the accrued interest calculation uses half of the annual coupon rate.

---

following formula: $y = \dfrac{-2\dfrac{M}{365} + 2\sqrt{\left(\dfrac{M}{365}\right)^2 - \left(2\dfrac{M}{365} - 1\right)\left(1 - \dfrac{1}{P}\right)}}{2\dfrac{M}{365} - 1}$. All terms are as defined in the text, except p, which is the price per $1 face value.

MARKETS IN ACTION   Salomon Scandals

8.1

Paul Mozer, the managing director under Vice-Chairman John Meriwether, reported to Meriwether on April 27, 1991 that he had broken the Treasury's 35% limit on a dealer's bid in new Treasury notes auctioned on February 21, 1991. Mozer told Meriwether that he submitted an unauthorized bid for 35% of the $9 billion 5-year note auction in a customer's name, Warburg. When the Fed contacted Salomon to inquire about the Warburg bid, Mozer instructed Thomas Murphy to indicate to the Fed that that bid should have been in the name of Mercury Asset Management, an affiliate of S.G. Warburg.

The Fed decided that the relationship between Warburg and Mercury was close enough to limit the combined bids of both entities to 35% of the auction. The Treasury sent a letter to Paul Mozer and S.G. Warburg, plc, the parent of Mercury and S.G. Warburg.

In an effort to prevent further investigation by the Treasury, Mozer contacted Mercury and requested that it not respond to the Treasury letter. In the meantime, Murphy also tried unsuccessfully to set up a meeting between Mozer and an acquaintance of his at S.G. Warburg, who had received the Treasury letter.

Mozer notified Meriwether on April 27, 1991 of the Treasury's letter. Meriwether immediately notified Tom Strauss of the violation. The next day, Meriwether, Strauss (the Salomon President), and Donald Feuerstein (Salomon's chief legal counsel) discussed the issue. They decided to report it to Salomon's Chairman John Gutfreund on April 29, 1991. The four executives discussed how best to report the matter, but did not reach a decision on how to approach the government.

In addition, in the May 22, 1991 auction of $12 billion in 2-year notes, Mozer submitted a $4.2 billion bid in the firm's account, a $2 billion bid for Tiger Investments, and a $4.3 billion bid for Quantum Fund. After the auction, the price of 2-year notes rose as dealers scrambled to buy notes to cover their short positions. Many dealers lost substantial sums of money to cover their positions. Some complained to the Fed about Salomon's large

inventory. The Fed asked Salomon to sell or loan its 2-year notes to ease the squeeze.

In early June, Salomon had not yet reported to the government Mozer's unauthorized bids in February auction and the Treasury was reportedly upset about Salomon's possible involvement in the May squeeze, an unpredicted shortage of supply and high demand for the notes.

In early July, the SEC and the Justice Department issued a subpoena for Salomon's documents for the May 1991 2-year note auction. After weeks of investigation, Salomon's outside counsel found four problems:

1. Salomon submitted an unauthorized bid of 4-year note auction on December 27, 1990.
2. Salomon fabricated bids for Warburg and Quantum.
3. Salomon submitted a $2.5 billion bid in the April 25, 1991 5-year note auction on behalf of Tudor Jones, $1 billion more than the client's authorization.
4. Salomon submitted a $2 billion bid in the May 22, 1991 2-year note auction on behalf of Tiger, $500 million more than Tiger's authorization.

The investigations led to the resignations of John Gutfreund and Thomas Strauss. The Board of Directors at the same meeting on August 18, 1991 also appointed Warren Buffett as the interim chairman of the firm. Furthermore, the Board fired Paul Mozer and Thomas Murphy. On August 19, 1991 Buffett accepted Meriwether's resignation.

John Meriwether set up his own hedge fund, Long Term Capital Management (LTCM), in 1994. During 1997–1998 Asian and Russian market crises, LTCM lost almost all its capital. Warren Buffett offered to rescue LTCM, but Meriwether didn't accept the offer. Eventually, a consortium of major Wall Street firms injected $3.6 billion of capital, took control of the operations, and gradually liquidated LTCM's positions. Many of the initial LTCM partners have set up their own asset management operations.

Sources: Jegadeesh (1993) and Williams (1992 and 1996).

Dealer Trading

Each morning dealers distribute to traders information about each issue such as the price, yield, dollar value of a basis point or dollar value of an 01 (DV01), and the yield value of a 32nd. The **DV01** is the change in the price of a bond resulting from a one-basis-point change in its yield. Frequently, the DV01 is expressed in dollars per million. The yield value of a 32nd is estimated by calculating the yield to maturity if the bond price changes by a 32nd. The difference between the initial yield and the new yield is the yield value of a 32nd. As an example, a 5 percent, 10-year note trading at par and yielding 5 percent has a value of a basis point (V01) of 0.07798 points, or a DV01 of $779.8 per $1 million dollars of par. This is calculated by taking the difference between the price at a yield of 5.00 percent (par) and the price at a yield of 4.99 percent (100.07798 percent of par).[12] The formula for the yield value of a 32nd is ($\frac{1}{32}$ × V01), which gives a yield value of a 32nd of 0.401 basis point. In the bills market, the DV01 is 0.01% × FV × ($\frac{n}{360}$). Therefore, the DV01 of a 90-day bill is $25.

A dealer generates profits from one or more of several sources. First, the bid-asked spread; the price spread varies from $\frac{1}{128}$ to $\frac{1}{32}$, depending on liquidity, volatility, and remaining maturity. Second, a dealer may profit from favorable market movements such as appreciation in the securities that the dealer has a long position and depreciation in the securities in which the dealer has a short position. Another source of profits comes from **carry**, or the difference between the interest earned on the securities held in inventory and the financing costs. A positive carry, meaning that interest income is more than interest expense, is a source of profit. Conversely, when interest expense is greater than interest income, the dealer has negative carry. For example, the carry is −12 basis points if the financing rate is 1.72% and the accrued interest is 1.60%.

Dealers frequently trade with each other through government interdealer brokers because of the speed and efficiency these brokers provide. Dealers give bids and offers to the brokers, who display the highest bid and lowest offer in a computer network linked to each trading desk. Traders responding to a bid or offer by "hitting" or "taking" pay a commission to the broker. Brokers keep the names of the dealers confidential. Major interdealer brokers include Cantor Fitzgerald, Garban, RMJ, Tullett & Tokyo Liberty, and Hilliard Farber. The quotes provided by the brokers represent prices in the interdealer market, also called the **inside market**. Figure 8.3 shows an example of a composite page from Tullet & Tokyo Liberty PLC. The quotations listed represent the best bid and offer at that time. A "+" after the price quote indicates half of a tick. A number 2 or 6 after the price quote represents $\frac{2}{8}$ or $\frac{6}{8}$ of a tick.

In addition to interdealer brokers, GovPX provides real-time information on transactions by the primary dealers. Specifically, it publishes the best bid and best offer, the size, yields, the last trade side (hit/take), and the last trade size. GovPX has a distribution network that includes Bloomberg, Reuters, Bridge, Telerate, and MoneyLine.

---

[12]Alternatively, a yield of 5.01 percent can be used. The price would be 99.92209 percent of par.

FIGURE 8.3 *Tullet & Tokyo Liberty Treasury Market Composite*

BILLS				+6¼	8/02	105.24	–272
3MO	3/11	4.40	–385	5⅞	9/02	104.19+	–23
6MO	6/10	4.41	–40	5¾	11/02	104.112	–14+
1YR	12/09	4.27	–265	5⅝	12/02	104.002	–036
WI3MO	3/18	4.385	–38	5½	1/03	103.216	–25
WI6MO	6/17	4.39	–385	5½	2/03	103.22+	–256
				5½	3/03	103.262	–29+
SHORT MATURITIES				5¾	4/03	104.286	–00
5⅜	1/00	100.26	–27+	5½	5/03	104.02	–052
5½	2/00	101.012	–02+	5⅜	6/03	103.26	–292
5½	3/00	101.042	–05+	5¼	8/03	103.10+	–13
5⅝	4/00	101.12+	–14	**5 YEAR**		99.19	–21
5½	5/00	101.102	–11+	6¼	2/07	110.226	–232
5⅜	6/00	101.062	–07+	6⅝	5/07	113.136	–142
5⅜	7/00	101.11	–12	6⅛	8/07	110.036	–04+
5⅛	8/00	100.33+	–00+	5½	2/08	106.17	–176
4½	9/00	100.00	–01	5⅝	5/08	107.112	–12
4	10/00	99.046	–06	**10 YEAR**		101.11	–12+
2 YEAR		100.122	–13	6⅝	2/27	119.22+	–25
6	8/00	102.086	–11	6⅜	8/27	116.162	–19
5¾	11/00	102.086	–10	6⅛	11/27	113.17	–19+
5⅜	2/01	101.252	–266	5½	8/28	106.01+	–042
5⅝	5/01	102.21+	–23+	**30 YEAR**		104.02	–04

Note: A snapshot at (2:27:17 P.M.) on Monday, December 14, 1998.

Source: Tullet & Tokyo Liberty.

Electronic Trading Systems

Electronic trading systems have rapidly become essential for both buying and selling in the government securities markets. They have changed the way dealers and investors do business. The market has moved from private networks or leased-line systems to the Internet because it offers substantial competitive advantages. Internet systems provide universal connectivity among all market participants without the costs of expensive private networks or the limitations of leased-line systems.

There are two major types of electronic trading systems in use in the government securities markets: dealer systems and cross-matching systems. Single-dealer systems provide an electronic venue where customers can trade with a specific dealer, while multidealer systems consolidate bids and offers from multiple dealers. Cross-matching systems provide real-time or periodic cross-matching sessions. Users can execute transactions electronically with multiple counterparties on an anonymous basis. In addition, as mentioned earlier, the Treasury Department allows customers to purchase Treasury securities through its Treasury Direct Web site.

Clearing and Settlement

The Treasury Department has offered new bills in book-entry form only since 1979, and new coupon securities since August 1986. The book-entry program has largely replaced physical government and agency securities with computer entries at Federal Reserve Banks. All treasuries held in physical form by depository institutions can be converted to book entry and for transfer by wire.

The Fedwire clears government securities. The Fedwire allows depository institutions to transfer securities and funds for their own accounts and for accounts of customers directly to one another and to depository institutions throughout the United States. The Clearing House Interbank Payment System (CHIPS) settles most international transactions.

For a trade in government securities, two transactions take place simultaneously. Suppose that a securities firm purchased a certain amount of a particular Treasury security from another firm. Assume that the buyer and the seller use two different clearing banks. The securities are transferred to the buyer over the Fedwire by decreasing the seller's clearing bank securities account at the Federal Reserve Bank and by increasing the buyer's clearing bank account by the same amount. Funds are transferred to the seller's account from the buyer's account. The market practice is delivery-versus-payment, so the buyer receives the purchased security and the seller the payment of funds at the same time. The Fedwire's operating hours for book-entry securities are 8:30 A.M. to 3:15 P.M. for transfer origination. The closing time for transfer reversals is 3:30 P.M. The Fed charges a fee for providing the service.

CONCLUDING SUMMARY

Four types of securities trade in the government securities markets. Treasury bills are discount money market instruments. Treasury notes and bonds pay interest every six months; hence, they are coupon securities. Since January 1997, the Treasury Department has auctioned inflation-indexed securities with maturity periods of 5, 10, and 30 years. The principal of an inflation-indexed security adjusts for inflation. Although deflation could cause the principal to decline, the Treasury will pay at maturity an amount that is no less than the par amount as of the date the security was first issued. In addition, Treasury strips, in which coupons trade separately from their underlying principal, have become an important segment of the marketplace.

Treasury securities are distributed through regularly scheduled auctions. The auction process begins with a public announcement by the Treasury Department. Market participants submit either competitive or noncompetitive bids. The Treasury awards all noncompetitive bids and accepts competitive bids that are at or below the high yield. On the issue date, purchasers pay, and the Treasury delivers the security. During the period immediately after the announcement and before the issue date, there is a when-issued market for the new security.

Once securities are issued, they mostly trade over-the-counter. The daily trading volume in the government securities markets averages about $360 billion. The transaction value for a coupon security is the sum of the quoted price and accrued interest. Buyers of a coupon Treasury pay the offer price plus the accrued interest from the last coupon date to the settlement date.

Key Terms

bid-to-cover ratio 191
carry 198
competitive bid 190
coupon roll 193
coupon stripping 180
Dutch auction 190
DV01 198
flight to liquidity 182
flight to quality 182
forward rate 186
high yield 190
inside market 198
invoice price 196

noncompetitive bid 190
short squeeze 194
single-price auction 190
spot rate 185
stop yield 190
tail 191
Treasury bills 180
Treasury bonds 180
Treasury Inflation-Protection Securities
    (TIPS) 180
Treasury notes 180
when-issued (WI) 191

Review Questions

1. The 6-month Treasury bill yield is 4.00 percent, and the 1-year bills yield 4.50 percent. The 1.5-year coupon Treasury with 4.50 percent coupon trades at 99:00 and the 2-year, 5.00 percent coupon Treasury at 101:00. Calculate the 1.5-year and 2-year spot rates.

2. Given the spot rates determined in the previous question, what is the implied forward rate on a 6-month bill one and one-half years from now?

3. The Treasury announced the auction of $10 billion of 30-year bonds on October 28, 1998, with an auction date of November 3, 1998, and an issue date of November 16, 1998. The auction results were released after the auction. The coupon rate was 5.250 percent and the high yield was 5.300 percent. The noncompetitive tenders amounted to $66,594,000, with all of these accepted. The total amount of competitive bids tendered was $16,215,097,000, with $9,934,570,000 accepted. What was the stop yield? What was the bid-to-cover ratio? What was the period of WI trading? What was the carry during this period?

4. In a negative carry environment, does the WI trade at a higher yield or a lower yield than a comparable outstanding Treasury security? Explain.

5. For the 26-week Treasury bills, quoted at a bid of 4.12 percent and an offer of 4.10 percent, why is the bid rate higher than the offer? How much do you pay if you purchase a par amount of $1 million?

6. What is the investment yield for the problem described in question 5?

7. Suppose an investor invests $1,000 on January 15 in a new inflation-indexed 10-year note with a 3 percent coupon. Assume the inflation rate is 1 percent during the first six months. What is the semiannual coupon payment on July 15? Suppose

that inflation accelerates during the second half of the year, so that it reaches 3 percent for the full year. What is the second semiannual interest payment?

8. A 2-year note carrying a coupon rate of 4 percent is quoted at a bid of 102:22 and an offer of 102:24. The number of days until settlement since the last coupon date is 72, and this coupon period has 182 days. A trader sells $5 million par amount. How much will the trader receive?

9. The on-the-run 2-year note with a 4.00 percent coupon trades at par. The overnight general collateral rate is 4.75 percent. This on-the-run 2-year note trades at 50 basis points special in the repo market. If a trader finances the purchase of this note with a repo, what is the carry?

10. The Treasury has announced an auction of $8 billion of 5-year notes. The total amount of noncompetitive tenders is $1 billion. Table 8.3 of the chapter lists the competitive bids. Who is awarded the security? At what yield?

Select Bibliography

Bond Market Association. *An Investor's Guide to U.S. Treasury Inflation-Indexed Securities.* New York: Bond Market Association, 1997.

Bond Market Association. *eCommerce in the Fixed-Income Markets: The 2001 Review of Electronic Transaction Systems.* New York: Bond Market Association, 2001.

Bureau of Public Debt, Department of Treasury. *Treasury Securities at a Glance.* Washington, D.C.: Department of Treasury, 2001.

Fabozzi, F. J. *Bond Markets, Analysis and Strategies,* 3rd ed. Upper Saddle River, N.J.: Prentice Hall, 2000.

Federal Reserve Bank of New York. *Basic Information on Treasury Securities.* 2000.

Federal Reserve Bank of New York. *Fee Schedule 2000.* 2000.

Jegadeesh, N. "Treasury auction bids and the Salomon squeeze." *Journal of Finance* 48, no. 4, September 1993, pp. 1403–1419.

J.P. Morgan Securities. *Government Bond Outlines,* 9th ed. April 1996.

Liaw, T. Pricing Treasury coupon rolls. *Corporate Finance Review,* March–April 1997, pp. 12–16.

Mester, L. "There's more than one way to sell a security: the Treasury's auction experiment." *Business Review,* Federal Reserve Bank of Philadelphia, July–August 1997, pp. 1–10.

Sundaresan, S. *Fixed Income Markets and Their Derivatives.* Cincinnati, Ohio: South-Western Publishing, 2001.

Williams, C. M., "Salomon and the Treasury securities auction." Boston, Mass.: Harvard Business School Publishing, 1992.

Williams, C. M., "Salomon and the Treasury securities auction: 1992 update." Boston, Mass.: Harvard Business School Publishing, 1996.

Municipal Bond Markets

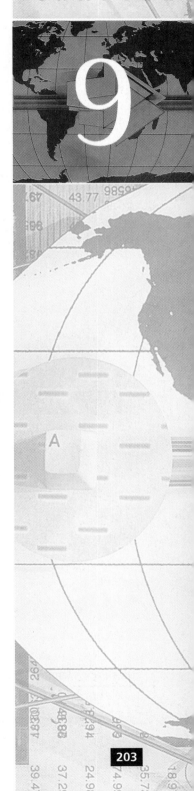

Municipal securities are debt instruments issued by states, cities, counties, and other government entities to raise money to fund projects that serve the public good. These securities fund bridges, highways, mass transit systems, sewage treatment plants, courthouses, and electricity-generating plants around the country, as well as certain types of private projects that serve important public purposes, such as low-income housing, private hospitals, colleges, and industrial facilities. The public service aspect of municipal bonds gives rise to their most distinctive characteristic: the interest they pay is generally free from federal income tax and, in some cases, is exempt from state and local taxes as well.

In addition to their tax advantages, municipal securities differ from Treasury securities and corporate debt in several other ways. For one thing, investors who purchase municipal securities are likely to hold them until maturity. Hence, there is a less active secondary market for municipal securities than for other debt instruments. Furthermore, municipal securities tend to be less uniform than other debt securities. With some 50,000 different issuers and as many as 1.5 million different issues, each with its own structural characteristics, both issuing and trading municipal securities can be complicated. Nonetheless, technological advances, in particular the growth of the Internet, have transformed these markets, just as they have changed other capital markets.

The objectives of this chapter are to provide an understanding of:
°   The various types of municipal securities.
°   The methods commonly used to float new municipal securities.
°   Insurance of municipal securities.
°   The use of technology for new issues and in trading.
°   The tax advantages of municipal securities.
°   The risks investors face when they invest in municipal securities.

MARKET OVERVIEW

At a little more than $1.5 trillion, the market for **municipal securities** is the smallest of the markets for debt instruments, being about half the size of the Treasury securities market and one-fourth as big as the corporate debt market. About 1.5 million municipal issues are outstanding. Annual issuance exceeded $100 billion for the first time in 1982 and then continued on an upward path until 2002 when it peaked at a record $430 billion. Since 1993 annual issuance has remained between $200 billion and $430 billion in most years, as Table 9.1 shows. As the table also shows, the vast majority of the funds raised—consistently more than 80 percent—have a maturity of longer than thirteen months.

Types of Municipal Securities

There are a variety of municipal securities. The most basic types are general obligation bonds and revenue bonds, but there are several variations as well. They differ mainly in the source of revenues that will be used to pay the principal and interest.

General obligation bonds (GOs) are municipal securities with the full faith and credit of the issuer backing the scheduled payments of principal and interest. Most GOs also have the added security that municipalities can raise property taxes to assure payment. Most regard these bonds, which must be

TABLE 9.1	Municipal Issuance, 1990–2001			
Year	Short Term ($ billions)	Long Term ($ billions)	Long Term as Percentage of Total (%)	Total ($ billions)
1990	34.8	128.0	78.6	162.8
1991	44.8	172.8	79.4	217.6
1992	43.0	234.8	84.5	277.8
1993	47.5	292.5	86.0	340.0
1994	40.3	165.1	80.4	205.4
1995	37.9	160.0	80.9	197.9
1996	41.5	185.1	81.7	226.6
1997	46.2	220.7	82.7	266.9
1998	34.7	286.2	89.2	320.9
1999	36.6	227.4	85.6	264.0
2000	41.0	200.4	83.3	241.4
2001	56.1	286.5	83.6	342.6
2002	72.3	358.4	83.2	430.7

Note: "Short term" refers to maturity of thirteen months or less.

Source: Data are from the Bond Market Association (http://www.bondmarkets.com).

approved by voters, as very safe. Additional fees, grants, and special charges secure certain GOs, known as double-barreled GOs.

Revenue bonds are municipal securities with payments secured by revenues derived from certain revenue-producing agencies or enterprises. Examples include water and sewage treatment facilities, hospitals, schools, and airports. Special authorities, created for this purpose, issue many of these bonds. The agency or authority often has the ability to levy charges and fees for its services. Usually, the yield is higher on a revenue bond than a general obligation bond because most think that revenues are less secure than taxes.

In addition to these two basic types, municipalities have issued a variety of other municipal securities. Several of them are special types of revenue bonds. Limited and special tax bonds are revenue bonds payable from the proceeds of a specific tax, such as a gasoline tax, a special assessment, or an ad valorem tax levied at a fixed rate (tax amount is in proportion to the value). Unlike GOs, which are backed by the general ability to raise taxes, these bonds are limited to the specific source of revenue.

Industrial revenue bonds are issued by a government agency to raise funds to develop industrial or commercial property for the benefit of private users. The money raised from this type of bond issue pays for the construction of the new facilities, which are then leased to the corporate guarantor. Hence, the safety of an industrial revenue bond depends on the creditworthiness of the corporate guarantor.

Housing bonds are a type of revenue bonds that are secured by mortgage payments on single-family houses. These bonds have the added protection that comes from federal subsidies for low-income families, Veteran Authority (VA) guarantees, and private mortgage insurance.

Moral obligation bonds are revenue bonds that, in addition to their primary source of revenues, are structured so that, in the event of a revenue shortfall, the state would make up the difference. The state has no legal obligation to do so, but the market perception is that failure to honor the moral pledge would have negative consequences for the state's own creditworthiness.

State and local authorities also issue **municipal notes**, which are short-term debt instruments with maturities ranging from about 60 days to one year. They are usually available in denominations of about $25,000. Municipalities use this type of financing as an interim step when they expect future revenues. For example, a municipality might issue tax anticipation notes while it waits for tax revenues to be paid. The safety of the issue depends on the security and the amount of the tax revenue the municipality expects to receive. A municipality sometimes issues bond anticipation notes (BANs) when it anticipates funds from a bond issue. For example, an issuer might delay a bond issue because of poor market conditions or because it wants to combine several projects into one larger issue. To tide it over while it waits, the municipality might issue BANs. Revenue anticipation notes are similar, issued in anticipation of revenues coming in from the state or federal government.

Major Investors

As Table 9.2 shows, individual investors directly own a third of all tax-exempt municipal securities. Although their direct ownership share has declined from almost half in 1990, individuals also own municipal securities indirectly through mutual funds and money market funds, and as the table also shows, percentages owned by these institutions have increased in recent years. Other major holders of tax-exempt securities include insurance companies.

NEW ISSUES

A municipality planning to market a new bond issue can choose between two strategies: a competitive bond sale or a negotiated bond sale. Each method has its own advantages and disadvantages.

Competitive Bidding

A municipality that chooses a **competitive bidding** process essentially will be selling its bonds at a public auction. After the municipality has solicited bids from various underwriters, they sell the bonds to the highest bidder; that is, the bid that produces the lowest financing costs for the municipality. To handle the bond sale and provide advice, the municipality usually hires a financial adviser. The financial adviser's responsibilities generally include preparing the preliminary and final official statements, recommending the structure of the issue, proposing a sale date, and evaluating the submitted bids. An **official statement**

TABLE 9.2 | *Municipal Securities Ownership*

	Total Amount Outstanding ($ billions)	Households (%)	Mutual Funds (%)	Money Market Funds (%)	Closed-end Funds (%)	Bank Personal Trust (%)	Banks (%)	Insurance Companies (%)	Others (%)
1990	1,184	48.5	9.5	7.1	1.2	6.8	9.9	11.6	5.4
1991	1,272	48.3	11.0	7.1	2.0	7.1	8.1	10.0	6.5
1992	1,302	44.9	12.9	7.4	3.0	7.4	7.5	10.3	6.6
1993	1,378	40.1	15.3	7.7	3.8	7.9	7.2	10.6	7.5
1994	1,342	37.4	15.4	8.5	4.0	8.5	7.3	11.5	7.5
1995	1,294	35.4	16.3	9.9	4.6	8.4	7.2	12.4	5.8
1996	1,296	33.4	16.5	11.1	4.8	8.0	7.3	13.5	5.4
1997	1,368	34.3	16.1	12.2	4.4	6.6	7.1	14.0	5.3
1998	1,464	30.5	17.3	13.8	4.2	6.4	7.5	14.8	5.5
1999	1,532	31.0	16.4	14.4	4.6	6.9	7.6	13.7	5.3
2000	1,568	31.3	15.6	16.5	4.4	6.7	7.7	12.4	5.4
2001	1,685	33.7	15.8	17.6	4.7	6.0	7.5	10.9	5.9
2002	1,783	34.6	15.6	15.9	4.6	5.7	6.8	10.3	6.6

Source: Data are from the Bond Market Association.

for a municipal bond issue is the equivalent of a prospectus for a stock or a corporate bond issue. It provides detailed financial information about the terms of the proposed issue, the issuer's financial status, and its operating data.

After the financial adviser designs the bond issue and the municipality approves it, notice of the bond sale is published. The notice includes such information as the specific date and time for submitting sealed bids, bidding by telephone or fax, minimum bids, and whether the security is book-entry. Underwriters or syndicates of underwriters review the specifications of the proposed bond issue and, if interested, submit sealed bids to the financial adviser. After the bidding closes, the financial adviser analyzes and compares the various bids to select the lowest-cost option.

Negotiated Deals

In contrast to the competitive bidding approach, in a **negotiated deal**, there is no open bidding. Instead, the first step for the municipality is the selection of the underwriter or underwriting syndicate. If an underwriter has successfully handled prior bond issues for the issuer, the municipality may simply use that underwriter again without soliciting other proposals. Otherwise, the municipal issuer will request proposals from several underwriters and make its selection after evaluating all of the proposals. In a negotiated deal, the underwriter handles most of the activities associated with the bond issue on behalf of the municipality. Usually, the issuer does not hire an independent financial adviser. The issuer and the underwriter then negotiate the costs and terms of the bond issue, including the interest rates, the underwriter's fees and charges, the original issue discount, and the issue date.

Advantages and Disadvantages of the Two Methods

Because of the perception of openness and the inherent competitiveness, many people believe that the competitive sale strategy is superior to the negotiated sale. Certainly, a competitive sale eliminates the opportunity for political influence. In competitive bidding, interested underwriters submit confidential sealed bids, so the issuer does not know in advance which underwriting firm will be selected. The use of an independent financial adviser to handle the bidding and evaluate the bids adds to the perception of independence and fairness. There are disadvantages to competitive bidding, however. For example, financial advisers usually advise an issuer to use a negotiated strategy if the bond issue is unusually large or complex. The competitive bidding method may also be inferior if only a few underwriters submit bids.

Certain disadvantages of the competitive sale are therefore advantages of the negotiated strategy. A major advantage of a negotiated bond sale is that the underwriter can better time the entry into the financial market. This flexibility can result in lower financing costs for the issuer. Another advantage is the assistance provided by the underwriter, who typically handles most of the administrative and technical aspects of the bond issue. The negotiated strategy also affords an underwriter the opportunity to sell the bond before an official public offering. This can be a significant advantage, particularly for issues that are complex or have low credit ratings.

At the same time, however, the negotiated sale strategy has some significant disadvantages. The most important is that the coupon rates and underwriter's fees are privately negotiated and are not determined by competitive bidding. On top of that, the underwriter may be selected on the basis of political or personal relationships, instead of merit.

Empirically, neither method seems to have a clear advantage. One study found no clear evidence as to whether competitive bidding or negotiated deals result in more money or lower costs for municipalities.[1] Another study that examined the overall financing costs of competitive and negotiated bonds sold by Pennsylvania school districts in 1993 concluded that the bond marketing strategy (competitive bidding or negotiated sale) was not a statistically significant factor in the determination of overall financing costs.[2]

Disclosure to Purchasers

Like issuers of corporate stock and bonds, issuers of municipal securities are required by the SEC to provide certain information to investors. SEC Rule 15c2-12 requires issuers to:[3]

1. Prepare official statements meeting the content requirements of the rule.
2. File certain financial information and operating data with national and state repositories each year.
3. Disclose any material events on a timely basis.

As explained previously, the final official statement sets forth information about the term of the issue, the financial status of the issuer, its operating data, and annual updating and event disclosure. The rule also requires the underwriters to review the preliminary official statement.

By requiring issuers to provide continuing disclosure throughout the life of each of their bond issues, the rule addressed investors' complaints that they could not obtain information about municipal securities in the secondary market. In addition to the obvious benefits to investors, continuing disclosure is beneficial to municipal issuers as well. To the extent that continuing disclosure enhances the liquidity of a security in the secondary market, investors may accept a lower yield at issuance that saves issuers interest costs. Reliable continuing disclosure can also help an issuer avoid potential liability due to incomplete publicly available information.

---

[1]The study was conducted by the Public Securities Association, which has been renamed The Bond Market Association.

[2]See Stevens and Wood (1998).

[3]The SEC adopted the rule on November 10, 1994.

To satisfy the continuing disclosure requirements, the issuer's financial information must be filed with each Nationally Recognized Municipal Securities Information Repository (NRMSIR) such as Bloomberg Municipal Repositories, DPC Data, J. J. Kenny Repository, and Thomson NRMSIR. The states also have information repositories.

In addition, the rule also requires the issuer to disclose any material event. An event or fact is material if it is likely to be significant to the deliberations of a reasonable investor. The event disclosure must be filed with each NRMSIR or the Municipal Securities Rulemaking Board (MSRB; **http:// ww1.msrb.org**) and with the appropriate state information repository in a timely manner.[4]

The three requirements outlined above apply only to issues of $1 million or more. Issues of less than that amount need not comply with any of the provisions of the rule. The rule also contains three general exemptions that apply if the securities are in minimum denominations of $100,000 or more:

1. A private placement exemption for securities sold to no more than thirty-five sophisticated investors (capable of judging the associated risk) who purchase for investment, not distribution.
2. An exemption for certain securities that the holder has a right to tender at a price of at least par at least as frequently as every nine months.
3. An exemption for securities with maturity of nine months or less.

Online Auctions

The new online auction/bidding systems that allow dealers and investors to bid directly on new issues. For example, Grant Street Group's (**http://www. grantstreet.com**) MuniAuction is an Internet-based electronic auction for new municipal bond issues conducted in real time. The issuer offers bonds for sale on the MuniAuction. Registered bidders can select from a variety of auctions and review the notice of sale and preliminary official statement online before entering the auction of choice. They visit the site at the scheduled auction time and submit bids to purchase all of the bonds or only a selected maturity—an option that is unavailable under the traditional system. Underwriters have the opportunity to view their status relative to other bidders or to modify their own bid, whereas previously they could submit only one final bid. The issuer can watch the auction in progress from its MuniAuction Web page, which lists the winning bids, as they are submitted, as well as winning bidders. MuniAuction also computes the true interest cost associated with the winning bids. Furthermore, online auctions are less expensive for the issuer, which

---

[4]Congress established the MSRB in 1975 to develop rules regulating securities firms and banks involved in underwriting, trading, and selling municipal securities. The MSRB sets standards for all municipal securities dealers. Like the New York Stock Exchange or the National Association of Securities Dealers, the MSRB is a self-regulatory organization that the SEC oversees.

TABLE 9.3	*Summary Comparison of Traditional Competitive Bid and MuniAuction Procedures*
Traditional Procedure	**MuniAuction**
Issuer's decision to sell bonds via competitive bids	Unchanged
Issuer or financial adviser mails notice of sale, preliminary official statement, and bid form to broker-dealers.	Unchanged, except unnecessary to send bid form
Underwriters assemble into bidding groups for purpose of making all-or-none purchase offers.	Some all-or-none bidding groups, more maturity-by-maturity bidders
Issuer or financial adviser responds to questions from broker-dealers.	Unchanged
Lead broker-dealer collects "price thoughts" from group members and clients and prepares bid.	Unchanged for all-or-none bids. Maturity-by-maturity bidders solicit institutional orders for specific maturities and then prepare bids.
Lead broker-dealer transcribes bid onto bid form of proposal to purchase and faxes, delivers, or calls in bid to issuer shortly before deadline.	All-or-none and maturity-by-maturity bidders enter bids on MuniAuction Webpage and submit them at any time during the auction.
Issuer opens and reads bids, announces winners, verifies true interest cost (TIC) calculation and resizes issue.	Issuer can view bids being submitted in real time on MuniAuction Observation Page. MuniAuction calculates TIC to determine winner and then produces report with rank ordering.
Issuer makes official award of bonds to winning broker-dealers.	Unchanged
Issuer or financial adviser finalizes offering size and mails it to lead broker-dealer.	Unchanged for all-or-none winner. Each maturity-by-maturity winner receives a reasonable supply of final offering size by mail.
At closing, lead broker-dealer's clearing agent wires funds to issuer who releases bonds.	Unchanged for all-or-none winner. If maturity-by-maturity wins, each winner's clearing agent wires proceeds to issuer.
Lead broker-dealer's clearing agent collects payments from investors and releases bonds to them.	Unchanged for all-or-none winners. Maturity-by-maturity clearing agent collects payments from winning bidders and releases bonds to them.

must pay gross commissions averaging 5 percent under the traditional system. Table 9.3 presents a summary comparison of the traditional competitive bidding process and the new MuniAuction system.

Form of Issuance

Before July 1983, issuers generally released municipal securities in certificate form with coupons attached. The issuer had no record of who owned its bonds. The owner clipped the coupons and collected interest from the issuer's paying agent. Transferring the bonds required physical delivery and payment.

After July 1983, municipal bonds have been issued in registered form. With a registered security, the holder is registered on the issuer's book. Today, a growing number of municipal bonds are issued in book–entry form, similar to the issuance of U.S. government securities. Ownership is recorded through data entry at a central clearing house. The investor's confirmation of purchase from a bank or brokerage firm provides the written record of the transaction. Registered and book–entry bonds offer a number of protections and convenience to bondholders, including protection from loss or theft, automatic payment of interest, notification of calls to pay off before maturity, and ease of transfer.

MUNICIPAL BOND INSURANCE

Almost half of new municipal securities come to market with bond insurance. The demand for insurance has increased in recent years as several major municipalities have experienced well-publicized fiscal problems, such as New York City's default in the mid-1970s, the default by the Washington Public Power Supply System (WPPSS) in 1984, and Orange County's bankruptcy in 1994 (see Box 9.1, p. 212). Insurance makes municipal bonds more attractive as an investment, because municipal bond insurers guarantee scheduled interest and principal payments. The guarantee covers 100 percent of the interest and principal for the full term of the issue. This level of assurance increases the marketability of the protected bonds and helps them retain their value.

Benefits to Investors

For investors, insurance offers three main benefits. First, each insured municipal is triple-A rated, the highest possible rating. Second, the insurance guarantees that investors will receive principal and interest payments without delay. If the issuer of the bond defaults, the insurance company makes funds available for scheduled payments on the next business day following the notification. Third, for new municipal bond issues, the insurance coverage is good for the life of the bond.

Benefits to Issuers

Most municipal issuers may benefit from insurance as long as their own credit is of investment-grade quality or higher.[5] The difference between what the issuer would have to offer as a yield on bonds carrying its own rating and what the market will accept as a yield on triple-A insured bonds represents gross interest cost savings. The gross savings minus the premium paid to the bond insurer are the net savings. While issuers with triple-B and single-A ratings would seem to have the most to gain, double-A and triple-A issuers also find insurance cost-effective. The Association of Financial Guaranty Insurors (http://www.afgi.org) has estimated that since the inception of municipal bond insurance in 1971, municipalities had saved $30 billion in borrowing costs through bond insurance by 2000. In 2000 alone, they saved about $2.3 billion.

For a smaller municipal issuer, buying insurance may be simpler and less expensive than applying for a credit rating from the major rating agencies. Insurance can also increase the marketability of an issue. Small or infrequent issuers are unknown to most municipal investors, and bond insurance may improve the market's acceptance of their securities.

---

[5]Insurers generally do not insure bonds issued by municipalities whose credit rating is below investment grade.

MARKETS IN ACTION   Orange County Bankruptcy

On December 6, 1994, Orange County, California—one of the wealthiest counties in the United States—filed for Chapter 9 bankruptcy protection. It was the first bankruptcy filing ever by a U.S. major municipality.

The Bankruptcy

A $1.7 billion loss in the county's investment pool precipitated the bankruptcy. The pool, managed by the county treasurer, Robert Citron, contained $7.4 billion—the operating and capital funds for the county, all of its school districts, thirty-one cities within the county, and various special districts such as water and sanitation districts. In an effort to maximize yield at the expense of liquidity and capital preservation, Citron leveraged the pool to three times its value, for a total of more than $21 billion, and invested more than 60 percent of the funds in derivative-related securities. Unfortunately, the pool incurred considerable interest rate exposure as a result of these investments, and when interest rates rose significantly in the second half of 1994, the investment pool suffered a $1.7 billion loss (23 percent).

The announcement of the loss and the bankruptcy filing created panic in several areas. The entities, whose funds were in the investment pool, wondered if they would be able to keep operating. Orange County bondholders, including many individual investors who depended on the interest payments for retirement income, feared the loss of their investments. Moreover, the municipal securities markets in general reeled from the news as investors worried that, if Orange County could collapse, what municipality might be next? Suddenly, municipal bonds, even from a very wealthy county, no longer seemed to be a safe investment.

The county called in securities firm Salomon Brothers (which later became part of Salomon Smith Barney, a division of Citigroup) to assess the damage and begin the clean-up. In one of the largest and most publicized securities auctions in Wall Street history, Salomon succeeded in liquidating the remaining $9 billion in securities over a thirty-day period. The sales proceeds exceeded initial estimates and unwound the web of leverage and derivatives that had exposed Orange County to potential future losses.

The Pool Investors

With the investment pool liquidated, the county next took steps to protect the entities that had invested their funds in the pool. The school district was a particular concern. They needed immediate cash to repay their short-term debt obligations, or they would become insolvent. The bankruptcy, which had thus far been confined to the county government, threatened to turn into a county-wide fiscal crisis.

In May 1995, the county reached an agreement with the pool investors, under which it agreed to distribute all of the cash from the litigation and promised to make whole the losses. In June 1995, the county successfully issued $279 million in new debt to provide funds for desperate school districts. This was the first time a bankrupt municipality had tried to issue new debt, but some innovative techniques, including giving the new bondholders priority under the bankruptcy code, enabled the county to find investors willing to purchase its debt.

The Noteholders

The crisis was by no means over, however. The county owed in excess of $1 billion in short-term general obligation debt with no means of repayment. The funds had been borrowed as part of Citron's scheme to maximize arbitrage earnings through leverage in the investment pool. As pointed out in the chapter text, the full faith and credit of the issuer backs the general obligation debt, meaning that as a last resort the issuer can always raise taxes to repay the debt. A basic tenet of the municipal securities market had been that a municipality would never default on general obligation debt. Later, however, California voters had approved Proposition 13, which severely restricted the ability of municipalities to raise taxes. Now the municipal markets watched anxiously as Orange County teetered on the precipice of defaulting on general obligation debt.

The county first obtained some breathing room by persuading the noteholders to roll over the debt for one year. Then the county devised what it thought would be a solution. It proposed a countywide sales tax increase for ten years, which would generate enough revenue to satisfy the county's obligations

MARKETS IN ACTION   Orange County Bankruptcy (continued)

and pay the claims in full. On June 27, 1995, the county put the tax increase to a vote, as required by Proposition 13, but the citizens of Orange County voted no by an overwhelming margin of 61 percent to 39 percent. In the wake of the measure's failure, unsecured noteholders were stranded with a potential recovery of as little as 25 cents on the dollar and with severely limited prospects for full repayment. The county's debt rating plummeted to default and speculative grade, as the ratings agencies saw no prospect for full repayment of the outstanding debt.

Finally, on July 18, 1995, Salomon Brothers announced a controversial plan to repay all of the noteholders in full. Under the plan, sufficient future tax revenues would be diverted from county agencies (cities, water and sanitation districts, and the transportation authority) to the county to pay off the county's obligations in full without impairing any agency's credit rating or service levels. In other words, all units of government in Orange County would contribute to solve the county's financial problems and avoid the negative ramification that would result for all, including the state of California,

if Orange County defaulted. Despite significant opposition from county agencies afraid of losing their tax dollars, the California state legislature approved the necessary legislation and Governor Pete Wilson signed it into law on October 9, 1995.

Conclusion
Although in the end all of Orange County's debt holders received payment in full, the crisis had exposed deficiencies in the oversight mechanisms, legal protections, and taxing authority of the municipal finance market. The conditions responsible for the county's catastrophic losses—a heavily leveraged portfolio with risky derivative securities—had persisted despite warnings by Citron's political opponent and supposedly close monitoring by rating agencies, law firms, accounting firms, and investment banks. The crisis had also called into question a basic assumption of the municipal securities markets—that general obligation debt, backed by the full faith and credit of the issuer, is safe and secure. Not surprisingly, then, the crisis contributed to the rising demand for municipal bond insurance.

Source: Orange County, California.

Municipal bond insurance is available in the secondary market as well. Municipal bond insurers provide insurance to traders, dealers, and institutional investors to improve the quality and marketability of municipal securities.

An insured bond typically bears a Statement of Insurance indicating that the insurer:[6]

> unconditionally and irrevocably agrees to pay for disbursement to the Bond-holders that portion of the principal [or accreted value in the case of capital appreciation bonds] of and interest on the Bonds which is then due for payment and which the issuer of the Bonds (the "Issuer") shall have failed to provide.

An Example from Orange County
Historically, credit-rating downgrades of unsecured municipal bonds have exceeded upgrades. In contrast, insured bonds maintain their triple-A ratings and liquidity regardless of the financial difficulties of the issuer. Orange

---

[6]This sentence is taken from the generic statement of insurance by Financial Guaranty Insurance Company.

County, California, whose spectacular bankruptcy Box Feature 9.1 describes, provides an example. When Orange County filed for bankruptcy in December 1994, it hurt the price and liquidity of uninsured bonds issued by the County. The insured bonds retained their rating and held their market value much better than their uninsured counterparts. The county's Transportation Authority Sales Tax Revenue 6 percent 2/15/08 bonds, both insured and uninsured, traded at $99.44 per $100 par value on October 31, 1994, before the bankruptcy filing. On December 16 of the same year, after the bankruptcy filing, the uninsured bond traded at $77.09 per $100 par value. The insured bond traded at $92.12 per $100 par value.[7]

Municipal Insurers

Municipal bonds are mostly insured by monoline insurers. The four largest municipal insurers are MBIA (**http://www.mbia.com**), AMBAC (**http://www.ambac.com**), Financial Security Assurance (**http://www.fsa.com**), and Financial Guaranty Insurance Company (**http://www.fgic.com**).[8] All these insurers carry a rating of Aaa by Moody's, AAA by Standard and Poor's, and AAA by FitchRatings. Bonds insured by these organizations receive the same triple-A rating.

Financial insurance companies must meet the requirements of insurance regulators in every state where they do business. They are also subject to intense scrutiny from rating agencies that evaluate and assign a rating to every transaction they insure. To test the adequacy of an insurer's capital resources, the rating agencies apply a computer-simulated stress test that measures its ability to pay claims.

For insurers, the most important measure of financial strength is the margin of safety. The margin of safety takes into account the full range of the insurer's claims-paying resources as well as the quality and diversification of risk in its portfolio. Rating agencies run a computer simulation to demonstrate how the bond insurer would fare in a prolonged economic depression to calculate the margin of safety. A measure of 1.2 to 1.3 is a minimum requirement for a triple-A rating.

SECONDARY MARKET

As mentioned earlier, most buyers purchase municipal securities and hold them until maturity. Hence, the secondary market is not very active, compared with the Treasury and corporate securities markets. Nevertheless, like those markets, it has felt the impact of new developments in technology.

Secondary Trading

The municipal market has historically traded over-the-counter, with market participants executing transactions through telephone contacts. With more than 50,000 different issuers and 1.5 million different issues, each with differ-

---

[7]This example is used in MBIA's marketing brochures, based on data obtained from J.J. Kenny.

[8]FGIC is a GE Capital company.

ent structural characteristics, the municipal market was not an ideal place to use electronic trading systems. In recent years, however, the market has changed. Technological advances, especially the growth of the Internet, now allow dealers and clients to interact through sophisticated systems for instantaneous electronic execution of transactions. The low cost of Internet access has also played a major role, allowing even the smallest individual investor access to tools and information sources that were, until recently, the private domain of institutional investors. Electronic trading will likely grow substantially over the next decade.

In secondary market trading, an odd lot is $25,000 or less in par value for retail investors. For institutions, anything less than $250,000 is an odd lot. Dealer spreads vary depending on factors such as liquidity, volatility, and market conditions. The retail spreads range from a quarter of a point for large blocks to several points for odd-lot sales of an inactive issue. For institutional investors, the spreads are no more than half of a point.

Information Sources

In the past, obtaining ongoing information about municipal issuers could be difficult, but the SEC's disclosure requirements have helped to alleviate this problem. As described earlier, Rule 15c2-12 requires municipal issuers to provide a continuous flow of information to bondholders and the securities markets. Several other sources of information are also available.

One good source of pricing information is the Standard & Poor's Blue List (**http://www.bluelist.com**). Other information sources include J. J. Kenny (**http://www.jjkenny.com**), Bonds Online (**http://www.bondsonline.com**), Electronic Municipal Statistics (E-Muni, **http://www.emuni.com**), and Thomson Municipal Market Monitor (**http://www.tm3.com**).

The Bond Market Association has also taken steps to improve the transparency of the municipal bond market. The association publishes daily trading volume on its Web site (**http://www.bondmarkets.com**). The association also cooperates with Bloomberg L.P. to publish municipal bond yields (**http://www.bloomberg.com/markets/psamuni.html**). They publish a benchmark for particular categories of municipal bonds. The yields are a composite of round-lot prices based on bonds that have coupons that reflect current market conditions.

TAX ADVANTAGES

Under federal income tax law, interest income from municipal securities is free from federal income taxes.[9] Therefore, municipal securities often trade at yields lower than those for comparable Treasury securities.[10] Table 9.4 (see p. 216) lists a sample of municipal yields. Note that the yield of an AAA municipal bond

---

[9] Any profit realized from the purchase or sale (or capital gain) is not exempt from tax. Only the accrued interest is tax-exempt.

[10] Interest income from Treasury securities is exempt from state and local taxation.

| TABLE 9.4 | *Municipal Yields (February 2001)* |

(1) Maturity	(2) AAA Municipal Yield (%)	(3) BBB Municipal Yield (%)	(4) Quality Spreads (3) − (2)
5 year	3.86	4.50	0.64
10 year	4.34	5.07	0.73
15 year	4.84	5.59	0.75
20 year	5.08	5.89	0.81
25 year	5.14	5.97	0.83
30 year	5.15	6.00	0.85

Source: Data are from J. J. Kenny Drake (http://www.kennydrake.com).

increases with maturity, as does the yield of a BBB bond. Note also that the yield differential between an AAA municipal and a BBB municipal widens as the maturity extends. The yield differential, also called the **quality spread**, is the result of differences in quality of these securities. In the table, the quality spread is 0.64 percent in the 5-year maturity segment, and widens to 0.85 percent in the 30-year segment. The reason is that investors have more concern about the credit risk in the long term. Thus, municipal securities of a lower quality have to offer a higher yield spread to compensate for such risk.

Equivalent Taxable Yield

As previously discussed, interest income from municipal securities is exempt from federal taxation.[11] One of the best ways to appreciate the tax-favored advantage of a municipal security is to compare it to a comparable taxable investment by converting the tax-exempt yield into an equivalent taxable yield. The equivalent taxable yield is calculated as follows:

$$9.1 \quad \text{Equivalent taxable yield} = \frac{tax\ exempt\ yield}{1 - marginal\ tax\ rate}.$$

For example, assume an investor is in the 35-percent federal tax bracket.[12] The investor has \$60,000 to invest and considers two investment alternatives: a tax-exempt municipal bond yielding 5.00 percent and a taxable corporate bond yielding 7.50 percent. Which investment is more advantageous? The investor can compare these two alternatives in several ways. One way is to use Equation 9.1 to obtain the equivalent taxable yield for the municipal bond:

$$9.2 \quad \text{Equivalent taxable yield} = \frac{5.00\%}{(1 - 0.35)} = 7.69\%.$$

[11]The following discussion deals with interest income only. Capital gains do not enjoy the tax-favored advantage.

[12]There are additional benefits if the municipal security is also state/local tax-free.

Obviously, the municipal bond provides an equivalent taxable yield of 7.69%, which is higher than the 7.50% a corporate bond provides.

A second approach is to convert the yield on the taxable corporate bond into an after-tax yield and then compare that yield with the municipal bond yield. The formula is

9.3   After-tax yield = (taxable yield) × (1 − marginal tax rate).

A 7.50 percent taxable yield can be converted to an after tax yield:

9.4   After tax yield = 7.50% × (1 − 0.35) = 4.88%.

Hence, the municipal bond provides a higher after tax return to investors.

Alternatively, a $60,000 investment in the municipal bond will earn the investor $3,000 a year with no federal income tax. The taxable bond invest-ment will produce $4,500 in interest income, but the investor would have to pay a 35 percent federal tax. Therefore the after-tax income is only $2,925. The investment in the municipal bond returns the investor $75 more.

The benefits from investing in tax-favored municipal securities are quite significant for investors who have high taxable income and are subject to a high marginal tax rate. Table 9.5 lists tax–exempt/taxable yield equivalents. As the table shows, a 5 percent tax-exempt yield is equivalent to a taxable yield of 5.88 percent for an investor in the 15 percent tax bracket. The equivalent

TABLE 9.5	*Tax-Exempt/Taxable Yield Equivalents*				
Tax Bracket	**15%**	**27%**	**30%**	**35%**	**38.6%**
Tax-Exempt Yield (%)	Equivalent Taxable Yield (%)				
3.0	3.53	4.11	4.29	4.62	4.89
3.5	4.12	4.79	5.00	5.38	5.70
4.0	4.71	5.48	5.71	6.15	6.51
4.5	5.29	6.16	6.43	6.92	7.33
5.0	5.88	6.85	7.14	7.69	8.14
5.5	6.47	7.53	7.86	8.46	8.96
6.0	7.06	8.22	8.57	9.23	9.77
6.5	7.65	8.90	9.29	10.00	10.59
7.0	8.24	9.59	10.00	10.77	11.40
7.5	8.82	10.27	10.71	11.54	12.21
8.0	9.41	10.96	11.43	12.31	13.03
8.5	10.00	11.64	12.14	13.08	13.84
9.0	10.5	12.33	12.86	13.85	14.66
9.5	11.18	13.01	13.57	14.62	15.47
10.0	11.76	13.70	14.29	15.38	16.29

taxable yield is 8.14 percent if the investor is subject to a marginal tax rate of 38.6 percent.

Residents of some states can obtain an additional benefit from investing in municipal securities. In addition to being free from federal tax, the interest income on municipal bonds is also free from state and local taxes if the bonds are issued in the state of residence. In other words, the investor can obtain a double exemption. For example, a resident of New York who buys a municipal bond issued by the state of New York will not pay New York State or local taxes on the investment. However, the same resident of New York who buys a municipal bond issued by a city in Connecticut will have to pay state and local tax on the interest income.[13] The tax rate varies from state to state, so the additional benefit investors receive from tax-favored municipal bond investments depends on the state of residence. For people living in a high-tax-rate state like New York, the additional tax benefits are significant. For those living in states that do not impose a state income tax, such as Alaska, Nevada, and Florida, the federal tax exemption is the only benefit available.

Other Aspects of the Taxation of Municipal Bonds

Even though the interest earned on a municipal bond is exempt from taxation, a holder can recognize a capital gain that is subject to federal income tax on the sale of such a bond. The amount of capital gain or loss is equal to the difference between the sale price of the bond and the purchase price (or tax basis).[14] As with stocks, there are two types of capital gains: long term (held for more than twelve months) and short term (held for twelve months or less).

In contrast, an investor may recognize a capital loss if the sale price is less than the tax basis (costs). In such a case, capital losses are first applied against capital gains of the same type to reduce the gains. Thus a long-term capital loss will first reduce other long-term capital gains, and a short-term capital loss will first reduce other short-term capital gains. Under the current tax law, any capital losses remaining after offsetting all available capital gains can then be used to reduce ordinary income by up to $3,000 per year. Any losses exceeding that amount may be carried forward to reduce capital gains or ordinary income in future years.

In the case where a tax-exempt bond is originally issued at a discount, the difference between the issue price and the par amount is an **original issue discount (OID)**. For example, if a 10-year bond with a $1,000 face amount and a stated coupon rate of 5 percent payable semiannually is issued for $925.61, the bond, for federal tax purposes, has $74.39 of OID. Because this is a tax-exempt bond, the OID is tax-free. However, the OID may increase the investor's tax basis in the bond for the purpose of calculating gain or loss if the investor trades the bond before maturity. The tax law provides that the

---

[13]State taxation of municipal bonds held by corporations is more complex and is beyond the scope of this text.

[14]The tax basis includes the purchase price, commissions, and fees.

investor's basis will increase over time based on a constant yield to maturity (CYM). The CYM on the bond is the yield to maturity that equates the price at issue to the present value of all future cash flows from the bond. For the bond described previously, the CYM is 6 percent, which can be calculated using the following equation:

9.5
$$\$925.61 = \sum_{t=1}^{20} \frac{\$25}{\left(1 + \dfrac{y}{2}\right)^t} + \frac{\$1,000}{\left(1 + \dfrac{y}{2}\right)^{20}}.$$

Solving for y gives a value of 6 percent. In Equation 9.5, a semiannual coupon (\$25) and semiannual yield ($y/2$) are used because the bond pays its coupon every six months. This 6 percent yield will enter into the accretion of the investor's basis. A sale price higher than the accreted basis will produce a capital gain, which is taxable. If a tax-exempt bond is purchased at a premium, whether at original issue or in the secondary market, the bond premium is amortized over the remaining term until maturity using the same CYM method.

When the municipal issuer redeems the bond prior to its maturity date at a fixed price, the bondholder should treat the transaction as a sale of the bond. Thus, the bondholder may recognize a capital gain or loss on such a sale. In some instances, if the purchase of a bond is financed by borrowed money, the interest expense is tax deductible. A taxpayer who borrows to purchase municipal bonds, however, may not deduct the interest expense incurred from federal income tax.

Taxable Municipal Securities

Some municipal bonds are subject to federal income tax because the federal government does not subsidize the financing of certain activities that do not provide a significant benefit to the general public. Bonds issued to finance investor-led housing, local sport facilities, and borrowing to replenish a municipality's underfunded pension plan are just a few examples of bond issues that are federally taxable. Taxable municipal securities offer yields comparable to those of other taxable securities.

RISKS

Investors in municipal securities face certain risks. The three main risks are default risk, market risk, and call risk.

Default Risk

A primary risk in the municipal bond market, as in other fixed-income markets, is **default risk** or credit risk, which is the possibility that the issuer will be unable to meet its financial obligations. Many consider municipal debt as having low default risk. According to a study by FitchRatings, general obligations,

TABLE 9.6	*Municipal Bond Ratings*		
Credit Risk	Standard and Poor's	Moody's	FitchRatings
Prime	AAA	Aaa	AAA
Excellent	AA	Aa	AA
Upper medium	A	A	A
Lower medium	BBB	Baa	BBB
Speculative	BB	Ba	BB
Very speculative	B, CCC, CC	B, Caa	B, CCC, CC, C
Default	D	Ca, C	DDD, DD, D

tax–backed, water/sewer, transportation, and public higher education bonds are among the least risky. The cumulative default rates (percentages of bonds that eventually defaulted) for these bonds range from 0.01 percent to 0.40 percent. The cumulative default rates in the health care, electric utilities, and multifamily sectors are in the range of 1 percent to 4 percent. The riskiest municipal sector is industrial development bonds, which have cumulative default rates close to 15 percent.[15]

Credit ratings can be used as an indicator of default probability. Rating agencies, such as Standard and Poor's, Moody's, and FitchRatings, grade municipal bonds. Municipal bonds that are rated at BBB or higher (by Standard and Poor's and FitchRatings) or at BAA (by Moody's) are investment grade. Bonds below these ratings are noninvestment grade or junk bonds. Table 9.6 shows the ratings by these agencies. FitchRatings estimates that 80 to 85 percent of the municipal market is rated investment grade or insured. FitchRatings also estimates that default rates for investment-grade bonds average from 0.31 to 0.33 percent. In contrast, municipal bonds rated below investment grade have substantially higher default rates, estimated at 3.05 to 4.06 percent.

Not all municipal bonds receive ratings. A Bond Market Association study that examined defaults from 1986 to 1991 found that nonrated municipal securities represented 23.5 percent of the total number of issues and 8 percent of the dollar volume during that time period. The default rate for the nonrated bonds averaged 1.1 percent from 1986 to 1991, and the default rate by dollar volume of issuance was 2.0 percent for the period.

Market Risk

The coupon rate for a fixed-rate municipal security does not change during the life of the bond. The market price, however, changes as market conditions change, giving rise to market risk, which is the risk that the market price will be more or less than the original purchase price. Prices of bonds increase when interest rates decline, and prices decline when interest rates rise. When interest rates fall, new issues come to market with lower yields than older securities,

---

[15]See Litvack and Rizzo (1999).

making the older securities worth more. When interest rates rise, new issues provide investors with higher yields than older securities, making the older ones worth less.

Market risk can be illustrated by a numerical example. Assume that one purchases a 10-year bond with a $1,000 face value and a stated coupon rate of 5 percent payable semiannually on the issue date of March 6, 2001, for $925.61. The yield of this bond is 6 percent, as shown in a previous section. Suppose that two months later the yield on the bond rises to 6.15 percent. The price of the security will decline to $915.97.[16]

Call Risk

Finally, investors in municipal securities face **call risk**, which is the possibility that the issuer will retire (call) all or a portion of the bond before maturity. Some municipal bonds allow the issuers to call all or a portion of the bonds at par or at a premium before the scheduled maturity date. Callable municipal bonds are likely to be called when they trade at a price above the initial price that occurs because of interest rate decline. By calling the bond and floating another issue, the municipality can save interest costs because the new issue will carry a lower coupon rate in the lower interest rate environment. Dealers often quote yield to call as well as yield to maturity on bonds that are likely to be called.

RECENT DEVELOPMENTS

Although the municipal securities markets have not been troubled by the default or bankruptcy of a major issuer in recent years, several other problems have surfaced. In particular, the abuses of yield burning and pay-to-play have received intense government scrutiny. The Municipal Securities Rulemaking Board has adopted new rules to prevent them from happening in the future.

Yield Burning

When a municipality issues a new municipal security to pay off an outstanding bond prior to its call date or maturity date, a financing structure called **advance refunding** is used. The sale of new bonds in advance of maturity or call of an old issue is to assure continuous funding. The municipality generally invests proceeds of the new issue in special government securities on a temporary basis. The interest income, together with the principal repayment on those invested securities, is then used to repay the old municipal issue. During this waiting period, federal law restricts the interest that can be earned on the escrow account to no more than the interest paid on the new issue. This is to prevent the municipality from engaging in tax arbitrage.

---

[16]This can be obtained from MS Excel function: PRICE("03/08/2001","01/08/2011",0.05,0.0615, 100,2,1). A detailed discussion of the price calculation appears in Chapter 10.

Since tax-exempt municipal rates are lower than most other yields, financial institutions managing the escrow account must make sure that the escrow account earns a below-market rate. To keep the earnings low, the Treasury Department issues a special low-interest security called State and Local Government Series (SLGS).[17] The Treasury offers SLGS securities for sale in book-entry form; these are nonmarketable. The interest rate earned on time deposit SLGS is 5 basis points below the estimated Treasury borrowing rate of comparable maturity. The SLGS demand deposit security is a one-day certificate of indebtedness. The principal and accrued interest are automatically rolled over each day until the municipality requests redemption. The average yield in the most recent auction of the 13-week Treasury bills, with certain adjustment, determines the interest rate on SLGS demand deposit securities.

In some cases, broker-dealers use this as an opportunity to overcharge the municipalities for open market Treasuries used in the escrow account. Since bond prices and yields move in opposite directions, when underwriters mark up the bonds, they "burn down" the yield. This is **yield burning**. The Internal Revenue Service has informed local governments across the country that their tax-exempt municipal bonds may be declared taxable if yield burning occurred on their watch.

Pay-to-Play

The practice of cozying up to government officials to win bond contracts is **pay-to-play**. In 1994, the MSRB passed a rule that barred securities firms and restricted many of their employees from making campaign contributions to public officials who select underwriters to sell municipal securities. In response, many Wall Street firms simply hired consultants and used their contacts and knowledge of state and local politics to help them win municipal bond deals.

The MSRB has adopted Rule G-37 and Rule G-38 to address these problems. Rule G-37 does not allow any broker-dealer to engage in municipal securities business with an issuer within two years after any contribution to an official of the issuer. In addition, Rule G-38 requires disclosure of all consultants hired by the broker-dealer during each calendar quarter.

CONCLUDING SUMMARY

The market for municipal securities consists of short-term notes and long-term bonds. More than four-fifths of the annual municipal issuance is long-term financing. This $1.5 trillion market has a high degree of fragmentation because there are more than 1.5 million different issues outstanding. Unlike the $3 trillion Treasury market, where there are about 200 or so issues outstanding

---

[17]The SLGS securities program was established in 1972 to prevent state and local governments from earning arbitrage profits in advance refunding by investing bond proceeds in higher yielding investments. The Treasury suspended the SLGS securities program on February 19, 2003.

and daily trading volume averages more than $360 billion, most municipal bonds are purchased and held until maturity.

One important characteristic of municipal securities is the tax-favored treatment of interest income. This tax-free status of interest income lowers the interest rate a municipality has to pay to raise capital to fund projects for the public good. Frequently, a municipality needs to float a new issue to pay off the maturing debt. But because of the subsidy on tax-free interest income, federal law restricts the interest that can be earned on the escrow account to no more than the interest paid on the new issue. However, some financial institutions managing the escrow account illegally "burn down" the yield in the account. This problem has received a great deal of media attention in recent years and has led to government investigations.

Another unique feature of the municipal market is that more than half of the newly issued municipal bonds have insurance, which offers benefits to both investors and issuers by reducing default risk. Regardless of credit rating, however, municipal securities are subject to market risk, meaning that their prices fluctuate as market conditions change. Additionally, investors also face call risk if there are provisions that allow the issuer to pay off a portion or all of the outstanding debt before its final maturity date.

Key Terms

advance refunding 221
call risk 221
competitive bidding 206
default risk 219
general obligation bonds (GOs) 204
municipal notes 205
municipal securities 204

negotiated deal 207
official statement 206
original issue discount (OID) 218
pay-to-play 222
quality spread 216
revenue bonds 205
yield burning 222

Review Questions

1. Briefly describe several important characteristics of the municipal market.
2. If you were the treasurer of a small county that planned to issue $10 million of municipal bonds, which method (competitive or negotiated sale) would you use to sell the new security? Why?
3. Under Rule 15c2-12, what are the requirements for a new issue? Are municipal issuers required to disclose material events? What is the rationale for such requirements?
4. Is the new Internet type of online auction or the traditional competitive sale method better for an issuer?
5. Why does financial insurance make municipal bonds more attractive as an investment?
6. Use any information source cited in the chapter to obtain price information on several municipal bonds issued by New York City.

7. Who is most likely to invest in municipal bonds? Is it a good investment policy for a university to invest in municipal securities?

8. Suppose you purchased $5,000 of a 10-year municipal zero-coupon bond when issued at 60 percent of the face value. You sold the bond after three years for a price of $4,000. Is the sale taxable? How much is taxable?

9. If the market anticipates that Congress will lower the marginal tax rates, what will happen to the price of municipal bonds?

10. Obtain the yields of triple-A rated 2-year, 5-year, 10-year, and 20-year municipal bonds and compare them with the yields of comparable Treasury securities. What are the yield spreads? What is the relationship between the spread and maturity?

Select Bibliography

Bond Market Association. *An Examination of Non-Rated Municipal Defaults: 1986–1991.* New York: Bond Market Association (previously known as the Public Securities Association), 1993.

Bond Market Association. *An Investors' Guide to Municipal bonds.* New York: Bond Market Association, 1999.

Bond Market Association. *eCommerce in the Fixed-Income Markets: The 2001 Review of Electronic Transaction Systems.* New York: Bond Market Association, 2001.

Crowder, W. J., and M. Wohar. "Are tax effects important in the long-run Fisher relationship? Evidence from the municipal bond market." *Journal of Finance* 54, No. 1, February 1999, pp. 307–317.

Latvack, D., and F. Rizzo. "Municipal default risk." New York: FitchRatings, 1999.

Leonard, P. A. "An empirical analysis of competitive and negotiated offerings of municipal bonds." *Municipal Finance Journal,* Spring 1996, pp. 37–67.

Moody's Investors Research. *Financial Guaranty: Industry Outlook.* January 2002.

Mysak, J., and M. R. Bloomberg. *Handbook for Muni Bond Issuers.* New York: Bloomberg Press, 1998.

Pauelz, A. V. Municipal bond issue structuring, in G. J. Miller (ed.), *Handbook of Debt Management,* New York: Marcel Dekker, 1996, pp. 401–431.

Stevens, L., and R. P. Wood. "Comparative financing costs for competitive and negotiated Pennsylvania school district bonds," *Journal of Public Budgeting, Accounting & Financial Management,* Winter 1998, pp. 529–551.

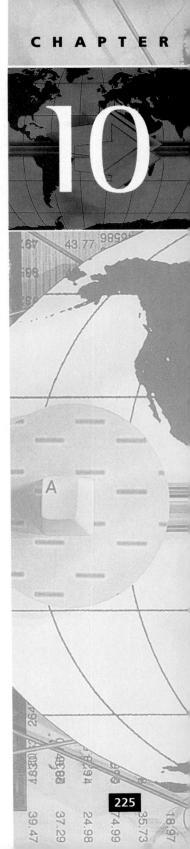

CHAPTER

10

Corporate Debt Markets

Corporations must raise capital to finance investments in facilities, equipment, research and development, and new technology. They do so through a variety of instruments, including commercial paper, time deposits, bankers' acceptances, medium-term notes, and various types of bonds. Of the $20 trillion outstanding in public and private debt in 2002, corporate debt securities accounted for more than $6.6 trillion—twice as much as U.S. government securities.

Fixed-income securities, whether Treasury, municipal, or corporate, play an important role in asset allocation. A portfolio that includes both fixed-income and stocks will generally provide a more stable performance over time than a portfolio limited to just one or the other. Like Treasury and municipal securities, corporate fixed-income securities or bonds offer current income and relative safety compared to stocks. Corporate bonds carry more risk than Treasury bonds, however, and they lack the tax-favored status of municipal bonds.

The objectives of this chapter are to provide an understanding of:
- The types of corporate debt securities.
- Bond market conventions and terminology.
- Regulatory issues when corporations sell debt securities in the private market.
- The importance of credit ratings in the bond market.
- The benefits of bond insurance.
- The valuation of various types of corporate debt securities.
- The risks facing bond investors.

MARKET OVERVIEW

Investors interested in corporate debt offerings can choose from a wide variety of instruments. These instruments, often called corporate **fixed-income securities**, pay investors fixed interest income at regular intervals and repay the principal at maturity (although some bonds do have a floating interest rate).[1] These debt instruments differ in terms of maturity, ranging from very short term, as short as a few days, to very long term, as long as a hundred years. Short-term (less than one year) instruments include commercial paper, most large time deposits, bankers' acceptances, and some medium-term notes. Some large time deposits and medium-term notes are long-term instruments, as are all bonds. Corporate debt instruments also differ in the returns they provide. Bonds pay investors fixed interest income at regular intervals and repay the principal at maturity. In contrast, the short-term instruments such as commercial paper and bankers' acceptances do not pay interest. The investor's return comes from the difference between the discount price and the face amount paid at maturity.

As noted earlier, the total amount of corporate debt securities outstanding was more than $6.6 trillion in 2002. The short-term instruments such as commercial paper, bankers' acceptances, and large time deposits, accounted for $2.6 trillion. The amount of long-term corporate debt securities was $4.0 trillion. The size of the corporate debt market is larger than the Treasury market, but the trading volume is much smaller. The average daily trading volume by primary dealers for corporate debt with maturities of more than one year was less than $20 billion in 2002.

TYPES OF CORPORATE DEBT INSTRUMENTS

Various types of corporate debt securities are available to allow corporations to match their financing requirements with investor needs. This section reviews the major types of corporate debt instruments: commercial paper, time deposits, bankers' acceptances, medium-term notes, and various types of bonds.

Commercial Paper

Commercial paper is a money market product and is a short-term unsecured promissory note. Corporations use it as an alternative to borrowing from banks. Interest rates on commercial paper are often lower than bank lending rates; and the savings, when large enough, provide an advantage over bank credit. Although both financial and nonfinancial firms issue commercial paper, financial companies account for most of the outstanding volume—80 percent at year-end 1999, for example, and 74 percent at year-end 2000.

Commercial paper is a cost-effective form of short-term funding, giving borrowers visibility in the institutional investor market and thereby facilitating

---

[1]Many people use the term *bonds* to include most fixed-income securities.

future capital market activities. Commercial paper programs raise floating-rate funds, although derivatives may be used to fix rates for a fixed term. The minimum borrowing amount is typically $50 million, and program sizes can range into the billions.

Commercial paper is usually issued in denominations of $100,000 or more. There are two methods of floating commercial paper. The issuer can either sell the paper directly to the buyer or sell the paper to a dealer firm, which in turn distributes it to investors. Most of the dealers are large securities firms or subsidiaries of commercial banks. Financial companies that have frequent and sizable borrowing needs often issue their commercial paper directly. By some estimates, direct issuers save a dealer fee of one-eighth of a percentage point, or $125,000 for every $100 million issued. Nonfinancial companies and smaller financial companies usually issue dealer-placed commercial paper. For these firms, the size and the frequency of their borrowings do not warrant maintaining a regular sales staff to issue the paper.

The maturity of commercial paper ranges from 1 day to 270 days, but most commonly it is 30 days or less. Because the maturity does not exceed 270 days, commercial paper is exempt from registration with the Securities and Exchange Commission (SEC). Commercial paper rates are quoted on a discount basis. The purchaser pays a discount price and receives the face amount when the paper matures. The return to the investor is the difference between the purchase price and the face amount. Table 10.1 lists sample commercial paper rates. The rates vary depending on the maturity, the credit quality of the issuer, market conditions, and investor demand.

For commercial paper, the convention is to assume a 360-day year. For example, the amount of discount for 7-day paper with $100,000 face value can be calculated as follows (from Table 10.1, the discount rate is 1.27 percent):

$$\boxed{10.1} \quad d = F \times r \times \frac{M}{360} = \$100,000 \times 0.0127 \times \frac{7}{360} = \$24.69,$$

TABLE 10.1 | *Commercial Paper Discount Rates*

Term	Financial Firms (%)	Nonfinancial Firms (%)
1-day	1.31	1.29
7-day	1.27	1.26
15-day	1.26	1.26
30-day	1.25	1.25
60-day	1.26	1.23
90-day	1.26	N/A

Note: The quotes are for AA-rated issuers. Data are as of February 27, 2003.

Source: Federal Reserve Release (http://www.federalreserve.gov/releases/CP).

where *d* denotes the dollar amount of discount, *F* the face value, *r* the discount rate, and *M* the number of days until maturity. As shown, the paper can be purchased at a discount of $24.69. That is, the purchaser pays $99,975.31 and receives $100,000 from the issuer after seven days.

Large Time Deposits

Large time deposits are certificates of deposits issued by commercial banks in denominations of $100,000 and up. Most are short term, although some have maturities of several years. Large commercial banks frequently rely on large time deposits for liquidity management. This market is very large, as Table 10.2 shows, the outstanding volume was more than $1.2 trillion in 2002. Table 10.2 also shows the outstanding commercial paper.

Bankers' Acceptances

A **bankers' acceptance (BA)** is a draft guaranteed by a bank for future payment, and is most commonly used in international trade where the parties desire a means of guaranteeing payments. For example, suppose that a U.S. importer wants to buy silk from China and pay for it sixty days later. One approach would be for the importer to borrow from its bank. However, short-term rates may be lower in the money markets. If so, and if the importer is not large enough to go into the open market on its own, it can choose the BA route. The importer will request its bank to issue a letter of credit for the amount of the purchase and send this letter of credit to the Chinese exporter. Upon export of the Chinese silk, the Chinese exporter draws a time draft (for payment at a stated future date) on the importer's U.S. bank and discounts this

TABLE 10.2 | *Outstanding Commercial Paper and Large Time Deposits 1990–2002 ($ billions)*

Year	Commercial Paper	Large Time Deposits
1990	558	547
1991	528	488
1992	545	415
1993	554	392
1994	600	411
1995	678	477
1996	779	591
1997	959	713
1998	1,161	806
1999	1,394	936
2000	1,602	1,052
2001	1,441	1,121
2002	1,369	1,203

Source: The Bond Market Association (http://www.bondmarkets.com).

draft at its local bank. This allows the Chinese merchant to obtain immediate payment for its silk. The Chinese bank, in turn, sends the time draft to the importer's U.S. bank, which then stamps "accepted" on the draft. The U.S. bank now guarantees payment on the draft, thereby creating an acceptance, and thus the BA.

If the Chinese bank does not want cash immediately, the U.S. bank will return the draft to that bank. The Chinese bank can hold the draft as an investment and present it to the U.S. bank for payment at maturity. If the Chinese bank wants cash immediately, the U.S. bank will pay it the discounted value and either hold the BA itself or sell it in the open market. Ultimately, the U.S. importer has to provide its bank with sufficient funds to pay off the acceptance at maturity. If the importer fails to do so, however, the U.S. bank still must honor the payment at maturity.

BAs resemble commercial paper in form. Both are short-term securities that trade at a discount and redeemed by the accepting bank at maturity for their full face value. There is one major difference, though. Commercial paper is backed by its issuers, while BAs carry the issuer's pledge to pay and are backed by the accepting bank. Therefore, BAs are less risky and thus generally sell at lower yields.

Medium-Term Notes

A **medium-term note (MTN)** is a corporate debt instrument with a maturity ranging from nine months to thirty years. Securities firms distribute MTNs for the issuers on a best efforts basis. In this case, the securities firms act as brokers helping to place the notes through their vast network of clients. The securities firms do not guarantee a price to the issuer. Unlike a typical bond issue where bonds are sold in large, discrete offerings, MTNs are sold in relatively smaller amounts on a continuous basis. Because the note offerings are ongoing, they are typically registered with the SEC under Rule 415 (shelf registration), which allows a corporation to issue securities up to an approved amount over a period of two years.[2] As Table 10.3 (see p. 230) shows, U.S. corporations issued $210 billion in MTNs in 2000, of which financial firms accounted for $190 billion.

General Motors Acceptance Corporation (GMAC) was one of the very first to issue medium-term notes and continues to be a major supplier in this market. Its SmartNotes program is a good example of MTNs. As shown in the prospectus summary (Table 10.4, see p. 231), GMAC offers the SmartNotes on an ongoing basis; they will mature on any day nine months to thirty years from the issue date, as selected by the purchaser and agreed to by GMAC. Smart-Notes are available on a weekly ongoing basis; every week there is a selection of rates and maturities. Table 10.5 (see p. 232) shows an example for the February 8–14, 2002 period. The program provides investors the opportunity to purchase an MTN directly from GMAC for a stated coupon and price. A

---

[2]This chapter later discusses shelf registration.

TABLE 10.3	Annual Issuance of Medium-Term Notes 1991–2001 ($ billions)

Year	Total Issuance	Issuance by Financial Corporations
1991	72	45
1992	74	50
1993	86	57
1994	88	70
1995	98	79
1996	93	81
1997	114	98
1998	149	128
1999	170	149
2000	210	190
2001	222	205

Source: Federal Reserve Statistical Release (http://www.federalreserve.gov/releases/medterm).

unique feature of this program is its survivor's option; the note holder has the option to elect to have GMAC purchase the notes from the holder's estate upon his or her death.

Bonds

A corporate **bond** is a loan; it reflects a promise by the company to pay the bondholder a fixed amount of interest (the coupon payment) periodically and to repay the money borrowed—the principal or redemption value—at a specific date in the future, the maturity date. Securities firms handle the underwriting, or distribution of bonds in the primary markets, for the issuer. Once the bonds are issued, dealers bid for bonds that investors wish to sell and offer bonds from their inventory to investors wanting to buy.

Bonds are long-term debt instruments; that is, they have maturities of longer than one year. Some bonds have very long-term maturities. During the low interest rate environment of the mid-1990s, various institutions including Coca-Cola, Walt Disney, IBM, and Yale University issued bonds with maturities as long as a hundred years. Chile's Empresa National Electricidad SA was the first Latin American company to sell bonds that mature in a hundred years.

Corporations issue a number of different types of bonds. The following discussion provides a brief review of each.

Convertible bonds have a feature that gives the bondholder the right to convert the par amount of the bond into a certain number of shares of the issuer's common stock. The ratio at which the par value is converted to shares of common stock is the conversion ratio. Suppose that a conversion provision gives the holder the right to convert $1,000 par amount into the issuer's common stock at $50 per share, the conversion price. The conversion ratio is hence 20 to 1. The share price substantially affects the value of a convertible. For example, if the shares of the issuer trade at $35 and the market price of the bond is $1,000, there would be no reason for an investor to convert. A

TABLE 10.4	*GMAC SmartNotes Prospectus Summary*
Issuer	**General Motors Acceptance Corporation (GMAC)**
Purchasing Agent	ABN AMRO Inc.
Title	SmartNotes.^{SM}
Amount	Up to $10,000,000,000 aggregate initial offering price.
Denomination	Unless otherwise specified in the applicable pricing supplement, the authorized denominations of the Notes will be $1,000 and any amount in excess thereof that is an integral multiple of $1,000.
Status	The Notes are unsecured and unsubordinated obligations of GMAC and will rate equally and ratably with all other unsecured and unsubordinated indebtedness of GMAC (other than obligations preferred by mandatory provisions of law).
Maturities	Due from nine months to thirty years from the date of issue, as specified in the applicable pricing supplement.
Interest	Each Note will bear interest from the Issue Date at a fixed rate, which may be zero in the case of a Note issued at an Issue Price representing a substantial discount from the principal amount payable upon the maturity date (a "Zero-Coupon Note"). Unless otherwise specified in the applicable pricing supplement: ° Interest on each Note (other than a Zero-Coupon Note) will be payable either monthly, quarterly, semi-annually, or annually on each Interest Payment Date and on the maturity date; and ° Interest on the Notes will be computed on the basis of a 360-day year of twelve 30-day months.
Principal	Unless otherwise provided in the applicable pricing supplement, the principal amount of the Notes will be payable on the maturity date of such Notes at the Corporate Trust Office of the Trustee or at such other place as GMAC may designate.
Redemption and Repayment	Unless otherwise provided in the applicable pricing supplement: ° the Notes will not be redeemable prior to the maturity date at the option of GMAC or repayable prior to the maturity date at the option of the holder; and ° the Notes will not be subject to any sinking fund. The pricing supplement relating to any Note will indicate whether the holder of such Note will have the right to require GMAC to repay a Note prior to its maturity date upon the death of the owner of such Note.
Form of Notes and Clearance	The Notes may be offered: ° in the United States only; ° outside the United States only; or ° in and outside the United States simultaneously as part of a global offering. Depending on where the relevant Notes are offered, the Notes will clear through one or more of The Depository Trust Company, Morgan Guaranty Trust Company of New York, Brussels office, as operator of the Euroclear System and Cedelbank, société anonyme or any successors thereto. Global Notes will be exchangeable for definitive Notes only in limited circumstances.
Tax Status	The Notes and payments thereon generally are subject to taxation by the United States and generally are not exempt from taxation by other U.S. or non–U.S. taxing jurisdictions. Non–U.S. Persons will be subject to U.S. Federal income tax and withholding tax unless they provide certain certifications or statements.
Trustee	J. P. Morgan Chase Bank, Institutional Trust Services, 450 West 33rd Street, 15th Floor, New York, New York 10001, under an Indenture dated as of September 24, 1996.
Selling Group Members	Broker-dealers and/or securities firms that have executed dealer agreements with the Purchasing Agent and have agreed to market and sell SmartNotes in accordance with the terms of these agreements along with all other applicable laws and regulations. You may call 1-800-501-2958 for a list of Selling Group Members or via the Internet access at http://www.smartnotes.com.

Source: GMAC SmartNotes (http://www.gmacfs.com/notes/smart/prospectus.htm).

| TABLE 10.5 | GMAC SmartNotes Program for the Period February 8–14, 2002 |

Coupon (%)	Payment	Maturity	Survivor's Option	Price
4.50	Monthly	2/15/04	Yes	100
5.10	Semiannual	2/15/05	Yes	100
5.75	Monthly	2/15/07	Yes	100

Note: Prices are quoted as a percentage of par. The medium-term notes are issued in $1,000 denominations. All interest and principal payments are made on the 15th of the month.

Source: GMAC SmartNotes (http://www.gmacfs.com/notes/smart/prospectus.htm).

convertible bond with a conversion price far higher than the market price of the stock generally trades at or close to its bond value, because the bond is not likely to be converted. On the other hand, when the share price is sufficiently higher than the conversion price, the convertible begins to trade more like equity, because the bondholder will convert it into shares of common stock.

With **exchangeable bonds**, the bondholders have the option of exchanging the debt for stocks of a second company or several companies, called the convert firm. A company might issue exchangeable bonds for several reasons. First, the issuing firm can capitalize on a security holding while delaying the recognition of capital gains. Another advantage is that the issuing firm collects the dividend income until the conversion option is exercised. Third, this can be a more efficient way of divesting a security holding, since a block sale tends to result in substantial negative market impact.

Callable bonds grant the issuer the right to pay off the debt before maturity. Exercising the call provision becomes attractive to the issuer when the yield drops sufficiently to make up for the cost of calling the bonds. The cost to call includes a call premium, administrative expenses, and the expenditures arising from floating a new issue to refund the retired debt. Most call provisions provide for a call premium of one-half of the coupon rate. That means the issuer has the right to pay the bondholders the par amount plus one-half of the annual coupon payment to retire the bond. For example, the issuer has to pay $1,030 per bond if it calls the bond with a 6% coupon. The call feature is a disadvantage to investors who must give up the higher-yielding bonds. Therefore, investors generally demand a higher yield from callable bonds.

Puttable bonds contain a put provision, granting investors the right to put the bonds back to the issuer at par. Investors will choose to exercise the right to put back the bond when the yield rises (and the price falls). Clearly, a puttable bond protects investors from downside risk. Therefore, investors will accept a lower yield when purchasing a puttable bond.

Junk bonds, also called high-yield bonds, have credit ratings of BB (by Standard and Poor's) or lower. Most regard these bonds as non-investment grade or speculative grade.[3] Before the 1980s, most junk bonds resulted from

---

[3]A later section covers credit ratings.

a decline in the credit quality of former investment-grade issues (known as **fallen angels**). Then Michael Milken of the securities firm Drexel Burnham Lambert convinced many investors that the risk-adjusted returns for portfolios of junk bonds were quite high. Milken argued that the credit risk of these bonds was more than compensated for by their high yields. Underwriters, notably Drexel Burnham, soon began to issue new bonds for issuers that were less than investment grade. The new-issue junk bond market took off.

A **foreign currency bond** is a debt security issued in a currency other than the issuer's national currency. By issuing foreign currency bonds, issuers can take advantage of international interest rate differentials. Issuers often convert the foreign currency into their home currency by way of a currency swap. A currency swap is a financial contract in which counterparties exchange initial principal amounts of two currencies at the spot exchange rate and swap fixed or floating rate interest in these currencies. Bonds issued by foreign issuers in the United States in U.S. dollars are Yankee bonds. Those issued in British pounds in England are Bulldogs. Yen-denominated bonds issued by non-Japanese issuers are Samurai bonds. Foreign currency bonds have a much different risk and return profile than domestic bonds. Not only is their price affected by movements in a foreign country's interest rate, but they also change in value depending on the foreign exchange rate.

Global bonds are tailor-made to appeal to investors internationally. The first global bond was offered by the World Bank (**http://www.worldbank .org**) in 1989.[4] Global bonds have several key characteristics:

- The bonds have legal eligibility for primary market sale in the world's major bond markets.
- The bonds can be settled and cleared on any of several systems such as Euroclear (**http://www.euroclear.com**) and Clearstream (**http:// www.clearstream.com**).
- An extended period of dialogue with investors worldwide sets the offering price.
- Selected international syndicates of bond dealers distribute the bonds.

Asset-backed securities, another type of bond, are backed by certain collateral assets, which are usually illiquid and private in nature. The idea behind securitization is to make these assets available for investment to a much broader range of investors. Bank of America issued the first mortgage-backed pass-through security in 1977. The securitization concept has since been applied to other asset types such as credit card receivables, auto loans, loans for mobile homes, and commercial property mortgage loans. In addition, several municipalities such as New York City and Jersey City have moved to securitize tax liens. Other innovative structures include securities backed by future royalties from record sales (see Box 10.1 on p. 234), high-leveraged loans, junk bonds,

---

[4]World Bank debt instruments include Eurobonds, global bonds, and domestic issues in selected markets.

MARKETS IN ACTION   David Bowie Bonds

10.1

In 1997, British rock legend David Bowie—who wrote the song "The Man Who Sold The World"—issued $55 million of bonds backed by royalties from 25 albums he recorded before 1990. Bowie's intellectual assets lent themselves uniquely to an asset-backed deal, because the star owns most of his hits.

The first-ever rock n' roll bonds offered a 7.9-percent coupon for 10 years. The bond carried A3 rating from Moody's. Prudential Insurance purchased the entire issue for its general account. The bonds offered yield higher than most asset-backed securities by at least half a point. The yield also beat the 6.37% yield then offered on 10-year Treasury bonds.

Minneapolis law firm Dorsey & Whitney, which specializes in asset-backed offerings, polled individual investors to see which celebrity-backed bonds they would consider buying. Oprah Winfrey and Steven Spielberg topped the list, and golfer Tiger Woods also made the list.

Sources: *Business Week Online* (March 11, 2002) and *Hollywood Reporter* (April 28–May 4, 1998).

and tobacco settlements. Chapter 13 provides a comprehensive coverage of securities backed by various types of assets.

PRIVATE PLACEMENTS AND SHELF REGISTRATION

Completing a public security issue is a costly and lengthy process. The amount of time needed depends on the readiness of the company, the availability of the information required in the registration statement, and market conditions. The costs include direct expenses, road shows, underwriting spreads, registration fees, listing fees, and management time. Both the time and costs associated with a public security issuance can be significantly reduced through private placements and shelf registration, however.

Private Placements and Rule 144A

A **private placement** does not go through the SEC's registration process. A private issue can save legal and registration expenses that can run up to several hundred thousand dollars. Securities acquired in a private placement (called restricted securities) are subject to holding period requirements, however. The period of time an investor must hold the security is one year when trading limited quantities of restricted securities and two years when trading unlimited amounts.

Until 1990, these holding period restrictions seriously dampened the liquidity of the private market. In that year, the SEC adopted Rule 144A, which allows the trading of privately placed securities among qualified institutional buyers without the holding period restriction. Since the rule became effective, securities firms have committed considerable capital and personnel to trading Rule 144A securities. As a result, the volume of private placement debt, most of it consisting of Rule 144A securities, has grown rapidly and now accounts for a significant portion of the debt market.

Most Rule 144A issues carry registration rights. That means that non-investment-grade borrowers can rush out Rule 144A deals quickly to reap the benefits of a strong market and go through the process of SEC registration later. Once SEC reporting requirements are satisfied, the securities are upgraded. Generally, Rule 144A deals are $100 million or more in size to provide liquidity for resale.

Shelf Registration

Many fixed-income issuers can save time by taking advantage of the SEC's shelf registration rule (Rule 415), which allows certain issuers to file a single registration document indicating the intent to sell a specified amount of a given class of securities within the next two years. In essence, the securities can be thought of as sitting on a shelf, from which they can be removed and sold to the public quickly—often in just days or even hours.

This means that once the issuer's nonprice terms are decided, the issue can be placed on the market immediately. Consequently, the pricing risk, or the risk that the securities will be priced above market value, shifts from the issuer to the underwriter and the syndicate. Even so, the lead underwriter often will step up to bid for the issue in order to retain the prestige associated with being the lead firm in the syndicate. In effect, the shortened new-issue process benefits issuers at the expense of underwriters. This is because they shift not only the pricing risk but also the waiting risk, or the risk that market conditions will change before the securities are issued, to the underwriter. In addition, the underwriter faces increased due diligence risk, or the risk that the underwriter will not have time to conduct due diligence and correctly value the security. Another risk underwriters face is when the inventory of unsold bonds has grown due to unfavorable interest rate movements. To make matters worse, the underwriter's financing costs move up with a rise in interest rates.

CREDIT RATINGS AND BOND INSURANCE

The credit rating assigned to the issue, as well as whether the issuer obtains insurance for the issue, directly affects the interest rate that an issuer of bonds must pay. A **credit rating** is a rating agency's opinion of the ability of a security issue to meet its financial commitments on a timely basis. Credit ratings do not measure other risks in fixed-income investment such as market risk, the risk of loss in market value arising from an increase in interest rates. Additionally, as opinions of credit strength, ratings do not measure a security's potential for price appreciation.

In the United States, major rating agencies include Standard and Poor's (**http://www.standardandpoors.com**), Moody's (**http://www.moodys .com**), and FitchRatings (**http://www.fitchratings.com**). Each of these agencies assigns its ratings based on an in-depth analysis of the issuer's financial condition and management, the characteristics of the debt, and the specific revenue sources securing the bond. Issue credit ratings can be either long term or short term. Obligations having an original maturity of less than 365 days generally receive short-term ratings. Rating methodologies and related publications from these agencies can be found at their Web sites.

Long-Term Credit Ratings

Long-term credit ratings focus on fundamental factors that influence the issuer's long-term ability to meet its debt payments. Thus, the ratings measure the ability of an issuer to generate cash in the future, and they assess the level and predictability of an issuer's future cash generation in relation to its commitments to repay debt holders. In other words, long-term issue credit ratings are based on the likelihood of payment, the nature and provisions of the obligation, and the protection afforded by the obligation in the event of bankruptcy or reorganization.

The rating definitions are expressed in terms of default risk. The highest ratings are AAA (S&P and FitchRatings) and Aaa (Moody's). Bonds rated in the BBB (Baa) category or higher are investment grade, while securities with ratings in the BB category or lower are below investment-grade. Non-investment-grade bonds are high-yield or junk bonds. Table 10.6 shows long-term credit ratings used by the three major agencies. It is important to note that the ratings reflect the total expected credit loss over the life of the bonds. They are an assessment of the likelihood that the issue will default and the amount of loss if default occurs.

Moody's publishes an annual bond default study that tracks the actual default and credit loss experience of corporate bond issuers by rating category since 1920. The 2001 study shows that the average one-year default rate for Aaa-rated bonds during that period was zero. By contrast, 6.8 percent of bonds rated B defaulted within one year. The study also shows that over ten-year

TABLE 10.6	*Long-Term Credit Ratings*		
Credit Risk	**Standard & Poor's**	**Moody's**	**FitchRatings**
Investment Grade			
Highest quality	AAA	Aaa	AAA
High quality	AA	Aa	AA
Upper medium grade	A	A	A
Medium grade	BBB	Baa	BBB
Non-Investment Grade			
Somewhat speculative	BB	Ba	BB
Speculative	B	B	B
Highly speculative	CCC	Caa	CCC
Most speculative	CC	Ca	CC
Imminent default	D	C	C
Default	D	C	D

periods, only 0.82 percent of bonds rated Aaa missed payments. The ten-year default rate for bonds rated B was dramatically higher at 43.9 percent.

Short-Term Credit Ratings

Rating agencies use a separate system to rate securities that mature in less than one year, such as commercial paper, bank deposits, or money market funds. Table 10.7 shows the ratings used by the three rating agencies. The highest ratings indicate that the issuer has sufficient access to funds to meet the payments on all of its short-term obligations, even under periods of market stress. The lower ratings, such as Not Prime by Moody's, represent the opinion that the issuer may not have sufficient access to bank lines of credit or other forms of backup funding to meet all of its short-term obligations in periods of market stress. A higher rating implies a higher degree of investor protection.

Bond Insurance

As with municipal bonds, the credit quality of corporate bonds can be enhanced by bond insurance. Bond insurance provides investors with guaranteed payment of principal and interest in the event an issuer cannot meet its financial obligations. The guarantee is unconditional and irrevocable, regardless of whether the underlying rating of the issuer is downgraded. Bond or financial insurance has been used to bridge the difference between the need of issuers and the demand of investors. Issuers of guaranteed securities can obtain funds at reduced interest rates, broaden and diversify their sources of funds, and gain access to both domestic and international capital markets. Investors not only obtain triple-A assurance of timely payment, but also benefit from extensive credit analysis, due diligence, and post issuance monitoring by the bond insurers.

Financial insurance provides issuers with an attractive alternative to other sources of financing from banks, governmental agencies, and other financial institutions. Insurance allows issuers to reduce their borrowing costs significantly over the life of the transaction because all issues insured by those major

TABLE 10.7	Short-Term Credit Ratings		
Credit Risk	**Standard & Poor's**	**Moody's**	**FitchRatings**
Investment Grade			
High grade	A-1	Prime-1	F1
Good grade	A-2	Prime-2	F2
Satisfactory grade	A-3	Prime-3	F3
Non-Investment Grade			
Speculative	B	Not Prime	B
High default risk	C		C
Default	D		D

insurance companies are rated triple-A. This often results in a lower interest rate. Issuers realize increased marketability for their transaction since insured securities appeal to a broader range of investors. Issuers also benefit from the reduced volatility of prospective costs of funds by virtue of the stable trading spreads on insured triple-A paper. Financial insurance can provide market access to smaller, less-well-known issuers and expand the marketability of securities issued by larger, better-known entities. Insured transactions can also help develop cross-border funding opportunities by attracting investors from outside the issuer's domestic market.

MARKET CONVENTIONS

Once issued, most bonds trade over-the-counter via a network of telephone and proprietary computer links that connect interested parties. In recent years, the Internet has provided an additional venue for trading corporate fixed-income securities. According to a recent survey conducted by the Bond Market Association (**http://www.bondmarkets.com**), the number of electronic systems for trading corporate bonds has increased from just seven in 1997 to thirty-two in early 2001.

Some corporate bonds issued in the United States are listed on an exchange such as the New York Stock Exchange (**http://www.nyse.com**). Many eurobonds are listed on the London Stock Exchange (**http://www.londonstock exchange.com**) and the Luxembourg Stock Exchange (**http://www. bourse.lu**). Companies seek listing to gain access to large international investors. Regardless of whether the bonds are traded over-the-counter or through an exchange listing, the market conventions discussed in this section are similar.

Dealers and Investors

Bond dealers make a market for bonds, meaning that the dealers have traders whose responsibility is to specialize in a group of bonds and to be prepared to quote a buying price (bid) or selling price (offer). The bid-offer spreads represent one source of profits for dealers. Such market making ensures liquidity for bond investors, thereby allowing them to buy and sell bonds more easily at close-to-market prices.

Major bond investors include financial institutions, pension funds, and mutual funds around the world. Those investors and dealers comprise the institutional market in which large blocks of fixed-income securities are traded. A trade of $1 million in the institutional market is a small ticket. Trades involving several hundred million dollars take place regularly. Individuals invest in corporate bonds mainly through mutual funds; direct purchases or sales of bonds by individual investors are very limited. In the retail market, bond trades are much smaller, usually under $1 million.

Bond Market Basics

In the fixed-income market, a **coupon** is the percentage interest to be paid on a bond in the course of one year. The interest is commonly paid semiannually, although it can also be payable monthly, quarterly, or annually. For example, if a bond has a face value of $1,000 and a 7 percent coupon, $70 in interest will be paid to the bondholder over one year.

The maturity date is the date when the bond is redeemed. For example, if a bond has a maturity date of December 15, 2015, then the buyer of the bond should expect to be paid off in full at that date. The settlement date is the date when the seller receives the payment and the buyer receives the bond. In the United States, the corporate bond market has a practice of settling three business days after the trade date, that is, T + 3.[5] After the settlement date, the accrued interest belongs to the buyer.

The quoted price for corporate bonds is often based on a percentage of par. For example, suppose that a bond dealer offers to sell a bond at 105:20. This means the dealer wants to sell at a price equal to 105 percent plus $^{20}/_{32}$ of 1 percent of the face value. More specifically, the price offered is 105.625 percent of the face value. For every $1,000 par amount, the price is $1,056.25.

The bid price is the price a dealer will pay for the bond. The offer (asked) price is the price at which the dealer will sell. The difference between the bid and the offer is the bid-asked spread. For example, if a dealer quotes the bond at a bid of 105:16 and an offer of 105:20, the bid-asked spread is 4 ticks. This implies a spread of $^4/_{32}$ of 1 percent (0.125 percent). This means that the dollar spread for the dealer is $12.50 per bond (assuming $1,000 par amount).

But an investor purchasing the bond at the asked price will usually have to pay more than $1,056.25. In addition to the quoted price, the buyer has to pay for the accrued interest, the interest that has accrued since the last payment date. The clean price plus any accrued interest is the so-called dirty price. This is the price the buyer actually pays for the bond. For the bond just described, suppose that it has been 61 days since the coupon was last paid and the next payment will be made in 122 days. Thus, there are 183 days in this coupon period. The accrued interest is equal to

10.2 $$\$1,000 \times 3.50\% \times \frac{61}{183} = \$11.67.$$

Therefore, the total purchase price for the bond is $1,056.25 + $11.67 = $1,067.92.

A bond's **current yield** is its annual coupon divided by its clean price. The formula is

10.3 $$current\ yield = \frac{coupon}{price}.$$

Since the bond in our example has a clean price of $1,056.25 and pays an annual coupon of $70, its current yield is 6.63 percent. Investors do not rely just on current yield for their investment decisions. Most investors also look at yield to maturity (discussed next) and at duration and convexity, which we cover in a later section.

Yield to maturity (or yield) is the rate that discounts future cash flows of the bond to the market price.[6] As you recall from the present value concept, the yield (the discount rate) and the present value are inversely related.[7] As the yield rises, the bond price (present value) declines. Conversely, a lower yield implies a higher bond price. From the present value concept, it is clear that a bond selling at par has a yield equal to the coupon rate. The yield to maturity is higher than the coupon rate when the bond trades at a discount. The yield to maturity is lower than the coupon rate if the bond sells at a premium above the face value. The quoted price of the bond in the previous example is $1,056.25; hence, the yield is lower than 7 percent. As the bond matures, the price will approach par. Therefore, an investor buying this bond at a premium will suffer a capital loss. Conversely, if the bond trades at a discount, the investor will be rewarded with a capital gain.

Finally, the term "bond spread" refers to the interest rate differential between two bonds. The spread is calculated simply by subtracting one bond yield from another, often the yield on a comparable Treasury security. For example, if the bond discussed previously yields 6.63 percent and a comparable Treasury yields 5.23 percent, then the spread is 1.40 percent or 140 basis points.

VALUATION OF CORPORATE BONDS

As the previous section observed, the price of a fixed-income security is the present value of all future cash flows from the security. These future cash flows include the periodic coupons and the face value at maturity. The discount rate is the yield to maturity. Hence, the value of a bond depends on the size of the coupon payments, the length of time remaining until the bond matures (current maturity), and the yield on the bond. As noted in Chapter 8, "Government Securities Markets," each cash flow should be discounted at an appropriate spot rate. Valuation theory does not recommend discounting all cash flows from different time points by the same rate—yield to maturity—as is conventionally done. The market, however, has become accustomed to using yield to maturity. Also, the efficiency of the market works to ensure that both yield to maturity

---

[6]As discussed in Chapter 8, yield to maturity is a means of quoting prices. The best valuation approach is based on the spot rate curve.

[7]The next section covers bond valuation.

and the spot rate method arrive at the same valuation; if not, there would be arbitrage opportunities. Therefore, we will use yield to maturity in the following discussions.

Bond Valuation Basics

The market prices a bond at the present value of the stream of dollar flows, which are the periodic interest payments plus the redemption value at maturity. The purpose is to determine the price that a bond will command, given the yield to maturity at which the bond trades. For example, assume that a 5-year bond has a coupon rate of 6.00 percent, pays interest twice a year, and trades at a yield of 6.20 percent. This means that every six months investors will receive a $30 interest payment for every bond with a par of $1,000. In addition, investors are paid the par amount when the bond matures. Table 10.8 shows the cash flows for this bond as well as the present value of each cash flow. The sum of the component present values equals $991.51. This is the value of the bond in the given market environment and is also the price a buyer would be willing to pay.

Table 10.9 (see p. 242) documents the price changes that will occur if the yield rises to 6.40 percent or decreases to 6.00 percent. As we have seen, at a yield of 6.20 percent, the price is $991.51. The price increases by $8.49 to $1,000.00 if the yield declines to 6.00 percent. If the yield rises to 6.40 percent, the price declines by $8.40 from $991.51 to $983.11. Note that the same

TABLE 10.8	Bond Cash Flows and Price		
Term	Cash Flow	Yield	Present Value
1	30.00	0.031	29.10
2	30.00	0.031	28.22
3	30.00	0.031	27.37
4	30.00	0.031	26.55
5	30.00	0.031	25.75
6	30.00	0.031	24.98
7	30.00	0.031	24.23
8	30.00	0.031	23.50
9	30.00	0.031	22.79
10	30.00	0.031	22.11
10	1000.00	0.031	736.91
		price =	991.51

Note: Term in the first column is the semiannual period, cash flow represents the semiannual coupon and par amount at maturity, and yield in the third column is the semiannual yield.

TABLE 10.9	Changes in Price for a Given Change in Yield			
		PRESENT VALUE		
Term	Cash Flow	At 3.1%	At 3.0%	At 3.2%
1	30.00	29.10	29.13	29.07
2	30.00	28.22	28.28	28.17
3	30.00	27.37	27.45	27.29
4	30.00	26.55	26.65	26.45
5	30.00	25.75	25.88	25.63
6	30.00	24.98	25.12	24.83
7	30.00	24.23	24.39	24.06
8	30.00	23.50	23.68	23.32
9	30.00	22.79	22.99	22.59
10	30.00	22.11	22.32	21.89
10	1000.00	736.91	744.09	729.80
	price =	991.51	1000.00	983.11

amount of change in yield, in this example 0.20 percent, does not lead to the same amount of change in price. This is because the price and yield relationship is convex, as will be explained later. Given an equal-size change in yield, the price will change by a larger amount for a yield decrease than an increase.

In general, the price of an M-year bond with a semiannual coupon of C and a redemption value of F is calculated as

10.4

$$P = \sum_{t=1}^{2M} \frac{C}{\left(1 + \frac{y}{2}\right)^t} + \frac{F}{\left(1 + \frac{y}{2}\right)^{2M}} =$$

$$C\left[\frac{1}{\frac{y}{2}} - \frac{1}{\frac{y}{2}\left(1 + \frac{y}{2}\right)^{2M}}\right] + \frac{F}{\left(1 + \frac{y}{2}\right)^{2M}}.$$

The semiannual yield ($\frac{y}{2}$) is used in the denominator because the coupon is paid every six months. The bond has a maturity of M years, thus, there are a total of $2M$ semiannual periods. As an example, we can use this formula to recalculate the price of the bond discussed previously. As shown next, the price is $991.51 at a yield of 6.20 percent, $1,000.00 at 6.00 percent, and $983.11 at 6.40 percent.

$$10.5 \qquad P = \$30 \times \left[\frac{1}{\frac{0.062}{2}} - \frac{1}{\frac{0.062}{2}\left(1 + \frac{0.062}{2}\right)^{2 \times 5}} \right] +$$

$$\frac{\$1,000}{\left(1 + \frac{0.062}{2}\right)^{2 \times 5}} = \$991.51.$$

$$10.6 \qquad P = \$30 \times \left[\frac{1}{\frac{0.060}{2}} - \frac{1}{\frac{0.060}{2}\left(1 + \frac{0.060}{2}\right)^{2 \times 5}} \right] +$$

$$\frac{\$1,000}{\left(1 + \frac{0.060}{2}\right)^{2 \times 5}} = \$1,000.00.$$

$$10.7 \qquad P = \$30 \times \left[\frac{1}{\frac{0.064}{2}} - \frac{1}{\frac{0.064}{2}\left(1 + \frac{0.064}{2}\right)^{2 \times 5}} \right] +$$

$$\frac{\$1,000}{\left(1 + \frac{0.064}{2}\right)^{2 \times 5}} = \$983.11.$$

Bond Valuation in Practice

The valuation method presented in the previous section was simplified. In reality, bonds trade every business day, so it is necessary to count the days since the last coupon payment date to the settlement date and the number of days from the settlement date to the next coupon date. One way to calculate the price of the bond is to calculate the value of the bond on the next coupon date and then discount that to obtain the present value on the settlement date. Figure 10.1 (see p. 244) depicts this approach. As the figure shows, we first have to compute the proportion coupon (*PC*) that accrues from the settlement date to the next coupon date. We also find the value on the next coupon date of the future cash flows (*V*). The sum of these two components (*PC* plus *V*) is then discounted to obtain the value on the settlement date.

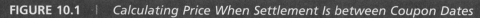

FIGURE 10.1 | *Calculating Price When Settlement Is between Coupon Dates*

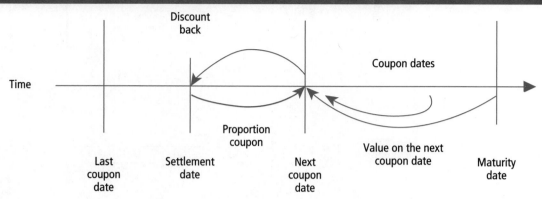

In real life, it is not practical to use this simplified formula (10.4). Instead, bond traders use Bloomberg or software like Microsoft® Excel® to calculate the price. The function in Excel is:

10.8   PRICE("settlement date", "maturity date", coupon rate, yield, redemption value, coupon frequency, day count basis).

The coupon frequency refers to the number of coupon payments in one year. The frequency is 1 for an annual payment, 2 for semiannual, 4 for quarterly, and 12 for monthly. The day count basis could be $^{30}/_{360}$, $^{actual}/_{365}$, $^{actual}/_{actual}$, or another convention.[8] For example, assume that a bond has a coupon rate of 6.00 percent and a maturity date of October 31, 2015. The bond has a yield of 5.85 percent, and the trade settles on September 9, 2003. The day count basis is $^{actual}/_{actual}$. The price is $101.28 per $100 face value:

10.9   Price = PRICE("9/9/2003", "10/31/2015", 0.06, 0.0585, 100, 2, 1) = $101.28.

Sometimes, a trader may need to calculate the yield given the price and other specifics of the bond. On Excel, the function to obtain the yield is as follows:

10.10   YIELD("settlement date", "maturity date", coupon rate, price, redemption value, coupon frequency, day count basis).

---

[8]The numerator represents the number of days in a month, and the denominator denotes the number of days in a year. Therefore, 30/360 assumes a 30-day month and a 360-day year. A day count basis of actual/actual means that the accrued interest calculation uses the actual number of days in the month and in the year.

If the price is known but the yield is not, the yield to maturity can be obtained by:

10.11
$$\text{Yield} = \text{YIELD}(\text{``9/9/2003''}, \text{``10/31/2015''},$$
$$0.06, 101.28, 100, 2, 1) = 0.0585.$$

Valuation of Zero-Coupon Bonds

Zero-coupon bonds pay the redemption value on the maturity date. There are no periodical coupon payments. The price of such a security is just the present value of the par amount to be received at maturity. For example, the value of a 7-year zero-coupon bond traded at a yield of 6.00 percent is equal to $1,000/(1+0.06)^7$ which is \$665.06 per \$1,000 par amount. In general, the formula is

10.12
$$P = \frac{F}{\left(1 + \dfrac{y}{N}\right)^{N \times M}},$$

where P denotes the bond price, F is the face value, y is yield to maturity, N is number of compounding periods in a year, and M is maturity in years.

Valuation of Perpetual Bonds

A bond that pays a regular coupon perpetually commands a price equal to the present value of those future payments. There is no maturity date, so there is no final redemption value. There is, however, an infinite number of coupon payments. The valuation formula is

10.13
$$P = \sum_{t=1}^{\infty} \frac{C}{\left(1 + \dfrac{y}{N}\right)^t}.$$

where C is the coupon and the other notations are the same as in the previous equation. The formula can be simplified to $p = 2C/y$, where $2C$ is the annual coupon. For example, assume a perpetual bond carries a coupon rate of 6.00 percent and trades at a yield of 5.85 percent. For every \$1,000 par value, the market will price it at \$1,025.64. Of course, if the trade settles between coupon dates, the approach depicted in Figure 10.1 can be used to obtain the price.

The Settlement Value

So far in this section we have discussed the clean price, which captures a large portion of the value to be settled. On the settlement date, however, as we have noted in a previous section as well as in Chapter 8, the buyer also has to pay to the seller the accrued interest that has accumulated between the last coupon date and the settlement date of this trade. For example, assume that a bond has a coupon rate of 6.00 percent and a maturity date of October 31, 2015. The bond trades at a yield of 5.85 percent or a price of $101.28 per $100 face value. The last coupon was paid 122 days ago, and the next coupon date is 61 days away. The settlement value is more than $101.28 for every $100 redemption value, because the buyer must also pay the seller the accrued interest for 122 days. The total trade value is the sum of the quoted clean price (P) plus the accrued interest (AI). This trade value (V) can be calculated as:

10.14 $$V = P + AI = \$101.28 + \$3 \times \left(\frac{122}{183}\right) = \$103.28.$$

Hence to purchase $100,000 of this bond, a buyer has to pay $103,280 for the purchase.[9]

DURATION AND CONVEXITY

As a previous section explained, credit ratings measure an issuer's ability to honor its interest and repayment obligations. This section focuses on two other types of risks that bond investors face: uncertainty with respect to the level of interest rates and uncertainty as to the shape of the yield curve. An investor purchasing a bond faces **reinvestment risk**, the risk that the investor will have to reinvest future coupon income at a yield less than the yield to maturity at which she purchased the bond. There is also a **price risk**, the risk that an investor might have to sell the bond before maturity at a price lower than anticipated. In that case, the yield to maturity earned by the investor may differ from the returns anticipated at the time of the purchase. Therefore, it is necessary to determine the sensitivity of a bond's price to a small change in yield. Duration and convexity are two measures commonly used for this purpose.

Duration

Macaulay duration is the time-weighted average of the discounted future cash flows. Put differently, it is the weighted average life of a bond where the weights are based on the present value of the individual cash flows, relative to the market price of the bond. For example, recall the 5-year, 6 percent bond discussed previously that trades at a price of $991.51. The duration is 4.39 years, as Table 10.10 shows. Present value calculations are based on the yield to maturity at which the bond trades; which, in this example, we shall assume to be 6.20 percent. In Table 10.10, the first column represents the semiannual periods. The second column lists the coupon payment every six months and the redemption value of $1,000 when the bond matures after five years (ten semiannual periods). The third column uses a semiannual yield of 3.10 percent to calculate the present value of each cash flow. The total present value of cash flows is the price of the bond. In the next column, weights for each period are

---

[9]The buyer has to pay commissions as well.

TABLE 10.10	Duration			
Term (t)	Cash Flows	Present Value	Present Value/Price	t (present value/price)
1	30.00	29.10	0.029	0.029
2	30.00	28.22	0.028	0.057
3	30.00	27.37	0.028	0.083
4	30.00	26.55	0.027	0.107
5	30.00	25.75	0.026	0.130
6	30.00	24.98	0.025	0.151
7	30.00	24.23	0.024	0.171
8	30.00	23.50	0.024	0.190
9	30.00	22.79	0.023	0.207
10	30.00	22.11	0.022	0.223
10	1000.00	736.91	0.743	7.432
	price =	991.51	sum =	8.78
			duration =	4.39

Notes: 1. The 5-year bond is trading at a yield to maturity of 6.20 percent.
2. In the first column, t represents semiannual periods. Therefore, the duration of 8.78 semiannual periods is divided by 2 to obtain a duration of 4.39 years.

determined by dividing the present value of each cash flow by the market price. For example in year 3 (period 6), the present value of the coupon is $24.98, and this is divided by the price of $991.51 to arrive at 0.025 in column 4. In column 5, each period is multiplied by the weights listed in column 4. For example, period 4 is multiplied by 0.027 to obtain 0.107 in column 5. The procedure is performed every period, and the values are summed. The final answer is 8.78 semiannual periods (4.39 years).

In general, the Macaulay duration (D_m) formula can be stated as

10.15
$$D_m = \frac{\dfrac{C_1}{\left(1 + \dfrac{y}{2}\right)^1}}{P} \times 1 + \frac{\dfrac{C_2}{\left(1 + \dfrac{y}{2}\right)^2}}{P} \times 2 + \cdots +$$

$$\frac{\dfrac{C_{2M}}{\left(1 + \dfrac{y}{2}\right)^{2M}}}{P} \times 2M + \frac{\dfrac{F}{\left(1 + \dfrac{y}{2}\right)^{2M}}}{P} \times 2M, \text{ or}$$

$$D_m = \sum_{t=1}^{2M} \frac{\dfrac{C_t}{\left(1 + \dfrac{y}{2}\right)^t}}{P} \times t + \frac{\dfrac{F}{\left(1 + \dfrac{y}{2}\right)^{2M}}}{P} \times (2M),$$

where y is the yield to maturity in annual terms, C is the periodic coupon, F is the face value, and M is the maturity of the bond in years. The semiannual analysis is used throughout the calculation; the answer should be divided by 2 to convert the figure to annual terms.

Microsoft Excel can be used to calculate the Macauley duration. The syntax is

10.16	DURATION("settlement", "maturity", coupon, yield, frequency, basis).

As an example, suppose a bond pays a 6.00 percent coupon, trades at a 5.85 percent yield, and matures on October 31, 2015. On September 9, 2003, this bond has a duration of 8.64 years.

Duration and Yield

Duration and yield have an inverse relation, because the present value is part of duration. Thus, higher yields lead to lower present values. For the example in Table 10.10, if the yield rises to 7.00 percent, the duration would decrease to 4.38 years, as Table 10.11 shows.

Duration and Coupon Rates

The duration and the coupon rate have inverse relation. The higher the coupon rate, the smaller the duration is. This is because higher-coupon-rate bonds give higher cash flows before maturity and thus tend to weight duration toward the earlier years. Conversely, lower-coupon-rate bonds pay less cash

TABLE 10.11 | Duration and Yield to Maturity

Term (t)	Cash Flows	Present Value	Present Value/Price	t (present value/price)
1	30.00	28.99	0.030	0.030
2	30.00	28.01	0.029	0.058
3	30.00	27.06	0.028	0.085
4	30.00	26.14	0.027	0.109
5	30.00	25.22	0.026	0.132
6	30.00	24.41	0.025	0.153
7	30.00	23.58	0.025	0.172
8	30.00	22.78	0.024	0.190
9	30.00	22.01	0.023	0.207
10	30.00	21.27	0.022	0.222
10	1000.00	708.92	0.740	7.397
	price =	958.38	sum =	8.75
			duration =	4.38

Notes: 1. The 5-year bond is assumed to trade at a yield of 7.00 percent.
2. In the first column, t represents the semiannual periods. Therefore, the duration of 8.75 semi-annual periods is divided by 2 to obtain a duration of 4.38 years.

flow before maturity, so duration is weighted closer to maturity. For example, if the coupon rate for the bond described in Table 10.10 increases from 6.00 percent to 7.00 percent, the duration will decrease from 4.39 to 4.32 years (see Table 10.12). At the extreme, a zero-coupon bond has the same maturity and duration because there is only one payment, and it is at maturity.

Duration and Price Sensitivity

The popularity of duration as a measure of risk derives from its use in estimating the change in a bond's value arising from a small change in its yield to maturity. Before using duration as a proxy for the bond price change due to a small change in yield, it is common (and more accurate) to derive the **modified duration** (D_{mod}). The formula is

10.17
$$D_{mod} = D_m \frac{1}{(1 + y)}.$$

Once we have obtained the modified duration, we can multiply the modified duration by the change in yield $(\Delta y/(1 + y))$ to determine the percentage change in the value of a bond $(\%\Delta P)$:

10.18
$$\%\Delta P = -D_{mod} \times \frac{\Delta y}{(1 + y)}.$$

Modified duration indicates the percentage change in the price of a bond for a given change in yield. As an example, the 5-year, 6 percent bond that trades

TABLE 10.12 | Duration and Coupon Rates

Term (t)	Cash Flows	Present Value	Present Value/Price	t (present value/price)
1	35.00	33.95	0.033	0.033
2	35.00	32.93	0.032	0.064
3	35.00	31.94	0.031	0.093
4	35.00	30.98	0.030	0.120
5	35.00	30.05	0.029	0.145
6	35.00	29.14	0.028	0.169
7	35.00	28.27	0.027	0.191
8	35.00	27.42	0.027	0.212
9	35.00	26.59	0.026	0.231
10	35.00	25.79	0.025	0.249
10	1000.00	736.91	0.713	7.127
	price =	1033.95	sum =	8.63
			duration =	4.32

Note: The 5-year bond is assumed to pay 7.00 percent semiannual coupon and trade at a yield of 6.20 percent.

at a yield of 6.20 percent has a modified duration of 4.134. When the yield increases to 6.40 percent, the price will decrease roughly by

$$\boxed{\text{10.19}} \qquad \%\Delta P = -4.134 \times \frac{0.2\%}{(1 + 6.20\%)} = -0.7785\%$$

Based on the proxy, the bond price will decrease from $991.51 by 0.7785 percent to $983.79. This is very close to the actual price of $983.11 when the yield rises to 6.40 percent. Thus, the proxy overestimates the price by $0.68 per bond. On the other hand, the price will increase from $991.51 by 0.7785 percent to $999.23 when the yield declines from 6.20 percent to 6.00 percent (from point X to point Y in Figure 10.2). Compared with the actual price of $1,000, the proxy underestimates the price by $0.77. The discrepancy between the estimated change in the bond price and the actual change is due to the convexity of the price-yield relationship, as Figure 10.2 shows.

As noted, the percentage price change calculation was just an approximation because it failed to account for the convexity of the price-yield relationship. Because of the shape of the price-yield curve, for a given change in yield, the gain in price for a drop in yield will be greater than the fall in price due to an equal rise in yield. Mathematically, the duration is the first derivative of price with respect to yield, and convexity is the second derivative. Put differently, convexity is the rate of change of duration with yield, and it accounts for

FIGURE 10.2 | *Convexity of Price-Yield Curve*

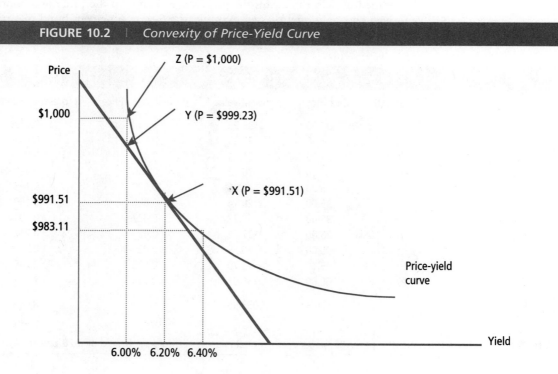

the fact that as the yield decreases, the slope of the price-yield curve and duration will increase. Similarly, as the yield increases, the slope of the curve will decrease, as will the duration.

CONCLUDING SUMMARY

The chapter has provided a comprehensive overview of the corporate fixed-income market. Many types of securities are traded in the corporate debt market, including commercial paper, large time deposits, bankers' acceptances, medium-term notes, and bonds. Corporations issue a variety of bonds. Convertible bonds can be converted into common stock. Exchangeable bonds can be converted to the common stock of another corporation. Callable bonds give the issuer the right to pay off the outstanding debt before maturity, while puttable bonds grant investors the right to put back the bonds to the issuer when interest rates rise. Junk bonds are non-investment-grade bonds. Global bonds and foreign currency bonds raise funds from major international markets.

Understanding the conventions of the bond market is also very important. The market uses a number of basic terms such as settlement, maturity, redemption value, clean price, accrued interest, current yield, yield to maturity, and coupon date. For example, the settlement date is the day the seller receives money and the buyer receives the securities. A seller failing to deliver on the settlement date provides free financing to the buyer and will not receive the accrued interest. The calculation of accrued interest is based on day count conventions. In the capital market, the assumption is a 365-day year, whereas the money market where commercial paper and bankers' acceptances are traded uses a 360-day year.

Although Treasury securities are assumed to be free from default risk, default risk is an important element in the corporate sector. Investors and traders rely on credit ratings to gauge the credit quality of a security. The three major rating agencies are Moody's, Standard & Poors, and FitchRatings. Corporate issuers of less than sound financial status often purchase financial insurance to raise the rating of their securities.

The valuation of bonds depends on their maturity, coupon rate, and yield to maturity. Bonds trade every day, so the valuation of a fixed-income security is determined not only by the quoted price but also by the accrued interest, which requires counting the days in the coupon period and the number of days since the last coupon date to the settlement date. Financial software such as Microsoft Excel provides a simple approach to such a calculation, as the chapter has presented. Furthermore, duration and convexity assist in examining price volatility and approximate accuracy when yield changes by a small amount.

Key Terms

bankers' acceptance (BA) 228
bond 230
callable bond 232
commercial paper 226
convertible bond 230
coupon 239
credit ratings 235
current yield 239
exchangeable bond 232
fallen angel 233
fixed-income securities 226

foreign currency bond 233
global bond 233
junk bond 232
Macaulay duration 246
medium-term note (MTN) 229
modified duration 249
price risk 246
private placement 234
puttable bond 232
reinvestment risk 246

Review Questions

1. What is commercial paper? What are its advantages?

2. A bankers' acceptance has seven days until maturity when the accepting bank will pay the face amount of $1 million to the holder of the paper. The acceptance trades at a discount of 5.12 percent. What is the price of the acceptance?

3. Define and compare callable bonds and puttable bonds.

4. A company owns a huge block of common stock of another firm. Selling the large block of shares in the open market will depress the stock price. The company decides to issue exchangeable bonds instead to raise the necessary funds. Describe the rationale for this approach.

5. A tobacco settlement will pay municipalities every year for a number of years. Some cash-strapped municipalities want to use the settlement agreement to raise large sums of money. Describe a mechanism that they can use to accomplish this.

6. Suppose that a bond that pays a 5.60 percent coupon semiannually matures on December 15, 2020. The bond trades at a yield of 6.11 percent, and the trade settles on January 18, 2003. What is the yield to maturity? What is the price of the bond? What is the current yield?

7. Continue question #6. Calculate the prices at ten different yields, five higher than 6.11 percent and five lower.

8. Continue question #6. What is the duration? Calculate the duration of the bond at various yields around 6.11 percent. What is the relationship between duration and yield?

Select Bibliography

Campbell, C. J. "Private security placements and resales to the public under SEC Rule 144," *Corporate Finance Review* 2, no. 1, July/August 1997, pp. 11–16.

Capell, K. "Care to buy some David Bowie bonds?" Business Week Online, March 11, 2002.

Fabozzi, F. J. *Bond Markets, Analysis and Strategies.* Upper Saddle River, N.J.: Prentice Hall, 2000.

Fisher, M. "Forces that shape the yield curve: Parts 1 and 2," Federal Reserve Bank of Atlanta, working paper, 2001.

Kendall, L. T., and M. J. Fishman, eds. *A Primer on Securitization.* Cambridge, Mass.: MIT Press, 1996.

Liaw, K. T. *The Business of Investment Banking.* New York: John Wiley & Sons, 1999.

Sherman, J., and M. Pollack. "Strike up the bond." *Hollywood Reporter,* April 28–May 4, 1998, p. 16.

Stigum, M., and F. L. Robinson. *Money Market and Bond Calculations.* Chicago: Irwin Professional Publishing, 1996.

Sundaresan, S. *Fixed Income Markets and Their Derivatives.* Cincinnati, Ohio: South-Western Publishing, 2001.

Tuckman, B. *Fixed Income Securities: Tools for Today's Markets.* New York: John Wiley & Sons, 2002.

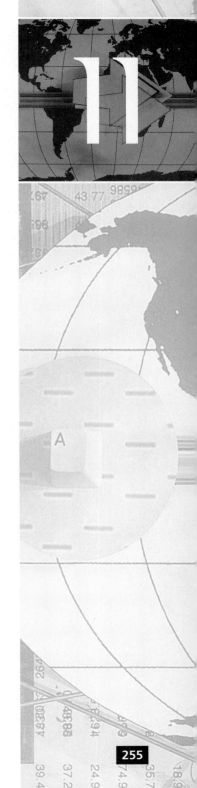

Stock Markets

Stock markets are essential to economic development. The stock market provides a place where corporations can go to raise long-term capital to finance a multitude of projects. Stocks also offer investors the opportunity to obtain capital gains from ownership of business enterprises, as well as to receive current dividend income. Stock ownership has expanded dramatically in the past decade as individuals have assumed more responsibility for providing for their retirements. In addition, low-cost online trading has opened the world of equities to millions of people who might not have otherwise considered investing in the stock market. This chapter will examine both the primary and the secondary stock markets. Corporations issue stocks in the primary market. In the secondary market, investors express their opinions, based on certain valuation techniques, about the future profitability of a company through the trades that they make. The aggregate of these trades gives the market consensus about the price of the stock. Investors use several approaches to determine the value of a stock, including fundamental analysis, technical analysis, and the efficient market hypothesis.

The objectives of this chapter are to provide an understanding of:
- Stock market trends and stock market indexes.
- Exchange versus over-the-counter markets.
- Trading mechanics.
- Transactions costs.
- Fundamental analysis and valuation techniques.
- Technical analysis.
- The efficient market hypothesis.

MARKET OVERVIEW

Corporations can raise long-term funds by issuing bonds or stock. As we saw in Chapter 10, corporate bonds are a form of debt. In contrast, stock represents an ownership interest in the corporation. There are two types of stocks: common stock and preferred stock. Common stockholders have the right to vote on important matters affecting the corporation such as the election of directors and to receive dividends (if the corporation pays them). Preferred stock is a hybrid between bonds and common stock. The preferred stockholder usually receives a fixed dividend. Because the dividend does not change, the price of preferred stock is more stable than that of common stock. Preferred stockholders have a claim on assets that is senior to that of common stockholders, but they usually do not have voting rights.

By purchasing common stock, an investor becomes an owner of the corporation. Stock ownership allows the shareholder to share in the earnings of the corporation in the same way a part owner of a local golf shop shares in the earnings of that business. Because stock represents an ownership interest, the firm does not have a legal obligation to make payouts such as dividends. Its interest payments to bondholders, however, are a legal obligation. These characteristics make stock investments riskier than investments in bonds, but potentially more rewarding.

Primary and Secondary Markets

The stock markets consist of a primary and a secondary market. Companies issue new securities to raise money in the **primary market**. The first time a company offers its stock for sale to the public is called an initial public offering (IPO).[1] Subsequently, the company may issue additional shares to raise more capital.

Investors trade outstanding shares in the secondary market. Although corporations do not raise capital directly in the secondary market, this market plays an important role in the process. After all, investors would be very reluctant to purchase stock in the primary market if they had no easy way of later selling these securities for cash. The **secondary market** provides a place for investors to trade securities that have already been issued. It allows investors to shift their assets into different securities and different markets. The secondary market also provides pricing information, thus making a firm's valuation transparent.

The bear market that started in 2000 led to cutbacks and layoffs by investment banks. To make matters worse, investors shied away from the market after the scandals of Enron and WorldCom. To restore investor confidence, the New York Stock Exchange has proposed adding new listing standards to improve corporate governance and accountability (see Box Feature 11.1).

---

[1]Chapter 4 describes the issuing process in detail.

MARKETS IN ACTION   NYSE's New Rules to Restore Investor Confidence   11.1

The NYSE has proposed to add new listing standards to restore investor confidence in the stock markets in the wake of Enron and WorldCom. These standards will further the availability of honest and well-intentioned directors, officers, and employees to perform their duties effectively. These changes will also allow shareholders to better monitor the performance of companies and directors in order to reduce the instances of lax and unethical behavior.

Important changes to the listing requirements on the NYSE include:

1. Increasing the role and authority of independent directors: independent directors must comprise the majority of the board; boards must convene regular executive sessions in which non-management directors meet without management directors; and listed companies must have an audit committee, nominating committee, and compensation committee, each comprised solely of independent directors.

2. Tightening the definition of independent directors: the board must affirmatively determine that the director has no material relationship with the listed company.

3. Focusing on good corporate governance: listed companies must adopt corporate governance guidelines, and code of business conduct and ethics.

4. Giving shareholders more opportunity to monitor and participate in the governance of their companies: listed companies must publish a code of business conduct and ethics, and shareholders must be given the opportunity to vote on equity-based compensation plans.

5. Establishing new control and enforcement mechanisms: each CEO must certify annually that the company has established and complied with procedures to give investors complete and accurate information.

Source: New York Stock Exchange (http://www.nyse.com).

Stock Exchanges versus Over-the-Counter Market

The transactions among investors in the secondary market take place at organized exchanges or in the over-the-counter market. The organized exchanges have trading floors where traders execute buy and sell orders for their clients. The **over-the-counter (OTC)** market does not have a trading floor; instead, traders execute transactions through a computerized telecommunications network.

By far the most important organized exchange is the New York Stock Exchange (NYSE; **http://www.nyse.com**). To be listed on the NYSE, a company must meet extensive requirements as to the distribution of its stock, its size, and its financial status. As Table 11.1 (see p. 258) shows, the minimum requirements are 2,000 shareholders, 1.1 million shares of public float (stock owned by the public) with a market value of $100 million, earnings of $2.5 million in the most recent year, operating cash flow of $25 million, or a market capitalization of $1 billion. The American Stock Exchange (AMEX) is also an organized exchange, but its size is much smaller than the NYSE, and as Table 11.2 (see p. 259) shows, its listing requirements are less stringent. In addition,

TABLE 11.1 | *NYSE Listing Criteria*

Distribution and Size:

1. Round-lot holders	2,000
Or	
Total shareholders	2,200
Average monthly trading volume	100,000 shares
Or	
Total shareholders	500
Average monthly trading volume	1 million shares
2. Public shares	1.1 million outstanding
3. Market value of public shares	
Public companies	$100 million
IPOs, spin-offs, carve-outs	$60 million

Financial Criteria:

4. Earnings	
Most recent year	$2.5 million
Each of two preceding years	$2 million
Or	
Most recent year	$4.5 million
Or	
5. Aggregate operating cash flow for three years (for companies with capitalization of no less than $500 million and $200 million in revenues)	$25 million
Or	
6. Revenues for the last fiscal year and	$250 million
Market capitalization	$1 billion

Note: A round-lot holder is a shareholder who owns 100 or multiple of 100 shares.

Source: New York Stock Exchange (http://www.nyse.com/listed/listed.html).

there are several regional exchanges such as the Philadelphia Stock Exchange, the Boston Stock Exchange, and the Pacific Stock Exchange.

The Nasdaq, an electronic quotation system, conducts the most important OTC market (Nasdaq is an acronym for the National Association of Securities Dealers Automated Quotations). Table 11.3 shows the listing requirements for the Nasdaq National Market and the Nasdaq SmallCap Market. In the past, most companies whose stocks traded on the Nasdaq (**http://www.nasdaq.com**) were smaller companies that did not qualify for listing on the NYSE. However, many large technology companies originally listed on the Nasdaq have chosen to remain there even though they now could qualify for NYSE listing. Some examples include Microsoft, Dell, and Intel. In 1998, the Nasdaq merged with AMEX.

TABLE 11.2	AMEX Listing Requirements	
Financial Guidelines:		
Pre-tax income		
Most recent year or		$750,000
2 of most recent 3 years		$750,000
Market value of public float		$3 million
Price		$3
Stockholder's equity		$4 million
Alternative Financial Guidelines:		
Market value of public float		$15 million
Price		$3
Operating history		3 years
Shareholder equity		$4 million
Distribution Guidelines:		
Public float		500,000
Public stockholders		800
Or		
Public float		1 million
Public stockholders		400
Or		
Public float		500,000
Public stockholders		400
Average daily volume		2,000

Source: American Stock Exchange (http://www.amex.com). The listing requirements are listed under "Listing Process" for equities.

Stock Market Indexes

Stock market indexes and averages can play an important role in investors' analysis of the performance of the stock market. They can also be used as benchmarks for comparison. The Dow Jones Industrial Average, the Nasdaq Composite, the S&P 500, and the Wilshire 5000 are all commonly reported indexes. In many instances, portfolio managers use these indexes as performance benchmarks. Each index has different characteristics that affect its usefulness as a benchmark. Understanding the construction of an index is important to understanding why its value changes and can also be useful in determining how to build an appropriate benchmark for evaluation.

The most popular stock market index is the **Dow Jones Industrial Average (DJIA)**, a price-weighted index consisting of 30 large industrial stocks. The composition of the DJIA changes from time to time to reflect changes in the economy and the relative importance of industries or of companies within an industry. For example, on November 1, 1999, the DJIA added Home Depot, Intel, Microsoft, and SBC Communications to reflect

TABLE 11.3	Nasdaq Listing Requirements

NASDAQ NATIONAL MARKET

Requirements	Criterion 1	Criterion 2	Criterion 3
Net tangible assets	$6 million	$18 million	N/A
Market capitalization, or	N/A	N/A	$75 million, or
Total assets, or			$75 million, or
Total revenues			$75 million
Pretax income	$1 million	N/A	N/A
Public float	1.1 million shares	1.1 million shares	1.1 million shares
Operating history	N/A	2 years	N/A
Market value of public float	$8 million	$18 million	$20 million
Minimum bid price	$5	$5	$5
Shareholders	400	400	400
Market makers	3	3	4

THE NASDAQ SMALLCAP MARKET

Requirements	Criterion
Net tangible assets, or	$4 million, or
Market capitalization, or	$50 million, or
Net income	$750,000
Public float	1 million shares
Market value of public float	$5 million
Minimum bid price	$4.00
Market makers	3
Operating history, or	1 year, or
Market capitalization	$50 million

Source: Nasdaq Stock Market (http://www.nasdaq.com/services/insidenasdaq.stm). The listing requirements are listed under "Listing and Legal Requirements."

both the importance of technology and changes in the retail sector of the economy. Although the DJIA is the most widely reported market index, it has little use as a performance benchmark because of its narrow makeup and price weighting.

The **Nasdaq Composite** is a market value-weighted index of stocks that trade in OTC market. In recent years, the growth of the technology giants that trade in this market has made the Nasdaq Composite an index of technology performance.

The **S&P 500 Index** is a market value-weighted index of NYSE and AMEX-Nasdaq stocks. It consists of 400 industrial companies, 20 transportation companies, 40 utility firms, and 40 financial companies. Because it is much broader than the DJIA, many use the S&P 500 as a performance benchmark for large cap stocks (companies with a market capitalization greater than $5 billion). Many mutual funds report the performance of the S&P 500 in their quarterly reports to provide investors with a benchmark for comparison.

The **Wilshire 5000** is a market value-weighted index that consists of stocks on the NYSE and the AMEX-Nasdaq. Although it began with 5,000 stocks, the index currently consists of more than 7,000 stocks. Many consider the Wilshire 5000 as an index for the entire stock market.

There are also a number of foreign indexes that market participants watch. The Nikkei Stock Average Index is a price-weighted index of 225 stocks on the Tokyo Stock Exchange (http://www.tse.or.jp). The Nikkei provides a gauge of the performance of Japanese stocks similar to the use of the DJIA in the United States.

The **Financial Times Stock Exchange 100 (FTSE 100)** is a market value-weighted index of the 100 largest stocks that trade on the London Stock Exchange (http://www.londonstockexchange.com). The CAC 40 is an index of stocks traded on the Euronext Paris (http://www.euronext .com/fr). The primary stock market index of Germany is the Xetra/DAX, which is based on the 30 most actively traded shares on the Deutsche Boerse (http://www.deutsche-boerse.com).

The **Hang Seng Index** is a widely followed index of Hong Kong's stock market. The index currently consists of 33 stocks representative of the market. These stocks represent approximately 70 percent of the total stock market capitalization of the Stock Exchange of Hong Kong (http://www. hkse.com.hk).

Recent Developments

Recently, changes in technology have revolutionized the way the stock markets work. The emergence of the Internet has led to a number of new institutions and services, such as online brokers, online road shows, and online delivery of securities research. Low-cost online trading has attracted millions of investors. More than 60 million Americans now own stocks, and many of them made their first stock purchase after online trading became a national phenomenon in the mid- and late-1990s. Other advances in technology have allowed buyers and sellers to meet and negotiate prices directly without the use of a broker. Many of these changes have increased the speed of transaction handling.

Foreign Securities

The major U.S. stock markets—the NYSE, AMEX, and Nasdaq—list hundreds of foreign stocks. Foreign stocks can trade in the United States in the form of **American depositary receipts (ADRs)**, which are certificates representing shares of foreign companies traded in the United States. A broker creates these receipts when he or she purchases shares of a foreign company in its local stock market and deposits these shares with a local custodian in the foreign country. The U.S. depositary bank then issues depositary receipts for trading in the United States. ADRs allow U.S. investors to invest in foreign firms without the problems of settling overseas trades or currency exchange. Investors trade ADRs in U.S. dollars, and receive dividends in U.S. dollars as well. Foreign companies must also register ADRs with the Securities and Exchange Commission. Chapter 12 provides a complete coverage of ADRs and other types of depositary receipts.

TRADING MECHANICS

Secondary markets such as the NYSE and Nasdaq not only allow investors to trade stocks at the current price at a moment's notice, but also allow them to put in a number of different types of orders that specify the buy or sell price. Investors can also borrow money to finance their purchases and to sell stocks they do not own. Regular trading hours are from 9:30 A.M. TO 4:00 P.M. During these hours, if the market experiences extreme volatilities, trading will be halted. Box Feature 11.2 provides details for when and how long trading is to be halted.

Brokers, Market Makers, and Specialists

A market needs several different types of individuals or institutions—brokers, market makers, and specialists—to facilitate the transactions in order to function smoothly. **Brokers** simply help others to complete transactions and earn a commission for their efforts. Unlike market makers and specialists, brokers do not put their own capital at risk by holding inventory of securities.

There are several types of brokers. Commission brokers are employees of a firm that holds a membership on an exchange. These brokers buy and sell for customers of the firm. When an order is placed with the firm, the firm may contact its commission broker on the floor of the exchange, who will then go to the appropriate post on the floor and buy or sell shares as instructed. **Floor brokers** are independent members of an exchange who act as brokers for other members. During busy times, a member firm may need the services of a floor broker to handle most of its orders.

MARKETS IN ACTION   NYSE Circuit Breakers

11.2

In response to the market breaks in October 1987 and October 1989, the New York Stock Exchange instituted several circuit breakers to reduce market volatility and promote investor confidence.

The circuit breakers work as follows. The trigger levels for a market-wide trading halt for various amounts of time are set at 10%, 20%, and 30% of the DJIA, calculated at the beginning of each calendar quarter, with each trigger value rounded to the nearest 50 points.

Under the rule, market trading would halt if the DJIA has dropped:

1. 10%: trading would be halted for one hour if it occurred before 2 P.M., and for 30 minutes if it occurred between 2 P.M. and 2:30 P.M., but would not halt trading at all after 2:30 P.M.
2. 20%: trading would be halted for two hours if it occurred before 1 P.M., for one hour if it occurred between 1 P.M. and 2 P.M., and close the market for the rest of the day after 2 P.M.
3. 30%: at any time, trading would be halted for the remainder of the day.

Source: New York Stock Exchange (http://www.nyse.com).

Market makers play a more active role in the smooth functioning of the market by ensuring that a buyer exists for those who wish to sell and vice versa. Market makers use their own capital to purchase an inventory of the securities for which they are market makers. With this inventory of securities, the market maker is in a position to provide liquidity to the market by purchasing from sellers and selling to buyers. Market makers exist in both auction markets such as the NYSE and in OTC markets.

On exchanges such as the NYSE, market makers also serve as specialists. **Specialists** differ from market makers in that specialists maintain a fair and orderly market. Unlike market makers, who do not have to undertake a transaction, specialists are under obligation to buy from sellers when other buyers cannot be found, and to sell to buyers when there is a shortage of sellers. During periods of market turmoil, such as the October 19, 1987, stock market crash, or when a specialist's stock is subject to a takeover rumor, the specialist may need to take detrimental positions in a security, simply to provide liquidity to the market. These positions can cause the specialist's firm to lose substantial sums of money in a very short period of time. Specialists have an incentive to perform their job well because they are subject to a quarterly rating system used by the NYSE. This system, which allows customers and floor brokers to rate the ability of specialists to create and maintain a continuous liquid market for their stocks, plays an important role in determining new stock allocations by the NYSE.

One valuable piece of information held by a specialist is the limit-order book, which contains limit orders (orders specifying a particular buy or sell price) placed by brokers. This information is valuable because it allows the specialist to know what traders think. Even though this information may give the specialists an advantage over other market participants, they cannot use this information to trade ahead of clients, a practice known as front running.

Specialists earn their income by providing both the broker function (helping others to complete transactions) and the dealer function (buying and selling from their own inventory). For an actively traded stock, the specialist has little need to act as a dealer and therefore derives most of his or her income from the broker function. For stocks that have low trading volume and high price volatility, the specialists will need to provide more of the dealer function and therefore earn most of their income from the bid-asked spread. A specialist can deal in more than one stock, but there will only be one specialist per stock. In general, specialists balance the risks of market making by specializing in some high-volume, low-risk stocks and some higher risk securities.

Types of Orders

Once investors have decided what to purchase or sell, they must decide what price they want to accept. Investors who will accept the current price offered in the market can use a market order. With a **market order**, the investor instructs the broker to buy or sell at the best available price in the market. If the investor wishes to buy or sell only at a certain price, a **limit order** specifying that price can be placed with a broker. Once the price reaches the limit, the order must be filled at the limit price or a better price. For example, if an investor places a buy limit order at $40, the stock must be purchased at a price of $40 or less. When using a limit order, the investor needs to specify how long the order is in effect and how the transaction should be handled. An investor can specify that the limit order be transacted immediately, "fill or kill." The order can also be good for part of the day or the full day, or it can be an open-ended order that is good until canceled.

An investor can also use several other types of orders. With a **stop loss order**, the investor directs that a stock should be sold if the price drops to a given level. Once the stock reaches that price, the stop loss order becomes a market order; this means that if the price falls rapidly, the investor may receive a lower price than is given in the stop loss order. For example, if an investor enters a stop loss order to sell at $40, the sell price could be lower than $40 if the price falls rapidly. When using a stop loss order or a limit order for protection, the investor should be aware of the differences. In the case of a limit order, the transaction price must be at the limit price or better. Therefore, in a market where the price of the stock falls rapidly, a sell limit order may never be executed if the price drops quickly through the limit price. With a stop loss order, however, when the stock reaches the set price, the order becomes a market order and will be executed at the best available price in the market at that time.

Margin Transactions

An investor can either pay for a securities purchase in cash or buy on margin. Buying on margin means that the investor borrows some of the cost of the stock and uses the stock as collateral for the loan. Not all securities can be purchased on margin. The Federal Reserve Board (the Fed) determines which securities meet eligibility for margin purchases. In general, all securities listed on national exchanges and OTC securities that the Fed has approved are marginable. Even when the Fed has determined that a security is marginable, a brokerage house may choose not to allow an investor to purchase a security on margin. The Fed also sets margin requirements. Brokerage houses must meet the requirements, but often impose stricter borrowing limits on their customers.

Buying on margin has the effect of leveraging the purchase; that is, the rate of return (both positive and negative) on the margin transaction will be greater than on a cash purchase. For example, current margin requirements are 50 percent, which means that an investor can borrow up to 50 percent of the value of the stock. Thus, to purchase $20,000 of stock, the investor needs $10,000 in cash and can borrow the rest. By borrowing $10,000 to purchase $20,000 in stock, the investor will achieve a rate of return on his money that is twice that of a cash purchase. For example, if the stock price rises by 5 percent, then the investor will realize a 10 percent return. If the stock price falls by 5 percent, the investor will realize a 10 percent loss. This is the leverage effect. In this case, the leverage factor is 2; that is, returns are twice that of a cash purchase. Table 11.4 shows an example of different returns for different levels of margin.

TABLE 11.4	Returns and Margin		
	CASH PURCHASE (100% MARGIN)	**BORROW 25% (75% MARGIN)**	**BORROW 50% (50% MARGIN)**
Number of shares at $100	200	200	200
Cost of investment	$20,000	$20,000	$20,000
Less borrowing	0	5,000	10,000
Equity	$20,000	$15,000	$10,000
Return if stock price rises to $120/share			
Value of stock	$24,000	$24,000	$24,000
Less cost	20,000	20,000	20,000
Capital gains	$4,000	$4,000	$4,000
Return on equity	(4,000/20,000) = 20%	(4,000/15,000) = 26.67%	(4,000/10,000) = 40%
Return if stock price falls to $70/share			
Value of stock	$14,000	$14,000	$14,000
Less cost	20,000	20,000	20,000
Capital loss	−$6,000	−$6,000	−$6,000
Return on equity	(−6,000/20,000) = −30%	(−6,000/15,000) = −40%	(−6,000/10,000) = −60%

Another important concept relating to margin is the investor's equity. Assume that an investor has purchased with **initial margin**, which is the amount an investor must put up in cash to purchase a security. If the price of the security falls, the investor's equity will fall, and the investor may receive a margin call from his or her broker, with a notification that the investor must place additional funds in the account. The amount that one must add to bring the equity account back to the initial margin level is the **variation margin**. If the customer elects not to place the necessary funds into the account, the brokerage house can sell some of the security until the margin requirement is met.

If the price of the security falls, but not sufficiently to require a margin call, the account becomes a restricted account. To purchase additional stocks, the investor will have to put up initial margin for the new purchase. If the seller sells shares in a restricted account, the investor can withdraw only 50 percent of the proceeds.

If the price of the stock purchased on margin rises, however, the increased value leads to excess equity. The investor can either withdraw this Reg T excess, as some call it, or use it to buy additional securities without putting up additional cash.

Short Selling

Investors who think that a particular stock's price will probably fall can engage in a **short sale** and sell stock that they do not own. In a short sale, the investor instructs the broker to sell short, for example, 500 shares of IBM stock at $100. Because the investor does not own the stock, the broker must borrow the shares from another investor. The investor must eventually replace the borrowed shares, but if the price declines, the investor can purchase the replacement shares at the lower price, thereby earning a profit. To ensure that short sales do not cause market prices to fall, short sales can be made only on an uptick trade. An uptick trade means that the last transaction was higher than the previous one. Short sales can also be made when the last trade results in an unchanged price if the previous trade was at a higher price. This is referred to as a zero uptick. Although short selling might seem to be a desirable strategy, especially in bear market, investors should consider several factors before engaging in short sales. One factor is the role dividends play in a short sale. The short seller has responsibility for any dividends that the lender of the stock would have received. Second, short sellers are subject to margin requirements. The short seller must post the same margin as an investor who purchased the stock. Finally, unlike the purchase of a security, where the amount paid for the stock is the limit of potential loss, there is no limit to the potential loss in a short sale. This makes short selling extremely risky.

Off-Exchange Trading and Electronic Communications Networks

In addition to trading on the exchanges, exchange-listed stocks may also trade over the counter in the third market. This market is popular because its trading hours are not fixed. Furthermore, many institutions have dispensed with brokers and exchanges altogether for transactions in exchange-listed stocks. Trades of this type, in which the buyer and the seller deal directly with each other, take place in the fourth market. Electronic communications networks (ECNs) such as Instinet and Island facilitate most of these transactions. ECNs are computerized trade-matching systems that unite the best bid and offer prices. Instead of people executing trades over the computer, which is how Nasdaq works, or through a specialist on an exchange floor, as in the case of the NYSE and the AMEX, ECNs operate like a giant auction house.

TRANSACTIONS COSTS

Successful trading requires not only the ability to select securities that will outperform the market but also the ability to implement this strategy in a cost-effective manner. The difference in returns between a paper portfolio and an actual portfolio is the implementation shortfall. This shortfall occurs because investors face both direct and hidden costs when implementing their portfolio strategy. These costs have made execution techniques an important part of investment returns.

Direct Costs of Trading

When investors buy or sell securities, they incur one of two direct costs, depending on the market in which the transaction takes place. In an auction market, buyers and sellers meet to negotiate a price, and investors use brokers to help complete the transaction. Thus, the direct cost is the commission paid to the broker for finding the other end of the transaction. In a dealer market, where dealers or market makers stand ready to buy or sell securities from their own accounts, the direct cost to the investor is the bid-asked spread, or the difference between the price at which a dealer sells a security and the price at which the dealer buys it. A number of factors determine the size of the bid-asked spread, including the trading volume, the security's price volatility, and the number of other dealers trading this security. The greater the trading volume in a security, the narrower the bid-asked spread, because dealers will have an easier time managing their inventories. Likewise, lower price volatility should lead to lower inventory risk and should therefore narrow the spread.

Hidden Costs

Most people view the costs of trading as simply the direct costs of the transaction, but the hidden costs are often much more significant. In addition to the direct costs of trading, trading costs have three other components:

- **Impact cost** is the cost of buying liquidity. Impact cost can be measured by looking at the change in price between the time of placement of an order to a broker and the time of execution of the trade.

- **Timing cost** refers to the costs incurred when an entire order is too large to be presented to the market for a single execution. In that case, the buyer or the seller parcels out smaller orders over time, and the transaction may be completed over a number of days. During that time, the price may move away from the target price. Timing cost can be thought of as the cost of seeking liquidity.

- **Opportunity cost** is the cost of not executing a trade. These costs can occur for a number of reasons, including movements in price away from the target range. Opportunity costs are especially hard to measure because the portfolio's actual performance does not reflect the gains or losses of the unpurchased securities.

All three of these costs cannot be directly observed and so are difficult to measure. In addition, note that tradeoff occurs between impact and timing costs. A trader can reduce impact costs on a large order by dividing it into smaller trades, but doing so can increase the timing costs.

Costs and Types of Trades

Different types of trading costs have different effects depending on the type of trader. **Information traders** attempt to profit by trading on information that the market doesn't know about. For information traders, time is extremely important, as they attempt to trade before the market incorporates the information into the security's price. Therefore, impact costs are relatively unimportant to the information trader who tries to acquire a position in the security before the information reaches the market. Information traders will choose to buy the security as long as the costs of executing the trade are less than the expected price movement due to the information.

Value traders trade because they believe there is a discrepancy between the market price and the equilibrium value. Value traders supply liquidity to the marketplace because they generally buy when the price falls and sell when the price rises; thus, they tend to have low hidden transactions costs.

Passive managers, who track some market indices, are somewhere between information and value traders. Because passive managers buy and sell securities simply to maintain the relationship between their portfolio and the chosen index, they neither supply nor buy liquidity from the market.

In general, information traders have the highest transactions costs because of the necessity of executing trades quickly. These costs can reduce the returns to an information strategy. Value investors, on the other hand, tend to buy out-of-favor securities and thus generally have lower impact costs. Finally, the cost of passive management tends to fall between the costs of information investing and value investing.

FUNDAMENTAL ANALYSIS

Investment management styles can basically be classified as active or passive. Passive managers seek to replicate the returns of some index, such as the S&P 500. Active managers seek to add value to a portfolio by selecting securities that will outperform the market or by adjusting the composition of the portfolio based on their forecasts of the overall direction of the market. In general, active managers can be classified by the type of analysis they perform—fundamental or technical. **Fundamental analysis** examines financial statements and economic fundamentals to determine the value of a security and its growth prospects. Technical analysis, which the next section covers, identifies patterns in a security's price and volume. Technical analysts believe that trends can be identified and that these trends will tend to persist.

Types of Fundamental Analysts and Investors

Analysts who use fundamental analysis may take either a top-down or a bottom-up approach. The top-down approach begins with an analysis of the aggregate economy. The analyst uses this information to determine which industries will prosper given the general economic outlook. Finally, the analyst tries to identify which companies will be the top performers in the best industries by analyzing companies' financial statements to determine their overall financial health, growth prospects, and value of their stocks. With the bottom-up approach, the analyst begins at the company level and works up to the aggregate economy to make sure that the outlook for the economy will support the company and its industry. This section later covers the types of information used in economics, industry, and company analysis.

Whether analysts use a top-down or a bottom-up approach, they usually fall into one of two camps—value investors or growth investors. **Value investors** seek out companies that they believe the market has incorrectly undervalued. **Growth investors** care less about value and more about the growth rate of earnings. Growth investors do not only look for companies with accelerating earnings growth but also for firms whose growth exceeds the expectations of other investors. A third type of investor is a hybrid who looks for growth at a reasonable price (GARP). Keep in mind that all three types of investors care about both the price of a security and the rate at which earnings will grow. The difference lies in the emphasis. Value investors place greater emphasis on the price paid relative to the firm's earnings. That is, they look for firms that are inexpensive relative to their current level of earnings, not for firms with superior growth prospects. Growth investors, on the other hand, place a great deal of emphasis on the earnings growth relative to the market price. That is, growth investors will pay more for a company that they believe has superior growth prospects that the stock price does not reflect. GARP investors tend to take a more balanced view of the importance of earnings growth and stock price.

A fourth style of investing is that of sector rotation. Investors who follow a sector rotation strategy rotate the portfolio into different industry sectors in order to prosper from perceived mispricings. In addition to shifting between sectors, investors may shift between value and growth stocks, or between small and large capitalization stocks.

Finally, some investors attempt to outperform the market through the use of market timing. With this strategy, the investor adjusts the stock/bond mix or the risk of the portfolio based on market forecasts. When investors expect the market to rise, the investor increases the portfolio's percentage of stocks or shifts into higher risk stocks, which are likely to rise faster than the market. When investors expect the market to fall, the investor will reduce the percentage of stocks or decrease the risk of the portfolio. Many consider market timing as the most unreliable method for attempting to beat the market, because of the difficulty in predicting the overall market's movement.

Economic Analysis

As mentioned before, top-down investing begins with an analysis of the overall economy. Analysts use various types of economic information including the following:

- Interest rate forecasts: Interest rates determine the cost of doing business for firms; therefore, interest rate forecasts can be important in determining business expansion and profitability. In addition, interest rates determine the return on assets such as bonds, which serve as substitutes for stocks. Thus, an increase in interest rates makes bonds more attractive relative to stocks.

- Shifts in the yield curve: The yield curve represents a plot of the yield to maturity and the term to maturity for bonds with the same risk characteristics (usually Treasury securities). Shifts in the yield curve often indicate future economic activity. For example, an inverted (downward-sloping) yield curve has been a good predictor of recessions.

- GDP forecasts: The growth in Gross Domestic Product (GDP) represents the income of the aggregate economy and so can be important in determining demand for products.

- ° Leading economic indicators: Leading indicators are variables that change before GDP changes and therefore may provide some indication of the direction of the economy in the coming months. They include unemployment claims, new orders for plant and equipment, and changes in the money supply.

- ° Demographic shifts: Changes in the size and age of the population can have profound implications for investing. For example, an aging population may benefit businesses that cater to an older population, such as pharmaceutical companies.

Industry Analysis

Once an analyst has determined the overall outlook for the economy, analysis usually shifts to the industry level. Industry analysis looks at the profitability and future growth prospects of an industry in order to determine which industries will offer the best investment opportunities. Professor Michael Porter of the Harvard Business School has provided a framework for analyzing the profitability of an industry. Porter has identified five factors that determine industry competitiveness:

1. Bargaining power of buyers
2. Bargaining power of suppliers
3. Threat of new entrants
4. Threat of substitutes
5. Rivalry among existing competitors

These five competitive forces determine industry profitability because they influence the components of return on an investment. An industry will be more profitable when these factors are favorable. For example, an industry whose products have few substitutes and where entry into the industry is difficult will tend to be more profitable than industries that face less favorable conditions.

Another method of analyzing the future profitability of an industry is to look at the industry life cycle, or at the five phases an industry passes through over its lifetime:[2]

1. Pioneering and development
2. Rapid accelerating growth
3. Mature growth
4. Stabilization and market maturity
5. Deceleration of growth and decline

Industries in the first or second stage of the industry life cycle will tend to see improving profitability, whereas industries in the fourth or fifth stage will tend to see stable or even declining profitability. The industry life cycle can be dif-

---

[2]Of course, such industry analysis also considers external factors such as technology, government policies, regulation, and social and demographic factors.

ficult to use these days because many firms are in a number of lines of business, which may be in different phases of the industry life cycle. For example, Intel Corporation began as a manufacturer of computer memory. However, as the industry matured and the company began to lose business to foreign competition, it moved into the microprocessor industry, an industry that was not as mature.

Competitive Strategies for a Firm

In addition to his work on industry competitiveness, Porter has also identified generic strategies that a firm can pursue. According to Porter, a firm's success depends on how well it pursues its strategy. Firms that try to be all things to all people usually do not succeed. First, a firm can choose to be a cost leader or a differentiator. Firms that follow a cost strategy hope to attain greater profitability by achieving cost savings in excess of the discount offered to customers. Firms that follow a differentiation strategy hope to attain greater profitability by charging a price in excess of the added costs of differentiating their products. Finally, a firm must decide on its focus or the breadth of the market that it will target, using either cost leadership or differentiation. A firm can try to focus on a narrow segment of the market or target a broader segment.

According to Porter, a firm can pursue four basic strategies. A firm can choose to take a cost leadership role in a very broad market, as Wal-Mart has, or it can choose to follow a broad differentiation strategy, as Coca-Cola has. A firm can also choose to use cost leadership or differentiation in a fairly narrow market. A good example of a firm that follows a cost focus strategy is GEICO, the direct marketer of automobile insurance. Rather than target all drivers, GEICO chooses to focus only on "good drivers." An example of a firm that follows a differentiation focus strategy is Cray, the maker of supercomputers. Both GEICO and Cray have chosen to ignore much of the market and to target only a smaller, and hopefully more profitable, subset of the market.

Valuation Approaches for Fundamental Analysis

In addition to performing general economic, industry, and company analysis, an analyst needs to determine the value of the company's stock. Several different valuation methods can be used. Discounted cash flow models look at the present value of future cash flows, such as dividends or earnings, to determine the value of a firm's equity. Relative valuation approaches compare the "relative value" of a security against stocks in the same industry or against the industry average.

Discounted Cash Flow   Discounted cash flow models are based on the principle of present value. Under this approach, value is the present value of the expected future cash flows:

11.1
$$Value = \sum_{t=1}^{n} \frac{CF_t}{(1+r)^t},$$

where CF_t denotes the expected cash flow in period t, n denotes the life of the asset, and r denotes the discount rate that reflects the riskiness of the cash flow. For stocks, the cash flow will be dividends. The riskiness of the projected cash flows determines the discount rate, with lower rates for safer assets and higher rates for riskier ones. Analysts using discounted cash flow methodologies face two problems: (1) deciding which cash flows to use and how to forecast these cash flows, and (2) determining an appropriate discount rate.

Once the analyst has determined the appropriate cash flows to use in the valuation model, a discount rate needs to be determined, based on the general level of interest rates, the expected inflation rate, and the uncertainty of the future cash flows. Estimation of the discount rate usually entails adding a risk premium and the expected inflation rate to the risk-free rate of interest. The risk premium can be determined using historical data or a theoretical model such as the capital asset pricing model (discussed in the next section).

The basic discounted cash flow model assumes that the cash flows from the asset terminate at some given date. This makes the basic model perfectly suited for valuing fixed income assets that have a terminal life. When valuing the stock of a firm, however, there is no maturity date, and the cash flows (dividends, earnings) from the stock can change over time.

Two variations of the basic discounted cash flow model can be used. They differ in the assumption they make about the growth of the cash flow stream. The constant growth model assumes that the cash flow stream will grow at a constant rate indefinitely. The multistage growth model assumes that the cash flow will grow at an above-normal rate for a short, definable period of time, and then slow to its normal growth rate.

If one assumes the growth rate to be constant indefinitely, the present value of the stock is

11.2
$$P_0 = \frac{D_0(1 + g)}{k - g} = \frac{D_1}{k - g},$$

where P_0 is the value of the stock, D_0 is the current dividend, D_1 is the dividend to be paid next year, g is the expected dividend growth rate, and k is the discount rate. This model assumes that the company pays dividends, the dividend growth rate is constant, and the discount rate is larger than the dividend growth rate. For example, suppose that a company just paid a dividend of $0.60 per share, that the dividend payments will grow at an annual rate of 12 percent indefinitely, and that the discount rate is 16 percent. The value of the stock is therefore

11.3
$$P_0 = \frac{\$0.60(1 + 12\%)}{16\% - 12\%} = \$16.80.$$

For a mature company with stable growth, the constant growth model is appropriate. Small firms, however, often show initially high growth that is not sustainable forever. In such a case, a two-stage or more growth model is appropriate. Suppose a firm currently pays a dividend of $0.60 per share that is expected to grow by 30 percent for the next two years and then slow to 10 percent thereafter. If the discount rate is 15 percent, the market will value the stock at $18.31 per share:

11.4

$$P_0 = \frac{D_1}{(1 + k)} + \frac{D_2}{(1 + k)^2} + \frac{\dfrac{D_2(1 + g)}{(k - g)}}{(1 + k)^2}$$

$$P_0 = \frac{\$0.60(1 + 30\%)}{(1 + 15\%)} + \frac{\$0.60(1 + 30\%)^2}{(1 + 15\%)^2} +$$

$$\frac{\dfrac{\$0.60(1 + 30\%)^2(1 + 10\%)}{15\% - 10\%}}{(1 + 15\%)^2} = \$18.31.$$

The present value of all future dividends is $18.31. This means that the current stock value is $18.31 per share. The stock is undervalued if it trades at a level lower than the calculated value. Conversely, the stock is overpriced if it trades at a level higher than the value. The stock trades at its fair value if the current market price is $18.31 per share.

Capital Asset Pricing Model   The discount rates used in the dividend growth models come from the **capital asset pricing model (CAPM)**, which provides a linkage between the risk of a stock and the required rate of return that investors demand. Under the CAPM, the total risk of a stock consists of two components: systematic risk and company-specific risk. **Systematic risk**, which is not diversifiable, is a measure of the stock's risk relative to an average stock. Company-specific risk is diversifiable. The investors' required rate of return for a stock is the discount rate we used in the dividend growth models. According to the CAPM, the required rate of return for a stock can be estimated using the following formula:

11.5

$$E(R) = R_f + \beta(R_m - R_f),$$

where $E(R)$ denotes the required rate of return, R_f denotes the risk-free rate, R_m denotes the return on the market portfolio, and β (beta) is the systematic risk of the stock. Many use the return on the 90–day Treasury bills as the risk-free rate, and the S&P 500 return as a proxy for the market return. The graphic representation of the relationship between risk and return identified in the equation is called the **security market line**. As shown in Figure 11.1 (see p. 274), the required rate of return increases with the systematic risk of the stock. The security market line begins at R_f on the vertical axis, meaning that investors can expect to earn the risk free-rate if the stock has a beta of zero. Every point on the security market line implies that the rate of return investors expect to earn is the same as the required rate of return determined by the

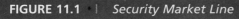

FIGURE 11.1 · | *Security Market Line*

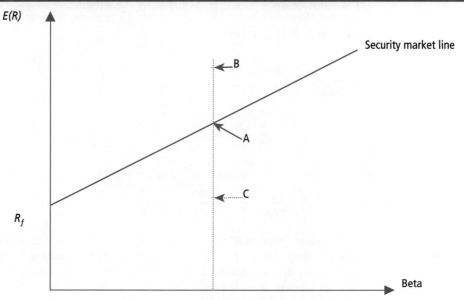

riskiness of the stock and market conditions. In other words, every security represented by a point (point A) on the security market line trades at its fair value. Any point (point B) that lies above the security market line implies an underpricing of the stock, as investors expect to earn a rate that is higher than the required rate of return. Conversely, any point (point C) below the security market line indicates an overpricing of the stock, because the rate of return investors expect to receive is lower than the required rate of return.

For example, suppose that the 90-day Treasury bills yield 5 percent and the S&P 500 index returns investors 11 percent annually. Assume that the beta of a stock is 1.2. The rate of return investors demand on this stock will be:

11.6 $$E(R) = 5\% + 1.2(11\% - 5\%) = 12.2\%.$$

This 12.2 percent is the discount rate that can be used to calculate the present value of future dividends in the dividend growth model.

Relative Valuation   The relative valuation approach compares a security with other similar securities. The assumption is that other firms in the industry have similar valuations. Relative valuation measures include the price-to-earnings ratio, price-to-book ratio, and price-to-sales ratio. For example, if the average firm in the industry has a price-to-earnings ratio of 25, then a firm with earnings of $4 per share will have a projected price of $100 per share. Many investors use the price-to-earnings ratio because it measures the cost of $1 of the company's earnings. Value investors often use this measure as they seek out companies selling for prices that are cheap relative to their earnings. Investors must be careful not to use a relative valuation measure such as the price-to-earnings ratio to compare firms in different industries. For example, industries that use a great deal of capital in manufacturing process, such as the automobile industry, have historically had lower price-to-earnings ratios than other industries. Table 11.5 provides a summary of the various relative value measures.

TECHNICAL ANALYSIS

Technical analysis assumes that prices tend to move in trends that persist for certain periods, and that these trends can be detected by charts. This approach is a dramatic departure from fundamental analysis or the efficient market hypothesis (discussed in the next section), which asserts that the market price fully reflects all relevant information. Many academicians equate technical analysis with mysticism. Conversely, technicians often criticize fundamentalists and market efficiency theorists as "divorced from the reality of the markets."

Charting is at the heart of technical analysis. Chartists often use the concepts of support and resistance to describe whether the market is a trading or a trending market. Prices generally move within the support-resistance range (trading range). Traders buy at support and sell at resistance. A breakout above a resistance point signals an upward trending market, while a breakout below a support level indicates that the market trends downward. As Figure 11.2 (see p. 276) shows, chartists would predict a bull market if the price breaks out of the resistance at point A. Conversely, the price will continue to move downward if it breaks out of support at point B. Volume is an essential supporting factor. A new high on heavy volume is bullish, while a new high on light trading volume may indicate a temporary move that is usually not sustainable.

There is no single magical technique for identifying trends and trading ranges. Technicians generally combine several methods. When they confirm one another, the signal is valid. When they contradict one another, it is better

TABLE 11.5	*Summary of Relative Valuation Approaches*	
Method	Advantages	Disadvantages
Price to earnings	Widely reported and easy to compute.	Cannot be used when a firm does not report earnings. Most P/E ratios use historical earnings rather than future earnings.
Price to book value	Can be used even if the firm does not report earnings.	Influenced by accounting methods. Cannot be used when a company records negative book value.
Price to sales	Can be computed for even the most troubled company.	Fails to recognize the cost side. It does not provide a measure of profitability.
Price to cash flow	Can be used for firms that have negative earnings but positive cash flows.	Fails to recognize amortization and depreciation.

FIGURE 11.2	*Support and Resistance*

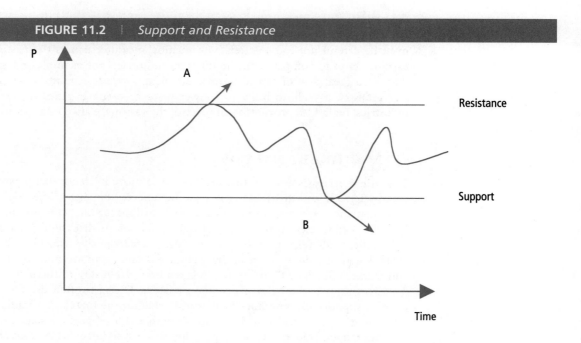

to pass up a trade. This section provides a brief description of several indicators frequently used by technicians.

Mutual Fund Cash Ratio

Mutual funds hold cash for several reasons. One obvious reason is for possible shareholder redemptions. Second, the money from new purchases of funds may not have been invested. Third, fund managers might build up their cash position if they have a bearish outlook. Some technicians interpret the mutual fund cash ratio (cash/assets) as a contrarian indicator. Technicians who use this approach consider mutual funds to be a proxy for the institutional investor group and assume mutual funds are generally wrong at market timing. Therefore, a rise in the cash ratio is a bullish sign and a decline in the cash ratio is a bearish signal.

Additionally, a high cash ratio can be considered a bullish sign because it means that mutual funds have potential buying power, which they will have to use for investment. Alternatively, a low cash ratio would mean that institutions have bought heavily and are left with little potential buying power.

Short Interest Ratio

Short interest is the total number of shares that have been shorted but not yet covered; that is, short sellers have not yet bought back the securities they sold short. Technicians compute a short interest ratio (SIR) as the outstanding short interest divided by the average daily trading volume on the exchange. For example, if the short interest totals 750 million shares and the average daily trading volume is 500 million shares, the SIR is 1.5. This means that the short interest equals about 1.5 day's trading volume. The SIR can also be computed for an individual stock.

Technicians interpret the SIR contrary to the short-seller's belief. Traders selling short expect stock prices to decline, so to these traders an increase in the SIR could be a bearish sign. On the contrary, technicians consider a high SIR bullish because it indicates potential demand for the security by those who have sold short and have not covered the sales. Recent experience suggests that technicians using this technique would be bullish if the SIR approaches 3.0 and bearish if it declines toward 2.0.

Options Ratio

The put/call ratio is also a contrarian indicator.[3] Technicians reason that a higher put/call ratio indicates a more pervasive bearish attitude, which to them is a bullish indicator. The ratio is typically less than 1 because investors tend to be relatively more bullish than bearish and avoid selling shorts or buying puts. A ratio approaching 0.70 indicates a buy signal. In contrast, a put/call ratio of 0.40 or lower is considered a bearish sign. A put/call reading of between 0.40 and 0.70 is neutral.

Odd-Lot Theory

The odd-lot technique focuses on the trading activities of small investors (an odd lot is less than 100 shares; small investors often trade odd lots because they cannot afford to purchase larger quantities). Most small investors do not engage in short selling except when they feel especially bearish. Technical analysts interpret heavy short selling by individuals as a signal that the market is close to a trough. Small investors get pessimistic only after a long decline in prices, just when the market is about to turn around.

Another assumption of the odd-lot behavior is that small investors are unsophisticated and frequently make mistakes in market reversals. Small investors often are successful but frequently miss key market turns. Specifically, the odd-lot investors are generally in the money as the market goes up. As the market continues upward, however, small investors get greedy and buy strongly just before the market reverses direction. Similarly, small investors are also assumed to be strong sellers right before the market bottoms out.

Investment Advisory Opinions

Technicians practicing this approach reason that most investment advisory services tend to be trend followers. Technicians develop a trading rule based on the number of bearish advisory recommendations as a percentage of the number of services expressing an opinion. A bearish sentiment index of 60 percent indicates a pervasive bearish attitude by advisory services; contrarians would

---

[3]A put option contract grants the buyer the right to sell to the seller of the contract the underlying security at the specified price anytime up to the expiration date. A call option contract grants the buyer the right to purchase the underlying security at the specified price anytime up to the expiration date.

consider this a bullish sign. Conversely, a decline of the bearish sentiment index to below 20 percent indicates a sell signal.

Short Sales by Specialists

Market participants watch short sales by exchange specialists closely because specialist operations consistently generate high returns. Specialists regularly engage in short selling as part of their market-making function, but they will be more aggressive in executing shorts when they feel strongly about the market direction.

The specialist short sale ratio is the ratio of short sales by specialists to the total short interest. Technicians view a decline of this ratio below 30 percent as a bullish sign because it means that specialists have attempted to minimize their participation in short selling. In contrast, a reading of 50 percent or higher is a bearish sign.

Moving Average

Moving average is very popular among technical practitioners. The **moving average (MA)** is easy to formulate and is less open to interpretation than other methods. The MA is the arithmetic average price of a security or an index over the past predetermined number of days. As each day passes, the practitioner drops the earliest day and includes the most recent one. Connecting each day's MA produces an MA line. The most important message of a simple MA is the direction of its slope. When it falls, it shows bearish sentiment. When it rises, it signals a bull market. When the market is bullish, prices rise above an MA. When the bears dominate, prices fall below an MA. Hence, a buy signal occurs when the security price crosses above the MA and continues to move upward. A sell signal occurs when the security price crosses below the MA and trends downward. There are no valid signals when the MA changes direction but the price does not cross the MA. When price fluctuates in a broad sideways pattern, the MA at times gives false signals. For this reason, technicians always use other indicators to confirm the direction of price.

Alternatively, a more complicated scheme involves the use of several MAs. For example, a technician might plot 4-week, 13-week, and 50-week MAs on the same graph. A buy signal comes when the shorter-term 4-week and 13-week averages cross the 50-week MA from below. A sell signal occurs when the two shorter averages fall through the 50-week MA. The two shorter MAs filter false signals.

Filter Trading Rule

According to the **filter trading technique**, when a security's price moves up by x percent above a previous low, it should be bought and held until the price falls by y percent below a previous high, at which time the trader should sell the stock. A trader using this rule believes that if the security's price rises x percent from some base, a positive breakout has occurred, and the price will continue to rise. In contrast, a y percent decline from some peak is a breakout on the downside. In this case, the trader will expect a downward trend and will sell any holdings and might also decide to sell short.

The specification of x percent and y percent will determine the frequency of trading. A small percentage specification will result in a large number of transactions. A large percentage specification might miss certain market movements. Studies have found that filter rules may be effective when the filter is small, in the range of 1 to 5 percent.

Breadth of Market

The breadth of market indicator measures the strength of advances over declines.[4] The advance/decline (A/D) line shows the difference between the number of advancing issues and the declining issues each day, ignoring the unchanged. For example, if 1,234 stocks traded higher for the day and 891 stocks declined, the A/D is +343. A trader creates a cumulative A/D line by adding each day's A/D to the previous day's total, and then compares the cumulative A/D with the DJIA. A rising cumulative A/D line supported by a higher DJIA signals a strengthening market. Conversely, a declining line coupled with a lower DJIA signals market weakness. Additionally, if a new high in the DJIA parallels a new high in the A/D line, then the rally has broad support. When the DJIA reaches a new high but the cumulative A/D line only goes up to a lower peak than the previous run, it shows few stocks have moved up and the bull run may come to an end. Similar analysis applies on a down market.

Momentum and Rate of Change

Momentum and rate of change (RoC) show when the trend speeds up or slows down. Momentum subtracts a past price from today's price, while RoC divides today's price by a past price. They can be expressed as

| 11.7 |

$$Momentum = P_t - P_{t-N}, \text{ and } RoC = \frac{P_t}{P_{t-N}},$$

where P_t is today's closing price and P_{t-N} is the close N days ago. For example, a 10-day momentum equals today's closing price minus the closing price 10 trading days ago. A 10-day RoC divides today's price by the closing price 10 days ago. A short time window is used to detect short-term market changes, while a long time window is used for trend following.

When momentum or RoC rises to a new high, it signals that stock prices are likely to rally higher. Conversely, when momentum or RoC falls to new low, this indicates lower prices. When prices rise but momentum or RoC declines, the market is near its top, and it is time to take profits or consider short selling. Reverse this approach during downtrends.

---

[4]Advances measure the number of securities that have increased in price and declines measure the number of securities that have declined in price.

Barron's Confidence Index

Barron's Confidence Index (BCI) is the ratio of Barron's average yield on 10 top-grade corporate bonds ($\gamma_{top\text{-}10}$) to the average yield on Dow Jones 40 bonds (γ_{DJ}). Specifically, the formula is

11.8

$$BCI = \frac{\gamma_{top-10}}{\gamma_{DJ}}.$$

The BCI measures the relative yield ratio between top-quality bonds and a large cross section of bonds. The BCI is always less than 1 because top-quality firms always pay lower interest rates. Technicians believe that the BCI gives a bullish signal when the index rises above 95 percent and gives a bearish signal when the index falls below 85 percent. The reasoning is that during periods of prosperity investors will invest more in lower-quality bonds for added yield. This causes a decrease in the average yield for the large cross section of bonds (relative to the average yield of the top-quality bonds), leading to an increase in the BCI value. Conversely, during periods when investors are pessimistic about the economic outlook, the BCI falls.

MARKET EFFICIENCY

The question of the efficiency of stock markets is important to stock valuation. If stock markets are efficient, the market price reflects all relevant information and provides the best estimate of value. The process of valuation becomes one of justifying the market price. If the stock markets are inefficient, the market price may deviate from the true value. In this case, stock valuation will aim at obtaining a reasonable estimate of the true value. Those who do valuation well will earn higher returns than other investors.

Efficient Market Defined

An **efficient market** is one in which the market price reflects all relevant information about the security. The market price is an unbiased estimate of the security's true value. Although the market price may deviate from the true value of the security, there is an equal chance that the price will be greater or less than the true value.

Key to the definition of market efficiency are certain assumptions about what information is available to investors and what information is reflected in prices. There are three levels of market efficiency, determined by the information reflected in the price. Under **weak-form efficiency**, current market prices fully reflect all past market prices and data. Thus, technical analysis that uses past prices and volumes would not be useful in finding undervalued or overvalued stocks. Under **semi-strong form efficiency**, the current market price reflects all public information. In other words, fundamental analysis is of no use. Finally, under **strong-form efficiency**, the market price reflects all information, public and private. If strong-form efficiency holds, no one will be able to consistently find mispriced securities. Even inside, private information will be of no use.

Conditions for Market Efficiency

Markets do not become efficient automatically. The actions of profit-maximizing investors—analyzing mountains of data and reports every day, and trading on deviations of the market price and the estimated true value—make the market efficient. Conditions that will create an efficient market include the following:

1. The availability of information to all market participants at the same time without costs
2. No transaction costs, taxes, or other barriers to trading
3. Market demand and supply determine the stock prices. Trading by any individual trader does not impact the market price.
4. All participants pursuing profit maximization.

Clearly, all four conditions are not strictly true in the real world. Information is not free and is generally available to corporate insiders at an earlier time than to others. Second, there are transactions costs and trading barriers. Yet those are relatively minor and would not lead to major price distortions today. Third, most investors do not affect the market price, but some do. Thus, basic assumptions are not strictly true in the real world, and therefore a distinction exists between a perfectly efficient and an economically efficient market. A perfectly efficient market is one in which prices always reflect all known information and prices adjust instantaneously to new information. In an economically efficient market, prices might not adjust to new information right away, but over the long run, speculative profits cannot be earned after factoring in transactions costs.

An efficient market is a self-correcting mechanism. Profit-maximizing investors constantly seek out ways of beating the market and thus make it efficient. Yet, if investors believed wholeheartedly in the efficiency of the market, they would stop looking for inefficiencies. That would lead to the market becoming inefficient again. Inefficiencies appear regularly but disappear quickly as investors find them and trade on them.

Implications of Market Efficiency

Asset allocation and security selection are two important parts of the investment process. If the financial markets are efficient, asset allocation is still important because investing money in various asset classes will influence the overall risk and return relationship. If the markets are efficient, however, then security selection is less important. Many investors who buy and sell stocks do so under the assumption that the stocks they buy are worth more than the price they pay, while the stocks they sell are worth less than the selling price. But if the markets are efficient, then trading in an attempt to outperform the market will effectively be a game of chance rather than one of skill. In an efficient market, investors are better off buying a diversified portfolio and following a passive investment strategy.

CONCLUDING SUMMARY

The aim of this chapter has been to provide students with a reference to all major aspects of the stock market. Issuance of new stocks occurs in the so-called primary market, in which investment banks purchase the whole block of a new security and resell it to institutional and individual investors.

Once the stock is listed on an exchange, trading in the secondary market begins. Investors can use several types of orders to execute trades. Investors can also borrow from the brokerage firm to leverage transactions. Such use of margin is subject to the requirements on initial margin and maintenance margin. Investors base their trades on certain valuation techniques, including fundamental analysis, technical analysis, and the efficient market hypothesis. Fundamental analysts study the economy, the industry, and the earning potentials of the company to value the stock. Technicians, on the other hand, examine the past trading volumes and prices to predict the future trend. Under the efficient market hypothesis, the stock price reflects all relevant information about the company, and therefore it is not possible to consistently spot mispriced securities.

Key Terms

American depositary receipt (ADR) 261
Barron's Confidence Index (BCI) 280
broker 262
capital asset pricing model (CAPM) 273
Dow Jones Industrial Average (DJIA) 259
efficient market 280
filter trading technique 278
Financial Times Stock Exchange 100 (FTSE 100) 261
floor broker 262
fundamental analysis 268
growth investor 268
Hang Seng Index 261
impact cost 267
information trader 267
initial margin 265
limit order 263
market maker 263
market order 263

moving average (MA) 278
Nasdaq Composite 260
opportunity cost 267
over-the-counter (OTC) 257
primary market 256
S&P 500 Index 260
secondary market 256
security market line 273
semi-strong form efficiency 280
short interest 276
short sale 265
specialist 263
strong-form efficiency 280
stop loss order 264
systematic risk 273
technical analysis 275
timing cost 267
value investor 268
value trader 268
variation margin 265
weak-form efficiency 280
Wilshire 5000 261

Review Questions

1. Describe the main differences between trades over the electronic communications networks and conventional broker-assisted trades.

2. What are the primary functions of a specialist?

3. In addition to commissions, what are the other components of transactions costs?

4. Suppose that the 90-day Treasury bills yield 6 percent and the return on the market portfolio as represented by the S&P 500 index is at 12 percent. An investor purchases a stock that has a beta value of 1.5 and expects to earn a return of 14 percent from the stock in one year. Is this a good buy? Explain.

5. Suppose the stock mentioned in the previous question just paid an annual dividend of 60 cents per share. Investors expect dividends to grow at a rate of 10 percent a year indefinitely. What is the value of the stock according to the constant dividend growth model?

6. What are the main assumptions required of the constant growth model?

7. If you believe that all market participants trade on the filter trading technique, how can you profit from it? Explain.

8. Discuss your investment strategies if you believe in the efficient market hypothesis.

9. Some market participants frequently use the price-to-earnings ratio to determine the overpricing or underpricing of a stock. Indicate when it is appropriate to use this approach.

10. What does value investing mean?

Select Bibliography

Baird, R., and C. McBurney. *Electronic Day Trading to Win*. New York: John Wiley & Sons, 1999.

Damodaran, A. *The Dark Side of Valuation*. New York: Financial Times Prentice Hall, 2001.

English, J. *Applied Equity Analysis: Stock Valuation Techniques for Wall Street Professionals*. New York: McGraw-Hill, 2000.

Grandmont-Gariboldi, N., and L. Soenen. "On the significance of the incremental returns from hedging international portfolios." *Emerging Markets Review* (1)3, pp. 271–286.

Hooke, J. C. *Security Analysis on Wall Street*. New York: John Wiley & Sons, 1998.

Liaw, K. T. *The Business of Investment Banking*. New York: John Wiley & Sons, 1999.

Lo, A. W., H. Mamaysky, and J. Wang. "Foundations of technical analysis: Computational algorisms, statistical inference, and empirical implementation." *Journal of Finance* 55(n4), 2000, pp. 1705–1765.

Penman, S. H. *Financial Statement Analysis and Security Valuation*. New York: McGraw-Hill, 2000.

Porter, M. E. *Competitive Advantage: Creating and Sustaining Superior Performance*. New York: Free Press, 1985.

Schwager, J. D. *Stock Market Wizards: Interviews with America's Top Stock Traders*. New York: Harper Business, 2001.

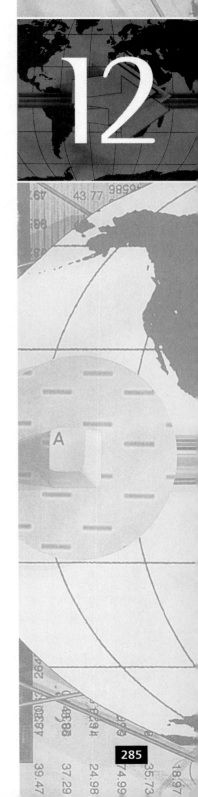

Depositary Receipts Markets

With the decline in the value of U.S. stocks since 2000, Americans have increasingly shown more interest in the benefits of diversification, including global diversification. Investing directly in global stocks can be difficult, however. Investors will likely have to pay taxes to foreign governments, will face foreign exchange risk, and may encounter less stringent accounting standards. Another problem is simply the mechanical difficulty of making trades in countries whose market hours do not correspond to those in the United States. Market hours in Europe overlap only partly with the U.S. trading day, and Asian hours do not overlap at all. As a result, Americans seeking exposure to foreign stocks increasingly turn to American depositary receipts (ADRs), which present an efficient, cost-effective, and liquid way to make specific foreign investments. ADRs—quoted in U.S. dollars with dividends paid in the same—can be purchased through any U.S. broker.

The objectives of this chapter are to provide an understanding of:
- The mechanics of establishing and maintaining unsponsored and sponsored ADR programs.
- Basic types of ADR programs.
- . U.S. securities regulations governing the listing and trading of ADRs.
- Advantages of ADRs to investors and issuers.
- The use of ADRs in acquisitions and privatizations.
- International securities in London.
- The euro depositary receipts (euroDR) market.

MARKET OVERVIEW

A depositary receipt is a negotiable certificate that represents ownership of shares in a foreign corporation. Depositary receipts traded in the United States are American depositary receipts (ADRs). Each ADR represents a specific number of underlying shares deposited at a local custodian in the issuer's home market.

Although ADRs are the most common type of depositary instruments, there are several other types as well. Global depositary receipts (GDRs) differ from ADRs in that their offerings take place in two or more markets outside the issuer's home country. Since the advent of the European Economic and Monetary Union (EMU), a market in euro depositary receipts (euroDRs) has developed. EuroDRs represent ownership of shares in a corporation based in a country outside the EMU. In addition, in yet another example of the globalization of capital markets, Singapore depositary receipts (SDRs) enable non-Singaporean companies to establish a presence in Singapore. Although most depositary receipts involve ownership of equity, foreign companies have also issued American depositary debentures (ADDs) evidencing ownership of debt instead of equity. Sweden's LM Ericsson was the first to do so in 1993. Most of these instruments will be examined in this chapter, although the main focus will be on ADRs.

The growth of ADRs over the last decade is a testament to their popularity. The total number of ADRs has increased from 836 in 1990 to 1,558 in 2001, but declined slightly to 1,436 in 2002. In 2000, the dollar value of transactions in exchange-traded ADRs exceeded $1 trillion for the first time. ADRs are also accounting for a growing percentage of U.S. investments in foreign equities. According to NYSE projections, U.S. investors will double the non-U.S. component of their equity portfolio from 5% to around 10% within the next few years.

STRUCTURE OF DEPOSITARY RECEIPTS FACILITIES

ADR programs are either unsponsored or sponsored. The foreign company doesn't support an unsponsored program, while the companies themselves establish sponsored programs. Sponsored and unsponsored programs for the same security cannot exist simultaneously because sponsored and unsponsored ADRs for the same foreign security might trade at different prices, creating confusion. The prices might be different in part because in a sponsored program the issuer reimburses the depositary for its expenses, whereas ADR holders bear such expenses in an unsponsored program.

Unsponsored Programs

A bank often initiates an **unsponsored ADR** program in response to investor demand. The issuer has no control over the program because there is typically no deposit agreement between the issuer and the depositary bank.

Registration of the underlying shares is not a requirement, but the ADRs must be registered with the Securities and Exchange Commission (SEC). The **depositary bank** and the issuer together submit an application to the SEC under Rule 12g3-2(b) seeking exemption from the full reporting requirements (the next section discusses eligibility for exemption).

Upon receipt of SEC approval, the depositary bank files Form F-6, which is a limited disclosure registration statement. The foreign issuer is not a signatory to the document and generally has no obligation or liability in connection with the registration of the ADRs. Once approved, the unsponsored ADRs can be traded only in the over-the-counter market. The SEC requires that material public information in the issuer's home country be supplied to the commission and made available to U.S. investors. The depositary will mail the issuer's annual reports and certain public information to U.S. investors upon request. The SEC does not require this material to be translated into English or to be adjusted for differences between the accounting standards used and the United States's generally accepted accounting principles (GAAP).

Unsponsored programs offer several advantages to the issuers. They provide an inexpensive and simple way of expanding the investor base in the United States. The SEC compliance and reporting requirements are minimal. Other depositary banks can duplicate an unsponsored program by filing a Form F-6 with the SEC without the consent of the issuer. Also, an unsponsored program can be converted to a sponsored facility. To do so, the issuer "buys out" the unsponsored facility by contacting the depositary bank of the unsponsored program, having it exchange its ADRs for the new sponsored ADRs, and paying the cash-out fee to the depositary.

Sponsored Programs

To establish a **sponsored ADR** program, the issuer usually selects a team consisting of lawyers, accountants, investment bankers, and investor relationships firms (see Box 12.1, p. 288). The issuer also chooses a depositary bank to implement and manage the ADR program on an ongoing basis. Major depositary banks include Bank of New York (**http://www.bankofny.com**), Morgan Guaranty (**http://www.jpmorgan.com**), and Citibank (**http://www.citibank.com**). The issuer works with the depositary bank to select a custodian to safe keep the underlying shares in the issuer's home market. The issuer, the depositary bank, and—in most cases—the ADR holders enter into a **deposit agreement** that sets forth the terms of the program. Based on the contract, the depositary bank performs the specified services on behalf of the issuer and investors.

The creation of ADRs comes about once the depositary's custodian in the issuer's home market receives the deposit of the underlying shares. The depositary then issues depositary receipts to investors. For example, suppose that an investor wishes to purchase new ADRs. The investor's U.S. broker contacts a foreign broker to purchase shares in the foreign corporation's local market. The foreign broker then deposits the purchased shares at a local custodian. The

MARKETS IN ACTION   ADR Participants

12.1

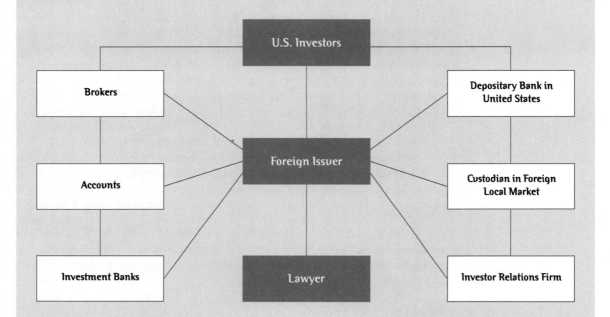

Foreign Issuer
° Determine its objectives
° Appoint U.S. depositary bank, lawyers, investment bank, and investor relations firm
° Determine program type
° Obtain approval from Board of Directors, shareholders, and regulators
° Provide financial information to accountants
° Develop investor relations plan

U.S. Depositary Bank
° Advise on ADR structure
° Appoint custodian
° Assist with ADR registration requirements
° Coordinate with lawyers, accountants, and investment bankers to ensure the completion of all program implementation steps
° Prepare and issue depositary receipts

° Enlist market makers
° Send ADR program announcement to brokers and traders

Brokers
° Execute and settle trades

Custodian
° Receive and safe keep underlying shares
° Confirm deposit of underlying shares
° Communicate with U.S. depositary bank on corporate actions and related issues
° Transmit dividend payments

Investor Relations Firm
° Develop a plan to promote the ADR program
° Help in road show
° Place tombstone advertisement announcing program establishment

MARKETS IN ACTION   ADR Participants (continued)

Lawyers
- Advise on type of DR structure
- Draft and negotiate deposit agreement
- File appropriate registration statements or establish exemptions with SEC
- File registration statements to list on U.S. exchanges (Levels II and III)

Investment Bankers
- Advise on type of ADR structure
- Obtain CUSIP number
- Obtain DTC, Euroclear, Clearstream, and PORTAL eligibility as needed
- Arrange and conduct road show
- Line up market makers
- Price and launch securities

Accountants
- Prepare financial statements in accordance with (or reconciled to) U.S. Generally Accepted Accounting Principles (GAAP) for Exchange Act registered securities

Investors
- Evaluate investment objectives and decide on asset allocation
- Select an ADR if it meets his/her investment objectives

Sources: Bank of New York (2003), Citigroup (2001), and Bankers Trust (1997).

custodian instructs the depositary bank to issue ADRs evidencing ownership of the deposited shares. The depositary bank then delivers the ADRs to the broker who initiated the trade, and the broker delivers the ADRs to the customer's account. The ADRs have been created. Upon establishment of the ADR program, the depositary acts as the liaison between the foreign issuer and U.S. investors.

The parties involved reverse the steps in order to cancel the ADR program. The broker receives ADRs from customers and delivers them to the depositary for cancellation. The depositary instructs the local custodian to release the underlying shares to the local broker who purchased the shares.

An important step in establishing an ADR program, whether sponsored or unsponsored, is the determination of the ratio of underlying shares to the ADR. ADR shares are established as a multiple or a fraction of the underlying shares. There are several important considerations in setting the ratio. First, the issuer will want to conform to the price range of industry peers in the United States. Second, each exchange has average price ranges for listed shares. In addition, some institutional and individual investors also have preferences for shares traded in certain ranges. Upon setting the ratio, the price of the ADRs should reflect the dollar-equivalent price of the shares in the home market. For example, suppose the ratio has been set at 1 to 1. Assume the price of the underlying shares in the home market is $15.25, and the ADR sells for $15.75. Arbitrageurs will buy shares and issue ADRs until the arbitrage profits disappear. In contrast, if the underlying shares trade at a higher level, arbitrageurs will buy the ADRs, cancel them, and sell the underlying shares in the local foreign market.

Although all sponsored programs follow the general form just described, a foreign company can issue several different types of sponsored ADRs—Level I, Level II, Level III, or Rule 144A. The choice depends on the needs and wishes of the issuer.

Level-I ADRs   Level-I ADRs are the easiest and least expensive way for a foreign company to gauge interest in its securities and to begin building a presence in the United States. The issuer must obtain a Rule 12g3-2(b) exemption from the SEC and must also file a Form F-6 and sign a deposit agreement. The issuer has greater control over a Level-I program than over an unsponsored program because the issuer and one exclusive depositary bank execute a deposit agreement. The agreement defines the responsibilities of the depositary, including its responsibilities for responding to investor inquiries, maintaining stockholder records, and mailing annual reports and other materials to shareholders.

Exchanges do not list Level-I ADRs, which trade in the over-the-counter market. Quotes are available in the pink sheets, and brokers wishing to trade in these securities can contact the listed market makers in the particular security.[1] The main advantages of these ADRs are their low cost and their ability to coexist with a Rule 144A ADR facility (called a **side-by-side program**). A side-by-side program allows the foreign issuer to combine the benefits of a publicly traded program with the efficiency of a private offering as a capital-raising tool. Also, a Level-I program is easy to set up; one can be established in as little as nine weeks. It is relatively inexpensive to upgrade the program to Level-II or Level-III as well.

Level-II ADRs   Level-II ADRs, listed on one of the national exchanges, must comply with the SEC's full registration and reporting requirements. The issuer must file with the SEC a Form F-6 for registering the ADRs and a Form 20-F to meet the reporting requirements (financial statements must be partially reconciled to U.S. GAAP). Compliance allows the issuer to list its ADRs on the New York Stock Exchange, the American Stock Exchange, and the Nasdaq; each of which has its own reporting and disclosure requirements. Table 12.1 shows how the number and annual dollar volume of exchange-listed ADRs has grown since the 1990s.

Full registration and listing increase liquidity and marketability and enhance the issuer's name recognition in the United States. The issuer can also monitor the ownership of its shares in the United States. Because the issuer must comply with the rigorous SEC requirements, it is well-positioned to upgrade and make a public offering in the U.S. market. The issuer may be qualified to use a short-form registration statement if it has filed timely, periodic reports with the SEC for a specified time period.

---

[1]Since April 1, 1998, the OTC Bulletin Board has not been available for Level-I ADRs. For a Level-I ADR to be eligible for the OTC Bulletin Board, the issuer must register the securities underlying the ADRs with the SEC under Section 12 of the Securities and Exchange Act of 1934. The ADRs will then be eligible for real-time quotation on the same basis as U.S. equity securities included on the Bulletin Board.

				Annual Dollar Volume of
Year	Total Number of ADRs	Sponsored ADRs	Exchange-Listed ADRs	Exchange Listed ADRs ($ billions)

TABLE 12.1 | *ADR Programs*

Year	Total Number of ADRs	Sponsored ADRs	Exchange-Listed ADRs	Annual Dollar Volume of Exchange Listed ADRs ($ billions)
1990	836	352	176	75
1991	886	418	186	94
1992	924	481	215	125
1993	986	574	256	201
1994	1,124	745	317	248
1995	1,209	866	357	276
1996	1,301	992	426	341
1997	1,358	1,066	457	503
1998	1,415	1,138	505	563
1999	1,438	1,175	532	667
2000	1,534	1,287	608	1,185
2001	1,558	1,332	623	752
2002	1,436	1,250	553	550

Source: Bank of New York (http://www.bankofny.com). Data are obtained from "DR Market Statistics."

On the other hand, a Level-II program is more expensive and time-consuming to set up and maintain than a Level-I facility. Another disadvantage is that the SEC does not permit a public offering of ADRs under a Level-II program; thus, a foreign company cannot use Level-II to raise capital in the United States.

Level-III ADRs   Companies wanting to raise capital use a sponsored Level-III facility. **Level-III ADRs** are similar to those issued under Level-II. In both programs, the issuer initiates the program, signs a deposit agreement with one depositary bank, lists on one of the U.S. exchanges, and files Forms F-6 and 20-F with the SEC. The major difference is that a Level-III program allows the issuer to make a public offering. To do so, the issuer must file a Form F-1 (similar to Form S-1 for U.S. companies) to register the shares underlying the Level-III ADRs. The reporting requirements are more onerous for Level-III than for Level-I or Level-II programs. Financial statements must be fully reconciled to the U.S. GAAP. The costs can be substantial; they include listing, legal, accounting, investor relations, and road shows. Establishment of a Level-II or Level-III program usually takes fifteen weeks or more, depending on individual program specifics.

In summary, a Level-I facility allows a foreign issuer to enjoy the benefits of a publicly traded security. Companies wanting to list shares on a U.S. exchange use Level-II programs, and companies wishing to raise capital use Level-III. Each higher level of ADR program reflects additional SEC registration requirements and increases the visibility and attractiveness of the ADR to institutional and retail investors.

Rule 144A ADRs   As an alternative to Level-III programs, foreign companies can access the U.S. capital market by issuing ADRs under Rule 144A, called **Rule 144A ADRs**, to accredited investors, thereby avoiding SEC registration and reporting requirements. Under Rule 144A, there is no holding period restriction if one resells to a **qualified institutional buyer (QIBs)**, defined as an institution that owns and invests on a discretionary basis at least $100 million in securities of an unaffiliated entity. In the case of registered broker-dealers, the requirement is $10 million.

Through Rule 144A ADRs, foreign companies have access to the U.S. private placement market and may raise capital without conforming to the full burden of SEC registration and disclosure. Issuing Rule 144A ADRs is considerably less costly than initiating a Level-III program. Establishment can take as little as seven weeks. In addition, the National Association of Securities Dealers has established an electronic trading system for Rule 144A ADRs, called Private Offerings, Resales and Trading through Automated Linkages (PORTAL). This system provides a market for privately traded securities. The system is available to both investors and market makers. Essentially, it allows institutions to claim Rule 144A ADRs as liquid securities for regulatory purposes.

Rule 144A ADRs offer both advantages and disadvantages to issuers. Rule 144A ADRs do not have to conform to full reporting and registration requirements. They can be launched on their own or as part of a global offering. There are two disadvantages, however. First, Rule 144As cannot be created for a class of shares already listed on a U.S. exchange. In addition, they can be traded only among QIBs; consequently, the market certainly is not as liquid as the public equity market. Table 12.2 provides a summary of the different filings required of different ADR programs by the SEC.

TABLE 12.2	*ADR Filing Requirements and Trading*		
Type of ADRs	SEC Filing	Exchange Listing and Trading	Raising Capital
Unsponsored	Form F-6 12g3-2(b)	Over the counter	No
Sponsored			
Level-I	Form F-6 12g3-2(b)	Over the counter	No
Level-II	Form F-6 Form 20-F	NYSE, Amex, Nasdaq	No
Level-III	Form F-6 and Form F-1 Form 20-F	NYSE, Amex, Nasdaq	Yes
Rule 144A	N/A	Private placement market	Yes

Note: For reporting purposes, Level-II financial statements must be partially reconciled to U.S. GAAP, and Level-III financial reports must be fully reconciled to U.S. GAAP.

Global Depositary Receipts   A global depositary receipt (GDR) allows an issuer to raise capital through a global offering in two or more markets at the same time. Citibank offered the first GDRs in 1990 on behalf of South Korea's Samsung. GDRs can be issued in either the public or private market in the United States and other countries. Most GDRs include a U.S. tranche and an international tranche. The U.S. tranche is structured as either a Level-III ADR or as a private placement under Rule 144A. The international tranche is placed outside the United States pursuant to Regulation S. As explained in the next section, Regulation S provides conditions under which securities offered or sold to investors outside the United States may not be subject to SEC registration requirements. Regulation S GDRs may be converted to Level-I only after satisfaction of the distribution compliance period. The Luxembourg or London exchange generally lists GDRs placed in Europe. In London, quotes appear on London's SEAQ International.

A Note on Trading Foreign Ordinaries   Americans who wish to invest in foreign ordinaries—stocks in overseas companies that do not trade on U.S. markets—find that they are not easily accessible. Only a handful of options are open to U.S. investors. Merrill Lynch (**http://www.ml.com**) and Charles Schwab (**http://www.schwab.com**) provide clients such access online or through a broker. Intltrader (**http://www.intltrader.com**) provides online access to quotes and trading in overseas companies as well. Investors should be aware, though, that to minimize the risk posed by differing trading hours or thinly traded foreign ordinaries, market makers often widen their bid–asked spreads. They bid less to buy shares and ask more to sell them during off hours.

U.S. SECURITIES REGULATION OF DEPOSITARY RECEIPTS

As the previous section indicated, publicly traded ADRs must be registered with the SEC. If the ADRs represent new shares, the registration must cover both the ADRs and the newly issued shares. For securities offered overseas, Regulation S provides a safe harbor exemption.

Registration of ADRs for Outstanding Shares

When outstanding shares back the ADR, either an unsponsored or a sponsored program, the broker or the issuer uses Form F-6 to register the ADRs under the Securities Act of 1933.[2] The simplified registration procedure is available only where the issuer of the deposited shares has obtained an exemption under Rule 12g3-2(a) or (b). The general eligibility requirements for an exemption are as follows:

- The ADR holder can withdraw the deposited securities at any time subject only to the temporary delay caused by closing transfer books.
- The relevant fees, taxes, and similar charges have been paid.

---

[2]Appendix C lists the complete SEC Form F-6.

○   The issuer reports pursuant to requirements of Section 13(a) or 15(d) of the Securities Exchange Act of 1934, or the deposited shares have an exemption by Rule 12g3-2(b) unless the issuer concurrently files a registration statement on another form for the deposited securities.

Under Rule 12g3-2(a), a foreign issuer has an exemption from the reporting requirements of the Securities Exchange Act of 1934 if it does not have a class of equity securities held by at least 300 persons resident in the United States. This exemption is unlikely to be available if the ADR program is successful, however, so the issuer usually must satisfy the reporting requirements of Section 12(g) or qualify for an exemption under Rule 12g3-2(b). Under Rule 12g3-2(b), a foreign issuer receives an exemption if it meets the following requirements:

○   Its ADRs or underlying securities do not have a listing on a U.S. exchange or quoted on the Nasdaq.

○   It submits to the SEC certain information that was made available to its shareholders or to foreign government authorities in the foreign local market.

○   It provides the SEC the same information during each subsequent fiscal year.

The requirement that the ADR should be unlisted means that the exemption is available only for unsponsored and Level-I programs; it is unavailable for Level-II and Level-III programs.

Registration of ADRs for New Shares

When ADRs represent new shares (as in a Level-III program) or shares distributed by a statutory underwriter, both the ADRs and the deposited shares must be registered with the SEC.[3] As mentioned previously, Form F-6 is available only for the registration of ADRs. The underlying securities must be registered on Form F-1, F-2, or F-3. The forms differ primarily with respect to the amount of information that a foreign issuer does not have to disclose in full if the issuer has already provided the information or provides it through Form 20-F and any other 1934 act filings.[4] Unless the foreign issuer has shares registered or reports under the 1934 act, Form F-1 must be used.

Regulation S

Regulation S, which applies to GDRs, provides two types of safe harbor exemptions for securities offered overseas without registration. One is the issuer safe harbor, which addresses offers and sales by issuers, their affiliates, and securities professionals involved in the initial offerings of securities. The second is the resale safe harbor, which addresses resales by securities profes-

---

[3] A statutory underwriter is a person who took the securities from the foreign issuer with a view toward distribution, causing resale of the securities and possibly the original sale of securities by the issuer, which is in violation of sections 5 and 12(1) of the 1933 act.

[4] Appendix D includes the complete SEC Form 20-F.

sionals such as brokers. Two general conditions must be satisfied to take advantage of these safe harbors: (1) any offer or sale must be made in an offshore transaction, and (2) no direct selling efforts may be made in the United States.

Regulation S and Rule 144A are closely related (they are related, but not similar). The SEC has maintained the position that foreign issuers may undertake private placements in the United States (Rule 144A) at the same time they make an offshore Regulation S offering without violating that regulation's prohibition against U.S. direct selling efforts. Substantial care must nevertheless be taken to avoid spillover of such securities into the U.S. public markets.

In the 1990s, the SEC has identified abusive practices in offshore Regulation S securities transactions. Therefore, in 1998 the SEC adopted amendments to Regulation S to prevent further abuses of the rule, but also to allow continued reliance on Regulation S in legitimate offshore offerings. The amendments adopted include the following:

- The classification of equity securities placed offshore by U.S. issuers under Regulation S is that of restricted securities within the meaning of Rule 144, so resales are under restriction.

- The distribution compliance period (restricted period under Regulation S) for these securities is one year (lengthened from forty-one days).

- Issuers must change from Form 8-K reporting to quarterly reporting on Form 10-Q.

The SEC indicated that to avoid undue interference with offshore offering practices of foreign issuers, these amendments apply to equity securities of U.S. issuers, but not to the equity securities of foreign issuers.

ADVANTAGES OF DEPOSITARY RECEIPTS

The ADR market provides several distinct benefits for investors, brokers, market makers, and issuers. ADRs greatly simplify the trading of foreign equities. Without ADRs, a U.S. investor who wished to purchase a foreign security would have to find a broker with capabilities in the specific foreign market where the security trades. A single trade would involve multiple parties, currency concerns, and settlement delays.

Investors benefit in other ways as well. The depositary bank collects dividends, converts the currency, and issues prompt payments in U.S. dollars or additional ADRs in the case of a stock dividend. An ADR program also helps investors avoid the regulations of countries that prohibit physical delivery of shares overseas. ADRs, registered in the United States, have records to protect ownership rights. With book-entry systems, investors save because they do not have to pay fees for safekeeping and insurance of securities.

Restrictions exist that prevent many institutional investors from investing in securities not traded on a U.S. exchange; therefore, listed ADRs represent a way for them to add international exposure to their portfolios. Similarly, institutions that invest only in the United States because they have no custodian

TABLE 12.3	*Major ADR Investors*

Investor
Barclays Global Investors
Brandes Investment Partners
Capital Guardian Trust Company
Capital International, Inc.
Capital Research & Management
Fidelity Management & Research
Invesco Capital Management
J.P. Morgan Investment Management
Janus Capital Corporation
Lazard Asset Management
Merrill Lynch Asset Management
Putnam Investment Management
Smith Barney Investment Advisors
Scudder Kemper Investments
Templeton Investment Counsel
Wellington Management Company

Source: J.P. Morgan Chase (http://adr.com) and Citibank (http://wwss.citissb.com/adr_info/index.htm).

facilities or arrangements abroad can invest in ADRs. Table 12.3 lists major ADR investors.

Another significant advantage ADR holders have over holders of foreign shares is that information is more readily available. The Bank of New York publishes an ADR Index that tracks the performance of ADRs in the United States (**http://160.254.123.37/adr_index_landing.jsp**). In addition, there are four regional subindices: the Europe ADR Index, the Asia ADR Index, the Latin America ADR Index, and the Emerging Markets ADR Index. J.P. Morgan Chase also publishes detailed information about the ADR market, company, and industry data (**http://adr.com**).

Securities dealers and brokers find ADRs attractive as well. ADRs standardize widely varying securities practices. The simplification of processing has reduced settlement risk. Securities in ADR form are easily transferable, and automated book-entry systems for clearing are well-established. The T+3 settlement cycle minimizes losses from fails.[5] The depositary can also prerelease ADRs to help bridge timing differences in settlement cycles in different nations.[6] In a prerelease, the depositary with the knowledge that the trade of underlying shares has been executed issues an ADR before an overseas custodian receives a physical deposit of the underlying shares.

---

[5]Fails occur when delivery of the security and/or payment of funds are not completed on settlement date.

[6]A depositary bank can use the same prerelease mechanism to provide ADRs to brokers against cash collateral rather than the underlying shares. This will artificially inflate the number of ADRs outstanding in the United States.

For foreign companies, ADRs provide the most effective means of entering the U.S. market, the largest in the world. An ADR program provides a simple means of diversifying a company's shareholder base. It enhances the company's visibility and name recognition in the United States. As a result of global demand and trading, the program may increase liquidity and local share price. An ADR program can also be used to help build a stronger financial presence in the United States. Features such as dividend reinvestment plans help ensure a continual stream of investment into an issuer's program. As mentioned earlier, ADR ratios are often adjusted to ensure that an ADR trades in a comparable range with its peers in the U.S. market. In addition, ADRs provide an easy way for U.S. employees of non–U.S. companies to invest in their companies' employee stock purchase programs. These benefits have motivated foreign companies to launch ADRs in the United States. During the 1995–2000 period, ADR offerings raised more than $132 billion in capital. Companies from many countries including the United Kingdom, Australia, Japan, Hong Kong, Mexico, Brazil, France, the Netherlands, Germany, Russia, Chile, China, and Taiwan have issued ADRs in the United States. Table 12.4 lists the top ten issuers with the most actively traded ADRs in 2001.

ADRS IN ACQUISITIONS AND PRIVATIZATIONS

As we have noted throughout this text, consolidation and globalization are two trends affecting financial services. As part of these trends, several foreign companies have used their ADRs as an acquisition currency (see Table 12.5 for some examples, p. 298). Many of these acquirers had established ADR programs before the acquisition. Both listed (Level-II and Level-III) and Rule 144A ADRs may be used to fund an acquisition.

Using ADRs can be advantageous for an acquisition in several ways. First, an active ADR program provides a liquidity option and transparent pricing for

TABLE 12.4 | *Most Active ADR Programs by Dollar Volume in 2001*

Company	Country
Nokia Corporation	Finland
Royal Dutch Petroleum Company	Netherlands
BP plc	United Kingdom
Teva Pharmaceutical	Israel
Taiwan Semiconductor	Taiwan
Unilever	Netherlands
Vodaphone Group	United Kingdom
Telefonos de Mexico	Mexico
Elan Corporation	Ireland
Glaxo SmithKline	United Kingdom

Source: Bank of New York, *Depositary Receipts: 2001 Year-End Market Review.*

TABLE 12.5	Foreign Acquisitions Using ADRs as Acquisition Currency			
Year	U.S. Target	Foreign Acquirer	Country	Size ($ billions)
1998	Amoco	British Petroleum	United Kingdom	54.3
1998	Chrysler	Daimler-Benz	Germany	40.5
1998	DSC Communications	Alcatel Alsthom	France	5.1
1996	Providian (insurance)	Aegon NV	Netherlands	3.5
1997	Equitable of Iowa	ING Group	Netherlands	2.6
1996	Fresenius	Fresenius AG	Germany	2.2
1996	New World Communication	News Corporation	Australia	2.2
1996	Varity Corporation	Lucas plc	United Kingdom	2.0
1997	Heritage Media	News Corporation	Australia	1.4
1997	Dauphin Deposit	Allied Irish Bank	Ireland	1.3

Sources: Bank of New York, Citigroup, and *Wall Street Journal* (various issues).

investors. Second, these ADR exchanges are in the form of tax-free stock swaps. Thus, a stock swap merger or acquisition results in a pool of new ADR investors. Third, by using ADRs, the acquirers can avoid taking on additional debt, thereby preserving capital and enhancing financial flexibility. The eventual success of the merger may in part depend on an employee stock purchase plan that the ADR programs make available conveniently. A listed program could also offer the advantage of enabling employee plans that hold company shares to continue without "cashing out" the existing employees.

Another significant contribution of the depositary receipt market is the raising of funds for privatization programs. The number of privatizations using depositary receipts in their global offerings has steadily increased in recent years. Examples include:

○ Compania Anonima Nacional Telefonos de Venezuela raised $904 million.

○ Deutsche Telekom raised $1.1 billion.

○ Eni (an Italian oil and gas company) raised $678 million.

○ Russia's Gazprom raised $429 million.

○ Telefonica del Peru raised $918 million.

○ Egypt's Commercial International Bank raised $117 million.

INTERNATIONAL SECURITIES IN LONDON

More international companies choose to list securities on the London Stock Exchange than on any other exchange in the world. London is a liquid market; its huge investment capital and efficient dealing have attracted hundreds of companies from around the world.

To list on the London exchange, a company must meet the following:

° A three-year's trading record.
° A market valuation of more than £700,000.
° A minimum of 25 percent of its shares in public hands.
° Issuance of a prospectus that complies with the exchange's listing rules.

International securities trade on the electronic, screen-based quotation system, SEAQ International. There are about fifty registered international market makers displaying quotes for over 1,000 securities from thirty-six countries. These quotes are usually in the home currency of each country, and transactions settle through the home market or one of the international clearing systems.

Companies from countries around the world including Argentina, Brazil, Hungary, India, Poland, South Africa, South Korea, and Taiwan have issued depositary receipts in London.

THE EURODR MARKET

On January 4, 1999, the eleven first-round participating nations of the European Monetary Union (EMU) switched to the euro.[7] Greece joined in 2000. The euro's introduction has led to a dramatic acceleration in cross-border investment. The euroDR market has been established to facilitate this trend. A **euroDR** is a negotiable certificate evidencing ownership of ordinary shares in a corporation from a country outside the EMU. Each euroDR denotes euro depositary shares representing a specific number of underlying shares remaining on deposit in the issuer's home market. The euroDRs trade in euros. Zagrebacka Bank, Croatia's largest commercial bank issued the first euroDR listed on the London Stock Exchange in January 1999. Table 12.6 (see p. 300) compares the features of the euroDRs, GDRs, and listed ADRs.

The process of issuing euroDRs in the euroland is similar to that for ADRs in the United States. To issue a new euroDR, the European broker must contact a broker in the issuer's home market to purchase shares through the stock exchange in the local market. The broker in the issuer's home market deposits the shares with a local custodian; then the custodian instructs the depositary bank to issue euroDRs that represent ownership of the shares deposited. The depositary bank issues euroDRs and delivers them through the clearing agency to the broker who initiated the trade. The broker then delivers euroDRs to the customer's account. A euroDR has been created.

---

[7]Only European Union countries with sound monetary and fiscal policies are admitted to the EMU. The Maasstricht Treaty requires a low inflation rate, stable exchange rates, comparably low interest rates, and a sustainable level of government debt for participation in EMU.

TABLE 12.6 | *GDRs, EuroDRs, and Listed ADRs*

	GDRs	EuroDRs	Listed ADRs
Investment vehicle	Private placement	Public listing in EU	Public offering in United States
Investor base	Institutional investors in Europe and U.S. QIBs	All investors in EU	All investors in United States
Listing and trading	Traded over the counter between institutions	EU exchanges	U.S. exchanges
Currency	U.S. dollars	euro	U.S. dollars
Visibility	Limited in the EU	Broad exposure in euroland	Broad exposure in United States

The cancellation process is the opposite. The investor contacts the European broker and requests sale of the euroDRs. The broker may either sell in the secondary market or cancel the existing program. To cancel the existing euroDR facility, the broker delivers the euroDRs to the depositary bank for cancellation and instructs a broker in the issuer's local market to sell the underlying shares. Investors receive the proceeds of the sale. The euroDR program has been canceled.

CONCLUDING SUMMARY

ADRs are a cost-effective way for foreign companies to improve their visibility and raise capital in the United States. ADRs provide U.S. investors an additional venue to make specific foreign investments without the problem of differing settlement processes and securities custody.

There are several types of ADR programs. The foreign issuer does not initiate an unsponsored ADR facility, and typically there is no deposit agreement between the issuer and the depositary bank. ADRs issued by an unsponsored program cannot be traded on an exchange, but it is an inexpensive way of expanding the investor base in the United States. Sponsored facilities issue four types of ADRs: Level-I, Level-II, Level-III, and Rule 144A ADRs. Level-I ADRs trade over the counter. The main advantage of a Level-I program is that it can support a side-by-side program. Level-II ADRs are listed on exchanges and comply with registration and reporting requirements. A sponsored Level-III facility represents a new issue of securities that raises capital for the foreign issuer. Rule 144A ADRs are an alternative to Level-III for raising capital. Issuers utilize GDRs to raise capital in two or more markets simultaneously.

Issuers of ADRs must comply with U.S. securities laws, including the Securities Act of 1933 and the Securities Exchange Act of 1934. The 1933 act governs registration of new securities issuance while the 1934 act requires registration of broker-dealers and reporting of issuers. For ADR issuers, Regulation S, Rule 144A, and Rule 12g3-2(b) provide certain exemptions.

Depositary receipts and international securities are well-established in London. The 1999 European Economic and Monetary Union has effectively brought about a merger of capital markets of the countries that joined the union. The euro's introduction has led to a dramatic acceleration in cross-border investment and global financial market integration. The euroDR market has become an important segment of that investment.

Key Terms

deposit agreement 287
depositary bank 287
depositary receipt 286
euroDR 299
foreign ordinaries 293
global depositary receipt (GDR) 293
issuer safe harbor 294
Level-I ADR 290
Level-II ADR 290

Level-III ADR 291
qualified institutional buyer (QIB) 292
Regulation S 294
resale safe harbor 294
Rule 144A ADR 292
side-by-side program 290
sponsored ADR 287
unsponsored ADR 286

Review Questions

1. Discuss how ADRs benefit U.S. investors and foreign issuers.
2. The latest development in the depositary receipts markets is the euroDR. How are euroDRs similar to GDRs and ADRs? What are the differences?
3. What is a side-by-side program?
4. Describe the registration and reporting requirements for different types of ADR facilities.
5. Both Level-II and Level-III ADRs are exchange-listed. What are the major differences between them?
6. Regulation S provides for issuer safe harbor and resale safe harbor. Describe how a foreign company could take advantage of Regulation S safe harbors.
7. ADR shares are a multiple or a fraction of the underlying shares. What are important considerations in setting the ratio?
8. Many foreign companies have used ADRs as an acquisition currency when acquiring U.S. companies. How do foreign companies benefit from using ADRs as an acquisition currency?

Select Bibliography

Bank of New York. *Depositary Receipt: 2002 Year-end Market Review.* New York: Bank of New York, 2003.

Bank of New York. *The Global Equity Investment Guide.* New York: Bank of New York, 2003

Bankers Trust. *Depositary Receipt Handbook.* New York: Bankers Trust (now Deutsche Bank), 1997.

Brancato, C. K. *Getting Listed On Wall Street.* Burr Ridge, Ill.: Irwin, 1996.

Citigroup. *ADR Information.* New York: Citigroup, 2001.

Coyle, R. J. (ed). *The McGraw-Hill Handbook of American Depositary Receipts.* New York: McGraw-Hill, 1995.

Darby, R. "ADRs shine again." *Investment Dealers Digest,* August 12, 1996, pp. 12–17.

Hubbard, D. J., and R. K. Larson. "American depositary receipts: Investment alternatives or quicksand?" *CPA Journal,* July 1995, 65(n7), pp. 70–73.

Muscarella, C. J. "Stock split: Signaling or liquidity? The case of ADR solo-splits." *Journal of Financial Economics,* September 1996, v42n1, pp. 3–26.

New York Stock Exchange. *An International Marketplace.* New York: New York Stock Exchange, 2002.

Ogden, J. "Should all those foreign companies be listing on the NYSE?" *Global Finance,* July 1996, pp. 54–58.

Securities and Exchange Commission. *Final Rule: Offshore Offers and Sales (Regulation S).* Washington, D.C.: Securities and Exchange Commission, February 1998.

Webb, S. E. "An examination of international equity markets using American depositary receipts." *Journal of Business Finance & Accounting,* April 1995, 22(n3), pp. 415–430.

Mortgage- and Asset-Backed Securities Markets

Historically, the financial institution that originated mortgages maintained and serviced those mortgages. Thus, the originating institution received the income from a mortgage but also assumed the risk that the borrower might default or that interest rates might change. Starting in the 1970s, however, banks and thrifts began to transform themselves from mortgage lenders into mortgage originators only. Securitization—the pooling and repackaging of relatively homogeneous assets into securities—made this transformation possible. Various forms of credit enhancement are available that upgrade the credit of the securitized instruments to a level higher than that of the underlying assets, and the instruments are then sold to investors.

Securitization began in 1977 with mortgage pass-throughs, but as investors became increasingly comfortable with the technique, it spread to other asset classes. Today, through the use of innovative structures, securitization has been applied to various types of assets including credit card receivables, home equity loans, auto loans, sports facility financing, tax liens, commercial loans, and junk bonds. This chapter first provides a general overview of securitization and its advantages and disadvantages and then examines specific examples of assets that have been successfully securitized.

The objectives of this chapter are to provide an understanding of:
- The structure and basic elements of securitized instruments.
- The benefits and costs of securitization.
- Mortgage-backed securities.
- Asset-backed instruments.
- Collateralized bond/loan obligations.
- Asset-backed commercial paper.

MARKET OVERVIEW

Since Bank of America issued the first mortgage-backed security (a security backed by a pool of mortgages) in 1977, the market for asset-backed securities has grown dramatically. Today, the market encompasses trillions of dollars, and the securitization process has taken on a global presence. The benefits that securitization brings to both issuers and investors has fueled this growth.

For issuers, securitization provides more cost-efficient funding for operations and greater flexibility in balance sheet management. For investors, securitized instruments present opportunities to participate in previously unavailable asset classes. Asset-backed securities offer investors a broad selection of fixed-income alternatives with higher yields than Treasury securities and higher credit ratings and fewer downgrades than corporate bonds.

As a result, there has been an explosion of new securitized instruments, including securities backed by high-yield bonds, known as **collateralized bond obligations (CBO)**, and securities backed by commercial loans, called **collateralized loan obligations (CLO)**. In another innovative move, a number of Wall Street firms have pitched so-called tobacco bonds to cities and states that have been promised large settlements from tobacco companies. The annual payments from the tobacco companies through the year 2025 and beyond back these settlement bonds (see Box 13.1 for more on the tobacco bonds).

Asset-backed securities are complex financial instruments that only institutional investors buy. Information on these securities is not widely available in the popular press. Several institutions, however, do provide securitized analytics and data. They include the Bond Market Association (**http://www.bond markets.com**), Wall Street Analytics (**http://www.wsainc.com**), and Asset-Backed Alert (**http://www.abalert.com**).

STRUCTURE AND BASIC ELEMENTS

The typical securitization process begins with the originator transferring assets or receivables to a trust called a **special purpose vehicle (SPV)**. The SPV acts as an intermediary between the originator and investors by acquiring the assets or receivables from the originator and then issuing securities backed by these assets. The SPV continues to hold the assets for the beneficial interest of the security holders. Various techniques are available to enhance the creditworthiness of the assets so that the credit of the securities backed by the assets raises to investment-grade levels. The process from pooling the assets together until closing is quite lengthy. Steps that must be taken include company and asset pool analysis, distribution of the term sheet, investor due diligence, the rating agency's credit analysis, deal pricing, and distribution. Figure 13.1 (see p. 306) depicts the basics of a securitized transaction, and Figure 13.2 (see p. 307) shows a timeline for the steps in the process. The remainder of this section discusses each element of the process in more detail.

MARKETS IN ACTION   Tobacco Bonds

13.1

In November 1994, Mississippi filed the first state lawsuit against the tobacco industry. Many states thereafter initiated similar legal actions. Antismoking sentiment quickly spread across the country as the news media published a series of stories that probed how much the tobacco industry officials knew of the dangers of smoking and withheld this information from the public. The Senate Commerce Committee came close to brokering a $500 billion settlement, but negotiations fell apart in April 1998 after RJR Nabisco balked.

The cigarette companies then began to negotiate with individual states. As Florida, Minnesota, Mississippi, and Texas reached settlements of $40 billion, the attorneys general of several key states tried to salvage some sort of master agreement. Eventually, the other forty-six states agreed to drop pending lawsuits in return for payments of $206 billion. The total settlement came to $246 billion, to be paid over the next twenty-five years. Moreover, the payments could go on indefinitely. As long as participating manufacturers sell cigarettes, payments will continue.

Many states are now looking to monetize their settlements. Some states and municipalities favor securitization because they have concerns about the lengthy payout schedule of the settlement and the

business risks still facing the tobacco industry. In their view, it is better to transfer that risk to bondholders. Proponents argue securitization is a way to diversify the tobacco settlement windfall. In November 1999, New York City and Nassau County (New York) became the first to issue so-called tobacco bonds backed by their share of the master settlement issuing $709 million and $300 million, respectively. Payments from the four tobacco companies secure the bonds, which are not considered city debt. The city avoided state debt constraints and shielded itself from responsibility for the debt should the cigarette manufacturers' payments stop or significantly decrease. Because the proceeds will be used for capital spending, the bonds are tax-exempt.

Such tobacco bonds are more complex than typical asset-backed securities. Tobacco bonds combine the elements of corporate, asset-backed, and municipal securities, with payments tied to cigarette sales (corporate), issuers borrowing based on the anticipated stream of money from the settlements (asset-backed), and municipalities issuing these tobacco bonds (municipal).

Sources: National Conference of State Legislators, National Association of Attorneys General, and LATimes.com (March 27, 2003).

Originator and Collateral

The originator that makes the loan and creates the asset that will become the underlying collateral may be a finance company, credit card issuer, or securities firm. In structuring the program, it is essential that the originator achieve a **true sale** in the transfer of assets to the SPV. In other words, the originator cannot retain any interest in the assets and must transfer the full title.

The collateral for a securitized instrument can be either existing or future income-producing assets. In an **asset-backed securitization**, the originator sells an existing pool of assets, such as existing mortgages, to the SPV. In this case, because the assets have already been transferred in a true sale, investors who purchase the securities do not assume any originator performance risk, or the risk that the originator will fail to remain in business and produce the assets. Nevertheless, the originator's creditworthiness may still be a concern for

FIGURE 13.1 | *Basic Structure for the Creation of an Asset-Backed Security*

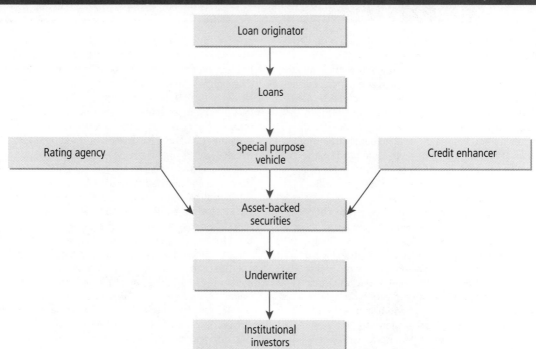

investors if, as often happens, the originator continues to service the collateral. If so, the originator's bankruptcy would likely affect the quality of its service.

In a **future cash-flow securitization**, the originator sells assets to the SPV before the assets have come into existence. The SPV then issues the securities and uses the proceeds to make a prepayment to the originator. In this case, investors assume the originator performance risk because the interest and principal on the securities will be paid only if the originator stays in business and creates the assets.

Servicing

Servicing includes the collection of payments and other steps necessary to ensure that the debtors meet their obligations and to protect the interests of investors. Many securitization programs retain the originator as the servicer. This is most likely when the assets involve extensive administrative responsibilities or require timely servicing in order to produce cash flows. Most programs also provide for the appointment of an independent backup servicer if certain events, such as the originator's bankruptcy, occur. To ensure that the originator's retention of some control over the assets will not prevent the transfer from being a true sale, the originator's role must be clearly limited to that

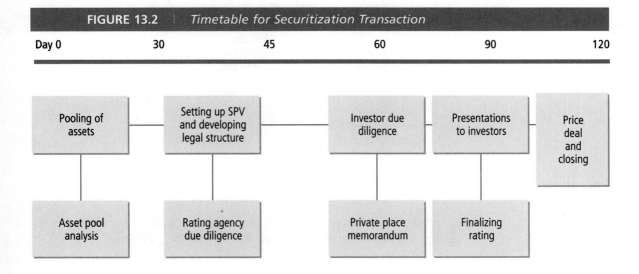

| FIGURE 13.2 | *Timetable for Securitization Transaction* |

Day 0   30   45   60   90   120

of a collection agent for the trust, and the originator must be paid a reasonable servicing fee.

Special Purpose Vehicle

A primary factor that mitigates the risk of a securitization transaction is that the trusts that serve as SPVs generally have bankruptcy protections. Constraints in the documents setting up the transaction restrict the business activities of the SPV to those associated with the securitization. These documents also prohibit the SPV from incurring additional debt or otherwise transferring or encumbering the assets.

Credit Enhancement

Securitized instruments have several levels of credit enhancement to mitigate the potential loss arising from the credit risk of the underlying assets. The amount and type of credit enhancement depend on the historical loss experience of similar loans and the rating sought by the issuer. Internal credit enhancements often include overcollateralization, excess spread, or a reserve account. External credit enhancement may be in the form of a bank letter of credit, a surety bond, or a financial guarantee from a bond insurance company. Table 13.1 (see p. 308) lists major bond insurers. The party providing this enhancement must be an entity with a rating at least as high as the desired transaction rating.

Credit Rating

Credit ratings provide investors with an indication of credit risk and the likelihood that they will be repaid on time and in full. In analyzing a securitization program, rating agencies examine the legal and structural protections

TABLE 13.1	Bond Insurance Companies	
Company	**Web Site**	
ACA Financial Guaranty Corporation	http://www.aca-insurance.com	
Ambac Assurance Corporation	http://www.ambac.com	
AXA Re Finance S.A.	http://www.axa-re.com	
Financial Guaranty Insurance Co.	http://www.gecapital.com	
Financial Security Assurance	http://www.fsa.com	
MBIA Insurance Corporation	http://www.mbia.com	
RAM Reinsurance Company Ltd.	http://www.pmigroup.com	
XL Capital Assurance	http://www.xlca.com	

Source: Association of Financial Guaranty Insurors.

provided to investors. In future cash-flow transactions, the agencies also review the generation and business risks applicable to the origination.

BENEFITS AND COSTS

Asset securitization provides originators/issuers with several advantages. The originator can tap into new sources of funding at a lower all-in cost of capital because the resulting securities present a better credit quality than the originator itself. To the extent that the originator continues to service the underlying assets, this generates a steady stream of servicing fees. As the originator removes assets from its balance sheet, the originator reduces its exposure to interest rate risk. In addition, the credit risk associated with those assets passes on to the investor. The transfer of title to the assets to the SPV is of particular value to banks as originators, as it eliminates the bank's need to comply with any applicable risk-based capital requirements related to the asset.[1] As such, it permits the bank to lend additional funds to its customers. Furthermore, if the originator is at or near the debt/equity ratio acceptable to the market or permitted under financial covenants in outstanding indentures, securitization will allow the originator to raise additional needed capital without incurring balance sheet debt and triggering a breach of these financial covenants. A securitization is also an effective way to divest excess or nonessential assets.

Another benefit obtainable only through securitization is the pricing efficiency and transparency resulting from the underwriting process and secondary market trading of the asset-backed securities. Without securitization there is at best infrequent and subjective valuation of the underlying asset. Moreover, by packaging individually illiquid loans into marketable securities, the selling financial institution increases the liquidity of its assets. Table 13.2 summarizes the advantages of securitization as compared with individual loans.

---

[1]See Chapter 3 for detailed coverage on risk-based capital requirements.

TABLE 13.2 │ *Advantages of Securitization Compared with Individual Loans*	
Individual Loans	**Asset-Backed Securities**
Illiquid	Liquid, active secondary markets for most
Periodic valuation	Pricing efficiency and transparency
Originator assesses risk	Rating agencies and credit enhancers assess risk
Local investor base	National/global markets
Higher cost of funding	Lower costs
No servicing fee generated	Additional fee income if the originator acts as servicer
Assets remain on the originator's balance sheet; additional loan origination requires additional capital	Assets are removed from the originator's balance sheet; additional funds are available to support more loan origination
Unwanted assets remain on the originator's balance sheet	The originator can sell unwanted assets and use the proceeds to expand its core business
Subject to debt/equity ratio constraints	Provide access to needed capital without incurring balance sheet debt

There are also disadvantages to issuers and originators, though. The up-front expenses and effort required for a first-time securitization are likely to exceed the expenses and effort associated with a bank borrowing or other debt offering.[2] Another disadvantage is the required disclosure of asset data. Investors and rating agencies in particular require the disclosure of a significant amount of information concerning the assets, which the originator may be reluctant to provide. In addition, these parties typically require detailed servicing reports monitoring the performance of the assets on at least a monthly basis.

MORTGAGE-BACKED SECURITIES

Securitization began with **mortgage-backed securities (MBS)**, which are debt instruments backed by residential or commercial mortgages. Today, the MBS market is still the largest market for securitized instruments. Through MBS market, mortgage lenders can access a larger reservoir of capital that makes financing available to homebuyers at lower costs. Mortgage securitization began with simple mortgage pass-throughs but now includes a number of other instruments developed to meet the needs of investors and rectify some perceived shortcomings of pass-throughs.

Mortgage Pass-Throughs

The first and most basic mortgage securities are pass-throughs, which represent a direct ownership interest in a pool of mortgage loans. With **mortgage pass-throughs**, the monthly mortgage payments, net of servicing and insurance

---

[2]However, those costs can be amortized over the life of the transaction. In addition, the follow-up transactions can be completed more easily and with lower transaction costs.

fees, pass along to the investors. Hence, the investors continue to receive payments as long as the mortgages are outstanding. As the next section explains, however, homeowners have the option of prepaying the outstanding balance—a possibility that has considerable ramifications for investors.

Although some private institutions issue various types of mortgage securities known as private-label MBS, the Government National Mortgage Association (Ginnie Mae or GNMA), the Federal Home Loan Mortgage Corporation (Freddie Mac or FHLMC), or the Federal National Mortgage Association (Fannie Mae or FNMA) issues and/or guarantees most pass-through MBS. These MBS are agency pass-throughs, and market participants consider the payments of interest and principal are secure. Nevertheless, the cash flow on these instruments may vary from month to month depending on the **prepayment rate**, the rate at which homeowners pay off their outstanding mortgage balances before maturity date, of the underlying mortgages. As Table 13.3 shows, total outstanding agency MBS amounted to more than $3 trillion in 2002. Daily trading volume peaked at more than $150 billion in 2002.

The market does not call for ratings for agency pass-throughs, as an agency can provide two types of guarantees. With **fully modified pass-throughs**, the agency guarantees the timely payment of both interest and principal. With **modified pass-throughs**, in addition to the timely payment of interest, the agency guarantees that the scheduled principal repayment will be made as collected but no later than a specified date. These mortgage securities trade in terms of their assumed average life rather than their maturity. The average life is the average amount of time that will elapse from the date of purchase until repayment of the principal, based on an assumed prepayment projection.

TABLE 13.3	*Outstanding Agency Mortgage-Backed Securities (in $ billions)*			
Year	GNMA	FNMA	FHLMC	Total
1990	403.6	299.8	321.0	1,024.4
1991	425.3	372.0	363.2	1,160.5
1992	419.5	445.0	409.2	1,273.7
1993	414.1	495.5	440.1	1,349.7
1994	450.9	530.3	460.7	1,441.9
1995	472.3	583.0	515.1	1,570.4
1996	506.2	650.7	554.3	1,711.2
1997	536.9	709.6	579.4	1,825.8
1998	537.4	834.5	646.5	2,018.4
1999	582.0	960.9	749.1	2,292.0
2000	610.5	1,057.8	823.3	2,490.6
2001	589.5	1,290.4	948.4	2,828.3
2002	536.2	1,538.3	1,082.1	3,156.6

Source: Bond Market Association.

The MBS market differs from other fixed-income markets in several ways. In the MBS market, one identifies a pass-through by a pool prefix, which indicates the type of pass-through, and a pool number, which gives information on the specific mortgage collateral and the issuer. In contrast, a TBA (to be announced) trade does not specify the pool information or the precise amount to be delivered. On a TBA trade, the investor could receive up to three pools, with pool numbers being announced shortly before the settlement date. The option of what pool to deliver rests with the seller, as long as it satisfies the Bond Market Association's guidelines for standards of delivery and settlement for MBS. TBA trades give yet another advantage to the seller. The Bond Market Association delivery variance permits an under- or over-delivery tolerance of 0.01 percent on the TBA trades of Fannie Mae, Freddie Mac, and Ginnie Mae pass-through securities. The 0.01 percent variance applies to each $1 million within a TBA trade larger than $1 million.

Prepayment Risk

As we noted previously, homeowners have the option of paying off the outstanding balance of their mortgages. The uncertainty about whether and when the borrower will exercise this option complicates the processes of projecting cash flows from a pass-through and of valuing a pass-through.

Many factors affect prepayments, including the prevailing mortgage rate, seasonal factors, and the economic environment. The prevailing mortgage rate affects prepayment in several ways. When the spread between the current rate and the rate homeowners pay widens, homeowners are more likely to refinance. The path by which the mortgage rate reached its current level is also important. The first time the rate drops to an attractive refinancing level, prepayment will speed up. If rates are volatile, however, the next time mortgage rates move down, prepayments will not increase.

The seasonal pattern, in which home buying increases in the spring and summer and declines in the fall and winter, also influences prepayments. Prepayments mirror this pattern as homebuyers sell their existing homes (pay off existing mortgages) and buy new ones (take on new mortgages). Economic activity also affects housing turnover and hence influences the number of prepayments. A growing economy provides higher incomes and more job opportunities. This increases family mobility and hence housing turnover, which speeds up prepayments. Prepayments slow down in a weak economy.

Projecting the cash flows from a pass-through requires making assumptions about future prepayments. The most widely used prepayment assumption is the **prepayment speed assumption (PSA)** developed by the Bond Market Association. The PSA assumes that the prepayment rate for new mortgage loans begins at 0.2 percent per annum in the first month and increases by 0.2 percent per annum each month as the mortgages age, eventually reaching a constant rate of 6.00 percent at 30 months. Market practice is to quote both projected and historical prepayment rates as a percentage of the PSA. For example, a 60 percent PSA means the prepayment rate is 60 percent of the PSA

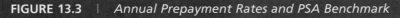

FIGURE 13.3 | *Annual Prepayment Rates and PSA Benchmark*

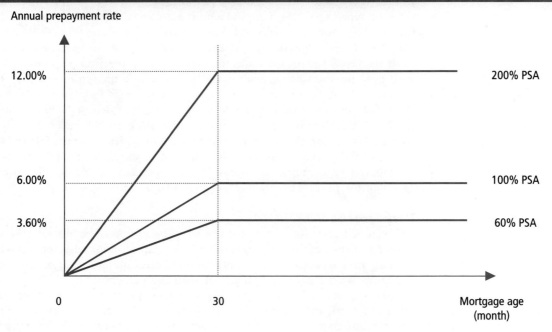

benchmark, and a 200 percent PSA indicates twice the benchmark prepayment speed. Figure 13.3 shows the annual prepayment rates for a 60 percent, 100 percent, and 200 percent PSA.

To estimate the amount of prepayment in the upcoming month, the prepayment rate can be converted to a concept called the single monthly mortality (SMM) rate using the following conversion formula:

13.1   For months $1 \leq t \leq 30$, SMM = $1 - (1 - 0.02\% \times t)^{1/12}$.

For months $t > 30$, SMM = $1 - (1 - 6\%)^{1/12} = 0.00514$.

Table 13.4 shows the SMM for months 1 to 30 based on 100 percent PSA. As an example, a prepayment rate of 6.00 percent can be converted to an SMM of 0.514 percent. A 0.514 percent SMM means that approximately 0.514 percent of the remaining mortgage balance, less the scheduled principal payment for the month, will be prepaid this month. Suppose the remaining balance is $200 million and the scheduled principal payment is $5 million. The estimated prepayment for the month will be $1,002,300 [= 0.00514 × ($200m − $5m)].

TABLE 13.4	*Single Monthly Mortality Rate and PSA Benchmark*	
Month	100% PSA Prepayment (per annum, %)	Single Monthly Mortality Rate (%)
1	0.2	0.01668
2	0.4	0.03340
3	0.6	0.05014
4	0.8	0.06691
5	1.0	0.08372
6	1.2	0.10055
7	1.4	0.11742
8	1.6	0.13432
9	1.8	0.15125
10	2.0	0.16821
11	2.2	0.18521
12	2.4	0.20223
13	2.6	0.21929
14	2.8	0.23638
15	3.0	0.25351
16	3.2	0.27066
17	3.4	0.28785
18	3.6	0.30507
19	3.8	0.32232
20	4.0	0.33961
21	4.2	0.35692
22	4.4	0.37428
23	4.6	0.39166
24	4.8	0.40908
25	5.0	0.42653
26	5.2	0.44402
27	5.4	0.46154
28	5.6	0.47909
29	5.8	0.49668
30	6.0	0.51430

The prepayment calculations are important in valuing MBS. The procedure used in most valuation modeling of MBS first specifies the interest rate process, and uses the process in Monte Carlo simulation procedures to simulate interest rate paths. Analysts use the empirical model of prepayment behavior to project the cash flows each month along each path. They then calculate the present value of total cash flows along each path by the appropriate spot rates (explained in detail in Chapter 8). Analysts repeat this process for numerous paths. The average present value on all interest rate paths is the theoretical value. If the average present value is greater than the market price, the security is underpriced. On the other hand, the MBS is overpriced if the average present value is smaller than the market price. When the market price equals the average present value, the security is fairly priced.[3]

Collateralized Mortgage Obligations

As investors found the prepayment risk of the pass-through MBS undesirable, their growth slowed. To rejuvenate the ABS market, Wall Street devised the **collateralized mortgage obligation (CMO)**, which alters the prepayment risk of MBS. A CMO does not eliminate prepayment concerns, but instead transfers this risk among different classes called tranches. This broadens the appeal of the security to various traditional fixed-income investors.

A CMO is a security backed by a pool of mortgages or mortgage passthroughs, and its structure redistributes the cash flows from the pool of collateral over a series of tranches. Each tranche has a different maturity date, cash-flow features, and risk exposure. Typically, CMO issuers first pay the interest to the bondholders in each tranche. The principal payments from the underlying collateral retire the classes of bonds on a priority basis. Many call the final tranche of a CMO the **accrual bond** or the Z-bond. Holders of these securities do not receive cash until the full payment of all earlier tranches. This type of CMO is a sequential pay CMO.

Over time a planned amortization class (PAC) and targeted amortization class (TAC) have emerged, designed to reduce the prepayment risk of certain tranches by establishing a sinking fund structure. A PAC structure separates the collateral's principal into PAC bonds and the companion bonds. The amortization schedule for the PAC bonds remains fixed within a certain range of prepayment speeds. The companion bonds absorb the prepayment risk for the PAC bonds. This structure leads to stable average lives for the PAC bonds. The companion bonds, on the other hand, have more volatile lives than otherwise similar sequential bonds. Similar to a PAC structure, a TAC receives a specified monthly prepayment. Non-TAC classes receive a distribution of any excess prepayment.

Congress further stimulated the CMO market when they passed the Tax Reform Act of 1986, which allowed mortgage security pools to elect the tax status of a **real estate mortgage investment conduit (REMIC)**. REMIC is a pass-through tax entity that can hold mortgages and can issue multiple classes of pass-through certificates to investors. Since 1986, most CMOs have been issued in REMIC form.

---

[3]Prepayments also affect MBS valuation by reducing both the duration and the convexity of the MBS. This increases the likelihood that the MBS will have negative duration and convexity. Negative duration implies that price decreases as the interest rate declines. This will occur when mortgages get paid off at a fast rate, causing the amount of interest payments to drop rapidly. Negative convexity will result in price compression when the rate declines. This topic is beyond the scope of this chapter.

Stripped Mortgage-Backed Securities

A **stripped mortgage-backed security** is a pass-through that divides the cash flow from the underlying collateral on a pro rata basis across the security holders. For example, the cash flow on a 7 percent pass-through security could be redistributed to create one new security with an 8 percent coupon (called the premium strip) and another with a 6 percent coupon (called the discount strip).

Securities may also be partially stripped so that each class receives some interest and some principal. With the securities completely stripped, all the interest is allocated to one class of security, known as **interest only (IO)**, and the entire principal to another, called **principal only (PO)**. The PO security trades at a discount. The yield an investor will realize depends on the prepayment rate; the faster the prepayments, the higher the yield. Upon prepayment of a mortgage, it redeems in full at par. When mortgage rates decline, prepayments speed up, accelerating payments to the PO investors. The unanticipated larger amount of cash flow will now be discounted at a lower interest rate. As a result, the price of a PO rises with declining mortgage rates. When mortgage rates rise, prepayments slow down, resulting in a lower cash flow. Coupled with a higher discount rate, the price of a PO falls with rising mortgage rates.

In contrast, IO holders receive only interest on the amount of principal outstanding. If mortgage rates decline, prepayments speed up. The smaller amount of principal outstanding will result in a decline in income for IO investors. Although the cash flow will be discounted at a lower rate, the net effect is typically a lower price for the IO. On a reverse interest rate trend, the expected cash flow improves, but the cash flow is subject to a higher discount rate. The net effect may be either a rise or a fall in IO value, depending on the magnitude of the change.

Callable Pass-Throughs

A recent development in the mortgage security market is the **callable pass-through**, created by separating a mortgage pass-through into a callable class and a call class. The callable class investor will receive all of the principal and interest from the underlying mortgage loans. In contrast, the call class holder has the right to call the underlying pass-through at a stated price (usually par plus accrued interest) from the callable class holders after a specified period of time has passed.

The callable class holder is long a bond and is short a call option.[4] But rather than just being short a series of call options to a number of mortgage borrowers who may or may not exercise the option to pay off their mortgages early, the callable class is also short one call option to the call class investor. The call class investor will call the underlying pass-through from the callable class holder in a much more efficient way than the mortgage borrowers. Hence, the

---

[4]This is similar to a callable bond. A call option gives the holder the right to purchase the underlying asset at a pre-specified price until the expiration date.

callable class holder will have a lower return relative to the pass-through investors if rates decline.

ASSET-BACKED INSTRUMENTS

The market uses the term **asset-backed securities (ABS)** to refer to securities backed by nonmortgage assets such as installment loans, leases, receivables, home equity loans, tax liens, revolving credit, commercial loans, and high-yield bonds. The total amount outstanding of these instruments has grown from $316 billion in 1995 to more than $1.5 trillion in 2002. Several factors foster this growth. In 1992, the SEC amended its rules to permit the shelf registration and public sale of investment-grade asset-backed securities. In 1994, Congress adopted amendments to the Secondary Mortgage Market Enhancement Act of 1984 to provide an exemption from state securities laws for highly rated securities backed by certain financial assets similar to the exemption already enjoyed by mortgage-backed securities. Then, in August 1996, Congress approved legislation to allow the creation of Financial Asset Securitization Trusts (FASITs). FASITs are similar to REMICs. They permit greater flexibility such as allowing the replacement of prepaid loans after the initial sale of the security, the pooling of mixed asset types, and the inclusion of construction loans. With the advent of FASITs, many of the benefits of REMIC treatment have extended to nonmortgage asset securitization.

Credit Card Receivables

The market for securities backed by credit card receivables has grown significantly, from $153.1 billion in 1995 to more than $397 billion in 2002. This growth has happened because of the widespread use of credit cards by consumers and the wider acceptance of cards by merchants and service providers.

Credit card securitizations have evolved from a stand-alone trust to a master trust structure. With a **stand-alone trust**, the trust buys a single pool of receivables, which it uses as collateral for a single security. When the issuer wants to issue another security, it must create a new pool of card accounts and sell those receivables to a separate trust. This structure was in place from the first credit card securitization in 1987 until 1991, when the master trust became the preferred vehicle. Under the **master trust** structure, the seller can sell multiple securities from the same trust, all of which share the credit risks as well as the cash flows from one large pool of credit card receivables.[5] For example, an issuer could transfer the receivables from one million credit card accounts to a trust, then issue multiple securities in various denominations and sizes. The issuer transfers more accounts to the same trust when it needs more financing. It can then issue more securities. Such a structure benefits the issuer

---

[5]These receivables are under the control of the seller and are from accounts designated by the seller.

because issuing a new series from a master trust entails less cost and effort than creating a new trust for every issue.

The seller's interest is trust assets not allocated to any series of securities. The size of the seller's interest is equal to the difference between the total principal receivable balance of the trust portfolio and the principal balance of all outstanding securities issued through the trust. The seller's interest fluctuates as the amount in the trust portfolio increases or decreases. The seller's interest serves two key purposes. First, this ownership interest acts as a buffer in instances when account payments exceed account purchases. Second, it absorbs reductions in the receivable balance due to receivable dilution or readjustment of noncomplying receivables.[6]

The typical trust setup has three different cash-flow periods: revolving, controlled amortization or controlled accumulation, and early amortization. During the revolving period, monthly principal collections are allocated between the seller and the investor interest on a pro rata basis. At the end of the revolving period, the controlled amortization (or accumulation) period begins. Ordinarily, the controlled accumulation or controlled amortization period starts one year before the expected payment date. In the case of a controlled amortization period, principal collections are not reinvested but rather paid to investors in twelve equal controlled amortization payments. If principal collections exceed the controlled amount, the excess will be reinvested in new receivables or paid to the seller. If the issue has a controlled accumulation period, the issuer establishes a principal funding account. The account receives a deposit of the controlled payments every month until the expected maturity date. At the end of the accumulation period, investors will be repaid in a single bullet payment.

Finally, severe asset deterioration or problems with the seller or the servicer triggers early amortization. Once triggered, the deal automatically enters the early amortization period and repays investors immediately.

Common forms of credit enhancement in credit card securitization are excess spread, a cash collateral account, a collateral invested account, and subordination.[7] The yield on credit cards is relatively high and is usually enough to cover the interest payment to investors in addition to servicing fees and any charge-off during the month. The remaining yield is the excess spread. Available excess spread may be shared with other series, used to pay fees to credit enhancers, deposited into a spread account for the benefit of the investors, or released to the seller.

---

[6]Dilution is any reduction to the receivables balance due to reasons other than losses or an obligor's cash payment, such as merchandise returns or rebates.

[7]The letter of credit was a common form of enhancement from the inception of credit card securitization until 1991. It is an unconditional, irrevocable commitment from a bank to provide a cash payment, up to the face amount of the letter of credit, to the trustee in the event that there is a shortfall in cash needed to pay interest, principal, or servicing. Banks discontinued this form of enhancement when rating agencies downgraded several banks providing letters of credit and the transactions they enhanced became downgraded as a result.

A cash collateral account is a segregated trust account, funded at the outset of the deal by a third-party bank. It can be drawn on to cover shortfalls in interest, principal, or servicing expense for a particular series if the excess spread falls to zero. The bank invests the cash in the account in high-quality, short-term securities.

The collateral invested account is an uncertificated ownership interest in the trust, subordinate in payment rights to all investor certificates. It serves the same purpose as the cash collateral account. With the collateral invested account drawn upon, it can be reimbursed from future excess spread.

Another common form of enhancement is a senior/subordinate structure that has two types of investor ownership in the trust: senior participation in the form of Class-A certificates and subordinate participation in the form of Class-B certificates. Class B will absorb losses allocated to class A that other forms of credit enhancements, discussed previously, do not already cover. Draws on the subordinate certificates may be reimbursed from future excess spread. Principal collections will be allocated to the subordinate investors only upon full repayment of the senior certificates.

Automobile Loan Receivables

Since the inception of the asset-backed securities market, automobile loan securitization has been a vital part of the total volume. Strong vehicle sales, attractive funding rates, and investor demand for short-term, highly rated securities have driven the outstanding volume from $59.5 billion in 1995 to $221.7 billion in 2002. The vast majority of securitized auto loans originate with the loan application sent to the finance company by a dealer. A very small portion involves loans directly originated by the issuer. The quality of auto loans depends on the vehicle age, the down payment, the advance rate, depreciation, the term distribution of loans, and geographic diversification.[8]

There are two main structures in auto loan securitization: a grantor trust and an owner trust. A **grantor trust** requires principal distributions on the underlying securities to be made on a pro rata basis. Hence, the senior and subordinate classes in a grantor trust will normally have the same average life. In contrast, in an **owner trust**, the deal documents stipulate how cash flows are allocated.

The primary forms of credit enhancement are reserve accounts, overcollateralization, subordination, excess spread, and bond insurance. Most auto loan securitizations use reserve or spread accounts, which an initial deposit and excess spread (up to a required amount) typically fund. Subordination and overcollateralization are similar because both represent a seller's interest in the underlying receivables. If collections are insufficient to make scheduled payments, funds otherwise payable to the seller or to junior bondholders will pay senior bondholders.

---

[8]The advance rate is the loan balance as a percentage of the manufacturer's suggested price.

Sports Finance

Because of the dramatic increase in sports facility construction, its financing has become an important component of the public finance debt market. Sports facilities have become an integral part of the overall economic development plans for a number of municipalities. Stadiums and arenas often serve as anchor tenants for a municipality's comprehensive development and revitalization plans. Many municipalities have aggressively attempted to maintain or lure major league and minor league sports franchises by constructing facilities.

Three basic methods finance these facilities. The traditional method is through tax-supported debt. State and local governments pledge to support the projects in various ways, including general obligation bonds, lease-backed bonds, and dedicated tax bonds. The second method is through project finance debt. Stadiums and arenas may also be supported by revenues generated from a management company, a dedicated tax, or other public-sector commitment. The last method is by asset-backed debt. An asset-backed structure is attractive because it isolates the collateral from the credit risk of the various parties. Table 13.5 lists examples of sport facilities financed by revenue-supported securitization.

In securitized financing, collateral may include naming rights, contributions by founding partners, luxury suites, and concessionaire and club seat agreements, as well as broadcast revenues. Asset-backed transactions may be structured with one or multiple classes of debt. The size of the credit enhancement typically reflects the liquidity and credit risks posed by the various contractually obligated revenue streams to ensure timely interest payments and ultimate repayment of principal. Credit enhancement may comprise overcollateralization, reserve accounts, and third-party support, as well as issuer equity investments.

Student Loans

Three primary sources back student loan securitizations: the Federal Family Education Loan Program (FFELP), the Federal Direct Student Loan Program

TABLE 13.5 | *Examples of Sports Facility Financing*

Facility	City	Type of Financing
Pepsi Center	Denver	New
American Airlines Arena	Miami	New
America West Arena	Phoenix	Refunding
Pacific Bell Park	San Francisco	New
Pro Player Stadium	Miami	Refunding
The FleetCenter	Boston	New
ALLTEL Stadium	Jacksonville	New
USTA National Tennis Center	New York	New

Source: Fitch IBCA, *Changing Game of Sports Finance*. New York: FitchRatings, April 1999.

(FDSLP), and alternative loans. Under the FFELP, private lending institutions fund loans and the U.S. government insures them. In contrast, through FDSLP, U.S. government funds student loans directly. Alternative loan programs refer to loans funded by private lending institutions with or without an insurance guarantee from a private institution.

The FFELP is the largest of the three programs. Under this program, private institutions fund loans to borrowers.[9] Private guarantee agencies insure these loans up to the federal default reimbursement limit, currently at 98 percent.[10] If default occurs, the guarantee agency reimburses the defaulted loans to the lending institutions but will receive reimbursement from the Department of Education.

Under the FDSLP, the U.S. government funds student loans directly to eligible students with money borrowed from the Department of Treasury. The objective was to make federal government student loan lending more cost-efficient as a result of direct government involvement. But the program has not been as successful as anticipated. In addition, the majority of schools that have participated in the FDSLP are trade schools, whose graduates historically have the highest default rate of all school types.

The third way is to fund student loans by private institutions. These loans may or may not be insured by private third parties. The insurer has responsibility to pay if the insured loans default. The largest private guarantor is the Education Resources Institute, Inc.

A widely used vehicle for issuing student loan asset-backed securities is the owner trust. This structure permits principal collections to be used to pay interest on the bonds, providing the needed liquidity in the early years of a student loan transaction.[11] Society National Bank (later renamed Key Bank U.S.A., N.A.) first used this structure in 1993. It was a $200 million transaction with a three-tranche sequential pay structure.

In a senior/subordinated structure, the underlying loans support both the senior and subordinated bonds. Additionally, reallocation of subordinated cash flows also supports the senior bonds. As a result, issuers have achieved a higher rating on the senior tranches, resulting in lower overall funding costs. Payments of principal can be either pro rata or sequential. In a pro rata structure, principal on the subordinated tranche can be paid before the full payment of the senior tranche, if funds are available. In a sequential pay structure, no principal can be paid to the subordinated tranche until the senior tranche has been retired.

Student loan securitized instruments generally have reserve accounts because there has to be liquidity in order to make interest payments on the

---

[9]The PLUS program requires some credit evaluation, but it comprises a relatively minor portion of the FFELP.

[10]Loans disbursed prior to October 1, 1993, have a guarantee at 100 percent.

[11]The life cycle of a student loan begins with the in-school period, which generally runs from one to four years. Once the student graduates, the loan enters a six-month grace period; thereafter, the loan goes into repayment phase.

bonds before receiving reimbursement of defaulted claims. The reserve account contains liquid collateral and earns an interest rate generated by the investment in highly rated securities. The reserve account may be funded out of proceeds of the bond issuance.

Tax Liens

Municipalities take advantage of the asset-backed securities market to securitize municipal assets for sale to investors. Tax liens are the most prominent of these assets, and the market for their securitized instruments continues to grow. A tax lien is a lien placed by a municipality on real property for nonpayment of taxes. Many states have already implemented a statutory procedure that allows municipalities to sell the accrued taxes, plus interest and penalties, annually in a public auction. Tax certificates, awarded at auction, represent a first priority lien position against a property for the amount of unpaid taxes. There is a statutory holding period during which the property owner may extinguish the lien by paying the outstanding taxes plus penalties and interest. If the property owner fails to pay by the end of the holding period, the tax certificate holder can file for a tax deed or follow alternative procedures necessary to obtain title to the property.

Many tax lien securitizations have a structure of a Delaware business trust designed in part to obtain a higher rating for the bonds than would be possible were the originator or the municipality itself to act as issuer.[12] Although the originator or municipality has beneficial ownership of the trust property, legal title to the liens and other collateral rests with the trust. The parties involved treat the transfer of the collateral to the trust as a true sale.

Credit enhancement has primarily been in the form of overcollateralization. Transactions have also included rated subordinate tranches, cash accounts to fund servicer working capital requirements, and liquidity reserves to cover bond interest in case of a shortfall in collections.

Other Types of Assets

Most income-producing assets can be securitized if reliable performance data exist. In addition to those already covered, other asset classes include trade receivables, lease receivables, record and film royalties, nonperforming loans, project finance receivables, aircraft finance receivables, utility receivables, toll-road receivables, franchise loans, and legal settlement funds. Moreover, high-yield bonds and bank loans have also been securitized, as discussed in the subsequent section.

---

[12]In 1988, Delaware enacted the Delaware Business Trust Act. Under the act, a Delaware business trust (DBT) is an unincorporated entity under which trustees and beneficial owners manage the property in the trust. The act affords the parties to a DBT great flexibility to create management structure by contract. The act eliminates several uncertainties associated with common law trusts. The act provides that a DBT is a separate legal entity whose trustees and beneficial owners may have the same limitation of personal liability as directors and stockholders of a Delaware corporation. In addition, the act provides that the property of a DBT will be protected from claims of creditors of beneficial owners of the DBT.

COLLATERALIZED BOND/LOAN OBLIGATIONS

The collateralized bond obligation and collateralized loan obligation markets started in the late 1980s with the repackaging of high-yield, speculative-grade bonds or loans into highly rated paper. Collateralized bond obligations (CBOs) are bonds collateralized by a portfolio of high-yield bonds. Portfolios of syndicated high-yield or investment-grade loans back collateralized loan obligations (CLOs). In both cases, cash flows from the underlying financial instruments pay off investors in rated securities.

Collateralized Bond Obligations

A **market value CBO** is an investment vehicle that can be used to capitalize on the arbitrage opportunities that exist between high-yield bonds and the lower-cost funds of highly rated debt. The transaction is generally structured with multiple classes of rated debt and a layer of unrated equity and invests in a pool of investments that is diverse in obligator, industry, and asset class. To gauge the performance of the transaction, the asset manager will mark to market the value of each investment on a regular basis, usually weekly or biweekly. Furthermore, the amount of debt that can be outstanding as a percentage of the current market value of the assets is the limit for the CBO. This limitation is based on the price volatility and liquidity of the assets in the pool. If the value declines below the acceptable levels, the asset manager will have to take corrective actions. If not, the assets will be liquidated and the proceeds will be paid to investors.

Cash-flow CBOs, on the other hand, are based on a pool of assets with predictable cash flows. As such, these structures can only include investments that meet minimum credit quality, tenor (the length of time until a loan is due), and expected recovery characteristics. The ongoing market price of collateral assets is not important in a cash-flow deal. Instead, it is the ability of each asset to pay scheduled principal and interest that makes these deals successful.

Bank Collateralized Loan Obligations

A CLO is a security backed by loans. Spread arbitrage derived from an asset mix of high-yield and distressed loans often motivates nonbank participants to issue CLOs. In bank CLOs, the motivation is to reduce capital requirements and fund low-yielding assets. The underlying collateral consists mostly of investment-grade and some non-investment grade corporate loans. There are generally several tranches of rated securities, as well as an unrated equity tranche retained by the issuing bank. The subordinated tranche or the equity absorbs the first losses from default. Hence, the most senior tranche holds the least credit risk and receives a higher rating than the subordinated tranches.

Banks that have securitized loans view the use of CLOs as an efficient capital management and funding tool. For example, assume a bank has a $500 million pool of loans with an average loan rating of BBB and an adequate level of diversification. The CLO issuance could be as high as 97 percent and could receive an investment-grade rating. The remaining 3 percent of the pool could be held as equity. From a presecuritization capital perspective, the issuing bank would be required to hold capital equivalent to 8 percent of $500 million, or $40 million. After securitization, the required capital would be $15 million. Thus, CLOs free up $25 million of capital. For investors, CLOs offer an asset class with limited correlation to consumer assets, which dominate the asset-backed securities market.

Credit Enhancement

One of the most common forms of credit enhancement is subordination. In the multi-tranche or senior/subordinated CBO/CLO, the subordinated tranches support the senior tranches. Holders of the senior tranches have priority of payment over the holders of any junior debt tranche. Therefore, junior debt tranches have ratings lower than the senior debt. However, the junior debt carries a higher yield. If overcollateralization is the only credit enhancement in a senior/subordinated structure, the overcollateralization amount is the estimated level of credit losses that the structure will probably withstand without causing a loss to the holders of the rated senior debt. For example, suppose a collateral pool with a total par value of $200 million supports a cash-flow transaction involving the issuance of $160 million of rated senior debt. This "80/20" structure consists of 80 percent senior debt and 20 percent unrated supporting debt or equity. The level of overcollateralization is 125 percent, which equals the ratio of assets over the amount of senior debt. If there was an issuance of subordinated debt in the amount of $14 million and equity in the amount of $6 million, overcollateralization for the $14 million junior class would be provided by the equity investment.

Cash collateral or reserve accounts are another form of credit enhancement. Cash reserves often appear in the initial phase of a cash-flow transaction. Cash proceeds from the sale of CBO/CLO securities can be used to purchase the underlying collateral or to fund reserve accounts. Cash reserves may not be the most efficient form of credit support, however. Interest owed on the CBO/CLO securities is typically higher than the interest earned on these reserves, so allocation of cash to reserve accounts can result in negative carry.[13]

Another method of credit enhancement involves insuring the rated securities with a financial guarantee insurance policy. The insurance transfers the credit risks associated with the underlying assets from the holders of the rated securities to the insurance company. Fully insured debt has a rating that is the same as that of the insurer.

ASSET-BACKED COMMERCIAL PAPER

Asset-backed commercial paper (ABCP) programs provide a valuable, flexible alternative for companies seeking short-term financing. ABCP programs have become a significant segment of the commercial paper market. An

---

[13]Carry is the difference between interest income and interest expense.

ABCP conduit is a bankruptcy-remote special purpose company that raises funds by issuing commercial paper to purchase trade receivables or term assets from one or several sellers. Commercial banks or finance companies establish many of the ABCP programs to provide trade receivables financing for their customers. Other ABCP programs come about as a means of financing credit card portfolios or other types of receivables.

The ABCP market is a significant segment of the capital markets. The market has grown from just $50 billion in outstanding volume in 1991 to more than $700 billion by June 2002. The continued expansion of existing programs, the entrance of new programs into the market, and the proliferation of new asset types financed through such conduits have fueled this growth.

Fully versus Partially Supported Program

ABCP conduits are generally either fully or partially supported, depending on the level of their program-wide credit enhancement. A fully supported ABCP program uses a single external support facility, generally provided by a highly rated bank or group of banks, to provide 100 percent coverage against credit risk and liquidity risk. The credit support often takes the form of a letter of credit or an irrevocable revolving commitment to either purchase assets from the issuer or make loans to the issuer. The credit enhancer will absorb any credit losses on the assets. The main risk to investors in a fully supported program is that the rating of the support provider may be downgraded, resulting in a lower credit rating for ABCP.

The rise of bank risk-based capital standards has imposed significant costs on banks in fully supported programs. Risk-based capital standards require banks to maintain capital for the entire face amount of ABCP outstanding under certain ABCP programs because the regulators view such credit support as a direct credit substitute, and not merely a loan commitment. Consequently, the creation of partially supported programs has occurred to reduce capital requirements.

A partially supported ABCP program typically has two supporting facilities. The first, called the credit enhancement facility, covers losses on the receivables, up to a specified amount (usually 10 or 15 percent of the total amount of ABCP outstanding). The second, called the liquidity facility, primarily covers liquidity risk.

Single-Seller versus Multiseller Programs

ABCP programs can also be categorized as either single-seller programs or multiseller programs. A single-seller program is a bankruptcy-remote special purpose company that issues ABCP to fund the assets of a single originator or seller. Multiseller conduits combine the assets of several unrelated sellers into one diverse portfolio of assets supporting the commercial paper issuance.

Credit Enhancement

ABCP conduits generally have two levels of credit protection: pool-specific and program-wide enhancement. Pool-specific support protects investors against losses, dilution, yield risk, obligator default, and servicing risks associated with an individual transaction. Many forms of pool-specific protection are available, including overcollateralization, recourse to the seller, third-party support, and excess spread. Such pool-specific credit enhancement covers defaults on a specific seller's receivables and cannot be used to fund losses in any other pools.

The program-wide credit enhancement is a fungible layer of credit protection provided by a third party. It can be drawn upon exhaustion of a transaction's pool-specific credit. The enhancement may be in the form of an irrevocable loan facility, a letter of credit, or a surety bond from an insurer. The rating of the third-party credit enhancer must be at least as high as that of the commercial paper. Program-wide enhancement provides the program sponsor with more flexibility in the application of its credit and investment policies and enhances its ability to meet the unique needs of its clients.

Liquidity Support

Liquidity support is an integral part of every ABCP program. Liquidity support is often in the form of either an asset purchase agreement or a loan agreement. Under an asset purchase agreement, the liquidity provider agrees to purchase nondefaulted assets when the ABCP facility needs liquidity. Under a loan agreement, the liquidity provider agrees to lend funds to the conduit. While credit enhancement covers asset defaults and dilution, liquidity providers commit to making funds available to the conduit for reasons other than credit deterioration of the portfolio assets to ensure timely payment to investors. Such noncredit events include market disruption, the issuer's inability to roll the commercial paper, or asset/liability mismatches.

Cash collections from pool assets or the proceeds from issuing new commercial paper typically repay maturing commercial paper. External liquidity replaces or supplements the collection of the program's assets, ensuring that the commercial paper will be repaid in full and on time; this external liquidity is critical when there is disruption to the issuance of new commercial paper.

CONCLUDING SUMMARY

Securitization is one of the most important financial engineering products. It benefits both originators and investors. For originators, securitization is an efficient way of financing operations at a lower cost and is a flexible tool in managing the balance sheet. For investors, securitized assets provide a broad selection of fixed-income alternatives previously unavailable. As a result, the market has grown to trillions of dollars.

The underlying collateral in a securitization transaction can be either existing or future income-producing assets. In an asset-backed securitization, the originator sells an existing pool of assets to the special purpose vehicle, thus removing the assets from the balance sheet of the originator. In contrast, in a future cash-flow securitization, the originator sells the assets to the SPV before the assets have come into existence. The proceeds from the issuance of the securities by the SPV provide funding for a prepayment to the originator.

A securitization transaction can be structured as a pass-through or as multiple classes. Securitized instruments expose investors to credit risk, so all asset-backed securities are credit-enhanced to provide investors with greater protection against losses. The amount and type of credit enhancement depend on the historical loss experience of similar loans and the rating sought by the issuer.

Successfully packaged and sold assets in the asset-backed securities market include mortgage loans, credit card receivables, auto loans, student loans, trade receivables, tax liens, sports facility revenues, tobacco settlement payments, commercial loans, and high-yield bonds. This technique has also been successful for asset-backed commercial paper. It provides a valuable, flexible alternative for companies seeking short-term financing.

Key Terms

accrual bond 314
asset-backed commercial paper
   (ABCP) 323
asset-backed securitization 305
asset-backed security (ABS) 316
callable pass-through 315
cash-flow CBO 322
collateralized bond obligation
   (CBO) 304
collateralized loan obligation
   (CLO) 304
collateralized mortgage obligation
   (CMO) 314
fully modified pass-through 310
future cash-flow securitization 306
grantor trust 318
interest only (IO) 315

market value CBO 322
master trust 316
modified pass-through 310
mortgage-backed security (MBS) 309
mortgage pass-through 309
owner trust 318
prepayment rate 310
prepayment speed assumption
   (PSA) 311
principal only (PO) 315
real estate mortgage investment conduit
   (REMIC) 314
special purpose vehicle (SPV) 304
stand-alone trust 316
stripped mortgage-backed security 315
true sale 305

Review Questions

1. Discuss the significance of creating a special purpose vehicle in asset securitization.

2. Why is credit enhancement common in the asset-backed market?

3. What are the advantages to banks of securitized financing?

4. Compared with other fixed-incomes securities, what are the unique features of mortgage-backed securities?

5. Assume a $500 million pool of mortgages backs a new MBS issue. The projected prepayment speed is 140 percent PSA. What is the amount of prepayment, in addition to the scheduled repayment of principal, in the first month?

6. In a declining interest rate environment, is it better to purchase POs or IOs? Why?

7. Discuss the main differences between market value and cash-flow CBOs.

8. What are the differences between a fully supported and a partially supported ABCP program? Why do banks prefer to credit enhance partially supported programs?

Select Bibliography

Border, S., and A. Sarker. "Securitizing property catastrophe risk." *Current Issues in Economics and Finance* 2(n9), Federal Reserve Bank of New York, August 1996, pp. 1–6.

Britt, P. "Asset securitization," *America's Community Banker,* April 1996, 5(n4), pp. 10–14.

Davison, A., L. L. Wolff, and A. Sanders. *Securitization: Structuring and Investment Analysis.* New York: John Wiley & Sons, 2003.

Deloitte & Touche. "The 1996 tax changes," New York: Deloitte Touche Tohmatsu, August 1996.

Fabozzi, F. J. *Bond Markets, Analysis and Strategies.* Upper Saddle River, N.J.: Prentice Hall, 2000.

———. *Accessing Capital Markets Through Securitization.* New York: John Wiley & Sons, 2001.

Grant Thornton, LLP. "Tax provisions in August 1996 laws: Provisions affecting financial services business." Chicago: Grant Thornton, LLC, 1997.

Henderson, J. *Asset Securitization: Current Techniques and Emerging Market Applications.* London: Euromoney Publications Plc, 1997.

Hu, J. C. *Basics of Mortgage-Backed Securities.* New York: McGraw-Hill, 1997.

Kendall, L. T., and M. J. Fishman, eds. *A Primer on Securitization.* Cambridge, Mass.: MIT Press, 2000.

Lockwood, L. J. "Wealth effects of asset securitization," *Journal of Banking and Finance,* 20(n1), January 1996, pp. 151–164.

Milbank, Tweed, Hadley & McCloy. "Capital markets updates: 1997—the year of the FASIT?" London: Milbank, Tweed, Hadley & McCloy, 1997.

Nirenberg, D. Z., C. J. Burke, and S. L. Kopp. "FASITs—the Small Business Act's new securitization vehicle." *Journal of Taxation,* 85(n5), November 1996, pp. 1–11.

Rosenthal, J. A., and J. M. Ocampo. *Securitization of Credit: Inside the New Technology of Finance.* New York: John Wiley & Sons, 1988.

Schwarcz, S. L. *Structured Finance: A Guide to the Principles of Asset Securitization.* New York: Practicing Law Institute, 1993.

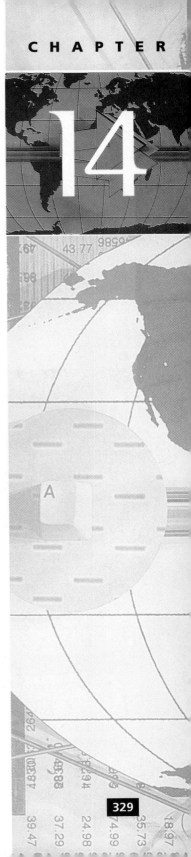

Financial Derivative Markets

Derivatives have received a great deal of attention, mainly because of their role in the bankruptcies of institutions such as Orange County, Barings, Long Term Capital Management, and Enron. Reports of major losses associated with derivatives have contributed to the controversy that surrounds these instruments. Critics fear that these new, complex, high-tech financial products could set off a financial disaster that would paralyze the world's financial markets and force governments to intervene to restore stability at taxpayers' expense. Many others, however, argue that financial derivatives serve a useful purpose in risk management.

Although some derivatives were developed primarily to provide the potential for high returns, most were developed to manage or hedge against risk. Through derivatives, the risks of traditional financial instruments can be efficiently unbundled into smaller components; these can then be traded separately to meet specific risk management objectives. Not only does the trading of individual risk components improve market efficiency, but through breaking down risk in this way, an organization can choose the risks that it is comfortable with and minimize those that it is not. Thus, when used correctly, derivatives can save costs and increase returns.

As our understanding of financial markets and risk management grows, new derivatives are constantly being created to meet the needs of global markets. In this chapter, after a brief introduction to derivatives in general, we will examine some of the most common financial derivatives, including forward contracts, futures, options, swaps, and credit derivatives.

The objectives of this chapter are to provide an understanding of:
- Forward contracts.
- Futures contracts.
- Options.
- Interest rate and currency swaps.
- Credit derivatives.

MARKET OVERVIEW

Simply put, a **derivative security** is a contract with its value derived from an asset or an index. Such a derivative can be created by means of an agreement; the types of derivative products that can be developed are limitless. The tremendous growth of the derivatives market and reports of scandals associated with derivatives trading have resulted in a great deal of confusion about these instruments. Critics fear that those structured finance style deals could help companies hide debt and pad profits, as evidenced by the collapse of Enron (see Box 14.1).

Derivatives trade both on the exchanges and in the over-the-counter (OTC) market. Exchange-traded derivatives have more standardization and offer greater liquidity than OTC contracts, which are tailored to meet the needs of particular buyers and sellers. Common financial derivatives include futures, options, swaps, and credit derivatives. A futures contract represents the right to buy or sell a standard quantity and quality of an asset or a security at a specified date and price. Futures trade on exchanges and are marked to mar-

MARKETS IN ACTION   Enron's Bankruptcy and Derivatives Trading

14.1

On December 2, 2001, Enron filed for bankruptcy—the nation's largest bankruptcy. Just months before the filing, Enron was one of the most valuable companies in America. In 2000, Enron had $101 billion in revenues and a stock market capitalization of $63 billion. Yet in a sickeningly swift spiral, the powerful trading company tumbled into bankruptcy. Much of the blame for Enron's collapse focused on the complex trading on structured products and the partnerships set up to inflate earnings, hide Enron's problems, and personally benefit the executives. These off-balance sheet structures grew increasingly complex and risky. Then the end came quickly because Enron had overextended itself and because customers and investors had lost confidence in its secretive and complex financial maneuvers. Furthermore, Enron's collapse was also attributable to a slew of bad investments, including overseas projects ranging from a water business in England to a power distributor in Brazil.

The Enron bankruptcy wiped out its stock-market value. Billions of its bonds traded at pennies for the dollar. Its biggest lenders J.P. Morgan Chase and Citigroup, each had more than $1 billion in exposure. Other losers included Enron's customers who traded everything from electricity gas to weather derivatives. Another poignant aspect of Enron's failure is the damage to its own employees who invested heavily in Enron stock.

In the aftermath of Enron's collapse and subsequent scandals at WorldCom and Global Crossing, Congress passed the sweeping Sarbanes-Oxley Act in July 2002 to overhaul U.S. securities laws. The Securities and Exchange Commission has also pursued several separate initiatives. In addition, congressional investigators will continue to examine issues relating to "structured finance" that includes allegedly deceptive tax and accounting strategies sold by big banks to corporate clients. The aim is to put an end to concocting elaborate structured-finance schemes with no legitimate business purpose other than tax and accounting manipulation.

Sources: Enron, American Institute of Certified Public Accountants, and *Wall Street Journal* (various issues).

ket daily. An option represents the right to buy or sell an asset during a given time for a specified price, called the strike price. An option to buy is a call, while an option to sell is a put. A swap is a simultaneous buying and selling of the same security or obligation. Under an interest rate swap agreement, the two counterparties agree to exchange interest payments for a certain period of time. A currency swap involves the exchange of currencies and related interest obligations. Finally, credit derivatives are contracts used to transfer credit risk from one party to another.

Risks Associated with Derivatives

Although derivatives can be used to help manage risks of other instruments, they also have risks of their own:

- Market risk, or the instrument's sensitivity to changes in market conditions, such as fluctuations in interest rates or currency exchange rates. The market risk of leveraged derivatives may be considerable, depending on the degree of leverage and the nature of the security.

- Liquidity risk, or the chance that the instrument cannot be sold at a reasonable price within a reasonable time frame. Because many derivatives are customized instruments, their liquidity risk may be substantial. Liquidity may decrease or evaporate entirely during unfavorable markets.

- Credit risk, or the risk that the counterparty will fail to service or repay a debt. This risk mainly involves OTC instruments arranged with particular counterparties. Exchange-traded derivatives are not subject to risk related to the counterparty's creditworthiness.

- **Hedging risk**, or the possibility that the use of derivatives may limit total returns. Several types of derivatives, including futures, options, and swaps, can be used as hedges to reduce specific risks. If the anticipated risks do not develop, however, the hedges limit the total return.

Note that the risks associated with derivatives are neither new nor unique. They are the same kinds of risks associated with traditional debt, equity, or currency instruments.

Notional Principal

In dealing with derivatives, it is necessary to distinguish between the notional principal and the amount actually at risk. When we speak of the size of a particular derivative contract, we refer to the notional principal. The **notional principal** is the amount used to calculate the payoff; that is, the amount that is the basis for calculating interest and other payments. It is not a measure of risk. Using the notional principal as a representation of the amount of risk can be misleading.

For interest rate instruments, the notional principal typically does not change hands; it is simply a quantity used to calculate payments and therefore involves less exposure to market and credit risks. Foreign exchange products

| TABLE 14.1 | Notional Principal of OTC Derivatives |

Year	Total Outstanding ($ trillion)
1990	3.4
1991	4.4
1992	5.3
1993	8.4
1994	11.3
1995	17.7
1996	25.4
1997	28.7
1998	50.9
1999	58.2
2000	63.0
2001	69.2
2002	99.8

Note: Derivative market data include interest rate swaps, currency swaps, and interest rate options.

Source: ISDA Market Survey (http://www.isda.org).

generally involve the exchange of principal, and show sensitivity to price changes in the underlying markets. Table 14.1 shows the notional principal outstanding. The amount has grown from less than $3.5 trillion in 1990 to almost $100 trillion by 2002.

Although notional principal is the most commonly used volume measure in derivative markets, it is not an accurate measure of credit exposure. A useful proxy for the actual exposure of a derivative instrument is its replacement-cost credit exposure, or the cost of replacing the contract at the current market value should the counterparty default before the settlement date. Together the replacement costs of all outstanding contracts make up the gross market value.[1] Even the gross market value exaggerates the actual credit exposure, however, because it excludes netting and other risk-reducing arrangements.

FORWARD CONTRACTS

A **forward contract** is an agreement to buy or sell an asset on a certain future date for a certain price. Forward contracts trade in the OTC market, usually between two financial institutions or a financial institution and its clients. One party takes a long position and agrees to buy the underlying asset on a specific

---

[1]For example, in June 1998, the total derivatives volume was about $70 trillion, but the gross market value was $2.4 trillion. A BIS report entitled "The global OTC derivatives market at end-June 1998" provided the data.

date for a specific price. The other party assumes a short position and agrees to sell on the same date for the same price. The price specified in a forward contract is the delivery price.

The payoff from a long position in a forward contract on one unit of an asset is the difference between the spot price of the asset at maturity of the contract (S_T) and the delivery price (E), that is, the payoff is equal to $S_T - E$. For example, assume that the spot price of gold at the maturity of a forward contract is $300 per ounce and the delivery price is $290. The payoff for a long position is $10. Similarly, the payoff for a short position in a forward contract on one unit of an asset is $E - S_T$. In this example, the short position will lose $10.

Forward Prices and Spot Prices

Forward prices and spot prices have relationships with each other. Consider forward contracts on gold, for example. Suppose the spot price is $290 per ounce and the one-year risk-free rate is 5 percent. Assuming, for simplicity, that there are no storage costs, the reasonable value for the one-year forward price will be $304.50 per ounce. Now suppose the one-year forward price is $310 instead. A trader can arbitrage by making the following transactions:

1. Borrow $290 at 5 percent for one year.
2. Buy one ounce of gold.
3. Short a one-year forward contract to sell the gold for $310 one year from now.

The interest on the $290 loan is $14.50, assuming annual compounding. Therefore, the trader nets $5.50 per ounce. As investors attempt to profit from such arbitrage opportunities, the supply of the one-year forward contracts will increase, and the forward price will decrease. Conversely, if the forward price is less than $304.50 per ounce, the reverse effect will cause the forward price to increase. Eventually, the one-year forward price will be $304.50 per ounce. Any other price will lead to an arbitrage opportunity.

Credit Risk

Implicit in any forward contract is the credit risk that the counterparty might not honor the obligation. If the spot price moves toward the forward price without much volatility during the life of the forward contract, the credit risk associated with the forward contract is negligible. If the spot price of the asset is highly volatile, the credit risk will be greater because it is possible that one party will owe a large settlement amount to the other party at the maturity date. Furthermore, there is not a good secondary market for forward contracts. To close or reverse a position, a holder must make an opposite trade with the same counterparty. If instead the holder were to arrange the second contract with a different counterparty, the holder would have two contracts and two separate counterparties and would face credit risk on both.

FUTURES CONTRACTS

Like forward contracts, futures represent agreements to buy or sell a certain asset at a specified date and price. A **futures contract** represents the right to trade a standard quantity and quality of an asset at a specified date and price. Futures differ from forward contracts in that the size, delivery procedures, expiration dates, and other terms of the futures are the same for all contracts. This standardization allows futures to trade on exchanges, which provides liquidity to market participants.

Futures have a number of useful applications. They can be used to hedge risk in the spot or cash market. By taking a position opposite to the position held in the spot market, it is possible to reduce or even eliminate risk. In addition, because futures are essentially costless, they can be used to speculate on the future price of a commodity. Furthermore, because the futures contract is based on delivery of some asset or commodity in the spot market, there should be a relationship between the two prices. If these prices get out of line, an opportunity to arbitrage the difference between the two prices will exist. When some stock market index is the basis of the spot and futures contracts for the arbitrage opportunity, for example, we refer to this opportunity as index arbitrage. Finally, futures can be used to adjust the risk of a portfolio.

Basis

In the futures market, **basis** represents the difference between the cash market price and the futures price:

14.1   Basis = Current Cash Price − Futures Price.

Basis, which can be either positive or negative, indicates the likely future direction of the cash price. When the basis is positive, the cash market price is higher than the futures price. When the basis is negative, the cash market price is lower than the futures price. As the contract approaches expiration, the basis becomes smaller. At the expiration, the basis of a contract will be zero because the futures price at expiration must equal the cash market price, as both panels of Figure 14.1 show. In Figure 14.1A, the futures price is above the spot price prior to the delivery month. In Figure 14.1B, the futures price is below the spot price prior to the delivery month. In both cases, however, the spot and futures prices ultimately come together. This phenomenon, in which the futures price and the underlying spot market price approach each other until they finally coincide on the last day of trading, is a convergence.

Notice also in Figure 14.1 that although the basis of a contract will equal zero at expiration, it can fluctuate during the life of the contract. The widening or narrowing of the basis can affect the effectiveness of a hedge. This type of risk is a **basis risk**. If the asset to be hedged and the asset underlying the futures contract are the same, the basis should be zero at the expiration of the futures contract.

FIGURE 14.1A | *Spot Price and Futures Price*

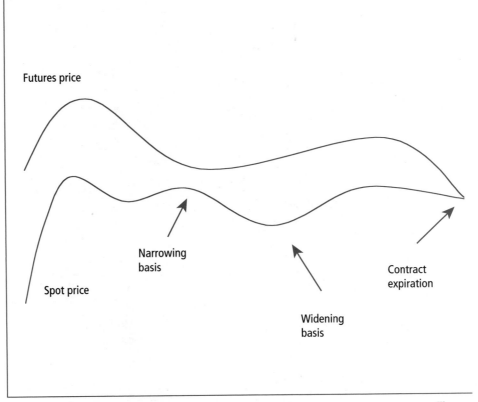

Futures Pricing

The value of a futures contract is determined by the underlying asset and the principle of arbitrage. **Arbitrage** occurs when it is possible for investors to earn a guaranteed profit without using any of their own money. This opportunity arises when the relationship between the cash and futures prices gets out of line. In principle, the value of a futures contract should be equal to the current cash market price plus any costs of carrying the commodity, such as interest, storage, and insurance costs. When the prices of the two markets get out of line, arbitrageurs will drive the prices back to their equilibrium state by purchasing in the market where the price is too low and simultaneously selling in the market where the price is too high. For example, suppose the price of gold

FIGURE 14.1B | Spot Price and Futures Price

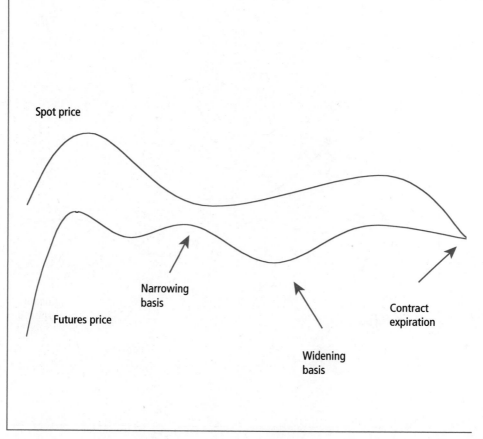

in the spot market is $300 per ounce. If the interest rate is 6 percent per year, then the futures price for a contract that expires in one year should be $318 ($300 × 1.06). If the futures price is less than $318, for example, $310, then the futures price is too low relative to the cash market price. To earn an arbitrage profit, an investor would buy the futures contract at $310 and sell short gold in the spot market for $300. The money from the short sale would be invested at the 6 percent interest rate. At the end of the period, the investor will have $318 in the bank, but will need only $310 to settle the futures contract. The gold will then be used to close out the short position. In this case, the investor will earn a guaranteed $8 without investing any money. This is an arbitrage profit. A similar result will occur if the futures price is too high relative to the cash market price.

Trading Futures Contracts

As mentioned earlier, there is a standardization of futures contracts, making it possible for these contracts to trade on the open market. Unlike forward contracts (negotiated in the OTC market), futures can be purchased and sold on exchanges such as the Chicago Board of Trade (http://www.cbot.com) and the Chicago Mercantile Exchange (CME; http://www.cme.com).

Trading takes place during trading hours in a designated physical location known as the pit, where traders make bids to buy or offers to sell futures contracts using a system of open outcry. A bid or offer is available to all other traders in the pit. Traders also use a system of hand signals to express their desire to buy or sell (see Box 14.2). In addition, there are electronic trading systems, such as the CME's GLOBEX, which provides access to the CME's electronic markets around the clock.

A market participant can choose to buy or sell a futures contract. Upon buying a contract, the purchaser agrees to take delivery of the asset at the agreed-on price (some contracts may be settled in cash, as explained later). The purchase of a futures contract is a long futures position. A long futures position will be profitable if the price of the underlying asset rises. Upon selling a futures contract, the seller agrees to make delivery of the asset at the agreed-on price. The sale of a futures contract is a short futures position. A short futures position will be profitable if the price of the asset falls.

Each futures exchange operates a clearinghouse, which plays a vital role in the smooth functioning of the market. A clearing member carries and guarantees the accounts of individual members, clearing firms, and nonmember customers doing business through the exchange to the clearinghouse. The essential purpose of the clearinghouse is to guarantee performance to all participants in the market. It assumes the position of buyer to every seller and

MARKETS IN ACTION   Hand Signals   14.2

1. Numbers
Holding your hand to your chin conveys single numbers. Holding your hand to your forehead indicates tens. Hence, three fingers on your forehead and then two on your chin would be thirty-two.

2. Buy or Sell
When your palms are facing you, the order will be taken as a buy. Palms facing away indicates you are working on a sell.

3. Cancel an Order
Making a slashing motion across your throat means cancel the bid or offer.

4. Complete an Order
The thumbs-up sign means the bid or offer you were working on is filled.

Source: Chicago Mercantile Exchange (http://www.cme.com)

seller to every buyer. Thus, all participants have the exchange clearinghouse as their counterparty. As a result, the original parties to the contract need not deal with each other. Their contractual obligations are with the clearinghouse.

Listing and Standardization of Futures Contracts

Many types of futures contracts trade on the exchanges. The underlying asset can be a physical commodity, a foreign currency, an interest-bearing asset, or an index. Commodity futures include agricultural, petroleum, and metallurgical futures contracts. Futures on foreign exchange cover all major currencies such as the British pound, euro, Japanese yen, and Swiss franc. Major interest rate futures cover Treasury bills, notes, and bonds, and Eurodollars. Furthermore, the major market indexes and the S&P 500 index are among the actively traded futures. Finally, investors can trade futures contracts based on individual stocks or weather as well.

Each exchange determines what contracts to offer based on the likely demand for the contract. Whenever there is a sufficiently active cash market for a commodity—so that a number of individuals or institutions could benefit from a futures contract in that asset—an exchange may decide to introduce a new contract. For each new contract, the exchange must specify in some detail the exact nature of the agreement between the buyer and the seller of the contract. Specifications include the underlying asset, contract size, delivery arrangements, the quoting of prices, daily price movement, and position limits. Sometimes there are alternatives specified for the asset that will be delivered and for the delivery arrangements. Typically, the seller makes a choice between these alternatives.

Standardizing contracts in this manner reduces transactions costs. Participants need not negotiate all the terms of a contract; the only item negotiated at the time of a futures transaction is the futures price. Such standardization, and the guarantee provided by the clearinghouse, make all futures contracts for the same item and maturity date perfect substitutes for one another. Consequently, a party to a futures contract can always liquidate a futures commitment before maturity through an offsetting transaction.

For example, a trader can liquidate a long position in Treasury bond futures by selling a contract for the same maturity date. The clearinghouse assumes the responsibility for collecting funds from traders who close out their positions at a loss and passes those funds along to traders with opposing positions at a profit. Most futures contracts liquidate in this manner before they mature, with only a very small percentage of all futures contracts held to maturity.

Margin Requirements and Daily Settlement

Another safeguard that contributes to the smooth functioning of the futures market is the requirement for **margin**, which is a cash deposit a trader must post with a broker in order to trade a futures contract. Margin requirements vary from contract to contract and may vary by broker. Margin can be posted in cash, a bank letter of credit, or in a short-term U.S. Treasury security. A trader faces three types of margin: initial margin, maintenance margin, and variation margin. Initial margin is the amount a trader must deposit before trading any contracts. In many cases, the initial margin is 5 percent or less of the underlying asset's value. Although 5 percent seems rather small, a system of daily settlement or marking to market is used. As a result, a futures contract settles at the end of every business day. The value in the margin rises by the amount of the gain if the futures price increases and declines by the amount of loss when the futures price decreases. This brings the value of the contract back to zero. When the equity in a trader's account falls below the maintenance margin level, she will receive a margin call, which will require the placing of additional funds into the account. The amount that needs to be deposited is the variation margin and must be sufficient to raise the account balance to the required level. If the investor does not provide the variation margin, the broker closes out the position by selling the contract.

Closing a Position

A trader can close out a futures position in three ways: delivery, offset, and an exchange for physicals. As mentioned earlier, many futures contracts call for the delivery of some assets. Delivery entails completion of the futures contract by the physical delivery of the specified commodity. In recent years, exchanges have introduced contracts that allow for cash settlement, whereby traders make payments to settle any differences in losses or gains. In general, traders rarely use physical delivery or cash settlement to close out a futures position.[2]

The most common method for closing out a futures position is offset (a reversing trade). In offset, the trader simply engages in a position opposite to the one she holds, thus leaving her with a net position of zero. For example, if a trader owns one September wheat contract, she can close the position by selling one September wheat contract.

A trader can also close a position through an exchange for physicals. In an exchange for physicals, two traders agree to simultaneously exchange a cash commodity and futures contracts based on that commodity.

Delivery

It is common to refer to a futures contract by its delivery month. The exchange specifies the precise period during the month when delivery can be made. If the party that is short the futures contract chooses to deliver the underlying asset, he must have the broker issue a notice of intention to deliver to the exchange clearinghouse. The notice will specify how many contracts will be delivered, where delivery will be made, and what grade will be delivered in the case of commodities. The exchange then uses some predetermined method for selecting the long futures party to receive delivery. If the notices are transferable, the long party has a period of time in which to find another long party

---

[2]Some financial futures only settle in cash, because it is inconvenient or impossible to deliver the underlying asset.

who will take delivery. The party taking delivery then has responsibility for all warehousing costs.

For interest rate futures such as futures on Treasury notes or bonds, the short may choose which acceptable issue to deliver and when to deliver during the delivery month. The short will select from all the deliverable issues the one that is **cheapest to deliver**; that is, the least expensive security that meets the qualification requirements for delivery. For each of the acceptable coupon Treasuries, the short calculates the return that can be earned by buying that issue, shorting the Treasury futures, and delivering the issue at the settlement date. The calculated return is the so-called **implied repo rate**. The cheapest-to-deliver issue is then the one among all acceptable issues with the highest implied repo rate.[3]

Hedging, Speculation, and Arbitrage

Futures contracts can be used for three different purposes: hedging, speculation, and arbitrage. Hedgers concern themselves with reducing or eliminating risk. Speculators show interest in profiting from movements in the price of the futures contract. Arbitrageurs attempt to profit from price discrepancies in the cash and futures markets.

Hedging entails the reduction of risk by taking an opposite position in the futures market from the trader's cash market position. For example, a farmer who owns wheat (long) would like to gain protection from a decline in the price of wheat. By taking a short position in wheat futures, the farmer can reduce the risk associated with a fall in the price of wheat. If the price of wheat falls, the farmer will sell the wheat for less in the cash market, but he will profit from his wheat futures position. Similarly, a bread manufacturer would like to be protected from an increase in the price of wheat. To protect itself from rising wheat prices, the manufacturer would buy wheat futures. If the price of wheat rises, the value of the futures contract will also rise, thus leading to a gain on the futures position. This gain will offset some or all of the additional cost of purchasing the wheat.

Because futures contracts come in standard in sizes, it is necessary to determine the **hedge ratio** or the number of contracts needed to hedge a position in the spot market. The following factors are usually important determinants of the hedge ratio:

1. The size of the spot or cash market position.
2. The size of the futures contract.
3. The sensitivity of the spot price and the futures price to some external factor such as changes in the interest rate.

---

[3]Shorting an interest rate futures contract with the intention to deliver is similar to a reverse repurchase agreement. As with a reverse repo, a trader who buys a Treasury security while selling a futures contract has temporary possession of the security, while committing to sell it at the futures price on the delivery date.

The first two factors are obvious. The larger the size of the spot market position relative to the size of the futures contract, the greater the number of contracts that will be necessary to hedge the risk. The third factor adjusts the number of contracts for the different sensitivities of spot prices and futures prices. For example, suppose you wish to hedge the purchase of 180-day T-bills with a 90-day T-bill futures contract. Because of the difference in maturities, the price of 180-day T-bills will be twice as sensitive to a change in interest rates as the futures contract. In this case, approximately twice as many futures contracts must be used to hedge the risk. As another example, suppose a portfolio manager wishes to hedge the adverse effect of a stock market correction. The manager can hedge by using an S&P 500 stock index futures contract. If the volatility of the portfolio is different from that of the S&P 500 index, however, then the number of contracts used for the hedge will need to be adjusted. If the portfolio is more (less) volatile than that of the S&P 500 index, then the number of contracts used to hedge the risk will need to be adjusted upward (downward).

Speculators differ from hedgers in that they attempt to earn profits by assuming the risks of holding only the futures contract. Speculators profit when prices move in the direction they predicted. Futures can be an extremely useful tool for speculation because of the low costs (only a small margin requirement) and the ease of entering and exiting the market. For example, a speculator profits from a long (short) position in a futures contract if the price of the underlying asset rises (falls). Speculators play an important role in the futures market because they are often the parties that assume the other half of transactions needed by hedgers.

Speculators fall into one of three categories based on how long they hold their position. Scalpers have the shortest time horizon. Generally, scalpers try to get a feel for the trading among other market participants and may hold their positions for only a few seconds or a few minutes. Scalpers can be useful to the market because their constant trading tends to provide liquidity to the market. Day traders try to profit from price movements over the course of a trading day. The name arose because day traders typically do not hold their positions overnight. Position traders have the longest time horizon of the three, holding their positions for weeks or even months. There are two types of position traders: those who hold outright positions and those who hold spread positions. With a spread position, the trader takes both long and short positions to bet on the spread between these contracts. If the spread moves in the anticipated direction, the trader gains. The trader will lose if the spread moves in the opposite direction.

Finally, as we noted earlier, arbitrageurs attempt to profit by finding mispricings between the cash and the futures markets. If the futures price is too high relative to the cash market price, then the arbitrageur will sell futures and buy in the cash market. If the futures price is too low relative to the cash market price, the arbitrageur will buy the futures and sell in the cash market.

OPTIONS

An **option** gives the holder of the option the right, but not the obligation, to buy an asset, in the case of a call option, or sell an asset in the case of a put option, at a pre-specified price during a specific time period. The price at which the security is bought or sold is the exercise or strike price. Because the option does not obligate the holder to transact, it provides unique payoff possibilities. When used in different combinations, options allow the creation of almost any contingent payoff imaginable.

There are two fundamental types of options: American options and European options. An American option allows the holder to exercise the option any time up to expiration. A European option allows the holder to exercise only at expiration.

Options trade on many different exchanges. The underlying assets include stocks, currencies, stock indexes, and many different futures contracts. Options trade on hundreds of different individual stocks. One contract gives the buyer the right to buy or sell 100 shares at the strike price. For currency options, the size of one contract depends on the currency. The two most popular stock index options are those on the S&P 100 and the S&P 500. In a futures option, the underlying asset is a futures contract. There are also OTC options, tailored by a financial institution to meet the needs of a corporate client. This section focuses on exchange-traded stock options.

Buying a Call Option

Buying a **call option** gives the holder the right, but not the obligation, to purchase the security at the exercise price during the specified time period. Because the call holder has no obligation to purchase the underlying security, the most the holder can lose is the premium paid for the option. If the stock's price is above the exercise price at the expiration of the call option, the option is in-the-money. If the stock's price is less than the exercise price, the option is out of the money. When the asset price and the exercise price are equal, the option is at-the-money. When the call option is in-the-money, the intrinsic value of the call will be the difference between the stock's price and the exercise price. When the call is out of the money, the call will not have any intrinsic value.

Figure 14.2A shows the payoff picture for the call buyer. A person purchases a call option because he believes that the price of the underlying asset will rise. As the price of the stock rises above the exercise price, the investor will profit. For every dollar that the price of the stock rises above the exercise price, the call buyer earns one dollar.[4]

---

[4]Of course, this is on a per unit basis. The actual profits have to be adjusted for the size of the contract.

FIGURE 14.2A | *Payoff Diagrams for Calls and Put Options*

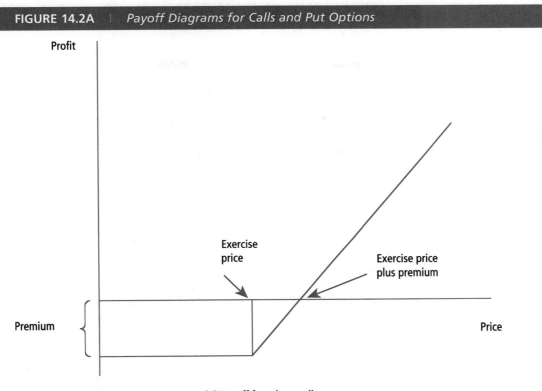

(A) Payoff for a long call

Selling a Call Option

The seller or writer of a call option gives the option holder the right to buy the stock from him at the exercise price during the specified time period. This means that the seller or writer of the call has an obligation to deliver shares should the buyer of the option choose to exercise this right. People sell call options because they believe that the price of the stock will not rise prior to expiration of the option. In this case, the seller will not have to deliver the shares of stock but will receive the option premium from the buyer. Figure 14.2B (see p. 344) illustrates the payoff for a call seller. Notice that it is the mirror image of the payoff diagram for a call option buyer. For every dollar that the price of the stock rises above the exercise price, the call writer loses one dollar.

Buying a Put Option

A **put option** gives the buyer the right to sell the underlying asset at the exercise price during the specified time period. Investors purchase put options when they believe the price of the underlying asset will fall. If the price does

FIGURE 14.2B | *Payoff Diagrams for Calls and Put Options*

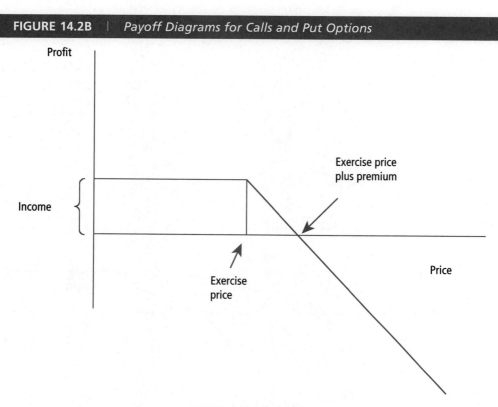

(B) Payoff for a short call

fall, the option buyer will profit from the put purchase by selling the asset at the exercise price. Put buying is similar to selling an asset short except that the most the buyer can lose is the put premium. Also, because the holder pays a premium to own the option, the profits will differ from the profits from a short sale by the amount of the premium. Figure 14.2C illustrates the payoff for the purchase of a put option.

Again, the profits from the option are tied to the price of the stock relative to the exercise price of the option. The put buyer earns profits as the price of the stock declines. For every dollar the stock price falls below the exercise price, the put buyer earns a dollar per share.

Selling a Put Option
The seller or writer of a put option receives a premium from the put buyer for giving the buyer the right to sell the stock to him at the exercise price. People sell put options when they believe that the price of the stock will remain above the exercise price; if they are correct, they will receive the premium and will

FIGURE 14.2C | *Payoff Diagrams for Calls and Put Options*

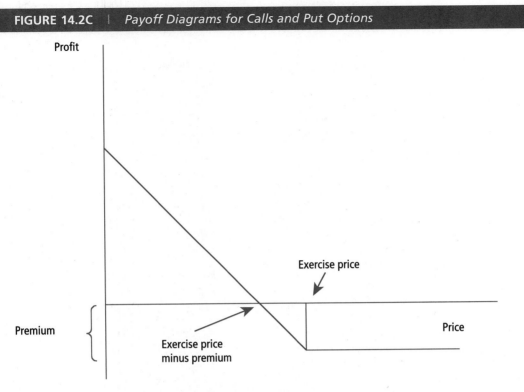

(C) Payoff for a long put

not have to buy shares of the stock. A put option can also be sold in an effort to purchase the stock at a price lower than the current market price. If the price falls, the put holder may exercise the option, which means that the put seller will have to buy shares of the stock at the exercise price. Figure 14.2D (see p. 346) shows the payoff for the sale of a put option.

As with call options, the profits from selling a put are the opposite of those from buying a put. Therefore, for every dollar that the stock's price falls below the exercise price, the put writer will lose one dollar. By combining put and call options with different exercise prices and with different positions in the underlying asset, it is possible to create almost any payoff diagram imaginable.

Options Pricing

The intuition behind options pricing lies in the fact that the value of a call option perfectly correlates with the value of the stock. Therefore, by purchasing the stock and writing call options in the correct proportions, an investor

| FIGURE 14.2D | *Payoff Diagrams for Calls and Put Options* |

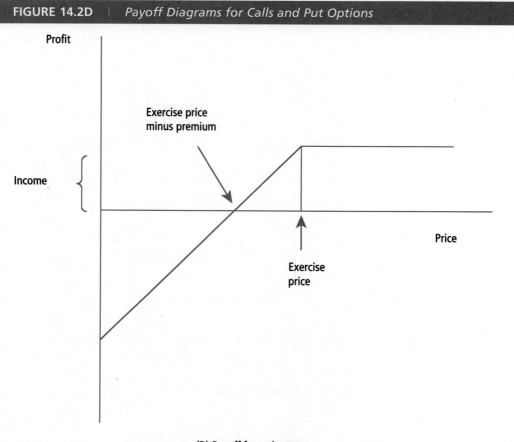

(D) Payoff for a short put

can create a riskless portfolio. This riskless portfolio must earn the risk-free rate of interest; otherwise, an arbitrage opportunity will exist. The number of call options that must be written for every share of stock purchased is the hedge ratio.

In 1973, Fischer Black and Myron Scholes produced the first satisfactory option-pricing model. The model says that a European call option's value (C) depends on five factors:

1. The current price of the stock (S).
2. The exercise or strike price of the option (E).
3. The time until the option expires (T).
4. The volatility of the stock's returns (σ^2).
5. The risk-free rate of interest (r).

The model can be expressed as follows:

14.2 $$C = S \times N(d_1) - E \times e^{-rT} \times N(d_2),$$

where

$$d_1 = \frac{\ln(S / E) + (r + 0.5\sigma^2) \times T}{\sigma\sqrt{T}}$$

$$d_2 = d_1 - \sigma\sqrt{T}, \text{ and}$$

$N(x)$ is the cumulative probability distribution function for a standardized normal variable.

An interesting aspect of the **Black/Scholes model** is that only the volatility of the stock's returns needs to be estimated; the other four factors are known. Table 14.2 summarizes the effect of changes in these variables on the price of an option.

One can find the price of a put option by applying the same concept of arbitrage. This relationship is known as put-call parity (P is the put value):

14.3 $$p = C - S + Ee^{-rT}.$$

Intuitively, by purchasing a call option and writing a put option, it is possible to create a payoff that is identical to purchasing the stock and borrowing an amount of money equal to the present value of the exercise price.

Let's consider a numerical example where the stock price six months from the expiration of an option is \$21, the strike price is \$20, the risk-free rate is 6 percent per annum, and the variance of the stock's returns is 20 percent per year. Hence,

$$d_1 = \frac{\ln(1.05) + (0.06 + 0.5 \times 0.2) \times 0.5}{\sqrt{0.2} \times \sqrt{0.5}} = 0.40727,$$

$$d_2 = 0.40727 - 0.31623 = 0.09104,$$

and

$$Ee^{-rT} = 20 \times e^{-0.03} = 19.4089.$$

TABLE 14.2 | *Effects of Changing One Variable on the Price of an Option*

Variable	Call	Put
Stock price	Positive	Negative
Exercise price	Negative	Positive
Time to expiration	Positive	Positive
Volatility	Positive	Positive
Risk-free rate	Positive	Negative

Therefore, if the option is a European call, its value is:

14.4

$$C = 21 \times N(0.40727) - 19.4089 \times N(0.09104)$$
$$= 21 \times 0.6591 - 19.4089 \times 0.5359$$
$$= 3.43987.$$

The put value will be:

14.5

$$P = 3.43987 - 21 + 19.4089 = 1.84877.$$

Measuring Volatility

There are two methods for estimating volatility of a stock's returns: historical volatility and implied volatility. The historical approach uses historical data and assumes that past volatility is a good indicator of the current volatility. In this case, interested parties collect historical return data and then compute the annualized variance. The implied volatility approach, on the other hand, assumes that the Black/Scholes model correctly prices options. Thus, the option price in the market implies the volatility. Here, different volatilities are substituted into the formula until the Black/Scholes price equals the current market price for the option. Estimating the implied volatility for options with different exercise prices will usually yield slightly different estimates. In this case, the trader uses the average of the estimates.

INTEREST RATE AND CURRENCY SWAPS

In the previous two sections, we examined two of the most commonly used exchange-traded derivatives: futures and options. In contrast, swaps represent privately negotiated or OTC securities. In a swap, two or more institutions (the counterparties) contract to exchange cash flows in the future according to some prearranged formula. Although options and futures have a long history, swaps are a relatively new tool. The first currency swaps appeared in the late 1970s when currency traders developed swaps techniques to circumvent British control over the movement of foreign currency. The first interest rate swap—an agreement between IBM and the World Bank—occurred in 1981.

The swaps market has grown tremendously over the past two decades. In the late 1980s, the value of outstanding swaps hovered around $1 trillion. By the mid-1990s, this number had grown to more than $10 trillion. By some estimates, the current level is about $50–$60 trillion. Much of this growth is a by-product of volatility in the financial markets. In many cases, market participants create swaps to hedge volatility in the financial markets. Although swaps share some of the same characteristics as exchange-traded derivatives such as futures and options, there is one big difference. Because counterparties negotiate swaps individually, the exchange clearinghouse does not guarantee the transactions. This can lead to default or counterparty risk, if the counterparty cannot honor its swap obligations. At the same time, by bypassing the floor of the exchange and negotiating contracts directly, parties can maintain a level of privacy unavailable with the use of exchange-traded derivatives. Another advantage is that unlike exchange-traded derivatives, swaps are subject to almost no government regulation. This is probably another major reason for the explosive growth in the swaps market.

A simple way to view a swap is as a series of forward contracts. In a forward contract, two parties agree to exchange some asset for a cash payment at some later date. If the forward agreement were to be settled by cash rather than by an asset-for-cash exchange, then the contract would consist of an exchange of cash flows on the expiration date. This is exactly what a one-period swap agreement is. If the contract is for more than one period, as is the case in most swaps, then the swap consists of a series of forward contracts, with each forward contract expiring on the date that cash flows are to be exchanged.

Interest Rate Swaps

The simplest swap is the plain vanilla **interest rate swap**, in which a fixed interest rate exchanges for a floating interest rate. The swap is based on an amount of unexchanged principal, known as the notional principal.

As an example, suppose that Firm A has a fixed-rate debt obligation and Firm B has a floating-rate debt obligation. Firm A wishes to convert its obligation to a floating rate, and Firm B wishes to have a fixed-rate obligation. On April 3, 2001, the two firms agree to a $100 million three-year plain vanilla interest swap. As Figure 14.3 (see p. 350) shows, Firm A agrees to pay Firm B a fixed rate of 10 percent and receives a floating interest rate of LIBOR (London InterBank Offered Rate) plus 2 percent. By swapping cash flows, each party has been able to create the type of debt obligation it desires. Table 14.3 (see p. 350) shows the cash flows from this transaction. In this example, we assume that the LIBOR rate used on the floating-rate loan is the rate at the beginning of the period. Therefore, on October 3, 2001, Firm A receives $4.5 million and pays $5.0 million. The net cash flow is therefore −$.5 million to Firm A. On April 3, 2002, Firm A receives a larger cash flow because interest rates have risen. Notice that on April 3, 2003, there is no exchange of cash flow because the amount received by Firm A exactly equals the amount paid.

In the previous example, Firms A and B negotiated the terms of the swap directly. In many cases, however, a swap broker or a swap dealer assists in completing the swap. A swap broker simply acts as a go-between, bringing the two counterparties together. A swap dealer transacts for its own account to help complete the transaction.

Figure 14.4 (see p. 351) shows a swap transaction when a swap dealer stands between the two parties to facilitate the swap. In this example, Firm A can borrow short term at LIBOR +2%, and Firm B can borrow at a fixed rate of 10 percent. However, Firm A would like a fixed-rate loan and Firm B would

FIGURE 14.3 | *Plain Vanilla Interest Rate Swap*

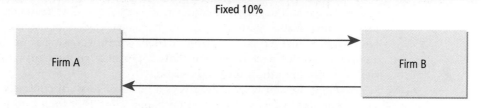

Fixed 10%

Firm A

Firm B

Floating: LIBOR + 2%

TABLE 14.3 | *Interest Rate Swap Cash Flows*

Date	LIBOR Rate (%)	Floating Cash Flow ($ millions)	Fixed Cash Paid ($ millions)	Net Cash Flow ($ millions)
April 3, 2001	7.00			
October 3, 2001	7.20	+4.5	−5.0	−0.50
April 3, 2002	7.60	+4.6	−5.0	−0.40
October 3, 2002	8.00	+4.8	−5.0	−0.20
April 3, 2003	8.20	+5.0	−5.0	0.00
October 3, 2003	8.40	+5.1	−5.0	+0.10
April 3, 2004	8.60	+5.2	−5.0	+0.20

Note: Cash flows to Firm A (the floating rate receiver) in a $100 million three-year interest rate swap upon payment of a fixed rate of 10 percent and the reception of LIBOR + 2 percent.

like a floating-rate loan tied to LIBOR. By entering into an interest rate swap, Firms A and B can convert their loans as desired. In this case, the swap dealer comes between the two and keeps a quarter percent of the money on both sides of the cash flow for a total of half a percent.

In most instances, it is unlikely that two companies will wish to engage in opposite positions of the same swap at the same time. In this case, large financial institutions will enter into a swap agreement without having an offsetting counterparty, which is warehousing interest rate swaps.

A plain vanilla interest rate swap can be viewed as an exchange of cash flows from two bonds. One bond represents a fixed-rate bond, and the other represents a floating-rate note tied to LIBOR. Therefore, the value of the swaps agreement is simply the difference between the values of the two bonds. For the counterparty that receives the floating rate and paying the fixed rate, the value of the swap is

14.6

$$V_{swap} = V_{floating} - V_{fixed},$$

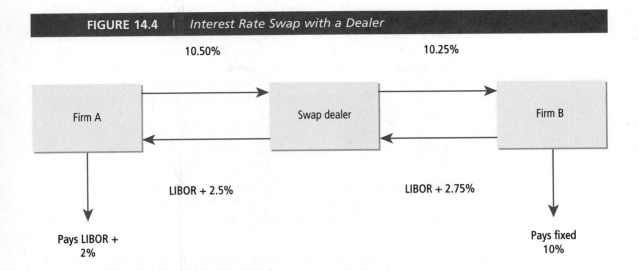

FIGURE 14.4 | *Interest Rate Swap with a Dealer*

where V_{swap} denotes the value of the swap agreement, $V_{floating}$ denotes the value of the floating-rate bond underlying the swap, and V_{fixed} denotes the value of the fixed-rate bond. Likewise, for the counterparty receiving the fixed rate and paying the floating rate, the value of the swap is the value of the fixed-rate bond less the value of the floating-rate bond. The values of the two bonds can be found by computing the present value of the cash flows.

Currency Swaps
A plain vanilla **currency swap** is more complicated than a plain vanilla interest rate swap because there is actually an exchange of cash. Therefore, the swap involves three sets of cash flows rather than one cash flow as in an interest rate swap. The first cash flow entails an exchange of cash; for example, dollars for euros. The second set of cash flows entails the exchange of periodic interest payments denominated in the appropriate currency. Finally, the principal exchanged in the first set of cash flows is itself exchanged. For example, suppose the spot exchange rate between euros and U.S. dollars is 1.10 euros per dollar. If the interest rate is 8 percent in Germany and 10 percent in the United States, Firm X, which holds €22 million and would like to exchange them for dollars, could enter into a currency swap agreement with Firm Y, as Figure 14.5 (see p. 352) shows. Notice that this currency swap involves three sets of cash flows. The two additional sets of cash flows are the exchanges of principal at the beginning and end of the period. The annual interest payments in Figure 14.5 represent the amount of money in dollars (euros) times the U.S. (German) interest rate.

In the absence of default risk, a currency swap, like an interest rate swap, can be valued as the difference between two bonds. In the case of a currency swap, however, the two bonds are from different countries, denominated in different currencies. Therefore, we must use the spot exchange rate so that both bonds have a denomination in the same currency. If one of the bonds is a U.S. bond, then the value of the swap to the receiver of U.S. dollars and a payer of foreign dollars will be

14.7

$$V_{\text{swap}} = V_{\text{dollars}} - S_0 V_{\text{foreign}},$$

where V_{swap} is the value of the currency swap contract, V_{dollars} is the value of the dollar bond, S_0 is the current spot exchange rate expressed as the number of dollars per unit of foreign currency, and V_{foreign} is the value of the foreign

FIGURE 14.5 | *A Currency Swap*

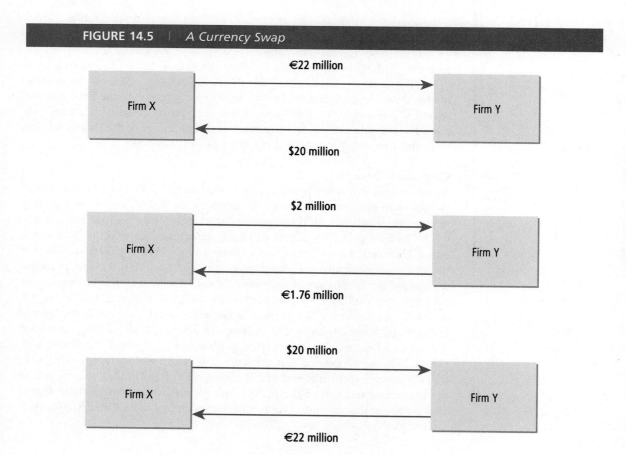

bond denominated in the foreign currency. Thus, $S_0 V_{\text{foreign}}$ is the dollar value of the foreign bond underlying the currency swap. The value of a currency swap can then be determined from the term structure of interest rates in the domestic currency, the term structure of interest rates in the foreign currency, and the spot exchange rate.

CREDIT DERIVATIVES

Credit risk is the possibility that a counterparty will fail to service or repay a debt. Such risk affects both debtors and creditors. For debtors, the cost of debt rises as the credit rating of the debt worsens. For investors (bondholders), the bond value will decline, because there must be a greater risk premium for holding the bond. Commercial banks take on credit risk when they make loans. To protect against credit risk, banks traditionally have set standards for their loans and diversified across industries and geographic areas. Some choose to securitize some of their loans and sell off pieces to other investors. But securitization requires homogeneous assets; assets with widely different characteristics and terms are difficult to securitize. Credit derivatives allow users to isolate, price, and trade firm-specific credit risk by unbundling a debt instrument or a basket of instruments and transferring each component risk to those best suited to or most interested in managing it.

A **credit derivative** is a privately negotiated contract with payoffs linked to a credit-related event, such as a default or credit rating downgrade. For example, a bank concerned about the credit of a major customer can protect itself against loss by transferring the credit risk to another party while keeping the loan on its book. This mechanism can be used for any debt instrument or for a basket of instruments. Credit derivatives offer a flexible way of managing credit risk and provide opportunities to enhance yield by purchasing credit synthetically.

Existing derivatives techniques have also been used for emerging market debt and have further been applied to corporate bonds and syndicated bank loans. In addition, investors have shown interest in using these products for yield enhancement. The four most commonly used instruments are: credit default swaps, credit spread options, total return swaps, and credit-linked notes.

Credit Default Swaps

A credit default swap is the most straightforward type of credit derivatives. It is an agreement between two counterparties that allows one party to be long a third-party credit risk, and the other to be short the same credit risk. Put differently, one counterparty sells insurance against the default of a third party and the other buys insurance against that event. In exchange for paying a premium, the buyer of the swap essentially has the right to a put on a specified asset (the reference bond) against the seller of the swap if the specified default occurs. The premium can be paid as a lump sum at the beginning of the contract or as periodic payments over the life of the contract. The seller of the swap pays the buyer only if the third party defaults.

For example, suppose that a dealer and an investor enter into a three-year credit default swap. They specify the reference asset, which is a particular credit risky bond issued by a third-party corporation or sovereign. The bond has a remaining maturity of three years and trades at par. The dealer agrees to make regular fixed (premium) payments for three years to the investor. In exchange, the dealer has the right to put the bond to the investor in exchange for the bond's par value. The credit default swap is therefore a contingent put; the third party must default to activate the put.

The premium is typically expressed in basis points of the notional amount. The decrease in the price of the security below par, after the reference credit has defaulted, determines the contingent payment. For example, in June 1997, an international bank that already had a basket of twenty loans totaling more than $500 million to mostly investment-grade companies wanted to lend more money to the same companies.[5] J.P. Morgan sold the bank the right to require J.P. Morgan to pay off any of the loans if a borrower went bankrupt.[6] J.P. Morgan could either retain the default risks in its portfolio and collect the premium or sell them to institutional investors such as insurance companies, hedge funds, or other banks. Meanwhile, J.P. Morgan's client retained the actual loans and customer relationships. Figure 14.6 depicts the transaction.

This transaction was actually a put option on a portfolio of loans or bonds. The client bank had the right to sell the default loans to J.P. Morgan at par. In a similar manner, bond investors can use this type of credit options to hedge against a decline in the price of a bond. As an example, suppose an institutional investor has a portfolio of five-year Italian government bonds. The investor pays the counterparty a premium of, for instance, 15 basis points a year. If Italy defaults on its debt, the counterparty must make a payment, which will be par less the market price. Of course, the notional principal and maturity can be tailored to provide the exact amount and tenor of protection required.

Credit default swaps have other applications as well. Consider a specialized heavy equipment company that expects to sell all of its products over the next several years to just a few customers. If a customer goes bankrupt, the equipment will be left in inventory, and the company will have no one else to sell it to. To hedge against this risk, the company can buy a credit swap on a notional principal that compensates for the loss of the sale. As another example, in project finance, an equity sponsor to a large project may want to hedge the portion of sovereign risk not guaranteed by an export credit agency-backed

[5] As reported in "Dizzying new ways to dice up debt," *Business Week*, July 21, 1997, pp. 102–103.

[6] After its merger with Chase Manhattan, the firm received the new name of J.P. Morgan Chase.

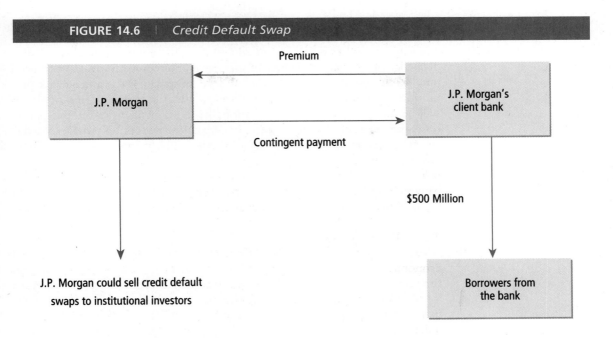

FIGURE 14.6 | *Credit Default Swap*

facility. It could enter into a credit default swap with a notional principal equal to the amount not covered by the guarantee.

Credit Spread Options

Credit spread options focus on the yield differential between credit-sensitive instruments and the reference security. Credit spread options have a relationship with bonds, priced and traded at a spread over a benchmark instrument of comparable maturity. The yield spread represents the risk premium that the market demands for holding the issuer's bonds relative to a U.S. Treasury security, LIBOR, or any other relevant benchmark. For example, an investor sells an option on the credit spread of a BBB-rated corporate bond with a three-year maturity to a bank in exchange for a premium up front. The option gives the bank the right to sell the bond to the investor at a certain strike price. The credit spread over a three-year Treasury sets the strike price here. On the expiration date, if the actual spread of the corporate bond is less than the strike price, the option expires worthless. If the spread is higher, then the bank delivers the underlying bond, and the investor pays the price whose yield spread over the benchmark equals the strike price.

Credit spread options can also be used by bond issuers to hedge against a rise in the average credit risk premium. As an illustration, suppose a Baa-rated company plans to issue $50 million of two-year bonds in three months. The interest rate the company anticipates paying is the current spread of 70 basis points over the two-year Treasury notes. If the average risk premium for Baa-companies increases before the bonds' issuance, the interest payments will rise. To hedge against the widening of the spread, the company could purchase a put option with a strike at the current level of spread. If the average risk premium rises above the strike rate in three months, the higher interest payments will be offset by gains from the option. Since payments from the put option offset the increased borrowing cost, purchasing the put option provides a hedge against increases in the credit premium. Alternatively, suppose that the credit risk premium falls. The put option has no payoff, but the company saves financing costs at a lower spread. Thus, purchasing the put option allows the company to insure against an increase in the credit risk premium while maintaining the benefits of lower funding costs if the spread declines.

Total Return Swaps

A **total return swap** is a contract that allows an investor to receive the total economic return of an asset without actually owning the asset. One party pays the total return on a notional amount of principal to another party in return for a periodic fixed- or floating-rate payment. The underlying reference benchmark for the payment can be any financial asset, a basket of assets, or an index.

Banks use total return swaps as a way of transferring the risk exposure of an asset to another interested party. Investors seeking exposure to a bank portfolio use these swaps to enhance their yield. For example, a bank might agree to pay the total return on a $250 million loan portfolio to an insurance company in exchange for semiannual payments of LIBOR plus 45 basis points. This allows the bank to reduce its exposure to the credit risk of the portfolio without selling the loans. Banks often want to keep loans on their books to avoid jeopardizing their client relationships or breaching client confidentiality. Meanwhile, the insurance company has obtained exposure to the portfolio without acquiring the loans.

Credit-Linked Notes

A **credit-linked note** is a security in which the coupon or the price of the note links to the performance of a reference asset. It offers borrowers a hedge against credit risk and investors a higher yield for buying a credit exposure. The creation of credit-linked notes occurs through a special purpose company or trust collateralized with AAA-rated securities. Investors buy the securities from the trust, which pays a fixed- or floating-rate coupon during the life of the notes. At maturity, investors receive par unless the reference credit defaults; in that case, the investors will receive the recovery value. For example, an automobile financing company may use debt to fund a portfolio of auto loans. To reduce its credit risk, the company creates credit-linked notes that pay lenders a higher coupon rate and the principal if automobile loan delinquency is below, say, 5 percent. If the default rate exceeds 5 percent, however, investors will receive payments based on a formula with potential loss of interest and principal.

CONCLUDING SUMMARY

The tremendous growth of the derivative markets and reports of major losses associated with derivatives trading have resulted in a great deal of confusion about these complex financial instruments. Critics fear that derivatives have posed and will continue to pose a great danger to the global financial system. Others, however, point out that financial derivatives serve an important purpose. Derivatives offer the opportunity for organizations to transfer risks to others who can and will manage these risks, thereby improving market efficiency.

This chapter has described several of the most common types of derivative securities. Futures and options trade on many different exchanges. They are standardized, and the exchange clearinghouse guarantees the performance of the contract. Other types of derivatives, such as forward contracts, swaps, and credit derivatives, trade in OTC markets.

The common types of futures contracts cover index, currency, interest rates, and commodities. Assets such as stocks and futures contracts are the underlying assets for options contracts. Swaps include interest rate swaps, currency swaps, and others. The market for credit derivatives, used to manage credit risks, has grown rapidly. Commonly used credit derivatives include credit default swaps, credit spread options, total return swaps, and credit-linked notes.

Key Terms

arbitrage 335
basis 334
basis risk 334
Black/Scholes model 347
call option 342
cheapest to deliver 340
credit derivative 353
credit-linked note 356
credit spread options 355
currency swap 351
derivative security 330
forward contract 332

futures contract 334
hedge ratio 340
hedging 340
hedging risk 331
implied repo rate 340
interest rate swap 349
margin 338
notional principal 331
option 342
put option 343
speculator 341
total return swap 356

Review Questions

1. Explain the differences between credit risk and market risk. How can each type of risk be hedged?

2. Companies A and B have received offers of the following rates per annum on a $50 million three-year loan:

	Fixed Rate	Floating Rate
Company A	9.00%	LIBOR + 0.25%
Company B	10.00%	LIBOR + 0.75%

   Company A requires a floating-rate loan; Company B wishes a fixed-rate loan. Design an interest rate swap that will net a swap dealer, acting as intermediary, 10 basis points and appear equally attractive to both companies.

3. A financial institution finds that its assets are mostly fixed-rate loans, whereas its liabilities are mostly floating-rate deposits. How can interest rate swaps be used to manage this type of interest rate risk?

4. Explain the main differences between a currency swap and an interest rate swap.

5. Assume a stock price is currently at $28 per share and the strike price for a call option is $25. The call option has three months until expiration. The estimation of the volatility of this stock's returns is 25 percent. What is the minimum value of the call option?

6. Assume you purchase 500 shares of ABC stock at $25 per share. At the same time, you also purchase five three-month calls and five puts on the stock at a strike of $25. The premiums paid for the calls and puts are $2 and $1, respectively. Assume that you liquidate all positions on the option expiration date. What are your gains or losses?

7. Briefly explain when a short hedge is appropriate, using futures contracts.

8. What are the main differences between futures and forward contracts?

9. ABC Company has issued a five-year bond at LIBOR + 0.5 percent. Is there an interest rate risk associated with the purchase of this bond? Is there a credit risk associated with holding the bond? How can these risks be managed?

Select Bibliography

Anson, M. J. P. *Credit Derivatives.* New Hope, Penn.: Frank J. Fabozzi Associates, 1999.

Das, S. *Swaps & Derivative Financing.* Chicago: Probus Publishing, 1994.

Dattatreya, R. E., and S. Peng. *The Structured Note Market.* Chicago: Probus Publishing, 1995.

Galitz, L. *Financial Engineering: Tools and Techniques to Manage Financial Risks.* Burr Ridge, Ill.: Irwin Professional Publishing, 1995.

Hull, J. C. *Options, Futures, and Other Derivatives.* Upper Saddle River, N.J.: Prentice Hall, 2002.

Jarrow, R., and S. Turnbull. *Derivative Securities.* Cincinnati, Ohio: South-Western, 1999.

McDonald, R. L. *Derivatives Markets.* Boston, Mass.: Addison-Wesley, 2002.

Siems, T. F. "10 myths about financial derivatives." *CATO Policy Analysis,* no. 283, September 11, 1997.

Stigum, M. L. *Money Market Derivatives and Structured Notes.* New York: McGraw-Hill, 1996.

Tavakoli, J. M. *Credit Derivatives: A Guide to Instruments and Applications.* New York: John Wiley & Sons, 1998.

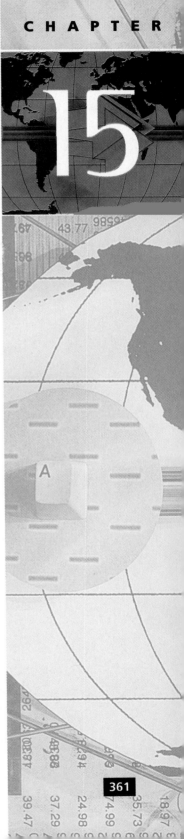

Foreign Exchange Markets

The foreign exchange market is vital to international trade and to the integration of the global capital markets. Whenever we drive a BMW, wear Italian shoes, or have a Beck's Beer before dinner, we use products originally purchased with foreign exchange. Foreign exchange is a general term that refers to money denominated in the currency of another nation or group of nations. It can take the form of foreign currency notes, foreign currency–denominated bank deposits, or claims denominated in foreign currency. Thus, within the United States, any money denominated in any currency other than the U.S. dollar is foreign exchange. This chapter first describes the basic mechanics of foreign exchange trading, including the conventions used for quoting exchange rates. Various instruments, including forward contracts, futures, options, and currency swaps trade in the foreign exchange market. Foreign exchange trading also involves risks; the chapter concludes with an examination of how they can be managed.

The objectives of this chapter are to provide an understanding of:
- The mechanics of foreign exchange trading.
- Spot rate and forward contracts.
- Currency swaps and over-the-counter currency options.
- Exchange-traded currency futures and options.
- Risk management in foreign exchange trading.

MARKET OVERVIEW

Since the early 1970s, the global foreign exchange market has experienced tremendous growth. Today, this market is the largest in the world, with average daily trading volume in excess of $1 trillion, far exceeding the trading volume in stocks or bonds. The growth of the foreign exchange market reflects the continuing expansion of international trade and the globalization of finance and investment. Several developments have stimulated these trends. First, the international monetary system underwent a fundamental transformation from a fixed exchange rate system to a floating rate system. Many countries have now adopted floating exchange rate regimes. Hence, the exchange rate matters. Second, financial deregulation occurs throughout the world. Many governments have lifted foreign exchange controls and restrictions.[1] Third, a similar trend toward trade liberalization has taken place as governments not only remove restrictions on trade but also take positive steps to encourage it, such as the adoption of the North America Free Trade Agreement (NAFTA), the formation of the European Union, and China's entry into the World Trade Organization (WTO). Fourth, advances in information technology have made it possible to transmit vast amounts of market data worldwide. New technology also provides the computing power needed to analyze these data to identify and exploit market opportunities and to quickly and reliably execute financial transactions.

Foreign Exchange Centers and Vehicle Currency

The foreign exchange market is a global market with participants buying and selling currencies worldwide via communications systems such as telephones, telexes, computers, and news wires. Although trading takes place throughout most of each day in all major financial centers, most transactions take place in London, New York, Chicago, and Tokyo.

London's preeminence reflects its leading position as an international financial center. Not only are a large number of foreign exchange dealers located in the United Kingdom, but London also benefits from its proximity to major European financial centers and its time zone. Its trading hours overlap with those of other financial centers in Europe, North America, and Asia. London's morning hours overlap with late hours in the Middle East and Asia. Its afternoon hours correspond to the morning sessions in North American markets.

Although London captures the largest share of foreign exchange trading, the U.S. dollar is by far the most widely traded currency. The widespread use of the U.S. dollar reflects its many roles as a reserve currency held by many central banks, an investment currency in many capital markets, a transaction currency in international trade, and an invoice currency in many contracts. Furthermore, many use the dollar as a **vehicle currency** in foreign exchange

---

[1]Some nations, especially developing countries, may still impose restrictions on foreign exchange transactions.

transactions. When trading a pair of currencies, traders often trade each of the two currencies against a common third currency as a vehicle, rather than trading the two currencies directly against each other. The most commonly used vehicle currency is the U.S. dollar. As an example, suppose a trader wants to shift funds from Swedish krona to Philippine pesos. The trader will sell krona for U.S. dollars and then sell the dollars for pesos, rather than selling krona directly for pesos. Frequently, traders utilize this approach because the dollar-krona and the dollar-pesos markets are more active and liquid than the krona-pesos market.

Market Participants

Participants in the foreign exchange market include dealers (commercial and investment banks), brokers, individuals, corporations, and central banks. Large commercial banks have traditionally played a dominant role as major dealers in the foreign exchange market, which is largely an over-the-counter (OTC) market. Like dealers in the OTC stock market, foreign exchange dealers regularly quote both bids and offers for particular currencies and stand ready to make a two-sided market for their customers. These market-making activities contribute to the functioning of the market by increasing liquidity, providing price information, and maintaining continuity of trading. About two-thirds of the total volume in the foreign exchange market represents trading among foreign exchange dealers themselves, with the remaining one-third accounted for by the dealers' transactions with customers. In recent years, investment banking firms and other financial institutions have begun to compete directly with commercial banks as dealers in the OTC market. Thus, they are now also part of the network of the foreign exchange market. Although still called the interbank market in foreign exchange, it is more accurately an interdealer market.

Bankers also facilitate the smooth functioning of the market by helping the would-be parties to a transaction find each other. A broker is an intermediary acting as an agent for one or both parties in the transaction in return for a fee or commission. Unlike dealers, brokers do not take positions or face the risk of holding an inventory subject to exchange rate fluctuations. In the OTC market, the activity of brokers is mostly in the dealers market.

The range of financial and nonfinancial customers includes smaller commercial banks and investment banks that do not act as major dealers, corporations that buy or sell foreign exchange because of international trade, money managers, pension funds, and individuals. For these intermediaries and end-users, the foreign exchange transaction is part of the payment process for completing a commercial, an investment, a speculative, or a hedging activity.

Finally, central banks participate in the foreign exchange market to monitor the market and to intervene for purposes of policy implementation. When a central bank uses its foreign exchange reserves to buy its own country's currency, it uses the intervention to decrease the supply of the currency and thus increasing its value in the foreign exchange market. Conversely, when a central bank sells its own currency for foreign currency, the objective is to increase the supply of its currency and thus lower its exchange rate. A striking example of central bank intervention was the Group of Five's effort to depreciate the dollar in September 1985. The central banks of France, Germany, Japan, the United Kingdom, and the United States sold billions of U.S. dollars, resulting in a 35 percent depreciation of the dollar in ten months. More recently, the U.S. Federal Reserve and other central banks intervened to prop up the Japanese yen in 1998 in the midst of the Asian financial crisis. Another recent intervention was the coordinated action by the U.S. Federal Reserve and the Canadian, Japanese, British, and several other European central banks to end a slump in the euro in September 2000 (see Box 15.1).

MECHANICS OF FOREIGN EXCHANGE TRADING

As mentioned earlier, most foreign exchange transactions take place in the OTC market. In the United States, for example, more than 90 percent of foreign exchange trading activities are OTC transactions. No official restrictions

MARKETS IN ACTION   The Euro

15.1

The euro is the common currency of the members of the European Monetary Union (EMU). The euro began trading in January 1999 at $1.17, but it steadily lost value against the dollar. The accompanying table shows the euro rate at the end of each month from January 1999 until the intervention in September 2000. The sliding euro prompted the world's most powerful central banks to step in on September 22, 2000, to bolster the euro to prevent a global economic downturn.

Date	USD/EUR
January 4, 1999	1.1812
January 29, 1999	1.1371
February 26, 1999	1.0995
March 31, 1999	1.0808
April 30, 1999	1.0564
May 28, 1999	1.0422
June 30, 1999	1.0310
July 30, 1999	1.0661
August 31, 1999	1.0581
September 30, 1999	1.0643
October 29, 1999	1.0518
November 30, 1999	1.0100
December 31, 1999	1.0070
January 31, 2000	0.9757
February 29, 2000	0.9643
March 31, 2000	0.9574
April 28, 2000	0.9089
May 31, 2000	0.9328
June 30, 2000	0.9545
July 31, 2000	0.9266
August 31, 2000	0.8878

Source: *Statistics: Releases and Historical Data*, The Federal Reserve Board.

or rules govern the hours or conditions of trading in the United States. Instead, market participants have developed these procedures. These procedures include the conventions for quoting exchange rates and the actual mechanics of conducting trades.

Exchange Rate Quotes

Every foreign exchange transaction involves two currencies: a base currency and a terms currency. A trader always buys or sells a fixed amount of the base currency and adjusts the amount of the terms currency as the exchange rate changes. The exchange rate is the price, the number of units of one nation's currency that must be rendered to obtain one unit of another nation's currency. Thus, there is an exchange rate for every national currency traded in the U.S. foreign exchange market. Table 15.1 lists several exchange rates as of December 11, 2002.

As the table shows, the dollar-yen exchange rate was 123.40, meaning that one U.S. dollar (USD) could be exchanged for 123.40 Japanese yen (JPY). This can also be expressed as JPY/USD, the amount of Japanese yen needed to purchase one U.S. dollar. This way of quoting the exchange rate is called European terms. The name means that the quotation is a direct quote from the perspective of someone in Europe (or, in this case, Japan); thus, it gives the amount of domestic currency (yen) per unit of foreign currency (dollars). Notice that the quotation is indirect from the U.S. perspective; that is, it quotes the amount of foreign currency (yen) per unit of domestic currency (dollars). In this example, the U.S. dollar is the base currency, and the Japanese yen is the terms currency. Most currencies are quoted in European terms. The exceptions are the euro, the British pound sterling, and the currencies of several former Commonwealth countries. These exceptions exist because the pound was formerly not a decimal currency and it was easier to quote it in terms of other currencies. The quotes of these currencies are usually in American terms, meaning a direct quote from the perspective of someone located in the United

TABLE 15.1 | *Cross Currency Rates*

	USD	GBP	CHF	JPY	CAD	AUD	EUR
EUR	0.9914	1.5613	0.6783	0.8034	0.6367	0.5564	
AUD	1.7817	2.8059	1.2191	1.4438	1.1443		1.7972
CAD	1.5571	2.4520	1.0653	1.2617		0.8739	1.5705
JPY	123.40	194.34	84.43		79.26	69.26	124.47
CHF	1.4616	2.3017		1.1844	0.9387	0.8203	1.4742
GBP	0.6350		0.4345	0.5146	0.4078	0.3564	0.6405
USD		1.5748	0.6842	0.8103	0.6422	0.5613	1.0087

Note: USD = U.S. dollar, GBP = British pound, CHF = Swiss franc, JPY = Japanese yen, CAD = Canadian dollar, AUD = Australian dollar, EUR = euro. Quotes under JPY are JPYx100.

Source: Bloomberg, December 11, 2002.

States. Thus, they are quoted in terms of the number of dollars (domestic currency) per unit of the foreign currency (pounds or euros). For example, the exchange rates for the sterling and the euro were 1.5748 and 1.0087, respectively, on December 11, 2002.

There is a reciprocal relationship between European and American term quotes. For example, the USD/GBP was 1.5748 (American terms). In European terms, the exchange rate would be just the reciprocal of 1.5748, or

15.1
$$\frac{GBP}{USD} = \frac{1}{\left(\dfrac{USD}{GBP}\right)} = \frac{1}{1.5748} = 0.6350.$$

Table 15.1 also lists several cross-exchange rates. A **cross-exchange rate** is an exchange rate between a currency pair where neither currency is the U.S. dollar. The cross-exchange rate can be calculated from the U.S. dollar exchange rates for the two currencies. For example, the JPY/GBP cross rate can be calculated from the JPY/USD and USD/GBP:

15.2 $JPY / GBP = (JPY / USD) \times (USD / GBP)$, *or numerically*

15.3 $194.33 = 123.40 \times 1.5748$

Bid and Offer

Market participants think in terms of how much it costs to buy or sell the base currency. A dealer's bid price is the amount of terms currency that the dealer will pay for one unit of the base currency; the offer price is the amount of terms currency the dealer will charge for a unit of the base currency. The differential is the dealer's spread. For example, a market maker's pound-dollar quote of 1.5748-52 indicates a bid price of $1.5748 per pound and an offer of $1.5752 per pound. The differential, USD 0.0004 per pound, represents the dealer's spread. Note that in trader jargon, in the quote 1.5748-52, the "1.57" is the big picture, and assumed to be known by all traders. Hence, a trader would ordinarily respond "48 to 52" when asked for a quote on the British pound.

Direct Dealing and Trading through Brokers

Dealers trade with each other both directly and through brokers. In the past, almost all trades were made by telephone or by telex, but now electronic dealing systems account for a very large portion of the direct trading among dealers. The dealers use computers to communicate with each other and to make and record transactions.

A direct dealing scenario might proceed like this. Trader Jane asks market maker Jim for quotes for buying and selling $10 million Swiss francs (CHF). Jane asks the rates on "spot dollar-swissie on ten dollars." Jim responds that dollar-swissie is 1.4616-21 or simply 16-21. This means that Jim wants to buy $10 million at a rate of CHF 1.4616 per dollar and sell $10 million at the rate of CHF 1.4621 per dollar. If Jane wants to buy and agrees with Jim's offer price, she will respond by saying "Done, I buy ten dollars at 1.4621." Jim might finish up with "Agreed." The trade is done.

The traditional role of a broker is to act as a go-between in foreign exchange trades. Until 1992, voice or live brokers handled almost all brokering in the OTC foreign exchange market. Voice brokers communicate with their client dealers via dedicated telephone lines. A live broker maintains close contact with many dealers and keeps informed about the prices each dealer quotes. When a customer calls, the broker will give the best price available— the highest bid if the customer wants to sell and the lowest offer if the customer wants to buy. With a broker, a trader who asks to see a quote may have the choice not only of hitting the bid or taking the offer, but also of joining either side of the quotes, or of improving either the bid or the offer being quoted in the broker's market.

The OTC spot market started to use electronic brokerage systems in 1992. In these systems, participants trade through a network of linked computer terminals. To trade, a trader keys an order into the system. If the order can be filled from other orders outstanding, and it is the best price from institutions acceptable to that trader's institution, the deal will be completed. If a new order cannot be matched with outstanding orders, the new order will be entered into the system and other participating users will have access to it. The order may be matched later, or it can be withdrawn.

Foreign Exchange Payment and Settlement System

Executing a foreign exchange transaction requires two transfers of currency, because it involves the exchange of one currency for another. The transfers engage the payment and settlement systems of both nations involved. In terms of the number of transactions, most payments in the United States are made with cash or checks, but the electronic funds transfer systems account for more than 80 percent of the value of payments. The two electronic funds transfer systems in the United States are CHIPS (Clearing House Interbank Payments System) and Fedwire.

Other countries also have interbank funds transfer systems. In the United Kingdom, the pound sterling leg of a foreign exchange transaction often settles through CHAPS (Clearing House Association Payments System). In the euro zone, the system is TARGET.

SPOT RATE AND FORWARD CONTRACTS

A wide variety of foreign exchange instruments trade in the OTC market. This section examines spot transactions, outright forwards, and foreign exchange swaps. The next section discusses the other OTC instruments—OTC currency swaps and OTC currency options.

Spot Market Trading

A **spot transaction** is an exchange of one currency for another with settlement in two business days, known as the value date. The spot rate is the current market price. As described earlier, in the OTC market the market practice is to quote U.S. dollars in European terms against most other currencies. Hence, the dollar is often the base currency.

In the interbank market, most trading goes through the dollar and involves cross-exchange rates. Remember that a cross-exchange rate is an exchange rate in which the dollar is neither the base currency nor the terms currency. For example, suppose a bank customer wants to trade out of British pounds and into Japanese yen. The bank frequently handles this trade for its customer by selling British pounds for U.S. dollars and then selling U.S. dollars for Japanese yen. As shown earlier, the value for USD/GBP and JPY/USA in Table 15.1 determined the cross rate for JPY/GBP of 194.33 on December 11, 2002.

Certain banks specialize in making a direct market between nondollar currencies. Their direct quotes are generally consistent with cross-exchange rates. If not, a triangular arbitrage is possible. **Triangular arbitrage** is the process of trading out of the U.S. dollar into a second currency, then trading it for a third currency, which is in turn traded for U.S. dollars. The purpose is to earn an arbitrage profit via trading from the second to the third currency when the direct exchange rate between the pair is not in alignment with the cross-exchange rate.

To illustrate a triangular arbitrage, assume the cross rates for JPY/USD and USD/GBP are 123.40 and 1.5748, as Table 15.1 shows.[2] A trader observes that a dealer makes a direct market between the yen and the pound, with a quote of 194.04. The trader calculates the cross rate at 194.33. A triangular arbitrage profit is available if the trader makes the following trades. A sale of $10 million for yen will yield 1,234,000,000 yen. This amount of yen will be resold for pounds. The amount of pounds the trader receives is 1,234,000,000/194.04 = £6,359,513. The trader sells the pounds for U.S. dollars to yield 6,359,513 × 1.5748 = $10,014,961 U.S. dollars. The arbitrage profit is $14,961; that is, the trader receives $10,014,961 for an initial outlay of $10,000,000.

Outright Forwards

Assume that ABC Company has located a new foreign supplier of fiber optics. On December 11, 2002, the company receives a quote of 400,000 Swiss francs (CHF) for a shipment. The price looks attractive given the current spot rate of 1.4616 CHF per dollar, or a cost of $273,672.69. Since the foreign supplier will need a few weeks to complete the manufacturing and shipment will take additional time, ABC Company believes that a payment date of January 30, 2003, seems reasonable. The chief financial officer believes that the current exchange rate is one of the best in recent memory, and he has concern that the rate may change before he has to make the payment. Any depreciation of the dollar

---

[2]For simplicity, we will ignore the bid-offer spread in this example.

before payment will increase the ultimate cost of this material. To avoid this potential for a price hike, the company contacts its bank's foreign exchange desk to book a forward contract.

An **outright forward** transaction is a single purchase or sale of one currency for another. The trade will settle on a preagreed date, often three or more business days after the trade date.[3] The specific forward exchange rate may be the same as the spot rate but is generally different. Though the exchange rate at which the execution of the forward transaction takes place is fixed at the outset, no money necessarily changes hands until the transaction takes place. ABC Company would book a forward contract for settlement on January 30, 2003, to eliminate the uncertainty in the exchange rate.

An outright forward is a flexible instrument. The contract can be tailored and customized to meet the specific needs of a customer with respect to maturity, size, and currency. Because those instruments do not have common standardized features, however, they tend to be less liquid and more difficult to reverse. The standard contract periods are one, two, three, six, and twelve months (called **straight dates**). Customers can obtain odd-date or broken-date contracts for periods falling between standard dates.

If the foreign exchange market is efficient, the forward rate will move toward an equilibrium point at which the interest rate differential between the two currencies will be offset by a premium or discount in the forward rate. Take Eurocurrency for example. Money can flow quickly and in large volume from one **Eurocurrency** (a deposit claim on a currency but deposited in a bank outside the country) to another. Thus, Eurodeposit rates (interest rates on Eurocurrency), spot exchange rates, and forward exchange rates are interdependent with identical yields across currencies. This condition is the **interest rate parity**. It can be expressed as:

15.4

$$F = S \frac{(1 + r_f)}{(1 + r_s)},$$

where F is the forward rate expressed as units of foreign currency per dollar, S is the spot exchange rate expressed as units of foreign currency per dollar, $r_\$$ is the Eurodollar deposit rate, and r_f is the other Eurocurrency deposit rate.

If the interest rate parity condition does not hold, a covered interest arbitrage opportunity will present itself. For example, if six-month Eurodollar deposits pay interest of 6 percent per year and six-month Euroyen deposits pay interest of 3 percent a year, and there is no premium or discount on the forward yen against the dollar, there would be an arbitrage opportunity. It would pay to borrow yen at 3 percent, sell the yen spot for dollars, and simultaneously resell dollars forward for yen in six months. At the same time, the dollars are invested at a rate of 6 percent for six months. This arbitrage process will result

---

[3]Note that spot trading is T + 2.

in an appreciation of the yen relative to the dollar until the establishment of equilibrium.

Forward rates are usually quoted in premiums or discounts from the spot rate. We measure the premium or discount in points, which is the amount of foreign exchange that will neutralize the interest rate differential between two currencies for the applicable period. For any currency pair, if the base currency earns a lower interest rate than the terms currency, the base currency will trade at a forward premium, or above the spot rate. Conversely, if the base currency earns a higher interest rate than the terms currency, the base currency will trade at a forward discount, or below the spot rate. We use the following formula for calculating the points:

$$\boxed{15.5} \quad points = (spot\ rate) \times \left[\frac{1 + r_t \times \dfrac{forward\ days}{360}}{1 + r_b \times \dfrac{forward\ days}{360}} - 1 \right].$$

where r_t denotes the terms currency interest rate and r_b denotes the base currency interest rate. For example, suppose that we want to calculate the forward premium or discount points for a 181-day dollar-yen forward. Let's assume that the Eurodollar interest rate is 5 percent and the Euroyen interest rate is 3 percent. Assume also the spot rate is 123.40. Hence, the points are:

$$\boxed{15.6} \quad points = (123.40) \times \left[\frac{1 + 3\% \times \dfrac{181}{360}}{1 + 5\% \times \dfrac{181}{360}} - 1 \right] = -1.22.$$

The six-month outright forward discount for dollar-yen would be 1.22 yen per dollar. Hence, the six-month outright forward rate would be 122.18 yen per dollar.

Foreign Exchange Swaps

The use of a foreign exchange (FX) swap can be illustrated by the following example. High Tech, Inc. decides on December 11, 2002, to expand its operations in Asia by establishing a subsidiary in Tokyo. The subsidiary will buy material from High Tech, repackage it to meet local market requirements, and distribute the product throughout Asia. The subsidiary will be operational and financially self-supporting in nine months. High Tech will initially loan the subsidiary 200 million yen to cover all startup costs and initial operating expenses. The CFO is uncomfortable with the currency risk involved with this conversion into yen, as these funds will have to be reconverted back into dollars when the loan is repaid. High Tech can tap into the FX swap market to avoid this type of risk. High Tech can buy 200 million yen at the current exchange rate of 123.40, or $1,620,745.54. At the same time, High Tech can enter into an arrangement to sell 200 million yen for delivery nine months later. If the exchange rate specified in the contract is 123.00, the forward leg of the swap will give High Tech $1,626,016.26.

In an **FX swap**, the two counterparties agree to exchange two currencies at a particular rate on one date, called the near date, and to reverse the payments on a specified subsequent date, called the far date.[4] Effectively, it is either a spot transaction and an outright forward transaction going in the opposite direction, or else two outright forwards with two different settlement dates. If both the near and far dates are within one month from the deal date, it is a **short-dated swap**. If one or both dates are one month or more from the deal date, it is a **forward swap**.

There are two types of FX swaps: buy/sell and sell/buy. In buy/sell FX swap, one purchases the base currency on the near date and sells on the far date. In a sell/buy FX swap, the trader sells the base currency on the near date and repurchases it on the far date. For example, if a trader purchases a fixed amount of yen spot for dollars and sells yen six months forward for dollar, it is a buy/sell yen swap.

CURRENCY SWAPS AND OTC CURRENCY OPTIONS

The foreign exchange products just discussed have been in use for many years. In recent decades, two newer products for use in OTC trading have sprung up: currency swaps and OTC currency options.

Currency Swaps
Currency swaps allow companies to exploit the global capital markets more efficiently. In a **currency swap,** the two counterparties exchange equal initial principal amounts of two currencies at the spot rate, then exchange a stream of interest payments in the swapped currencies, and finally reexchange the initial principal amounts at maturity. Sometimes, instead of exchanging interest payments, one counterparty pays the other a difference check to cover the net obligation.

For example, consider a U.S.-based company that has raised money by issuing a Swiss franc-denominated Eurobond (a bond sold to investors in several countries without being subject to the full regulation of any single country) with fixed semiannual coupon payments of 6 percent on 100 million Swiss francs.[5] The company has received 100 million Swiss francs (ignoring transactions costs) and wants to use the funds to finance its U.S. operations. The

---

[4]An FX swap differs from a currency swap. In an FX swap, the counterparties exchange and reexchange the two currencies involved. In a currency swap, the two counterparties exchange and reexchange the currencies and stream of interest payments in two different currencies.

[5]One good reason to do this is that there are investors with Swiss franc funds who look to diversify their portfolios with U.S. credits such as this company's. They will buy the U.S. company's Eurobonds at a lower yield than the company can issue bonds in the United States.

company has to convert the money from Swiss francs into U.S. dollars and pays its liability for the coupon payments in U.S. dollars every six months. The company can accomplish this by entering into a currency swap contract with a dealer.

The process works as follows. The company agrees to exchange the 100 million Swiss francs at inception into U.S. dollars, receive the Swiss franc coupon payments to pay its Eurobond investors, make U.S. dollar payments tied to a preset index, and reexchange the U.S. dollar notional into Swiss francs at maturity. Figure 15.1 depicts the process.

FIGURE 15.1 | *A Currency Swap Example*

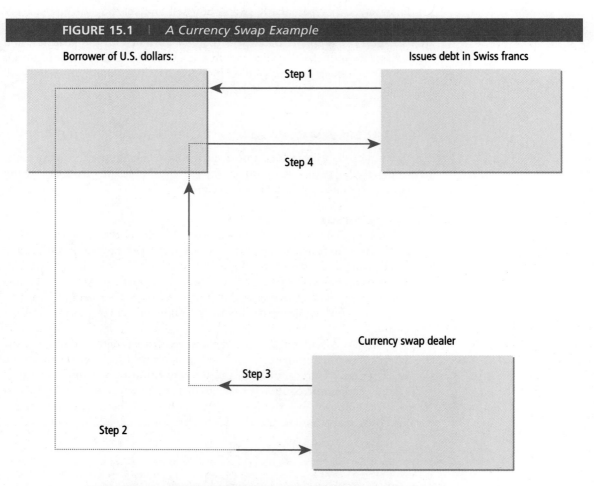

Step 1: The company issues debt in the Eurobond market to raise Swiss francs.
Step 2: The Swiss francs are swapped for dollars for the company's use during the life of the loan.
Step 3: The dollars are swapped back for Swiss francs to pay the periodic interests and loan.
Step 4: The loan is paid off in Swiss francs.

There are various forms of currency swaps. In a fixed-for-fixed currency swap, the interest rates on the periodic interest payments are set for the life of the swap. In a fixed-for-floating swap, the interest rate in one currency changes with market conditions while the interest rate in the other stays the same. In floating-for-floating currency swaps, both interest rates float.

OTC Currency Options

A **currency option** contract gives the buyer of the contract the right to buy or sell a specified amount of one currency for another on or before a specified date. A call option is the right, but not the obligation, to buy the underlying currency, and a put option gives the right to sell the underlying currency for another. The right will be exercised only if it is in the holder's interest to do so. Every option, when exercised, involves two sides: the purchase of one currency and the sale of another. Thus, a call option to buy yen for dollars is also a put option to sell dollars for yen.

The price at which the underlying currency may be bought or sold is the exercise or strike price. The option premium is the price of the option that the buyer pays to the option writer for the right. The buyer of an option contract pays a premium in exchange for insurance against adverse movements in the underlying spot exchange rate while retaining the right to profit from any favorable movements. The potential gain for the option buyer is the risk that the option seller faces.

Options can be written either European style or American style. European options can be exercised only on the expiration date, whereas American options can be exercised anytime up to the expiration date. Most trading in the OTC interbank market involves European options.[6] The value of a European option at expiration is its **intrinsic value**, which is the amount by which the strike exchange rate is more advantageous than the spot rate to the option holder. If the intrinsic value is positive, the option is in-the-money. If the spot exchange rate and the strike exchange rate are the same, there is no intrinsic value and the option is at-the-money. On the other hand, if the strike rate is less advantageous than the spot rate, there is no intrinsic value and the option is out-of-the-money. On the expiration date, the option holder will exercise the option only if the intrinsic value is positive.

As an example of the use of an option contract, suppose on December 18, 2002, ABC Imports agrees to buy certain materials from a Japanese company that cannot be delivered for six months. At the current exchange rate, ABC Imports would expect to pay $600,000 (equivalent to 74,040,000 yen, assuming an exchange rate of 123.40) upon receipt of this merchandise. The CFO of ABC is uneasy with the transaction. A forward contract would prevent a change in the purchase price, but the uncertainty of getting good delivery from an unknown source proves to be a stumbling block. In addition, financial markets in Asia have been unstable for sometime, which has the CFO thinking that

---

[6]American options are standard on some of the exchange-traded products.

a devaluation of the yen is possible. Given the circumstances, the CFO considers purchasing a Japanese yen call option. For an $8,000 premium, ABC has the right to buy yen at a rate of 123.40 (the strike price) or better. Table 15.2 presents three possible outcomes.

The value of a European option can be estimated by using the Black/Scholes model. Under certain assumptions, the spot exchange rate, the interest rate on the base currency, the interest rate on the terms currency, the strike rate at which the option can be exercised, and the volatility of the exchange rate together will determine the value. Among these factors, traders pay special attention to the volatility because it is the only variable not known in advance and it is critically important in pricing options. Volatility is a statistical measure of the tendency of the spot exchange rate to vary over time. There are different measurements of volatility, including historical volatility, future volatility, and implied volatility. Historical volatility is the actual volatility of an exchange rate that occurred during some defined past period of time. Future volatility is the expected variance of the exchange rate over the life of the option. Finally, **implied volatility** is the variability in an exchange rate implied by the current option premium. It is the market's estimate of future volatility.

In the OTC market, dealers express their quotes and execute transactions in terms of implied volatility. The technique used in the market is to solve the Black/Scholes formula backwards: take the price of an option in the market as given and calculate the volatility implied by that market price. Table 15.3 lists several examples of implied volatility rates for foreign currency options published by the Federal Reserve Bank of New York on July 31, 2002.

Another important parameter calculated from the Black/Scholes formula is the **delta**, or the hedge ratio, which measures how much the price of an option changes with a small change in the value of the underlying currency. For example, assume a trader sold a (European call option on euro)/(put option on dollars) with the face amount of $10 million, and the delta is 0.5. The trader could hedge her option risk by taking an opposite spot position (purchase of euros and sale of dollars) equal to 50 percent of the option's face amount, or $5 million.

TABLE 15.2	Possible Outcomes Using Currency Option Contract		
Market Exchange Rate at Maturity (JPY/USD)	Action Taken by ABC Imports	Dollar Costs	
125.40 (or > 123.40 strike)	Let option expire. Buy yen on the spot market.	74,040,000/125.40 = $590,430.62.	
123.40 (= 123.40 strike)	Buy yen at spot, as it equals the strike price.	74,040,000/123.40 = $600,000.00.	
121.40 (or < 123.40 strike)	Exercise the option and buy yen for 123.40.	74,040,000/123.40 = $600,000.00.	

Note: The cost figure does not include the $8,000 premium.

TABLE 15.3	*Implied Volatility Rates for Foreign Currency Options*							
Implied Volatility	1 Week	1 Month	2 Month	3 Month	6 Month	12 Month	2 Year	3 Year
EUR	11.0	10.9	10.8	10.9	10.9	10.9	10.9	11.0
JPY	10.5	9.9	9.5	9.4	9.2	9.1	9.1	9.2
CHF	11.6	11.5	11.3	11.4	11.2	11.2	11.2	11.2
GBP	8.8	8.8	8.6	8.5	8.5	8.5	8.8	9.1
CAD	9.9	8.8	7.8	7.6	7.1	7.0	6.9	6.8
AUD	11.3	11.5	11.2	11.2	11.0	11.0	10.9	10.6
GBPEUR	6.4	6.5	6.4	6.3	6.3	6.3	6.0	5.7
EURJPY	8.5	8.9	8.9	8.9	9.0	9.1	9.2	9.2

Source: Rates for July 31, 2002, published by the Federal Reserve Bank of New York.

For European options, there is an important relationship between call and put. The put-call parity indicates that the price of a European call (or put) option can be deduced from the price of a European put (or call) option on the same currency, with the same strike and expiration. When the strike exchange rate is the same as the forward rate, the call and the put will have the same value. When the strike is different from the forward exchange rate, the difference between the value of the put and that of the call will equal the difference in the present values of the two currencies.

EXCHANGE-TRADED CURRENCY FUTURES AND OPTIONS

In addition to the OTC instruments discussed in the previous sections, currency futures and options on foreign currencies and on currency futures trade on exchanges in Chicago, Philadelphia, and New York. Most participants in the futures and options markets are either hedgers or speculators. Hedgers are market participants who want to transfer risk. Speculators take a position in the hope of generating a profit. If a speculator takes a long position and the market price goes up, the position is profitable.

Exchange-Traded Currency Futures

A foreign exchange futures contract is an agreement to buy or sell a specific quantity of a particular foreign currency at a specified price on a specific future date. A futures contract month, also called the **delivery month**, identifies the month and year in which the futures contract reaches maturity. Hence, a foreign exchange futures contract is similar to a forward contract. Nevertheless, there are several important differences. First, futures contracts trade on exchanges, but forward contracts trade in the OTC market. Second, futures contracts are standardized in terms of contract size and maturity, and they are subject to the trading rules of the exchange. Forward contracts, on the other hand, can be customized between parties. Third, futures contracts are marked to market daily at the settlement price. The **settlement price** is a price representative of the futures transaction price at the close of the daily trading on the exchange. The buyer of a futures contract in which the settlement price is higher (lower) than the previous day's level has a positive (negative) settlement for the day because the contract holder can purchase the underlying asset at a price specified in the contract. A higher (lower) settlement price means the futures price of the underlying asset has increased (decreased). As a result, a long position is worth more (less). On the other side, the margin of the seller of the futures contract will be decreased (or increased) exactly the amount the long's margin account has changed. Thus, the sum of the long's daily settlement and the short's daily settlement is zero. In other words, this is a zero-sum game. Unlike futures contracts, forward contracts do not require initial margin or maintenance margin. Forwards require cash payments only at maturity. Fourth, two counterparties trade the forward contracts directly. In futures trading, the clearinghouse becomes the buyer to every seller and the seller to every buyer. In this way, the exchange drastically reduces counterparty risk.

These differences are significant. The fact that there is a clearinghouse and daily marking to market means that credit risk has reduced. In the futures market, a contract can be canceled simply by making a reverse transaction that nets out the position. In contrast, if the holder of a forward contract wants to close a position, he needs to trade a second contract. If the trader trades with a different counterparty the second contract, there will be two contracts and two counterparties, with credit risk on both.

The currency futures market began on May 16, 1972, in the United States. Since the first trading at the Chicago Mercantile Exchange (CME; **http://www.cme.com**), trading activities in currency futures have expanded rapidly.[7] Currency futures now trade on the CME, the Singapore Exchange (**http://www.ses.com.sg**), the Tokyo International Financial Futures Exchange (**http://www.tiffe.or.jp**), the London International Financial Futures Exchange (**http://www.liffe.com**), and other exchanges. Table 15.4 lists currency futures and options that trade at the CME.

Exchange-Traded Currency Options

Prior to 1982, all currency options contracts were traded in the OTC market, as discussed in the previous section. In December 1982, the Philadelphia Stock Exchange (PHLX) began trading options on foreign currency. Currently, these options trade generally in a March, June, September, and December expiration cycle with original maturity of 3, 6, 9, and 12 months.

Exchange-traded currency options are standardized contracts. Trades clear through the exchange clearinghouse, which guarantees the performance of both the buyer and the seller of a contract. The seller receives the premium and must deposit the initial margin and to make additional payment if the

---

[7]The CME currency futures go through a physical trade in a March, June, September, and December cycle. The physical delivery is made on the third Wednesday of the delivery month.

TABLE 15.4 | *Sample Futures and Options Contracts at the Chicago Mercantile Exchange*

Currency Futures	Size of Futures Contract (in foreign currency)	Options on Futures
Australian dollar	100,000	Yes
Brazilian real	100,000	Yes
British pound	62,500	Yes
Canadian dollar	100,000	Yes
E-mini euroFX	62,500	
EuroFX	125,000	Yes
E-mini Japanese yen	6,250,000	
Japanese yen	12,500,000	Yes
Mexican peso	500,000	Yes
New Zealand dollar	100,000	Yes
Russian ruble	500,000	Yes
South African rand	2,500,000	Yes
Swiss franc	125,000	Yes
Cross Rates		
British pound/Swiss franc	125,000 pounds	
British pound/Japanese yen	125,000 pounds	
EuroFX/British pound	125,000 euros	Yes
EuroFX/Japanese yen	125,000 euros	Yes
EuroFX/Swiss franc	125,000 euros	Yes

Source: Chicago Mercantile Exchange (http://www.cme.com).

exchange rate moves in the adverse direction. The options give the holder the right to exercise at the strike exchange rate, but there is no obligation to deal. As a result, options protect the owner from downside risk, but provide unlimited potential for gains. The premium depends on the selected strike rate, interest rates, the spot market for the currency, volatility, and the tenor of the transaction.

The buyer of a call option contract on a certain currency profits if the currency appreciates. The seller (also called the writer) of the call option has a profit-loss schedule opposite to the buyer's. A put option contract grants the holder the right to sell the named currency at the prespecified exchange rate (strike price). Therefore, a put holder gains if the currency depreciates and loses if the currency appreciates. The market trades both American and European options. Because American option can be exercised anytime during the contract, they are more valuable than European options. The profit-loss schedules, however, are the same at the expiration date. Figure 15.2 (see p. 378) depicts the profit-loss schedules for various positions at the expiration of a contract on USD/EUR. As Figure 15.2A shows, purchasing a call results in a profit if the spot rate at the contract expiration date rises above the strike. Otherwise, the buyer of the call loses the amount of the premium paid for the contract. The

FIGURE 15.2 | *Option Profit-Loss Graphs*

A: LONG A CALL

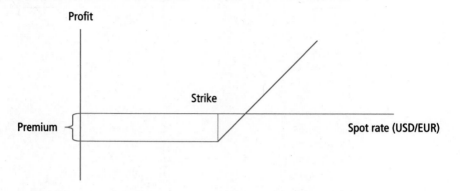

B: SHORT A CALL

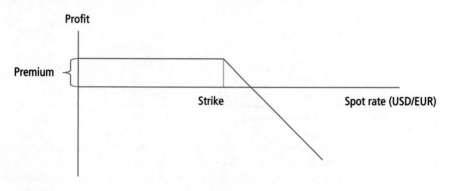

C: LONG A PUT

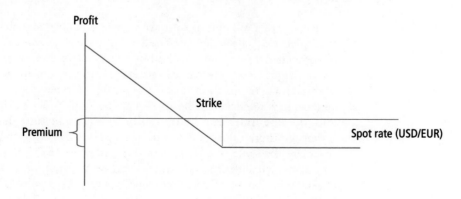

| FIGURE 15.2 | *Option Profit-Loss Graphs* (continued) |

D: SHORT A PUT

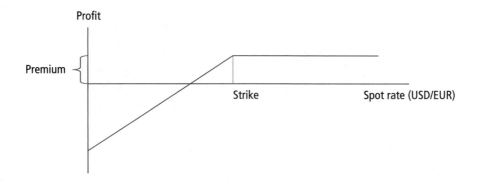

profit possibilities for the seller of the call are the exact opposite of the buyer's, as seen in Figure 15.2B. Figures 15.2C and 15.2D show the profit or loss possibilities for a put buyer and a put seller.

The CME trades American options on the currency futures contracts (see Table 15.4, p. 377). With these options, the underlying asset is a futures contract on the specified foreign currency. These options also trade in a March, June, September, and December cycle. The options on currency futures behave very similarly to options on the physical currency since the futures price converges to the spot rate as the futures contract nears maturity. Exercise of an option results in a long futures position for the call buyer or the put writer and a short position for the put buyer or the call writer. If the futures position is not reversed or offset prior to the futures expiration date, receipt or delivery of the specified currency will result or be required.

RISK MANAGEMENT IN FOREIGN EXCHANGE TRADING

The risks in trading foreign exchange include market risk, credit risk, liquidity risk, legal risk, and operational risk. The success of any institution trading in the foreign exchange market depends on how well it manages these risks. Managing risk is a constant part of doing business.

Market Risk

Market risk is a price risk that consists of exchange rate risk and interest rate risk. Exchange rate risk is inherent in foreign exchange trading. Every time a dealer or a trader takes a position, that position is immediately exposed to the risk that the exchange rate may move against it. Trading foreign exchange entails interest rate risk as well. An uncovered outright forward position can change in value, not only because of a change in the spot rate but also because of a change in interest rates, since a forward exchange rate reflects the interest rate differential between the two currencies. In an FX swap, there is no shift in foreign exchange exposure, and the market risk is interest rate risk. All other types of transactions, including currency swaps, currency options, and futures, are also subject to interest rate risk.

To manage market risk, most institutions have long maintained volume or position limits on the maximum open position that each trader or group can carry overnight and intraday. In addition, there frequently is a limit on the estimated potential losses (the concept of value at risk, or VaR). For example, a trader might have a position limit of $5 million and also a VaR limit of $100,000.

Credit Risk

Credit risk arises from the possibility that the counterparty to a trade will be unable to make the agreed payment when it comes due. Between the time of the trade and the time of the settlement, both parties extend credit and accept credit risk. Involved parties manage this risk by knowing the customer and by setting credit limits for each customer. Credit risk includes settlement risk and sovereign risk.

Settlement risk, also known as **Herstatt risk**, is particularly important in foreign exchange trading. Such risk arises in part because the two legs of a foreign exchange transaction often settle in two different time zones, with different business hours. Settlement risk can be reduced by using netting and exchange clearing arrangements to modify the settlement process. Another element of credit risk is sovereign risk, which is the political, legal, and other risk associated with a cross-border payment. The risk arises when governments interfere with international transactions in their currencies. To limit this type of risk, most participants establish ceilings for individual countries, monitor regulatory changes and credit ratings, or employ credit derivatives (discussed in the preceding chapter).

Other Risks

Other risks in foreign exchange trading include liquidity risk, legal risk, and operational risk. Liquidity risk occurs when a participant finds that it cannot liquidate positions without loss. Given the size, breadth, and depth of the foreign exchange market, liquidity risk is less of a concern for major currencies.

Legal risk is the risk of loss if a contract cannot be enforced. It may occur because the counterparty is not legally capable of making a binding agreement. This risk has increased with the growth in currency derivatives, since many securities laws and regulations were enacted before the introduction of these products.

Finally, foreign exchange trading is subject to operational risk. This is the risk of losses from inadequate systems, human errors, lack of proper oversight policies and procedures, and employee dishonesty.

CONCLUDING SUMMARY

An understanding of the foreign exchange market is essential to firms that operate globally because they are exposed to foreign currency fluctuations. The market has grown from an estimated daily turnover of $150 billion in 1985 to more than $1 trillion a day in recent years. Indeed, a daily foreign exchange trading volume of $1.5 trillion or $2 trillion is not unheard of.

The ratio at which the exchange of one currency for another occurs for settlement in two business days is the spot exchange rate. Most currencies are quoted in European terms; that is, the amount of foreign currency that will be exchanged for one U.S. dollar. In contrast, the euro, the British pound, and the currencies of several former Commonwealth countries are quoted in American terms, which is merely the reciprocal of the rate derived using European terms.

In addition to the spot market, there are outright forwards, FX swaps, OTC options, currency swaps, and exchange-traded futures and options. These instruments can be used for various purposes.

Trading in the foreign exchange market is subject to market risk, credit risk, liquidity risk, and operational risk. Proper management of these risks is key to success in foreign exchange trading.

Key Terms

American terms 365	implied volatility 374
base currency 365	interest rate parity 369
cross-exchange rate 366	intrinsic value 373
currency option 373	legal risk 380
currency swap 371	outright forward 369
delivery month 375	settlement price 376
delta 374	settlement risk 380
Eurocurrency 369	short-dated swap 371
European terms 365	spot transaction 368
exchange rate 365	straight date 369
FX swap 371	terms currency 365
forward swap 371	triangular arbitrage 368
Herstatt risk 380	vehicle currency 362

Review Questions

1. If one sells 10 million yen in the spot market, how many dollars will be received, based on the quotes in Table 15.1? When would settlement normally take place?

2. What is the interest rate parity condition?

3. Restate the following one-, three-, and six-month outright forward bid-asked quotes in forward points.

	Bid–asked
Spot	1.2431–1.2436
One-month	1.2432–1.2442
Three-month	1.2448–1.2463
Six-month	1.2488–1.2502

4. Who are the market participants in the foreign exchange market?

5. What is triangular arbitrage? What condition will give rise to a triangular arbitrage opportunity?

6. Calculate the forward premium or discount points for a 181-day dollar-yen forward. The Eurodollar interest rate is assumed to be 6 percent and the Euroyen interest rate to be 4 percent. Assume that the current spot rate is 126.40.

7. Suppose that the annual interest rate in the United States is 5 percent and that in Switzerland it is 7 percent. The spot exchange rate is 1.654 Swiss francs per U.S. dollar. The one-year forward rate is 1.700 Swiss francs per U.S. dollar. Does interest rate parity hold? If not, how can you arbitrage from this situation?

8. Suppose you plan to attend a private school in London after you graduate from college two years from now and the tuition is very expensive. There is a slight possibility, though, that you might stay in the United States for your graduate studies, instead of going to London. After studying this chapter, you think you would like to lock in today's exchange rate if you do go. How can you accomplish this?

9. Most newspapers print foreign exchange quotes every business day. What is the exchange rate for EUR/USD today? Is this American terms or European terms?

10. Suppose the cross-exchange rate JPY/EUR is 194.34. At the same time, the JPY/USD is 122.40 and the EUR/USD is 1.0087. Is there an arbitrage opportunity here? How?

Select Bibliography

Baker, J. C. *International Finance: Management, Markets, and Institutions.* Upper Saddle River, N.J.: Prentice Hall, 1998.

Fabozzi, F. J., and A. Franco. *Handbook of Emerging Fixed Income and Currency Markets.* New Hope, Penn.: Frank J. Fabozzi Associates, 1998.

Kawaller, I. G. "Comparing futures and forwards for managing currency exposures," Chicago: Chicago Mercantile Exchange, 2000.

Krugman, P. R. *Currencies and Crises.* Cambridge, Mass.: MIT Press, 1995.

Luca, C. *Trading in the Global Currency Markets.* Upper Saddle Rivers, N.J.: Prentice Hall, 2000.

National Futures Association. *Buying Options on Futures Contracts.* 2000.

Stephens, J. J. *Managing Currency Risks Using Financial Derivatives.* New York: John Wiley & Sons, 2001.

Walmsley, J. *The Foreign Exchange and Money Market Guide.* New York: John Wiley & Sons, 2000.

INTERNATIONAL FINANCIAL CENTERS

The Euromarket

After World War II, the U.S. dollars became the world's primary trading currency, replacing the British pound sterling. During the postwar period, Communist countries such as Soviet Union and China needed dollar reserves to support their international transactions because their own currencies could not be converted into dollars. As Cold War tensions intensified, the Communist governments became concerned that the U.S. government might freeze their deposits in U.S. banks, so they transferred their dollar deposits from the U.S. banks to European banks (the first transfers were to the Eurobank in Paris and the Moscow Narodny Bank in London). These U.S. dollar deposits in European banks came to be known as Eurodollars. In time, the term Eurocurrency arose to refer to any currency deposited outside its country of origin; the term has been used even if neither the currency nor the country of deposit is "European." Eventually, the market has applied the "Euro" concept to securities as well, and various financial instruments denominated in a currency different from the home currency of the country of issuance developed. These include Eurobonds, Eurocommercial paper, and Euro medium-term notes. All of these instruments trade in the Euromarket and will be examined in this chapter.

The objectives of this chapter are to provide an understanding of:
- Eurocurrencies.
- Eurobonds.
- Floating rate notes.
- Eurocommercial paper and Euro medium-term notes.

MARKET OVERVIEW

The Euromarket originated in London and spread from there to other European centers, and later to financial centers throughout the world. Today, **Euromarket** is an offshore money and capital market, with trading around the clock in all major financial centers. The currency of denomination used in transactions is not the official currency of the country where the transaction takes place. Major centers of Euromarket activities include London, New York, Paris, Brussels, Frankfurt, Luxembourg, Tokyo, Hong Kong, and Singapore. Although dollar-denominated instruments constitute a major segment of the Euromarket, the euro, the British pound sterling, and Japanese yen are also important Eurocurrencies.[1]

The Euromarket has grown to such prominence for several reasons. Certainly, a major reason for its impressive growth is the absence of regulation. Because the essence of the "Euro" concept is the mismatch between a financial instrument's country of issuance and the currency in which the security is denominated (or between the country where the currency deposits are and their country of origin), Euromarket activities are outside of the jurisdiction of national regulatory authorities (see Box 16.1 for an example of how the creation of Eurodollars occurs). Thus, U.S. banks can avoid U.S. banking regulations by accepting dollar-denominated deposits and making dollar-denominated loans outside the United States. In the 1960s, for example, U.S. banks turned to the newly developing Euromarket to escape the imposition of reserve requirements, deposit insurance, and legal lending limits, as well as the interest equalization tax.[2] In addition, during the same period the lifting of foreign exchange restrictions in Western Europe, which allowed multinational corporations to shift their borrowing to the currency with the lowest interest rate, also stimulated the development of the Euromarket.

The explosive growth of the Euromarket did not begin until the late 1970s, however. Then changes in U.S. monetary policy, coupled with spiraling inflation, caused interest rates to skyrocket. Concerned about the effects of inflation on their savings, investors began to take their money out of U.S. banks and deposit it in foreign banks.[3] During the same period, surplus oil revenues from the OPEC countries and new wealth from emerging countries poured into the

---

[1] It is important not to confuse Eurocurrencies and Euro instruments with the euro, the currency of the members of the European Economic and Monetary Union (EMU). Although the euro is an important Eurocurrency, the "Euro" concept itself does not refer to any particular currency. Eurocurrencies existed long before the advent of the euro, which the EMU members gradually adopted between 1999 and 2002; indeed, the deutsche mark and the French franc, which were among the currencies replaced by the euro, were previously important Eurocurrencies.

[2] It was a 15 percent tax imposed on interest received from foreign borrowers. Its purpose was to restrict foreign debt issues sold into the U.S. market. Its actual effect, however, was to stimulate the development of the Euromarkets and drive the dollar-based financing to London. The government eliminated this tax in 1974.

[3] Regulation Q imposed a ceiling on the interest rate that U.S. banks could pay their depositors. This regulation was put into effect in 1966 and eliminated in 1986.

MARKETS IN ACTION   The Creation of Eurodollars

16.1

An Italian automobile firm sells sports cars worth U.S. $10 million to an importer in the United States. The Italian automaker receives a U.S.-dollar check drawn on J.P. Morgan Chase, New York. The firm initially deposits this check in a checking account for dollar working capital use. But to earn a higher rate of interest on the $10 million, the Italian firm decides to place funds in a time deposit with a bank in France. Ten million Eurodollars have been created.

The $10 million dollar account in the French bank has substituted the dollar account held at J.P. Morgan Chase in New York. Note that no U.S. dollars left New York, but ownership of the dollar deposit has moved from an Italian company to a French bank.

Euromarket. Blue chip multinationals increasingly tapped into the Euromarket for floating-rate loans. The introduction of international banking facilities in the United States in 1981 extended the Euromarket into the United States. An **international banking facility** is a U.S. status similar to an offshore banking unit that permits a bank to operate in offshore transactions. Banking regulations do not apply to international banking facilities, which can be used only by non–U.S. residents. Market participants also call the dollar deposits in these facilities Eurodollars.

Finally, the success of currency swaps and improvements in clearing operations have contributed to the rise of the Euromarket. A significant proportion of the funds raised through the sale of Euro issues swaps into other currencies. By using currency swaps, borrowers can raise funds in almost any currency and then swap to the desired currency and the desired form of interest liabilities. In addition, technological developments have provided the infrastructure needed for the market's explosive growth. Without electronic clearing systems such as Euroclear and Cedel (which has been renamed Clearstream), the market could not have grown to its current size because physical delivery of bearer certificates is too inefficient and risky.

EUROCURRENCY

Eurocurrency is a currency on deposit outside its country of origin or in international banking facilities in the United States. In addition to various financial instruments to be discussed in later sections, Eurocurrency comes in several forms for financial institutions: time deposits, certificates of deposit (CDs), call money, and interbank placements. Eurocurrency time deposits are nonnegotiable whereas CDs are negotiable. Call deposits are equivalent to demand deposits in the U.S. domestic market. Interbank placements are the Euromarket equivalent of the federal funds market. The existence of interbank placements permits smaller banks to acquire Eurocurrencies without the need to have a large network to attract deposits from multinational corporations. Box 16.2

provides an example of effective annual cost for a Eurodollar (the dominant Eurocurrency) loan.

Banks in the Eurodollar market compete with banks in the United States to attract dollar-denominated funds. Since the Eurodollar market is relatively free of regulation, banks in this market can operate on narrower margins or spreads between dollar borrowing and lending rates than can banks in the United States. This is because regulatory initiatives such as stricter capital standards, deposit insurance, and more intense supervisory scrutiny have raised the cost of depository intermediation in the United States. In short, the Eurodollar market has grown up largely as a means of avoiding the regulatory costs in the U.S. domestic market.

Eurodollar Certificates of Deposits

Banks usually issue Eurocurrency certificates of deposit (CDs) in denominations of at least $1 million with a maturity ranging from overnight to five years. The most significant segment of the Eurocurrency CD market consists of Eurodollar CDs, which are bank deposit liabilities denominated in U.S. dollars but not subject to U.S. banking regulations. Foreign monetary authorities generally have reluctance to regulate the Eurodollar business because to do so would drive the business away. For the most part, banks offering Eurodollar deposits reside outside the United States; although, as mentioned earlier, under international banking facilities banks in the United States have offered Eurodollar deposits to non–U.S. residents since 1981.

Most Eurodollar CDs are fixed-rate, typically with a maturity from three to six months. Market practice is to quote the Euro CD rate as a simple yield, with the assumption of a 360-day year. For example, at an interest rate of 5 percent, a 3-month (90-day) Eurodollar CD with a par value of $5 million at maturity will pay:

MARKETS IN ACTION   Effective Annual Cost of Eurodollar Loan

16.2

Citibank has arranged a syndicated Eurodollar loan of $800 million for IBM. The upfront syndication fee is 1 percent. Thus, the net proceeds to IBM are

$$800,000,000 - \$800,000,000 \times 0.01 = \$792,000,000.$$

The interest rate on the Eurodollar loan is LIBOR + 0.75%, with LIBOR reset every six months. If the initial LIBOR is 2.25%, the first interest payment is

$$800,000,000 \times \{(2.25\% + 0.75\%)/2\} = \$12,000,000.$$

Therefore, the effective annual rate for the first six months of the Eurodollar loan is

$$\{\$12,000,000/\$792,000,000\} \times 2 \times 100 = 3.03\%.$$

$$\boxed{16.1} \qquad \$5,000,000\left(1 + \frac{0.05 \times 90}{360}\right) = \$5,062,500.$$

Banks issue floating-rate Eurodollar CDs as well, usually with longer maturities. Some Eurodollar CDs, known as "tranche" CDs, are issued in large aggregate amounts (usually between $10 million and $30 million). Dealers then divide these CDs into a number of smaller ($10,000 to $25,000) certificates. These smaller certificates can then be sold through brokers or the issuing bank's retail sales operation.

Banks issue Eurodollar CDs to fund international lending and to raise funds to transfer to their home head offices for domestic lending. Large U.S. banks continually compare the effective costs of raising funds in the United States and in the Eurodollar market. They substitute domestic CDs for Eurodollar CDs when the effective cost is lower in the United States, and vice versa. The effective cost is the interest paid adjusted for the costs of holding non–interest-bearing required reserves at the Federal Reserve and paying deposit insurance premium to the Federal Deposit Insurance Corporation.

Because of the absence of government regulations, the effective cost of Eurocurrency deposits can be less than the effective cost of alternative domestic sources of funds. For example, suppose that a bank can raise $5 million in the Eurodollar market at a rate of 5 percent or in the U.S. market at a rate 25 basis points lower, or 4.75 percent. These domestic deposits carry a 3-percent reserve requirement, however, and a 0.23 percent deposit insurance premium. Thus, the effective cost of the domestic funds is

$$\boxed{16.2} \qquad \frac{0.04750 + 0.0023}{1 - 0.03} = 5.134\%$$

Although the domestic CD pays a lower interest rate, its effective cost is 13.4 basis points higher than the cost of the Eurodollar CD because Euro CDs are not subject to either deposit insurance premiums or reserve requirements.

Eurodollar Futures and Options Contracts

In December 1981, the Chicago Mercantile Exchange (CME; **http://www. cme.com**) introduced the Eurodollar futures contract. The contract represents a $1 million, 3-month **London Interbank Offered Rate (LIBOR)** deposit (see Table 16.1 for the contract specifications, p. 390). The final settlement price for Eurodollar futures contracts is based on a rate fixed by the British Bankers Association (BBA) using the following procedure:

- At 11:00 A.M. London time, sixteen BBA-designated banks provide quotes that reflect their perception of the rates at which U.S. dollar deposits are available.

- The BBA eliminates the four highest and the four lowest rates and then takes the average of the remaining eight rates.

TABLE 16.1	*Eurodollar Futures Contract Specification*

A. One contract represents a Eurodollar time deposit having a principal value of $1 million with a maturity of 3 months.

B. One point = 0.01 = $25.00.

C. Contract listings:
  March
  June
  September
  December

D. Trading venues:
  Floor   no price limits
  GLBX2   200 points price limit

E. Minimum fluctuation:
  Floor   regular   0.01   = $25.00
            half tick   0.005   = $12.50
            quarter   0.0025 = $ 6.25
  GLBX2   regular   0.01   = $25.00
            half tick   0.005   = $12.50

Source: Chicago Mercantile Exchange (http://www.cme.com).

° The average, rounded out to the fifth decimal place, is the fixing for the day.

Eurodollar futures are cash settled, so there is no delivery of a cash instrument upon expiration. The Eurodollar futures rate is stated as a discount rate. For example, if the rate is 5.12 percent, the futures price would be stated as $100 - 5.12 = 94.88$. For a Eurodollar deposit that has a principal value of $1 million and a three-month maturity, the dollar price would be:

$$\boxed{16.3} \quad p = F\left(1 - \frac{d \times t}{360}\right) = \$1,000,000\left(1 - \frac{0.0512 \times 90}{360}\right) = \$987,200$$

where p = dollar price,
  F = face value,
  d = settlement rate, and
  t = number of days.

If LIBOR is 5.08 percent on the contract final settlement date, then the long position would gain while the short position would lose. This is because the contract holder is now entitled to purchase a three-month Eurodollar deposit at a price of $987,200, but the deposit is worth:

$$\boxed{16.4} \quad p = \$1,000,000\left(1 - \frac{0.0508 \times 90}{360}\right) = \$987,300.$$

Since Eurodollar futures are cash settled, the short has to pay the long the difference: $987,300–$987,200, or $100 per contract.

The CME also offers bundles and packs, which are prepackaged series of contracts that enable traders to rapidly execute strip positions in a single transaction rather than having to construct the same positions with individual contracts.[4] A **bundle** is the simultaneous sale or purchase of a consecutive series of Eurodollar contracts. The first contract in any bundle is usually the first quarterly contract in the strip. For example, a three-year bundle consists of the first twelve Eurodollar contracts. Bundles are quoted on the basis of the net average price change of the contracts in the bundle relative to the previous day's settlement price. For example, assume a three-year bundle trade takes place at a price quotation of +2. This means an agreement exists between the buyer and the seller that among the nearest twelve Eurodollar contracts the average net change in the contracts' prices is 2 ticks. A **pack** is a simultaneous purchase or sale of an equally weighted consecutive series of Eurodollar futures, but the number of contracts remains the same at four.

The CME lists options of Eurodollar futures contracts as well. One options contract represents one Eurodollar futures contract. A call option entitles the buyer to purchase a Eurodollar futures contract anytime, up to the option expiration date, at the strike price. Thus, the option value increases with the futures price. In contrast, a put option holder has the right to sell a Eurodollar futures contract to the seller at the strike price, so the value of the put increases when the futures price declines.

Forward Rate Agreements

A **forward rate agreement (FRA)** is a forward contract between two parties to exchange an interest rate on a Eurodollar deposit at a given future date. An FRA can be used to hedge future interest expense or investment income. For example, a borrower can purchase an FRA as protection against an increase in the general level of interest. If the rate rises, the seller of the FRA will pay to the borrower the difference between the interest rate fixed in the FRA and the prevailing market interest rate. For example, assume that Company ABC has taken out a six-month loan with a bank, with interest payments linked to the three-month LIBOR.[5] The interest rate fixed for the three-month period starting today is 5 percent. The future trend of the three-month LIBOR is

---

[4]The term *strip* comes from the practice of using two or more consecutive quarterly futures contracts in combination with a Eurodollar cash position.

[5]The benchmarks for the money and capital markets in the euro zone after the advent of the European Economic and Monetary Union are EURIBOR and EONIA. **Euro Interbank Offered Rate (EURIBOR)** is the euro interbank term-deposit rate offered by one prime bank to another prime bank in the euro zone. EONIA (Euro OverNight Index Average) is the weighted average rate of all overnight unsecured lending transactions in the interbank market within the euro area.

uncertain. Company ABC buys a 3 × 3 FRA, with a three-month hedging period, starting in three months at a rate of 5.20 percent. Now suppose that over the next three months the three-month LIBOR rises to 6.10 percent. Without the FRA, Company ABC would be subject to 90 basis points higher interest for this period. With the FRA, the seller of the agreement will be responsible for the interest payments in excess of 5.20 percent.

Alternatively, an investor can protect investment income against falling interest rates by selling an FRA. If interest rate falls below the agreed threshold, the buyer of the FRA will pay to the investor the reduced return. For example, assume that Company XYZ knows that in two months it will have $5 million to invest. The current interest level is 5.05 percent, but the company has concerns that interest rates will go down in the short term, which would reduce its investment return. Company XYZ hedges this risk by selling a 2 × 3 FRA at 5.00 percent. Two months later the market interest rate has fallen to 4.85 percent, so the company faces a corresponding 15 basis points loss of income. With the FRA, the buyer of the agreement compensates the company for its 15 basis points loss, safeguarding its investment returns.

Because FRAs are cash settled, the forward rate is established when the contract is first entered. On the settlement date, the contract is cash settled, based on the value of LIBOR at that time. One can calculate the cash settlement as follows:

16.5
$$CS = NP \times (LIBOR - f)\left(\frac{t}{360}\right)$$

where CS = amount of cash settlement
NP = notional principal
f = forward rate
t = number of days of the deposit.

As an example, suppose that the notional principal of a 3 × 3 FRA is $5 million, the forward rate is 5.05 percent, and the three-month LIBOR on the settlement date is 5.12 percent. The net cash settlement will be:

16.6
$$CS = \$5,000,000 \times (5.12\% - 5.05\%) \times \frac{90}{360} = \$875.$$

EUROBONDS

Eurobonds are bonds denominated in a currency different from the currency of the country where they are issued. The Eurobond market took off in the 1960s and has grown significantly in recent years. The volume was less than $300 billion in 1992, but surpassed the $1 trillion mark in 1998. The U.S. dollar is the most widely used currency, but the deutsche mark, French franc, British pound sterling, and Japanese yen also accounted for significant volumes in the 1990s. Today, the dollar, euro, sterling, and yen are the most widely used currencies.

For issuers, a key attraction of the Eurobond market is that, by selling outside the country of origin, the issuer can often escape local regulation and securities law. For companies in the United States, Eurobond issues are not subject to the registration and disclosure requirements of the Securities and Exchange Commission. For investors, an important advantage is that the interest income is not subject to withholding tax. In addition, Eurobond issuers tend to be highly creditworthy borrowers. Both corporate and sovereign borrowers use the Eurobond market. The Eurobond market received a big boost from the introduction of two electronic clearing systems: Euroclear **(http:// www.euroclear.com)** in 1968 and Cedel **(http://www.clearstream.com)** in 1971. Before that, trading in Eurobonds was costly and risky. Eurobonds are bearer bonds; whoever holds the bonds owns them. If someone stole the bonds, the original bondholder does not own the bonds anymore because there is no proof of ownership. Electronic clearing and safekeeping eliminated this problem.

Eurobonds issuers generally do not register them with any particular regulatory agency, although the bonds may list in London or Luxembourg or on other exchanges. Listing aims mainly at attracting institutional investors, which often cannot purchase unlisted securities. Table 16.2 summarizes the main features of Eurobonds.

Yields on Eurobonds

The majority of Eurobonds (called **Euro straights**) pay a fixed-rate coupon with a stated redemption date. These bonds pay interest only once a year on a basis of 30/360; that is, the calculation of accrued interest assumes that each

TABLE 16.2 | *Major Features of Eurobonds*	
Issuer	Top-quality borrowers
Currency	Any widely used international currency
Average issuing size	U.S. $50–500 million
Type	Bearer
Regulation	Not subject to regulation by any sovereign governments
Tax	No withholding tax
Interest payments	Annual for fixed rates, semiannual or quarterly for floating-rate notes
Listing	London or Luxembourg
Security covenants	Unsecured
Investors	Institutional and individual
Structure	Bullets are common
Issuing procedures	Placed through an international syndicate
Trading	Over the counter; spreads vary among currencies
Settlement	Book-entry via Euroclear and Clearstream

month has 30 days and each year 360 days. Because these fixed-rate straight bonds pay interest annually, instead of semiannually, investors should expect a higher yield. The formula for calculating the equivalent yield on a Eurobond that would be necessary to equal the yield of a U.S. semiannual coupon bond is:

16.7
$$y = r(1 + r/4),$$

where y is the annual equivalent yield and r is the yield for a semiannual coupon bond. For example, to be equivalent to a U.S. bond with a 10-percent yield, a Eurobond would have to yield 10.25 percent.

The formula can be adjusted as follows to calculate the U.S. semiannual bond yield equivalent to a Eurobond yield:

16.8
$$r = 2\left[(1 + y)^{0.5} - 1\right]$$

For example, suppose that a Eurobond yields 10 percent. Then the U.S. bond equivalent yield is 9.76 percent.

Other Types of Eurobonds

In addition to fixed-rate straight bonds, there are several other types of Eurobonds including floating-rate notes (discussed in the next section), convertible bonds, zero-coupon bonds, bonds with attached warrants, and dual-currency bonds. Many Eurobonds have attached warrants. A popular type, called a debt warrant, allows the holder to purchase additional debt at a fixed price. These warrants are basically interest rate call options and are attractive to investors who expect interest rates to decline. A typical debt warrant allows the holder to purchase additional bonds with the same maturity bearing a lower coupon rate (than the host bonds). In addition, some Eurobonds contain currency warrants or commodity warrants. A **currency warrant** permits the holder to exchange one currency for another at a predetermined rate; thus, it protects the bondholder against a depreciation of the currency in which the cash flows are denominated. Similarly, a **commodity warrant** allows the warrant holder to purchase the commodity from the issuer at the specified price.

Convertible Eurobonds generally pay a fixed rate but may, at the option of the holder under certain conditions, be converted to shares of common stock. Alternatively, they may be converted from one currency of denomination to another.

Dual-currency bonds pay interest in one currency, with the bond redeemed in another currency. Thus, they resemble a portfolio of annuities (periodic coupons) and a zero-coupon bond (face amount at maturity) in two different currencies. The exchange rate may be specified at the time of the bond's issuance; otherwise, it is the prevailing market rate at the time when the bond pays interest. Issuers in the Euromarket started to float a zero-coupon Eurobond (called a **streaker bond**) in the early 1980s. The advantage of a streaker bond is that investors receive a guaranteed yield if they hold the bond until maturity, so there is no reinvestment risk. Another innovation is the **global bond**, which is a hybrid between a Eurobond and a foreign bond. The World Bank pioneered the global bond in September 1989, when it placed 10-year notes ($1.5 billion issue) in the United States and other markets simultaneously.

FLOATING-RATE NOTES

Floating-rate notes (FRNs) are simply Eurobonds with a variable rate coupon. The coupon resets periodically, ensuring that the FRN pays coupons in line with market interest rates. Consequently, the market value of an FRN is typically close to the issuing price before the resetting of the coupon. The FRN trades at par at coupon reset. The most significant variations in value tend to be due to unanticipated changes in the creditworthiness of the issuer or the guarantor. Changes in interest rates have less effect. In times of falling interest rates, investors tend to turn to fixed-coupon bonds to secure their yields, whereas issuers prefer FRNs, as they do not want to be locked into high financing costs. The reverse situation applies in times of rising interest rates.

Coupon Reset
The rate on an FRN is generally quoted as a margin over or under a specific benchmark rate. The coupon resets periodically, based on the benchmark rate, usually LIBOR, plus a margin that reflects the issuer's credit rating. Less commonly used benchmarks are LIBID (London Interbank Bid), which is the rate London banks offer to borrow from each other, and LIMEAN, which is the midpoint between LIBOR and LIBID.

Most issues carry a margin over LIBOR, though a few issues of very high quality may carry a margin below. For example, if the three-month LIBOR is 4.50 percent on the coupon reset date and the issue carries a 10 basis points margin above the rate, then the coupon for the following three months will be set at 4.60 percent. At about the same time, the payment of the accrued interest occurs. The process repeats after three months.

Other Types of FRNs
Several variations on the basic FRN are available. Perpetual FRNs have no fixed maturity date. A collared floater is a floating-rate debt with a cap and a floor on its interest rate. The coupon may float within the range. To attract investors, the minimum coupon often is set higher than the prevailing rates at that time. If market interest rates soar above the maximum rate, the market value of the FRN will fall. Conversely, the market value will appreciate when interest rates plummet.

Discount Margin
The quote for the yield on an FRN is not on an absolute basis, as with a yield to maturity. Instead, the yield quote is in terms of its spread (discount margin)

in relation to a chosen benchmark such as LIBOR or LIBID. Pricing an FRN involves discounting all future "unknown" cash flows back to their present value. Since future coupons reset periodically and are unknown before the reset, the calculation requires a forecast of the future path of interest rates. Specifically, to apply the bond equation to an FRN, the trader must forecast the value of the reference benchmark on each of the remaining reset dates. Assume that all coupons after the next one occur at equal intervals.[6] One can calculate the clean price of an FRN (the FRN price excluding accrued interest) as:

16.9

$$p = d_{sn}\left[\sum_{n=1}^{N-1} d^n C_n + Rd^{N-1}\right] - AI$$

where d_{sn} = the discount factor from settlement to next coupon date,
   d = discount factor for future cash flows,
   C_n = coupon at n,
   R = redemption value,
   N = total number of future coupons,
   AI = accrued interest.

When the clean price is above or below the FRN's redemption value, the differential amortizes over the life of the instrument and converts into a percentage per annum. One can then add or subtract this percentage from the stated margin against the benchmark.

EUROCOMMERCIAL PAPER AND EURO MEDIUM-TERM NOTES

Eurocommercial paper (Euro CP) and Euro medium-term notes (Euro MTN) represent a significant sector of the Eurocapital market. Euro CP is a short-term bearer, unsecured zero-coupon security with a maturity in the range of 7 to 365 days. The vast majority of Euro CPs is dollar-denominated. Their many advantages have enabled them to obtain a larger and larger portion of the international debt market.

Eurocommercial Paper

The Euro CP market expanded considerably after the early 1980s. Initially, only private corporations with the highest credit ratings issued Euro CPs. These high-grade Euro CPs were attractive because they offered a higher rate than Euro CDs. Soon, though, less creditworthy borrowers issued lower-grade or even unrated paper at even higher yields. After several defaults in 1989–1990, investors began to pay more attention to credit ratings. Table 16.3

---

[6]This method takes leap years into account.

TABLE 16.3	*Short-Term Credit Ratings*
STANDARD AND POOR'S	**MOODY'S**
A-1 Issuer has strong capacity to meet its financial commitments. A plus sign (+) indicates issuer's capacity is extremely strong.	**Prime-1** Issuer has superior ability to pay senior short-term debt obligations.
A-2 Issuer has satisfactory capacity to meet its financial commitments.	**Prime-2** Issuer has a strong ability to pay senior short-term obligations.
A-3 Issuer has adequate capacity to meet its financial commitments.	**Prime-3** Issuer has an acceptable ability to pay senior short-term obligations.
B Issuer is vulnerable and has significant speculative characteristics.	**Not Prime** Issuer's rating does not fall within any of the Prime rating categories.
C Issuer is currently vulnerable to nonpayment and is dependent upon favorable conditions to meet its financial commitments.	

Sources: Moody's and Standard and Poor's.

summarizes the short-term issuer credit ratings used by Standard and Poor's and Moody's.

The expansion of the Euro CP market threatened wholesale banks' business of providing short-term credit to major industrial and government borrowers. Hence, banks introduced note issuance facilities. A **note issuance facility (NIF)** is a standby credit agreement with a bank that permits a borrower to obtain financing on specific terms if the borrower does not succeed in selling its short-term paper to investors. With a NIF, a borrower retains all the benefits of a Euro CP program and also secures a committed bank facility. For example, suppose that BDX Company enters into an agreement with a bank for a $300 million revolving credit facility for seven years. The lead bank syndicates the credit facility with other banks. BDX Company can withdraw or repay funds at any time without penalty. The company also obtains a rating for its Euro CP. It can issue the Euro CP to the syndicate at the rate the dealer group offers. If the CP market is not attractive, the banks are ready to make the loan. Thus, for a modest fee, the borrower has obtained both the lower rate of the Euro CP market and a guaranteed assurance that funds will be available. Most NIFs have tender panels, in which a group of banks and dealers bid for the Euro CP at an auction.

Euro CP can also be issued through **revolving underwriting facilities (RUF),** under which members of the tender panel and the placement agents can bid whatever rate they want; they participate largely on a best efforts basis. The borrower can replace them if their participation is not satisfactory, however. The aim is to obtain competitive money market rates through aggressive bidding. A well-known issuer may be able to obtain bids at LIMEAN or lower, thus saving 20 or 30 basis points over bank loans. If the fees for the RUF do not exceed the cost savings, the issuer comes out ahead.

Euro MTN

The **Euro medium-term notes (Euro MTN)** market began in 1985 and had exceeded $500 billion in outstanding volume by 1996. The growth of the market can be attributed to three factors: cost, speed, and flexibility. The costs of setting up a Euro MTN program have declined so that the one-time upfront costs are not much higher than the costs for a stand-alone Eurobond that the issuer must pay for every issue. Issuers thus benefit from continuous offerings. Although the issuer has to prepare a similar amount of documentation for Eurobonds and Euro MTN, several different instruments can be issued under a single form of documentation in the MTN market, thereby lowering both costs and the time needed for an issue. Pricing supplements for plain vanilla MTN deals are typically only a few pages long. In addition, the MTN market gives issuers tremendous flexibility because a variety of issues may be done with the same documentation.

For these reasons, the Euro MTN market has become the predominant way of issuing international debt. The short maturities have cut into the traditional commercial paper domain. Increased transparency and dealer rivalry have also greatly improved the competitiveness of secondary trading.

CONCLUDING SUMMARY

Two factors have contributed to the development and success of the Euromarket: the Cold War and the desire to avoid regulation. The Euromarket began during the Cold War, when Communist countries withdrew their money from U.S. banks and deposited it in European banks. Although the Cold War ended more than a decade ago, the Euromarket has continued to grow because Eurocurrencies and Euro instruments are largely free of regulation. For example, dollar deposits outside the United States or at international banking facilities in the United States are not subject to the Fed's reserve requirements or to deposit insurance premium. Today, the Euromarket is a global financial market with trading activities in all major financial centers around the world.

A Eurocurrency is any currency on deposit outside its country of origin or in international banking facilities in the United States. The most important Eurocurrencies are the U.S. dollar, the euro, the British pound sterling, and the Japanese yen. Eurodollars dominate the market. Among the most important Eurodollar products are Eurodollar certificates of deposits, Eurodollar futures and options contracts available at the Chicago Mercantile Exchange, and forward rate agreement, which can be used to protect against increases in future interest rates or to lock in interest income.

Other Euro instruments include Eurobonds, floating rate notes, Euro-commercial paper, and Euro medium-term notes. Eurobonds have denominations in a currency different from the currency of the country where they are issued. Floating-rate notes are Eurobonds that pay a variable coupon rate. The rate on an FRN is generally quoted as a spread over a specific benchmark such as LIBOR. Euro medium-term notes are medium term debt instruments. Eurocommercial paper provides an alternative to short-term bank financing at an attractive market interest rate.

Key Terms

bundle 391
commodity warrant 394
currency warrant 394
Euro Interbank Offered Rate
    (EURIBOR) 391
Euro medium-term note
    (Euro MTN) 398
Euro straight 393
Eurobonds 392
Euromarket 386
floating-rate note (FRN) 395

forward rate agreement (FRA) 391
global bond 395
international banking facility 387
London Interbank Offered Rate
    (LIBOR) 389
note issuance facility 397
pack 391
revolving underwriting facility (RUF)
    397
streaker bond 394

Review Questions

1. Describe the factors that have contributed to the development and growth of the Euromarket.
2. Assume that a three-month Eurodollar CD pays 4.88 percent. What is the amount of money the depositor will receive at maturity?
3. What is LIBOR? Describe the process of setting the LIBOR.
4. In Eurodollar futures, what is the value, per contract, if the price increases by 5 points?
5. Your company in one month will have $10 million to invest for three months. What trade, buy or sell, would you execute in FRAs to lock in a certain interest rate? How does an FRA work?
6. A Eurobond's coupon rate is 8.25 percent, paid once a year. What is its U.S. bond equivalent yield?
7. Assume an investor has a choice of buying either a U.S. bond or a Eurodollar bond issued by the same top-quality company. The U.S. bond yields 8.25 percent, and the Eurobond yields 8.40 percent. Which should the investor purchase? Why?
8. A floating-rate note's quote is in terms of its "discount margin," in relation to a benchmark. Describe the determination of the discount margin.

Select Bibliography

Canals, J. *Universal Banking.* Oxford: Oxford University Press, 1997.

Fabozzi, F. J., S. Mann, and S. Mann. *Floating Rate Securities.* New Hope, Penn.: Frank J. Fabozzi Associates, 2000

Friedel, M., and M. Jansberg. "Why issue Eurobonds rather than an EMTN programme? A statistical comparison," Bussum, the Netherlands: Zanders & Partners, 2002.

Goodfriend, M. "Eurodollars," in *Instruments of the Money Markets.* Richmond, Va.: Federal Reserve Bank of Richmond, 1998.

Ho, T. S. Y. (Ed.) *Fixed Income Solutions: New Techniques for Managing Market Risks.* Chicago: Irwin Professional Publishing, 1996.

Steil, B. (Ed.). *International Financial Market Regulation.* New York: John Wiley & Sons, 1994.

Stigum, M. and F. L. Robinson. *Money Market and Bond Calculations.* Chicago: Irwin Professional Publishing, 1997.

Thompson, V. *Mastering the Euromarkets.* Chicago: Irwin Professional Publishing, 1996.

Walter, I. and R. C. Smith. *Global Banking.* Oxford: Oxford University Press, 1997.

European Economic and Monetary Union

The advent of the European Economic and Monetary Union (EMU) has transformed the face of Europe. It has removed different currencies, monetary policies, and (to a degree) fiscal policies from EMU member countries; and has effectively brought about a merger of the capital markets of the participating countries.

The twelve countries that make up the EMU form a block that rivals the United States in population and gross domestic product (GDP). In 2001, the combined population of the EMU was 304 million, versus 284 million for the United States. Their combined GDP was about $8 trillion, compared to $10 trillion for the United States. Together, the EMU countries account for 20 percent of the world's trade. The emergence of this formidable economic power has profound effects not only on European capital markets but also on the global capital marketplace. After a brief history of the EMU, this chapter examines those effects.

The objectives of this chapter are to provide an understanding of:
- The main responsibilities of the European Central Bank.
- Government debt markets.
- Corporate fixed-income markets.
- Equity markets.
- Repurchase agreement markets.
- Asset securitization.
- The United Kingdom's plans and the London market.

MARKET OVERVIEW

In January 2002, the twelve members of the **European Economic and Monetary Union (EMU)**—Austria, Belgium, Finland, France, Germany, Greece, Ireland, Italy, Luxembourg, the Netherlands, Portugal, and Spain—gave up their venerable national currencies as euro notes and coins began to circulate. The shift to a single currency within these countries has brought dramatic changes to the way Europeans do business with each other and with the rest of the world. The euro has already benefited the European economy in numerous ways. With only one common currency, businesses operating in the euro-zone save on transaction costs and can plan without currency uncertainty. Travelers within the EMU no longer have to exchange money, saving both time and expenses. Estimates of the savings on currency conversion alone range from 0.5 percent (by the European Commission) to 0.8 percent (by the Ifo Institute for Economic Research in Germany) of the euro area's GDP per year. In addition, the European Commission (**http://europa.eu.int/comm**) estimates that the reduction in risk and uncertainty will boost GDP by 5 percent over the next decade. Record keeping is simpler and less costly with only one currency. Another benefit is market transparency. Prices in different countries are much more readily comparable. This enhances competition and has driven down prices. Furthermore, the euro has partially replaced the dollar as an accounting unit in international trade and as a reserve currency. Consequently, the European economy is now less dependent on the rate of the dollar. Finally, the introduction of the euro has led to lower interest rates in the EMU countries than they would otherwise have experienced.

The introduction of the euro also entailed some costs, estimated to be as high as $100 billion to $150 billion. Not only were costs incurred for the withdrawal of national currencies and introduction of euro notes and coins, but securities laws and market practices had to be adjusted, market professionals had to be retrained, and the back-office operations of all businesses had to be restructured. Calculations made by the European Commission suggest that the payback period is about five years. Furthermore, after the elimination of EMU national currencies, bank revenues from foreign exchange trading have declined. Potentially, too, the EMU countries may encounter problems as a result of surrendering their national instruments for exchange rate and interest rate policies. Table 17.1 summarizes the benefits and costs of the euro, and the next section explains how Europe came to adopt a single currency.

A Brief History of the European Economic and Monetary Union

Origins of the European Economic and Monetary Union can be traced back to the European Economic Community (EEC). In July 1968, its six founding members—Belgium, France, Germany, Italy, Luxembourg, and the Netherlands—abolished all customs duties between them. Over the next decade, the EEC's membership grew: Denmark, Ireland, and United Kingdom joined in 1973;

TABLE 17.1	Advantages and Disadvantages of the Euro	

Advantages	Disadvantages
One common currency	Cost of introduction
No need to change money	Decline of foreign exchange trading
Price transparency	Loss of benchmark for prices
Simplification of recordkeeping	Requirement of maintaining a low deficit
Euro as a reserve currency and as an accounting unit in trade	Surrender of monetary policy Interest rate dependence on deficits in other countries
Lower interest rates	

Greece joined in 1981; and Spain and Portugal joined in 1986. In January 1993, the EEC became the European Union (EU). Two years later, Austria, Finland, and Sweden joined the EU, bringing the total to fifteen countries.[1]

The plan for the EMU itself was launched in the late 1980s. In 1988, the Hanover Summit appointed Jacques Delors to look into the practical aspects of a single currency. He delivered his report in 1989, and an intergovernmental conference that concluded in Maastricht in December 1991 endorsed the Delors plan for a monetary union.

To ensure that the union would include only countries with sound monetary and fiscal policies, the plan laid out several requirements for admission. These were incorporated into the **Maastricht Treaty**, the member nations signed in 1992. To participate in the union, a nation must have a low inflation rate, stable exchange rates, low interest rates, and a sustainable level of government debt. Specifically, the treaty established the following requirements:

○ Low inflation rate. Inflation rates observed over a period of more than one year must be within 15 percent of the three best-performing member countries.

○ Exchange rate stability. The exchange rate must have remained within the normal fluctuation band of the Exchange Rate Mechanism of the European Monetary system for at least two years.

○ Low interest rates. The average nominal interest rate on long-term government bonds, observed over a period of more than one year, must be within 2 percent of the rates of the three best member states.

○ Sustainable government debt. A member state's budget deficit (including federal and local government) should not exceed 3 percent of GDP (except under exceptional circumstances), and the ratio of public debt to GDP should be no higher than 60 percent or should approach that value at a satisfactory speed.

---

[1]Ten countries have been invited to join the EU on May 1, 2004: Cyprus (Greek part), the Czech Republic, Estonia, Hungary, Latvia, Lithuania, Malta, Poland, Slovakia and Slovenia. (http://userpage.chemie.fu-berlin.de/adressen/eu.html)

The Maastricht Treaty assumed that participation in the monetary union would be irrevocable—it included no provisions for a country that wanted to leave the union.

In May 1998, eleven countries that met the entry requirements decided to join the single currency. The initial members were Austria, Belgium, Finland, France, Germany, Ireland, Italy, Luxembourg, the Netherlands, Portugal, and Spain. Denmark and the United Kingdom decided not to join at that time, and Greece and Sweden did not qualify for membership. (Greece later met the requirements and joined in 2001.)

Stability and Growth Pact

Upon admittance to the EMU, a nation must continue to meet the stability and growth pact. According to the Maastricht Treaty, the upper limits for budget deficits and for public debt continue to apply. In the event of non-compliance, the treaty provides a mechanism for sanctions.

Every member state is subject to restrictions on its annual deficit and total outstanding debt. If an EMU member reports a budget deficit of more than 3 percent, the sanctions impose a non–interest-bearing deposit in the amount of 0.2 percent of GDP, plus 0.1 percent for each additional percentage point over the target. The maximum amount to be paid is 0.5 percent of GDP for a deficit ratio of 6 percent. If the budget deficit does not drop below 3 percent after two years, the deposit will be retained and distributed among the member states that have adhered to the budgetary guidelines.

The Council of Economics and Finance Ministers (ECOFIN) decides if a deficit is excessive, with a two-thirds majority needed before sanctions may be imposed on a member state. The country being charged cannot vote. The sanction mechanism will not be applied in the event of a recession with a 2 percent or more decline in GDP. If GDP falls by 0.75 percent to 2 percent, the finance ministers will have to decide whether an exemption should be granted.

The Transition to the Euro

The **euro** officially came into being on January 1, 1999 (see Box 17.1 for a summary of the steps that led to its adoption).[2] During a three-year transition period, from January 1, 1999, to December 31, 2001, member countries had no requirements or prohibitions to use the euro. Although national currencies still could be used for retail transactions, individuals and companies could use the euro as the unit of account for banking transactions, credit cards, and bank cards. In the eurozone, the prices of all listed securities were quoted, traded, and settled in euros as of January 4, 1999.

On December 31, 1998, the EMU countries fixed their exchange rates irrevocably to the euro, and effectively among each other as well. During the

---

[2]The EU countries selected *euro* as the name for the new currency in 1995. Robert Kalina, an Austrian, designed the euro bills and notes.

MARKETS IN ACTION   The Main Stages toward the Euro

17.1

March 1957	The Treaty of Rome establishes the European Economic Community (EEC)
January 1973	Admission of United Kingdom, Ireland, and Denmark to the EEC
March 1979	Creation of European Monetary System (EMS)
January 1981	Admission of Greece
January 1986	Admission of Spain and Portugal
July 1987	The Single European Act establishes the goal of a single market by 1992
February 1992	Signing of the Treaty on European Union in Maastricht
January 1993	The EEC becomes the European Union (EU)
January 1994	Establishment of European Monetary Institute (EMI)
January 1995	Admission of Sweden, Finland, and Austria
December 1995	The European Council adopts the "Maastricht scenario" for euro introduction
December 1996	The European Council determines the legal framework for the introduction of the euro
June 1997	Confirmation of the Stability and Growth Pact
May 1998	Choice of the first-round participating countries (eleven countries)
July 1998	Nomination of board of European Central Bank
January 1999	Introduction of the euro
January 2002	Introduction of euro notes and coins
July 2002	Withdrawal of national notes and coins of participating countries (EMU countries withdrew their national currencies by July 2002)

Sources: *EMU Factsheet*, J.P. Morgan, 1999; *Euro Background*, Andersen Consulting, 1999; and *The Wall Street Journal Interactive Edition*, January 5, 1999.

three-year transitional period, these fixed rates were the only valid rates for the conversion of the euro into EMU national currencies (see Table 17.2, p. 406). The value of the euro against leading currencies on the same date was: 1.1743 U.S. dollar, 132.4554 yen, and 1.6129 Swiss francs per euro.

During the transitional period (1999–2001), converting between two EMU national currencies required a **triangular conversion**. The initial amount of a national currency first had to be converted into euros; then, the euro amount converted into the target national currency. The intermediate result in euros could be rounded to no less than three decimals. For example, the triangular conversion of 1,000 Austrian shillings (ATS) to German marks (DEM) took two steps. First, 1,000 ATS converted to 72.673 euros, which then converted to 142.14 DEM (see Table 17.2 for the exchange rate fixings).

Converting between an EMU national currency and another currency required a **bilateral conversion**: one simply multiplied the EMU national

TABLE 17.2	Irrevocable Fixed Exchange Rates in the Euro

Country	Currency (symbol)	Fixed euro rate
Austria	Schilling (ATS)	13.7603
Belgium	Franc (BEF)	40.3399
Finland	Mark (FIM)	5.94573
France	Franc (FRF)	6.55957
Germany	Mark (DEM)	1.95583
Greece	Drachma (GRD)	340.750
Ireland	Punt (IEF)	0.787564
Italy	Lira (ITL)	1936.27
Luxembourg	Franc (LUF)	40.3399
Netherlands	Guilder (NLG)	2.20371
Portugal	Escudo (PTE)	200.482
Spain	Peseta (ESP)	166.386

Sources: *Financial Times* (http://www.ft.com), Bloomberg Online (http://www.bloomberg.com), and European Central Bank (http://www.ecb.int).

currency by the conversion rate. For example, to convert U.S. dollars (USD) to French francs (FRF), the USD amount first converted into a euro amount by applying a USD/EUR exchange rate. The euro amount then converted into an FRF amount by using the conversion rate. On April 1, 1999, the USD–euro exchange rate was 1.07890. Hence $1,000 was worth 1,078.90 EUR. When multiplied by the conversion rate of 6.55957, the amount comes to 7,077.12 FRF.

During the transitional period, the exchange rates of the euro continued to float against other noneuro currencies and still do so today. Hence, there still is exchange rate risk between the euro and other currencies. As with other currencies, economic and political developments are crucial in determining the value of the euro against other currencies. The European Central Bank (**http://www.ecb.int**) publishes reference exchange rates for the euro on a daily basis.

EUROPEAN CENTRAL BANK

The **European Central Bank (ECB)** determines monetary policy for the EMU. Established on June 1, 1998, the ECB began determining policy for the EMU on January 1, 1999. Together with the central banks of the EU nations, the ECB is part of the European System of Central Banks (ESCB). The term **Eurosystem** refers to the ECB and the national central banks of the member states that have adopted the euro. The primary objective of the Eurosystem is to maintain price stability. Its basic tasks include the following:

° Defining and implementing EMU monetary policy.

- Conducting foreign exchange operations.
- Holding and managing foreign exchange reserves.
- Promoting the smooth operation of payment systems.

The ESCB has three decision-making bodies: the Executive Board, the Governing Council, and the General Council.

The Executive Board has six members and has responsibility for the implementation of monetary policy in accordance with the guidelines set by the Governing Council. To ensure independence, the member states set strict rules for the appointment of the board members. Members of the board have eight-year long appointments and are ineligible for a second term. An exception was made for the first appointments to ensure that all members of the board would not retire at the same time; starting in 2002, at least one member leaves each year. Table 17.3 lists the first board members.

The Governing Council consists of the board members and the presidents of the central banks of the EMU countries. This body decides on interest rates. The General Council includes the president and vice president of the ECB and the presidents of the central banks of all EU member states. Its responsibilities include deciding on whether a country has met the EMU admissions criteria.

Monetary Policy

In determining the monetary policy for the eurozone, ECB's main objective—as specified in the Maastricht Treaty—is to maintain price stability (inflation below 2 percent). To achieve this objective, the ECB focuses its monetary strategy on the growth of the money supply and other indicators of future inflation, as well as on the euro's exchange rates against major currencies.

The ECB's policy tools include open market operations, standing facilities, and reserve requirements (see Table 17.4, p. 408). Open market operations aim to provide banks with longer-term liquidity. The ECB's most important money market interest rate is the basic repo rate, or the interest rate on a basic repurchase agreement. Through repurchase transactions, the ECB provides liquidity to the banking system in exchange for collateral. Banks repurchase the collateral at the end of the basic repo term, which is typically two weeks. Banks that

TABLE 17.3	*First-term Board Members of the ECB*

Name	Responsibility	End of term
Wim Duisenberg	President	2006
Christian Noyer	Vice President	2002
Sirkka Hamalainen	Executive Board Member	2003
Otmar Issing	Executive Board Member	2006
Tommaso Padoa Schioppa	Executive Board Member	2005
Eugenio Domingo Solans	Executive Board Member	2004

Source: *European Central Bank*, (http://www.ecb.int).

TABLE 17.4 | *Policy Tools of the ECB*

Type	Instrument	Maturity	Frequency
Open market operations	Basic repos	2 weeks	Weekly
	Longer-term repos	3 months	Monthly
Standing facilities	Marginal lending	Overnight	Daily
	Deposit	Overnight	Daily
Reserve requirements		1 month	Monthly

do not want to trade repos on a weekly basis can use longer-term repos with a maturity of three months.

The ECB uses **standing facilities**, such as marginal lending or deposit facilities, to cope with shocks in the money market on a day-to-day basis. With the marginal lending facility, liquidity can be provided overnight against collateral. The rate for this facility, was at 4.5 percent at the beginning of 1999, constitutes the ceiling for the money market rate. On the other hand, a bank's cash surplus at the end of the business day can be deposited with the ECB. The deposit rate, was at 2 percent in the beginning of 1999, sets the floor for the money market rate.[3]

Finally, commercial banks in the EMU must hold cash reserves. The reserve requirements are 2 percent of the value of the outstanding deposits and money market paper. The ECB pays market interest rate on these reserves.

Management of Foreign Exchange Reserves

The ECB holds foreign exchange and supervises the management of foreign exchange reserves by the participating central banks. To prevent conflicts between the ECB and the national central banks, the banks must obtain the ECB's permission to manage their reserves. The ECB's own reserves have been set at a maximum of 50 billion EUR. At the start of 1999, the ECB had reserves of 39.5 billion EUR because four EU countries had not yet joined the EMU.

Before the advent of the euro, each individual country needed to hold a significant amount of reserves. With the EMU, this need has diminished. Consequently, the EMU nations held $210 billion of surplus reserves in 1999. The member nations have gradually converted the surplus reserves into euro investments or sold them off, with the proceeds transferred to member states.

Payment System

The euro payment system is called **TARGET (Trans-European Automated Real-time Gross-settlement Express Transfer system)**. It consists of fifteen national real-time gross settlement systems and the ECB payment

---

[3]During an adjustment period, from January 4 to January 21, 1999, the ECB narrowed the interest rate corridor to 50 basis points. The marginal lending rate was 3.25 percent and the deposit rate was 2.75 percent.

mechanism. The ECB and users developed TARGET to achieve three objectives: provide a reliable mechanism for the settlement of cross-border payments, increase efficiency of intra-EMU cross-border payments, and serve the needs of the ECB's monetary policy.

TARGET is a real-time gross settlement system, with each payment handled individually. The sending national central bank receives confirmation of each payment order in real time. The system settles transactions between banks immediately and irrevocably.

GOVERNMENT DEBT MARKETS

Several factors have made the eurozone a low-interest-rate environment. As we have seen, participating countries not only are subject to the same monetary policy and fiscal discipline, but they must also continue to meet the requirements stipulated in the stability and growth pact. The stability pact requires a budget deficit of no more than 3 percent of GDP and a debt stock of less than 60 percent of GDP. Violators can be fined.[4] In addition, as mentioned earlier, the ECB has set a target for inflation of no higher than 2 percent. Nevertheless, one currency does not mean a single yield curve for all government security markets. Clearly, different sovereign borrowers may have different credit ratings and pay different interest rates in line with their credit quality, although the huge spreads Italian and Spanish bonds offered over German bonds in the past are over.[5] The tighter range of credit ratings also reflects the narrower spreads between different issuers, as Table 17.5 shows.

TABLE 17.5 | *Credit Ratings at the Introduction of the EMU*

Member State	Moody's	Standard & Poor's
Austria	Aaa	AAA
Belgium	Aa1	AA+
France	Aaa	AAA
Finland	Aaa	AA
Germany	Aaa	AAA
Ireland	Aaa	AA+
Italy	Aa3	AA
Luxembourg	Aaa	AAA
Netherlands	Aaa	AAA
Portugal	Aa2	AA–
Spain	Aa2	AA

[4]A country does not have to pay fines if GDP declines by 2 percent or more. For a contraction of GDP of 0.75 percent to 2 percent, fines are discretionary.

[5]Of course, size and liquidity also affect yields.

Before the EMU, many global fixed-income investors traded in European bond markets on the basis of an interest rate **convergence play**. For example, traders made a bundle betting on the once-weak bonds of Italy and Spain. Fears of political and currency glitches kept government bonds in those countries virtually in the junk category and thus created wide spreads over the **Bunds** (German government bonds). Italian 10-year bonds had a yield of 12.09 percent in July 1995, and the yield dropped to 6.52 percent in July 1997. Spanish 10-year bonds that yielded 11.25 percent in 1995 were traded at 6.23 percent two years later. During the same time span, the yield on the German 10-year bonds declined from 6.79 percent to 5.57 percent. Hence, the Italian-German spread declined from 5.30 percent to 0.95 percent, and the Spanish-German spread dropped from 4.46 percent to 0.66 percent.

Since the introduction of the euro, such plays (based on convergence of government yields) have largely been eliminated. Variations in credit spreads have continued, but they are far less volatile than the spread movements of the past. As a result, investors have looked elsewhere for opportunities. The bond markets of the countries that stayed out initially, such as Sweden, provide one such opportunity. More attention has been paid to the so-called fast-track countries for the same reason. Barclays Capital publishes Euro Government Bond Indices that can be used as a performance benchmark. Table 17.6 presents a sample of these indices.

TABLE 17.6 | *Euro Government Bond Indexes*

	Index
Euro (All)	122.73
Austria	123.39
Belgium	124.10
Finland	123.58
France	121.54
Germany	122.05
Greece	120.07
Ireland	125.00
Italy	123.33
Netherlands	122.67
Portugal	123.42
Spain	122.97

Notes: 1. Luxembourg is not listed here because it has very little government debt. 2. The requirements for inclusion in the indexes are fixed rate government bonds with a maturity of at least one year and a minimum outstanding balance of €2 billion. 3. The index is a total return index, with a base on December 31, 1997 (index = 100).

Source: Barclays Capital, January 31, 2003.

Redenomination and Reconvention

From January 1, 1999, onward, EMU countries have issued all of their new government debt in euros. The existing government debt denominated in the national currency or the European currency unit (ECU) went under a process of redenomination in euros during the conversion weekend.[6] Given the high cost involved, the EMU decided that nongovernment issuers could choose if and when to redenominate their outstanding debt.

To integrate the EMU bond market, it proved necessary to develop new conventions for trading bonds. These conventions include the day count basis, the number of business days, the settlement date, and the number of coupon payments.

The day count basis for the calculation of effective yield and accrued interest, starting on January 1, 1999, is the number of actual days that have elapsed in relation to the number of actual days in the year for which interest is due (Actual/Actual). For money market instruments, the day count is on the basis of Actual/360. The business day is defined as the day on which the payment transfer system, TARGET, is operational. If the coupon date falls on a date that TARGET is closed, the holder of the debt instrument will receive interest payment the first subsequent business day. The standard settlement date for internationally traded bonds is the trade day (T) plus three business days (T+3). Finally, coupon payments are made annually, except in Italy where payments occur semiannually. These conventions apply to newly issued government and nongovernment debt as well as to outstanding government debt. Outstanding nongovernment debt in general remains under the old conventions.

CORPORATE FIXED-INCOME MARKETS

Since 1999, euro corporate bonds have become a major asset class in global capital markets. Several factors have contributed to this development. As we have seen, the euro capital market has a uniform set of market conventions. The average issue size of euro-denominated bonds is larger than in the previous national bond markets. Some investors in the past tended to underweigh the smaller European bond markets in global bond portfolios, either because the overall market was too small or because individual bond issues within that market were too small and illiquid. However, both of those factors changed after the introduction of the euro.

In addition, the absence of foreign exchange risk has prompted European investors to shift investments back to the EMU from other markets. The Eurobond market has benefited from the euro as well, especially since the euro

---

[6]ECU is an index of foreign exchange consisting of European currencies.

has proved to be a strong challenger to the U.S. dollar. Foreign issuers now seek to diversify their capital structures by issuing euro-denominated Eurobonds.

Many investors in Europe traditionally sought yield through currency speculation, rather than through credit. These investors now must seek other yield opportunities. The corporate debt market has become an important source of yield as investors move down the credit curve. This trend began even before the euro's arrival in 1999. For example, ratings assigned by Standard & Poor's to European companies in 1997, didn't cluster around the traditional AAA/AA categories, but instead around the A/BBB level.[7]

Mergers and Acquisitions and Banking Relationships

Merger and acquisition (M&A) activities have also contributed to the corporate bond market in the eurozone. Since the advent of the euro, a battle for corporate control has swept through Europe. The surge in M&A activity can be attributed to several factors:

° Increased cross-border trade. The single currency has reduced the need for companies to have manufacturing facilities in the same countries as their clients. Companies look to reap economies of scale by having access to as many markets in the eurozone as possible.

° Differences in taxation and labor laws. Regional variations such as taxation and labor laws still remain. Companies located in countries with favorable environments are attractive acquisition candidates.

° Greater competition. Cross-border competition has grown as companies compete for business on a pan-European basis. Companies that were sector leaders in a country may use acquisitions to become sector leaders in the eurozone.

° The equity culture. European managers now focus more on efficiency and shareholder value. Investors are also more comfortable with equity investing. Hence, the equity markets in the eurozone have expanded; increased M&A activity is a natural consequence.

° Privatization. EMU governments have taken steps to deregulate and privatize state-owned enterprises to meet restrictions on their borrowing requirements.

° Availability of capital. The eurozone's booming capital markets provide unprecedented fuel for companies' M&A ambitions.

Europe is now the fastest growing region for M&A business. Major M&A advisory powerhouses include Morgan Stanley, Goldman Sachs, J.P. Morgan Chase, Merrill Lynch, Credit Suisse First Boston, Deutsche Bank, NM Rothschild, UBS Warburg, and Lazard. Clearly, U.S. houses dominate the field. U.S. investment banks have also brought debt to European deal making.

---

[7] *The Euro* reported this (Euromoney Publications, October 1998).

European investors are hungry for higher yields than the rates they can earn from government bonds, which has opened the gates for raising large sums of money in the capital market. American buyout firms such as Kohlberg Kravis & Roberts; Clayton, Dubilier & Rice; and Hicks, Muse, Tate, & Furst have opened offices in Europe or expanded existing operations.

There are also expectations that companies will shift a portion of their funding sources from banks to the debt and equity markets. In the past, similar to their counterparts in Japan, European companies relied overwhelmingly on banks for their capital needs. In Germany, for example, well over 90 percent of corporate financing was met by long-term bank borrowing. Even in France, the most developed corporate bond market in the eurozone, the number was 60 percent. By contrast, the U.S. corporate sector relies on banks for just about one-third of its long-term borrowing needs. Now, however, increased competition has begun to undermine traditional relationships between companies and "house banks." Bankers lending to corporations in Europe has become far more competitive and less profitable. Bankers have cut back their direct corporate lending. The deeper and wider capital market created by the euro will make it increasingly attractive for corporations to satisfy their financial requirements directly in the capital market.

The High-Yield Debt Market

Before the EMU became a reality, many anticipated that it would lead to a period of significant growth in the high-yield debt market. Since the introduction of the euro, yields on European government debt have dropped as European economies align themselves under the EMU. As a result, investors have an increased appetite for other fixed-income products such as junk bonds. As we have noted, they no longer can capitalize on fluctuations on currency exchange rates and intercountry interest rate differentials. Thus, with the elimination of currency risk, investors have focused on credit risk. Fixed-income analysis has played a more prominent role as investors look for third party, sector-specific expertise.

The growth of the high-yield market has resulted in greater liquidity and transparency. This greater liquidity has resulted from the increased issuance and demand for bonds, coupled with secondary market support provided by underwriters. Increased trading volume will lead to greater price transparency. Although certain institutional investors cannot invest in high-yield debt, the recent innovation of collateralized bond obligations, securitizing highly leveraged loans and junk bonds, has expanded the investor base.

As the credit rating of issues falls, the number of potential corporate issuers will increase, affording more companies access to the capital market. For investors, the increase in the number of issues and products provides more diversified credit risk and portfolio holdings. The growth of high-yield debt is likely to be at the expense of the bank loan market as corporations take advantage of alternative, more flexible forms of financing.

EQUITY MARKETS

The launch of the monetary union has had a significant impact on European equity markets. As we have seen, the introduction of the euro eliminated currency risk for investors within the eurozone, enabling them to further diversify their portfolios across eurobloc markets without assuming additional currency risk. This has encouraged them to switch from domestic equities toward a broader exposure. Like the corporate bond and high-yield bond markets, the equity markets have attracted investors looking for higher yields than they can obtain on government bonds in the EMU's low interest rate environment. In addition, the growth of private pension funds and the issuance of new equities has enabled investors to diversify away from their predominant holdings in bonds to more balanced portfolios.

As the equity markets have developed, they have attracted investors from outside the eurozone. Furthermore, the expected increase in GDP has stimulated the equity markets as companies seek equity finance to fuel their growth. We have already noted the increase in the amount of M&A activity. In addition, the size of M&A transactions has increased. Multibillion-dollar deals are now common. Realistically, transactions of this magnitude cannot be done with cash; Europeans use stock to finance these mega deals.[8] Just as important is the emergence of an equity culture in Europe. Compared to bank lending, it is easier for companies to access the equity market and to tap into a much larger retail investor sector.

As the equity markets transform from a group of single markets to one single euro equity market, average dealing costs and spreads have come down. In addition, there has been significant convergence in stock valuations throughout Europe in recent years. The single currency will help this trend continue. Most believe that full convergence throughout the eurozone will not happen, however, as long as investors have different valuation methods. Other factors inhibiting full convergence are national differences in taxes, accounting standards, and regulatory environments.

Structural Forces Affecting the Supply of Equities

Structural forces have transformed the equity markets of the eurozone in both the supply side and the demand side. On the supply side, several structural forces affect the supply of equities in the eurozone: underdeveloped equity markets, changing bank relationships, privatization, and corporate financing requirements for expansion.

The equity market in the eurozone is underdeveloped compared with the United States and the United Kingdom. Countries in the EMU accounted for about one-quarter of world GDP at the introduction of the euro but they contributed less than one-sixth to total global equity market capitalization. Within

---

[8]There is also a convincing tax argument in favor of stock deals, in that the capital gains tax defers until the shareholder sells the stock. And using stock avoids goodwill.

the eurozone itself, national stock markets vary greatly in size and development. For example, the FT/S&P World Index did not include Portugal until May 1, 1998. Prior to that, the Index treated it as a developing economy. Structural reforms within the eurozone should encourage a more diverse range of companies to realize the benefits of obtaining a public listing.

Changing bank relationships are likely to cause traditional cross-shareholdings to unwind. Maximizing shareholder value has started to become a high priority for management. Companies increasingly seek to optimize their capital structure. Over time, the purpose of cross-shareholdings between banks and the corporate sector will be undermined, and the role of bank lending as the key source of financing will be reduced as companies seek more equity financing.

Financing requirements for expansion and privatization play a pivotal role in the growth of the equity markets. For many industries—including water, electricity, and telecommunications—the demand for capital is so great that governments have little alternative but to limit their involvement. For example, in 1997 Oxera (**http://www.oxera.co.uk**), a consulting firm in the United Kingdom, estimated that by 2020 the growth in global demand for electricity will triple, requiring $3 trillion in further investments. According to estimates by Nomura Securities, the market capitalization of utility companies in the eurozone would be about €800–900 billion if they privatize. The transport sector is likely to add an additional €200 billion.[9]

Structuring Forces Affecting the Demand for Equities

On the demand side, the main structural factors affecting the demand for equities are pension fund growth, the development of equity culture, and shifts in asset allocation.

Pension plans in the EMU countries rely predominantly on state-provided defined benefit schemes. These are usually "**pay-as-you-go**" systems: current payroll taxes pay pensions to current retirees. The problem with these schemes is that as the population ages, the number of younger workers entering the workforce will not be sufficient to support the increasing pension obligations. Currently, four workers in Europe support every retiree, but projections indicate this number will fall to only two by 2040. Possible solutions range from raising the retirement age to cutting benefits and reducing the extent to which pension benefits can be indexed. Whatever measures governments choose, private pension schemes such as defined contribution plans will likely grow in coming years as a way of reducing reliance on state benefits.

Traditionally, European pension funds have invested predominantly in fixed-income instruments, but this allocation has shifted toward equity. As we have discussed, the supply of government debt is restricted by the limitation on government deficits. The low and stable inflation environment, the low level of

---

[9]See *The Euro: Strategic Issues for Equity Investors,* Nomura International plc (London, U.K.), December 1998.

yields, and the single currency have forced pension managers to look for other investments. Finally, rules that set limits for specific asset classes or currencies restricted most institutional investors in Europe prior to the EMU. The monetary union has widened the universe of eligible investments, although certain restrictions on asset classes remain.

Although the introduction of the euro and the establishment of a single monetary policy has gradually led to further country convergence and greater focus on sector analysis, country factors still remain important. One reason for this is that although the ECB sets a single interest rate across the whole eurozone, national governments still maintain independent fiscal policies. Consequently, regional differences in tax policies and accounting principles, the impact of monetary policy, and labor market rigidities persist:

°   Taxes remain a major obstacle to a true single market and to the development of a sector approach to portfolio investment. In the EMU, fiscal policy is the only instrument that national governments have left. The temptation for governments to engage in tax competition will be irresistible, particularly in a market where labor lacks mobility.

°   Accounting principles are not yet uniform across the eurozone. Progress has been made as several member states have permitted companies to prepare financial statements according to international accounting standards. Shareholders will benefit from greater transparency, but the emergence of uniform accounting principles will take several years.

°   Having the same monetary policy does not necessarily mean that the EMU countries will be equally sensitive to the effects of that policy. For example, the International Monetary Fund found that in Austria, Belgium, and Germany a rise in interest rates could take three years to take full effect. In contrast, the same interest rate move would affect France, Italy, and Spain in half the time.

°   Labor mobility is likely to be limited across borders for years to come. Portability of pensions, recognition of professional qualifications, availability of suitable housing, and education facilities will not change substantially in the short term.

Online Trading in Europe

Internet stock trading has taken off in Europe. A growing number of investors have abandoned traditional brokerages and their higher fees for convenience and, for some, the excitement of Internet trading. By some estimates, cybertraders in Europe could number 10 million in a few years. Having share prices quoted in a single currency since the advent of the euro has encouraged this trend. Local ebrokers have offered low commissions to gain market share. Traditional securities firms have also moved quickly onto the Internet.

American brokerage houses have been aggressively beefing up their operations in Europe. Charles Schwab bought a British discount brokerage, Share-

Link, in 1995, and claims to have launched Europe's first fully automated online service in December 1998. E*Trade has signed licensing agreements with local players in the United Kingdom and with partners elsewhere in Europe. In January 1999, it set up a French joint venture, CPR–E*Trade. Online brokerages also compete to provide ever-more sophisticated information such as stock research, historical data, and breaking news. Retail investors have access to much of the data found on a broker's terminal.

REPURCHASE AGREEMENT MARKETS

A repurchase agreement (repo) is a sale and an agreement to repurchase the same security at a higher price that reflects the financing cost at a future date. Although a repo in format is a security transaction, in essence it is a collateralized loan to finance the purchase of the underlying security. Security market participants enter into repo transactions because they have cash and want a short-term investment or because they have securities and need funding. Most repo transactions have a maturity of three months or less. One-day transactions are overnight repos, while longer maturities are term repos. An open repo is an overnight repo that rolls over automatically until terminated by either party.

The development of a repo market in Europe has been slow for several reasons. One reason is that most companies need board approval, so repo brokers and dealers have to persuade the treasurer who in turn has to explain to the board. This is a slow process. Another reason is that, before the EMU, European securities were in many different currencies with a great variety of issuers and structures. The repo market therefore was neither liquid nor transparent, which again hindered development. The strength of the banking relationships and the low pressure that treasurers are under to perform in the short term also has deterred the growth of a repo market.

Now the EMU has provided the impetus for the development of a repo market. With a single currency in the eurozone, securities are now more homogeneous. In addition, the issuance of nongovernment securities has been concentrated in investment-grade instruments from financial institutions. As discussed previously, the issuance of corporate debt instruments will likely grow and expand to a wider credit spectrum. The growth in corporate debt and high-yield paper will increase the collateral used in fixed-income repo transactions.

As repo volume increases, some countries will benefit more than others. The larger and more liquid markets will be more active. Smaller countries, which previously had only domestic repo markets, are likely to see more interest from outside investors. Before the EMU, most repo desks were set up on a country basis. In a single currency environment, they have to change to operate more like U.S. Treasury repo desks. Repos are divided into specials and general collateral, with different traders concentrating on different segments of the yield curve. As repo-trading volume increases and the market becomes more competitive and efficient, spreads will narrow.

ASSET SECURITIZATION IN EUROPE

The markets for securitized instruments—asset-backed securities (ABS) and mortgage-backed securities (MBS)—in the United States have been very successful. They provide businesses with access to new sources of capital at lower costs, even after taking into account upfront analysis, structuring, and credit enhancement costs. Also, securitization provides a crucial source of funding for companies with limited access to other forms of credit, because ABS are rated on their own merit, independent of the issuing company's financial standing. The market in Europe presents great potential, as corporations and financial institutions begin to take advantage of the benefits of securitization.

MBS in Germany

The only country in the EMU with a well-developed MBS market is Germany, with its Pfandbrief market. **Pfandbriefe** are asset-backed bonds. Unlike ABS in the United States, the underlying assets for Pfandbriefe remain on the book of the issuers. There is no special-purpose vehicle. The issuer has to manage the pool of assets to make sure its value and cash flows cover all Pfandbrief liabilities. Pfandbriefe are also not subject to prepayment risks. Table 17.7 compares Pfandbriefe and MBS.

In the past, Pfandbriefe were available in sizes from DM 50 million to DM 300 million, with a maturity ranging from 2 to 15 years. The small size and the fact that they were relatively unknown outside Germany made them unattractive to international investors. Since the introduction of Jumbo Pfandbriefe in May 1995, demand for this high-grade German paper has spread throughout Europe. Pfandbriefe are the largest individual component of the European nongovernment bond sector.

Several factors have contributed to the growing reputation of the Pfandbrief market. One of these is the enhanced liquidity. The average size of

TABLE 17.7	*Pfandbriefe and MBS*	
	Pfandbriefe	**MBS**
Balance-sheet treatment	On balance sheet	Off balance sheet
Source of principal and interest payment	Issuer's cash flow	Underlying mortgage cash flow
Collateral	Secured by a substitutable pool of assets of equal amount and of equal average maturity	Secured by a nonsubstitutable pool of assets
Pool loans	Heterogeneous	Homogeneous
Principal redemption	Bullet form	Amortization and prepayment

a Jumbo issue rose from €798 million in 1996 to over €1 billion in 1999. Another important characteristic is the growing internationalization of the Jumbo sector. Issuers have reached out to new investors by launching Pfandbriefe in other currencies and incorporating novel features. Jumbo issues now have prices in line with internationally accepted fixed-price reoffer mechanisms and underwritten by a syndicate of banks. Also, an increasing number of issues have ratings, with the vast majority carrying a triple-A rating. This has increased demand from international investors, many of whom are restricted from buying nonrated bonds.

Pfandbriefe are subject to strict legal and supervisory regulations. They are very safe debt instruments, second only to the **Bunds** (German government bonds). This has earned them the nickname "**Baby Bunds.**" Because of their excellent credit quality, Pfandbriefe are eligible for collateral borrowing from the Deutsche Bundesbank and for repo transactions with the ECB.

Securitization in Europe

Other than Denmark and Germany, issuance of ABS and MBS in Europe has lagged far behind the United States. Other European countries have only recently established frameworks that allow the development of their own asset-backed market. Securitization has developed slowly in Europe for several reasons. In the past, due to favorable funding rates and excess capital, many financial institutions did not have strong incentives to remove assets from their balance sheets. The lack of a legal and regulatory framework also hindered development. Differences in mortgage terms from country to country diminished the appeal of MBS from one country to investors in other countries. Before the EMU, currency differences presented another barrier to cross-border transactions. Additionally, many European investors focused on government debt, rather than spread products.

The EMU is likely to foster a more rapid development of securitization. The introduction of a single currency has a major impact. It shifts investor attention from government securities to spread products. As noted, several countries have made legal and regulatory changes that facilitate securitization. Also, the Bond Market Association (**http://www.bondmarkets.com**) has set up a European Securitization Forum (**http://www.europeansecuritiza tion.com**) to promote securitization in Europe. Furthermore, advances in computer technology have made prepayment analysis and options adjusted spread calculations more accessible to market participants. To reach the full potential, however, Europe needs to set up the equivalent of Ginnie Mae, Fannie Mae, or Freddie Mac. These entities have played a critical role in the growth of the mortgage market in the United States. The establishment of a pan-European housing finance agency would likely have a similar effect in Europe.

THE LONDON MARKET

The United Kingdom decided not to join the monetary union at the first opportunity. The British government decided in 1997 that whatever the decision the matter should be put to a referendum. The government set out five economic tests that would have to be met before it would decide to join:

1. The U.K. economy has achieved sustainable convergence with the economies of the single currency.
2. There is sufficient flexibility in the U.K. economy to adapt to change and other unexpected economic events.
3. Joining the single currency would create better investment conditions in the United Kingdom.
4. The membership would benefit the U.K. financial services industry.
5. Joining the single currency would be good for employment.

These tests are challenging. However, the U.K. government worked closely with the business community and various public sectors to ensure that necessary preparations were in place to deal with the euro from January 1, 1999, and to take forward detailed planning for possible U.K. entry if they decided to do so. The process for the United Kingdom to join the EMU would take about 40 months from the day they would make that decision (see Figure 17.1).

As Figure 17.1 shows, the key stages in the decision process are: (1) a government decision to join the single currency, (2) a referendum, (3) joining the EMU, (4) the introduction of euro coins and notes, and (5) the end of the changeover when sterling withdraws from circulation. By some estimates, it would take about four months from a decision to a referendum. A positive referendum would result in joining. The amount of time required depends on a number of factors, including the readiness of the business sector. A rough esti-

FIGURE 17.1 | *Key Stages for United Kingdom's Joining of the EMU*

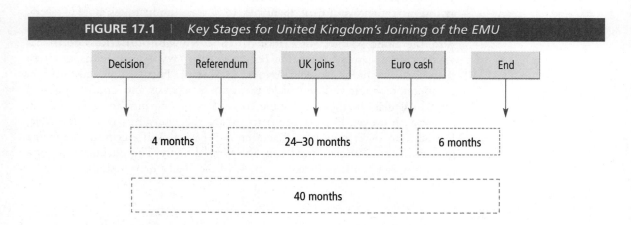

mate is about twenty-four to thirty months. The final phase, from the introduction of euro notes and coins to the withdrawal of sterling, has been set at six months.

London Stock Exchange

Though the United Kingdom has not joined the monetary union, it plays a pivotal role in the dynamics of the European capital markets. The London Stock Exchange (LSE; **http://www.londonstockexchange.com**) is one of the world's top three stock exchanges. London is the most international of the world's great financial centers. It is the natural apex of the global financial triangle that also includes New York and Tokyo. More than 500 international banks and 170 global securities firms have offices in London, providing an unrivaled pool of financial expertise for international clients. A third of the world's institutional equity holdings are managed in Europe, and London provides access to the largest pool of institutional equity capital in the world.

There are more than 2,250 U.K. companies with market capitalization of over £1 trillion and more than 500 international companies with a capitalization in excess of £2 trillion listed on the LSE. The LSE currently offers four market models for trading U.K. shares—SETS, SEAQ, SEAQ Auctions, and SEATS PLUS—and one market model for trading overseas shares. SETS is an electronic limit order book used to trade the blue-chip stocks, including all FTSE 100 and all UK FTSE Eurotop 300 stocks. SEAQ is a quote-display system used as the price reference point for telephone execution between market participants and registered market makers. The majority of Official List stocks trade on SEAQ.[10] SEATS PLUS is the trading service used for all AIM securities and some small Main Market stocks. SEAQ International is the LSE's quote-display system for overseas securities.

European Alliance

On September 10, 1998, the LSE announced a plan to offer a series of euro-denominated capital market products. These products include euro depositary receipts, euro-denominated Eurobonds, and euro convertible bonds. They trade on SEAQ International. On December 7, 1998, the LSE listed the first depositary receipt designed to be denominated in euro. The issuer was Croatia's largest commercial bank, Zagrebacka Banka. This program allowed the company to list and to trade a global depositary receipt in ECU until January 4, 1999, when it converted to the euro.

As noted previously, the LSE and Deutsche Bourse entered into an alliance to collaborate in July 1998, with the ultimate aim of creating a European stock exchange.[11] The aim of the alliance is to establish a single European market. The LSE and Deutsche Bourse established the alliance against a background of

---

[10]Official list is the U.K. Listing Authority's list of all listed securities.

[11]The merger of the exchanges in Amsterdam, Brussels, and Paris created Euronext in September 2002.

change within the financial services industry in Europe.[12] In particular, as we have seen, investment patterns have changed, with a switch toward equities, a move towards investing by sector rather than by country, and an increasing focus on reducing transaction costs. At the same time, investors look for increased liquidity, transparent markets, and a less duplicative regulatory regime. They also look for reductions in costs, especially in relation to trading and settlement, regulatory compliance, and technology overheads. Against this backdrop, the alliance aims to achieve the following:

- One market for the most liquid European securities, with harmonized rules and regulations and a standardized membership admission procedure.
- One common system of electronic, continuous trading for these securities.
- One pan-European market to ensure open access by a worldwide network of participants.
- Development of facilities to deliver common clearing and settlement and other value-added services, according to customer demand.

The alliance of the LSE, Deutsche Bourse, and other European exchanges will create a competitive market that reflects the requirements of market users, including investors, intermediaries, and issuers, and will be positioned to compete effectively in the increasingly global financial services market.

Alternative Investment Market and techMARK

The LSE launched **Alternative Investment Market (AIM)** in June 1995. AIM is the section for young and fast-growing companies. As of January 2003, 850 companies listed on the AIM, and these companies raised more than $10 billion. In November 1999, the LSE launched **techMARK** to list innovative technology companies and to meet their unique requirements. As of September 2002, there were about 200 techMARK companies.

CONCLUDING SUMMARY

This chapter has presented an overview of the European Monetary Union and the alliance of stock exchanges. The EMU unites twelve member states' economies under a single currency—the euro. To join the EMU, a country must maintain price stability, exchange rate stability, a low government deficit, and a low interest rate level. After joining, every EMU nation continues to be subject to the growth and stability pact.

The euro was introduced in a three-year transitional period starting in 1999. By July 2002, all national currencies had withdrawn, and the euro became the only legal tender in the euroland. The introduction of the euro,

---

[12]NMAX in Amsterdam, EURO.NM Belgium in Brussels, Neuer Market in Frankfurt, and Le Noveau Marche in Paris have also joined forces to create EURO.NM to promote a pan-European network of markets for fast-growing companies.

which has become the world's second major reserve currency, has created a new investment and commercial environment. The euro has eliminated currency risk within the eurobloc. In the new commercial environment throughout the EMU, price transparency has created a new competitive arena and has already led to the consolidation of financial institutions in the eurozone.

Participating countries are subject to the same monetary policy and fiscal discipline. With the single currency, EMU corporate bonds have become a major asset class in global capital markets. The fixed-income market has grown due to global bond portfolio rebalancing, changing banking relationships, and mergers and acquisitions. The equity market has also grown substantially. Both supply and demand are favorable for strong growth in the equity market.

The United Kingdom has decided to stay out of the monetary union for now. Nevertheless, it continues to play a pivotal role in the dynamics of the European capital market. The London Stock Exchange has formed an alliance with Deutsche Bourse and has taken steps to expand the alliance to include all European stock exchanges. In September 2002, the exchanges in Amsterdam, Brussels and Paris merged to create Euronext. Through the alliance, investors will benefit from the improved liquidity, pricing transparency and harmonized settlement practices. Also, online stock trading has taken off in Europe. The ultimate objective is one European stock market and an integrated European settlement system to increase liquidity and lower costs for issuers and investors.

Key Terms

Alternative Investment Market
  (AIM) 422
Baby Bunds 419
bilateral conversion 405
Bund 410
convergence play 410
euro 404
European Central Bank (ECB) 406
European Economic and Monetary
  Union (EMU) 402

Eurosystem 406
Maastricht Treaty 403
pay-as-you-go 415
Pfandbriefe 418
standing facility 408
TARGET (Trans-European Automated
  Real-time Gross-settlement Express
  Transfer system) 408
techMARK 422
triangular conversion 405

Review Questions

1. What are the convergence criteria (i.e., the entry requirements for admission to the EMU)? What are their implications for the government securities markets?

2. The European Central Bank is in charge of the implementation of monetary policy in the EMU. Describe the ECB's policy tools.

3. Twelve countries have joined the EMU. What are the benefits and costs of participating?

4. What are the consequences if a country decides to leave the EMU?

5. Why is reconvention necessary?

6. During 1999–2002 transitional period, the EMU official policy was "no compulsion, no prohibition." How was a member state's national currency converted to another state's currency during that period? Illustrate the process by way of a numerical example.

7. Why has merger and acquisition activity increased as a result of the EMU?

8. The MBS and ABS markets in Europe will likely enter a period of faster growth as a result of the EMU. Why haven't the European MBS and ABS markets developed more quickly in the past?

9. The London Stock Exchange and Deutsche Bourse have formed an alliance. Other exchanges have expressed an interest in joining. What are the benefits of such an alliance of European stock exchanges?

10. Pfandbriefe are the largest nongovernment bond markets in Europe. What are Pfandbriefe? What are the main differences between Pfandbriefe and MBS in the United States?

Select Bibliography

Bear Stearns International (U.K.). *European Monetary Union.* London: Bear Stearns International, 1999.

Chabot, C. *Understanding the Euro: The Clear and Concise Guide to the New Trans-European Currency.* New York: McGraw-Hill, 1998.

Deutsche Bank. *European Monetary Union: What It's All About.* Frankfurt, Germany, 1998.

Ehrmann, M., and M. Fratzscher. "Interdependence between the euro area and the US: What role for EMU?" ECB Working Paper No. 200, December 2002.

European Commission. *The Impact of the Introduction of the Euro on Capital Markets.* Brussels: European Commission, 1997.

European Securitization Forum. *European Securitization: A Resource Guide.* New York: The Bond Market Association, 2000.

ING. *The International Role of the Euro.* Economics Department of ING Bank, 1998.

Lemmen, J. *Integrating Financial Markets in the European Union.* Williston, Vt.: Edward Elgar Publishing, 1998.

Liaw, K. T. *The Business of Investment Banking.* New York: John Wiley & Sons, 1999.

Morgan Stanley. *Global Equity and Derivative Markets.* June 1998.

Nomura International Plc. *The Euro: The Die Is Cast.* London: Nomura International Plc, November 1998.

Steil, B. (ed). *The European Equity Markets.* London: Royal Institute of International Affairs, 1996.

Temperton, P. (ed). *The Euro.* New York: John Wiley & Sons, 1999.

Japanese Capital Markets

In recent years, the Japanese capital markets have undergone a dramatic reshaping. Facing a prolonged decline in the equity market and a serious banking crisis, the Japanese government instituted a series of financial reforms that have come to be known as the Japanese "Big Bang." In undertaking these reforms, the government had two goals: to revitalize the Japanese economy and to upgrade Japanese financial markets so that they would rival the financial markets of New York and London by 2001. Unfortunately, the reforms have fallen short of anticipated results, the economy has not yet recovered, and the financial markets are still in a state of malaise. The chapter will examine the reforms and the impact they have had on Japan's capital markets, and will also explore some possible explanations as to why the Big Bang has failed to have the desired effects on the Japanese economy.

The objectives of this chapter are to provide an understanding of:
* Financial system reforms.
* The banking sector.
* Japanese government bonds.
* Corporate debt markets.
* Stock markets.
* The mutual fund business.

MARKET OVERVIEW

Although Japan is the world's third largest economy and capital market—behind the United States and the European Monetary Union—for more than a decade it has experienced an economic recession and depressed securities markets. The origins of Japan's problems can be traced to the bubble economy of the 1980s, when the Nikkei-225 stock average soared to close to 40,000 and real estate prices reached ever greater heights. Convinced that prices would continue to climb, commercial real estate developers borrowed excessively to fuel real estate investments. Homebuyers took on huge mortgages. Unfortunately, in 1990 the bubble collapsed. The ensuring sharp decline in real estate values—to 70 to 80 percent below their highs in the 1980s—resulted in huge losses. According to the Ministry of Finance, by 1998 bad real estate loans amounted to 77 trillion yen ($642 billion), causing a serious deterioration in the capital base of the borrowers and of financial institutions that had lent to them.[1]

The stock market's decline added to the difficulties because the Ministry of Finance allowed Japanese banks to use 45 percent of their **hidden reserves** (unrealized gains on equity holdings) to meet international capital requirements. By some estimates, Japanese banks directly or indirectly owned 30 percent of Japanese industrial companies either through subsidiaries and affiliates or through cross-holding arrangements. Hence, the decline in the equity market decreased the banks' capital and lending ability. As bank lending dropped, bankruptcies increased, and consumer confidence declined.

As the 1990s wore on, the problems not only persisted but intensified. Stock prices continued to fall—in March 2003, the Nikkei-225 average reached a twenty-year low—and levels of nonperforming loans continued to rise. Another concern was the failure of several major financial institutions including Hokkaido Takushoku Bank, Yamaichi Securities, Nissan Mutual Life, Long-Term Credit Bank of Japan, and Nippon Credit Bank. Monetary policy failed to help. As Box 18.1 shows, the **Bank of Japan (http://www.boj.or.jp)** has kept the official discount rate at or below 0.5 percent since September 1995. At the same time, these low rates reduced the returns earned by the 1,200 trillion yen ($10 trillion) in private savings in Japan. With an increasingly aging population that would be dependent on these savings for retirement, Japanese policymakers realized the need for higher returns. Adding to their sense of urgency was the scheduled introduction of the euro in 1999, which they feared might challenge the yen's place as an international currency.

Facing these myriad problems, the Japanese government undertook a series of steps aimed at revitalizing the economy, maintaining the value of the yen, and restructuring the financial system. The centerpiece of these reforms was the Big Bang, which aimed at nothing less than a structural revolution that would lead to a more Western-style financial system. As of early 2003, the

---

[1]The assumption is that the exchange rate is U.S. $1 = JPY ¥ 120.

MARKETS IN ACTION   History of Discount Rate Changes*

18.1

	Official Discount Rate (%)		Official Discount Rate (%)
January 1976	6.50	October 1989	3.75
March 1977	6.00	December 1989	4.25
April 1977	5.00	March 1990	5.25
September 1977	4.25	August 1990	6.00
March 1978	3.50	July 1991	5.50
April 1979	4.25	November 1991	5.00
July 1979	5.25	December 1991	4.50
November 1979	6.25	April 1992	3.75
February 1980	7.25	July 1992	3.25
March 1980	9.00	February 1993	2.50
August 1980	8.25	September 1993	1.75
November 1980	7.25	April 1995	1.00
March 1981	6.25	September 1995	0.50
December 1981	5.50	February 2001	0.35
October 1983	5.00	March 2001	0.25
January 1986	4.50	September 2001	0.10
March 1986	4.00		
April 1986	3.50		
November 1986	3.00	Source: *Statistics: Official Discount Rates*, Bank of Japan, 2003.
February 1987	2.50	*The table lists the new rate and the month when the rate
May 1989	3.25	change occurred.

desired results of these reforms have not been realized yet and market observers are not optimistic in the short term.

THE REFORMS

During the 1990s, the Japanese government undertook a series of reforms aimed at addressing the nation's economic problems. The reforms began in 1992 with measures aimed at reducing fraud in the securities industry, but the government undertook the most important steps in 1998 when it introduced a comprehensive plan to revitalize the economy and launched the Big Bang reforms.

The Securities Industry

The Japanese securities industry experienced unprecedented growth and profits in the 1980s. The transaction volume surged from 3.528 trillion yen ($29.4 billion) in 1980 to 40.824 trillion yen ($340.2 billion) by 1987 but then declined to 23.302 trillion yen ($194.2 billion) in 1990 after the crash.

Commissions and fees rose to a peak of 45.085 billion yen ($375.7 million) in 1989. Financial liberalization, the high valuation of the yen, and low interest rates fueled this extraordinary growth. The markets were stimulated in 1983 when the Ministry of Finance (**http://www.mof.go.jp**) relaxed its restrictions and permitted banks to sell long-term public bonds, to deal in public bonds the next year, and to trade in futures and options some time later. Securities companies received permission to expand into transactions in certificates of deposits, yen-denominated banker's acceptances, and commercial paper issued overseas.

In 1991, however, scandals roiled markets involving several major firms. The top management at Yamaichi Securities and Nomura Securities, two of Japan's top securities firms, had to resign when investigators discovered that the firms had compensated customers for trading losses and made payoffs to alleged racketeers. As a result of the scandals, there is now an explicit prohibition against compensation by a brokerage firm to its customers for trading losses.

In 1992, the government amended Securities and Exchange Law to include several reform measures. One amendment required the Ministry of Finance to establish a market surveillance committee to monitor securities firms and enforce mandatory disclosure and antifraud rules. The second amendment broadened the definition of security to include:

° Debt security issued by the government, municipalities, and corporations.

° Stock issued by corporations.

° Beneficial certificates under a securities investment trust or loan trust.

° Securities issued by foreign governments or companies that have characteristics resembling the domestic issues.

° Any other security designated by cabinet order.

In addition, the Ministry relaxed rules on private placement. An exemption from disclosure requirements is available when the issuer sells the new securities to qualified institutional investors only.

The Comprehensive Plan

In July 1998, the Japanese government announced the **Comprehensive Plan for Financial Revitalization**, the so-called total plan, to revitalize the financial system and help the banks recover from their bad loans. First, the plan created the Financial Supervisory Agency to serve as a watchdog for Japan's banks. Second, in the belief that full disclosure was an important prerequisite to the disposal of bad loans, the plan established new disclosure standards, comparable to those adopted by the SEC in the United States. By 1998, many banks had already begun the process of removing bad loans from their balance sheets by selling off the loans or the underlying real estate collateral. To assist the banks in this process, the government allocated 30 trillion yen ($250 billion) to serve as deposit guarantees. Of this amount, a special account of the Deposit Insurance Corporation (DIC; **http://www.dic.go.jp**) received a 17 trillion yen allocation to provide full protection of depositors. A new Financial Crisis Management Account of the DIC received the remaining 13 trillion yen to enhance the capital base of financial institutions (the DIC will be discussed later, in the section on the banking system).

The Big Bang

Although the banking reforms initiated under the Comprehensive Plan were crucial to Japan's recovery, policymakers realized that Japanese securities companies faced an increasingly competitive market environment both at home and abroad due to the globalization of the financial markets and advances in information technology. To ensure that Japan's capital markets could continue to be successful in the global economy, in November 1996 Prime Minister Hashimoto announced plans for major reforms—reforms so all-encompassing that they came to be known as Japan's **Big Bang**. After some preliminary steps in 1997, the government implemented the main reform measures from 1998 through 2000.

Three principles provided the foundation for these reforms:

1. Free—The promotion of free competition to ensure that the market determines the cost of services.
2. Fair—The full and timely disclosure of material information to ensure that the playing field is the same for all participants.
3. Global—The adoption of global standards in law, accounting, and taxation to ensure that Japanese companies can compete successfully in the increasingly integrated global capital marketplace.

The reform measures focused on four general areas: deregulation of financial products, promotion of free competition, lifting of trade restrictions, and the establishment of a reliable framework and rules for fair and transparent transactions.

Deregulation

The deregulation of financial products has expanded the menu of choices for borrowers and investors. One of the first steps was to lift the ban on derivatives. Trading of options on individual stocks began in July 1997 and the government gradually lifted restrictions on other derivatives. Another important step was the introduction of asset management accounts. Banks also received authorization to sell securities investment trusts or mutual funds (in December 1997) and insurance (in 2001). Over-the-counter sales of investment trusts managed by banks and other financial institutions rapidly expanded after this measure; by September 1999, banks and other financial institutions managed investment trusts valued at 1.8 trillion yen ($15 billion).

Another deregulatory measure provided for special purpose vehicles, which are the issuers of asset-backed securities. Additionally, amendments of the Foreign Exchange Law that took effect on April 1, 1998, removed restrictions on cross-border capital transactions. For the first time, Japanese investors could freely invest in foreign currencies. At the same time, the government lifted restrictions on foreign investments in Japan, except for the rules governing mergers and acquisitions.

Promotion of Free Competition

Several measures aimed to promote free competition and thereby improve the quality of financial service. In an important change, the barriers preventing banks, securities companies, and insurance companies from engaging in each other's businesses were lifted. Now, by establishing a holding company, financial institutions can combine banking, securities, and insurance operations within one company, allowing the one-stop shopping and efficiency that have been seen in other countries where similar reforms have occurred. Daiwa was the first to set up a holding company, Daiwa Securities Group (**http://www.daiwa.co.jp**), which now oversees Daiwa's operations in retail, wholesale, research, trust banking, finance, and other units. Nikko Cordial (**http://www.nikko.co.jp**) and Nomura (**http://www.nomura.co.jp**) took similar steps.

Other measures also expanded the services that financial institutions can offer their clients. Since 1999, ordinary banks, which include city banks, regional banks, and foreign banks, have been allowed to issue ordinary bonds. Previously, only seven authorized banks could issue bank debentures. In addition, the amended Foreign Exchange Law provided for free competition in the foreign exchange business. Now all financial institutions can offer various types of foreign exchange services such as the sale and purchase of currencies and currency swaps. Previously, authorized foreign exchange banks had a monopoly on the foreign exchange business.

Lifting of Trading Restrictions

By removing various restrictions on securities trading, the Big Bang reforms have provided Japan with more diversified markets and channels for raising capital. Perhaps most importantly, the Big Bang lifted the rule that stocks could be traded only through stock exchanges, and permitted proprietary electronic trading systems. Consequently, broker-dealers are now free to trade listed securities through these systems. The reforms also lifted the ban on the trading and intermediating of unlisted or unregistered stocks by securities firms. As a result of these changes, the Tokyo Stock Exchange established a new market for promising start-ups, called **Mothers (Market for High Growth and Emerging Stocks)**, in November 1999, and the Osaka Stock Exchange established a Nasdaq-like stock market for Japan in June 2000.

In addition, trading has been encouraged by eliminating restrictions that prevented firms from competing by lowering brokerage commissions. The removal of these restrictions has led to not only lower commissions for investors but also to the expansion of Internet trading in Japan.

Ensuring Market Transparency

Realizing that the reforms just described would not have the desired effect unless investors could be sure that they received complete information, Japanese policymakers took several steps to enhance standards and require disclosure. With the proliferation of financial instruments, additional amendments to the Securities and Exchange Law broadened the definition of security beyond that established in 1992, and thus extended the law's reach to more instruments. There were new accounting standards implemented for various financial instruments.

As further protection for investors, the government enacted several measures to ensure that companies' published financial statements reflect their true financial condition. Tradable securities, such as derivatives and equities, must now be valued at the market price, not historic cost.[2] Since 1999, companies must publish consolidated accounts that include all associated operations over which they have influence.[3] Financial institutions must disclose information on their nonperforming assets on a consolidated basis, using standards equivalent to those used by the U.S. Securities and Exchange Commission. In addition, companies must disclose the true market value of their pension liabilities and indicate whether shortfalls exist. As further protection for customers of financial institutions, the government had already (in 1997) required them to maintain separate accounts for customer assets.

Additional Measures

The Japanese government also took additional measures to restore confidence in the banking sector. In October 1998, it enacted the Financial Function Early Strengthening Law and the Financial Revitalization Law. Through these laws, the government provided credit guarantees of up to 25 trillion yen ($208 billion) and 18 trillion yen ($150 billion), respectively, in addition to the 17 trillion already appropriated for the protection of deposits under the Comprehensive Plan. In December 1999, the government also announced that it would extend the special measures to fully protect deposits by one year, until the end of March 2002. By opening the Japanese capital markets to foreign investors; removing the barriers separating banks, securities firms, and insurance companies; and deregulating almost all aspects of its markets, the Japanese government set out to create a new financial system that could compete successfully with the other major financial systems of the world. When it enacted the Big Bang reforms, the government expected that the reforms would lead to the reorganization of the financial sector through mergers, the establishment of holding companies, and the expansion of foreign financial institutions into Japan. These changes in turn would improve the efficiency and profitability of Japan's financial institutions, allowing them to make new strategic investments for more advanced and diversified financial services to their customers. The remainder of this chapter will examine the individual aspects of Japan's

---

[2]The U.S. FASB 115 and FASB 133 require companies to report market value of securities.

[3]In the past, a parent company counted operations as subsidiaries only if it had more than 50 percent ownership. In reality, big companies often controlled these smaller affiliates with far smaller stakes and thus could shift unwanted losses to the affiliates. Now, if the parent company exercises control by financing the affiliate's debt or picking its board, the parent must treat the affiliate as a full-blown subsidiary.

financial system, with particular emphasis on how the Big Bang reforms have affected them.

THE BANKING SECTOR

As we have seen, a major reason for the Big Bang and other reforms was to foster the recovery of the Japanese banking sector, which has struggled with a mass of bad loans. To this end, the reforms encouraged competition by allowing branches of foreign banks to compete freely with Japanese banks, ending the monopoly certain banks held on foreign exchange business, and eliminating barriers that separated banks, securities firms, and insurance companies. Despite these changes, Japan still has five distinct categories of banks: city banks, regional banks, foreign-owned bank branches, trust banks, and long-term credit banks.

City banks are based in large cities and have nationwide branch networks. They traditionally provided short-term funds to large corporations. Until the Big Bang reforms, the city banks were the only banks licensed to conduct foreign exchange. The sources of funding for city banks are borrowings from the Bank of Japan, the interbank market, and corporate deposits. There are six city banks:

- Asahi Bank (**http://www.asahibank.co.jp**)
- Bank of Tokyo–Mitsubishi (**http://www.btm.co.jp**)
- Daiwa Bank (**http://www.daiwabank.co.jp**)
- Mizuho Holdings (**http://www.mizuho-fg.co.jp**)
- UFJ Bank (**http://www.ufjbank.co.jp**)
- Sumitomo Mitsui Banking Corp. (**http://www.smbc.co.jp**)

Regional banks provide financing within their prefectures (administrative districts). Their customers are mainly small and medium-sized corporations and individuals. Since regional banks have few loan clients outside large cities, they provide interbank loans on the so-called call market to city banks. Foreign-owned bank branches are similar to city banks or regional banks. They account for an insignificant share of the market, but are quite active in the derivatives market. Since the Big Bang, foreign bank branches have had permission to compete freely with Japanese banks. City banks, regional banks, and foreign bank branches together are known as "ordinary banks."

Trust banks have license to engage in banking and trust activities. They obtain their funding from individual and corporate deposits held in trusts. There are more than 30 trust banks. Long-term credit banks provide long-term funding to corporations. They have authorization to issue debentures, but they cannot take deposits from borrowers or the government.

In addition, Japan has many smaller banking institutions such as mutual banks, credit associations, credit cooperatives, and credit federations of agricultural cooperatives and fishery cooperatives. These institutions have traditionally provided funding to their members, and their sources of funds are primarily deposits and savings by members. Finally, there are several government banks and the post office. The Japanese postal savings system is not a bank, but has a sizable portion of all Japanese deposits.

Bank Regulation

The Ministry of Finance, the Bank of Japan, the Deposit Insurance Corporation, and the Resolution and Collection Bank all regulate Japanese banks. The Ministry of Finance (MOF) is the primary bank regulator. It establishes bank standards and has the sole responsibility for bank licensing and the enforcement of bank regulations.

Before April 1, 1998, the Bank of Japan (BOJ) was under the control of the MOF. Now the independent BOJ has regulatory powers comparable to those of independent central banks in other countries. The BOJ's responsibility is to maintain price stability and ensure the stability of the financial system, thereby laying the foundation for sound economic growth. The BOJ closely monitors trends in loans and deposits of individual financial institutions, and its staff members regularly visit banks to carry out on-site examinations of their financial conditions and management policies.

The Japanese established the Deposit Insurance Corporation (DIC) in 1971 to protect depositors and maintain the stability of the banking sector. The DIC collects premiums from participating banks, pays insurance claims, and purchases assets from failing or failed institutions. The deposit insurance ceiling is 10 million yen ($83,333) per deposit, which does not cover Interbank deposits, deposits in foreign currency, and deposits in foreign banks or in overseas branches of Japanese banks. The DIC is under the supervision of the Ministry of Finance (MOF), which must approve all applications for financial assistance from distressed financial institutions. The Resolution and Collection Bank (RCB), established in 1995 and modeled after the U.S. Resolution Trust Corporation, receives and manages the assets of failed financial institutions.

Recent Problems in the Banking Sector

As we have seen, since the early 1990s, Japanese banks have faced enormous problems created by bad loans and the stock market's prolonged decline. Structural problems have compounded these difficulties. One problem is that the Japanese government has tremendous power over the banking sector and traditionally has directed banks to fund targeted firms. In return, the banks were protected from competition. To protect the banking industry, the MOF created disincentives to the issuance of stocks and bonds. All bonds had to be collateralized. Likewise, regulations on equity issuance made the stock market an expensive pool to tap. Hence, bank loans have remained the major source of corporate funding, far outpacing the stock and bond markets as sources of capital.

The second structural problem is the **keiretsu**, a conglomerate of Japanese businesses that cooperate to achieve common goals. Several keiretsu have a large bank at their center, with the rest consisting of insurance, trading, construction, finance, and real estate companies. The bank is both the lender to the other businesses in the keiretsu and their shareholder. The other businesses are also the shareholders of the bank and the primary beneficiaries of its low-cost loans.[4] Government industrial policy and the inherent conflicts of interest in the keiretsu structure are barriers to an efficient and competitive banking industry.

Faced with these difficulties, the Japanese government has proposed several short-term fixes, such as lowering the official discount rate (to 0.10 percent in 2001) and providing stimulus packages. The Big Bang reforms are the long-term solutions. Many banks have already taken steps to sell their nonperforming loans. Most of the buyers are foreign entities. In addition, some banks have initiated modest downsizing and branch closings. Consolidation is the trend of the future. Deregulation has succeeded in breaking down the barriers between banks and other financial companies such as brokerages and insurers. As a result, such companies have been seeking alliances with both domestic and foreign partners to remain competitive. As an example, in September 2000, Dai-Ichi Kangyo Bank, Fuji Bank, and Industrial Bank merged to form Mizuho Holdings, creating a bank with more than $1 trillion in assets.

JAPANESE GOVERNMENT BONDS

The Japanese government issues three types of securities: short-term Treasury bills, coupon bonds, and zero-coupon bonds. **Japanese government bonds (JGB)** are available with various maturity periods. JGBs have original maturity periods of 2 to 30 years. Payment of coupons occurs semiannually. Also offered are 3-year zero-coupon bonds that pay the principal at maturity. Table 18.1 lists the types of Japanese government securities and their issuing frequency. And as Table 18.2 shows, yields on all types of government securities have been much lower in Japan than in the United States in recent years.

Both medium- and long-term bonds are numbered serially and are referred to by number rather than by the maturity and coupon. As an example, in March 2001 the most recently issued 10-year bond, which had a coupon rate of 1.40 percent and a maturity of March 21, 2011, was referred to as JGB #229.

The Benchmark Issue
The Japanese government relies heavily on long-term financing. As of March 2003, for example, long-term (10 years and over) accounted for 274 trillion yen ($2.28 trillion) of the total 492 trillion yen ($4.1 trillion) in outstanding marketable government bonds. Medium-term bonds (two to six years) and

[4]Until its abolishment in 1993, the Interest Rate Law set maximum ceilings for short-term and long-term deposit and loan rates. The Ministry of Finance would ensure low financing costs and the political allocation of funds to strategic industries.

| TABLE 18.1 | Types of Japanese Government Securities |

Type	Maturity	Issuing Frequency
Treasury bills	3-month, 6-month, 1-year	Monthly
Discount bonds	3-year	Bimonthly
Medium-term bonds	2-year, 5-year and 10-year	Monthly
Long-term bonds	15-year	Quarterly
	20-year	Every other month
	30-year	Semiannual

Source: Ministry of Finance (Japan).

| TABLE 18.2 | Japanese Yield Curve (February 4, 2003) |

	Japanese Government Bills/Bonds			
	Coupon (%)	Maturity Date	Price (% of par)	Yield (%)
3 months	0.000	05/06/03	100.000	0.002
6 months	0.000	07/10/03	99.999	0.002
1 year	0.100	03/22/04	100.078	0.029
2 years	0.100	02/20/05	100.099	0.050
5 years	0.300	12/20/07	100.124	0.274
10 years	0.900	12/20/12	100.381	0.858
15 years	2.600	03/20/18	119.987	1.064
20 years	1.700	12/20/22	105.431	1.353
30 years	1.400	12/20/32	96.958	1.549

Source: Bloomberg (http://www.bloomberg.com/markets/rates/japan.html).

short-term securities (up to one year) accounted for 104 trillion ($866 billion) and 35 trillion yen ($291 billion), respectively.

For years, the 10-year bond has been the benchmark issue; that is, it is the most actively traded issue in the secondary market and has the most liquidity, similar to the on-the-run issue in the U.S. government securities market. For example, in early June 1999, the benchmark issue was JGB #203 with a maturity of June 2008, not the most recently issued JGB #210 with a maturity of December 2010. The benchmark issue generally has several characteristics:

° A coupon rate close to the prevailing market rate.

° A large outstanding amount.

° A wide distribution.

° A current maturity of close to 10 years.

The benchmark issue usually retains its status for several months until a new benchmark emerges. Since there is a large liquidity premium for the benchmark—from 10 to 100 basis points—the transition can be costly and usually takes several weeks.

Japanese Government Bond Auctions

Japanese government traditionally offered treasury securities through a syndicated underwriting system, in which the syndicate members commit to purchase the unsold portion of the offering at the average of the successful bid prices. Almost all of the securities companies and financial institutions in Japan belong to an underwriting syndicate. Competitive bidding was introduced in April 1989. Under this method, a bidder submits a sealed bid and pays his own bid price if the bid is accepted by the Ministry of Finance. With few exceptions today, most government bonds are issued through a competitive auction.

The auction process begins with the auction announcement. The MOF approves the issue and sets the coupon reference rate in the auction announcement. For example, on March 6, 2001, the MOF announced the auction of 15-year floating-rate bonds. The auction date was March 13 and the issue date was March 31. The amount of the offering was 800 billion yen ($6.67 billion). In addition, the MOF set the reference rate used for the first coupon at 1.40 percent.

At 8:30 A.M. on the day of the auction, the MOF announces the terms of the issue, set after consultation with the syndicate representatives. Financial institutions submit bids between 11:30 A.M. and 1:30 P.M. Any syndicate member can bid up to 30 percent of the auction amount. Large banks and securities firms submit most of the bids. The auction result is announced at 2:30 P.M. The issue date usually occurs on the twentieth of the month after the auction. There is no when-issued market in the pre-auction period. Dealers cannot start trading the bonds on a when-issued basis until after the auction date. The maturity typically occurs on the twentieth day or the next business day of the last month of the quarter, and the first coupon payment is made six months after the final month of that quarter.

Compared to the U.S. market, Japanese government bond auctions have a higher average **coverage ratio**, which is the ratio of the total amount of bids submitted to the auction amount. According to Hamao and Jegadeesh (1998), the average coverage ratio in Japan is 4.03, almost twice the ratio of 2.16 for the 10-year note auctions in the United States. A possible explanation is that most consider the 10-year Japanese bond the benchmark bond; the secondary market is very liquid. The higher levels of auction participation in Japan lead to a narrower price range for accepted bids. The average yield range for successful bids for 10-year bonds in Japan is 0.12 percent, compared to 0.24 percent in the United States. The more competitive bidding process and the tighter price range tend to produce lower auction profits for the dealers than are normal in the United States.

Hamao and Jegadeesh (1998) also found that when big Japanese securities houses win larger amounts in bond auctions, their average profits are significantly negative. The securities firms recoup their losses by using the bonds as part of a tying strategy. They bid aggressively when they can sell government bonds to their clients in combination with other products they underwrite.

Interestingly, U.S. firms seem to be better at processing information about the values of Japanese government bonds than Japanese firms are. When big U.S. investment banks win a larger proportion of the auction, their profits are positive and significantly above zero. U.S. firms have been participating in Japanese government bond auctions since 1989, when competitive bidding began. Today, active U.S. firms include Goldman Sachs, Merrill Lynch, Morgan Stanley, and Smith Barney.

Secondary Market Trading

Secondary market trading of Japanese government bonds is primarily over-the-counter. The Tokyo Stock Exchange also lists government bonds, but exchange transactions are usually conducted by retail investors.

During the past two-and-one-half decades, the government bond trading has expanded significantly as the government has taken steps to gradually open up the market. For example, banks could not sell government bonds until 1977 and could not buy and sell government bonds (known as **bank dealing**) until 1984. The establishment of the Japan Bond Trading Corporation and the introduction of bank dealing contributed to the rapid growth in the interdealer market, which in turn led to rapid growth in the government bond market and the overall fixed-income market. Today, the Big Three (Daiwa, Nomura, and Nikko) claim the top positions in government bond trading. In 1985, the bond futures market began trading. Options on government bond futures were introduced in 1990.

Clearing and Settlement

Japan has tried to improve its settlement system. In 1997, it adopted a T+3 settlement system for government securities. Before that, JGBs settled in principle on the fifth, tenth, fifteenth, twentieth, twenty-fifth, and the last day of every month as a market practice. Under that system, the average period between trade and settlement was around seven days. Note that the settlement cycle for U.S. government bonds is T+1.

Paperless Trading

The MOF announced that trading of government bonds would go paperless starting in 2003. To accomplish this, the MOF adopted a new book-entry transfer system. Under the new system, government bonds are traded by entering the trades into the books maintained at financial institutions. By making the transactions paperless, the new book-entry transfer system will eliminate the loss and forgery of JGB certificates (see Box 18.2 for MOF's announcement on a warning against a fictitious certificate).

CORPORATE DEBT MARKETS

As we have seen, traditionally Japanese corporations have relied heavily on bank loans for their financing needs rather than issuing debt. As a consequence, the corporate debt market has remained relatively underdeveloped and has consisted, in large part, of bank debentures. In recent years, this situation has begun to change, as a result of both the problems in the Japanese banking sector and the structural reforms occurring in Japan's capital markets.

Increasingly, corporations turn to the debt markets for their financing needs. The banking crisis—which has caused many banks to lend less and to demand stricter covenants from their corporate borrowers—as well as deregulation has spurred this shift. Big banks such as Norinchkin can now underwrite bonds. To shore up their securities business, they encourage their corporate clients to refinance their loans in the bond market instead of rolling over their bank loans.

Another factor that has contributed to the growth of the corporate debt market is the low interest rate environment that has prevailed in Japan during the 1990s and 2000s. In the quest for higher yield, both retail and institutional investors have shifted money from bank deposits into the bond market. Most of the bond issues have been fixed-rate bonds with a maturity of 3 to 5 years. With investors hungry for higher coupons, top-rated companies have been able to extend maturity to 10 to 20 years.

MARKETS IN ACTION   Ministry of Finance News Release
Warning of Fictitious Certificate

18.2

On October 6, 2000, the Ministry of Finance sent out the following news release to alert the public about a fictitious certificate that the Japanese Minister of Finance had allegedly issued:

A "Kanpukin Zandaka Kakuninsho" is a fictitious certificate which has allegedly been issued by the Japanese Minister of Finance to certify the existence of a remaining balance on a Japanese government bond refund. It claims to confirm that the Japanese Minister of Finance will exchange the amount specified for an equivalent amount of Japanese government bonds.

Although some of the perpetrators who attempted to receive money by using a "Kanpukin Zandaka Kakuninsho" have already been arrested by the police since 1984, the fraudulent use of such a fictitious certificate has been occurring repeatedly.

Please note that the Japanese Ministry of Finance has never issued such "Kanpukin Zandaka Kakuninsho," and that such a certificate could never exist legally.

Source: Ministry of Finance (Japan).

Maintaining a high credit rating is important. Since a credit rating downgrade helped sink Yamaichi Securities in 1997, the Japanese financial industry has paid considerable attention to credit ratings. Major Japanese rating agencies include Nippon Investors Service, Japan Bond Rating Institute, Japan Credit Rating Agency, and Mikuni & Co. In addition, Moody's, Standard and Poor's, and FitchRatings provide credit ratings in Japan as well.

Several other changes have also contributed to the growth of the corporate bond market. A shelf registration rule introduced in 1987 permitted issuers to come to the market faster. Equity-linked securities, such as convertible bonds and bonds with warrants, have been popular. The market has also seen an increase in structured deals such as dual-currency bonds and callable bonds. International issuance has also increased.

Another healthy development has been an increase in the use of spread-based pricing. In the past, most bonds in Japan were priced on a coupon basis. A triple-A bond might be priced at almost the same level as an A-rated bond. Spread-based pricing has resulted in a larger supply of bonds and a more efficient allocation of funds.

The growth of the bond market has increased demand for underwriting services. Major bond underwriters include Nomura Securities, Daiwa Securities, Bank of Tokyo-Mitsubishi, Sanwa Bank, Mizuho Holdings, Merrill Lynch, and Goldman Sachs.

Despite all of the changes that have occurred, bank debentures are still a significant part of the corporate fixed-income market. Even here, though, changes have occurred. In the past, only seven banks were allowed to issue bank debentures, but since the Big Bang reforms, all ordinary banks can issue bonds.[5]

Foreign Bonds

Foreign bonds are bonds issued in Japan by foreign institutions or outside Japan by Japanese institutions. **Samurai bonds** are yen-denominated bonds issued in the Japanese market under domestic regulations. Major samurai issuers include supranational institutions, sovereign governments, governmental institutions from various countries, and corporate issuers. The first samurai issuers were the Asian Development Bank (1970), the World Bank (1971), Australia (1972), and Sears Roebuck (1979). The samurai bond market has grown rapidly in recent years, due to an effective hedging strategy and the low interest rate environment. Non–Japanese borrowers use samurai bonds to hedge against foreign exchange risk. Foreign institutions may also tap into the samurai market and simultaneously swap the issue into another currency to take advantage of the lower costs of funding in Japan.

Until January 1996, bonds issued in Japan by foreign institutions had to have a minimum credit rating of Baa3/BBB−. Packer and Reynolds (1997) observe that the elimination of the minimum credit rating requirement

---

[5]Long-Term Credit Bank of Japan and Nippon Credit Bank failed in 1998.

increased foreign bond issues in 1996 by 507 billion yen, or 23 percent of the growth from 1995 to 1996.

Government-guaranteed bonds issued in foreign markets are quite significant. In the 1990s, the annual issuance was in the range of 600–800 billion yen ($5–6.67 billion). The issuers include Japan Development Bank, Export-Import Bank of Japan, Japan Finance Corporation for Municipal Enterprises, Japan Finance Corporation for Small Business, Hokkaido-Tohoku Development Finance Public Corporation, Japan Highway Public Corporation, Tokyo Metropolitan Government, Yokohama City, Electric Power Development Company, and Kansai International Airport Company.

Yield Quotes

Yields in the Japanese bond market are quoted on a simple yield basis.[6] One can calculate simple yield as follows:

18.1

$$y = \frac{c \times F + \dfrac{F - P}{M}}{P}$$

Where y = simple yield,
 c = annual coupon rate,
 F = par amount,
 P = clean price, and
 M = years to maturity.

As is clear from this expression, the simple yield is the coupon rate if the bond trades at par. If an investor purchases the bond at a premium, the simple yield earned will be less than the coupon rate, because the drag to par will lead to a capital loss as the bond approaches maturity. Conversely, if an investor purchases the bond at a discount, then the simple yield will exceed the coupon rate as the drag to par produces capital gains.

STOCK MARKETS

Japan now has two main stock exchanges, including the Tokyo Stock Exchange (TSE, **http://www.tse.or.jp**) and the Osaka Securities Exchange (**http://www.ose.or.jp**). The TSE is the largest exchange in Japan, accounting for 85 percent or more of trading volume in recent years. Its development over the past half century, as Table 18.3 shows, provides a guide to the progress of the Japanese securities market.

---

[6]This is different from the yield-to-maturity concept used in the United States. A yield-to-maturity is an interest rate that discounts all future incomes of the bond to the current market price of the bond.

TABLE 18.3	Milestones in the Growth of the Tokyo Stock Exchange
1951	Margin trading introduced
1956	Bond trading started
1966	Japanese government bonds listed for the first time since World War II
1969	Tokyo Stock Price Index (TOPIX) introduced
1970	Trading in convertible bonds began
1971	Book-entry clearing system for stocks introduced
1973	Yen-denominated foreign bonds listed and foreign stock section opened
1977	Ad valorem brokerage commission system introduced
1982	Computer-assisted Order Routing and Execution System introduced
1985	Trading in 10-year government bond futures started
1988	Trading in TOPIX futures started
1989	Trading in TOPIX options and U.S. T-bond futures started
1990	Trading in options on government bond futures started and Floor Order Routing and Execution System introduced
1991	Central Depository and Clearing System began operation
1994	Partial deregulation of commission schedule
1997	Equity options introduced
1998	Partial deregulation of brokerage commissions and abolition of restriction on off-exchange trading for listed securities
1999	Liberalization of brokerage commissions, abolition of the fixed number of members, and establishment of Market of High Growth and Emerging Stocks
2000	Hiroshima and Niigata stock exchanges merged into TSE
2001	Tokyo Stock Exchange Inc. established after demutualization of TSE

Source: Tokyo Stock Exchange.

Although the Securities and Exchange Law governs the issuance and trading of securities in Japan, the exchanges themselves establish the listing requirements. Stocks of companies that do not meet the exchange listing requirements trade over-the-counter (OTC). In October 1991, the securities industry launched Japanese Association of Securities Dealers Automated Quotations (Jasdaq; **http://www.jasdaq.co.jp**) to integrate computerized trading of OTC securities.

TSE Listing Requirements for Domestic Stocks

A company that wishes to issue a security must first file a registration statement with the Ministry of Finance. After issuance, the company must disclose specified matters in annual reports filed with the ministry. Additional requirements must be met to list on the TSE.

Companies applying for an initial listing on the TSE must meet various requirements as to the number of shares, number of shareholders, history of incorporation, shareholder's equity, and dividends. The TSE conducts a rigorous examination of the applicant. If satisfied, the TSE accepts the listing application with the approval of the MOF.

The TSE requires listed companies to provide an immediate notice of any material information. The TSE also requires listed companies to file various documents on matters relating to shareholder rights.

The TSE assigns domestic stocks into either the **First Section** or the **Second Section**. The requirements for the First Section are much more stringent. Newly listed stocks are generally assigned to the Second Section. At the end of each year the TSE examines the listed companies to determine whether they should be reassigned from one section to the other.

TSE Listing Requirements for Foreign Companies

A foreign company seeking listing at the TSE is subject to a listing examination by the TSE in accordance with its regulations. When the TSE determines it appropriate to list stock of the applicant after the examination, it will announce the approval. Following the announcement, the applicant's stock will list and trade on the exchange.

Once accepted, foreign companies are assigned to the Foreign Section at the exchange. On December 19, 1973, Dow Chemical became the first foreign company to list on the TSE. No other companies listed their shares until after 1985. In recent years, the number of foreign companies listed on the TSE has declined.

Market of the High-Growth and Emerging Stocks

In November 1999, the Tokyo Stock Exchange established a new market called Mothers (market of the high-growth and emerging stocks) to provide venture companies access to funds at an early stage of their development and to provide investors with more diversified investment products.

Trading on the TSE

In the past, members generally could not trade listed securities off the floor of the exchange. As we have seen, Big Bang reforms have lifted these restrictions. Listed securities now can trade off the exchange. Trading hours are 9:00 A.M. to 11:00 A.M. for the morning session and 12:30 P.M. to 3:00 P.M. for the afternoon session. Stocks may be traded on the floor of the exchange or by using the Computer-assisted Order Routing and Execution System (CORES).

The TSE sets the minimum price change for listed shares. The individual share price determines the minimum price fluctuation: the higher the share price, the higher the minimum. In addition, there is a daily price limit on each stock. The previous day's closing prices determine the daily price limits for individual stocks. The price limits range from about 7 percent to 30 percent of the closing price on the previous day. Generally, a higher percentage applies to a lower-priced stock, and a lower percentage applies to a higher-priced stock.

Settlement and Clearing

For settlement of domestic shares, the TSE opens a settlement account at Japan Securities Depository Center (JASDEC) and uses its Central Depository and Book Entry Transfer System. The TSE's wholly owned subsidiary Japan

Securities Clearing Corporation (JSCC) handles the practical aspects of securities settlement for its members.

Settlement works as follows. Transactions on the TSE generally settle on a T+3 basis (meaning settlement on three business days after the trade day). Transactions made on the ex-dividend or ex-rights date settle T+4. Cash settlements and special agreements can be arranged between buyers and sellers. A special agreement has to be settled within 14 business days. On trade date, members receive the trade report upon execution of orders. Member firms compare the reports with their internal records. At the same time, Tosho Computer System Corporation (a subsidiary of the TSE) compiles the trade data. On T+1, member firms report any errors or discrepancies to the TSE for correction. On the morning of T+2, the Tosho Computer System compiles the post-trade data for net settlement between counterparties. By 8:00 P.M., the TSE provides JASDEC with transfer instructions effective on T+3. Book entries, from net-selling member's account to the net-buying member's account, carry out the settlement. The book-entry transfers for settlement are completed at 9:00 A.M. on T+3. If the net-selling firm does not have sufficient stock in its account, it must make up the deficiency by 3:00 P.M. The settlement of funds on a net basis takes place on T+3.

Margin Trading

To trade on margin, a customer at the TSE must open a margin account. There are two types of margin transactions: standardized margin transactions and negotiable margin transactions. For standardized margin transactions, the exchange rules regulate eligibility, the lending fee, and the settlement period. Securities companies may borrow securities and cash needed for standardized margin transactions from securities finance corporations, in arrangements called loan transactions. In contrast, the lending fee and settlement period are negotiated between the seller and the buyer if margin transactions are negotiable. Margin requirements are at least 30 percent of the trade value.

Futures Trading

Futures trading takes place at two exchanges. The TSE lists Japanese government bond futures, which are contracts to trade the underlying bond at a set point in the future for an agreed price. In addition, futures trade at the Tokyo International Financial Futures Exchange (TIFFE, **http://www.tiffe.or.jp**). Contracts traded include three-month Euroyen futures, three-month Euroyen LIBOR futures, options on three-month Euroyen futures, and U.S. dollar–Japanese yen currency futures. The TIFFE links with the London International Financial Futures and Options Exchange (LIFFE; **http://www.liffe.com**), so the trading time extends from the TIFFE's opening to the LIFFE's close.

THE MUTUAL FUND BUSINESS

Although mutual funds, or investment trusts as the Japanese call them, have been available since 1951, they still account for only a small portion of the

1,200 trillion yen ($10 trillion) in private savings. In 1989, their best year up to that time, mutual fund assets totaled 59 trillion yen ($492 billion). Growth in fund assets ended with the stock market crash in 1990. Nevertheless, the mutual fund business will likely grow significantly in the future. Two developments fuel this optimism. In October 2000, Japanese firms adopted defined contribution pension plans similar to U.S. 401(k) plans—a move that should spark demand for mutual funds. At the same time, the reforms have led to increased competition in the mutual fund business, so the number and variety of funds offered are likely to increase.

Today, Japanese mutual funds have two main structures: unit investment trusts and open-end mutual funds. Unit trusts have closed periods during which there are no new investments or redemptions. Open-end funds accept continuous inflows of money and redemptions. The prolonged downturn of the stock market since 1990 has led investors to switch from equity funds to bond funds. Currently, bond funds and money market funds are the most important segments of the mutual fund industry in Japan.

The mutual fund market has changed rapidly as a result of the deregulation of fund distribution and the internationalization of Japanese capital markets. The 1998 amendments to the Foreign Exchange Law effectively abolished foreign exchange controls. Foreign firms have increased sales of foreign-sponsored, Japan-based funds or offshore funds. Banks and insurance companies have also begun to offer funds. Those forces have enhanced competition and eroded the dominance of the securities industry over the fund business.

Banks and Insurers in Mutual Fund Business

As a result of the Big Bang reforms, banks and insurance companies can now sell mutual funds directly to their clients. The reforms replaced an unwieldy system (established in 1996) that permitted banks to sell mutual funds only through "room renting," whereby a fund company would rent space in a bank branch. Most banks simply rented space to their affiliated investment management companies, although several banks, including Sumitomo and Sanwa (UFJ Bank), also rented space to foreign firms. In 1997, under the room renting system, banks and insurers had only 5 percent of the mutual fund market, compared to 90 percent for securities firms. Now, however, with their branch networks, banks should substantially increase their share. Moody's Investors Service believes that the market share of banks and insurers will climb to 40 percent by 2005, while the share of securities houses will decline to 55 percent.

Increased Competition from Foreign Fund Providers

Another objective of the Big Bang reforms has been to open up Japan's financial markets. Competition from abroad will increase as foreign money managers start to benefit from the changes. Foreign firms are well-positioned to compete for the Japanese savings and retirement market. Foreign funds have good performance records and a superior level of disclosure. Japanese investors have also moved from relationship-based banking to product-based investment. As a result, for the first time in April 1998, foreign-sponsored funds took in more assets than their Japanese counterparts.

CONCLUDING SUMMARY

For the last decade, Japan has faced serious financial challenges. Bad loans have saddled the banking industry. The prolonged decline in the equity market and in real estate values has seriously affected the banks' capital and lending ability. On top of these problems, the banking sector has structural issues. The keiretsu networks lead to conflicts of interest as the banks provide cheap capital to affiliated businesses in the keiretsu, rather than pursuing profitability. The Japanese government has set aside trillions of yen to fix the crippled banking system and unveiled stimulus packages to jump-start the economy.

The Japanese government bond market is the third largest government bond market in the world, with an outstanding volume of 492 trillion yen. In contrast to the U.S. Treasury market, the benchmark issue in Japanese government bonds is not necessarily the current issue.

The Tokyo Stock Exchange is the center of Japanese stock market activities. The equity market has experienced a long-term decline since 1990. The losses experienced in the equity market have created a market environment in which investors simply deposit money at post offices and earn very low interest.

To revive the financial system and provide an increased level of market returns for private savings, Japan introduced a series of financial system reforms called the Big Bang. The Big Bang aims to revitalize Tokyo as an international financial center that rivals New York and London. Japan hopes that the reform will restore its economic vitality, enabling the nation to cope with its rapidly aging population, and strengthening the yen's status as an international currency.

Key Terms

bank dealing 437
Bank of Japan 426
Big Bang 429
city bank 432
Comprehensive Plan for Financial
   Revitalization 428
coverage ratio 436
First Section 442
hidden reserve 426

Japanese government bond (JGB) 434
keiretsu 433
Mothers (Market for High Growth and
   Emerging Stocks) 430
regional bank 432
samurai bond 439
Second Section 442
trust bank 432

Review Questions

1. What is the estimated amount of bad loans in Japan? What is the main cause of the problem?

2. What are the primary reasons for the crisis in the Japanese banking industry?

3. Japan's Big Bang was a three-year process of financial reforms. During what time period were the reform measures implemented? What were the main objectives of the reforms?

4. The 10-year bonds account for about 80 percent of Japanese government bond market. How does the auction process work? Is it different from or similar to the process in the United States?

5. One factor contributing to the dominance of the 10-year bonds is their status as a benchmark. Describe the characteristics of a benchmark issue.

6. There is no pre-auction when-issued trading in the Japanese government bond market. How might this handicap dealers' hedging strategies? How does it affect the trading activities for the outstanding issue?

7. Compare the benchmark issue in Japan and an on-the-run issue in the United States.

8. Yields in the Japanese fixed-income market are quoted on a simple yield basis. What is the main difference between such a yield and the yield to maturity concept used in the United States?

9. A 10-year Japanese government bond trades at a price of 102 percent of par. The issue has a coupon rate of 1.80 percent and a current maturity of 9.5 years. What is the simple yield?

10. How does one determine opening stock prices on the Tokyo Stock Exchange? How are prices set during a trading session?

11. Mutual fund investing is insignificant in Japan. Why? What recently introduced measures might revive the mutual fund business in Japan?

Select Bibliography

Bank of Japan. "Japanese financial institutions' efforts to address their management tasks." Bank of Japan research paper, Bank Examination and Surveillance Department, June 2002.

Craig, V. V. "Japanese banking: A time of crisis." *FDIC Banking Review,* Vol. 11, No. 2, 1998, pp. 9–17.

Essex, M., and R. Pitchford. *The Reuter's Guide to World Bond Markets.* New York: John Wiley & Sons, 1997.

Hall. M. J. B. *Financial Reform in Japan.* Williston, Vt.: Edward Elgar Publishing, 1999.

Hamao, Y., and N. Jegadeesh. "An analysis of bidding in the Japanese government bond auctions." *Journal of Finance,* Vol. 53, No. 2, April 1998, pp. 755–772.

Ito, H., and A. Z. Szamosszegi. *A Cure for Japan's Sick Banks.* Washington, D.C.: Economic Strategy Institute, June 1998.

Ministry of Finance (Japan). *Financial System Reform.* Tokyo: Ministry of Finance, 1997.

Moody's Investors Service. "Japanese fixed income investment trusts: Facing the 'Big Bang' in deregulation," New York: Moody's Investors Service, June 1998.

Packer, F., and E. Reynolds. "The samurai bond market," *Current Issues in Economics and Finance,* Vol. 3, No. 8. Federal Reserve Bank of New York, June 1997, p. i–6.

Patrick, H. T., and Y. C. Park (eds). *The Financial Development of Japan, Korea, and Taiwan.* Oxford: Oxford University Press, 1994.

Schaede, U. "The Japanese financial system from postwar to the new millennium," Boston, Mass.: Harvard Business School Publishing, 2000.

Securities and Exchange Council. *Comprehensive Reform of the Securities Markets.* Tokyo: Securities and Exchange Council, June 1997.

Shirakawa, M., K. Okina, and S. Shiratsuka. "Financial market globalization: present and future." Tokyo: Bank of Japan, December 1997.

Weinstein, D.E., and Y. Yafeh. "On the costs of a bank-centered financial system: Evidence from the changing main bank relations in Japan." *Journal of Finance,* vol. 53, No. 2, April 1998, pp. 635–672.

Emerging Financial Markets

During the early to mid-1990s, many investors in search of high yields and high growth potential, as well as geographic diversification, discovered that the securities of developing countries could be attractive prospects. However, the crises that roiled emerging markets around the world—in Mexico in 1994–1995, Southeast Asia in 1997, Russia in 1998, and Brazil in 1999—soon dampened their initial optimism. Each crisis started with a local currency devaluation, but in each case the impact went far beyond the initial country affected. In a phenomenon known as market contagion, problems in one emerging market caused investors to lose confidence in other emerging markets (although Argentina's default on its external debt in 2001 did not spill over to other emerging markets). Their rush to withdraw funds from those markets set off further devaluations and declining values. Clearly, investments in emerging markets involve many risks. Nonetheless, many still believe that emerging markets offer great opportunities for yield enhancement and portfolio diversification in the long term.

The objectives of this chapter are to provide an understanding of:
- Risk factors of emerging markets.
- Emerging market debt instruments, especially Brady bonds.
- Emerging market indexes and derivatives.
- The crises in Mexico, Southeast Asia, Russia, and Brazil.

MARKET OVERVIEW

The term **emerging market** refers to the securities markets of a developing country and the use that country makes of international capital markets. Countries considered to be emerging markets generally possess some, but not necessarily all, of the following characteristics:

° A low per capita gross domestic product.

° Recent liberalization of economic and political systems.

° A lack of well-developed capital market.

° Nonmembership in the Organization of Economic Cooperation and Development (OECD).

Examples of emerging markets include Argentina, Brazil, India, Mexico, the People's Republic of China, Poland, and Russia. Some consider Greece, Portugal, Singapore, and Turkey to be emerging markets, but these countries possess fewer of the aforementioned characteristics. Many also refer to most countries in Africa, some Central American nations, and a number of the former Soviet republics as preemerging markets.

In addition to the specific risk factors that we will examine, emerging markets present a more general problem for investors: Information about issuers or securities, particularly local instruments, is not as readily available as with the world's more advanced markets. Today, this problem is less significant than in the past because many securities firms and other institutions have worked to provide investors with accurate and timely information. In general, market participants can turn to several sources, including the Emerging Market Traders Association (**http://www.emta.org**), the International Finance Corporation (**http://www.ifc.org**), and the International Monetary Fund (**http://www. imf.org**). Major rating agencies such as Moody's (**http://www.moodys .com**) and Standard & Poor's (**http://www.standardandpoors.com**) regularly update their assessments of credit ratings for many emerging countries. For securities from emerging markets listed in the United States as American depositary receipts, information is widely available in the United States.[1]

RISK FACTORS

As the various crises of the 1990s and early 2000s make clear (see Box 19-1), emerging markets entail considerable risk as well as the potential for high yields. Any investors considering committing capital to an emerging market should be aware of six primary risks:

° Volatility risk and risk of contagion effects.

° Liquidity risk.

---

[1]Chapter 12 covers American depositary receipts in detail.

MARKETS IN ACTION Significant Emerging Market Events in the 1990s and 2000s

19.1

1990 Mexico and Venezuela complete their Brady Plan restructurings.	1999 Brazil devalues the real. Ecuador defaults on its Brady bonds.
1991 Argentina adopts the Convertibility Plan, linking the peso to the U.S. dollar.	2000 Ecuador reschedules 97 percent of its Brady bonds.
1993 Argentina completes its Brady Plan restructuring.	Moody's upgrades Mexico's rating to investment grade.
1994 Brazil introduces the Real Plan, ending its hyperinflation.	Russia announces London Club restructuring. Ecuador adopts dollarization.
Brazil completes its Brady Plan restructuring. Mexico devalues its currency in December (Tequila Crisis).	2001 Mexico redeems its Series A discount bonds. Argentina defaults on its external debt. IMF proposes sovereign bankruptcy regime.
1995 Mexican rescue package stabilizes markets.	2002 Brazil receives $30 billion IMF package.
1997 Asian financial crisis begins. South Korea recovery package announced.	Argentina defaults on Series D of World Bank guaranteed bonds.
1998 Russian ruble devalues and Russia defaults on a number of debt instruments. Trading volume of emerging market instruments drops significantly in the aftermath of the Russian crisis.	

Source: Emerging Market Traders Association.

- ° Clearance and settlement risk.
- ° Political risk.
- ° Currency risk.
- ° Limited disclosure and insufficient legal infrastructure.

Volatility Risk and Risk of Contagion Effects

High volatility is a characteristic of emerging markets. Emerging markets are immature and sometimes vulnerable to scandal. They often lack the legal and judicial infrastructure to enforce the law. Accounting, disclosure, trading and settlement practices may at times seem overly arbitrary and naive. Against this backdrop, many emerging markets have had to cope with unprecedented inflows and outflows of capital in recent years. The sudden withdrawal of highly speculative, short-term capital has the potential of taking with it much of a market's price support. Such sudden flights of capital, triggered by events in one emerging market, can spread instantly to other markets through contagion effects—even when those markets have quite different conditions. When Mexico's currency collapsed in 1994–1995, the panic quickly spread to other Latin markets through the so-called **tequila effect**. Similarly, the financial crisis that started in Southeast Asia in 1997 spilled over to other markets and eventually led to the crisis in Russia and Brazil in 1998 and 1999, respectively.

Liquidity Risk

Many emerging markets are small and illiquid. A country's entire market capitalization may be less than that of a single large U.S. company. Many of the public companies may be closely held family businesses. In several markets, shares of only several hundred companies trade and total daily trading volume may reach only a few million shares. Such thin trading often leads to higher costs because large transactions have a significant impact on the market. Thus, buyers of large blocks of shares may have to pay more to complete the transaction, and sellers may receive a lower price. In addition, in Russia and parts of Latin America, it is sometimes difficult to sell shares in a falling market because of underdeveloped and corrupt stock markets.

Clearance and Settlement Risk

Inadequate settlement procedures also rank high on the list of emerging market risks. Often, stock exchange officials and regulators did not perceive this risk until the transaction volume increased and statistics showed high fail rates in the 1990s. A fail occurs when a trade fails to settle on the settlement date. The fail rates in emerging markets are much higher than those in the developed markets. When such problems occur, a purchaser can miss an attractive opportunity if a securities purchase cannot be completed, and a seller can experience losses if the security price declines after the trade and the counterparty is not held accountable for the fail.

Trading in Brady bonds (described in the next section) is not subject to the same risk. The Emerging Market Traders Association has developed many standard market practices for trading Brady bonds, and the Emerging Market Clearing Corporation has helped reduce counterparty risk and improve efficiency by assuming trades and effecting settlement on behalf of most major dealers.

Political Risk

Many emerging countries have undergone major changes in their governmental, economic, and financial institutions. Certainly, some nations face political risks as coups, assassinations, or paralyzing power struggles. Governments may grapple with long-standing political and social problems, and at times make a sudden retreat toward socialism that is unfavorable to a free and competitive financial market. Progress can also be stalled by the economic reversals that have often afflicted emerging economies.

Equally important is that the government may change the tax policy for capital gains, dividends, and interests earned by foreign investors. Governments may also restrict repatriation of earnings or change the conditions under which funds may be repatriated. Restrictions may take the form of new foreign exchange regulations or limitations on the convertibility of the local currency.

Several advisory services and financial publications rank political risks. Also, *Institutional Investor-International* periodically publishes the results of surveys of sovereign political risk. *Euromoney* regularly publishes political risk ratings as well.

Currency Risk

Fluctuations in the foreign exchange markets can have a dramatic effect on profits earned abroad. Falling local currencies could turn high profits from underwriting, trading, mergers and acquisitions, or privatization programs into losses. Currency devaluations and stock market downturns, as happened in Mexico (1994–1995), Asia (1997–1998), Russia (1998), and Brazil (1999), can produce steep losses. One of the primary causes of currency risk in emerging markets has been runaway inflation. The common causes of currency devaluation are a large current account deficit, high levels of short-term debt, and an overvalued currency.

Disclosure and Property Right Risk

Most emerging markets lack legal structures for investor protection. Indeed, in many developing countries, the perception exists that protecting investors is less important than expanding the securities markets. Nevertheless, investor protection is the key to maintaining confidence in the capital markets. More and more countries have moved toward better investor protection and full, accurate, and timely financial reporting and disclosure. In addition, many have taken steps to ensure fair securities issuance and trading practices. Despite this progress, many emerging countries still lack a general law of contracts, stringent corporate accounting standards, and banking regulations that protect depositors. Furthermore, the laws that do exist may not be enforced by the justice system. Pursuing one's rights through the courts of an emerging country can be a hopeless cause.

Therefore, capital market participants should always remember that they must deal with limited disclosure and imperfect fundamental data in emerging markets.

EMERGING MARKET DEBT: BRADY BONDS

In 2001, the total trading volume of emerging market debt was $3.5 trillion, a substantial decline from its peak of $6 trillion in 1997 but still far above its 1992 level of $730 billion. Major emerging market debt instruments include loans, Brady bonds, non–Brady sovereign and corporate bonds, local market instruments, and options and warrants. Local market instruments are securities issued in a domestic market, subject to local regulations and denominated in the local currency. In 2001, they accounted for $1.5 trillion of the trading volume.

The most liquid emerging market debt, however, is for Brady bonds, which accounted for $573 billion of the total trading volume in 2001. Because of the significance of Brady bonds in global capital markets, this discussion will focus on them. **Brady bonds** (named after Nicholas Brady, a former secretary of the U.S. Department of Treasury) are securities issued between 1990 and 1997 in an attempt to solve the debt crisis that many developing countries faced by the end of the 1980s. The countries had borrowed heavily from commercial banks for development purposes, but rising interest rates and a global recession made it impossible for them to repay the loans. Under a plan devised by then Secretary Brady, the commercial bank loans were converted into bonds with some reduction in the amount owed, and the debtor nations were given more time to repay the principal. The creditor banks received some, but not all, of the amounts the borrowers owed. Because the U.S. government bonds back most of the Brady bonds, purchasers received some guarantee of payment. As for the debtor nations, their debt was reduced. In return, the countries had to accept certain conditions and agree to make reforms required by the International Monetary Fund and the United States (Chapter 21 examines the crisis that led to the issuance of Brady bonds in more detail).

Since 1990, when Mexico became the first nation to issue Brady bonds, there have been more than $160 billion worth of the bonds issued. All major Brady restructurings had been announced or completed by 1997. In addition to Mexico, Argentina, Brazil, Bulgaria, Costa Rica, the Dominican Republic, Ecuador (which defaulted on its Brady bonds in 1999), Ivory Coast, Jordan, Nigeria, Panama, Peru, the Philippines, Poland, Russia, Uruguay, Venezuela, and Vietnam have all issued Brady bonds.

Much of the Brady debt will eventually be exchanged or bought back. In recent years, there have been many conversions and redemptions of Bradys, and the amount has declined. Bradys accounted for one-third of the total volume in emerging market debt instruments in 2001, compared to more than half from 1992 to 1996.[2] Top dealers in Brady bonds include J.P. Morgan Chase, Citigroup, Bear Sterns, Morgan Stanley, Merrill Lynch, ING, ABN AMRO, and Credit Suisse First Boston. Major interdealer brokers in Bradys include Euro Brokers, Garban Securities, and RMJ Securities. Interdealer brokering has expanded because it allows big dealers to trade huge positions without revealing themselves.

Characteristics of Brady Bonds

Brady bonds come in many types and with various options, but there are several consistent characteristics. The similarity stems from the fact that the plan gave the creditor banks alternatives for restructuring the debt: (1) exchanged the original face value of the loans for new 30-year par bonds that paid below-market fixed interest rates, (2) converted the loans into new 30-year bonds that carried a discount from face value (usually a 35 percent discount) and paid a floating interest rate of LIBOR + $^{13}\!/_{16}$ percent, or (3) carried the full principal amount of the loans on their books while providing new lending of at least

---

[2] See Eng and Lees (1997) for details.

25 percent of the old loans over several years. The bonds issued under the first and second alternatives were the Brady bonds.

Also, 30-year zero-coupon U.S. Treasury bonds and other high-quality assets collateralize the principal and semiannual interest payments of many Brady bonds. The debtor countries used their foreign reserves to purchase this collateral enhancement. If a Brady bond with a collateralized principal defaults, holders can only collect the principal when the bond matures. Some Brady bonds have embedded warrants whose value is tied to the world price of raw products native to the debtor country. The vast majority of outstanding Brady bonds are in U.S. dollars. Although some bonds exist in other currencies, these nondollar issues tend to be relatively illiquid.

The first Mexican issue ($48 billion) of Brady bonds illustrates these characteristics. The banks received two options for converting their loans into tradable securities. Mexican par bonds, issued in March 1990, had 29¾-year maturities and fixed 6¼-percent coupons. The discount bonds gave a 35 percent discount on the face value of the debt, but offered a floating rate of LIBOR + $^{13}/_{16}$ percent.

Both types of bonds were in dollars and had their principal backed by zero-coupon U.S. Treasury bonds. In addition, a rolling interest guarantee covered 18 months of interest payments.

Structures of Brady bonds have become more complex over time, but they still exhibit the same basic characteristics. A major feature added to later issues was a buyback option that allows a country to repurchase part of its debt at an agreed-on discount, thereby enabling it to engage in a debt reduction program. In 1995, Argentina repurchased some of its par and discount bonds in the secondary markets. In April 1996, Mexico completed a $1.75 billion swap deal to repurchase mainly par bonds in exchange for a 30-year uncollateralized global bond, which represents pure sovereign risk. In 2000, Brazil closed a $5 billion exchange offer. In 2001, Mexico redeemed its Series A discount bonds. In many of these buyback deals, investors from Europe, Asia, and the United States exchanged Brady bonds for unsecured, higher-yield 30-year global bonds.

Types of Brady Bonds

There are several types of Brady bonds: par or discount bonds, front loaded interest reduction bonds, debt conversion or new money bonds, interest arrears capitalization and capitalization bonds (C-bonds).

Most outstanding Brady bonds are par or discount bonds. As we have seen, **par bonds** are fixed-rate bonds issued at par. **Discount bonds** are floating-rate debt, issued at a discount. Both have their principal backed by zero-coupon U.S. Treasury bonds. Par and discount bonds have long-term maturities and are the most liquid Brady bonds. They also have bullet amortization (these bonds were issued at the original face value of the sovereign loan). Several countries including Mexico, Venezuela, and Nigeria attached to their par and discount bonds the right to recover a portion of the debt or to reduce their debt service if the country's debt service capability improves. These rights, known as oil warrants, link payments with oil export prices and thus to the country's oil export receipts.

Front loaded interest reduction bonds are medium-term step-up bonds that pay below-market interest rates for the initial five to seven years, and then pay a floating rate until maturity. These bonds provide partial interest collateral in the form of cash, with the collateral rolled over for subsequent periods upon timely interest payments. These bonds are less liquid than par or discount bonds, but they have a much shorter life on average as amortization payments typically begin after five to seven years.

Debt conversion bonds are short-term floating-rate bonds issued without collateral. Creditors exchanged loans for the bonds at par and provided additional funds to the issuing nations at a floating rate of interest. The bonds were a positive development, as the issuing countries had the ability to service their debt obligations but did not want to pay until the introduction of debt conversion bonds.

Interest arrears capitalization bonds were created when commercial banks rescheduled interest in arrears on Brazilian, Argentine, and Ecuadorian debt. The interest created new short-term floating-rate bonds. The issuance of these bonds occurred prior to the rescheduling of the principal in the Brady format.

Brazil issued capitalization bonds (C-bonds) in 1994. The initial maturity was 20 years; Brazil initially offered the bonds with a fixed below-market coupon rate that would rise to 8 percent during the first six years. An important feature is that these bonds capitalize (add to principal) the interest difference between the current step coupon rate and the notional 8 percent. Therefore, interest accrues on both the principal and any capitalized interest. Both capitalized interest and principal payments are made after a 10-year grace period.

Valuation

Brady bonds have three distinct features: principal collateral, interest collateral, and the sovereign portion. When evaluating a Brady, it is necessary to strip out the credit enhancements attached to it in order to understand and analyze the risk and relative valuation ascribed by the market to each sovereign issuer. Removing the value of the U.S. Treasury strips and the interest guarantee will produce the yield of the unenhanced income stream, based on the credit quality of the issuing nation. Table 19.1 lists foreign currency ratings of emerging countries by Moody's.

EMERGING MARKETS INDEXES AND DERIVATIVES

Although the emerging markets are an increasing part of today's investment opportunities, so far they have only been considered primarily by global institutional investors. Individuals have invested in emerging markets mainly through mutual funds or exchange-traded, closed-end funds. For those who

TABLE 19.1	*Sovereign Foreign Currency Ratings: Bonds and Notes (2003)*	
Country	Long-term	Short-term
Argentina	CA	NP
Brazil	B2	NP
Bulgaria	B1	NP
Chile	Baa1	P-2
China	A3	P-2
Colombia	Ba2	—
Croatia	Baa3	P-3
Czech Republic	A1	P-1
Dominican Republic	Ba2	NP
Ecuador	Ba1	NP
Egypt	Ba1	NP
Hong Kong	A3	P-1
Hungary	A1	P-1
India	Ba1	NP
Indonesia	B3	NP
Jordan	Ba3	NP
Kazakstan	Baa3	NP
Korea	A3	P-2
Latvia	A2	P-1
Lithuania	Baa1	P-2
Mexico	Baa2	P-2
Pakistan	B3	NP
Panama	Baa1	P-2
Peru	Ba3	NP
Philippines	Ba1	NP
Poland	A2	P-1
Romania	B1	NP
Russia	Ba2	NP
Singapore	Aaa	P-1
Slovak	A3	P-2
Slovenia	Aa3	P-1
South Africa	Baa2	P-2
Taiwan	Aa3	P-1
Thailand	Baa3	NP
Turkey	B1	NP
Uruguay	B3	NP
Venezuela	Caa1	NP

Source: *Ratings List: Government Bonds and Country Ceilings*, Moody's, February 2003.

wish to participate, several indexes track the performances of emerging markets. In addition, exchange-traded derivatives are available and can be used to participate in the potential of emerging markets without owning emerging market assets. These derivatives can be used to hedge certain risks when investing in emerging markets as well.

Emerging Market Indexes

One widely used source in benchmarking emerging markets is Standard & Poor's (**http://www.standardandpoors.com**) Emerging Market Data Base (EMDB).[3] The EMDB provides information and indexes on stock markets in developing countries. S&P's emerging market indexes include Global (S&P/ IFCG), Investable (S&P/IFCI), and Frontier (S&P/IFCG Frontier). The S&P/ IFCG includes securities without accounting for the stock's availability to foreign investors. Typically, an S&P/IFCG index covers about 70 to 75 percent of a market's total capitalization. The S&P/IFCI indexes further screen stocks for foreign ownership restrictions, factoring in minimum market capitalization and liquidity. Stocks included in these indexes are assigned weights, representing the amount that foreign institutional investors may purchase. The Frontier indexes tend to cover relatively small and illiquid securities. S&P calculates these indexes on a monthly basis.

Morgan Stanley (**http://www.morganstanley.com**) also publishes many emerging market indexes. These include Emerging Markets (EM), EM Europe, EM Latin America, EM Asia, and EM Far-East. J.P. Morgan Chase (**http:// www.jpmorganchase.com**) also publishes several emerging market indexes. The Emerging Market Bond Market Index Plus (EMBI+) tracks total returns for traded debt instruments in emerging markets. The Emerging Market Local Markets Index tracks total returns for local currency denominated money market instruments in 10 emerging markets.

Emerging Market Derivatives

The Chicago Mercantile Exchange (**http://www.cme.com**) lists many emerging market products. Among them are options contracts on Brady bonds, including Mexican par bonds, Argentine floating-rate bonds, Brazilian C-bonds, and Brazilian eligible interest bonds. In addition, there are options on country indexes such as Mexican IPC Stock Index Options and Dow Jones Taiwan Stock Index Options.

MEXICO'S PESO CRISIS

In the early 1990s, the Mexican economy seemed poised to enter a period of sustained growth. Inflation, which had been in triple figures only a few years earlier, was down to single digits. Government finances showed a slim budget

---

[3]The International Finance Corporation launched the EMDB in 1981. Standard & Poor's acquired it in January 2000.

surplus, and the country's foreign exchange reserves ticked upwards as foreign investors poured more than $33 billion into the economy in 1993 alone. Furthermore, many thought that the North American Free Trade Agreement (NAFTA), which took effect in early 1994, would encourage foreign investors to take advantage of Mexico's privileged access to the U.S. market.

Nevertheless, some market observers questioned certain aspects of Mexico's glittering economic performance. One concern was the widening inequality in income. At the same time, some economists worried about Mexico's exchange rate policy. The central bank kept the exchange rate within a preset band that allowed for small daily slippage against the dollar—a system known as a **crawling peg**. If market forces pushed the peso too close to the limit of the band, the Mexican central bank would intervene or raise the upper limit of the band daily by a pre-announced amount, which allowed for a gradual depreciation of the peso. Nevertheless, many observers believed that the peso became overvalued. They pointed to Mexico's account deficit, which had ballooned to $20 billion in 1993 (from $6 billion in 1989), and had reached 6.5 percent of GDP. At the same time, economic growth slowed to less than 1 percent. Yet Mexican officials firmly dismissed any suggestion of devaluation.

Origin of the Crisis

In 1994, a series of political crises compounded Mexico's growing economic problems: a rebellion in the southern province of Chiapas that began early in the year; the assassination of the ruling party's presidential candidate, Luis Donalso Colosio, on March 23; the resignation of the minister of the interior (Jorge Carpizo) and the kidnapping of a prominent businessman (Alfredo Harp) in June; and finally, in mid-November, accusations by Colosio's brother, Deputy Attorney General Mario Ruiz Massieu that his superior obstructed the investigation of his brother's murder.

With each crisis, investor confidence declined, and the Mexican markets became more turbulent. The stock market plummeted not only because of panic selling but also because mutual fund managers faced with redemptions by clients had to raise money by selling shares. Interest rates on peso-denominated treasury bills, known as **Cetes**, soared. Capital bled steadily out of the country, and foreign exchange reserves fell as the government intervened in the foreign exchange markets in an effort to maintain the value of the peso. In the month after Colosio's assassination, Mexico lost nearly $11 billion in reserves; another $2.5 billion was lost in three weeks in June.

In an effort to bolster investor confidence, Mexico's NAFTA partners, the United States and Canada, offered billions of dollars in lines of credit. Meanwhile the Mexican government started converting a huge amount of public debt from Cetes to **Tesobonos**, which were short-term treasury paper denominated in U.S. dollars. By April 1994, the total Tesobonos outstanding had reached $21 billion. A growing number of investors sold their Cetes and bought Tesobonos instead.

With investor confidence on the slide, speculators saw their chance to make money by attacking the peso. The November political crisis gave them an opportunity. Within a month, Mexico had lost another $5.5 billion in reserves. On December 20, 1994, the Mexican government gave up and devalued the peso by 15 percent, to about four pesos per dollar. Two days later, on the morning of December 22, with reserves reduced to less than $6 billion, the government announced that it would abandon the exchange rate target band and allow the peso to float.

The financial crisis that followed quickly cut the peso's value in half, sent inflation soaring, and set off a severe recession in Mexico. The trouble quickly spread to other Latin American countries. Very soon virtually every debt issue with an "emerging market" label came under pressure. The spread of the malaise to emerging markets that had little to do with Mexico came to be known as the tequila effect.

U.S. and International Responses

As the Mexican government's access to credit dried up, market participants increasingly worried about the large quantity of short-term Tesobonos due to mature in 1995. Nearly $10 billion worth of Tesobonos would mature in the first quarter of 1995, and another $19 billion were due before the end of 1995. Yet Mexico's reserves were less than $6 billion at the beginning of January 1995 and had dwindled to $3.48 billion by the end of that month.

The U.S. government made several efforts to help Mexico resolve the crisis. By early 1995, it was clear that the situation was urgent and that without either a sudden restoration of investor confidence or a substantial loan from other nations, Mexico would likely default on its dollar-denominated obligations. The Clinton administration judged that it was in the interest of the United States to intervene. On January 2, 1995, there was a commitment for an $18 billion line of credit for Mexico, half from the U.S. government and half from other major governments and large banks. Investors, however, still had reservations to roll over Mexican debt because the credit line was smaller than the amount of Tesobonos coming due in the next few months.

On January 12, 1995, the Clinton administration proposed a larger package—$40 billion in loan guarantees. Under this plan, Mexico would have borrowed dollars to roll over its maturing obligations, with the United States guaranteeing repayment if Mexico defaulted. But the U.S. Congress would not approve the package. By January 31, the situation was desperate. Mexico needed cash quickly to avoid default, but congressional approval of the support package was nowhere in sight. Therefore, the Clinton administration announced a package centered on $20 billion from the **Exchange Stabilization Fund**, a stock of money kept for foreign exchange market intervention.[4] The $20 billion came with $17.8 billion from the IMF and a

---

[4]To avoid the need for a special congressional vote authorizing the assistance, the Clinton administration used the Exchange Stabilization Fund.

short-term loan of $10 billion from the Bank for International Settlements and other commercial banks. In exchange, Mexico would put up crude oil as collateral and also had to meet a number of conditions including further budget cuts and more privatization to balance its books. (See Chapter 21 for a discussion of Mexico after the crisis and its capital markets today.)

ASIAN FINANCIAL CRISIS

Even more serious than the Mexican crisis was the crisis that swept through Asia in 1997 and 1998. Like the Mexican crisis, the **Asian crisis** began with currency devaluation (in Thailand) and spread through contagion effects to many countries in East and Southeast Asia. Ultimately, markets worldwide felt the impact of the crisis.

Origin of the Crisis

The causes of the crisis were complex and varied slightly from country to country. Nonetheless, all of the affected countries shared three common features: a large current account deficit, high levels of short-term debt, and an overvalued currency. In most countries, lax regulation of financial markets, a speculative bubble, and corruption in government and financial circles exacerbated these problems.

In the 1990s, most East Asian currencies were tied directly or indirectly to the U.S. dollar. But in 1995, the dollar appreciated against the Japanese yen. From a low of less than 80 yen in April, the dollar climbed to more than 100 yen by yearend and finished 1996 around 116. During the same period, China gained an international edge through structural reforms and an effective devaluation of the yuan in 1994. As a result, most Asian countries suddenly lost competitiveness against Japan and China in major world markets. Current account deficits ballooned. Furthermore, East Asian countries saved at a high rate of 30 percent, but invested at a rate of 40 percent of GDP. That meant that external capital had to be borrowed from abroad. One economy after another had already opened up and deregulated its financial sector. Since international interest rates were lower than domestic rates, it was very worthwhile for Asian firms to obtain offshore loans. Indeed, many banks and finance companies could borrow hard currency, exchange it for local money, and lend the money domestically at higher rates.

By 1997 the private sector accounted for well over half of Thai and Indonesian foreign debt and a staggering 90 percent of South Korea's external obligations. The borrowers took an immense risk for themselves if exchange rates depreciated, particularly as the offshore loans were usually short term and needed to be rolled over regularly. But because many Asian currencies had been so stable for so long, the borrowers had begun to take exchange rate stability for granted. Even worse, the quality of their investments was in doubt. At first, capital had flowed into industry, often to the point of building huge excess capacity. But as the boom continued, much of it poured into speculative real estate and stock market bubbles that swelled across the region. Inflows of capital from overseas not only fueled the speculative frenzy but also encouraged an explosion of domestic credit. Slack financial regulation and cronyism made matters worse.

The Thai baht came under increasing pressure in early 1997 when a bond default by a major property developer and the collapse of Thailand's biggest finance company began to reveal the colossal extent of highly leveraged exposure to the crumbling real estate sector. In February 1997, Moody's announced that it considered downgrading Thailand's foreign currency debt. Persistent devaluation rumors had already persuaded some Thai companies to hedge their currency exposure. Hedge funds and other speculators saw a chink in the baht's armor and pounced. To defend the value of the currency, the Thai central bank imposed capital controls by ordering domestic banks not to lend to offshore parties. In May, the Bank of Thailand spent $4 billion in reserves to defend the baht in the spot foreign exchange market. On June 30, Prime Minister Chavalit assured the nation that there would be no devaluation. Two days later, the central bank said it would no longer defend the peg and would move to a managed float. The baht plunged, setting off an emerging market panic that would last nearly two years and drag down a trail of other currencies.

Within a week the Indonesian rupiah started to slide, and the Philippine and Malaysian central banks had to intervene aggressively to defend the peso and the ringgit, respectively. On July 11, the Philippine central bank gave up its defense of the peso after spending $2 billion of its $10 billion reserves on intervention. On the same day, the Indonesian central bank said it would widen the currency band in which the ringgit moved. On August 14, the bank abolished the band and the rupiah immediately plunged. On August 28, Malaysia imposed restrictions on selling stocks short, but that proved to be a disastrous step. Long-term investors read the move as a hint of further market and capital controls and sold off their shares. Traders sold Malaysian currency and the ringgit slumped.

In October, the crisis shifted to other emerging markets. On October 17, after months of dogged intervention to hold its currency above 28.50 to the dollar, Taiwan's central bank abruptly abandoned its defense. The next trading day the Taiwanese dollar fell through the powerful psychological barrier of 30 to the U.S. currency for the first time in a decade.

Taiwan's unexpected move raised questions about Hong Kong's commitment to its rigid currency peg, at around 7.8 to the U.S. dollar. But the Hong Kong Monetary Authority did not waver; instead, it drew on its huge foreign reserves and pushed the overnight rate to as high as 300 percent from 6 percent to hammer short sellers. The Hong Kong stock market dropped off a cliff, however, with the Heng Seng index plunging 1,200 points or 10 percent on October 23. In just four days, it had lost nearly one-fourth of its value.

South Korea had the biggest debt problem in the region. Controls were lax, and companies commonly borrowed as much as four times or even five times their capital. By mid-1997, South Korea's short-term borrowing alone amounted to three times the country's foreign exchange reserves. Some Koreans talked about economic crisis as early as January when the country's fourteenth largest **chaebol** (conglomerate) collapsed. The default sparked a chain of corporate failures. By the end of October 1997, the banking system was on the brink of collapse, and the won plummeted. Eventually, the IMF arranged a support package of more than $58 billion—the biggest international rescue package in history.

Indonesia was the next to suffer. Indonesia's private debt problem, amounting to an estimated $74 billion, claimed its first victim on January 12, 1998, when Hong Kong's Peregrine Investment Holdings collapsed under a mountain of bad loans to Indonesian borrowers. The crisis also had political implications, forcing the resignation of President Suharto in May 1998. A deal in early June between foreign banks and Indonesian companies to reschedule the massive corporate debt could not keep the Indonesian markets from plunging, as the rupiah fell below 15,000 to the dollar.

Even Japan was not immune. After the devaluations of other currencies in the region, Japan's export competitiveness evaporated. At the same time, Japanese banks had an estimated loan exposure to the region of around $150 billion, little of which would be repaid. In late November 1997, Yamaichi Securities, the fourth largest brokerage, failed. It was Japan's biggest ever corporate failure and the news drove the yen to a five-year low. In May 1998, the yen was well over 130 to the dollar. On May 29, the dollar rocketed to a seven-year high of 139 yen. A week later it broke 140.

The Aftermath

In an effort to curb the worst effects of the crisis, the IMF arranged support packages for Thailand ($17.2 billion), Indonesia ($43 billion), and South Korea ($58 billion), and augmented a credit to the Philippines to support its exchange rate and other economic policies. Nonetheless, the countries all experienced severe recessions. Governments had tried to counter the weakness of their currencies by selling their foreign exchange reserves and raising interest rates, which in turn slowed economic growth. The enormous capital outflows exacerbated the problems. In late 1997 and 1998, for example, Indonesia, Malaysia, the Philippines, and South Korea experienced net capital outflows of more than $80 billion. In 1998, Korea and Malaysia experienced GDP growth of −5.8 percent and −7.5 percent, respectively, and in Indonesia and Thailand, the rates were worse than −10 percent. (See Chapter 20 for a discussion of Asian capital markets since the crisis.)

Initially, many economists had confidence that the Asian financial crisis could be confined primarily to countries in East and Southeast Asia. They were wrong. A rush out of equities into U.S. government bonds and other more stable investments caused declines in stock markets worldwide. Asian panic became the catalyst for a much wider pruning of bullish stock market values. On October 23, 1997, for example, Wall Street closed down more than 2 percent, while British, Japanese, French, and Dutch stocks lost more than 3 percent.

Frankfurt dropped 4.7 percent and New Zealand more than 5 percent. There was more trouble to come. On October 27, 1997, the Dow Jones Industrial Average closed down more than 550 points, or 7.2 percent—at the time it was the largest one-day point drop in Wall Street's history. Canadian stocks fell more than 6 percent. The carnage was even worse in Latin America, where stocks in Brazil, Mexico, and Argentina all lost more than 12 percent.

In 1998, as we describe in the next section, the turmoil spread to Russia, setting off yet another meltdown in equity markets worldwide and causing huge losses for banks and securities firms. One of the casualties was the hedge fund Long Term Capital Management (see Chapter 5 for a discussion of how the Federal Reserve facilitated a $3.625 billion rescue of the fund by a consortium of banks and investment houses).

RUSSIA FINANCIAL CRISIS

As the Asian crisis swept through country after country, emerging markets worldwide became susceptible to contagion effects, as foreign investors and lenders rushed to withdraw their funds from developing countries. Russia, with its high levels of external debt and an economy heavily dependent on exports of raw materials, proved particularly vulnerable, and in August 1998, it not only had to devalue the ruble, but also effectively defaulted on its debt.

Origin of the Crisis

By August 1998, the Russian economy felt the impact of the Asian crisis in several ways. Russia's chief exports are oil and other raw materials, but with many countries around the world experiencing economic downturns, prices of these commodities declined. In particular, falling oil prices had caused a sharp dropoff in Russia's hard currency inflows.

At the same time, Russia's external debt had ballooned to $180 billion (including more than $70 billion inherited from the Soviet Union), a level that was clearly unsustainable. Foreign lenders recognized the dangers and started to reduce their exposure to Russia. Those who still would lend to Russia only offered short-term loans at high interest rates.

In an effort to maintain stability, the Russian central bank followed a policy of pegging the ruble to the U.S. dollar within a narrow band. At the same time, the bank allowed free movement of capital. By August 1998, the bank spent $1 billion per week to defend the exchange rate. Obviously, with Russia's hard currency inflows already reduced as a result of the drop in oil prices, continued interventions at that rate would soon deplete the country's hard currency reserves. On August 17, the Russian central bank gave in and raised the upper limit of the band to 9.5 rubles to the dollar. On August 27, with the black market rate already at 15 rubles to the dollar, the bank ceased its efforts to peg the currency and allowed the ruble to float.

The Aftermath

The crisis had worldwide effects. Along with the devaluation of the ruble, the Russian government declared a 90-day moratorium on its debt payments while it renegotiated the terms. Although there was never a formal announcement of default, the slow pace of the negotiations and the fact that certain interest payments had already been missed suggested to observers that Russia had de facto defaulted on its debt. In the aftermath, yet another wave of selling sent stock markets plunging around the world.

In Russia, the effects were even more painful. On the eve of the crisis, many of the country's 1,500 banks had high exposure to devaluation. Gambling that the ruble would not be devalued, many banks had taken out loans in foreign currencies and sold foreign exchange forward contracts to Western banks. Furthermore, most banks also owned Russian government treasury bills (known as GKOs) as assets. Thus, the steps taken by the government hurt the banks on both sides of their balance sheets. The sudden devaluation made their liabilities impossibly expensive, and the moratorium on the payment of government debt made their assets almost worthless. Although the moratorium temporarily protected the banks from their foreign creditors, it also froze their assets, making it impossible for banks to meet the demands of their depositors. The result was an almost complete paralysis of the banking sector and a collapse of the payment system. Companies could not pay their suppliers and employees, and individuals could not withdraw their money for daily use.

The Russian economy suffered. Private consumption plunged as a result of the problems in the banking sector, and investment declined due to the flight of foreign investors and the lack of domestic savings to replace the foreign capital. Although exports often rise in the wake of a devaluation, that did not happen in Russia's case because demand for oil and other raw materials remained low. Imports, however, declined by 45 percent from August to September 1998; any imported goods became much more expensive, causing the consumer price index to rise sharply.

As for the government debt, the Russian government indicated that it could service its own Eurobonds and IMF loans in full, but it asked its creditors for partial forgiveness of the old Soviet debt and for more time to repay the remainder. In December 1998, the government began to slip into arrears on $32 billion of dollar-denominated bonds known as principal arrears notes (PANs) and interest arrears notes (IANs). PANs and IANs were Soviet era debt that had been restructured and securitized in 1997 after negotiations with its **London Club** of private creditors. Note that, with regard to Russian creditors, many often use the terms Paris Club to refer to their sovereign creditors and London Club their private creditors. More negotiations ensued, and in February 2000, the Russian government and its creditors reached an agreement under which approximately 36 percent of the bond value was written off, with the rest reissued as sovereign Russian Eurobonds. (Chapter 20 discusses the Russian economy and Russian capital markets since the crisis.)

BRAZIL'S REAL DEVALUATION

Brazil's economic crisis in late 1998 and 1999 followed a familiar pattern: an overvalued currency, a growing current account deficit, and ballooning debt. Russia's de facto default in August 1998 heightened investors' concerns about all emerging market debt, and Brazil's growing budget deficit added to their worries. Though Brazil had a large amount of domestic short-term debt falling due, few creditors wanted to roll it over. In August the country's main stock exchange, Sao Paolo's **Bovespa**, sank nearly 40 percent. Money flowed out of the country's foreign exchange market, forcing the central bank to pump in reserves to support its currency, the real (like the Mexican and Russian systems, Brazil allowed its currency to move within a narrow band and intervened whenever the real approached either edge of the band). In the first two weeks of September, the central bank used an estimated $15 billion of its foreign exchange reserves to support the real. Nevertheless, the foreign exchange market lost $2 billion on September 10, panicking the traders at the Bovespa, which dropped 16 percent in a single day.

On another front, President Fernando Henrigue Cardoso's commitment to fiscal discipline was in doubt. The president failed to sell to his wobbly majority in the congress a key reform of the social security system designed to halt the snowballing deficit. Adding to the costly defeat, Itamer Franco, the newly elected governor of the state of Minas Gerais, announced that his state government called for a debt moratorium and would cease servicing the state's $15 billion debt to the federal government for 90 days. This announcement further threatened the fiscal integrity of the federal government. Governors in the populous states of Rio de Janeiro and Rio Grande do Sul expressed support for a debt moratorium. The states refused to service their debt; they feared the federal government's fiscal crisis could spin out of control. The possibility of default led to increasing capital outflows. The Brazilian central bank began waving warning flags as its dollar reserves declined at a rate of $2 billion a day.

President Cardoso and his advisers decided that the solution was devaluation. Because Cardoso had earlier pledged not to devalue, his about-face not only reinforced the negative market expectations, but destroyed the government's credibility. Recognizing this, the head of the central bank, Gustavo Franco, resigned. Instead of stopping the outflow of dollars, the devaluation speeded it up. On January 13, 1999, the central bank widened the band in which the real could move, effectively devaluing the real by 9 percent against the U.S. dollar. The new system lasted only two days as it resulted in an immediate outflow of $2.9 billion. On January 15, finding it impossible to continue to defend the currency, the central bank allowed the real to float freely. The result was a panic-driven massive depreciation of the real's exchange rate by 60 percent in a few days. Meanwhile, the Bovespa had plunged 10 percent on January 13 and another 9.97 percent on the next day. As in other countries we have examined, the crisis plunged Brazil into a recession. Per capita GDP in 1999 was only $3,400, almost a 33 percent decline from its 1997 level of $5,022.

CONCLUDING SUMMARY

The 1990s witnessed several episodes of financial and currency turmoil, including the Tequila Crisis following Mexico's peso devaluation in 1994–1995, the severe crisis that swept through Asia in 1997–1998, Russia's default in 1998, and Brazil's real devaluation in early 1999. Although all of the affected countries suffered severe economic downturns as a result of the crises, the economic effects of such exchange rate instability devastated Asia in particular.

Although economists disagree widely about the appropriate cure for such crises, they seem to have reached greater consensus on the causes. Economists suggest unsustainable foreign exchange policies were at least partially responsible for the exchange rate instability. An unsustainable exchange policy makes a country vulnerable to abrupt shifts in investor confidence, and a sudden rise in investor expectations of a crisis can force a policy response that validates the original expectations. Other contributing factors to the turmoil included inadequate supervision of the banking and financial sectors, the rapid transmission of the crisis through structural links, and spillover effects among the countries. Other possible lesions include the following:

- Large and persistent current account deficits are potentially malign.
- Excessive reliance on short-term capital inflows invariably leads to financial disasters.
- Pegged exchange rates are untenable in a world of unfettered capital mobility.
- A well-regulated financial system is a necessity.
- The corporate governance system should be subject to strict market discipline.
- Transparency about the financial and corporate sectors always helps.

Key Terms

Asian crisis 461
Bovespa 466
Brady bonds 454
Cetes 459
chaebol 463
crawling peg 459
debt conversion bond 456
discount bond 455
emerging market 450

Exchange Stabilization Fund 460
front loaded interest reduction
   bond 456
interest arrears capitalization bond 456
London Club 465
par bond 455
tequila effect 451
Tesobonos 459

Review Questions

1. What are the potential benefits that emerging markets offer to global investors?

2. Document the trend in the trading volume of emerging market instruments. A good source of data is the Emerging Market Traders Association.

3. Compared to financial markets in developed countries, what are the unique characteristics of risks in emerging financial markets?

4. What are Brady bonds? What is the floor value of a typical Brady bond? Why?

5. Suppose an institutional investor intends to allocate a certain amount of funds to invest in several emerging markets. What are the benefits of this strategy? Are there any barriers in implementing such a strategy?

6. Summarize the causes of the Mexico's peso crisis in 1994–1995.

7. The objective of issuing Tesobonos was to ensure that foreign capital would stay in Mexico by assuring investors that their interests would be protected. Why, then, did the large amount of Tesobonos contribute to the crisis?

8. Briefly explain the main causes of the Asian financial crisis.

9. Briefly explain the causes of the Russian financial crisis.

10. During the crises, international capital often flowed to the United States. Why? Such flight-to-quality increased the problems in the economies directly affected by the crises. Why?

Select Bibliography

Beim, D. O., and C. W. Calomiris. *Emerging Financial Markets*. New York: McGraw-Hill, 2000.

Dornbusch, R. "Emerging markets crises: Origins and remedies." Working paper, Boston, Mass.: Massachusetts Institute of Technology, 1999.

D'Souza, J., and W. L. Megginson. "The financial and operating performance of privatized firms during the 1990s," *Journal of Finance* 54:4, August 1999, pp. 1397–1438.

Edwards, S., and J. A. Frankel (eds.). *Preventing Currency Crisis in Emerging Markets*. Chicago: University of Chicago Press, 2002.

Journal of Emerging Markets. Various issues.

Kim, K. A. "Corporate governance and the role of the securities regulator in the aftermath of the Asian financial crisis," *Review of Pacific Basin Financial Markets and Policies* 2:4, December 1999, pp. 515–519.

Lamfalussy, A. *Financial Crisis in Emerging Markets: An Essay on Financial Globalization and Fragility*. New Haven, Conn.: Yale University Press, 2000.

Malkiel, B., and J. P. Mei. *Global Bargain Hunting*. New York: Simon & Schuster, 1998.

Oh, J., and D. Park. "Financial reforms and financial crisis," *Review of Pacific Basin Financial Markets and Policies* v2n3, September 1999, pp. 265–284.

Patel, S., and A. Sarkar. "Stock market crises in developed and emerging markets," research paper, Federal Reserve Bank of New York, 1998

Pesenti, P., and C. Tille. "The economics of currency crises and contagion: An introduction," *Economic Policy Review* 6:3, Federal Reserve Bank of New York, September 2000, pp. 3–16.

Stiglitz, J. E. "Reforming the global economic architecture: Lessons from recent crises," *Journal of Finance* 54:4, August 1999, pp. 1508–1522.

Tudor, G. *Rollercoaster: The Incredible Story of the Emerging Markets.* New York: Reuters, 2000.

van Wincoop, E. "Asia crisis postmortem: Where did the money go and did the United States benefit?" *Economic Policy Review*, 6:3, Federal Reserve Bank of New York, September 2000, pp. 51–70.

Asian and Russian Markets

As we saw in Chapter 19, a financial crisis swept through many developing nations of East and Southeast Asia in 1997 and 1998. In 1998, Russia faced a similar crisis. In each case, the unbalanced nature of the nation's financial reforms in the early 1990s contributed to the crisis. Rapid deregulation of the rules on external sources of financing led to large inflows of foreign capital. A large portion of these funds was invested in risky projects, which would set the stage for a crisis if, as occurred in country after country, the currency should happen to weaken. Since the crisis, most of the affected countries have implemented reforms to prevent a recurrence of the problems. In this chapter, we look at the changes that have occurred in the developing countries of Asia and in Russia since the crisis and also provide a brief survey of their capital markets.

The objectives of this chapter are to provide an understanding of capital markets in the following countries and economies:
- China
- Hong Kong
- Indonesia
- Malaysia
- Singapore
- South Korea
- Taiwan
- Thailand
- Russia

MARKET OVERVIEW

Since the financial crisis, most of these nations have maintained restrictions on flows of foreign exchange. Some of them still peg their currencies to the U.S. dollar, some peg the currency at a fixed rate, and others allow the currency to move within a narrow band. Table 20.1 compares the exchange rates at the beginning of 1997 before the crisis with those at the beginning of 2003. As the table shows, these currencies, relative to the U.S. dollar, were still weaker than the 1997 levels.

Our examination of capital markets in Asia and Russia will focus on their stock markets because the bond markets, especially the corporate bond sector, are insignificant and still underdeveloped in most of these nations. (The most important emerging market debt instruments are Brady bonds, which we covered in Chapter 19.) The stock markets resemble the U.S. markets in some ways—for example, as Table 20.2 shows, each market has its representative index, the equivalent of the Dow Jones Industrial Average—but differ from them in others. The Asian and Russian markets are much smaller than the U.S. market. Other differences include daily limits on price movements, regulated minimum tick size, and separate morning and afternoon sessions. Several countries also limit the percentage of foreign ownership of companies in certain industries.

CHINA

The People's Republic of China (PRC) is the most populous country in the world, with a population of more than 1.25 billion. Since 1979, when China began to open its economy to the rest of the world and initiate reforms, its economic performance has been impressive. In 2001, its gross domestic prod-

TABLE 20.1	*Exchange Rates Between Asian and Russian Currencies and U.S. Dollar*		
Currency	Symbol	Exchange Rate in January 1997	Exchange Rate in January 2003
Chinese yuan	CNY	8.3260	8.2775
Hong Kong dollar	HKD	7.7397	7.7994
Indonesian rupiah	IDR	2369.30*	8750
Malaysian ringgit	MYR	2.4900	3.8000
South Korea won	KRW	854.07	1176.45
Singapore dollar	SGD	1.4061	1.7363
Taiwan dollar	TWD	27.477	34.571
Thai baht	THB	25.726	42.773
Russian ruble	RUB	5.6088*	31.80

*Data for Indonesian rupiah and Russian ruble in January 1997 are from Oanda Corporation.

Source: *Exchange Rates*, Federal Reserve Bank of St. Louis, 2003.

TABLE 20.2 | *Asian and Russian Market Indexes*

Country	Representative Stock Market Index
China	Shanghai Composite
Hong Kong	Hang Seng
Indonesia	Jakarta Composite
Malaysia	KLSE Composite
Singapore	Straits Times
South Korea	Seoul Composite
Taiwan	Taiwan Weighted
Thailand	SET
Russia	Moscow Times

uct (GDP) reached $5.2 trillion, although per capita GDP, at $4,091, remained low. The reforms have reduced, if not completely eliminated, the rigidities of the former central planning system. As a result, China has undergone a fundamental change from complete reliance on state-owned enterprises to a mixed economy where private enterprise also plays an important role. The private sector will account for an increasingly higher percentage of the economy in the coming years.

China became more fully integrated into the world economy in 2001 when it became a member of the **World Trade Organization (WTO; http://www.wto.org).** As a condition for membership in the WTO, China agreed to institute a series of reforms. China benefits from entering the WTO in many ways. It increases the speed of its economic reform process, improves its external economic relations, and brings in foreign competition, which will benefit the country's long-term growth prospects. However, this also poses significant risks to the Chinese government as it exacerbates the problems China is already having in managing its transition to a market economy. In the coming years (2002–2006) the country will slash tariff and non-tariff barriers, as well as open up sectors of the economy that have long been off-limits to foreigners, such as banking, insurance, and telecommunications. China promises to protect foreign intellectual property and get rid of a raft of local content requirements that have hobbled foreign manufacturers.

The Stock Market

China has two national stock markets: the Shanghai Stock Exchange (**http://www.sse.com.cn**) and the Shenzhen Stock Exchange (**http://www.sse.org.cn**). The Shanghai exchange opened in 1990 and the Shenzhen exchange in 1991. On July 1, 1999, China's Securities Law, which sets out the basic rules governing the securities markets, went into effect.

A unique feature of China's stock markets is that companies may issue A-shares and B-shares. Only Chinese residents may purchase **A-shares** that are denominated in **renminbi** (the Chinese currency). **B-shares** were exclusively for foreign investors, but in February 2001, the PRC government allowed Chinese residents to purchase B-shares (see Box 20.1 for detailed specifics of B-shares). B-shares are not convertible to A-shares, but both types of shares give their owners the same rights with one exception: dividends for B-shares are in foreign currencies. The result is a segmented market in which A-shares are much more numerous; more than a thousand companies have issued A-shares, but only a little over a hundred have issued B-shares.

B-shares provide foreign investors with access to China's equity market. B-shares trade on both exchanges. Before China's entry into the WTO, foreign brokerage firms were only able to trade B-shares through local brokers.

In addition to B-share transactions, foreign investors can participate in China's stock markets through several other alternatives, including shares listed in Hong Kong and New York. In Hong Kong, there are **Red Chip stocks**. The Hong Kong companies that issue these stocks typically derive considerable revenues from operations in China, or else Chinese corporations control these Hong Kong companies outright.

The Bond Market

The Chinese government has floated debt instruments since 1981. The government financed budget requirements with these instruments, which were purchased by state and collective enterprises and by local governments. Between 1981 and 1991, with the treasury bonds sold on an allocated basis, the central government set the coupon, price, maturity, and size of the issue. Since 1991, selected issues have been placed via an underwriting procedure.

During the 1980s, the government recognized the need to allow large, specialized banks to provide financing beyond that provided by the government. In 1985, therefore, these banks and other institutions began to issue bonds to individuals. Two years later, large state-owned companies began to issue enter-

MARKETS IN ACTION   China's B-Shares

20.1

The special characteristics of B-shares are:

° B-shares have denominations in renminbi, but trade in foreign currency (in U.S. dollars in the Shanghai bourse and Hong Kong dollars in Shenzhen).

° Dividends and other payments are calculated and declared in renminbi, but paid in foreign currency.

° B-shares can only be issued to foreign investors (the government lifted this rule to allow

Chinese residents to purchase B-shares in 2001).

° Dividends and capital gains from B-shares can be sent abroad despite China's strict foreign exchange control.

° Foreign securities houses can serve as dealers of B-shares while they cannot engage in the business of A-shares (after China's accession to the WTO, this ban has been gradually lifted).

Source: Ministry of Finance, People's Republic of China.

prise bonds. Shortly after that, companies began to issue construction bonds to finance the building of manufacturing or transport facilities.

By 1990, many institutions had issued various types of debt instruments. Nevertheless, government instruments, including treasury bonds, fiscal bonds, and special-purpose bonds, still dominate the fixed-income market. Secondary trading has been permitted since 1988, with trust and investment companies and securities firms participating as brokers or dealers. On June 3, 2002, China launched its first bond index, the Bank of China Bond Index. The index covers most of the bonds issued by the Ministry of Finance.

China is a major participant in the international capital markets. As a member of the International Monetary Fund (IMF) and the World Bank, China has qualified for commercial borrowing through syndicated bank loans and the sale of capital market securities. China's first international bond issue was a private placement of 10 billion yuan (renminbi) by the China International Trust and Investment Company (CITIC) in 1982. Since then, China has issued billions of bonds in most global financial centers. The first U.S. (Yankee) bond issue took place in 1993 when CITIC sold a 10-year bond in New York.

Foreign Exchange

The official Chinese currency is renminbi or yuan. Renminbi is the only legal tender in China; foreign currency can be exchanged in banks, but cannot circulate. China has an extensive array of regulations governing the inflow and outflow of capital. Residents borrowing abroad are subject to stringent controls. The loans must be approved by and registered with the State Administration of Foreign Exchange (SAFE). Since 1996, the government has relaxed its foreign exchange controls and permitted limited convertibility of renminbi in order to promote economic development and to attract foreign investments.

Foreign companies operating in China (called foreign-invested enterprises, or FIEs) must open a current account and a capital account with a designated foreign exchange bank. The companies use a current account for daily recurring transactions in the ordinary course of business. Current account transactions do not require SAFE's approval. The capital account is used for import and export capital, direct foreign investment and loans, and securities transactions. The companies must receive prior approval from the SAFE for all capital account transactions. The government permits current account items, including dividend payments and profits, to be freely converted into foreign currencies within the country. Removing those funds from the country (repatriation), however, is a capital account activity and thus requires the SAFE's approval.

Since 1995, all foreign companies must submit an annual Foreign Exchange Examination Report prepared by a public accounting firm registered in China. Any company that fails to submit this report cannot directly access foreign exchange centers and must obtain the specific approval of the local foreign exchange control authorities for each foreign exchange transaction.

HONG KONG

Hong Kong reverted to Chinese sovereignty on July 1, 1997, as a Special Administrative Region (SAR) of the PRC. China promised to grant Hong Kong a high degree of autonomy for at least 50 years.

Hong Kong has had a stock market since 1891. In 1989, the Securities and Futures Commission became the single securities market regulator. The Hong Kong Exchange (HKSE; http://www.hkex.com.hk) first listed derivative warrants in 1988, Chinese company shares (H shares) in July 1993, and stock options in 1995, and allowed short selling for the first time in 1994.

The Stock Market

In January 2003, 815 companies were listed on the Main Board of the exchange; 7 of these were Nasdaq stocks (Microsoft, Intel, Cisco, Dell, Amgen, Applied Materials, and Starbucks). During 1999, the exchange introduced a Primary Market Database that publishes summaries of information submitted to the exchange and selected listed company announcements. In November 1999, Hong Kong Exchange established an alternative market, Growth Enterprise Market (GEM), to provide capital-raising opportunities for growth companies that do not meet the listing requirements of the Main Board.

Trading takes place on weekdays in a morning session (10:00 A.M. to 12:30 P.M.) and an afternoon session (2:30 P.M. to 4:00 P.M.). The opening quotation rule governs the first bid or ask order entered into the trading system. The first bid must not be lower than the previous closing price minus eight spreads. The first ask must be higher than the previous closing price plus eight spreads. Table 20.3 lists the spreads for various stocks at different levels of prices.

The exchange charges a transaction levy of 0.007 percent of the amount of the consideration for each purchase or sale of securities, payable by both the buyer and the seller. In addition, there is a trading fee of 0.005 percent for every transaction. The government charges a transfer deed stamp duty of HK$5 and a trading tariff of HK$0.5 for each and every purchase or sale. Furthermore, each listed company levies a transfer fee of HK$2.50 per share certificate. Hong Kong does not require withholding on interest or dividends and does not impose capital gains tax.

The Bond Market

The Hong Kong bond market trades corporate bonds, government bonds, and supranational bonds. For corporate bonds, some are listed on the exchange, but most trade over-the-counter. Until the mid-1990s, the market for government securities was insignificant. The Hong Kong's government began to promote the debt market by issuing exchange fund bills and notes and by setting up an efficient central clearing system to facilitate secondary market trading. Since August 1996, exchange fund notes have been listed on the stock exchange, a development that has enhanced their liquidity in the secondary market and enlarged their investor base to include retail investors. Exchange fund paper

Price Range in HK$	Spread in HK$
All Securities Other than Debt	
0.01–0.25	0.001
> 0.25–0.50	0.005
> 0.50–2.00	0.010
> 2.00–5.00	0.025
> 5.00–30.00	0.050
> 30.00–50.00	0.100
> 50.00–100.00	0.250
> 100.00–200.00	0.500
> 200.00–1,000.00	1.000
> 1,000–9,995.00	2.500
Exchange Fund Notes and Hong Kong Mortgage Corporation Notes	
0.50–9,999.95	0.050
Other Debt Securities	
0.50–9,999.875	0.125

TABLE 20.3 | *Spreads at Various Levels of Prices in Hong Kong*

Source: Hong Kong Exchange.

can be used as margin collateral for trading in futures, index options, and stock options.

Another sign of development in the fixed-income market is the lengthening of the maturity profiles of issues. In addition, the Hong Kong Monetary Authority has taken steps to provide supporting infrastructure for the local debt market. This includes issuing the exchange fund bills and notes to generate an effective yield curve and establishing the Central Moneymarkets Unit (CMU) to enhance clearing and settlement capabilities. The implementation of a U.S. dollar payment clearing system, which made its debut in August 2000, has enhanced the development of the U.S. dollar debt market in Hong Kong.

The Derivatives Market
Both equity and derivative warrants are listed on the Hong Kong Exchange. In addition, Hong Kong has an established futures market. The Hong Kong Futures Exchange lists equity index products, equity products, and interest rate products. Index products include Hang Seng Index Futures and Options, Mini-Hang Seng Index Futures, MSCI China Free Index futures, and Dow Jones Industrial Average futures. Equity products include stock futures, stock options, and international stock futures and options. Interest rate products include HIBOR (Hong Kong Interbank Offered Rate) and Three-Year Exchange Fund Note futures.

Foreign Exchange

Hong Kong pegs its currency, the Hong Kong dollar, to the U.S. dollar. To maintain the stability of the exchange rate, the **Hong Kong Monetary Authority (HKMA; http://www.info.gov.hk/hkma),** Hong Kong's quasicentral bank, issues or redeems bank notes as necessary against U.S. dollars at the fixed exchange rate of HK$7.8 to US$1. The local currency increases when U.S. dollars are sold in exchange for Hong Kong dollars, and vice versa. The expansion or contraction of the monetary base thus causes local interest rates to fall or rise. After the depreciation of the Taiwan dollar in October 1997, the HKMA raised interest rates to defend the local currency. The consequences hit the local economy hard. Hong Kong's stock market plunged as speculators mounted several more attacks in 1998. To boost the market, on August 14, 1998, the government purchased large quantities of shares ultimately, owning 7.3 percent of the 33 companies that made up the Hang Seng Index.

Hong Kong has no foreign exchange controls, and cross-border remittances are readily permitted. These rules have not changed since Hong Kong reverted to China. Corporations in Hong Kong have total freedom to move capital and repatriate profits. There are no restrictions on the conversion and remittance of dividends and interest. The government generally makes no distinction between local and foreign companies and imposes no limitations on direct investments, except for certain regulated industries such as banking, insurance, and television.

INDONESIA

Indonesia had a population of more than 228 million, with a per capita GDP of less than $2,700 in 2001. Like Malaysia, Singapore, and Thailand, discussed later in this chapter, it is a member of the **Association of Southeast Asian Nations (ASEAN; http://www.asean.or.id).**[1] As described in Chapter 19, Indonesia suffered a significant downturn as a result of the crisis of 1997. Since then, it has made much progress in the recapitalization of banks via programs by the Indonesian Bank Restructuring Agency. The government has also taken steps to assist corporate debt restructuring solutions. In addition, the Indonesian government talked with the Paris Club of lenders to reschedule its debt.

The Stock Market

The Jakarta Stock Exchange (JSX; **http://www.jsx.co.id**) was established in 1991 and privatized in July 1992. In 1995, the exchange moved to a new building at Sudirman central business district and launched an automated trading system to replace the old manual one. The system integrates trading, clearing

---

[1]Its members are Brunei Darussalam, Cambodia, Indonesia, Laos, Malaysia, Myanmar, the Philippines, Singapore, Thailand, and Vietnam. The objective of ASEAN is to bring together the countries of Southeast Asia to cooperate in securing the region's peace, stability, and development.

and settlement, and depository and broker accounting functions. Shares can trade in round lots or odd lots. On the regular market, trading takes place in round lots of 500 shares. Block trading, odd lot trading, and cross trading occur in a negotiated market separate from the regular market. Cross trading occurs when there is a matching purchase and sale order by the same broker acting for different customers.

Trading takes place from 9:30 A.M. to 12:00 noon (Session I) and from 1:30 P.M. to 4:00 P.M. (Session II). Transactions generally follow a T+3 settlement cycle. In 2003, 302 companies listed their stocks on the exchange.

The Capital Market Executive Agency regulates the stock market. It has three principal responsibilities: approving new listings, supervising the capital markets, and monitoring listed companies. The Capital Market Bill, which took effect in 1996, established disclosure obligations for issuers, permitted the introduction of open-end mutual funds, and set rules for securities lending. The first rating agency started its business in 1994.

Foreign Exchange

Indonesia's official currency is the rupiah. Since 1986, the central bank, Bank Indonesia (**http://www.bi.go.id**), has attempted to maintain the currency within a narrow band.[2] As we saw in Chapter 19, Indonesia had to devalue its currency in 1997, but since then, Bank Indonesia has succeeded in maintaining the rupiah's stability.

Transfers of funds to and from foreign countries have no restrictions, but capital inflows require government approval. The Foreign Investment Law permits foreign investors to transfer home all current after-tax profits, certain costs, depreciation, and compensation. But for the purpose of recording invested capital and investment guarantees, statements reflecting investments in foreign currencies must be filed with Bank Indonesia.

Bank Indonesia must approve loans from abroad to state-owned companies and foreign-invested companies in advance. Earnings on approved investments can be freely transferred in the currency of the original investment. However, the remitting company must report the transfer to Bank Indonesia and also provide an annual balance sheet and profit-and-loss statement.

MALAYSIA

Malaysia had a population of almost 22 million, with a per capita GDP of more than $10,000 in 2001. Before the 1997 Asian financial crisis, Malaysia had achieved a high rate of economic growth and had enjoyed steadily improving living standards over a period of several decades. In the wake of the crisis, Malaysia adopted measures to restore market confidence and financial stability. In July 1998, the government implemented the National Economic Recovery

---

[2]N. Gelfand and M. Hilderbrand, *Indonesia,* Boston, Mass.: Harvard Business School Publishing, 1996.

Plan to provide a comprehensive framework for economic recovery and to counter the negative impact of the currency depreciation and the decline of the stock market. In addition, the government cut taxes to reduce the cost of doing business and to enhance the nation's competitiveness and productivity.

Recognizing that foreign direct investment had been instrumental in introducing management techniques and technological advances to the country, the government tried to encourage capital inflows by permitting foreign ownership of as much as 100 percent of manufacturing companies. Foreign ownership of up to 49 percent of telecommunications firms has also been permitted.

The Stock Market

The main stock market in Malaysia is the Kuala Lumpur Stock Exchange (KLSE; http://www.klse.com.my), with 874 listed companies as of February 2003. Among them, the Main Board listed 563, the Second Board listed 296, and the Mesdaq market listed 15. The government established the Malaysian Exchange of Securities Dealing and Automated Quotations (MESDAQ; http://www.klse.com.my/website/mesdaq/index.htm) to specialize in growth and technology companies. Initially, the KLSE linked to the Stock Exchange of Singapore with many companies listed on both exchanges. In 1990, however, such a relationship ended, and now companies list on either Malaysia or Singapore, not both.

Like many other Asian exchanges, the KSLE has a morning session (9:00 A.M. to 12:30 P.M.) and an afternoon session (2:30 P.M. to 5:00 P.M.). The brokerage commission has a 0.70 percent cap. Trading is generally in 1,000 units, called board lots, but for certain companies, trades of 200 shares are allowable in an effort to make highly priced or thinly traded securities more affordable to a larger segment of the investing public.

The KLSE has a rule for minimum price variations (or tick size). The minimum variation increases with the stock price. For example, for a stock priced up to ringgit 1.00, the minimum variation is 0.50 sen (1 ringgit = 100 sen), and for a stock priced at more than ringgit 100.00, the minimum variation is 50 sen. Thus, if the last price for a stock is ringgit 105.22, the next bid or offer must at least 50 sen above or below ringgit 105.22—that is, ringgit 105.72 or ringgit 104.72.

Securities transactions settle through a central depository system. A buyer receives securities on T+3. If the shares are not in the seller's account on T+3, the KLSE will initiate a buy-in against the seller on T+4.

The Bond Market

Debt instruments available include Malaysian treasury bills (maturity up to one year), Malaysian government securities (maturity more than one year), government investment issues, Bank Negara Malaysia bills, commercial paper, medium-term notes, and corporate bonds. In addition, there are Cagamas instruments, which include floating-rate bonds, fixed-rate bonds, Cagamas notes, and Islamic notes (medium-term debt securities issued under the Islamic principle of Al Mudharabah with a predetermined profit sharing ratio). All bond issues must be rated.

The Malaysian government has taken several measures to develop the bond market. In April 2000, for example, the Controller of Foreign Exchange granted general permission for the issuance of private debt securities so long as the issuer does not use the proceeds to finance investments abroad or to refinance offshore borrowings. In July 2000, the Securities Commission (SC) became the single regulator for all fund-raising activities. The government also established the National Bond Market Committee (NBMC) to help design appropriate strategies. The SC and the NBMC recommended new regulatory measures intended to facilitate the issuance process, broaden the investor base, establish a reliable benchmark yield curve, and enhance secondary market liquidity.

Foreign Exchange

Malaysia's official currency is the ringgit. The central bank, Bank Negara (**http://www.bnm.gov.my**), enforces the rules relating to foreign exchange control. Foreign investors who invest in Malaysian stocks and bonds but not real property must pay a repatriation levy to withdraw their funds from the country. The amount of the levy gradually decreases with the length of time the funds have been invested in Malaysia. In addition, all repatriated profits are subject to an additional 10 percent levy.

These measures reflect a considerable easing of the stringent restraints imposed after the 1997 crisis. In 1998, Bank Negara imposed measures to restrain speculation in the ringgit and to minimize the impact of short-term capital flows in and out of the country. As a result, Malaysia had increased its international reserves to more than $27 billion in 2001. There were also positive net inflows of foreign direct investment in 2001.

SINGAPORE

Singapore is an island state located at the tip of the Malay Peninsula. It gained independence from the British in 1959. The population is small (4.3 million in 2001), but the per capita income is high (US$23,000 in 2001).

The Stock Market

The **Singapore Exchange (SGX; http://www.ses.com.sg)** formed in December 1999 from the merger of the Stock Exchange of Singapore (SES), which had been established in 1973; and the Singapore International Monetary Exchange Limited (SIMEX), which was the first financial futures exchange in Asia. The Singapore Exchange was the first fully electronic and floorless exchange in Asia. On November 23, 2000, it became a public company, issuing 1 billion shares. The securities products traded on the SGX include equity and equity options, warrants, bonds, and depositary receipts. Shares mostly trade in board lots of 1,000 shares on the SGX. The tick size increases with the

stock price. Effective October 1, 2000, brokerage rates have been fully negotiable for all transactions on the SGX.

Each trading session at the exchange begins at 9:00 A.M. and runs until
5:00 P.M. Before the market opens, there is a preopen period (8:30 A.M. to
8:59 A.M.) for input of buy and sell orders. Then, during the noncancel period
(8:59 A.M. to 9:00 A.M.), a price is selected as the opening price, thereby maximizing the trading volume. Similarly, the closing price is set during the pre-
close period (5:00 P.M. to 5:05 P.M.) and a noncancel period (5:05 P.M. to
5:06 P.M.).

The Singapore Exchange conducts its operations through five wholly
owned subsidiaries:

1. Singapore Exchange Securities Trading Limited (SGX-ST; formerly
   known as the Stock Exchange of Singapore).
2. Central Depository Pte Limited (CDP).
3. Singapore Exchange Derivatives Trading Limited (SGX-DT; formerly
   SIMEX).
4. Singapore Exchange Derivatives Clearing Limited (SGX-DC).
5. Singapore Exchange IT Solutions Pte Limited.

The main board listed more than 500 companies in 2002. In addition, there
is the SGX Sesdaq that listed 89 small- to medium-sized companies as of
November 2002. Furthermore, the SGX Xtranet offers a venue for listing and
trading of structured products such as exchanged traded funds (ETFs). In July
2002, it introduced Singapore's first real estate investment trusts.

Singapore also has a well-established derivatives market. Futures, options,
warrants, swaps, and other derivatives actively trade at both the Singapore
Commodity Exchange and the Singapore Exchange.

The Bond Market

The Singapore bond market consists of government securities and corporate
fixed-income securities. The government issues its securities as a matter of policy rather than as a function of the government's need for financing. The
Singapore government usually runs a surplus, so it has no need to tap the capital market. Its principal objectives in issuing securities are to:

1. provide a liquid investment alternative for investors;
2. establish a liquid government bond market to serve as a benchmark for
   the corporate fixed-income market; and
3. encourage the development of skills relating to fixed-income securities
   and broaden the spectrum of financial services.

The Monetary Authority of Singapore issues treasury bills (3-month and 1-
year) and bonds (2-, 5-, 7-, 10-, and 15-year). Government securities clear and
settle electronically on a delivery-versus-payment (DVP) basis. Transactions
generally settle T+1. As of January 2003, the total outstanding volume of
Singapore government bills and bonds was S$58.25 billion (U.S. $33.5 billion).

After the 1997 crisis, the Monetary Authority implemented several bond market reforms. These included extending the yield curve of the government securities to 10 years (later to 15 years), allowing foreign companies to issue bonds in Singapore dollars, and instituting new offering mechanisms. As a result, the Monetary Authority now issues more short-end bills and long-term bonds. The Authority also increased the issue size from an average of S$1.5 billion to S$2.5 billion. The government has made selected new treasury bill issues eligible for the tax incentives such as an exemption from withholding on interest income for nonresidents.

The corporate sector consists of Asian dollar bonds and Singapore dollar bonds. Asian dollar bonds are issued in Singapore but denominated in a foreign currency, mostly in U.S. dollars, although some are in other currencies such as the yen, the euro, and the Australian dollar. Singapore dollar bonds are denominated in Singapore dollars. To promote the development of the fixed-income market, the government encourages government-linked companies to raise capital in the fixed-income market and introduced the Approved Bond Intermediary (ABI) scheme in February 1999. Deals arranged by an ABI qualify for tax incentives for interest and fee income.

Foreign Exchange

Singapore imposes no restrictions on foreign exchange. Companies can borrow and lend in all currencies, and Singapore allows free flows of capital and cross-border transfers of the Singapore dollar and other currencies. There are no restrictions on local borrowing by foreign firms, except that the funds must be used locally. Financial institutions must consult with the Monetary Authority of Singapore (**http://www.mas.gov.sg**) before extending Singapore dollar credit facilities to nonresidents if the funds are to be used outside Singapore or if the credit facilities exceed S$5 million and are to be used to acquire financial assets.

SOUTH KOREA

Prior to the 1997 economic crisis, many viewed the South Korean economy as a dramatic success story, powered by a bank-centered financial system and the chaebol conglomerate system. The South Korean economy traditionally relied heavily on the banking system to channel savings to industrial investments. Big corporate conglomerates known as chaebols, such as Samsung, Hyundai, and Daewoo, dominated the Korean economy.

The Asian financial crisis of 1997–1998 exposed weaknesses in South Korea's development model, including high corporate debt–equity ratios, massive foreign borrowing, and an undisciplined financial sector in which lending liberally supported industrial expansion without due regard for profitability. As first Thailand then Indonesia saw the exchange value of their currencies collapse, South Korea also fell victim to foreign investors' rush for the exits.

The Bank of Korea saw its international reserves dissipating rapidly; the bank had to devalue the won, averaging W1400/US$ in 1998, as compared to W804/US$ in 1996. In December 1997, South Korea signed a $58 billion International Monetary Fund package, including loans from the IMF, World Bank, and Asia Development Bank. Under the terms of the program, South Korea agreed to accelerate the opening of its financial and equity markets to foreign investment and to reform and restructure its financial and corporate sectors to increase transparency, accountability, and efficiency. By the end of 1998, it had recovered financial stability—rebuilding foreign exchange reserves to record levels by running a current account surplus of $40 billion that year. By year-end 2001, South Korea had completely repaid its IMF loan package and did it well ahead of schedule.

The Stock Market

The trading session at the **Korea Stock Exchange (KSE; http://www.kse .or.kr)** consists of a regular session and an off-hour session. The regular session runs from 9:00 A.M. to 3:00 P.M., and the off-hour trading begins at 3:10 P.M. and ends at 4:00 P.M. During off-hour trading, orders are executed at the closing price, except certain block orders, which may be executed within 7 percent from the closing price.

There are two types of transactions, depending on the settlement period: regular transactions and cash transactions. A regular transaction can settle either T+1 or T+2, while a cash transaction settles the same day. Stocks settle T+2. The interdealer market for government bonds uses T+1. Other debt securities are same-day settlements.

The stock-trading unit, a round lot, is 10 shares. At market opening and closing, the exchange pools over all customer orders and sets a price that minimizes the imbalance between the buying and the selling orders. The minimum price variation, or tick size, increases with the price of the stock. Furthermore, to avoid wide price fluctuations and foster an orderly market, the exchange sets a daily price change limit. Stock prices cannot move 15 percent above or below the previous day's closing price. The exchange added circuit breakers in December 1998. If the stock price index falls by 10 percent or more for more than one minute, stock trading halts for 20 minutes. Such a trading halt can only occur once a day.

Korea has an over-the-counter market as well. The Kosdaq (**http://www. kosdaq.or.kr**), modeled after the U.S. Nasdaq, was established in July 1996 to provide a computerized competitive trading system for small- and medium-sized enterprises and high-tech companies. As of February 2003, the Kosdaq listed 868 companies. The daily price change limit is 12 percent. There is no regulation on brokerage commissions. Online trading is popular for Kosdaq stocks. The online trading rate was 40 percent in 1999 and increased to 75 percent in 2000.

The Bond Market

The South Korean bond market comprises both public bonds and corporate bonds. Public bonds include government bonds, municipal bonds, and special bonds. In 1999, in an effort to improve the liquidity of the government bond market and thus facilitate the development of benchmark yields in various maturity segments, the Ministry of Finance and Economy designated 24 financial institutions as primary dealers of government securities. Corporate bonds are either debentures (unsecured bonds) or secured bonds. Most corporate bonds are issued in the form of fixed-rate coupons and guaranteed by financial institutions. The convertible bonds, bonds with warrants, and exchangeable bonds have emerged as new debt instruments.

Bonds trade during two sessions, which have the same hours as the stock exchange. The trading unit is 100,000 won (US$85) for bonds and the minimum quotation unit is one basis point. There is no price change limit in bond trading.

Futures and Options

Trading of the Korea Stock Price Index 200 (KOSPI 200) started in May 1996. The trading of the KOSPI 200 futures is under an order-driven, continuous trading system. The contract months are March, June, September, and December. The KSE imposes a circuit breaker that halts trading when a price reaches a specified trigger. For example, for a lead month contract, the trigger is 5 percent deviation from the close of the previous day. For program trading, when the price of a futures contract with the largest trading volume on the previous day moves 4 percent or more from the previous close for one minute, all orders for program trading are disclosed for 5 minutes before execution. This rule does not apply during the first 5 minutes and the last 40 minutes of the trading day. The last trading day of futures and options contracts is the second Thursday of each contract month. Trading hours are from 9:00 A.M. to 3:15 P.M.

Foreign Exchange

The South Korean currency is the **won**. The Ministry of Finance and Economy is in charge of foreign exchange regulation. The central bank, the Bank of Korea (**http://www.bok.or.kr**), sets foreign exchange controls as directed by the ministry. The bank announces the daily basic exchange rate (the average rate of transactions in the previous day), intervenes in foreign exchange market operations, authorizes and oversees foreign exchange banks, and other exchange policies.

Foreign-owned companies incorporated in Korea must report any foreign long-term loan agreement with the foreign parent company or with affiliated companies. Foreigners can purchase Korean stocks either through direct stock purchase or through indirect investment via beneficiary certificates and the Korea fund. There are no restrictions on the remittance of dividends, profits, interest, or principal.

TAIWAN

Taiwan is an island economy. Economically, Taiwan has done extremely well. In 1995, the Taiwanese government introduced a plan, called the **Asia–Pacific Regional Operations Center**, to promote Taiwan as a regional business hub. The goal was to establish Taiwan as an Asian financial center by developing the local financial services industry into a major provider of international cross-border financial services. To meet this goal, the Taiwanese government:

° Increased both the amount that each qualified foreign institutional investor (QFII) could invest in any company listed in Taiwan, and the total amount of any listed company that could be owned by such investors.

° Attempted to induce prestigious foreign securities firms to set up branches in Taiwan.

° Tried to speed up internationalization of the Taiwanese securities markets.

In recent years, the Taiwanese government has taken additional measures to continue to enhance the competitiveness of its financial markets. The government enacted and signed into law the Financial Market Modernization Act in 2002. Furthermore, the government also enacted the Financial Asset Securitization Act that provided the legal foundation for the issuance of the first asset-backed securities in January 2003.

The Stock Market

The Taiwanese government established the Taiwan Stock Exchange (TSE; http://www.tse.com.tw) in 1962. The number of companies listed on the exchange increased from 199 in 1990 to 584 in 2001. Although the stock market is not large, it is quite active. The annual turnover value ranks high internationally. In the peak of the market in late 1990s, the annual turnover value of the TSE was just lower than that of the New York Stock Exchange, Tokyo Stock Exchange, and London Stock Exchange, but substantially higher than that of other stock exchanges.

The trading hours at the Taiwan Stock Exchange are from 9:00 A.M. to 1:30 P.M. As at the Korea Stock Exchange, at the opening of each trading day, a call market sets the opening price to maximize the trading volume. After the opening, a continuous auction is in place until the end of the trading day. To maintain stability, the daily change has a maximum limit of 7 percent from the previous closing price. For bonds, the limit is 5 percent. The tick size increases with stock price, as Table 20.4 shows.

In addition to the Taiwan Stock Exchange, Taiwan has an over-the-counter market that began operation in 1994, and a Taiwan Futures Exchange (http://www.taifex.com.tw) that began operation in 1997.

The Bond Market

As in most emerging markets, the government bond sector accounts for most of the fixed-income market. The corporate bond market is relatively small. As

TABLE 20.4	*Taiwan Stock Tick Size*
Stock Price (Taiwan Dollar)	**Tick Size**
Less than 5	0.01
Between 5 and 15	0.05
Between 15 and 50	0.1
Between 50 and 150	0.5
Between 150 and 1,000	1.0
1,000 and above	5.0

Source: *Trading Mechanism*, Taiwan Stock Exchange (http://www.tse.com.tw).

a result, insurance companies and banks prefer the safety of sovereign bonds. By far the biggest purchasers of corporate bonds are local bond funds, which buy and hold the bonds until maturity. This practice is a major reason that the secondary bond market in Taiwan is very limited. Corporate bonds are subject to a 0.1% transaction fee. Also unpopular is the practice of dividing bond issues into small tranches. The bond funds purchase these as an entire block, thereby again stifling any secondary market liquidity. In recent years, due to the slump in the stock market, investors have purchased large sums of corporate bonds. However, trading in the secondary market is still not active.

In 1991, Asian Development Bank issued U.S. dollar denominated Dragon bonds in Taiwan. This was the first foreign bond issue in Taiwan. Other foreign entities floated additional Dragon bonds in subsequent years.

Foreign Exchange

The Taiwanese currency is the Taiwan dollar. Since 1987, there have been no restrictions on outward remittances for trade-related transactions (imports or exports of goods and services). All dividends, profits, interest, and principal can also be removed from the country without restrictions. Taiwanese corporations may remit abroad up to US$50 million per year and US$1 million per transaction without authorization. Any larger amounts must be approved by the Central Bank of China (CBC; **http://www.cbc.gov.tw**), Taiwan's central bank.

THAILAND

Thailand, with a population of more than 60 million, had a per capita GDP in 2001 of $6,200. Before the 1997 crisis, Thailand had enjoyed a long period of rapid economic growth, boosted by foreign investment. Months of speculative pressure on Thailand's baht currency led the government to devalue it in July 1997, marking the beginning of the Asian financial crisis. The Thai economy contracted 1.4 percent in 1997 and 10.4 percent in 1998. The $17.2 billion IMF economic recovery program and other measures that the government took afforded Thailand stability in the value of its currency in the second half of 1998 and helped replenish foreign reserves. Significant progress has been made over the past few years in stabilizing the economy and fostering an economic recovery. However, the recovery remains fragile because there are large sums of nonperforming loans in the banking sector and Thailand relies too heavily on exports (about 65 percent of its GDP).

The Stock Market

The Securities Exchange of Thailand (SET; **http://www.set.or.th/th/index.html**) opened for trading on April 30, 1975, renamed as The Stock Exchange of Thailand on January 1, 1991. On January 4, 1994, the SET opened with its index at a historic high of 1753.73. On February 21, 2003, the index was only at 359.53. The Securities and Exchange Act of 1992 provided a regulatory framework for the capital markets. Under the act, the Securities and Exchange Commission (SEC) is responsible for the supervision and regulation of the primary market while the secondary market remains the responsibility of the SET.

The trading hours at the exchange break up into a morning session and an afternoon session. Note that as in other exchanges, the SET has a preopening period to determine the opening price and an off-hour trading session after the close.

In 1997, the SET introduced new price limits for trading. The limit generally allows prices to fluctuate in a range of 30 percent from the previous closing price. Like several other emerging stock markets, Thailand also sets the bid–offer spread for stocks. The spread is at 0.10 baht for stock priced less than 10 baht and increases to 6.00 baht if the stock price is at 1,000 baht or higher. Brokerage commissions have been deregulated since October 1, 2000. Market forces, not regulatory measures, set the commissions. All fees are subject to a 7 percent value-added tax.

The SET introduced an automated trading system in 1996. On the main board, trading must be in round lots—100 shares if the price is not more than 500 baht and 50 shares if the price is more than 500 baht. Short selling was impermissible until January 1998. SET trading settles T+3 through the Thailand Securities Depository Company.

Small and medium-sized companies can raise capital through the Market for Alternative Investments. This market is not active, however. The number of listed companies was only 9 in 2002.

Foreign Exchange

The official currency of Thailand is the **baht**. The government has shifted some of the administration of foreign exchange regulations from the Bank of Thailand (**http://www.bot.or.th**) to commercial banks. The government has eased foreign exchange controls significantly in recent years. Thailand imposes no restrictions on the inflow and outflow of funds for equity investment. Generally, foreign shareholdings cannot exceed 49 percent in companies listed on the stock exchange. Many companies have imposed their own maximum limits, usually in the range of 25 to 30 percent. In addition, foreign ownership of banks and finance and credit institutions is typically limited to 25 percent. Capital, loans, dividends, and interest can be freely repatriated upon presentation of documentation to commercial banks. Local firms can invest up to $10 million abroad in a given year without approval of the Bank of Thailand.

RUSSIA

Russia, the largest republic of the former Soviet Union, had a population of 145 million and a per capita GDP of $4,570 in 2001. As we saw in Chapter 19, the Russian economy experienced a severe crisis in 1998. Exports fell and investors withdrew from Russia. Rising oil prices in 2000 and 2001 have helped the economy to recover. In 2000 and 2001, the current account surplus was sufficiently large, enabling Russia to pay down international debt and build up its international reserves, which stood at $33 billion in 2001.

The Stock Market
Russia's equity market is still in the early stages of development. There are several exchanges, including the Russian Trading System (RTS; **http://www. rts.ru**), the Moscow Interbank Currency Exchange (MICEX), and the Moscow Central Stock Exchange (MCSE; **http://www.mse.ru**).

The RTS is an interregional over-the-counter system, similar to the U.S. Nasdaq. Shares traded in the RTS subdivide into two trading categories: the RTS-1 is for mature, highly liquid stocks; the RTS-2 covers securities with less stringent requirements. The MICEX lists government, corporate, hard currency, and municipal bonds. It also provides advice about Russia's economy and financial conditions as well as trading tips and information about stocks. The MICEX also offers insurance against investment risks in case of settlement fails. Finally, the MCSE, established in June 1997, lists domestic securities.

The Bond Market
The Russian fixed-income market started during 1994–1995, when the government decided to shift its borrowing from the central bank to the capital market. The fixed-income market consists of sovereign (government) Eurobonds, MinFin bonds, sovereign ruble bonds, London Club debt, municipal and corporate Eurobonds, and local ruble bonds. Sovereign Eurobonds were first issued in 1996–1997 and were classified as Russian-era debt. Their initial maturity dates ranged from 2001 to 2028. **MinFin bonds** are U.S. dollar denominated bonds that carry a 3 percent coupon; the Ministry of Finance issued them in 1992 to compensate the holders of funds held in the foreign currency account of Vnesheconombank, the State Bank for Foreign Economic Affairs of the Soviet Union. Foreign investors held most of the $10 billion worth of MinFin bonds issued.

The sovereign ruble bond market consists of short-term zero-coupon bonds, known as **GKOs (Gosudarstvenniye Kratkosrochiniye Obligatsii)**, and medium-term floating-rate bonds, known as **OFZs (Obligatsii Federalnogo Zaima)**. The GKOs have a maturity of three months, six months, or one year. In August 1998, two-thirds of the market was frozen by Russian government. Later they were swapped into new ruble-denominated OFZs with maturities of two to four years.

As mentioned in Chapter 19, the London Club debt includes PRINs (principal arrears notes) and IANs (interest arrears notes). It represents restructured debt owed to London Club creditors. The total face value of PRINs and IANs is about $30 billion, with a floating-rate coupon and maturity in 2015 and 2020. An agreement between the Russian government and the London Club of commercial creditors created the debt, so that Russia could restructure its Soviet-era external debt.

Three municipalities, Moscow, St. Petersburg, and Nizhny Novgorod, issued Eurobonds before the crisis hit in 1998. Several corporations also issued Eurobonds prior to the crisis. In addition, institutions issued local ruble bonds as an instrument for payment. Although these are ruble denominated, investors are hedged against currency risk as principal payments are pegged to the dollar.

Foreign Exchange

The official currency of Russia is the **ruble**. Russia's foreign exchange regulations focus on two crucial issues: the dollarization of the domestic economy and capital flight. Russia's underground, or gray, economy is one of the largest in the world. Billions of U.S. dollars in $100 bills are imported every year to supply it. Since the ruble's devaluation and the nation's default on its debt in 1998, the Bank of Russia (**http://www.cbr.ru**) has made an effort to stop capital outflows. Empowered by an amendment to a law on banks and banking activities, the Bank of Russia imposed restrictions on commercial banks dealings with their offshore counterparts. Since September 1, 1999, Russian banks must maintain reserves of 50 percent against practically any risk exposure to offshore banks, including loans, portfolio investments, and correspondent account balances.

In July 1997, Russia introduced a tax on purchases of hard currency, which applies to individuals as well as corporations. It does not apply to withdrawals of foreign currency from foreign-currency credit cards or bank accounts. Hard-currency purchases by lending institutions from the Bank of Russia and other lending institutions are also exempt from the tax. Entities fully financed from the state budget are exempt from the tax as well.

CONCLUDING SUMMARY

This chapter has provided an overview of the stock, bond, and foreign exchange markets in China, Hong Kong, Indonesia, Malaysia, Singapore, South Korea, Taiwan, Thailand, and Russia. Most of these countries experienced severe financial crises during the 1990s. By early 2000s, they had begun to recover from the worst effects of the crisis, although foreign investment remained below the levels it reached in the early 1990s. Nevertheless, all have worked to build their capital markets.

As is clear from our discussions, most of these markets are still relatively small, with limited trading hours compared to the United States. These countries generally impose restrictions on foreign ownership of companies in certain industries such as telecommunications, airlines, and financial institutions. Some also have strict regulations on flows of capital from abroad. Until 2001, China had its B-shares exclusively for foreign investors. Bond markets in these countries are generally underdeveloped.

Key Terms

Asia-Pacific Regional Operations
    Center 486
A-share 473
Association of Southeast Asian Nations
    (ASEAN) 478
baht 488
B-share 473
GKO (Gosudarstvenniye
    Kratkosrochiniye Obligatsii) 490
Hong Kong Monetary Authority
    (HKMA) 478

Korea Stock Exchange (KSE) 484
MinFin bond 489
OFZ (Obligatsii Federalnogo
    Zaima) 490
Red Chip stock 474
renminbi 473
ruble 490
Singapore Exchange (SGX) 481
won 485
World Trade Organization (WTO) 473

Review Questions

1. What are B-shares in China? Who can purchase B-shares?

2. Briefly describe the various fees investors pay when trading in Hong Kong.

3. Visit the Web site of Bank Indonesia and obtain data on Indonesian interest rates. Compare them with the rates in the United States. How different are they? Why?

4. Why does the government of Singapore issue government securities even though it generally runs a surplus?

5. What was the purpose of the primary dealership system in South Korea?

6. What measures did the Taiwanese government take to establish Taiwan as an Asian financial center?

7. What is the relationship between the changes in baht exchange rates (against the U.S. dollar) and the stock market return in Thailand?

8. Briefly describe the Russian fixed-income market.

Select Bibliography

Beim, D. O., and C. W. Calomiris. *Emerging Financial Markets.* New York: McGraw-Hill, 2000.

Goldstein, M. *The Asian Financial Crisis: Causes, Cures and Systematic Implications.* Washington, D.C.: Institute for International Economics, 1998.

Haggard, S. *The Political Economies of the Asian Financial Crisis.* Washington, D.C.: Institute for International Economics, 2000.

Harwood, A., R. E. Litan, and M. Pomerleano, eds. *Financial Markets and Development: The Crisis in Emerging Markets.* Washington, D.C.: Brookings Institute, 1999.

Hertz, E. *The Trading Crowd: An Ethnography of the Shanghai Stock Market.* Cambridge: Cambridge University Press, 1998.

Keim, D. B., and W. T. Ziemba, eds. *Security Market Imperfection in World Wide Equity Markets.* Cambridge: Cambridge University Press, 2000.

Kelley, L., and Y. Luo, eds. China 2000: *Emerging Business Issues.* Thousand Oaks, Calif.: Sage Publications, 1999.

Williamson, J. *Exchange Rate Regimes for Emerging Markets: Reviving the Intermediate Option.* Washington, D.C.: Institute for International Economics, 2000.

Wong, K. A., and K. Yuanto. "Short-term senilities on the Jakarta Stock Exchange," *Review of Pacific Basin Financial Markets and Policies* 2n3, 1999, pp. 375–398.

Latin American Markets

As we saw in Chapter 19, both Mexico and Brazil experienced severe financial crises in the 1990s—Mexico in 1994 and 1995 and Brazil in 1999.
Although Argentina, the third largest country in Latin America, did not
entirely escape the contagion effects of these crises, it was not forced to devalue
its currency during the 1990s. Many attributed Argentina's successful defense
of its currency to its currency board arrangement, which pegged its currency
to the U.S. dollar. The benefits of Argentina's currency board would become
less apparent in more recent years, however.

Since the 1990s, the fortunes of Mexico, Brazil, and Argentina have
diverged. Mexico has recovered from the worst effects of the crisis of
1994–1995 and has even succeeded in repaying the loans it received from the
United States during the crisis. Brazil, however, has had less success in stabilizing its economy, and Argentina has faced a major financial crisis that forced it
to give up its currency board arrangement and devalue its currency in 2002.

**The objectives of this chapter are to provide an understanding of current
capital markets in Latin America's three largest nations:**

° Argentina
° Brazil
° Mexico

MARKET OVERVIEW

Together, Argentina, Brazil, and Mexico have a population of about 300 million—larger than the population of the United States and about 60 percent of the total population in Latin America and the Caribbean. Despite their large populations and considerable resources, these three nations have experienced several financial crises in recent decades as well as periods of growth. In addition to the recurrent crises, another aspect of Latin American economic life that requires some general comments is the use of currency boards and dollarization.

Recurrent Crises and Recovery

Certainly, the crises of the 1990s were not the first problems Latin America had experienced. As Chapter 19 explained, the most important emerging market debt securities are Brady bonds, initially issued to solve a debt crisis that began in Latin America (although it eventually affected other regions as well). The source of the debt crisis was the rapid increase in the price of oil that occurred when the Organization of Petroleum Exporting Countries (OPEC) raised oil prices beginning in the early 1970s. As a result, the OPEC countries amassed a tremendous amount of U.S. dollars, which they deposited in Eurodollar accounts. By 1976, these deposits amounted to nearly $100 billion. Eurobanks faced a huge problem: They had to lend these funds in order to generate income to pay interest on the deposits. Less-developed countries, or LDCs, as they were called then, were eager to borrow to foster economic development and to pay for oil imports.

When OPEC raised the price of oil again in the late 1970s, however, the high prices caused both inflation and unemployment to increase in the industrialized nations. Interest rates also soared. The result was a global recession that led to a decline in the demand for commodities, which were major exports for most LDCs. Faced with both a loss in income from the decline in exports and higher interest rates, the LDCs found it impossible to service their debt obligations. On August 20, 1982, Mexico asked its creditor banks to forgive $68 billion in loans. Argentina, Brazil, and other LDCs soon followed suit. Although various attempts by those countries and creditor banks to restructure the debt were made during the 1980s, none succeeded until the issuance of Brady bonds as described in Chapter 19 (see Box 21.1 for an interesting side effect of the crisis; that is, the first debt-for-equity swaps).

The restructuring of debt under the Brady plan and the economic and financial reforms that accompanied it enabled Argentina, Brazil, and Mexico to achieve a certain degree of success in the early 1990s, as foreign investors poured billions of dollars into Latin American economies. As we saw in Chapter 19, however, the era of growth and confidence proved to be short. It was soon followed by a series of emerging market crises, starting with Mexico in 1994.

MARKETS IN ACTION Debt-for-Equity Swaps

21.1

An important side effect of the crisis was the emergence of the first debt-for-equity swaps. In the midst of the crisis, a secondary market developed for LDC debt securities at prices discounted significantly from their face value. Multinational corporations purchased many of the LDC loans to engage in debt-for-equity swaps. Creditor banks would sell their loans for U.S. dollars at discounts to multinational corporations that wanted to make equity investments in subsidiaries or local firms in the debtor countries. The central bank of the relevant LDC would then buy the bank debt

from the corporation at a smaller discount than the corporation had paid, but in local currency. The corporation would then use the local currency to make investments in the debtor country. As an example, Volkswagen paid $170 million for $283 million face value of Mexican debt. The company then resold the debt to the Mexican central bank for the equivalent of $260 million in Mexican pesos. Figure 21.1 depicts a debt-for-equity swap program.

Sources: ARBI Transnational (San Francisco, CA) and Bradynet, Inc. (Miami, FL).

FIGURE 21.1 | *Debt-for-Equity Swap*

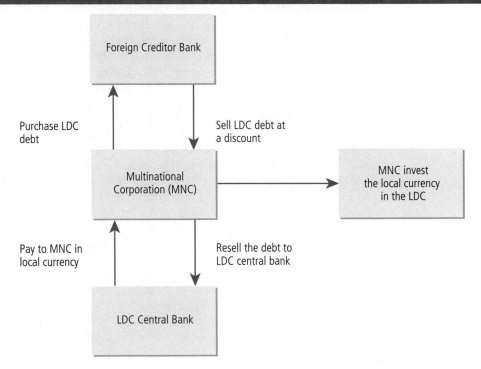

By 2000, recovery was under way in most Latin American countries, but its pace varied from country to country. Brazil's swift policy response to its currency crisis in 1999 stopped speculative capital outflows and enabled it to achieve economic recovery. Mexico's tight fiscal policy and flexible foreign exchange regime reassured external creditors and spurred growth. However, declining commodity prices, trade shocks triggered by Brazil's 1999 currency crisis, and reduced access to private financing hurt Argentina. Its problems culminated in 2001 and 2002 when it had to devalue its currency.

Overall, however, the market reforms and liberalization that began in the 1990s have made Latin American economies more resilient. Nonetheless, private capital inflows remain well below their peaks of the early 1990s. Only the strongest firms have access to international credit markets. Domestic long-term financing for midsize and small firms is virtually nonexistent. This lack of credit has created an unprecedented demand for multilateral development banks such as the International Finance Corporation (**http://www.ifc.org**) to provide financing for the private sector.

Currency Boards and Dollarization

As mentioned earlier, Argentina used a currency board arrangement to peg its currency to the U.S. dollar between 1991 and 2001. In the beginning of 2002, the Argentine peso started to lose its value. By early 2003, it had lost 70 percent of its value against the U.S. dollar. Although Argentina's experience with a currency board will be discussed in detail later, some general comments on currency boards may be useful at the outset. Under a **currency board** arrangement, a country sets its currency at par with another nation's currency, with the monetary base (the currency in circulation plus reserves in banks and other depository institutions) backed by reserves of the pegged foreign currency. The monetary base can expand only if reserves increase as a result of the nation running a balance of payment surplus. In that event, the expansion of the monetary base keeps the exchange rate fixed. Hence, market mechanism fully determines the interest rate. In fact, interest rates will follow those of the country of the pegged currency. The advantage of a currency board is that it stabilizes the nation's currency by imposing discipline on its rate of money creation. Hence, inflation should remain low. The disadvantage, of course, is that it makes the country dependent on the policies of the country of the pegged currency —even when those policies may not be suitable for its own economy. In addition, since monetary policy is no longer an option, a country with a currency board can use only fiscal policy to influence its macroeconomy.

A currency board is unofficial dollarization (or "euroization," as the case may be; although we will use the term *dollarization* for convenience, note in Table 21.1 that other currencies, especially the euro, are also in use). Some countries have what might be called semiofficial dollarization, in which the

TABLE 21.1	*Currency Board and Dollarization: Select Countries*	
Country	**System Began**	**Currency System Based On**
Currency Board		
Argentina	1991	U.S. dollar
Bermuda	1915	U.S. dollar
Brunei	1952	Singapore dollar
Bosnia	1997	Deutsche mark
Bulgaria	1997	Deutsche mark
Cayman Islands	1972	U.S. dollar
Djibouti	1949	U.S. dollar
Estonia	1992	Deutsche mark
Falkland Islands	1899	British pound
Faroe Islands	1940	Danish krone
Gibraltar	1927	British pound
Hong Kong	1983	U.S. dollar
Lithuania	1994	U.S. dollar
Dollarization		
Cook Islands	1995	New Zealand dollar
Cyprus, Northern	1974	Turkish lira
Greenland	Before 1800	Danish krone
Guam	1898	U.S. dollar
Kiribati	1943	Australian dollar, own coins
Liechtenstein	1921	Swiss franc
Marshall Islands	1944	U.S. dollar
Micronesia	1944	U.S. dollar
Monaco	1865	euro
Nauru	1914	Australian dollar
Northern Mariana Islands	1944	U.S. dollar
Palau	1944	U.S. dollar
Panama	1904	U.S. dollar
Puerto Rico	1899	U.S. dollar
Saint Helena	1834	British pound
Salvador	2000	U.S. dollar
Samoa, American	1899	U.S. dollar
San Marino	1897	euro, own coins
Tuvalu	1892	Australian dollar, own coins
Vatican City	1929	euro, own coins
Virgin Islands, UK	1973	U.S. dollar
Virgin Islands, U.S.	1934	U.S. dollar

Sources: Z. Bogetic, "Official or full dollarization: Current experiences and issues," International Monetary Fund, 1999; S.H. Hanke and K. Schuler, "Currency boards for developing countries," working paper, 1999; J. Kahn, "U.S. and IMF welcome Salvador's adoption of dollar," *New York Times*, November 25, 2000.

foreign currency is legal tender, but plays a secondary role to the domestic currency in paying wages, taxes, and everyday expenses. Official or full **dollarization** occurs when a foreign currency has exclusive or predominant status as full legal tender. Thus, the foreign currency is used for all expenses, including government payments. If a domestic currency even exists, it plays only a secondary role. As of 2003, Ecuador was the largest country to dollarize.

The main benefit of official dollarization is the credibility the nation obtains. With this credibility comes lower inflation, faster growth, deeper financial markets, government budgetary discipline, and lower interest rates. At the same time, there are disadvantages. As with a currency board, a country that dollarizes or euroizes can no longer conduct an independent monetary policy but have to accept the monetary policy of the United States or the European Monetary Union. Another disadvantage is the loss of **seigniorage**, which is the profit that a country earns when it issues currency. Seigniorage is equal to the difference between the value of the currency and the cost of printing that currency. For example, a $100 bill is worth $100, but costs only 4 cents to print. Thus, the seigniorage is $99.96.

ARGENTINA

Argentina had a population of 37 million and a per capita GDP of US$8,781 in 2001. With its abundant fertile land and other natural resources, Argentina was one of the world's wealthiest countries in the early 1900s. Since then, however, political and economic instability has prevented the nation from fulfilling this early promise. From 1930 until the early 1980s, Argentina vacillated between democratic elections and military coups. The nation further tarnished its image in the 1970s and 1980s by the so-called dirty war between the government and political dissidents, which resulted in the death or disappearance of thousands of citizens. More controversy ensued in 1982 when Argentina unsuccessfully attempted to wrest control of the Falkland Islands from the British.

The Mexican crisis of 1994–1995 had strong spillover effects on Argentina. In the three months following the devaluation of the Mexican peso, the Central Bank of Argentina (**http://www.bcra.gov.ar**) sold more than one-third of its foreign exchange reserves. Argentina's stock market index, the Merval, plummeted 50 percent between December 19, 1994, and March 8, 1995. Argentine bond prices fell 36 percent, and the interest rate jumped from 11 percent to 19 percent during the same time period.[1] In an effort to mitigate these contagion effects and to convince the international capital markets that it would not devalue its currency (the peso), the Argentine government instituted the following policies:[2]

---

[1]Emmons (1996).

[2]For details, see Ganapolsky and Schmukler (1998).

- December 28, 1994: Reserve requirements on U.S. dollar deposits lowered to provide more liquidity to the banking industry.
- January 12, 1995: Reserve requirements on peso deposits lowered, because of concerns that depositors withdrew their money from banks to exchange pesos for U.S. dollars.
- January 12, 1995: In an effort to restore market confidence, the central bank dollarized peso deposits held by financial institutions. The idea was to show that the central bank would have no incentive to devalue the peso.
- January 12, 1995: The central bank established a fund to purchase troubled financial institutions' nonperforming loans.
- March 10, 1995: The central bank allowed banks to use 50 percent of their cash as reserve requirements.
- March 28, 1995: A fund was set up to provide additional credit to troubled banks.
- April 4, 1995: The central bank established a deposit insurance system. The insurance covers up to $10,000 per person for all deposits up to 90 days and an additional $10,000 per person for time deposits of more than 90 days.

These measures succeeded in averting devaluation in 1995, and economic recovery was strong in the following two years, reaching almost 9 percent growth in 1997. After slowing to a 3.9 percent growth in 1998, the economy contracted for the subsequent three years. The recession began in the fourth quarter of 1998, following the Russian crisis. Brazil's devaluation of the real in early 1999 significantly affected Argentina's price competitiveness with neighboring nations. The continued difficulties forced its central bank to devalue the peso in 2002.

Stock Market

The **Buenos Aires Stock Exchange (BASE, http://www.merval.sba .com.ar)** is the major stock market in Argentina. The BASE, founded in 1854, was the first exchange in Latin America. A self-regulatory organization, called Mercados de Valores, regulates the activities of brokers and brokerage firms.

Individuals and entities residing in Argentina and, with certain limits, pension funds and mutual funds can invest in foreign securities as well. To provide Argentine investors more opportunities to build diversified portfolios, the government allows the issuance of Argentine depositary receipts, known as Cedears. **Cedears** are depositary receipts representing a class of shares or other securities of foreign companies in Argentina. They are similar to the American depositary receipts discussed in Chapter 12.

Stocks trade via a Concurrence Market, where trades occur on screen or in the traditional open outcry mode on the floor of the exchange. Share transactions normally settle on T+3. Forward transactions settle according to the contractual agreement between the parties, but cannot exceed 120 days. The exchange guarantees that the securities sold will be delivered only if the counterparty to the transaction has made the corresponding payment and that the payment will be effected only if the seller has delivered the securities—a practice called delivery-versus-payment. The seller has the option to authorize Merval (Mercado de Valores de Buenos Aires) to deliver the relevant securities without payment. For short sales, the short sellers can hold the position for up to 365 days. Merval may suspend new short sales at any moment.

Fixed-Income Market

In addition to the Concurrence Market, brokers and dealers may trade corporate and government bonds on the Continuous Trading Session for their own accounts or on behalf of customers. Merval guarantees the settlement of all trades executed in the Concurrence Market. Trades over the Continuous Trading Session can be with or without Merval's settlement guarantee.

Unlike the open outcry, the best-offer rule does not apply in the Continuous Trading Session, and trader's compensation as well as stock exchange fees are implicit in the agreed-on price. Fixed-income trades also settle T+3.

BRAZIL

Brazil is the fifth largest country in the world with a population of more than 170 million. The two major urban centers are Sao Paolo and Rio de Janeiro, with populations of 17 million and 11 million, respectively. The per capita GDP in 2001 was $2,923 (see Table 21.2 for the recent trends in GDP).

During the 1980s and early 1990s, chronic inflation plagued Brazil, though it was curbed to a large extent when the government adopted a new currency,

TABLE 21.2	*Brazil's Per Capita GDP*	
	Year	Per Capita GDP (U.S. dollars)
	1990	3,180
	1991	2,706
	1992	2,544
	1993	2,781
	1994	3,464
	1995	4,436
	1996	4,809
	1997	4,942
	1998	4,755
	1999	3,163
	2000	3,493
	2001	2,923

Source: Banco Central de Brazil.

the **real**, in 1994. Under the Real Plan (see Chapter 19), the government allowed the currency to appreciate and eliminated indexation, which had been widespread throughout the economy. The plan succeeded in its goal of achieving a rapid and sustained decrease in inflation. From 1980 to 1993, the average annual rate of inflation was about 450 percent, and it had reached more than 5,100 percent in June 1994 when the government launched the plan. By the end of 1995, inflation had dropped to 22 percent. Since 1995, it has remained much lower than the 1995 level. In 2002, it was about 10 percent.

As we saw in Chapter 19, Brazil experienced a major currency crisis in 1999, when it had to give up its efforts to maintain the real within a wide band. Since then, the real has floated freely. By February 2003, it had depreciated to 3.50 against the U.S. dollar; the exchange rate at the end of 1999 after the real was devalued had been 1.79.

Foreign portfolio investment in Brazil reflects the ups and downs of the economy. Outflows exceeded inflows in 1998 when investors anticipated the currency crisis that eventually materialized. The decline in inflows in 2002 reflects investors' concerns about the election of Lula da Silva as president. Under the Foreign Capital Law, foreign investments must be registered with the Central Bank of Brazil (**http://www.bcb.gov.br**). The registration forms the basis for future remittances abroad of cash dividends, capital gains, and repatriation of the investments. Since 1991, foreign institutional investors could invest directly in stocks, convertible debentures, and derivatives for hedge purposes. Since April 2000, foreign individual investors could invest in stocks, fixed-income securities, and derivatives, and can switch from one kind of instrument to another without any restrictions.

Stock Market

Brazil has several exchanges, but almost all equity trading takes place at the Bolsa de Valores de Sao Paolo (Bovespa, **http://www.bovespa.com.br**). The other exchanges have integrated to form the National Trading Electronic System, of which the Rio de Janeiro Stock Exchange is the hub. Since the restructuring of the Brazilian securities market in 2000, the Bovespa has been exclusively responsible for stock transactions, and the Rio de Janeiro exchange has had responsibility for government bond transactions. The Brazilian Clearing and Depository Corporation handles all clearing, settlement, and custody.

Trades at the Bovespa occur on the trading floor and via the electronic trading system. The electronic trading system (MEGA BOLSA) operates from 11:00 A.M. to 5:00 P.M. A preopening fixing occurs from 10:45 A.M. to 11:00 A.M. to set the opening price. The aftermarket trading session is exclusively for the electronic trading system and is from 5:45 P.M. to 7:00 P.M.

The Bovespa has also introduced trading through the Internet, called **Home Broker**. Investors can use Home Broker to place orders for immediate or programmed execution and to access their portfolio positions, market information, and price quotes. Investors can find a link to the brokerage house that trades through this mechanism at the Bovespa's Web site.

Starting December 2000, shares of companies that have adopted more stringent governance practices and disclosure requirements than those already required by Brazilian law trade under the Bovespa's New Market program. To qualify for the program, a company must meet the following requirements:

○   Only voting shares are listed.

○   The company has a minimum free float of 25 percent of total capital.

○   Any rights provided to majority shareholders in the event of the sale of the company will be extended to all shareholders.

○   Financial statements adhere to U.S. generally accepted accounting principles (GAAP) or International Accounting Standards.

○   The company must institute a lock-up period of six months before original shareholders can sell their shares.

○   The company must give shareholders a minimum 15-day notice when it calls a shareholders' meeting, instead of the 8 days required by Brazilian corporate law.

As mentioned, the Brazilian Clearing and Depository Corporation has responsibility for the clearance and settlement of trades executed in the cash, options, and forward markets. Settlement is a rolling cycle of three business days. The delivery of securities takes place on $T+2$, whereas payment occurs on $T+3$. Thus, the delivery-versus-payment system is not used. Table 21.3 summarizes the settlement cycle.

Fixed-Income Market

The fixed-income market in Brazil consists of both corporate and government securities. The public debt market includes central bank bonds and notes; national treasury bills, notes, and bonds; and privatization currency bonds. Private sector instruments include bank deposit certificates, bank deposit receipts,

TABLE 21.3	*Bovespa Settlement Summary*	
Date	**Action**
T+0	Trade date; last day for allocating trades among beneficial owners for options and forwards; last day for collateralizing positions in options and forward markets in other eligible assets different from cash.
T+1	Last day for trade allocation to the beneficial owner in the cash market; last day for providing cash collateral and margin requirements for options and forward markets.
T+2	Delivery of securities; at night, the Brazilian Clearing and Depository Corporation (CBLC) debits the shares from the seller's account and credits to the buyer's account. The securities remain blocked until the payment becomes final on T+3.
T+3	Last day for payment to CBLC; cash collateral charged to defaulters.
T+4	Last day for the clearing agent of the selling counterparty to provide for delivery, if securities have not been delivered on T+2.

Source: Sao Paolo Stock Exchange.

interbank certificates of deposit, corporate debentures, and Eurobonds. Table 21.4 provides a description of these instruments.

The central bank has taken several steps to improve liquidity in the domestic bond market. These measures include extending maturity and facilitating the replacement of floating-rate by fixed-rate instruments. Other important changes in recent years include concentrating maturity dates, permitting banks to maintain short positions, and introducing derivative instruments.

Mercosul

Brazil is one of the founding members of the Mercosul (or Mercosur in Spanish). **Mercosul** is a free trade association that Brazil, Argentina, Paraguay, and Uruguay established through the Treaty of Assuncion on March 26, 1991. The Mercosul is the fourth largest economic unit in the world, behind only the North America Free Trade Agreement (NAFTA) countries, the European Monetary Union, and Japan.

Mercosul's objective is to eliminate tariffs and other trade barriers among members. About 95 percent of all such trade is now tariff-free. The association also hopes to eliminate trade barriers between other Latin American nations. To that end, it admitted Chile as an associate member in 1996 and Bolivia in 1997. Free trade agreements and preferential arrangements are under negotiation with other countries.

TABLE 21.4	*Public and Private Debt in Brazil*
Public Debt	
Central bank bonds (Bonus do Banco Central, BBCs)	Discounted; 35- to 56-day maturity
Central bank notes (Notas do Banco Central, NBCs)	Issued as a monetary policy tool; 6- to 12-month maturity
National treasury bills (Letra do Tesouro Nacional, LTNs)	Discounted; 182-day maturity
National treasury notes (Notas do Tesouro Nacional, NTNs)	Floating or fixed rate; 90-day to 12-month maturity
National treasury bonds (Bonus do Tesouro Nacional, BTNs)	Fixed rate; up to 25-year maturity
Privatization currency bonds	Denominated in foreign currency and discounted. These are the restructured debt of a state-owned company. Investors receive company shares at redemption.
Private Debt	
Bank deposit certificates (CDBs)	Fixed or variable rate; minimum maturity of 30 days
Bank deposit receipts (RDBs)	Fixed or variable rate; minimum maturity of 120 days
Interbank certificates of deposits (CDIs)	Used as collateral for financial institutions' trading operations
Corporate debentures	Floating rate; maturity of at least 1 year
Eurobonds	Issued in foreign currencies outside Brazil

Sources: Banco Central de Brazil and Rio de Janeiro Stock Exchange.

MEXICO

Mexico had a population of 101 million and a per capita GDP of $8,454 in 2001. Like the other emerging markets we have examined, Mexico has had a turbulent economic history in recent decades. Periods of growth and reform have all too often been followed by financial crises and currency devaluations. Nonetheless, in the early 2000s, observers were cautiously optimistic about Mexico. The free market reforms and deregulation that had taken place over the last decade appeared to be having an effect.

The cycle of growth and crisis goes back to at least the 1980s. In 1987, for example, a sharp stock market decline led to a devaluation of Mexico's peso. Following the devaluation, the Mexican government tried to peg the peso at the new lower exchange rate and introduced a new program of stabilization and reform. The introduction of the **Pecto program** fostered macroeconomic stabilization. Under the program, wage bargaining and price setting were co-ordinated to support the overall macroeconomic strategy. As part of the Pecto, the peso exchange rate against the dollar crawled down slowly. Inflation slowly abated as the Pecto successfully reduced inflationary expectations.

The government started to deregulate the banking sector in 1988. The government gradually lifted and eventually abolished restrictions on the convertibility of the peso into foreign exchange, on both current and capital accounts (see Chapter 20 for an explanation of these terms). In 1989, the government abolished rules that forced the banks to finance the government and to lend to politically favored sectors. In addition, the government took steps to privatize commercial banks.

By the early 1990s, these reforms and the successful restructuring of Mexico's debt as Brady bonds had led to an economic recovery and inflow of foreign capital. Eventually, the inflow of capital exceeded the demands of the Mexican economy. Hence, the central bank, **Banco de Mexico (http:// www.banxico.org.mx)**, built up its stock of foreign exchange reserves. Since late 1992, the peso's exchange rate against the dollar had been quite stable. At the same time, even though Mexico's inflation rate had been reduced, it was still higher than the low levels of inflation in the United States. Thus, the stable exchange rate actually implied an appreciation in real terms. The prices of Mexican goods rose when converted into dollars. Hence, there was built-in pressure for the peso to depreciate. As we saw in Chapter 19, when Mexico encountered severe political and economic problems in 1994, a crisis ensued that culminated in the devaluation of the peso and a $50 billion international rescue package for Mexico.

In 2000, the Mexican economy was strong. Increasing exports on strong U.S. demand, steady inflows of foreign investments averaging more than $10 billion per year, and expanded domestic spending amid record low unemployment and rising real wages all contributed to the strong showing. Although the slowdown in the U.S. economy in 2001 led to a decline in Mexican economy, Mexico's economic fundamentals have remained sound. Mexico is well prepared to participate in the global recovery in the next few years.

The Stock Market

Mexico has only one stock exchange, the **Mexican Stock Exchange** (Bolsa Mexicana de Valores, BMV; http://www.bmv.com.mx). Traditionally, banks, family groups, and other insiders dominated the financial system and market trading, but legislation and reforms enacted in 1975 opened the market to all investors.

The main purpose of the stock exchange is to provide the infrastructure and services necessary to effectively handle the processes of issuing, offering, and trading securities. All shares of Mexican companies must be registered. A Mexican company typically issues three series of stocks: series A shares, which can be purchased only by Mexican nationals; series B shares, which may be owned by foreign investors; and series C shares, which do not have voting rights.

Private companies raised more than $31 billion by issuing stocks in the early 1990s. About 200 of the largest Mexican companies have listed their shares on the exchange. After a public offering, investors buy and sell those securities through brokerage firms. Since January 11, 1999, trading has been conducted via an electronic trading system, the BMV-Sentra Equities System.

As at other exchanges, a lot is the minimum quantity of shares normally exchanged in a transaction. For the stock market, a lot is 1,000 shares. An odd lot is less than 1,000 shares. At the exchange, odd lots cannot be traded in short sales. A tick, expressed as a fraction of the market price or nominal value, is the minimum amount by which the unit price of each security may vary. The Mexican exchange has an up-tick or zero-tick rule for short sales; that is, a short sale can happen only if the price is one tick above or equal to the last price.

Securities trade during the trading session, which runs from 8:30 A.M. to 3:00 P.M. for stocks, debentures, mutual funds, and warrants. For other debt instruments, trading hours run from 8:30 A.M. to 2:30 P.M. Settlement takes place T+2. Deferred settlements require approval of the National Banking and Securities Commission.

There are several market indices. The broadest indicator of the overall performance of the Mexican stock exchange is the Price and Quotations Index (IPC). The sample used to calculate the IPC consists of issuers from various sectors of the economy. The Indice Mexico (INMEX) is an index weighted by market capitalization of the issuers included. In contrast to the IPC, the weighting of any stock may not exceed 10 percent at the start of each calculation period. In addition, there is a mid-cap index (IMC30) and several sectoral indices.

In July 1993, the exchange established a second tier market to attract medium-sized companies. In addition, the Mexican Derivatives Exchange (MexDer) began operation in December 1998.

The Fixed-Income Market

A variety of debt instruments trade on the exchange. The three main government securities are federal treasury certificates (Cetes), federal government development bonds (Bondes), and investment unit bonds (Udibonos). **Cetes** are credit certificates that oblige the Mexican federal government to pay the bearer the face value at maturity. The government uses the funds raised through Cetes to finance public spending and to control the amount of money circulating in the economy. **Bondes** are long-term debt securities issued to finance federal government projects. Interest is payable every 28 or 91 days. **Udibonos** are linked to inflation and backed by the Mexican federal government. Interest is payable every six months.

In the private sector, companies issue various types of corporate debt instruments. Banks issue promissory notes with interest payable at maturity and a maturity of no more than 360 days. Market conditions determine the interest rate. National credit institutions issue development bank bonds to raise funds for a period of up to three years. Bank Saving's Protection Institute issues bank savings protection bonds to fund the saver's assistance programs. Bank Saving's Protection Institute pays interest every 28 days. Assistance Trust to the Rescue of Highways in Concession issues promissory notes for the highway indemnity program. The maturity ranges from 5 to 15 years. The bond pays interest every 182 days and the government guarantees it. In addition, there are banker's acceptances and commercial paper.

Foreign Exchange

Since 1995, the central bank, Banco de Mexico, has allowed the peso to float freely (it has depreciated from about 6 pesos to a U.S. dollar in 1995 to about 11 pesos to a U.S. dollar in March 2003). The central bank publishes daily a dollar–peso exchange rate, called the interbank 24-hour sell rate, which is the de facto official rate for all tax and reporting purposes. Market demand and supply determine the exchange rate. Since 1996, the Banco de Mexico has conducted monthly auctions of contracts that allow credit institutions to acquire the right to sell a predetermined amount of dollars against pesos to the central bank. Banco de Mexico will buy dollars against pesos from the put option holder on any bank business day while the contract is in effect. But unlike a traditional option, there is no fixed strike price. If the credit institution exercises the contract, the strike is the fixing exchange rate that the central bank determines through a survey from the previous business day.

The Exchange Commission also conducts a dollar-selling scheme to help reduce the volatility of the Mexican peso. The central bank auctions $200 million daily among Mexican credit institutions at an exchange rate equal to the fixing rate determined on the previous day multiplied by 1.02. The auction is conducted in three sessions: from 9:00 A.M. to 9:15 A.M., from 11:00 A.M. to 11:15 A.M., and from 1:00 P.M. to 1:15 P.M.

There are no restrictions on domestic or foreign currency held locally by nonresidents. Corporations, but not individuals, may have bank accounts in dollars. There are no exchange controls on incoming equity capital. Since 1999, however, customs law requires that all individuals entering Mexico with more than $20,000 in currency or checks must declare the amount.

CONCLUDING SUMMARY

This chapter has provided an overview of the financial markets in the three largest countries in Latin America: Argentina, Brazil, and Mexico. All of these countries have experienced both periods of growth and financial crises in recent decades. The LDC debt crisis of the 1980s, which the issuance of Brady bonds eventually solved, started in Mexico in 1982 and eventually moved to affect Argentina and Brazil. Both Mexico and Brazil experienced severe currency crisis in the 1990s. Argentina escaped the crises of the 1990s, but experienced its own crisis in 2001 and 2002.

From 1991 to 2001, Argentina had a currency board in which the exchange rate was fixed at 1 peso against 1 U.S. dollar. Eventually, however, the currency became unstable, and Argentina had to devalue the peso. As of early 2003, its currency still suffered from the effect of the crisis.

Brazil is the largest economy in Latin America. The most significant reform in the 1990s was the Real Plan, which effectively put an end to the inflationary spiral that had plagued the country. At that time, Brazil adopted the real as the official currency. The real has depreciated from about 1 real per U.S. dollar in 1994 to 3.5 real per U.S. dollar in March 2003. Stock trading takes place on the Sao Paolo Stock Exchange and bond trading on the Rio de Janeiro Stock Exchange. In December 2000, the Sao Paolo Stock Exchange introduced the New Market program for companies that meet more stringent requirements. The government has recently taken steps to improve liquidity in the fixed-income market.

Mexico has largely recovered from the financial crisis of 1994–1995. Since 1995, the peso has been floating against the U.S. dollar, but the central bank publishes an official exchange rate daily for tax and reporting purposes. To curb excessive volatility in the foreign exchange market, the central bank sells put options that give holders the right to sell U.S. dollars to the central bank at a certain rate.

Key Terms

Banco de Mexico 504	Home Broker 501
Bondes 506	Mercosul 503
Buenos Aires Stock Exchange 499	Mexican Stock Exchange 505
Cedear 499	Pecto program 504
Cetes 506	real 501
currency board 496	seigniorage 498
dollarization 498	Udibonos 506

Review Questions

1. How did oil-exporting countries contribute to the debt crisis of the less-developed countries (LDCs) in the early 1980s?
2. Describe the debt-for-equity swaps used for LDC debt.

3. What is a currency board arrangement? What is dollarization? Discuss the advantages and disadvantages of dollarization.

4. Describe Brazil's Real Plan. What were its objectives?

5. What ways is Mercosul similar to the European Monetary Union? In what ways is it different?

6. In the early 1990s, the Mexican peso exchange rate was quite stable, but there was built-in pressure to depreciate. Why?

7. Mexico issued tesobonos to maintain the level of reserves as a buffer to capital outflows. Why did the issuance of the tesonobos contribute to the 1994–1995 currency crisis?

8. Banco de Mexico auctions put options that allow credit institutions to sell U.S. dollars to the central bank. How does this system work?

Select Bibliography

Adams, J.A., Jr. *Mexican Banking and Investment in Transition.* Westport, Conn.: Quorum Books, 1997.

Balino, T.J.T., and C. Enoch. *Currency Board Arrangements: Issues and Experiences.* Washington, D.C.: International Monetary Fund, 1997.

Berg, A., and E. Borensztein. "The pros and cons of full dollarization," IMF Working Paper, March 2000.

Bevilaqua, A.S., and M.G.P. Garcia. "Debt management in Brazil: Evaluation of the Real Plan and challenges ahead." Washington, D.C.: National Bureau of Economic Research, 2000.

Calvo, G.A., M. Goldstein, and E. Hochreiter. *Private Capital Flows to Emerging Markets After the Mexican Crisis.* Washington, D.C.: Institute for International Economics, 1996.

Emmons, W. "ENTel and the privatization of Argentine telecommunications," Boston, Mass.: Harvard Business School Publishing, April 1996.

Ganapolsky, E.J.J., and S.L. Schmukler. "Crisis management in capital markets: The impact of Argentine policy during the tequila effect," World Bank Economists' Forum, 1999, Vol. 1, pp. 1– 28.

Harwood, A., R.E. Litan, and M. Pomerleano, eds. *Financial Markets and Development: The Crisis in Emerging Markets.* Washington, D.C.: Brookings Institute, 1999.

Loser, C. M., and M. Guerguil. "The long road to financial stability," *Finance & Development,* v37n1, International Monetary Fund, 2000.

The Salomon Smith Barney Guide to World Equity Markets 2000, London: Euromoney plc., 2000.

Schmitt-Grobe, S., and M. Uribe. "Dollarization and seignorate: How much is at stake?" Unpublished paper, University of Pennsylvania, 1999.

Welch, J.H. *Capital Markets in the Development Process: The Case of Brazil.* Pittsburgh, Penn.: University of Pittsburgh Press, 1992.

APPENDIX A:
Online Resources by Category

CENTRAL BANKS

Banco de Mexico http://www.banxico.org.mx

Bank of England (BOE)
http://www.bankofengland.co.uk

Bank Indonesia http://www.bi.go.id

Bank of Japan (BOJ) http://www.boj.or.jp

Bank of Korea http://www.bok.or.kr

Bank Negara http://www.bnm.gov.my

Bank of Russia http://www.cbr.ru

Bank of Thailand http://www.bot.or.th

Central Bank of Argentina
http://www.bcra.gov.ar

Central Bank of Brazil http://www.bcb.gov.br

Central Bank of China (CBC)
http://www.cbc.gov.tw

European Central Bank (ECB)
http://www.ecb.int

Federal Reserve System
http://www.federalreserve.gov

Hong Kong Monetary Authority
http://www.info.gov.hk/hkma

Monetary Authority of Singapore
http://www.mas.gov.sg

BANKS

ABN AMRO http://www.abnamro.com

Asahi Bank http://www.asahibank.co.jp

Bank of New York http://www.bankofny.com

Bank of Tokyo-Mitsubishi http://www.btm.co.jp

Citibank http://www.citibank.com

Citigroup http://www.citigroupgcib.com

Daiwa Bank http://www.daiwabank.co.jp

Deutsche Bank http://www.db.com

E*Trade Bank http://www.etradebank.com

HSBC Holdings http://www.hsbc.com

J.P. Morgan Chase
http://www.jpmorganchase.com

Mizuho Holdings http://www.mizuho-fg.co.jp

NetBank http://www.netbank.com

Nikko Cordial http://www.nikko.co.jp

Nomura http://www.nomura.co.jp

Sumitomo Mitsui Banking Corp.
http://www.smbc.co.jp

UBS http://www.ubs.com

UFJ Bank http://www.ufjbank.co.jp

SECURITIES FIRMS

Ameritrade http://www.ameritrade.com

Charles Schwab http://www.schwab.com

Credit Suisse First Boston http://www.csfb.com

Daiwa Securities Group http://www.daiwa.co.jp

E*Trade http://www.etrade.com

Goldman Sachs http://www.gs.com

Merrill Lynch http://www.ml.com

Morgan Stanley http://www.morganstanley.com

Quick & Reilly http://www.quick-reilly.com

INSURANCE COMPANIES

Automobile Insurance Companies
Allstate Group http://www.allstate.com

American International Group
http://www.aig.com

Berkshire Hathaway
http://www.berkshirehathaway.com

Farmers Insurance Group
http://www.farmersinsurance.com

Hartford Insurance Group
http://www.thehartford.com

Liberty Mutual Insurance
http://www.libertymutual.com

Nationwide Group http://www.nationwide.com

State Farm Group http://www.statefarm.com

Life and Health Insurance Companies
Aetna, Inc. http://www.aetna.com

American General Group http://www.agg.com

Equitable Group http://www.equitable.com

Hartford Insurance Group
http://www.thehartford.com

John Hancock Group
http://www.johnhancock.com

Metropolitan Insurance

Nationwide Group http://www.nationwide.com

New York Life http://www.newyorklife.com

Northwestern Mutual Group
http://www.northwesternmutual.com

Prudential Insurance http://www.prudential.com

TIAA CREF http://www.tiaa-cref.org

Reinsurance Companies
American Re-Insurance Company
http://www.amre.com

Arch Reinsurance Company
http://www.riskcapre.com

AXA Reinsurance Company
http://www.axa.com

Chubb Re http://chubbre.com

CNA Re http://www.cnare.com

GeneralCologne Re http://www.gcr.com

PMA Reinsurance Corporation
http://www.pmare.com

PXRE Reinsurance Company
http://www.pxregroup.com

SCOR Reinsurance Company
http://www.scor.fr/us/index.asp

St. Paul Re http://www.stpaul.com

Swiss Reinsurance http://www.swissre.com

Toa Re Insurance Company of America
http://www.toare.com

Trenwick America Reinsurance Corporation
http://www.trenwick.com

Financial Insurance Companies:
ACA Financial Guaranty Corporation
http://www.aca-insurance.com

AMBAC http://www.ambac.com

AXA Re Finance S.A. http://www.axa-re.com

Financial Guaranty Insurance Company
http://www.fgic.com

Financial Security Assurance
http://www.fsa.com

MBIA http://www.mbia.com

XL Capital Assurance http://www.xlca.com

EXCHANGES

American Stock Exchange
http://www.amex.com

Bolsa de Valores de Sao Paulo (Bovespa)
http://www.bovespa.com.br

Buenos Aires Stock Exchange (BASE)
http://www.merval.sba.com.ar

Chicago Board of Trade http://www.cbot.com

Chicago Mercantile Exchange (CME)
http://www.cme.com

Deutsche Boerse http://deutsche-boerse.com

Hong Kong Exchange (HKSE)
http://www.hkex.com.hk

Japanese Association of Securities Dealers
Automated Quotations (Jasdaq)
http://www.jasdaq.co.jp

Korea Stock Exchange (KSE)
http://www.kse.or.kr

Kosdaq http://www.kosdaq.or.kr

Kuala Lumpur Stock Exchange (KLSE)
http://www.klse.com.my

London International Financial Futures Exchange
http://www.liffe.com

London Stock Exchange
http://www.londonstockexchange.com

Luxembourg Stock Exchange
http://www.bourse.lu

MESDAQ http://www.klse.com.my

Mexican Stock Exchange (Bolsa Mexicana de
Valores, BMV) http://www.bmv.com.mx

Moscow Central Stock Exchange (MCSE)
http://www.mse.ru

Nasdaq http://www.nasdaq.com

New York Stock Exchange
http://www.nyse.com

Osaka Securities Exchange http://www.ose.or.jp

Paris Bourse http://www.euronet.com/fr

Russian Trading System RTS http://www.rts.ru

Securities Exchange of Thailand (SET)
http://www.set.or.th/th/index.html

Shanghai Stock Exchange
http://www.sse.com.cn

Shenzhen Stock Exchange
http://www.sse.org.cn

Singapore Exchange (SGX)
http://www.ses.com.sg

Stock Exchange of Hong Kong
http://www.hkse.com.hk

Taiwan Stock Exchange (TSE)
http://www.tse.com.tw

Tokyo International Financial Futures Exchange
http://www.tiffe.or.jp

Tokyo Stock Exchange http://www.tse.or.jp

CLEARING FIRMS

Clearstream http://www.clearstream.com

Emerging Market Clearing Corporation
(EMCC) http://www.e-m-c-c.com

Euroclear http://www.euroclear.com

Fixed Income Clearing Corporation
http://www.ficc.com

GovPX http://www.govpx.com

The National Securities Clearing Corporation
(NSCC) http://www.nscc.com

ELECTRONIC COMMUNICATIONS NETWORKS

Archipelago http://www.tradearca.com

Attain http://www.dom-sec.com

BRUT http://www.ebrut.com

B-Trade http://www.bloombergtradebook.com

Instinet http://www.instinet.com

Island http://www.island.com

NextTrade http://www.nextrade.com

INDUSTRY ASSOCIATIONS

Bond Market Association
http://www.bondmarkets.com

Emerging Market Traders Association
http://www.emta.org

European Securitization Forum
http://www.europeansecuritization.com

Hedge Fund Association http://www.thehfa.com

Insurance Information Institute
http://www.iii.org

International Swaps and Derivatives Association
http://www.isda.org

Investment Company Institute
http://www.ici.org

MuniAuction Association of Financial Guaranty
Insurors http://www.afgi.org

Municipal Securities Ruling Board
http://ww1.msrb.org

National Association of Securities Dealers
(NASD) http://www.nasd.org

National Credit Union Administration
http://www.ncua.gov

Securities Industry Association
http://www.sia.com

RATING AGENCIES

FitchRatings http://www.fitchratings.com

Moody's http://www.moodys.com

Standard and Poor's
http://www.standardandpoors.com

GOVERNMENT AGENCIES

Association of Southeast Asian Nations (ASEAN)
http://www.asean.or.id

Bank for International Settlements
http://www.bis.org

Department of the Treasury, Bureau of Public
Debt http://www.publicdebt.treas.gov

European Commission
http://europa.eu.int/comm

Federal Deposit Insurance Corporation
http://www.fdic.gov

Federal Reserve Bank of New York
http://www.ny.frb.org

International Finance Corporation
http://www.ifc.org

International Monetary Fund
http://www.imf.org

Japan Deposit Insurance Corporation (DIC)
http://www.dic.go.jp

Ministry of Finance http://www.mof.go.jp

National Association of Insurance Commissioners
(NAIC) http://www.naic.org

National Information Center
http://www.ffiec.gov/nic

Social Security Administration
http://www.ssa.gov

Treasury Direct
http://www.publicdebt.treas.gov/sec/sectdes.
htm

World Bank http://www.worldbank.org

World Trade Organization (WTO)
http://www.wto.org

OTHER INSTITUTIONS

Asset-Backed Alert http://www.abalert.com

Bloomberg http://www.bloomberg.com

Bonds Online http://www.bondsonline.com

Electronic Municipal Statistics (E-Muni)
http://www.emuni.com

Euromoney http://www.euromoney.com

Financial Times http://www.ft.com

GMAC SmartNotes
http://www.gmacfs.com/notes/smart/
prospectus.htm

Institutional Investor
http://www.iimagazine.com

Investors Network http://www.investornet.com

J. J. Kenny http://www.jjkenny.com

Lipper, Inc. http://www.lipperweb.com

Morgan Guaranty http://www.jpmorgan.com

Morningstar http://www.morningstar.com

Mutual Fund Investor Guide
http://www.investorguide.com

Mutual Fund Investor's Center
http://www.mfea.com

Oxera http://www.oxera.co.uk

Standard & Poor's Blue List http://bluelist.com

Thomson Municipal Market Monitor
   http://www.tm3.com

Value Line Mutual Fund Survey
   http://www.valueline.com

Van Hedge Fund Advisors
   http://hedgefund.com

Vcapital http://www.vcapital.com

VentureOne http://www.ventureone.com

Vfinance http://www.vfinance.com

Wall Street Analytics http://www.wsainc.com

APPENDIX B: SEC Form S-1

UNITED STATES
SECURITIES AND EXCHANGE COMMISSION
WASHINGTON, D.C. 20549

FORM S-1

REGISTRATION STATEMENT UNDER THE SECURITIES ACT OF

_____
(Exact name of registrant as specified in its charter)

_____
(State or other jurisdiction of incorporation or organization)

_____
(Primary Standard Industrial Classification Code Number)

_____
(I.R.S. Employer Identification Number)

_____
(Address, including zip code, and telephone number, including area code, of registrant's principal executive offices)

_____
(Name, address, including zip code, and telephone number, including area code, of agent for service)

_____
Approximate date of commencement of proposed sale to the public

If any of the securities being registered on this Form are to be offered on a delayed or continuous basis pursuant to Rule 415 under the Securities Act, check the following box: ☐

If this Form is filed to register additional securities for an offering pursuant to Rule 462(b) under the Securities Act, check the following box and list the Securities Act registration statement number of the earlier effective registration statement for the same offering. ☐

If this Form is a post-effective amendment filed pursuant to Rule 462(c) under the Securities Act, check the following box and list the Securities Act registration statement number of the earlier effective registration statement for the same offering. ☐

If this Form is a post-effective amendment filed pursuant to Rule 462(d) under the Securities Act, check the following box and list the Securities Act registration statement number of the earlier effective registration statement for the same offering. ☐

If delivery of the prospectus is expected to be made pursuant to Rule 434, check the following box. ☐

Calculation of Registration Fee

Title of Each Class of Securities to be Registered	Amount to be Registered	Proposed Maximum Offering Price Per Unit	Proposed Maximum Aggregate Offering Price	Amount of Registration Fee

Note: Specific details relating to the fee calculation shall be furnished in notes to the table, including references to provisions of Rule 457 (§230.457 of this chapter) relied upon, if the basis of the calculation is not otherwise evident from the information presented in this table. If the filing fee is calculated pursuant to Rule 457(o) under the Securities Act,

SEC 870 (3-03)   **Persons who are to respond to the collection of information contained in this form are not required to respond unless the form displays a currently valid OMB control number.**

only the title of the class of securities to be registered, the proposed maximum aggregate offering price for that class of securities and the amount of registration fee need to appear in the Calculation of Registration Fee table. Any difference between the dollar amount of securities registered for such offerings and the dollar amount of securities sold may be carried forward on a future registration statement pursuant to Rule 429 under the Securities Act.

GENERAL INSTRUCTIONS

I. Eligibility Requirements for Use of Form S-1

This Form shall be used for the registration under the Securities Act of 1933 ("Securities Act") of securities of all registrants for which no other form is authorized or prescribed, except that this Form shall not be used for securities of foreign governments or political subdivisions thereof.

II. Application of General Rules and Regulations

A. Attention is directed to the General Rules and Regulations under the Securities Act, particularly those comprising Regulation C (17 CFR 230.400 to 230.494) thereunder. That Regulation contains general requirements regarding the preparation and filing of the registration statement.

B. Attention is directed to Regulation S-K (17 CFR Part 229) for the requirements applicable to the content of the non-financial statement portions of registration statements under the Securities Act. Where this Form directs the registrant to furnish information required by Regulation S-K and the item of Regulation S-K so provides, information need only be furnished to the extent appropriate.

III. Exchange Offers

If any of the securities being registered are to be offered in exchange for securities of any other issuer, the prospectus shall also include the information which would be required by Item 11 if the securities of such other issuer were registered on this Form. There shall also be included the information concerning such securities of such other issuer which would be called for by Item 9 if such securities were being registered. In connection with this instruction, reference is made to Rule 409.

IV. Roll-up Transactions

If the securities to be registered on this Form will be issued in a roll-up transaction as defined in Item 901(c) of Regulation S-K (17 CFR 229.901(c)), attention is directed to the requirements of Form S-4 applicable to roll-up transactions, including, but not limited to, General Instruction I.

V. Registration of Additional Securities

With respect to the registration of additional securities for an offering pursuant to Rule 462(b) under the Securities Act, the registrant may file a registration statement consisting only of the following: the facing page; a statement that the contents of the earlier registration statement, identified by file number, are incorporated by reference; required opinions and consents; the signature page; and any price-related information omitted from the earlier registration statement in reliance on Rule 430A that the registrant chooses to include in the new registration statement. The information contained in such a Rule 462(b) registration statement shall be deemed to be a part of the earlier registration statement as of the date of effectiveness of the Rule 462(b) registration statement. Any opinion or consent required in the Rule 462(b) registration statement may be incorporated by reference from the earlier registration statement with respect to the offering, if: (i) such opinion or consent expressly provides for such incorporation; and (ii) such opinion relates to the securities registered pursuant to Rule 462(b). See Rule 411(c) and Rule 439(b) under the Securities Act.

PART 1—INFORMATION REQUIRED IN PROSPECTUS

Item 1.   Forepart of the Registration Statement and Outside Front Cover Page of Prospectus.

Set forth in the forepart of the registration statement and on the outside front cover page of the prospectus the information required by Item 501 of Regulation S-K (§229.501 of this chapter).

Item 2. Inside Front and Outside Back Cover Pages of Prospectus.

Set forth on the inside front cover page of the prospectus or, where permitted, on the outside back cover page, the information required by Item 502 of Regulation S-K (§229.502 of this chapter).

Item 3.   Summary Information, Risk Factors and Ratio of Earnings to Fixed Charges.

Furnish the information required by Item 503 of Regulation S-K (§229.503 of this chapter).

Item 4.   Use of Proceeds.

Furnish the information required by Item 504 of Regulation S-K (§229.504 of this chapter).

Item 5.   Determination of Offering Price.

Furnish the information required by Item 505 of Regulation S-K (§229.505 of this chapter).

Item 6.   Dilution.

Furnish the information required by Item 506 of Regulation S-K (§229.506 of this chapter).

Item 7.   Selling Security Holders.

Furnish the information required by Item 507 of Regulation S-K (§229.507 of this chapter).

Item 8.   Plan of Distribution.

Furnish the information required by Item 508 of Regulation S-K (§229.508 of this chapter).

Item 9.   Description of Securities to be Registered.

Furnish the information required by Item 202 of Regulation S-K (§229.202 of this chapter).

Item 10.   Interests of Named Experts and Counsel.

Furnish the information required by Item 509 of Regulation S-K (§229.509 of this chapter).

Item 11.   Information with Respect to Registrant.

Furnish the following information with respect to the registrant:

(a) Information required by Item 101 of Regulation S-K (§229.101 of this chapter), description of business;

(b) Information required by Item 102 of Regulation S-K (§229.102 of this chapter), description of property;

(c) Information required by Item 103 of Regulation S-K (§229.103 of this chapter), legal proceedings;

(d) Where common equity securities are being offered, information required by Item 201 of Regulation S-K (§229.201 of this chapter), market price of and dividends on the registrant's common equity and related stockholder matters;

(e) Financial statements meeting the requirements of Regulation S-X (17 CFR Part 210) (Schedules required under Regulation S-X shall be filed as "Financial Statement Schedules" pursuant to Item 16, Exhibits and Financial Statement Schedules, of this Form), as well as any financial information required by Rule 3-05 and Article 11 of Regulation S-X;

(f) Information required by Item 301 of Regulation S-K (§229.301 of this chapter), selected financial data;

(g) Information required by Item 302 of Regulation S-K (§229.302 of this chapter), supplementary financial information;

(h) Information required by Item 303 of Regulation S-K (§229.303 of this chapter), management's discussion and analysis of financial condition and results of operations;

(i) Information required by Item 304 of Regulation S-K (§229.304 of this chapter), changes in and disagreements with accountants on accounting and financial disclosure;

(j) Information required by Item 305 of Regulation S-K (§229.305 of this chapter), quantitative and qualitative disclosures about market risk;

(k) Information required by Item 401 of Regulation S-K (§229.401 of this chapter), directors and executive officers;

(l) Information required by Item 402 of Regulation S-K (§229.402 of this chapter), executive compensation;

(m) Information required by Item 403 of Regulation S-K (§229.403 of this chapter), security ownership of certain beneficial owners and management; and

(n) Information required by Item 404 of Regulation S-K (§229.404 of this chapter), certain relationships and related transactions.

Item 12.   Disclosure of Commission Position on Indemnification for Securities Act Liabilities.

Furnish the information required by Item 510 of Regulation S-K (§229.510 of this chapter).

PART II—INFORMATION NOT REQUIRED IN PROSPECTUS

Item 13.   Other Expenses of Issuance and Distribution.

Furnish the information required by Item 511 of Regulation S-K (§229.511 of this chapter).

Item 14.   Indemnification of Directors and Officers.

Furnish the information required by Item 702 of Regulation S-K (§229.702 of this chapter).

Item 15.   Recent Sales of Unregistered Securities.

Furnish the information required by Item 701 of Regulation S-K (§229.701 of this chapter).

Item 16.   Exhibits and Financial Statement Schedules.

(a) Subject to the rules regarding incorporation by reference, furnish the exhibits as required by Item 601 of Regulation S-K (§229.601 of this chapter).

(b) Furnish the financial statement schedules required by Regulation S-X (17 CFR Part 210) and Item 11(e) of this Form. These schedules shall be lettered or numbered in the manner described for exhibits in paragraph (a).

Item 17.   Undertakings.

Furnish the undertakings required by Item 512 of Regulation S-K (§229.512 of this chapter).

SIGNATURES

Pursuant to the requirements of the Securities Act of 1933, the registrant has duly caused this registration statement to be signed on its behalf by the undersigned, thereunto duly authorized, in the City of _____, State of _____, on _____, 20 _____ .

_____
(Registrant)

_____
By (Signature and Title)

Pursuant to the requirements of the Securities Act of 1933, this registration statement has been signed by the following persons in the capacities and on the dates indicated.

_____
(Signature)

_____
(Title)

_____
(Date)

Instructions.

1. The registration statement shall be signed by the registrant, its principal executive officer or officers, its principal financial officer, its controller or principal accounting officer and by at least a majority of the board of directors or persons performing similar functions. If the registrant is a foreign person, the registration statement shall also be signed by its authorized representative in the United States. Where the registrant is a limited partnership, the registration statement shall be signed by a majority of the board of directors of any corporate general partner signing the registration statement.

2. The name of each person who signs the registration statement shall be typed or printed beneath his signature. Any person who occupies more than one of the specified positions shall indicate each capacity in which he signs the registration statement. Attention is directed to Rule 402 concerning manual signatures and to Item 601 of Regulation S-K concerning signatures pursuant to powers of attorney.

INSTRUCTIONS AS TO SUMMARY PROSPECTUSES

1. A summary prospectus used pursuant to Rule 431 (§230.431 of this chapter), shall at the time of its use contain such of the information specified below as is then included in the registration statement. All other information and documents contained in the registration statement may be omitted.

    (a) As to Item 1, the aggregate offering price to the public, the aggregate underwriting discounts and commissions and the offering price per unit to the public;

    (b) As to Item 4, a brief statement of the principal purposes for which the proceeds are to be used;

    (c) As to Item 7, a statement as to the amount of the offering, if any, to be made for the account of security holders;

    (d) As to Item 8, the name of the managing underwriter or underwriters and a brief statement as to the nature of the underwriter's obligation to take the securities; if any securities to be registered are to be offered otherwise than through underwriters, a brief statement as to the manner of distribution; and, if securities are to be offered otherwise than for cash, a brief statement as to the general purposes of the distribution, the basis upon which the securities are to be offered, the amount of compensation and other expenses of distribution, and by whom they are to be borne;

    (e) As to Item 9, a brief statement as to dividend rights, voting rights, conversion rights, interest, maturity;

    (f) As to Item 11, a brief statement of the general character of the business done and intended to be done, the selected financial data (Item 301 of Regulation S-K (§229.301 of this chapter) and a brief statement of the nature and present status of any material pending legal proceedings; and

    (g) A tabular presentation of notes payable, long-term debt, deferred credits, minority interests, if material, and the equity section of the latest balance sheet filed, as may be appropriate.

2. The summary prospectus shall not contain a summary or condensation of any other required financial information except as provided above.

3. Where securities being registered are to be offered in exchange for securities of any other issuer, the summary prospectus also shall contain that information as to Items 9 and 11 specified in paragraphs (e) and (f) above which would be required if the securities of such other issuer were registered on this Form.

4. The Commission may, upon the request of the registrant, and where consistent with the protection of investors, permit the omission of any of the information herein required or the furnishing in substitution therefor of appropriate information of comparable character. The Commission may also require the inclusion of other information in addition to, or in substitution for, the information herein required in any case where such information is necessary or appropriate for the protection of investors.

APPENDIX C: SEC Form F-6

FORM F-6

REGISTRATION STATEMENT UNDER THE SECURITIES ACT OF 1933 FOR DEPOSITARY SHARES EVIDENCED BY AMERICAN DEPOSITARY RECEIPTS

_____
(Exact name of issuer of deposited securities as specified in its charter)

_____
(Translation of issuer's name into English)

_____
(Jurisdiction of incorporation or organization of issuer)

_____
(Exact name of depositary as specified in its charter)

_____
(Address, including zip code, and telephone number, including area code, of depositary's principal executive offices)

_____
(Address, including zip code, and telephone number, including area code, of agent for service)

It is proposed that this filing become effective under Rule 466
(check appropriate box)

☐ immediately upon filing

☐ on (Date) at (Time).

If a separate registration statement has been filed to register the deposited shares, check the following box. ☐

Calculation of Registration Fee

Title of Each Class of Securities to be Registered	Amount to be Registered	Proposed Maximum Aggregate Price Per Unit	Proposed Maximum Aggregate Offering Price	Amount of Registration Fee

GENERAL INSTRUCTIONS

I. **Eligibility Requirements for Use of Form F-6**

   A. *General.* Form F-6 may be used for the registration under the Securities Act of 1933 (the "Securities Act") of Depositary Shares evidenced by American Depositary Receipts ("ADRs") issued by a depositary against the deposit of the securities of a foreign issuer (regardless of the physical location of the certificates) if the following conditions are met:

   (1) The holder of the ADRs is entitled to withdraw the deposited securities at any time subject only to (i) temporary delays caused by closing transfer books of the depositary or the issuer of the deposited securities or the deposit of shares in connection with voting at a shareholders' meeting, or the payment of dividends, (ii) the payment of fees, taxes, and similar charges, and (iii) compliance with any laws or governmental regulations relating to ADRs or to the withdrawal of deposited securities;

   (2) The deposited securities are offered or sold in transactions registered under the Securities Act or in transactions that would be exempt therefrom if made in the United States; and

   (3) As of the filing date of this registration statement, the issuer of the deposited securities is reporting pursuant to the periodic reporting requirements of section 13(a) or 15(d) of the Securities Exchange Act of 1934 or the deposited securities are exempt therefrom by Rule 12g3-2(b) (§240.12g3-2(b) of this chapter) unless the issuer of the deposited securities concurrently files a registration statement on another form for the deposited securities.

   B. *Registration of Deposited Securities.* Form F-6 is available for registration of the Depositary Shares only. The registration of the deposited securities, if necessary, shall be on any other form the registrant is eligible to use. Alternatively, Depositary Shares may also be registered on any form used to register the deposited securities if such registration statement also conforms to the requirements of Parts I and II of Form F-6 and either the depositary or the legal entity created by the agreement for the issuance of ADRs signs the registration statement with respect to the disclosure and undertakings made in response to such requirements. The amount of fees charged need not be disclosed in the prospectus if the depositary makes and follows the undertakings in Item 4(c) and if the prospectus lists the various services for which fees may be charged, states that such fees may differ from those other depositaries charge, states that the fee schedule is available without charge from the depositary, and states that each registered holder of an ADR will receive thirty days notice of a change in the fee schedule.

II. **Amount of Securities; Filing Fee**

   An ADR evidences one or more Depositary Shares, as defined in Rule 405 (§230.405 of this chapter). The registration statement relates to Depositary Shares, not the number of physical certificates issued. For example, if an ADR is issued against a Depositary Share, which equals two common shares in a foreign issuer, the registration of 100,000 Depositary Shares represents 200,000 common shares. If the depositary issues a certificate for 10,000 Depositary Shares and another for 15,000 Depositary Shares, then 75,000 (100,000 minus 25,000) Depositary Shares (not 99,998) remain available for distribution undex the registration statement.

   Rule 457(k) (§230.457(k) of this chapter) describes the method of computing the filing fee.

III. **Application of General Rules and Regulations**

   A. Attention is directed to the General Rules and Regulations under the Securities Act, particularly Regulation C (§230.400 et seq. of this chapter). That Regulation contains general requirements regarding the preparation and filing of registration statements.

   B. The prospectus may consist of the ADR certificate if it includes the information required in Part I of this Form. Such prospectus need not conform to the requirements of Rule 420 (§240.420 of this chapter) except that the type shall be roman type at least as large as 5 1/2-point modern type.

   C. You must file the Form F-6 registration statement in electronic format via the Commission's Electronic Data Gathering, Analysis, and Retrieval (EDGAR) system in accordance with the EDGAR rules set forth in Regulation

S-T (17 CFR Part 232). For assistance with technical questions about EDGAR or to request an access code, call the EDGAR Filer Support Office at (202) 942-8900. For assistance with the EDGAR rules, call the Office of EDGAR and Information Analysis at (202) 942-2940.

If filing the registration statement in paper under a hardship exemption in Rule 201 or 202 of Regulation S-T (17 CFR 232.201 or 232.202), or as otherwise permitted, you must file the number of copies of the registration statement and of each amendment required by Securities Act Rules 402 and 472 (17 CFR 230.402 and 230.472), except that you need only file three additional copies instead of the ten referred to in Rule 402(b) (17 CFR 230.402(b)). You may also file only three additional copies instead of the eight referred to in Securities Act Rule 472(a) (17 CFR 230.472(a)).

PART I—INFORMATION REQUIRED IN PROSPECTUS

Item 1.   Description of Securities To Be Registered.

Furnish the information required by Item 12.E. of Form 20-F (§249.22 of this chapter).

Item 2.   Available Information.

State the information in either (a) or (b) below, whichever is applicable, and that the documents described therein can be inspected by holders of ADRs and copied at public reference facilities maintained by the Commission in Washington D.C.

(a) The foreign issuer furnishes the Commission with certain public reports and documents required by foreign law or otherwise under Rule 12g3-2(b) under the Securities Exchange Act of 1934.

(b) The foreign issuer is subject to the periodic reporting requirements of the Securities Exchange Act of 1934 and, accordingly, files certain reports with the Commission.

PART II—INFORMATION NOT REQUIRED IN PROSPECTUS

Item 3.   Exhibits.

Subject to the rules as to incorporation by reference, the exhibits specified below shall be filed as a part of the registration statement. Exhibits shall be appropriately lettered or numbered for convenient reference. Exhibits incorporated by reference may bear the designation given in the previous filing. Instruction 1 to Item 601 of Regulation S-K applies to this paragraph.

(a) A copy of the Deposit Agreement or Deposit Agreements under which the securities registered hereunder are issued. If the Deposit Agreement is amended during the offering of the Depositary Shares, such amendments shall be filed as amendments to the registration statement.

(b) Any other agreement, to which the depositary is a party relating to the issuance of the Depositary Shares registered hereby or the custody of the deposited securities represented thereby.

(c) Every material contract relating to the deposited securities between the depositary and the issuer of the deposited securities in effect at any time within the last three years.

(d) An opinion of counsel as to the legality of the securities being registered, indicating whether they will when sold be legally issued, and entitle the holders thereof to the rights specified therein.

(e) If the procedure in Rule 466 is being used, a certification in the following form:

Certification under Rule 466

The depositary, _____ represents and certifies the following:

(1) That it previously had filed a registration statement on Form F-6 (Name and File No.), which the Commission declared effective, with terms of deposit identical to the terms of deposit of this registration statement except for the number of foreign securities a Depositary Share represents.

(2) That is ability to designate the date and time of effectiveness under Rule 466 has not been suspended.

[Depositary] _____

By [Signature and Title] _____

Item 4. Undertakings.

Notwithstanding the provisions of Rule 415(a)(2) (§230.415(a)(2) of this chapter), the undertakings in Item 512(a) of Regulation S-K are not required. Furnish the following undertakings:

(a) The depositary hereby undertakes to make available at the principal office of the depositary in the United States, for inspection by holders of the ADRs, any reports and communications received from the Issuer of the deposited securities which are both (1) received by the depositary as the holder of the deposited securities; and (2) made generally available to the holders of the underlying securities by the issuer.

(b) If the amounts of fees charged are not disclosed in the prospectus, the depositary undertakes to prepare a separate document stating the amount of any fee charged and describing the service for which it is charged and to deliver promptly a copy of such fee schedule without charge to anyone upon request. The depositary undertakes to notify each registered holder of an ADR thirty days before any change in the fee schedule.

SIGNATURES

Pursuant to the requirements of the Securities Act of 1933, the registrant certifies that it has reasonable grounds to believe that all the requirements for filing on Form F-6 are met and has duly caused this registration statement to be signed on its behalf by the undersigned, thereunto duly authorized, in the City of _____

State of _____ on _____ , 20_____ .

[Legal entity created by the agreement
for the issuance of American Depositary Receipts for shares of _____

_____
By [Signature and Title]

[Registrant] _____

_____
By [Signature and Title]

Pursuant to the requirements of the Securities Act of 1933, this registration statement has been signed by the following persons in the capacities and on the dates indicated.

_____
[Signature]

_____
[Title]

_____
[Date]

Instructions.

1. The legal entity created by the agreement for the issuance of ADRs shall sign the registration statement as registrant. The depositary may sign on behalf of such entity, but the depositary for the issuance of ADRs itself shall not be deemed to be an issuer, a person signing the registration statement, or a person controlling such issuer. If the issuer of the deposited securities sponsors the ADR arrangement, the registration statement shall also be signed by the issuer and its principal executive officer or officers, its principal financial officer, its controller or principal accounting officer, at least a majority of the board of directors or persons performing similar functions, and its authorized representative in the United States.

2. The name of each person who signs the registration statement shall be typed or printed beneath his signature. Any person who occupies more than one of the specified positions shall indicate each capacity in which he signs the registration statement. Attention is directed to Rule 402 concerning manual signatures and Item 601 of Regulation S-K concerning signatures pursuant to powers of attorney.

APPENDIX D: SEC Form 20-F

UNITED STATES
SECURITIES AND EXCHANGE COMMISSION
WASHINGTON, D.C. 20549

FORM 20-F

OMB APPROVAL	
OMB Number:	3235-0288
Expires:	July 31, 2005
Estimated average burden hours per response 486.00	

(Mark One)

☐ REGISTRATION STATEMENT PURSUANT TO SECTION 12(b) OR (g) OF THE SECURITIES EXCHANGE ACT OF 1934

OR

☐ ANNUAL REPORT PURSUANT TO SECTION 13 OR 15(d) OF THE SECURITIES EXCHANGE ACT OF 1934

For the fiscal year ended _____

OR

☐ TRANSITION REPORT PURSUANT TO SECTION 13 OR 15(d) OF THE SECURITIES EXCHANGE ACT OF 1934

For the transition period from _____ to _____

Commission file number _____

_____
(Exact name of Registrant as specified in its charter)

_____
(Translation of Registrant's name into English)

_____
(Jurisdiction of incorporation or organization)

_____
(Address of principal executive offices)

Securities registered or to be registered pursuant to Section 12(b) of the Act.

Title of each class	Name of each exchange on which registered
_____	_____
_____	_____

Securities registered or to be registered pursuant to Section 12(g) of the Act.

_____
(Title of Class)

_____
(Title of Class)

Securities for which there is a reporting obligation pursuant to Section 15(d) of the Act.

_____
(Title of Class)

Indicate the number of outstanding shares of each of the issuer's classes of capital or common stock as of the close of the period covered by the annual report.   _____

_____

Indicate by check mark whether the registrant (1) has filed all reports required to be filed by Section 13 or 15(d) of the Securities Exchange Act of 1934 during the preceding 12 months (or for such shorter period that the registrant was required to file such reports), and (2) has been subject to such filing requirements for the past 90 days.

☐ Yes ☐ No

Indicate by check mark which financial statement item the registrant has elected to follow.

☐ Item 17 ☐ Item 18

(APPLICABLE ONLY TO ISSUERS INVOLVED IN BANKRUPTCY PROCEEDINGS DURING THE PAST FIVE YEARS)

Indicate by check mark whether the registrant has filed all documents and reports required to be filed by Sections 12, 13 or 15(d) of the Securities Exchange Act of 1934 subsequent to the distribution of securities under a plan confirmed by a court.   ☐ Yes ☐ No

GENERAL INSTRUCTIONS

A. Who May Use Form 20-F and When It Must Be Filed

(a) Any foreign private issuer may use this form as a registration statement under Section 12 of the Securities Exchange Act of 1934 (referred to as the Exchange Act) or as an annual or transition report filed under Section 13(a) or 15(d) of the Exchange Act. A transition report is filed when an issuer changes its fiscal year end. The term "foreign private issuer" is defined in Rule 3b-4 under the Exchange Act.

(b) A foreign private issuer must file its annual report on this Form within six months after the end of the fiscal year covered by the report.

(c) A foreign private issuer filing a transition report on this Form must file its report in accordance with the requirements set forth in Rule 13a-10 or Rule 15d-10 under the Exchange Act that apply when an issuer changes its fiscal year end.

B. General Rules and Regulations That Apply to This Form

(a) The General Rules and Regulations under the Securities Act of 1933 (referred to as the Securities Act) contain general requirements that apply to registration on any form. Read these general requirements carefully and follow them when preparing and filing registration statements and reports on this Form.

(b) Pay particular attention to Regulation 12B under the Exchange Act. Regulation 12B contains general requirements about matters such as the kind and size of paper to be used, the legibility of the registration statement or report, the information to give in response to a requirement to state the title of securities, the language to be used and the filing of the registration statement or report.

(c) In addition to the definitions in the General Rules and Regulations under the Securities Act and the definitions in Rule 12b-2 under the Exchange Act, General Instruction F defines certain terms for purposes of this Form.

(d) Note Regulation S-X, which applies to the presentation of financial information in a registration statement or report.

(e) Where the Form is being used as an annual report filed under Section 13(a) or 15(d) of the Exchange Act, provide the certification required by Rule 13a-14 (17 CFR 240.13a-14) or Rule 15d-14 (CFR 240.15d-14) exactly as specified in this form.

C. How To Prepare Registration Statements and Reports on This Form

(a) Do not use this Form as a blank form to be filled in; use it only as a guide in the preparation of the registration statement or annual report. General Instruction E states which items must be responded to in a registration statement and which items must be responded to in an annual report. The registration statement or report must contain the numbers and captions of all items. You may omit the text following each caption in this Form, which describes what must be disclosed under each item. Omit the text of all instructions in this Form. If an item is inapplicable or the answer to the item is in the negative, respond to the item by making a statement to that effect.

(b) Unless an item directs you to provide information as of a specific date or for a specific period, give the information in a registration statement as of a date reasonably close to the date of filing the registration statement and give the information in an annual report as of the latest practicable date.

(c) Note Exchange Act Rule 12b-20, which states: "In addition to the information expressly required to be included in a statement or report, there shall be added such further material information, if any, as may be necessary to make the required statements, in light of the circumstances under which they are made, not misleading."

(d) If the same information required by this Form also is required by the body of accounting principles used in preparing the financial statements, you may respond to an item of this Form by providing a cross-reference to the location of the information in the financial statements, in lieu of repeating the information.

(e) Note Item 10 of Regulation S-K which explains the Commission policy on projections of future economic performance, the Commission's policy on securities ratings, and the Commission's policy on use of non-GAAP financial measures in Commission filings.

(f) If you are providing the information required by this Form in connection with a registration statement under the Securities Act, note that Rule 421 requires you to follow plain English drafting principles. You can find helpful information in "A Plain English Handbook—How to create clear SEC disclosure documents" and in staff legal bulletins supplementing the Handbook. These documents are available on our Internet website, at www.sec.gov.

D. How To File Registration Statements and Reports on This Form

(a) You must file the Form 20-F registration statement or annual report in electronic format via our Electronic Data Gathering and Retrieval System (EDGAR) in accordance with the EDGAR rules set forth in Regulation S-T (17 CFR Part 232). The Form 20-F registration statement or annual report must be in the English language as required by Regulation S-T Rule 306 (17 CFR 232.306). You must provide the signatures required for the Form 20-F registration statement or annual report in accordance with Regulation S-T Rule 302 (17 CFR 232.302). If you have technical questions about EDGAR or want to request an access code, call the EDGAR Filer Support Office at (202) 942-8900. If you have questions about the EDGAR rules, call the Office of EDGAR and Information Analysis at (202) 942-2940.

(b) If you are filing the Form 20-F registration statement or annual report in paper under a hardship exemption in Rule 201 or 202 of Regulation S-T (17 CFR 232.201 or 232.202), or as otherwise permitted, you must file with the Commission (i) three complete copies of the registration statement or report, including financial statements, exhibits and all other papers and documents filed as part of the registration statement or report, and (ii) five additional copies of the registration statement or report, which need not contain exhibits. Whether filing electronically or in paper, you must also file at least one complete copy of the registration statement or report, including financial statements, exhibits and all other papers and documents filed as part of the registration statement or report, with each exchange on which any class of securities is or will be registered. When submitting the Form 20-F in paper, you must sign at least one complete copy of the registration statement or report filed with the Commission and one copy filed with each exchange in accordance with Exchange Act Rule 12b-11(d) (17 CFR 12b-11(d)). You must conform the unsigned copies when submitting the Form 20-F registration statement or report in paper. When submitting the Form 20-F in electronic format to the Commission, you may submit a paper copy containing typed signatures to each United States stock exchange in accordance with Regulation S-T Rule 302(c) (17 CFR 302(c)). See also Exchange Act Rule 12b-12(d) and Form 20-F's Instructions as to Exhibits for requirements concerning use of the English language and treatment of foreign language documents.

(c) When registration statements and reports are permitted to be filed in paper, they are filed with the Commission by sending or delivering them to our File Desk between the hours of 9 a.m. and 5:30 p.m., Washington, DC time. The File Desk is closed on weekends and federal holidays. If you file a paper registration statement or report by mail or by any means other than hand delivery, the address is U.S. Securities and Exchange Commission, Attention: File Desk, 450 Fifth Street, NW., Washington, DC 20549. We consider documents to be filed on the date our File Desk receives them.

E. **Which Items To Respond to in Registration Statements and Annual Reports**

   (a) *Exchange Act Registration Statements.* A registration statement filed under the Exchange Act on this Form must include the information specified in Part I and Part III. Read the instructions to each item carefully before responding to the item. In some cases, the instructions may permit you to omit some of the information specified in certain items in Part I.

   (b) *Annual Reports.* An annual report on this Form must include the information specified in Parts I, II and III. Read the instructions to each item carefully before responding to the item. In some cases, the instructions may permit you to omit some of the information specified in certain items in Part I. The instructions also may permit you to omit certain information if it was previously reported to us and has not changed. If that is the case, you do not have to file copies of the previous report with the report being filed on this Form.

   (c) *Financial Statements.* An Exchange Act registration statement or annual report filed on this Form must contain the financial statements and related information specified in Item 17 of this Form. We encourage you to provide the financial statements and related information specified in Item 18 of this Form in lieu of Item 17, but the Item 18 statements and information are not required. In certain circumstances, Forms F-2, F-3 or F-4 for the registration of securities under the Securities Act require that you provide the financial statements and related information specified in Item 18 in your annual report on Form 20-F. Consult those Securities Act forms for the specific requirements and consider the potential advantages of complying with Item 18 instead of Item 17 of this Form. Note that Items 17 and 18 may require you to file financial statements of other entities in certain circumstances. These circumstances are described in Regulation S-X.

   The financial statements must be audited in accordance with U.S. generally accepted auditing standards, and the auditor must comply with the U.S. standards for auditor independence. If you have any questions about these requirements, contact the Office of Chief Accountant in the Division of Corporation Finance at (202) 942-2960.

   (d) *Securities Act Registration Statements.* The registration statement forms under the Securities Act direct you to provide information required by specific items of Form 20-F. Some items of Form 20-F only apply to Securities Act registration statements, and you do not have to respond to those items if you are using Form 20-F to file an Exchange Act registration statement or an annual report. The instructions to the items of Form 20-F identify which information is required only in Securities Act registration statements.

F. **Definitions**

The following definitions apply to various terms used in this Form, unless the context indicates otherwise.

Affiliate—An "affiliate" of a specified person or entity refers to one who, directly or indirectly, either controls, is controlled by or is under common control with, the specified person or entity.

Beneficial owner—The term "beneficial owner" of securities refers to any person who, even if not the record owner of the securities, has or shares the underlying benefits of ownership. These benefits include the power to direct the voting or the disposition of the securities or to receive the economic benefit of ownership of the securities. A person also is considered to be the "beneficial owner" of securities that the person has the right to acquire within 60 days by option or other agreement. Beneficial owners include persons who hold their securities through one or more trustees, brokers, agents, legal representatives or other intermediaries, or through companies in which they have a "controlling interest," which means the direct or indirect power to direct the management and policies of the entity.

Company—References to the "company" mean the company whose securities are being offered or listed, and refer to the company on a consolidated basis unless the context indicates otherwise.

Directors and senior management—This term includes (a) the company's directors, (b) members of its administrative, supervisory or management bodies, (c) partners with unlimited liability, in the case of a limited partnership with share capital, (d) nominees to serve in any of the aforementioned positions, and (e) founders, if the company has been established for fewer than five years. The persons covered by the term "administrative, supervisory or management bodies" vary in different countries and, for purposes of complying with the disclosure standards, will be determined by the host country.

Document—This term covers prospectuses and offering documents used in connection with a public offering of securities and registration statements or prospectuses used in connection with the initial listing of securities.

> *Instruction: References to the "document" mean whatever type of document is being prepared using Form 20-F disclosure requirements, including, as applicable, a prospectus, an Exchange Act registration statement, and an annual report.*

Equity securities—The term "equity securities" includes common or ordinary shares, preferred or preference shares, options or warrants to subscribe for equity securities, and any securities, other than debt securities, which are convertible into or exercisable or redeemable for equity securities of the same company or another company. If the equity securities available upon conversion, exercise or redemption are those of another company, the disclosure standards also apply to the other company.

Group—A "group" is a parent and all its subsidiaries. References to a company's group mean the group of which it is a member.

Home country—This term refers to the jurisdiction in which the company is legally organized, incorporated or established and, if different, the jurisdiction where it has its principal listing.

Host country—This term refers to jurisdictions, other than the home country, in which the company is seeking to offer, register or list its securities.

> *Instruction: Note that, as used in this Form, the term "host country" means the United States and its territories.*

Pre-emptive issue—The term "pre-emptive issue" and references to "pre-emptive purchase rights" refer to offerings made to the company's existing shareholders in order to permit them to maintain their pro rata ownership in the company.

PART I

Item 1. Identity of Directors, Senior Management and Advisers

The purpose of this standard is to identify the company representatives and other individuals involved in the company's listing or registration.

A. *Directors and senior management.* Provide the names, business addresses and functions of the company's directors and senior management.

B. *Advisers.* Provide the names and addresses of the company's principal bankers and legal advisers to the extent the company has a continuing relationship with such entities, the sponsor for listing (where required by the host country regulations), and the legal advisers to the issue.

C. *Auditors.* Provide the names and addresses of the company's auditors for the preceding three years (together with their membership in a professional body).

Instructions to Item 1: If you are filing Form 20-F as an annual report under the Exchange Act, you do not have to provide the information called for by Item 1. You must provide this information, to the extent applicable, if you are filing a registration statement under either the Securities Act or the Exchange Act.

Instructions to Item 1.B: You only have to provide the information called for by Item 1.B if you are required to disclose the information in a jurisdiction outside the United States. These persons will not be considered "experts" or "sellers" under the Securities Act solely due to the fact that they are named in response to Item 1.B.

Item 2. Offer Statistics and Expected Timetable

The purpose of this standard is to provide key information regarding the conduct of any offering and the identification of important dates relating to that offering.

A. *Offer statistics.* For each method of offering, e.g., rights offering, general offering, etc., state the total expected amount of the issue, including the expected issue price or the method of determining the price and the number of securities expected to be issued.

B. *Method and expected timetable.* For all offerings, and separately for each group of targeted potential investors, the document shall state the following information to the extent applicable to the offering procedure:

    1. The time period during which the offer will be open, and where and to whom purchase or subscription applications shall be addressed. Describe whether the purchase period may be extended or shortened, and the manner and duration of possible extensions or possible early closure or shortening of this period. Describe the manner in which the latter shall be made public. If the exact dates are not known when the document is first filed or distributed to the public, describe arrangements for announcing the final or definitive date or period.

    2. Method and time limits for paying up securities; where payment is partial, the manner and dates on which amounts due are to be paid.

    3. Method and time limits for delivery of equity securities (including provisional certificates, if applicable) to subscribers or purchasers.

    4. In the case of pre-emptive purchase rights, the procedure for the exercise of any right of pre-emption, the negotiability of subscription rights and the treatment of subscription rights not exercised.

    5. A full description of the manner in which results of the distribution of securities are to be made public, and when appropriate, the manner for refunding excess amounts paid by applicants (including whether interest will be paid).

Instructions to Item 2: If you are filing Form 20-F as a registration statement or annual report under the Exchange Act, you do not have to provide the information called for by Item 2. You must provide this information if you are filing a registration statement under the Securities Act.

Item 3.   Key Information

The purpose of this standard is to summarize key information about the company's financial condition, capitalization and risk factors. If the financial statements included in the document are restated to reflect material changes in the company's group structure or accounting policies, the selected financial data also must be restated. See item 8.

A. *Selected financial data.*

    1. The company shall provide selected historical financial data regarding the company, which shall be presented for the five most recent financial years (or such shorter period that the company has been in operation), in the same currency as the financial statements. Selected financial data for either or both of the earliest two years of the five-year period may be omitted, however, if the company represents to the host county regulator that such information cannot be provided, or cannot be provided on a restated basis, without unreasonable effort or expense. If interim period financial statements are included, the selected financial data should be updated for that interim period, which may be unaudited, provided that fact is stated. If selected financial data for interim periods is provided, comparative data from the same period in the prior financial year shall also be provided, except that the requirement for comparative balance sheet data is satisfied by presenting the year end balance sheet information.

    2. The selected financial data presented shall include items generally corresponding to the following, except that the specific line items presented should be expressed in the same manner as the corresponding line items in the company's financial statements. Such data shall include, at a minimum, net sales or operating revenues; income (loss) from operations; income (loss) from continuing operations; net income (loss); net income (loss) from operations per share; income (loss) from continuing operations per share; total assets; net assets; capital stock (excluding long term debt and redeemable preferred stock); number of shares as adjusted to reflect changes in capital; dividends declared per share in both the currency of the financial

statements and the host county currency, including the formula used for any adjustments to dividends declared; and diluted net income per share. Per share amounts must be determined in accordance with the body of accounting principles used in preparing the financial statements.

3. Where the financial statements provided in response to Item 8 are prepared in a currency other than the currency of the host county, disclosure of the exchange rate between the financial reporting currency and the currency of the host county should be provided, using the exchange rate designated by the host country for this purpose, if any:

   (a) At the latest practicable date;

   (b) The high and low exchange rates for each month during the previous six months; and

   (c) For the five most recent financial years and any subsequent interim period for which financial statements are presented, the average rates for each period, calculated by using the average of the exchange rates on the last day of each month during the period.

B. *Capitalization and indebtedness.* A statement of capitalization and indebtedness (distinguishing between guaranteed and unguaranteed, and secured and unsecured, indebtedness) as of a date no earlier than 60 days prior to the date of the document shall be provided showing the company's capitalization on an actual basis and, if applicable, as adjusted to reflect the sale of new securities being issued and the intended application of the net proceeds therefrom. Indebtedness also includes indirect and contingent indebtedness.

C. *Reasons for the offer and use of proceeds.*

1. The document shall disclose the estimated net amount of the proceeds broken down into each principal intended use thereof. If the anticipated proceeds will not be sufficient to fund all the proposed purposes, the order of priority of such purposes should be given, as well as the amount and sources of other funds needed. If the company has no specific plans for the proceeds, it should discuss the principal reasons for the offering.

2. If the proceeds are being used directly or indirectly to acquire assets, other than in the ordinary course of business, briefly describe the assets and their cost. If the assets will be acquired from affiliates of the company or their associates, disclose the persons from whom they will be acquired and how the cost to the company will be determined.

3. If the proceeds may or will be used to finance acquisitions of other businesses, give a brief description of such businesses and information on the status of the acquisitions.

4. If any material part of the proceeds is to be used to discharge, reduce or retire indebtedness, describe the interest rate and maturity of such indebtedness and, for indebtedness incurred within the past year, the uses to which the proceeds of such indebtedness were put.

D. *Risk factors.* The document shall prominently disclose risk factors that are specific to the company or its industry and make an offering speculative or one of high risk, in a section headed "Risk Factors." Companies are encouraged, but not required, to list the risk factors in the order of their priority to the company. Among other things, such factors may include, for example: the nature of the business in which it is engaged or proposes to engage; factors relating to the countries in which it operates; the absence of profitable operations in recent periods; the financial position of the company; the possible absence of a liquid trading market for the company's securities; reliance on the expertise of management; potential dilution; unusual competitive conditions; pending expiration of material patents, trademarks or contracts; or dependence on a limited number of customers or suppliers. The Risk Factors section is intended to be a summary of more detailed discussion contained elsewhere in the document.

Instructions to Item 3:

1. *If you are filing Form 20-F as an annual report under the Exchange Act, you do not have to provide the information called for by Item 3.B or 3.C. If you are filing Form 20-F as a registration statement under the Exchange*

Act, you do not have to provide the information called for by Item 3.C. You must provide the information called for by Item 3 if you are filing a registration statement under the Securities Act.

2. *Throughout Form 20-F, the terms "financial year" and "fiscal year" have the same meaning. The term "fiscal year" is defined in Rule 405 under the Securities Act and Rule 12b-2 under the Exchange Act.*

Instructions to Item 3.A:

You may present the selected financial data on the basis of the accounting principles used in your primary financial statements. If you do this, however, you also must include in this summary any reconciliations of the data to U.S. generally accepted accounting principles and Regulation S-X, pursuant to item 17 or 18 of this Form. In that case, you only have to provide selected financial data on a basis reconciled to U.S. generally accepted accounting principles for (i) those periods for which you were required to reconcile the primary annual financial statements in a filing under the Securities Act or the Exchange Act, and (ii) any interim periods.

If you are unable to provide selected financial data for the earliest two years of the five-year period, submit the required representation to us before or at the time you file the document. Disclose in the document that data for the earliest two years have been omitted and explain the reasons for the omission.

Instructions to Item 3.B:

1. *If you are including the capitalization table called for by Item 3.B in a prospectus supplement for a shelf offering registered on Form F-3, the amounts shown in the table may be as of the date of the most recent balance sheet filed as part of the registration statement, if the information in the table is updated to reflect securities issued up to 60 days prior to the date of the supplement.*

2. *If you are not selling new securities in a firm commitment underwritten offering or an "all or none" best efforts offering, reflect the capitalization "as adjusted" for the net proceeds of the offering only in the following ways:*

   a. *In a best efforts "minimum/maximum" offering, reflect both the minimum and maximum proceeds; and*

   b. *In a rights offering or an offering of securities upon the exercise of outstanding warrants, reflect the proceeds only to the extent exercise is likely in view of the current market price.*

Instructions to Item 3.D: *Risk factors should be concise and explain clearly how the risk affects the issuer or the securities.*

Item 4.   Information on the Company

The purpose of this standard is to provide information about the company's business operations, the products it makes or the services it provides, and the factors that affect the business. The standard also is intended to provide information regarding the adequacy and suitability of the company's properties, plants and equipment, as well as its plans for future increases or decreases in such capacity.

A. ***History and development of the company.*** The following information shall be provided:

1. The legal and commercial name of the company.

2. The date of incorporation and the length of life of the company, except where indefinite.

3. The domicile and legal form of the company, the legislation under which the company operates, its country of incorporation and the address and telephone number of its registered office (or principal place of business if different from its registered office). Provide the name and address of the company's agent in the host country, if any.

4. The important events in the development of the company's business, e.g. information concerning the nature and results of any material reclassification, merger or consolidation of the company or any of its significant subsidiaries; acquisitions or dispositions of material assets other than in the ordinary course of business; any material changes in the mode of conducting the business; material changes in the types of products pro-

duced or services rendered; name changes; or the nature and results of any bankruptcy, receivership or similar proceedings with respect to the company or significant subsidiaries.

5. A description, including the amount invested, of the company's principal capital expenditures and divestitures (including interests in other companies), since the beginning of the company's last three financial years to the date of the offering or listing document.

6. Information concerning the principal capital expenditures and divestitures currently in progress, including the distribution of these investments geographically (home and abroad) and the method of financing (internal or external).

7. An indication of any public takeover offers by third parties in respect of the company's shares or by the company in respect of other companies' shares which have occurred during the last and current financial year. The price or exchange terms attaching to such offers and the outcome thereof are to be stated.

B. *Business overview.* The information required by this item may be presented on the same basis as that used to determine the company's business segments under the body of accounting principles used in preparing the financial statements. The following information shall be provided:

1. A description of the nature of the company's operations and its principal activities, stating the main categories of products sold and/or services performed for each of the last three financial years. Indicate any significant new products and/or services that have been introduced and, to the extent the development of new products or services has been publicly disclosed, give the status of development.

2. A description of the principal markets in which the company competes, including a breakdown of total revenues by category of activity and geographic market for each of the last three financial years.

3. A description of the seasonality of the company's main business.

4. A description of the sources and availability of raw materials, including a description of whether prices of principal raw materials are volatile.

5. A description of the marketing channels used by the company, including an explanation of any special sales methods, such as installment sales.

6. Summary information regarding the extent to which the company is dependent, if at all, on patents or licenses, industrial, commercial or financial contracts (including contracts with customers or suppliers) or new manufacturing processes, where such factors are material to the company's business or profitability.

7. The basis for any statements made by the company regarding its competitive position shall be disclosed.

8. A description of the material effects of government regulations on the company's business, identifying the regulatory body.

C. *Organizational structure.* If the company is part of a group, include a brief description of the group and the company's position within the group. Provide a listing of the company's significant subsidiaries, including name, country of incorporation or residence, proportion of ownership interest and, if different, proportion of voting power held.

D. *Property, plants and equipment.* The company shall provide information regarding any material tangible fixed assets, including leased properties, and any major encumbrances thereon, including a description of the size and uses of the property; productive capacity and extent of utilization of the company's facilities; how the assets are held; the products produced; and the location. Also describe any environmental issues that may affect the company's utilization of the assets. With regard to any material plans to construct, expand or improve facilities, describe the nature of and reason for the plan, an estimate of the amount of expenditures including the amount of expenditures already paid, a description of the method of financing the activity, the estimated dates of start and completion of the activity, and the increase of production capacity anticipated after completion.

Instruction to Item 4: Furnish the information specified in any industry guide listed in Part 9 of Regulation S-K (§229.802 of this chapter) that applies to you, except that if you furnish the information specified in Appendix A to Item 4.D of this form you do not need to furnish any additional information specified in Guide 2 relating to oil and gas operations.

Instructions to Item 4.A.4: If you are providing the information called for by Item 4.A.4 in an annual report, you only have to provide the required information for the period from the beginning of your last full financial year up to the latest practicable date.

Instructions to Item 4.B:

1. The reference in Item 4.B to "the body of accounting principles used in preparing the financial statements" means the accounting principles used in preparing the primary financial statements, not to accounting principles used only to prepare the U.S. GAAP reconciliation.

2. If you:

   (a) Are filing a registration statement on Form F-1 under the Securities Act or on Form 20-F under the Exchange Act,

   (b) Were not required to file reports under Section 13(a) or 15(d) of the Exchange Act immediately prior to filing that registration statement, and

   (c) Have not received (or your predecessor has not received) revenue from operations during each of the three fiscal years immediately prior to filing the registration statement:

   you must provide information about your plan of operations. Provide information comparable to the information required by Item 101(a)(2) of Regulation S-K.

Instructions to Item 4.D:

1. In the case of an extractive enterprise:

   (a) Provide material information about production, reserves, locations, developments and the nature of your interest. If individual properties are of major significance to you, provide more detailed information about those properties and use maps to disclose information about their location.

   (b) If you are giving reserve estimates in the registration statement or report:

      (i) Consult the staff of the Office of International Corporate Finance of the Division of Corporation Finance. That office may request that you provide supplementally a copy of the full report of the engineer or other expert who estimated the reserves. See Rule 418 of Regulation C (§ 230.418 of this chapter) and Rule 12b-4 of Regulation 12B (§ 240.12b-4 of this chapter) for information about submitting supplemental information to the Commission and requesting its return.

      (ii) In documents you file publicly with the Commission, do not disclose estimates of oil or gas reserves unless the reserves are proved (or in the case of other extractive industries, proved or probable) and do not give estimated values of those reserves, unless foreign law requires you to disclose the information. If these types of estimates have already been provided to any person that is offering to acquire you, however, you may include the estimates in documents relating to the acquisition.

      (iii) If you represent that the estimates of reserves you provide, or any estimated valuation of those reserves, are based on estimates prepared or reviewed by independent consultants, you must name those consultants in the document.

   (c) If oil and gas operations are material to your or your subsidiaries' business operations or financial position, provide the information specified in Appendix A to Item 4.D, located at the end of this Form.

Item 5.   Operating and Financial Review and Prospects

The purpose of this standard is to provide management's explanation of factors that have affected the company's financial condition and results of operations for the historical periods covered by the financial statements, and management's assessment of factors and trends which are anticipated to have a material effect on the company's financial condition and results of operations in future periods.

Discuss the company's financial condition, changes in financial condition and results of operations for each year and interim period for which financial statements are required, including the causes of material changes from year to year in financial statement line items, to the extent necessary for an understanding of the company's business as a whole. Information provided also shall relate to all separate segments of the company. Provide the information specified below as well as such other information that is necessary for an investor's understanding of the company's financial condition, changes in financial condition and results of operations.

A. *Operating results.* Provide information regarding significant factors, including unusual or infrequent events or new developments, materially affecting the company's income from operations, indicating the extent to which income was so affected. Describe any other significant component of revenue or expenses necessary to understand the company's results of operations.

1. To the extent that the financial statements disclose material changes in net sales or revenues, provide a narrative discussion of the extent to which such changes are attributable to changes in prices or to changes in the volume or amount of products or services being sold or to the introduction of new products or services.

2. Describe the impact of inflation, if material. If the currency in which financial statements are presented is of a country that has experienced hyperinflation, the existence of such inflation, a five year history of the annual rate of inflation and a discussion of the impact of hyperinflation on the company's business shall be disclosed.

3. Provide information regarding the impact of foreign currency fluctuations on the company, if material, and the extent to which foreign currency net investments are hedged by currency borrowings and other hedging instruments.

4. Provide information regarding any governmental economic, fiscal, monetary or political policies or factors that have materially affected, or could materially affect, directly or indirectly, the company's operations or investments by host country shareholders.

B. *Liquidity and capital resources.* The following information shall be provided:

1. Information regarding the company's liquidity (both short and long term), including:

   (a) A description of the internal and external sources of liquidity and a brief discussion of any material unused sources of liquidity. Include a statement by the company that, in its opinion, the working capital is sufficient for the company's present requirements, or, if not, how it proposes to provide the additional working capital needed.

   (b) An evaluation of the sources and amounts of the company's cash flows, including the nature and extent of any legal or economic restrictions on the ability of subsidiaries to transfer funds to the company in the form of cash dividends, loans or advances and the impact such restrictions have had or are expected to have on the ability of the company to meet its cash obligations.

   (c) Information on the level of borrowings at the end of the period under review, the seasonality of borrowing requirements and the maturity profile of borrowings and committed borrowing facilities, with a description of any restrictions on their use.

2. Information regarding the type of financial instruments used, the maturity profile of debt, currency and interest rate structure. The discussion also should include funding and treasury policies and objectives in terms of the manner in which treasury activities are controlled, the currencies in which cash and cash equivalents are

held, the extent to which borrowings are at fixed rates, and the use of financial instruments for hedging purposes.

   3. Information regarding the company's material commitments for capital expenditures as of the end of the latest financial year and any subsequent interim period and an indication of the general purpose of such commitments and the anticipated sources of funds needed to fulfill such commitments.

C. *Research and development; patents and licenses, etc.* Provide a description of the company's research and development policies for the last three years, where it is significant, including the amount spent during each of the last three financial years on company-sponsored research and development activities.

D. *Trend information.* The company should identify the most significant recent trends in production, sales and inventory, the state of the order book and costs and selling prices since the latest financial year. The company also should discuss, for at least the current financial year, any known trends, uncertainties, demands, commitments or events that are reasonably likely to have a material effect on the company's net sales or revenues, income from continuing operations, profitability, liquidity or capital resources, or that would cause reported financial information not necessarily to be indicative of future operating results or financial condition.

E. *Off-balance sheet arrangements.*

   1. In a separately-captioned section, discuss the company's off-balance sheet arrangements that have or are reasonably likely to have a current or future effect on the company's financial condition, changes in financial condition, revenues or expenses, results of operations, liquidity, capital expenditures or capital resources that is material to investors. The disclosure shall include the items specified in Items 5.E.1(a), (b), (c) and (d) of this Item to the extent necessary to an understanding of such arrangements and effect, and shall also include such other information that the company believes is necessary for such an understanding.

     (a) The nature and business purpose to the company of such off-balance sheet arrangements;

     (b) The importance to the company of such off-balance sheet arrangements in respect of its liquidity, capital resources, market risk support, credit risk support or other benefits;

     (c) The amounts of revenues, expenses and cash flows of the company arising from such arrangements; the nature and amounts of any interests retained, securities issued and other indebtedness incurred by the company in connection with such arrangements; and the nature and amounts of any other obligations or liabilities (including contingent obligations or liabilities) of the company arising from such arrangements that are or are reasonably likely to become material and the triggering events or circumstances that could cause them to arise; and

     (d) Any known event, demand, commitment, trend or uncertainty that will result in or is reasonably likely to result in the termination, or material reduction in availability to the company, of its off-balance sheet arrangements that provide material benefits to it, and the course of action that the company has taken or proposes to take in response to any such circumstances.

   2. As used in this Item 5.E., the term *off-balance sheet arrangement* means any transaction, agreement or other contractual arrangement to which an entity unconsolidated with the company is a party, under which the company has:

     (a) Any obligation under a guarantee contract that has any of the characteristics identified in paragraph 3 of FASB Interpretation No. 45, *Guarantor's Accounting and Disclosure Requirements for Guarantees, Including Indirect Guarantees of Indebtedness of Others* (November 2002) ("FIN 45"), as may be modified or supplemented, excluding the types of guarantee contracts described in paragraphs 6 and 7 of FIN 45;

     (b) A retained or contingent interest in assets transferred to an unconsolidated entity or similar arrangement that serves as credit, liquidity or market risk support to such entity for such assets;

(c) Any obligation under a derivative instrument that is both indexed to the company's own stock and classified in stockholders' equity, or not reflected, in the company's statement of financial position; or

(d) Any obligation, including a contingent obligation, arising out of a variable interest (as referenced in FASB Interpretation No. 46, *Consolidation of Variable Interest Entities* (January 2003), as may be modified or supplemented) in an unconsolidated entity that is held by, and material to, the company, where such entity provides financing, liquidity, market risk or credit risk support to, or engages in leasing, hedging or research and development services with, the company.

F. *Tabular disclosure of contractual obligations.*

1. In a tabular format, provide the information specified in this Item 5.F.1 as of the latest fiscal year end balance sheet date with respect to the company's known contractual obligations specified in the table that follows this Item 5.F.1. The company shall provide amounts, aggregated by type of contractual obligation. The company may disaggregate the specified categories of contractual obligations using other categories suitable to its business, but the presentation must include all of the obligations of the company that fall within the specified categories. A presentation covering at least the periods specified shall be included. The tabular presentation may be accompanied by footnotes to describe provisions that create, increase or accelerate obligations, or other pertinent data to the extent necessary for an understanding of the timing and amount of the company's specified contractual obligations.

Contractual obligations	Payments due by period				
	Total	Less than 1 year	1–3 years	3–5 years	More than 5 years
[Long-Term Debt Obligations]..................					
[Capital (Finance) Lease Obligations]..........					
[Operating Lease Obligations]....................					
[Purchase Obligations].............................					
[Other Long-Term Liabilities Reflected on the Company's Balance Sheet under the GAAP of the primary financial statements]					
Total..					

2. As used in this Item 5.F.1, the term *purchase obligation* means an agreement to purchase goods or services that is enforceable and legally binding on the company that specifies all significant terms, including: fixed or minimum quantities to be purchased; fixed, minimum or variable price provisions; and the approximate timing of the transaction.

G. *Safe harbor.*

1. The safe harbor provided in section 27A of the Securities Act and section 21E of the Exchange Act ("statutory safe harbors") shall apply to forward-looking information provided pursuant to Item 5.E and F, provided that the disclosure is made by: an issuer; a person acting on behalf of the issuer; an outside reviewer retained by the issuer making a statement on behalf of the issuer; or an underwriter, with respect to information provided by the issuer or information derived from information provided by the issuer.

2. For purposes of Item 5.G.1 of this Item only, all information required by Item 5.E.1 and 5.E.2 of this Item is deemed to be a "forward looking statement" as that term is defined in the statutory safe harbors, except for historical facts.

3. With respect to Item 5.E, the meaningful cautionary statements element of the statutory safe harbors will be satisfied if a company satisfies all requirements of that same Item 5.E.

Instructions to Item 5:

1. *Refer to the Commission's interpretive release (No. 33-6835) dated May 18, 1989 for guidance in preparing this discussion and analysis by management of the company's financial condition and results of operations.*

2. *The discussion should focus on the primary financial statements presented in the document. You should refer to the reconciliation to U.S. GAAP, if any, and discuss any aspects of the differences between foreign and U.S. GAAP, not otherwise discussed in the reconciliation, that you believe are necessary for an understanding of the financial statements as a whole.*

3. *We encourage you to supply forward-looking information, but that type of information is not required. Forward-looking information is covered expressly by the safe harbor provisions of Section 27A of the Securities Act and Section 27A of the Exchange Act. Forward-looking information is different than presently known data which will have an impact on future operating results, such as known future increases in costs of labor or materials. You are required to disclose this latter type of data if it is material.*

Instruction to Item 5.A:

1. *You must provide the information required by item 5.A.2 with respect to hyperinflation if hyperinflation has occurred in any of the periods for which you are required to provide audited financial statements or unaudited interim financial statements in the document. See Rule 3-20(c) of Regulation S-X for a discussion of cumulative inflation rates that trigger this requirement.*

Instructions to Item 5.E:

1. *No obligation to make disclosure under Item 5.E shall arise in respect of an off-balance sheet arrangement until a definitive agreement that is unconditionally binding or subject only to customary closing conditions exists or, if there is no such agreement, when settlement of the transaction occurs.*

2. *Companies should aggregate off-balance sheet arrangements in groups or categories that provide material information in an efficient and understandable manner and should avoid repetition and disclosure of immaterial information. Effects that are common or similar with respect to a number of off-balance sheet arrangements must be analyzed in the aggregate to the extent the aggregation increases understanding. Distinctions in arrangements and their effects must be discussed to the extent the information is material, but the discussion should avoid repetition and disclosure of immaterial information.*

3. *For purposes of paragraph Item 5.E only, contingent liabilities arising out of litigation, arbitration or regulatory actions are not considered to be off-balance sheet arrangements.*

4. *Generally, the disclosure required by Item 5.E shall cover the most recent fiscal year. However, the discussion should address changes from the previous year where such discussion is necessary to an understanding of the disclosure.*

5. *In satisfying the requirements of Item 5.E, the discussion of off-balance sheet arrangements need not repeat information provided in the footnotes to the financial statements, provided that such discussion clearly cross-references to specific information in the relevant footnotes and integrates the substance of the footnotes into such discussion in a manner designed to inform readers of the significance of the information that is not included within the body of such discussion.*

Instructions to Item 5.F:

1. *The company is not required to include the table required by Item 5.F.1 for interim periods. Instead, the company should disclose material changes outside the ordinary course of the company's business in the specified contractual obligations during the interim period.*

2. *Except for "purchase obligations," the contractual obligations in the table required by Item 5.F.1 should be based on the classifications used in the generally accepted accounting principles under which the company prepares its primary financial statements. If the generally accepted accounting principles under which the company pre-*

pares its primary financial statements do not distinguish between capital (finance) leases and operating leases, then present all leases under one category.

Item 6.   Directors, Senior Management and Employees

The purpose of this standard is to provide information concerning the company's directors and managers that will allow investors to assess such individuals' experience, qualifications and levels of compensation, as well as their relationship with the company. Information concerning the company's employees is also required.

A. *Directors and senior management.* The following information shall be disclosed with respect to the company's directors and senior management, and any employees such as scientists or designers upon whose work the company is dependent:

1. Name, business experience, functions and areas of experience in the company.

2. Principal business activities performed outside the issuing company (including, in the case of directors, other principal directorships).

3. Date of birth or age (if required to be reported in the home country or otherwise publicly disclosed by the company).

4. The nature of any family relationship between any of the persons named above.

5. Any arrangement or understanding with major shareholders, customers, suppliers or others, pursuant to which any person referred to above was selected as a director or member of senior management.

B. *Compensation.* Provide the following information for the last full financial year for the company's directors and members of its administrative, supervisory or management bodies:

1. The amount of compensation paid, and benefits in kind granted, to such persons by the company and its subsidiaries for services in all capacities to the company and its subsidiaries by any person. Disclosure of compensation is required on an individual basis unless individual disclosure is not required in the company's home country and is not otherwise publicly disclosed by the company. The standard also covers contingent or deferred compensation accrued for the year, even if the compensation is payable at a later date. If any portion of the compensation was paid (a) pursuant to a bonus or profit-sharing plan, provide a brief description of the plan and the basis upon which such persons participate in the plan; or (b) in the form of stock options, provide the title and amount of securities covered by the options, the exercise price, the purchase price (if any), and the expiration date of the options.

2. The total amounts set aside or accrued by the company or its subsidiaries to provide pension, retirement or similar benefits.

C. *Board practices.* The following information for the company's last completed financial year shall be given with respect to, unless otherwise specified, the company's directors, and members of its administrative, supervisory or management bodies.

1. Date of expiration of the current term of office, if applicable, and the period during which the person has served in that office.

2. Details of directors' service contracts with the company or any of its subsidiaries providing for benefits upon termination of employment, or an appropriate negative statement.

3. Details relating to the company's audit committee and remuneration committee, including the names of committee members and a summary of the terms of reference under which the committee operates.

D. *Employees.* Provide either the number of employees at the end of the period or the average for the period for each of the past three financial years (and changes in such numbers, if material) and, if possible, a breakdown of persons employed by main category of activity and geographic location. Also disclose any significant change in the number of employees, and information regarding the relationship between management and labor unions. If the company employs a significant number of temporary employees, include disclosure of the number of temporary employees on an average during the most recent financial year.

E. *Share ownership.*

   1. With respect to the persons listed in subsection 6.B, above, provide information as to their share ownership in the company as of the most recent practicable date (including disclosure on an individual basis of the number of shares and percent of shares outstanding of that class, and whether they have different voting rights) held by the persons listed and options granted to them on the company's shares. Information regarding options shall include: the title and amount of securities called for by the options; the exercise price; the purchase price, if any; and the expiration date of the options.

   2. Describe any arrangements for involving the employees in the capital of the company, including any arrangement that involves the issue or grant of options or shares or securities of the company.

Instruction to Item 6.C:

   1. *The term "plan" is used very broadly and includes any type of arrangement for compensation, even if the terms of the plan are not contained in a formal document.*

   2. *If the company is a listed issuer as defined in Exchange Act Rule 10A-3 (17 CFR 240.10A-3) and its entire board of directors is acting as the company's audit committee as specified in section 3(a)(58)(B) of the Exchange Act (15 U.S.C. 78c(a)(58)(B)), so state.*

   3. *If the company has a board of auditors or similar body, as described in Exchange Act Rule 10A-3(c)(3) (17 CFR 240.10A-3(c)(3)), the disclosure required by this Item 6.C. with regard to the company's audit committee can be provided with respect to the company's board of auditors, or similar body.*

Instruction to Item 6.E: If (a) any of the persons listed in subsection 6.B beneficially owns less than one percent of the class of shares and (b) that person's individual share ownership previously has not been disclosed to shareholders or otherwise made public, you may indicate, by an asterisk and explanatory footnote or similar means, that the person beneficially owns less than one percent of the class, instead of providing that person's individual share ownership.

Item 7.   Major Shareholders and Related Party Transactions

The purpose of this standard is to provide information regarding the major shareholders and others that control or may control the company. The standard also provides information regarding transactions the company has entered into with persons affiliated with the company and whether the terms of such transactions are fair to the company. These standards may require disclosure of related party transactions not required to be disclosed under the body of accounting principles used in preparing the financial statements. This standard is not intended to address the thresholds at which shareholders are required, on a continuing basis, to disclose their beneficial ownership of securities.

A. *Major shareholders.* To the extent that the following information is known to the company or can be ascertained from public filings, it should be provided as of the most recent practicable date, with references to the number of shares held in the company including shares beneficially owned.

   1. The following information shall be provided regarding the company's major shareholders, which means shareholders that are the beneficial owners of 5% or more of each class of the company's voting securities (unless the company is required to disclose a lesser percentage in its home country, in which case that lesser percentage applies):

      (a) Provide the names of the major shareholders, and the number of shares and the percentage of outstanding shares of each class owned by each of them as of the most recent practicable date, or an appropriate negative statement if there are no major shareholders.

      (b) Disclose any significant change in the percentage ownership held by any major shareholders during the past three years.

(c) Indicate whether the company's major shareholders have different voting rights, or an appropriate negative statement.

2. Information shall be provided as to the portion of each class of securities held in the host country and the number of record holders in the host country.

3. To the extent known to the company, state whether the company is directly or indirectly owned or controlled by another corporation(s), by any foreign government or by any other natural or legal person(s) severally or jointly, and, if so, give the name(s) of such controlling corporation(s), government or other person(s), and briefly describe the nature of such control, including the amount and proportion of capital held giving a right to vote.

4. Describe any arrangements, known to the company, the operation of which may at a subsequent date result in a change in control of the company.

B. *Related party transactions.* Provide the information required below for the period since the beginning of the company's preceding three financial years up to the date of the document, with respect to transactions or loans between the company and (a) enterprises that directly or indirectly through one or more intermediaries, control or are controlled by, or are under common control with, the company; (b) associates; (c) individuals owning, directly or indirectly, an interest in the voting power of the company that gives them significant influence over the company, and close members of any such individual's family; (d) key management personnel, that is, those persons having authority and responsibility for planning, directing and controlling the activities of the company, including directors and senior management of companies and close members of such individuals' families; and (e) enterprises in which a substantial interest in the voting power is owned, directly or indirectly, by any person described in (c) or (d) or over which such a person is able to exercise significant influence. This includes enterprises owned by directors or major shareholders of the company and enterprises that have a member of key management in common with the company. Close members of an individual's family are those that may be expected to influence, or be influenced by, that person in their dealings with the company. An associate is an unconsolidated enterprise in which the company has significant influence or which has significant influence over the company. Significant influence over an enterprise is the power to participate in the financial and operating policy decisions of the enterprise but is less than control over those policies. Shareholders beneficially owning a 10% interest in the voting power of the company are presumed to have a significant influence on the company.

1. The nature and extent of any transactions or presently proposed transactions which are material to the company or the related party, or any transactions that are unusual in their nature or conditions, involving goods, services, or tangible or intangible assets, to which the company or any of its parent or subsidiaries was a party.

2. The amount of outstanding loans (including guarantees of any kind) made by the company or any of its parent or subsidiaries to or for the benefit of any of the persons listed above. The information given should include the largest amount outstanding during the period covered, the amount outstanding as of the latest practicable date, the nature of the loan and the transaction in which it was incurred, and the interest rate on the loan.

C. *Interests of experts and counsel.* If any of the named experts or counselors was employed on a contingent basis, owns an amount of shares in the company or its subsidiaries which is material to that person, or has a material, direct or indirect economic interest in the company or that depends on the success of the offering, provide a brief description of the nature and terms of such contingency or interest.

Instructions to Item 7.B:

1. *If you are providing the information called for by Item 7.B in an annual report, you only have to provide the required information for the period from the beginning of your last fill fiscal year up to the latest practicable date.*

2. *In response to Item 7.B.2, if the lender is a bank savings and loan association, or broker dealer extending credit under Federal Reserve Regulation T, and the loans are not disclosed as nonaccrual, past due, restructured or potential problems under Industry Guide 3, your response may consist of a statement, if true, that the loans in question (A) were made in the ordinary course of business, (B) were made on substantially the same terms, including interest rates and collateral, as those prevailing at the time for comparable transactions with other persons, and (C) did not involve more than the normal risk of collectibility or present other unfavorable features.*

Instruction to Item 7.C: If you are filing Form 20-F as a registration statement or annual report under the Exchange Act, you do not have to provide the information called for by Item 7.C. You must provide this information if you are filing a registration statement under the Securities Act. Accountants who provide a report on financial statements that are presented or incorporated by reference in a registration statement should note Article 2 of Regulation S-X. That Article contains the Commission's requirements for qualifications and reports of accountants.

Item 8.   Financial Information

The purpose of this standard is to specify which financial statements must be included in the document, as well as the periods to be covered, the age of the financial statements and other information of a financial nature.

A. *Consolidated Statements and Other Financial Information.*

1. The document must contain consolidated financial statements, audited by an independent auditor and accompanied by an audit report, comprised of:

    (a) Balance sheet;

    (b) Income statement;

    (c) Statement showing either (i) changes in equity other than those arising from capital transactions with owners and distributions to owners; or (ii) all changes in equity (including a subtotal of all non-owner items recognized directly in equity);

    (d) Cash flow statement;

    (e) Related notes and schedules required by the comprehensive body of accounting standards pursuant to which the financial statements are prepared; and

    (f) If not included in the primary financial statements, a note analyzing the changes in each caption of shareholders' equity presented in the balance sheet.

2. The document should include comparative financial statements that cover the latest three financial years, audited in accordance with a comprehensive body of auditing standards.

3. The audit report(s) must cover each of the periods for which these international disclosure standards require audited financial statements. If the auditors have refused to provide a report on the annual accounts or if the report(s) contain qualifications or disclaimers, such refusal or such qualifications or disclaimers shall be reproduced in full and the reasons given, so the host country securities regulator can determine whether or not to accept the financial statements. Include an indication of any other information in the document which has been audited by the auditors.

4. The last year of audited financial statements may not be older than 15 months at the time of the offering or listing; provided, however, that in the case of the company's initial public offering, the audited financial statements also shall be as of a date not older than 12 months at the time the document is filed. In such cases, the audited financial statements may cover a period of less than a full year.

5. If the document is dated more than nine months after the end of the last audited financial year, it should contain consolidated interim financial statements, which may be unaudited (in which case that fact should be stated), covering at least the first six months of the financial year. The interim financial statements should include a balance sheet, income statement, cash flow statement, and a statement showing either (i) changes in equity other than those arising from capital transactions with owners and distributions to own-

ers, or (ii) all changes in equity (including a subtotal of all non-owner items recognized directly in equity). Each of these statements may be in condensed form as long as it contains the major line items from the latest audited financial statements and includes the major components of assets, liabilities and equity (in the case of the balance sheet); income and expenses (in the case of the income statement) and the major subtotals of cash flows (in the case of the cash flow statement). The interim financial statements should include comparative statements for the same period in the prior financial year, except that the requirement for comparative balance sheet information may be satisfied by presenting the year end balance sheet. If not included in the primary financial statements, a note should be provided analyzing the changes in each caption of shareholders' equity presented in the balance sheet. The interim financial statements should include selected note disclosures that will provide an explanation of events and changes that are significant to an understanding of the changes in financial position and performance of the enterprise since the last annual reporting date. If, at the date of the document, the company has published interim financial information that covers a more current period than those otherwise required by this standard, the more current interim financial information must be included in the document. Companies are encouraged, but not required, to have any interim financial statements in the document reviewed by an independent auditor. If such a review has been performed and is referred to in the document, a copy of the auditor's interim review report must be provided in the document.

6. If the amount of export sales constitutes a significant portion of the company's total sales volume, provide the total amount of export sales and the percent and amount of export sales in the total amount of sales volume.

7. Provide information on any legal or arbitration proceedings, including those relating to bankruptcy, receivership or similar proceedings and those involving any third party, which may have, or have had in the recent past, significant effects on the company's financial position or profitability. This includes governmental proceedings pending or known to be contemplated.

8. Describe the company's policy on dividend distributions.

B. *Significant Changes.* Disclose whether or not any significant change has occurred since the date of the annual financial statements, and/or since the date of the most recent interim financial statements, if any, included in the document.

Instructions to Item 8:

1. *This item refers to the company, but note that under Rules 3-05, 3-09, 3-10, 3-14 and 3-16 of Regulation S-X, you also may have to provide financial statements or financial information for entities other than the issuer. In some cases, you may have to provide financial statements for a predecessor. See the definition of "predecessor" in Exchange Act Rule 12b-2 and Securities Act Rule 405.*

2. *For offerings of securities (a) upon the exercise of outstanding rights granted by the issuer of the securities to be offered, if the rights are granted pro rata to all existing securityholders of the class of securities to which the rights attach; or (b) pursuant to a dividend or interest reinvestment plan; or (c) upon the conversion of outstanding convertible securities or upon the exercise of outstanding transferable warrants issued by the issuer of the securities to be offered, or by an affiliate of that issuer, the 15-month period referred to in Item 8.A.4 is extended to 18 months and the interim financial statements referred to in Item 8.A.5 shall be as of a date within 12 months of the date of the document. The provisions of this paragraph are not applicable if securities are to be offered or sold in a standby underwriting in the United States or similar arrangement.*

Instructions to Item 8.A.2:

1. *You do not have to provide a balance sheet for the earliest of the three-year periods specified in Item 8.A.2 if that balance sheet is not required by a jurisdiction outside the United States.*

2. *The financial statements must be audited in accordance with U.S. generally accepted auditing standards, and the auditor must comply with the U.S. and Commission standards for auditor independence. Note Article 2 of Regulation S-X, which contains requirements for qualifications and reports of accountants.*

Instruction to Item 8.A.3: *The circumstances in which we would accept an audit report containing a disclaimer or qualification are extremely limited. If you plan to submit this type of report, we recommend that you contact the staff of the Office of Chief Accountant in the Division of Corporation Finance well in advance of filing the document, to discuss the report.*

Instructions to Item 8.A.4:

1. *In calculating the 15-month requirement for the age of financial statements, determine the age based on the period of time that has elapsed between the date of the balance sheet and "the time of the offering or listing," which means the time the registration statement is declared effective. You may satisfy this requirement by providing audited financial statements covering a period of less than a full year.*

2. *The additional requirement that financial statements be no older than 12 months at the date of filing applies only in those limited cases where a nonpublic company is registering its initial public offering of securities. We will waive this requirement in cases where the company is able to represent adequately to us that it is not required to comply with this requirement in any other jurisdiction outside the United States and that complying with the requirement is impracticable or involves undue hardship. File this representation as an exhibit to the registration statement. If we waive the 12-month requirement, you must comply with the 15-month requirement in this item.*

Instructions to Item 8.A.5:

1. *Item 8.A.5 does not apply to annual reports on Form 20-F.*

2. *The third sentence of Item 8.A.5 explains that the required interim financial statements may be in condensed form using major line items from the latest audited financial statements. To determine which major line items must be included in condensed interim information, see Rules 10-01(a) (1) through (7).*

3. *The third sentence from the end of Item 8.A.5 requires you to include in the document interim financial information that has been published by the company if that information covers a more current period than the statements otherwise required by Item 8. This requirement does not apply to annual reports filed on Form 20-F. The requirement covers any publication of financial information that includes, at a minimum, revenue and income information, even if that information is not published as part of a complete set of financial statements. Whenever you provide more current interim financial information in response to this requirement:*

   (a) *Describe any ways in which the accounting principles, practices and methods used in preparing that interim financial information vary materially from the principles, practices and methods accepted in the United States, and*

   (b) *Quantify any material variations, unless they already are quantified because they occur in other financial statements included in the document.*

Instructions to Item 8.A.7:

1. *This Item also requires disclosure of any material proceeding in which any director, any member of senior management, or any of your affiliates is either a party adverse to you or your subsidiaries or has a material interest adverse to your or your subsidiaries.*

2. *If you are providing the information called for by Item 8.A.7 in an annual report, also describe the disposition of any previously reported litigation that occurred during the last fiscal year.*

Item 9.   The Offer and Listing

The purpose of this standard is to provide information regarding the offer or listing of securities, the plan for distribution of the securities and related matters.

A. *Offer and listing details.*

1. Indicate the expected price at which the securities will be offered or the method of determining the price, and the amount of any expenses specifically charged to the subscriber or purchaser.

2. If there is not an established market for the securities, the document shall contain information regarding the manner of determination of the offering price as well as of the exercise price of warrants and the conversion price of convertible securities, including who established the price or who is formally responsible for the determination of the price, the various factors considered in such determination and the parameters or elements used as a basis for establishing the price.

3. If the company's shareholders have pre-emptive purchase rights and where the exercise of the right of pre-emption of shareholders is restricted or withdrawn, the company shall indicate the basis for the issue price if the issue is for cash, together with the reasons for such restriction or withdrawal and the beneficiaries of such restriction or withdrawal if intended to benefit specific persons.

4. Information regarding the price history of the stock to be offered or listed shall be disclosed as follows:

   (a) For the five most recent full financial years: the annual high and low market prices;

   (b) For the two most recent full financial years and any subsequent period: the high and low market prices for each full financial quarter;

   (c) For the most recent six months: the high and low market prices for each month;

   (d) For pre-emptive issues, the market prices for the first trading day in the most recent six months, for the last trading day before the announcement of the offering and (if different) for the latest practicable date prior to publication of the document.

   Information shall be given with respect to the market price in the host market and the principal trading market outside the host market. If significant trading suspensions occurred in the prior three years, they shall be disclosed. If the securities are not regularly traded in an organized market, information shall be given about any lack of liquidity.

5. State the type and class of the securities being offered or listed and furnish the following information:

   (a) Indicate whether the shares are registered shares or bearer shares and provide the number of shares to be issued and to be made available to the market for each kind of share. The nominal par or equivalent value should be given on a per share basis and, where applicable, a statement of the minimum offer price. Describe the coupons attached, if applicable.

   (b) Describe arrangements for transfer and any restrictions on the free transferability of the shares.

6. If the rights evidenced by the securities being offered or listed are or may be materially limited or qualified by the rights evidenced by any other class of securities or by the provisions of any contract or other documents, include information regarding such limitation or qualification and its effect on the rights evidenced by the securities to be listed or offered.

7. With respect to securities other than common or ordinary shares to be listed or offered, outline briefly the rights evidenced thereby.

   (a) If subscription warrants or rights are to be listed or offered, state: the title and amount of securities called for; the amount of warrants or rights outstanding; provisions for changes to or adjustments in the exercise price; the period during which and the price at which the warrants or rights are exercisable; and any other material terms of such warrants or rights.

   (b) Where convertible securities or stock purchase warrants to be listed or offered are subject to redemption or call, the description of the conversion terms of the securities or material terms of the warrants shall include whether the right to convert or purchase the securities will be forfeited unless it is exercised before the date specified in the notice of redemption or call; the expiration or termination date of the warrants; the kind, frequency and timing of notice of the redemption or call, including where the notice will be published; and, in the case of bearer securities, that investors are responsible for making arrangements to prevent loss of the right to convert or purchase in the event of redemption or call.

B. *Plan of distribution.*

1. The names and addresses of the entities underwriting or guaranteeing the offering shall be listed.

2. To the extent known to the company, indicate whether major shareholders, directors or members of the company's management, supervisory or administrative bodies intend to subscribe in the offering, or whether any person intends to subscribe for more than 5% of the offering.

3. Identify any group of targeted potential investors to whom the securities are offered. If the offering is being made simultaneously in the markets of two or more countries and if a tranche has been or is being reserved for certain of these, indicate any such tranche.

4. If securities are reserved for allocation to any group of targeted investors, including, for example, offerings to existing shareholders, directors, or employees and past employees of the company or its subsidiaries, provide details of these and any other preferential allocation arrangements.

5. Indicate whether the amount of the offering could be increased, such as by the exercise of an underwriter's over-allotment option or "greenshoe," and by how much.

6. Indicate the amount, and outline briefly the plan of distribution, of any securities that are to be offered otherwise than through underwriters. If the securities are to be offered through the selling efforts of brokers or dealers, describe the plan of distribution and the terms of any agreement or understanding with such entities. If known, identify the broker(s) or dealer(s) that will participate in the offering and state the amount to be offered through each.

7. If the securities are to be offered in connection with the writing of exchange-traded call options, describe briefly such transactions.

8. If simultaneously or almost simultaneously with the creation of shares for which admission to official listing is being sought, shares of the same class are subscribed for or placed privately or if shares of other classes are created for public or private placing, details are to be given of the nature of such operations and of the number and characteristics of the shares to which they relate.

9. Unless otherwise described under the response to Item 10.C (Material Contracts), describe the features of the underwriting relationship together with the amount of securities being underwritten by each underwriter in privity of contract with the company or selling shareholders. The foregoing information should include a statement as to whether the underwriters are or will be committed to take and to pay for all of the securities if any are taken, or whether it is an agency or the type of "best efforts" arrangement under which the underwriters are required to take and to pay for only such securities as they may sell to the public.

10. If any underwriter or other financial adviser has a material relationship with the company, describe the nature and terms of such relationship.

C. *Markets.* The company shall disclose all stock exchanges and other regulated markets on which the securities to be offered or listed are traded. When an application for admission to any exchange and/or regulated market is being or will be sought, this must be mentioned, without creating the impression that the listing necessarily will be approved. If known, the dates on which the shares will be listed and dealt in should be given.

D. *Selling shareholders.* The following information shall be provided:

1. The name and address of the person or entity offering to sell the shares, the nature of any position, office or other material relationship that the selling shareholder has had within the past three years with the company or any of its predecessors or affiliates.

2. The number and class of securities being offered by each of the selling shareholders, and the percentage of the existing equity capital. The amount and percentage of the securities for each particular type of securities beneficially held by the selling shareholder before and immediately after the offering shall be specified.

E. *Dilution.* The following information shall be provided:

1. Where there is a substantial disparity between the public offering price and the effective cash cost to directors or senior management, or affiliated persons, of equity securities acquired by them in transactions during the past five years, or which they have the right to acquire, include a comparison of the public contribution in the proposed public offering and the effective cash contributions of such persons.

2. Disclose the amount and percentage of immediate dilution resulting from the offering, computed as the difference between the offering price per share and the net book value per share for the equivalent class of security, as of the latest balance sheet date.

3. In the case of a subscription offering to existing shareholders, disclose the amount and percentage of immediate dilution if they do not subscribe to the new offering.

F. *Expenses of the issue.* The following information shall be provided:

1. The total amount of the discounts or commissions agreed upon by the underwriters or other placement or selling agents and the company or offeror shall be disclosed, as well as the percentage such commissions represent of the total amount of the offering and the amount of discounts or commissions per share.

2. A reasonably itemized statement of the major categories of expenses incurred in connection with the issuance and distribution of the securities to be listed or offered and by whom the expenses are payable, if other than the company. If any of the securities are to be offered for the account of a selling shareholder, indicate the portion of such expenses to be borne by such shareholder. The information may be given subject to future contingencies. If the amounts of any items are not known, estimates (identified as such) shall be given.

Instruction to Item 9: If you are using this Form as a registration statement under the Exchange Act, provide only the information called for by items 9.A.4-7 and 9.C. If you are using this Form as an annual report, provide only the information called for by Items 9.A.4 and 9.C. If you are providing this information in a Securities Act registration statement, provide the information called for by the entire item.

Instruction to Item 9.A: When you are required to state the title of the securities, the title must indicate the type and general character of the securities, such as whether they are callable, convertible or redeemable and whether there is any preference or fixed rate of dividends.

Instructions to Item 9.B:

1. You may satisfy the requirement in Item 9.B.1 to provide the underwriters' addresses by giving the addresses of the lead underwriters for the offering.

2. If previously you have not been required to file reports under section 13(a) or 15(d) of the Exchange Act and any of the managing underwriters (or a majority of the principal underwriters) has been organized, reactivated or first registered as a broker-dealer within the past three years, disclose that fact. Also disclose, if true, that the principal business function of this underwriter will be to sell the securities being registered or that your promoters or founders have a material relationship with this underwriter. Give enough details to provide a clear picture of the underwriter's experience and its relationship with you, your promoters or founders, and their controlling persons.

Instruction to Item 9.F: Major categories of expenses include at least the following: registration fees, federal taxes, state taxes and fees, trustees' and transfer agents' fees, printing and engraving costs, legal fees, accounting fees, engineering fees, and any premiums paid to insure directors or officers for liabilities in connection with the registration, offer or sale of the securities you are registering.

Item 10.   Additional Information

The purpose of this standard is to provide information, most of which is of a statutory nature, that is not covered elsewhere in the document.

A. *Share capital.* The following information shall be given as of the date of the most recent balance sheet included in the financial statements and as of the latest practicable date:

1. The amount of issued capital and, for each class of share capital: (a) the number of shares authorized; (b) the number of shares issued and fully paid and issued but not fully paid; (c) the par value per share, or that the shares have no par value; and (d) a reconciliation of the number of shares outstanding at the beginning and end of the year. If more than 10% of capital has been paid for with assets other than cash within the past five years, that fact should be stated.

2. If there are shares not representing capital, the number and main characteristics of such shares shall be stated.

3. Indicate the number, book value and face value of shares in the company held by or on behalf of the company itself or by subsidiaries of the company.

4. Where there is authorized but unissued capital or an undertaking to increase the capital, for example, in connection with warrants, convertible obligations or other outstanding equity-linked securities, or subscription rights granted, indicate: (i) the amount of outstanding equity-linked securities and of such authorized capital or capital increase and, where appropriate, the duration of the authorization; (ii) the categories of persons having preferential subscription rights for such additional portions of capital; and (iii) the terms, arrangements and procedures for the share issue corresponding to such portions.

5. The persons to whom any capital of any member of the group is under option or agreed conditionally or unconditionally to be put under option, including the title and amount of securities covered by the options; the exercise price; the purchase price, if any; and the expiration date of the options, or an appropriate negative statement. Where options have been granted or agreed to be granted to all the holders of shares or debt securities, or of any class thereof, or to employees under an employees' share scheme, it will be sufficient so far as the names are concerned, to record that fact without giving names.

6. A history of share capital for the last three years identifying the events during such period which have changed the amount of the issued capital and/or the number and classes of shares of which it composed, together with a description of changes in voting rights attached to the various classes of shares during that time. Details should be given of the price and terms of any issue including particulars of consideration where this was other than cash (including information regarding discounts, special terms or installment payments). If there are no such issues, an appropriate negative statement must be made. The reason for any reduction of the amount of capital and the ratio of capital reductions also shall be given.

7. An indication of the resolutions, authorizations and approvals by virtue of which the shares have been or will be created and/or issued, the nature of the issue and amount thereof and the number of shares which have been or will be created and/or issued, if predetermined.

B. *Memorandum and articles of association.* The following information shall be provided:

1. Indicate the registor and the entry number therein, if applicable, and describe the company's objects and purposes and where they can be found in the memorandum and articles.

2. With respect to directors, provide a summary of any provisions of the company's articles of association or charter and bylaws with respect to: (a) a director's power to vote on a proposal, arrangement or contract in which the director is materially interested; (b) the directors' power, in the absence of an independent quorum, to vote compensation to themselves or any members of their body; (c) borrowing powers exercisable by the directors and how such borrowing powers can be varied; (d) retirement or non-retirement of directors under an age limit requirement; and (e) number of shares, if any, required for director's qualification.

3. Describe the rights, preferences and restrictions attaching to each class of the shares, including: (a) dividend rights, including the time limit after which dividend entitlement lapses and an indication of the party in whose favor this entitlement operates; (b) voting rights, including whether directors stand for reelection at staggered intervals and the impact of that arrangement where cumulative voting is permitted or required; (c) rights to share in the company's profits; (d) rights to share in any surplus in the event of liquidation; (e) redemption provisions; (f) sinking fund provisions; (g) liability to further capital calls by the company; and (h) any provision discriminating against any existing or prospective holder of such securities as a result of such shareholder owning a substantial number of shares.

4. Describe what action is necessary to change the rights of holders of the stock, indicating where the conditions are more significant than is required by law.

5. Describe the conditions governing the manner in which annual general meetings and extraordinary general meetings of shareholders are convoked, including the conditions of admission.

6. Describe any limitations on the rights to own securities, including the rights of non-resident or foreign shareholders to hold or exercise voting rights on the securities imposed by foreign law or by the charter or other constituent document of the company or state that there are no such limitations if that is the case.

7. Describe briefly any provision of the company's articles of association, charter or bylaws that would have an effect of delaying, deferring or preventing a change in control of the company and that would operate only with respect to a merger, acquisition or corporate restructuring involving the company (or any of its subsidiaries).

8. Indicate the bylaw provisions, if any, governing the ownership threshold above which shareholder ownership must be disclosed.

9. With respect to items 2 through 8 above, if the law applicable to the company in these areas is significantly different from that in the host country, the effect of the law in these areas should be explained.

10. Describe the conditions imposed by the memorandum and articles of association governing changes in the capital, where such conditions are more stringent than is required by law.

C. *Material contracts.* Provide a summary of each material contract, other than contracts entered into in the ordinary course of business, to which the company or any member of the group is a party, for the two years immediately preceding publication of the document, including dates, parties, general nature of the contracts, terms and conditions, and amount of any consideration passing to or from the company or any other member of the group.

D. *Exchange controls.* Describe any governmental laws, decrees, regulations or other legislation of the home country of the company which may affect:

1. The import or export of capital, including the availability of cash and cash equivalents for use by the company's group.

2. The remittance of dividends, interest or other payments to nonresident holders of the company's securities.

E. *Taxation.* The company shall provide information regarding taxes (including withholding provisions) to which shareholders in the host country may be subject. Information should be included as to whether the company assumes responsibility for the withholding of tax at the source and regarding applicable provisions of any reciprocal tax treaties between the home and host countries, or a statement, if applicable, that there are no such treaties.

F. *Dividends and paying agents.* Disclose any dividend restrictions, the date on which the entitlement to dividends arises, if known, and any procedures for nonresident holders to claim dividends. Identify the financial organizations which, at the time of admission of shares to official listing, are the paying agents of the company in the countries where admission has taken place or is expected to take place.

G. *Statement by experts.* Where a statement or report attributed to a person as an expert is included in the document, provide such person's name, address and qualifications and a statement to the effect that such statement or report is included, in the form and context in which it is included, with the consent of that person, who has authorized the contents of that part of the document

H. *Documents on display.* The company shall provide an indication of where the documents concerning the company which are referred to in the document may be inspected. Exhibits and documents on display generally should be translated into the language of the host country, or a summary in the host country language should be provided.

I. *Subsidiary Information.* Certain information relating to the company's subsidiaries must be provided in some countries, if the information is not otherwise called for by the body of generally accepted accounting principles used in preparing the financial statements.

Instructions to Item 10:

1. *In annual reports filed on Form 20-F:*

   (a) *You do not have to provide the information called for by items 10.A, 10.F and 10.G; and*

   (b) *If the information called for by Item 10.B has been reported previously in a registration statement on Form 20-F or a registration statement filed under the Securities Act and has not changed, you may incorporate that information by a specific reference in the annual report to the previous registration statement.*

2. *In registration statements filed under the Securities Act or the Exchange Act that relate to securities other than common equity, you do not have to provide the information called for by Items 10.A or 10.F.*

3. *The information referred to in Item 10.I is not required for registration statements and reports filed in the United States.*

Item 11.   Quantitative and Qualitative Disclosures About Market Risk

(a) Quantitative information about market risk.

(1) Registrants shall provide, in their reporting currency, quantitative information about market risk as of the end of the latest fiscal year, in accordance with one of the following three disclosure alternatives. In preparing this quantitative information, registrants shall categorize market risk sensitive instruments into instruments entered into for trading purposes and instruments entered into for purposes other than trading purposes. Within both the trading and other than trading portfolios, separate quantitative information shall be presented, to the extent material, for each market risk exposure category (i.e., interest rate risk, foreign currency exchange rate risk, commodity price risk, and other relevant market risks, such as equity price risk). A registrant may use one of the three alternatives set forth below for all of the required quantitative disclosures about market risk. A registrant also may choose, from among the three alternatives, one disclosure alternative for market risk sensitive instruments entered into for trading purposes and another disclosure alternative for market risk sensitive instruments entered into for other than trading purposes. Alternatively, a registrant may choose any disclosure alternative, from among the three alternatives, for each risk exposure category within the trading and other than trading portfolios. The three disclosure alternatives are:

   (i) (A) (*1*) Tabular presentation of information related to market risk sensitive instruments; such information shall include fair values of the market risk sensitive instruments and contract terms sufficient to determine future cash flows from those instruments, categorized by expected maturity dates.

   (*2*) Tabular information relating to contract terms shall allow readers of the table to determine expected cash flows from the market risk sensitive instruments for each of the next five years. Comparable tabular information for any remaining years shall be displayed as an aggregate amount.

(*3*) Within each risk exposure category, the market risk sensitive instruments shall be grouped based on common characteristics. Within the foreign currency exchange rate risk category, the market risk sensitive instruments shall be grouped by functional currency and within the commodity price risk category, the market risk sensitive instruments shall be grouped by type of commodity.

(*4*) See the Appendix to this Item for a suggested format for presentation of this information; and

(B) Registrants shall provide a description of the contents of the table and any related assumptions necessary to understand the disclosures required under paragraph (a)(1)(i)(A) of this Item 11; or

(ii) (A) Sensitivity analysis disclosures that express the potential loss in future earnings, fair values, or cash flows of market risk sensitive instruments resulting from one or more selected hypothetical changes in interest rates, foreign currency exchange rates, commodity prices, and other relevant market rates or prices over a selected period of time. The magnitude of selected hypothetical changes in rates or prices may differ among and within market risk exposure categories; and

(B) Registrants shall provide a description of the model, assumptions, and parameters, which are necessary to understand the disclosures required under paragraph (a)(1)(ii)(A) of this Item 11; or

(iii) (A) Value at risk disclosures that express the potential loss in future earnings, fair values, or cash flows of market risk sensitive instruments over a selected period of time, with a selected likelihood of occurrence, from changes in interest rates, foreign currency exchange rates, commodity prices, and other relevant market rates or prices;

(B) (*1*) For each category for which value at risk disclosures are required under paragraph (a)(1)(iii)(A) of this Item 11, provide either:

(i) The average, high and low amounts, or the distribution of the value at risk amounts for the reporting period; or

(ii) The average, high and low amounts, or the distribution of actual changes in fair values, earnings, or cash flows from the market risk sensitive instruments occurring during the reporting period; or

(iii) The percentage or number of times the actual changes in fair values, earnings, or cash flows from the market risk sensitive instruments exceeded the value at risk amounts during the reporting period;

(*2*) Information required under paragraph (a)(1)(iii)(B)(1) of this Item 11 is not required for the first fiscal year end in which a registrant must present Item 11 information; and

(C) Registrants shall provide a description of the model, assumptions, and parameters, which are necessary to understand the disclosures required under paragraphs (a)(1)(iii)(A) and (B) of this Item 11.

(2) Registrants shall discuss material limitations that cause the information required under paragraph (a)(1) of this Item 11 not to reflect fully the net market risk exposures of the entity. This discussion shall include summarized descriptions of instruments, positions, and transactions omitted from the quantitative market risk disclosure information or the features of instruments, positions and transactions that are included, but not reflected fully in the quantitative market risk disclosure information.

(3) Registrants shall present summarized market risk information for the preceding fiscal year. In addition, registrants shall discuss the reasons for material quantitative changes in market risk exposures between the current and preceding fiscal years. Information required by this paragraph (a)(3), however, is not required if disclosure is not required under paragraph (a)(1) of this Item 11 for the current fiscal year. Information required by this paragraph (a)(3) is not required for the first fiscal year end in which a registrant must present Item 11 information.

(4) If registrants change disclosure alternatives or key model characteristics, assumptions, and parameters used in providing quantitative information about market risk (e.g., changing from tabular presentation to value at risk, changing the scope of instruments included in the model, or changing the definition of loss from fair values to earnings), and if the effects of any such change is material, the registrant shall:

    (i) Explain the reasons for the change; and

    (ii) Either provide summarized comparable information, under the new disclosure method, for the year preceding the current year or, in addition to providing disclosure for the current year under the new method, provide disclosures for the current year and preceding fiscal year under the method used in the preceding year.

Instructions to Item 11(a).

1. *Under Item 11(a)(1):*

    A. *For each market risk exposure category within the trading and other than trading portfolios, registrants may report the average, high, and low sensitivity analysis or value at risk amounts for the reporting period as an alternative to reporting year-end amounts.*

    B. *In determining the average, high and low amounts for the fiscal year under instruction 1.A. of the Instructions to Item 11(a), registrants should use sensitivity analysis or value at risk amounts relating to at least four equal time periods throughout the reporting period (e.g., four quarter-end amounts, 12 month-end amounts, or 52 week-end amounts).*

    C. *Functional currency means functional currency as defined by generally accepted accounting principles (see, e.g., FASB, Statement of Financial Accounting Standards No. 52, "Foreign Currency Translation," ("FAS 52") paragraph 20 (December 1981)).*

    D. *Registrants using the sensitivity analysis and value at risk disclosure alternatives are encouraged, but not required, to provide quantitative amounts that reflect the aggregate market risk inherent in the trading and other than trading portfolios.*

2. *Under Item 11(a)(1)(i):*

    A. *Examples of contract terms sufficient to determine future cash flows from market risk sensitive instruments include, but are not limited to:*

        i. *Debt instruments—principal amounts and weighted average effective interest rates;*

        ii. *Forwards and futures—contract amounts and weighted average settlement prices;*

        iii. *Options—contract amounts and weighted overage strike prices;*

        iv. *Swaps—notional amounts, weighted average pay rates or prices, and weighted average receive rates or prices; and*

        v. *Complex instruments—likely to be a combination of the contract terms presented in 2.A.i. through iv. of this Instruction;*

    B. *When grouping based on common characteristics, instruments should be categorized, at a minimum, by the following characteristics, when material:*

        i. *Fixed rate or variable rate assets or liabilities;*

        ii. *Long or short forwards and futures;*

        iii. *Written or purchased put or call options with similar strike prices;*

        iv. *Receive fixed and pay variable swaps, receive variable and pay fixed swaps, and receive variable and pay variable swaps;*

        v. *The currency in which the instruments' cash flows are denominated;*

vi. *Financial instruments for which foreign currency transaction gains and losses are reported in the same manner as translation adjustments under generally accepted accounting principles (see, e.g., FAS 52 paragraph 20 (December 1981)); and*

vii. *Derivatives used to manage risks inherent in anticipated transactions;*

C. *Registrants may aggregate information regarding functional currencies that are economically related, managed together for internal risk management purposes, and have statistical correlations of greater than 75% over each of the past three years;*

D. *Market risk sensitive instruments that are exposed to rate or price changes in more than one market risk exposure category should be presented within the tabular information for each of the risk exposure categories to which those instruments are exposed;*

E. *If a currency swap (see, e.g., FAS 52 Appendix E for a definition of currency swap) eliminates all foreign currency exposures in the cash flows of a foreign currency denominated debt instrument, neither the currency swap nor the foreign currency denominated debt instrument are required to be disclosed in the foreign currency risk exposure category. However, both the currency swap and the foreign currency denominated debt instrument should be disclosed in the interest rate risk exposure category; and*

F. *The contents of the table and related assumptions that should be described include, but are not limited to:*

   i. *The different amounts reported in the table for various categories of the market risk sensitive instruments (e.g., principal amounts for debt, notional amounts for swaps, and contract amounts for options and futures);*

   ii. *The different types of reported market rates or prices (e.g., contractual rates or prices, spot rates or prices, forward rates or prices); and*

   iii. *Key prepayment or reinvestment assumptions relating to the timing of reported amounts.*

3. *Under Item 11(a)(1)(ii):*

   A. *Registrants should select hypothetical changes in market rates or prices that are expected to reflect reasonably possible near-term changes in those rates and prices. In this regard, absent economic justification for the selection of a different amount, registrants should use changes that are not less than 10 percent of end of period market rates or prices;*

   B. *For purposes of instruction 3.A. of the Instructions to Item 11(a), the term reasonably possible has the same meaning as defined by generally accepted accounting principles (see, e.g., FASE, Statement of Financial Accounting Standards No. 5, "Accounting for Contingencies," ("FAS 5") paragraph 3 (March 1975));*

   C. *For purposes of instruction 3.A. of the Instructions to Item 11(a), the term near term means a period of time going forward up to one year from the date of the financial statements (see generally AICPA, Statement of Position 946, "Disclosure of Certain Significant Risks and Uncertainties," ("SOP 94-6") at paragraph 7 (December 30, 1994));*

   D. *Market risk sensitive instruments that are exposed to rate or price changes in more than one market risk exposure category should be included in the sensitivity analysis disclosures for each market risk category to which those instruments are exposed;*

   E. *Registrants with multiple foreign currency exchange rate exposures should prepare foreign currency sensitivity analysis disclosures that measure the aggregate sensitivity to changes in all foreign currency exchange rate exposures, including the effects of changes in both transactional currency/functional currency exchange rate exposures and functional currency/reporting currency exchange rate exposures. For example, assume a French division of a registrant presenting its financial statements in U.S. dollars ($US) invests in a deutschmark (DM)-denominated debt security. In these circumstances, the $US is the reporting currency and the DM is the transactional currency. In addition, assume this division determines that the French franc (FF) is its functional currency* *according to FAS 52. In preparing the foreign currency sensitivity analysis disclosures, this registrant should report the aggregate potential loss from hypothetical changes in both the DM/FF exchange rate exposure and the FF/$US exchange rate exposure; and*

F. *Model, assumptions, and parameters that should be described include, but are not limited to, how loss is defined by the model (e.g., loss in earnings, fair values, or cash flows), a general description of the modeling technique (e.g., duration modeling, modeling that measures the change in net present values arising from selected hypothetical changes in market rates or prices, and a description as to how optionality is addressed by the model), the types of instruments covered by the model (e.g., derivative financial instruments, other financial instruments, derivative commodity instruments, and whether other instruments are included voluntarily, such as certain commodity instruments and positions, cash flows from anticipated transactions, and certain financial instruments excluded under instruction 3.C.ii. of the General Instructions to Items 11(a) and 11(b)), and other relevant information about the model's assumptions and parameters, (e.g., the magnitude and timing of selected hypothetical changes in market rates or prices used, the method by which discount rates are determined, and key prepayment or reinvestment assumptions).*

4. *Under Item 11(a)(1)(iii):*

A. *The confidence intervals selected should reflect reasonably possible near-term changes in market rates and prices. In this regard, absent economic justification for the selection of different confidence intervals, registrants should use intervals that are 95 percent or higher;*

B. *For purposes of instruction 4.A. of the Instructions to Item 11(a), the term reasonably possible has the same meaning as defined by generally accepted accounting principles (see, e.g., FAS 5, paragraph 3 (March 1975));*

C. *For purposes of instruction 4.A. of the Instructions to Item 11(a), the term near term means a period of time going forward up to one year from the date of the financial statements (see generally SOP 94-6, at paragraph 7 (December 30, 1994));*

D. *Registrants with multiple foreign currency exchange rate exposures should prepare foreign currency value at risk analysis disclosures that measure the aggregate sensitivity to changes in all foreign currency exchange rate exposures, including the aggregate effects of changes in both transactional currency/functional currency exchange rate exposures and functional currency/reporting currency exchange rate exposures. For example, assume a French division of a registrant presenting its financial statements in U.S. dollars ($US) invests in a deutschmark(DM)-denominated debt security. In these circumstances, the $US is the reporting currency and the DM is the transactional currency. In addition, assume this division determines that the French franc (FF) is its functional currency according to FAS 52. In preparing the foreign currency value at risk disclosures, this registrant should report the aggregate potential loss from hypothetical changes in both the DM/FF exchange rate exposure and the FF/$US exchange rate exposure; and*

E. *Model, assumptions, and parameters that should be described include, but are not limited to, how loss is defined by the model (e.g., loss in earnings, fair values, or cash flows), the type of model used (e.g., variance/covariance, historical simulation, or Monte Carlo simulation and a description as to how optionality is addressed by the model), the types of instruments covered by the model (e.g., derivative financial instruments, other financial instruments, derivative commodity instruments, and whether other instruments are included voluntarily, such ascertain commodity instruments and positions, cash flows from anticipated transactions, and certain financial instruments excluded under instruction 3.C.ii of the General Instructions to Items 11(a) and 11(b)), and other relevant information about the model's assumptions and parameters, (e.g., holding periods, confidence intervals, and, when appropriate, the methods used for aggregating value at risk amounts across market risk exposure categories, such as by assuming perfect positive correlation, independence, or actual observed correlation).*

5. *Under Item 11(a)(2), limitations that should be considered include, but are not limited to:*

A. *The exclusion of certain market risk sensitive instruments, positions, and transactions from the disclosures required under Item 11(a)(1) (e.g., derivative commodity instruments not permitted by contract or business cus-*

tom to be settled in cash or with another financial instrument, commodity positions, cash flows from anticipated transactions, and certain financial instruments excluded under instruction 3.C.ii. of the General Instructions to Items 11(a) and 11(b)). Failure to include such instruments, positions, and transactions in preparing the disclosures under Item 11(a)(1) may be a limitation because the resulting disclosures may not fully reflect the net market risk of a registrant; and

B. The ability of disclosures required under Item 11(a)(1) to reflect fully the market risk that may be inherent in instruments with leverage, option, or prepayment features (e.g., options, including written options, structured notes, collateralized mortgage obligations, leveraged swaps, and options embedded in swaps).

[end of Instructions to Item 11(a)]

(b) Qualitative information about market risk.

   (1) To the extent material, describe:

   (i)   The registrant's primary market risk exposures;

   (ii) How those exposures are managed. Such descriptions shall include, but not be limited to, a discussion of the objectives, general strategies, and instruments, if any, used to manage those exposures; and

   (iii) Changes in either the registrant's primary market risk exposures or how those exposures are managed, when compared to what was in effect during the most recently completed fiscal year and what is known or expected to be in effect in future reporting periods.

   (2) Qualitative information about market risk shall be presented separately for market risk sensitive instruments entered into for trading purposes and those entered into for purposes other than trading.

Instructions to Item 11(b).

1. For purposes of disclosure under Item 11(b), primary market risk exposures means:

   A. The following categories of market risk: interest rate risk, foreign currency exchange rate risk, commodity price risk, and other relevant market rate or price risks (e.g., equity price risk); and

   B. Within each of these categories, the particular markets that present the primary risk of loss to the registrant. For example, if a registrant has a material exposure to foreign currency exchange rate risk and, within this category of market risk, is most vulnerable to changes in dollar/yen, dollar/pound and dollar/peso exchange rates, the registrant should disclose those exposures. Similarly, if a registrant has a material exposure to interest rate risk and, within this category of market risk, is most vulnerable to changes in short-term U.S. prime interest rates, it should disclose the existence of that exposure.

2. For purposes of disclosure under Item 11(b), registrants should describe primary market risk exposures that exist as of the end of the latest fiscal year, and how those exposures are managed.

General Instructions to Items 11(a) and 11(b).

1. The disclosures called for by Items 11(a) and 11(b) are intended to clarify the registrant's exposures to market risk associated with activities in derivative financial instruments, other financial instruments, and derivative commodity instruments.

2. In preparing the disclosures under Items 11(a) and 11(b), registrants are required to include derivative financial instruments, other financial instruments, and derivative commodity instruments.

3. For purposes of Items 11(a) and 11(b), derivative financial instruments, other financial instruments, and derivative commodity instruments (collectively referred to as "market risk sensitive instruments") are defined as follows:

   A. Derivative financial instruments has the same meaning as defined by generally accepted accounting principles (see, e.g., FASB, Statement of Financial Accounting Standards No. 119, "Disclosure about Derivative Financial Instruments and Fair Value of Financial Instruments," ("FAS 119") paragraphs 5-7 (October 1994)), and includes futures, forwards, swaps, options, and other financial instruments with similar characteristics;

B. *Other financial instruments means all financial instruments as defined by generally accepted accounting principles for which fair value disclosures are required (see, e.g., FASB, Statement of Financial Accounting Standards No. 107, "Disclosures about Fair Value of Financial Instruments," ("FAS 107") paragraphs 3 and 8 (December 1991)), except for derivative financial instruments, as defined above;*

C. i.   *Other financial instruments include, but are not limited to, trade accounts receivable, investments, loans, structured notes, mortgage-backed securities, trade accounts payable, indexed debt instruments, interest-only and principal-only obligations, deposits, and other debt obligations;*

   ii. *Other financial instruments exclude employers and plans obligations for pension and other post-retirement benefits, substantively extinguished debt, insurance contracts, lease contracts, warranty obligations and rights, unconditional purchase obligations, investments accounted for under the equity method, minority interests in consolidated enterprises, and equity instruments issued by the registrant and classified in stockholders' equity in the statement of financial position (see, e.g., FAS 107, paragraph 8 (December 1991)). For purposes of this item, trade accounts receivable and trade accounts payable need not be considered other financial instruments when their carrying amounts approximate fair value; and*

D. *Derivative commodity instruments include, to the extent such instruments are not derivative financial instruments, commodity futures, commodity forwards, commodity swaps, commodity options, and other commodity instruments with similar characteristics that are permitted by contract or business custom to be settled in cash or with another financial instrument. For purposes of this paragraph, settlement in cash includes settlement in cash of the net change in value of the derivative commodity instrument (e.g., net cash settlement based on changes in the price of the underlying commodity).*

4. A.   *In addition to providing required disclosures for the market risk sensitive instruments defined in Instruction 2. of the General Instructions to Items 11(a) and 11(b), registrants are encouraged to include other market risk sensitive instruments, positions, and transactions within the disclosures required under Items 11(a) and 11(b). Such instruments, positions, and transactions might include commodity positions, derivative commodity instruments that are not permitted by contract or business custom to be settled in cash or with another financial instrument, cash flows from anticipated transactions, and certain financial instruments excluded under instruction 3.C.ii. of the General Instructions to Items 11(a) and 11(b).*

   B.   *Registrants that voluntarily include other market risk sensitive instruments, positions and transactions within their quantitative disclosures about market risk under the sensitivity analysis or value at risk disclosure alternatives are not required to provide separate market risk disclosures for any voluntarily selected instruments, positions, or transactions. Instead, registrants selecting the sensitivity analysis and value at risk disclosure alternatives are permitted to present comprehensive market risk disclosures, which reflect the combined market risk exposures inherent in both the required and any voluntarily selected instruments, position, or transactions. Registrants that choose the tabular presentation disclosure alternative should present voluntarily selected instruments, positions, or transactions in a manner consistent with the requirements in Item 11(a) for market risk sensitive instruments.*

   C.   *If a registrant elects to include voluntarily a particular type of instrument, position, or transaction in their quantitative disclosures about market risk, that registrant should include all, rather than some, of those instruments, positions, or transactions within those disclosures. For example, if a registrant holds in inventory a particular type of commodity position and elects to include that commodity position within their market risk disclosures, the registrant should include the entire commodity position, rather than only a portion thereof, in their quantitative disclosures about market risk.*

5. A.   *Under Items 11(a) and 11(b), a materiality assessment should be made for each market risk exposure category within the trading and other than trading portfolios.*

   B.   *For purposes of making the materiality assessment under instruction 5.A. of the General Instructions to Items 11(a) and 11(b), registrants should evaluate both:*

    i   *The materiality of the fair values of derivative financial instruments, other financial instruments, and derivative commodity instruments outstanding as of the end of the latest fiscal year; and*

    ii.   *The materiality of potential, near-term losses in future earnings, fair values, and cash flows from reasonably possible near-term changes in market rates or prices.*

    iii.   *If either paragraphs B.i. or B.ii. in this instruction of the General Instructions to Items 11(a) and 11(b) are material, the registrant should disclose quantitative and qualitative information about market risk, if such market risk for the particular market risk exposure category is material.*

  C. *For purposes of instruction 5.B.i. of the General Instructions to Items 11(a) and 11(b), registrants generally should not net fair values, except to the extent allowed under generally accepted accounting principles (see, e.g., FASB Interpretation No. 39, "Offsetting of Amounts Related to Certain Contracts" (March 1992)). For example, under this instruction, the fair value of assets generally should not be netted with the fair value of liabilities.*

  D. *For purposes of Instruction 5.B.ii. of the General Instructions to Items 11(a) and 11(b), registrants should consider, among other things, the magnitude of:*

    i.   *Past market movements;*

    ii.   *Reasonably possible, near-term market movements; and*

    iii.   *Potential losses that may arise from leverage, option, and multiplier features.*

  E. *For purposes of instructions 5.B.ii. and 5.D.ii. of the General Instructions to Items 11(a) and 11(b), the term near term means a period of time going forward up to one year from the date of the financial statements (see generally SOP 946, at paragraph 7 (December 30, 1994)).*

  F. *For the purpose of instructions 5.B.ii. and 5.D.ii. of the General Instructions to Items 11(a) and 11(b), the term reasonably possible has the same meaning as defined by generally accepted accounting principles (see, e.g., FAS 5, paragraph 3 (March 1975)).*

6. *For purposes of Items 11(a) and 11(b), registrants should present the information outside of, and not incorporate the information into, the financial statements (including the footnotes to the financial statements). In addition, registrants are encouraged to provide the required information in one location. However, alternative presentation, such as inclusion of all or part of the information in Management's Discussion and Analysis, may be used at the discretion of the registrant. If information is disclosed in more than one location, registrants should provide cross-references to the locations of the related disclosures.*

7. *For purposes of the instructions to Items 11(a) and 11(b), trading purposes has the same meaning as defined by generally accepted accounting principles (see, e.g., FAS 119, paragraph 9a (October 1994)). In addition, anticipated transactions means transactions (other than transactions involving existing assets or liabilities or transactions necessitated by existing firm commitments) an enterprise expects, but is not obligated, to carry out in the normal course of business (see, e.g., FASB, Statement of Financial Accounting Standards No. 80, "Accounting for Futures Contracts," paragraph 9 (August 1984)).*

[end of General Instructions to Items 11(a) and 11(b)]

  (c) Interim periods. If interim period financial statements are included or are required to be included by Article 3 of Regulation S-X (17 CFR 210), discussion and analysis shall be provided so as to enable the reader to assess the sources and effects of material changes in information that would be provided under Item 11 of Form 20-F from the end of the preceding fiscal year to the date of the most recent interim balance sheet.

Instructions to Item 11(c).

1. *Information required by paragraph (c) of this Item 11 is not required until after the first fiscal year end in which this Item 11 is applicable.*

  (d) Safe Harbor.

(1) The safe harbor provided in Section 27A of the Securities Act of 1933 (15 U.S.C. 77z-2) and Section 21E of the Securities Exchange Act of 1934 (15 U.S.C. 78u-5) ("statutory safe harbors") shall apply, with respect to all types of issuers and transactions, to information provided pursuant to paragraphs (a), (b), and (c) of this Item 11, provided that the disclosure is made by an issuer; a person acting on behalf of the issuer; an outside reviewer retained by the issuer making a statement on behalf of the issuer; or an underwriter, with respect to information provided by the issuer or information derived from information provided by the issuer.

(2) For purposes of this paragraph (d) of this Item 11 only:

    (i) All information required by paragraphs (a), (b)(1)(i), (b)(1)(iii), and (c) of this Item 11 is considered forward looking statements for purposes of the statutory safe harbors, except for historical facts such as the terms of particular contracts and the number of market risk sensitive instruments held during or at the end of the reporting period; and

    (ii) With respect to paragraph (a) of this Item 11, the meaningful cautionary statements prong of the statutory safe harbors will be satisfied if a registrant satisfies all requirements of that same paragraph (a) of this Item 11.

(e) Small business issuers. Small business issuers, as defined in § 230.405 of this chapter and § 240.12b-2 of this chapter, need not provide the information required by this Item 11, whether or not they file on forms specially designated as small business issuer forms.

General Instructions to Items 11(a), 11(b), 11(c), 11(d), and 11(e).

1. *Bank registrants, thrift registrants, and non-bank and non-thrift registrants with market capitalizations on January 28, 1997 in excess of $2.5 billion should provide Item 11 disclosures in filings with the Commission that include annual financial statements for fiscal years ending after June 15, 1997. Non-bank and non-thrift registrants with market capitalizations on January 28, 1997 of $2.5 billion or less should provide Item 11 disclosures in filings with the Commission that include annual financial statements for fiscal years ending after June 15, 1998.*

2. A. *For purposes of instruction 1. of the General Instructions to Items 11(a), 11(b), 11(c), 11(d), and 11(e), bank registrants and thrift registrants include any registrant which has control over a depository institution.*

    B. *For purposes of Instruction 2.A. of the General Instructions to Items 11(a), 11(b), 11(c), 11(d), and 11(e), a registrant has control over a depository institution if:*

       i. The registrant directly or indirectly or acting through one or more other persons owns, controls, or has power to vote 25% or more of any class of voting securities of the depository institution;

       ii. The registrant controls in any manner the election of a majority of the directors or trustees of the depository institution; or

       iii. The Federal Reserve Board or Office of Thrift Supervision determines, after notice and opportunity for hearing, that the registrant directly or indirectly exercises a controlling influence over the management or policies of the depository institution;

    C. *For purposes of instruction 2.B. of the General Instructions to Items 11(a), 11(b), 11(c), 11(d), and 11(e), a depository institution means any of the following:*

       i. An insured depository institution as defined in section 3(c)(2) of the Federal Deposit Insurance Act (12 U.S.C.A. Sec. 1813 (c));

          a. An institution organized under the laws of the United States, any State of the United States, the District of Columbia, any territory of the United States, Puerto Rico, Guam, American Samoa, or the Virgin islands, which both accepts demand deposits or deposits that the depositor may withdraw by check or similar means for payment to third parties or others and is engaged in the business of making commercial loans.

D. *For purposes of Instruction 1. of the General Instructions to Items 11(a), 11(b), 11(c), 11(d), and 11(e), market capitalization is the aggregate market value of common equity as set forth in General Instruction I.B.1. of Form S-3; provided however, that common equity held by affiliates is included in the calculation of market capitalization; and provided further that instead of using the 60 day period prior to filing referenced in General Instruction I.B.1. of Form S-3, the measurement date is January 28, 1997.*

Appendix to Item 11—Tabular Disclosures

The tables set forth below are illustrative of the format that might be used when a registrant elects to present the information required by paragraph (a)(I)(i)(A) of Item 11 regarding terms and information about derivative financial instruments, other financial instruments, and derivative commodity instruments. These examples are for illustrative purposes only. Registrants are not required to display the information in the specific format illustrated below. Alternative methods of display are permissible as long as the disclosure requirements of the section are satisfied. Furthermore, these examples were designed primarily to illustrate possible formats for presentation of the information required by the disclosure item and do not purport to illustrate the broad range of derivative financial instruments, other financial instruments, and derivative commodity instruments utilized by registrants.

Interest Rate Sensitivity

The table below provides information about the Company's derivative financial instruments and other financial instruments that are sensitive to changes in interest rates, including interest rate swaps and debt obligations. For debt obligations, the table presents principal cash flows and related weighted average interest rates by expected maturity dates. For interest rate swaps, the table presents notional amounts and weighted average interest rates by expected (contractual) maturity dates. Notional amounts are used to calculate the contractual payments to be exchanged under the contract. Weighted average variable rates are based on implied forward rates in the yield curve at the reporting date. The information is presented in U.S. dollar equivalents, which is the Company's reporting currency. The instrument's actual cash flows are denominated in both U.S. dollars ($US) and German deutschmarks (DM), as indicated in parentheses.

December 31, 19x1

			Expected Maturity Date					
	19x2	19x3	19x4	19x5	19x6	There-after	Total	Fair Value
Liabilities							(US$ Equivalent in millions)	
Long-term Debt								
Fixed Rate ($US)	$XXX	$XXX	$XXX	$XXX	$XXX	$XXX	$XXX	$XXX
Average interest rate	X.X%	X.X%	X.X%	X.X%	X.X%	X.X%	X.X%	
Fixed Rate (DM)	XXX	XXX	XXX	XXX	XXX	XXX	XXX	XXX
Average interest rate	X.X%	X.X%	X.X%	X.X%	X.X%	X.X%	X.X%	
Variable Rate ($US)	XXX	XXX	XXX	XXX	XXX	XXX	XXX	XXX
Average interest rate	X.X%	X.X%	X.X%	X.X%	X.X%	X.X%	X.X%	

			Expected Maturity Rate					
Interest Rate Derivatives	19x2	19x3	19x4	19x5	19x6	There-after	Total	Fair Value
							(In millions)	
Interest Rate Swaps								
Variable to Fixed ($US)	$XXX	$XXX	$XXX	$XXX	$XXX	$XXX	$XXX	$XXX
Average pay rate	X.X%	X.X%	X.X%	X.X%	X.X%	X.X%	X.X%	
Average receive rate	X.X%	X.X%	X.X%	X.X%	X.X%	X.X%	X.X%	
Fixed to Variable ($US)	XXX	XXX	XXX	XXX	XXX	XXX	XXX	XXX
Average pay rate	X.X%	X.X%	X.X%	X.X%	X.X%	X.X%	X.X%	
Average receive rate	X.X%	X.X%	X.X%	X.X%	-X.X%	X.X%	X.X%	

Exchange Rate Sensitivity

The table below provides information about the Company's derivative financial instruments, other financial instruments, and firmly committed sales transactions by functional currency and presents such information in U.S. dollar equivalents.[1] The table summarizes information on instruments and transactions that are sensitive to foreign currency exchange rates, including foreign currency forward exchange agreements, deutschmark (DM)-denominated debt obligations, and firmly committed DM sales transactions. For debt obligations, the table presents principal cash flows and related weighted average interest rates by expected maturity dates. For firmly committed DM-sales transactions, sales amounts are presented by the expected transaction date, which are not expected to exceed two years. For foreign currency forward exchange agreements, the table presents the notional amounts and weighted average exchange rates by expected (contractual) maturity dates. These notional amounts generally are used to calculate the contractual payments to be exchanged under the contract.

December 31, 19x1

| | Expected Maturity Date | | | | | | | |
	19x2	19x3	19x4	19x5	19x6	There-after	Total	Fair Value
On-Balance Sheet Financial Instruments								
	(US$ Equivalent in millions)							
$US Functional Currency[2]								
Liabilities								
Long-Term Debt								
Fixed Rate (DM)	$XXX	$XXX	$XXX	$XXX	$XXX	$XXX	$XXX	$XXX
Average interest rate	X.X	X.X	X.X	X.X	X.X	X.X	X.X	

| | Expected Maturity or Transaction Date | | | | | | | |
	19x2	19x3	19x4	19x5	19x6	There-after	Total	Fair Value
Anticipated Transactions and Related Derivatives[3]	(US$ Equivalent in millions)							
$US Functional Currency:								
Firmly committed transactions:								
Sales Contracts (DM)	$XXX	$XXX	—	—	—	—	$XXX	$XXX
Forward Exchange Agreements (Receive $US/Pay DM)								
Contract Amount	XXX	XXX	—	—	—	—	XXX	XXX
Average Contractual Exchange Rate	X.X	X.X	—	—	—	—	X.X	

Commodity Price Sensitivity

The table below provides information about the Company's corn inventory and futures contracts that are sensitive to changes in commodity prices, specifically corn prices. For inventory, the table presents the carrying amount and fair value at December 31, 19x1. For the futures contracts the table presents the notional amounts in bushels, the weighted aver-

---

[1] The information is presented in U.S. dollars because that is the registrant's reporting currency.

[2] Similar tabular information would be provided for other functional currencies.

[3] Pursuant to General Instruction 4 to Items 11(a) and 11(b) of Form 20-F, registrants may include cash flows from anticipated transactions and operating cash flows resulting from non-financial and non-commodity instruments.

age contract prices, and the total dollar contract amount by expected maturity dates, the latest of which occurs one year from the reporting date. Contract amounts are used to calculate the contractual payments and quantity of corn to be exchanged under the futures contracts.

December 31, 19x1

On Balance Sheet Commodity
  Position and Related Derivatives

	Carrying Amount	Fair Value
	(In millions)	
Corn Inventory	$XXX	$XXX[4]

Related Derivatives

	Expected Maturity 1992	Fair Value
Futures Contracts (Short)		
Contract Volumes (100,000 bushels)	XXX	
Weighted Average Price (Per 100,000 bushels)	$X.XX	
Contract Amount ($US in millions)	$XXX	$XXX

Item 12.   Description of Securities Other than Equity Securities

A. *Debt Securities.* If you are registering debt securities, provide the following information if it is relevant to the securities you are registering.

1. Information about interest, conversions, maturity, redemption, amortization, sinking funds or retirement.

2. The kind and priority of any lien securing the issue, as well as a brief identification of the principal properties subject to each lien.

3. Subordination of the rights of holders of the securities to other security holders or creditors. If the securities are designated in their title as subordinated, give the aggregate amount of outstanding indebtedness as of the most recent practicable date that is senior to the subordinated debt and briefly describe any limitations on the issuance of additional senior indebtedness, or state that there is no limitation.

4. Information about provisions restricting the declaration of dividends or requiring the creation or maintenance of any reserves or of any ratio of assets or requiring the maintenance of properties.

5. Information about provisions permitting or restricting the issuance of additional securities, the withdrawal of cash deposited against the issuance of additional securities, the incurring of additional debt, the release or substitution of assets securing the issue, the modification of the terms of the security and similar provisions. You do not need to describe provisions permitting the release of assets upon the deposit of equivalent funds or the pledge of equivalent property, the release of property no longer required in the business, obsolete property or property taken by eminent domain, the application of insurance monies, and similar provisions.

---

[4] Pursuant to General Instruction 4 to Items 305(a) and 305(b) of Regulation S-K, registrants may include information on commodity positions, such as corn inventory.

6. The general type of event that constitutes a default and whether or not you are required to provide periodic evidence of the absence of a default or of compliance with the terms of the indenture.

7. Modification of the terms of the security or the rights of security holders.

8. If the rights evidenced by the securities you are registering are or may be materially limited or qualified by the rights of any other authorized class of securities, provide enough information about the other class of securities so investors will understand the rights evidenced by the securities you are registering. You do not need to provide information about the other class of securities if all of it will be retired, as long as you have taken appropriate steps to ensure that retirement will be completed on or before the time you deliver the securities you are registering.

9. The tax effects of any "original issue discount" as that term is defined in Section 1232 of the Internal Revenue Code (26 U.S.C. 1232), including cases where the debt security is being sold in a package with another security and the allocation of the offering price between the two securities may have the effect of offering the debt security at an original issue discount.

10. The name and address of the trustee and the nature of any material relationship between the trustee and you or any of your affiliates, the percentage of the class of securities that is needed to require the trustee to take action, and what indemnification the trustee may require before proceeding to enforce the lien.

11. The names and addresses of the paying agents.

12. The currency or currencies in which the debt is payable. If the debt may be paid in two or more currencies, state who has the option to determine the currency conversion and what the basis will be for that determination.

13. Any law or decree determining the extent to which the securities may be serviced.

14. The consequences of any failure to pay principal, interest, or any sinking or amortization installment.

15. If the securities are guaranteed, the name of the guarantor and a brief outline of the contract of guarantee.

B. *Warrants and Rights.* If the securities you are registering are being offered pursuant to warrants or rights, provide the following information, in addition to the description of the securities the warrants or rights represent.

1. The amount of securities called for by the warrants or rights.

2. The period during and the price at which the warrants or rights are exercisable.

3. The amount of warrants or rights outstanding.

4. Provisions for changes or adjustments in the exercise price.

5. Any other material terms of the warrants or rights.

C. *Other Securities.* If you are registering securities other than equity, debt, warrants or rights, briefly describe the rights evidenced by the securities you are registering. The description should be comparable in detail to the description you would be required to provide for equity, debt, warrants or rights.

D. *American Depositary Shares.* If you are registering American depositary shares represented by American depositary receipts, provide the following information.

1. Give the name of the depositary and the address of its principal executive office.

2. Give the title of the American depositary receipts and identify the deposited security. Briefly describe the American depositary shares, including provisions, if any, regarding:

   (a) The amount of deposited securities represented by one unit of American depositary receipts;

   (b) Any procedure for voting the deposited securities;

   (c) The procedure for collecting and distributing dividends;

(d) The procedures for transmitting notices, reports and proxy soliciting material;

(e) The sale or exercise of rights;

(f) The deposit or sale of securities resulting from dividends, splits or plans of reorganization;

(g) Amendment, extension or termination of the deposit arrangements;

(h) The rights that holders of American depositary receipts have to inspect the books of the depositary and the list of receipt holders;

(i) Any restrictions on the right to transfer or withdraw the underlying securities; and

(j) Any limitation on the depositary's liability.

3. Describe all fees and charges that a holder of American depositary receipts may have to pay, either directly or indirectly. Indicate the type of service, the amount of the fees or charges and to whom the fees or charges are paid. In particular, provide information about any fees or charges in connection with (a) depositing or substituting the underlying shares; (b) receiving or distributing dividends; (c) selling or exercising rights; (d) withdrawing an underlying security; and (e) transferring, splitting or grouping receipts. Provide information about the depositary's right, if any, to collect fees and charges by offsetting them against dividends received and deposited securities.

Instructions to Item 12:

1. *You do not need to provide the information called for by this item if you are using this form as an annual report.*

2. *You do not need to include any information in a registration statement or prospectus in response to Item 305(a)(2) of the Trust Indenture Act of 1939, 15 U.S.C. 77aaa et seq., as amended if the information is not otherwise required by this Item.*

3. *If you are registering convertible securities or stock purchase warrants that are subject to redemption or call, include the following information in your description of the securities.*

    a. *Whether holders will forfeit the right to convert or purchase the securities unless they exercise that right before the date specified in the notice of redemption or call;*

    b. *The expiration or termination date of the warrants;*

    c. *The kinds, frequency and timing of the redemption or call notice, including the cities or newspapers in which you will publish the notice; and*

    d. *In the case of bearer securities, that investors are responsible for making arrangements to avoid losing the right to convert or purchase if there is a redemption or call, such as by reading the newspapers in which you will publish the redemption or call notice.*

4. *When you are required to state the title of the securities, the title must indicate the type and general character of the securities.*

PART II

Item 13. Defaults, Dividend Arrearages and Delinquencies

A. If there has been:

1. A material default in the payment of principal, interest, a sinking or purchase fund installment, or

2. Any other material default not cured within 30 days, relating to indebtedness of you or any of your significant subsidiaries, and if the amount of the indebtedness exceeds 5% of your total assets on a consolidated basis, identify the indebtedness and state the nature of the default. If the default falls under paragraph A.1 above, state the amount of the default and the total arrearage on the date you file this report.

B. If the payment of dividends is in arrears or there has been any other material delinquency not cured within 30 days, relating to:

   1. Any class of your preferred stock which is registered or ranks prior to any class of registered securities, or

   2. Any class of preferred stock of your significant subsidiaries, state the title of the class and the nature of the arrearage or delinquency. If the payment of dividends is in arrears, state the amount of this arrearage and the total arrearage on the date you file this report.

Instructions to Item 13:

   1. *If you previously have reported information called for by this item in a report on Form 6-K, you may incorporate the information by specifically referring in this report to the previous report.*

   2. *You do not have to provide the information called for by this Item if the default or arrearage relates to a class of securities held entirely by or for the account of you or any of your wholly owned subsidiaries.*

Instructions to Item 13.A: This requirement only applies to events that have become defaults under the governing instruments, i.e., after any grace period has expired and any notice requirements have been satisfied.

Item 14.   Material Modifications to the Rights of Security Holders and Use of Proceeds

A. If you or anyone else has modified materially the instruments defining the rights of holders of any class of registered securities, identify that class of securities and briefly describe the general effect of the modification on the rights of those security holders.

B. If you or anyone else has modified materially or qualified the rights evidenced by any class of registered securities by issuing or modifying any other class of securities, briefly describe the general effect of the issuance or modification on the rights of holders of the registered securities.

C. If you or anyone else has withdrawn or substituted a material amount of the assets securing any class of your registered securities, provide the following information.

   1. Give the title of the securities.

   2. Identify and describe briefly the assets withdrawn or substituted.

   3. Indicate the provisions in the underlying indenture, if any, that authorize the withdrawal or substitution.

D. If the trustees or paying agents for any registered securities have changed during the last financial year, give the names and addresses of the new trustees or paying agents.

E. *Use of proceeds.* If required pursuant to Rule 463 under the Securities Act, report the use of proceeds after the effective date of the first Securities Act registration statement filed by you or your predecessor. You must report the use of proceeds:

   (i) On the first Form 20-F annual report you file pursuant to sections 13(a) and 15(d) of the Exchange Act after the Securities Act registration statement is effective, and

   (ii) On each of your subsequent Form 20-F annual reports filed pursuant to sections 13(a) and 15(d) of the Exchange Act.

You may cease reporting the use of proceeds on the later of the date you disclose application of all the offering proceeds, or the date you disclose termination of the offering. If a required report on the use of proceeds relates to the first effective registration statement of your predecessor, you must provide the report.

Provide the information required by paragraphs E.1 through E.4 below in the first Form 20-F annual report you file pursuant to sections 13(a) and 15(d) of the Exchange Act. In subsequent Form 20-F annual reports, you only need to provide the information required by paragraphs E.2 through E.4 if that information has changed since the last Form 20-F annual report you filed.

1. The effective date of the Securities Act registration statement for which the use of proceeds information is being disclosed and the Commission file number assigned to that registration statement;

2. The offering date, if the offering has commenced, or an explanation of why it has not commenced;

3. If the offering terminated before any securities were sold, an explanation for the termination; and

4. If the offering did not terminate before any securities were sold, disclose:

    (a) Whether the offering has terminated and, if so, whether it terminated before all of the registered securities were sold;

    (b) The name(s) of the managing underwriter(s), if any;

    (c) The title of each class of securities registered and, if a class of convertible securities is being registered, the title of any class of securities into which the convertible securities may be converted;

    (d) For each class of securities (other than a class into which a class of registered convertible securities may be converted without additional payment to the issuer) the following information, provided for both the account of the issuer and the account(s) of any selling shareholder(s): the amount registered, the aggregate price of the offering amount registered, the amount sold and the aggregate offering price of the amount sold to date;

    (e) From the effective date of the Securities Act registration statement to the ending date of the reporting period, the amount of expenses incurred for the issuer's account in connection with the issuance and distribution of the registered securities for underwriting discounts and commissions, finders' fees, expenses paid to or for underwriters, other expenses and total expenses. Indicate if a reasonable estimate for the amount of expenses is provided instead of the actual amount of the expense. Indicate whether the payments were:

        (i) Direct or indirect payments to directors, officers, general partners of the issuer or their associates; to persons owning 10% or more of any class of the issuer's equity securities; and to affiliates of the issuer; or

        (ii) Direct or indirect payments to others;

    (f) The net offering proceeds to the issuer after deducting the total expenses described in paragraph E.4(e) of this Item;

    (g) From the effective date of the Securities Act registration statement to the ending date of the reporting period, the amount of net offering proceeds to the issuer used for construction of plant, building and facilities; purchase and installation of machinery and equipment; purchases of real estate; acquisition of other business(es); repayment of indebtedness; working capital; temporary investments (which should be specified); and any other purposes for which at least 5% of the issuer's total offering proceeds or $100,000 (whichever is less) has been used (which should be specified). Indicate if a reasonable estimate for the amount of net offering proceeds applied instead of the actual amount of net offering proceeds used. Indicate whether such payments were:

        (i) Direct or indirect payments to directors, officers, general partners of the issuer or their associates; to persons owning 10% or more of any class of the issuer's equity securities; and to affiliates of the issuer; or

        (ii) Direct or indirect payments to others; and

    (h) If the use of proceeds in paragraph E.4(g) of this Item represents a material change in the use of proceeds described in the prospectus, the issuer should describe briefly the material change.

Instruction to Item 14: *If you previously have reported information called for by this item in a report on Form 6-K, you may incorporate the information by specifically referring in this report to the previous report.*

Instruction to Item 14.B: *You should report any working capital restrictions or other limitations on the payment of dividends.*

Instruction to Item 14.C: You do not have to provide the information called for by Item 14.C. if the withdrawal or substitution is made pursuant to the terms of an indenture qualified under the Trust Indenture Act of 1939.

Item 15.   Controls and Procedures

(a) Where the Form is being used as an annual report filed under Section 13(a) or 15(d) of the Exchange Act, disclose the conclusions of the registrant's principal executive officer or officers and principal financial officer or officers, or persons performing similar functions, about the effectiveness of the registrant's disclosure controls and procedures (as defined in §§ 240.13a-15(c) and 240.15d-15(c)) based on their evaluation the controls and procedures as of a date within 90 days prior to the filing date of the report.

(b) Where the Form is being used as an annual report filed under Section 13(a) or 15(d) of the Exchange Act, disclose whether or not there were significant changes in the registrant's internal controls or in other factors that could significantly affect these controls subsequent to the date of their evaluation, including any corrective actions with regard to significant deficiencies and material weaknesses.

Item 16A.   Audit Committee Financial Expert

(a) (1) Disclose that the registrant's board of directors has determined that the registrant either:

    (i)   Has at least one audit committee financial expert serving on its audit committee; or

    (ii)   Does not have an audit committee financial expert serving on its audit committee.

(2) If the registrant provides the disclosure required by paragraph (a)(1)(i) of this Item, it must disclose the name of the audit committee financial expert and whether that person is independent, as that term is defined in the listing standards applicable to the registrant if the registrant is a listed issuer, as defined in 17 CFR 240.10A-3. If the registrant is not a listed issuer, it must use a definition of audit committee member independence of a national securities exchange registered pursuant to section 6(a) of the Exchange Act (15 U.S.C. 78f(a)) or a national securities association registered pursuant to section 15A(a) of the Exchange Act (15 U.S.C. 78o-3(a)) that has been approved by the Commission (as such definition may be modified or supplemented) in determining whether its audit committee financial expert is independent, and state which definition was used.

(3) If the registrant provides the disclosure required by paragraph (a)(1)(ii) of this Item, it must explain why it does not have an audit committee financial expert.

Instruction to paragraph (a) of Item 16A:

If the registrant's board of directors has determined that the registrant has more than one audit committee financial expert serving on its audit committee, the registrant may, but is not required to, disclose the names of those additional persons.

(b) For purposes of this Item, an "audit committee financial expert" means a person who has the following attributes:

(1) An understanding of generally accepted accounting principles and financial statements;

(2) The ability to assess the general application of such principles in connection with the accounting for estimates, accruals and reserves;

(3) Experience preparing, auditing, analyzing or evaluating financial statements that present a breadth and level of complexity of accounting issues that are generally comparable to the breadth and complexity of issues that can reasonably be expected to be raised by the registrant's financial statements, or experience actively supervising one or more persons engaged in such activities;

(4) An understanding of internal controls and procedures for financial reporting; and

(5) An understanding of audit committee functions.

(c) A person shall have acquired such attributes through:

(1) Education and experience as a principal financial officer, principal accounting officer, controller, public accountant or auditor or experience in one or more positions that involve the performance of similar functions;

(2) Experience actively supervising a principal financial officer, principal accounting officer, controller, public accountant, auditor or person performing similar functions;

(3) Experience overseeing or assessing the performance of companies or public accountants with respect to the preparation, auditing or evaluation of financial statements; or

(4) Other relevant experience.

(d) Safe Harbor.

(1) A person who is determined to be an audit committee financial expert will not be deemed an "expert" for any purpose, including without limitation for purposes of section 11 of the Securities Act of 1933 (15 U.S.C. 77k), as a result of being designated or identified as an audit committee financial expert pursuant to this Item 16A.

(2) The designation or identification of a person as an audit committee financial expert pursuant to this Item 16A does not impose on such person any duties, obligations or liability that are greater than the duties, obligations and liability imposed on such person as a member of the audit committee and board of directors in the absence of such designation or identification.

(3) The designation or identification of a person as an audit committee financial expert pursuant to this Item 16A does not affect the duties, obligations or liability of any other member of the audit committee or board of directors.

Instructions to Item 16A:

1. *Item 16A applies only to annual reports, and does not apply to registration statements, on Form 20-F.*

2. *If a person qualifies as an audit committee financial expert by means of having held a position described in paragraph (c)(4) of this Item, the registrant shall provide a brief listing of that person's relevant experience. Such disclosure may be made by reference to disclosures required under Item 6.A.*

3. *In the case of a foreign private issuer with a two-tier board of directors, for purposes of this Item 16A, the term board of directors means the supervisory or non-management board. In the case of a foreign private issuer meeting the requirements of 17 CFR 240.10A-3(c)(3), for purposes of this Item 16A, the term board of directors means the issuer's board of auditors (or similar body) or statutory auditors, as applicable. Also, in the case of a foreign private issuer, the term generally accepted accounting principles in paragraph (b)(1) of this Item means the body of generally accepted accounting principles used by that issuer in its primary financial statements filed with the Commission.*

4. *A registrant that is an Asset-Backed Issuer (as defined in §240.13a-14(g) and §240.15d-14(g) of this chapter) is not required to disclose the information required by this Item 16A.*

Item 16B.   Code of Ethics

(a) Disclose whether the registrant has adopted a code of ethics that applies to the registrant's principal executive officer, principal financial officer, principal accounting officer or controller, or persons performing similar functions. If the registrant has not adopted such a code of ethics, explain why it has not done so.

(b) For purposes of this Item 16B, the term "code of ethics" means written standards that are reasonably designed to deter wrongdoing and to promote:

(1) Honest and ethical conduct, including the ethical handling of actual or apparent conflicts of interest between personal and professional relationships;

(2) Full, fair, accurate, timely, and understandable disclosure in reports and documents that a registrant files with, or submits to, the Commission and in other public communications made by the registrant;

(3) Compliance with applicable governmental laws, rules and regulations;

(4) The prompt internal reporting of violations of the code to an appropriate person or persons identified in the code; and

(5) Accountability for adherence to the code.

(c) The registrant must:

(1) File with the Commission a copy of its code of ethics that applies to the registrant's principal executive officer, principal financial officer, principal accounting officer or controller, or persons performing similar functions, as an exhibit to its annual report;

(2) Post the text of such code of ethics on its Internet Web site and disclose, in its annual report, its Internet address and the fact that it has posted such code of ethics on its Internet Web site; or

(3) Undertake in its annual report filed with the Commission to provide to any person without charge, upon request, a copy of such code of ethics and explain the manner in which such request may be made.

(d) The registrant must briefly describe the nature of any amendment to a provision of its code of ethics that applies to the registrant's principal executive officer, principal financial officer, principal accounting officer or controller, or persons performing similar functions and that relates to any element of the code of ethics definition enumerated in Item 16B(b), which has occurred during the registrant's most recently completed fiscal year.

(e) If the registrant has granted a waiver, including an implicit waiver, from a provision of the code of ethics to one of the officers or persons described in Item 16B(a) that relates to one or more of the items set forth in Item 16B(b) during the registrant's most recently completed fiscal year, the registrant must briefly describe the nature of the waiver, the name of the person to whom the waiver was granted, and the date of the waiver.

Instructions to Item 16B.

1. *Item 16B applies only to annual reports, and does not apply to registration statements, on Form 20-F.*

2. *A registrant may have separate codes of ethics for different types of officers. Furthermore, a "code of ethics" within the meaning of paragraph (b) of this Item may be a portion of a broader document that addresses additional topics or that applies to more persons than those specified in paragraph (a). In satisfying the requirements of paragraph (c), a registrant need only file, post or provide the portions of a broader document that constitute a "code of ethics" as defined in paragraph (b) and that apply to the persons specified in paragraph (a).*

3. *If a registrant elects to satisfy paragraph (c) of this Item by posting its code of ethics on its website pursuant to paragraph (c)(2), the code of ethics must remain accessible on its website for as long as the registrant remains subject to the requirements of this Item and chooses to comply with this Item by posting its code on its website pursuant to paragraph (c)(2).*

4. *A registrant that is an Asset-Backed Issuer (as defined in §240.13a-14(g) and §240.15d-14(g) of this chapter) is not required to disclose the information required by this Item.*

5. *The registrant does not need to provide any information pursuant to paragraphs (d) and (e) of this Item if it discloses the required information on its Internet website within five business days following the date of the amendment or waiver and the registrant has disclosed in its most recently filed annual report its Internet address and intention to provide disclosure in this manner. If the registrant elects to disclose the information required by paragraphs (d) and (e) through its website, such information must remain available on the website for at least a 12-month period. Following the 12-month period, the registrant must retain the information for a period of not less than five years. Upon request, the registrant must furnish to the Commission or its staff a copy of any or all information retained pursuant to this requirement.*

6. *The registrant does not need to disclose technical, administrative or other non-substantive amendments to its code of ethics.*

7. *For purposes of this Item 16B:*

a. *The term "waiver" means the approval by the registrant of a material departure from a provision of the code of ethics; and*

b. *The term "implicit waiver" means the registrant's failure to take action within a reasonable period of time regarding a material departure from a provision of the code of ethics that has been made known to an executive officer, as defined in Rule 3b-7 (§240.3b-7 of this chapter), of the registrant.*

Item 16C. Principal Accountant Fees and Services.

(a) Disclose, under the caption Audit Fees, the aggregate fees billed for each of the last two fiscal years for professional services rendered by the principal accountant for the audit of the registrant's annual financial statements or services that are normally provided by the accountant in connection with statutory and regulatory filings or engagements for those fiscal years.

(b) Disclose, under the caption Audit-Related Fees, the aggregate fees billed in each of the last two fiscal years for assurance and related services by the principal accountant that are reasonably related to the performance of the audit or review of the registrant's financial statements and are not reported under paragraph (a) of this Item. Registrants shall describe the nature of the services comprising the fees disclosed under this category.

(c) Disclose, under the caption Tax Fees, the aggregate fees billed in each of the last two fiscal years for professional services rendered by the principal accountant for tax compliance, tax advice, and tax planning. Registrants shall describe the nature of the services comprising the fees disclosed under this category.

(d) Disclose, under the caption All Other Fees, the aggregate fees billed in each of the last two fiscal years for products and services provided by the principal accountant, other than the services reported in paragraphs (a) through (c) of this Item. Registrants shall describe the nature of the services comprising the fees disclosed under this category.

(e) (1) Disclose the audit committee's pre-approval policies and procedures described in paragraph (c)(7)(i) of Rule 2-01 of Regulation S-X.

   (2) Disclose the percentage of services described in each of paragraphs (b) through (d) of this Item that were approved by the audit committee pursuant to paragraph (c)(7)(i)(C) of Rule 2-01 of Regulation S-X.

(f) If greater than 50 percent, disclose the percentage of hours expended on the principal accountant's engagement to audit the registrant's financial statements for the most recent fiscal year that were attributed to work performed by persons other than the principal accountant's full-time, permanent employees.

Instructions to Item 16C.

1. *You do not need to provide the information called for by this Item 16C unless you are using this form as an annual report.*

2. *A registrant that is an Asset-Backed Issuer (as defined in § 240.13a-14(g) and § 240.15d-14(g) of this chapter) is not required to disclose the information required by this Item.*

Item 16D. Exemptions From the Listing Standards for Audit Committees

If applicable, provide the disclosure required by Exchange Act rule 10A-3(d) (17 CFR 240.10A-3(d)) regarding an exemption from the listing standards for audit committees. You do not need to provide the information called for by this Item 16D unless you are using this form as an annual report.

PART III
[See General Instruction E(c)]

Item 17.   Financial Statements

(a) The registrant shall furnish financial statements for the same fiscal years and accountants' certificates that would be required to be furnished if the registration statement were on Form 10 or the annual report on Form 10-K. Schedules designated by §§210.12-04, 210.12-09, 210.12-15, 210.12-16, 210.12-17, 210.12-18, 210.12-28, and 210.12-29 of this chapter shall be furnished if applicable to the registrant.

(b) The financial statements shall disclose an information content substantially similar to financial statements that comply with U.S. generally accepted accounting principles and Regulation S-X.

(c) The financial statements and schedules required by paragraph (a) above may be prepared according to U.S. generally accepted accounting principles. Alternatively, such financial statements and schedules may be prepared according to a comprehensive body of accounting principles other than those generally accepted in the United States if the following are disclosed:

   (1) An indication, in the accountant's report or in a reasonably prominent headnote before the financial statements, of the comprehensive body of accounting principles used to prepare the financial statements.

   (2) A discussion of the material variations in the accounting principles, practices, and methods used in preparing the financial statements from the principles, practices, and methods generally accepted in the United States and in Regulation S-X. Such material variations shall be quantified in the following format:

   (i) For each year and any interim periods for which an income statement is presented, net income shall be reconciled in a tabular format, substantially similar to the one shown below, on the face of the income statement or in a note thereto. Each material variation shall be described and quantified as a separate reconciling item, but several material variations may be combined on the face of the income statement if shown separately in a note. However, reconciliation of net income of the earliest of the three years may be omitted if that information has not previously been included in a filing made under the Securities Act or Exchange Act.

Net income as shown in the financial statements XXX

Description of items having the effect of increasing reported income
   Item 1 XXX
   Item 2, etc. XXX

Description of items having the effect of decreasing reported income
   Item 1 . . . . (XXX)
   Item 2, etc. . . . . (XXX)

Net income according to generally accepted accounting
principles in the United States. XXX

   (ii) For each balance sheet presented, indicate the amount of each material variation between an amount of a line item appearing in a balance sheet and the amount determined using U.S. generally accepted accounting principles and Regulation S-X. Such amounts may be shown in parentheses, in columns, as a reconciliation of the equity section, as a restated balance sheet, or in any similar format that clearly presents the differences in the amounts.

   (iii) For each period for which an income statement is presented and required to be reconciled to generally accepted accounting principles in the United States, provide either a statement of cash flows prepared in accordance with generally accepted accounting principles in the United States or with International Accounting Standard No. 7, as amended in October 1992; or furnish in a note to the financial statements a quantified description of the material differences between cash or funds flows reported in the primary financial statements and cash flows that would be reported in a statement of cash flows prepared in accordance with accounting principles generally accepted in the United States.

(iv) (A) Issuers that prepare their financial statements on a basis of accounting other than U.S. generally accepted accounting principles in a reporting currency that comprehensively includes the effects of price level changes in its primary financial statements using the historical cost/constant currency or current cost approach, may omit the disclosures specified by paragraphs (c)(2)(i), (c)(2)(ii), and (c)(2)(iii) of this Item relating to effects of price level changes. The financial statements should describe the basis of presentation, and that such effects have not been included in the reconciliation.

(B) Issuers that prepare their financial statements on a basis of accounting other than U.S. generally accepted accounting principles that translates amounts in financial statements stated in a currency of a hyperinflationary economy into the issuer's reporting currency in accordance with International Accounting Standards No. 21, "The Effects of Changes in Foreign Exchange Rates," as amended in 1993, using the historical cost/constant currency approach, may omit the disclosures specified by paragraphs (c)(2)(i), (c)(2)(ii), and (c)(2)(iii) of this Item relating to the effects of the different method of accounting for an entity in a hyperinflationary environment.

(C) If the method of accounting for an operation in a hyperinflationary economy complies with IAS 21, a statement to that effect must be included in the financial statements. The reconciliation shall state that such amounts presented comply with Item 17 of Form 20-F and are different from that required by U.S. generally accepted accounting principles.

(v) Issuers that prepare financial statements on a basis of accounting other than U.S. generally accepted accounting principles that are furnished for a business acquired or to be acquired pursuant to §210.305 of this chapter may omit the disclosures specified by paragraphs (c)(2)(i), (c)(2)(ii) and (c)(2)(iii) of this Item if the conditions specified in the definition of a significant subsidiary in §210.1-02(v) of this chapter do not exceed 30 percent.

(vi) Issuers that prepare financial statements on a basis of accounting other than U.S. generally accepted accounting principles that are furnished for a less-than-majority-owned investee pursuant to §210.309 of this chapter may omit the disclosures specified by paragraphs (c)(2)(i), (c)(2)(ii) and (c)(2)(iii) of this Item if the first and third conditions specified in the definition of a significant subsidiary in §210.102(v) of this chapter do not exceed 30 percent.

(vii) Issuers that prepare financial statements on a basis of accounting other than U.S. generally accepted accounting principles that allows proportionate consolidation for investments in joint ventures that would be accounted for under the equity method pursuant to U.S. generally accepted accounting principles may omit differences in classification or display that result from using proportionate consolidation in the reconciliation to U.S. generally accepted accounting principles specified by paragraphs (c)(2)(i), (c)(2)(ii) and (c)(2)(iii) of this Item; *Provided*, the joint venture is an operating entity, the significant financial operating policies of which are, by contractual arrangement, jointly controlled by all parties having an equity interest in the entity. Financial statements that are presented using proportionate consolidation must provide summarized balance sheet and income statement information using the captions specified in §210.1-02(aa) of this chapter and summarized cash flow information resulting from operating, financing and investing activities relating to its pro rata interest in the joint venture.

(viii) Issuers that prepare financial statements on a basis of accounting other than U.S. generally accepted accounting principles and which basis conforms with the guidance in International Accounting Standards No. 22, as amended in 1993, with respect to the period of amortization of goodwill and negative goodwill may omit the disclosures specified by paragraphs (c)(2)(i), (c)(2)(ii), and (c)(2)(iii) of this Item regarding the effects of differences attributable solely to the period of amortization. Goodwill and negative goodwill that is subject to the amortization period under IAS 22 is based on the amount determined in accordance with U.S. generally accepted accounting principles.

Instructions:

1. *If the variations quantified pursuant to paragraph (c) are significant, the registrant should consider presenting them on the face of the financial statements.*

2. *Earnings per share computed according to generally accepted accounting principles in the United States shall be presented if materially different from the earnings per share otherwise presented.*

3. *If the registrant presents its financial statements according to generally accepted accounting principles in the United States except for SFAS No. 131 and if it furnishes the information relating to categories of activity required by Items 4.B.1 and 4.B.2 of Form 20-F, then such financial statements will be considered to comply with this Item, even if the auditor's report is qualified for noncompliance with SFAS No. 131. Such report and financial statements, however, must comply with all other applicable requirements.*

4. *If the cash flows statement prepared under the basis of accounting used in the primary financial statements complies with International Accounting Standard No. 7 or U.S. generally accepted accounting principles, a statement to this effect must be included in the financial statements or the accountant's report. If the cash flows statement in the primary financial statements is prepared in accordance with either U.S. generally accepted accounting principles or International Accounting Standard No. 7 but such presentation departs from the comprehensive body of accounting principles otherwise followed in the financial statements, the reference to the departure in the accountant's report must identify the body of accounting standards used in preparing the cash flow statement. If a supplemental cash flows statement that complies with either International Accounting Standards or U.S. generally accepted accounting principles is furnished in a note to the financial statements, the body of accounting standards used in preparing the statement must be indicated. The basis of presentation must be consistent for all periods.*

5. *For purposes of this Item, a hyperinflationary economy is one that has cumulative inflation of approximately 100% or more over the most recent three year period.*

6. (a) *A business combination which would be deemed a uniting of interests under international Accounting Standards No. 22, as amended in 1993 ("IAS 22"), and was accounted for using that method in the primary financial statements may be deemed to be, for purposes of the reconciliation to U.S. generally accepted accounting principles, a pooling of interests. A business combination which would be deemed an acquisition under IAS 22 and was accounted for using that method in the primary financial statements may be deemed to be, for purposes of the reconciliation to U.S. generally accepted accounting principles, a purchase. This paragraph is not applicable for promoter transactions, leveraged buyouts, mergers of entities under common control, reverse acquisitions and other transactions not addressed by IAS 22. Once the method of accounting is determined, the reconciliation to U.S. generally accepted accounting principles should quantify differences between the balances in the primary financial statements and the amounts determined in accordance with U.S. generally accepted accounting principles as required by this Item.*

   (b) *To obtain relief from the reconciliation requirement regarding the method of accounting, or the amortization period of goodwill or negative goodwill, the primary financial statements should apply the respective provisions of IAS 22 to all business combinations consummated on or after January 1, 1995. Issuers can either retroactively adopt IAS 22 in the primary financial statements for all business combinations consummated prior to January 1, 1995, or provide a full reconciliation to U.S. generally accepted accounting principles for such prior business combinations.*

   (c) *If the method of accounting for a business combination and/or the provisions for amortization of goodwill or negative goodwill complies with IAS 22, a statement to that effect must be included in the financial statements. The reconciliation shall state that the amounts presented comply with Item 17 of Form 20-F and are different from that required by U.S. generally accepted accounting principles.*

Item 18.   Financial Statements

Provide the following information:

(a) All of the information required by Item 17 of this Form, and

(b) All other information required by U.S. generally accepted accounting principles and Regulation S-X unless such requirements specifically do not apply to the registrant as a foreign issuer. However, information may be omitted (i) for any period in which net income has not been presented on a basis reconciled to United States generally accepted accounting principles, or (ii) if the financial statements are furnished for a business acquired or to be acquired pursuant to §210.3-05 or less-than-majority-owned investee pursuant to §210.3-09 of this chapter.

Instruction to Item 18: All of the instructions to Item 17 also apply to this Item, except Instruction 3 to Item 17, which does not apply.

Item 19.   Exhibits

List all exhibits filed as part of the registration statement or annual report, including exhibits incorporated by reference.

Instruction to Item 19: If you incorporate any financial statement or exhibit by reference, include the incorporation by reference in the list required by this Item. Note Rule 12b-23 regarding incorporation by reference. Note also the Instructions to Exhibits at the end of this Form.

SIGNATURES

The registrant hereby certifies that it meets all of the requirements for filing on Form 20-F and that it has duly caused and authorized the undersigned to sign this registration statement [annual report] on its behalf.

_____

(Registrant)

_____

(Signature)*

Date:

*Print the name and title of the signing officer under this signature.

CERTIFICATIONS*

I, _____ , certify that:
[identify the certifying individual]

1. I have reviewed this annual report on Form 20-F of _____ ;
[identify registrant]

2. Based on my knowledge, this annual report does not contain any untrue statement of a material fact or omit to state a material fact necessary to make the statements made, in light of the circumstances under which such statements were made, not misleading with respect to the period covered by this annual report;

3. Based on my knowledge, the financial statements, and other financial information included in this annual report, fairly present in all material respects the financial condition, results of operations and cash flows of the registrant as of, and for, the periods presented in this annual report;

4. The registrant's other certifying officers and I are responsible for establishing and maintaining disclosure controls and procedures (as defined in Exchange Act Rules 13a-14 and 15d-14) for the registrant and we have:

    (a) designed such disclosure controls and procedures to ensure that material information relating to the registrant, including its consolidated subsidiaries, is made known to us by others within those entities, particularly during the period in which this annual report is being prepared;

    (b) evaluated the effectiveness of the registrant's disclosure controls and procedures as of a date within 90 days prior to the filing date of this annual report (the "Evaluation Date"); and

    (c) presented in this annual report our conclusions about the effectiveness of the disclosure controls and procedures based on our evaluation as of the Evaluation Date;

5. The registrant's other certifying officers and I have disclosed, based on our most recent evaluation, to the registrant's auditors and the audit committee of registrant's board of directors (or persons performing the equivalent function):

    (a) all significant deficiencies in the design or operation of internal controls which could adversely affect the registrant's ability to record, process, summarize and report financial data and have identified for the registrant's auditors any material weaknesses in internal controls; and

    (b) any fraud, whether or not material, that involves management or other employees who have a significant role in the registrant's internal controls; and

6. The registrant's other certifying officers and I have indicated in this annual report whether or not there were significant changes in internal controls or in other factors that could significantly affect internal controls subsequent to the date of our most recent evaluation, including any corrective actions with regard to significant deficiencies and material weaknesses.

Date: _____

_____
[Signature]

_____
[Title]

*Provide a separate certification for each principal executive officer and principal financial officer of the registrant. See Rules 13a-14 and 15d-14. The required certification must be in the exact form set forth above.

INSTRUCTIONS AS TO EXHIBITS

File the exhibits listed below as part of an Exchange Act registration statement or report. Exchange Act Rule 12b-32 explains the circumstances in which you may incorporate exhibits by reference. Exchange Act Rule 24b-2 explains the procedure to be followed in requesting confidential treatment of information required to be filed.

Previously filed exhibits may be incorporated by reference. If any previously filed exhibits have been amended or modified, file copies of the amendment or modification or copies of the entire exhibit as amended or modified.

If the Form 20-F registration statement or annual report requires the inclusion, as an exhibit or attachment, of a document that is in a foreign language, you must provide instead either an English translation or an English summary of the foreign language document in accordance with Exchange Act Rule 12b-12(d) (17 CFR 240.12b-12(d)) for both electronic and paper filings. You may submit a copy of the unabridged foreign language document along with the English translation or summary as permitted by Regulation S-T Rule 306(b) (17 CFR 232.306(b)) for electronic filings or by Exchange Act Rule 12b-12(d)(4) (17 CFR 240.12b-12(d)(4)) for paper filings.

Include an exhibit index in each registration statement or report you file, immediately preceding the exhibits you are filing. The exhibit index must list each exhibit according to the number assigned to it below. If an exhibit is incorporated by reference, note that fact in the exhibit index. For paper filings, the pages of the manually signed original registration statement should be numbered in sequence, and the exhibit index should give the page number in the sequential numbering system where each exhibit can be found.

1. The articles of incorporation or association and bylaws, or comparable instruments, as currently in effect and any amendments to those documents. If you are filing an amendment, file a complete copy of the document as amended.

2. (a) All instruments defining the rights of holders of the securities being registered. You do not have to file instruments that define the rights of participants, rather than security holders, in an employee benefit plan.

   (b) All instruments defining the rights of holders of long-term debt issued by you or any subsidiary for which you are required to file consolidated or unconsolidated financial statements, except that you do not have to file:

      (i) Any instrument relating to long-term debt that is not being registered on this registration statement, if the total amount of securities authorized under that instrument does not exceed 10% of the total assets of you and your subsidiaries on a consolidated basis and you have filed an agreement to furnish us a copy of the instrument if we request it;

      (ii) Any instrument relating to a class of securities if, on or before the date you deliver the securities being registered, you take appropriate steps to assure that class of securities will be redeemed or retired; or

      (iii) Copies of instruments evidencing script certificates for fractions of shares.

   (c) A copy of the indenture, if the securities being registered are or will be issued under an indenture qualified under the Trust Indenture Act of 1939. Include a reasonably itemized and informative table of contents and a cross-reference sheet showing the location in the indenture of the provisions inserted pursuant to sections 310 through 318(a) inclusive of the Trust Indenture Act.

3. Any voting trust agreements and any amendments to those agreements.

4. (a) Every contract that is material to you and (i) is to be performed in whole or in part on or after the date you file the registration statement or (ii) was entered into not more than two years before the filing date. Only file a contract if you or your subsidiary is a party or has succeeded to a party by assumption or assignment or if you or your subsidiary has a beneficial interest.

   (b) If a contract is the type that ordinarily accompanies the kind of business you and your subsidiaries conduct, we will consider it have been made in the ordinary course of business and will not require you to file it, unless it falls within one or more of the following categories. Even if it falls into one of these categories, you do not have to file the contract if it is immaterial in amount or significance.

(i) Any contract to which (A) directors, (B) officers, (C) promoters, (D) voting trustees or (E) security holders named in the registration statement are parties, unless the contract involves only the purchase or sale of current assets that have a determinable market price and the assets are purchased or sold at that price;

(ii) Any contract upon which your business is substantially dependent. Examples of these types of contracts might be (a) continuing contracts to sell the major part of your products or services or to purchase the major part of your requirement of goods, services or raw materials, or (b) any franchise or license or other agreement to use a patent, formula, trade secret, process or trade name if your business depends to a material extent on that patent, formula, trade secret processor trade name;

(iii) Any contract for the acquisition or sale of any property, plant or equipment if the consideration exceeds 15% of your fixed assets on a consolidated basis; or

(iv) Any material lease under which you hold part of the property described in the registration statement.

(c) We will consider any management contract or compensatory plan, contract or arrangement in which your directors or members of your administrative, supervisory or management bodies participate to be material. File these management contracts or compensatory plans, contracts or arrangements unless they fall into one of the following categories:

(i) Ordinary purchase and sale agency agreements;

(ii) Agreements with managers of stores in a chain or similar organization;

(iii) Contracts providing for labor or salesmen's bonuses or for payments to a class of security holders in their capacity as security holders;

(iv) Any compensatory plan, contract or arrangement that is available by its terms to employees, officers or directors generally, if the operation of the plan, contract or arrangement uses the same method to allocate benefits to management and nonmanagement participants; and

(v) Any compensatory plan, contract or arrangement if you are furnishing compensation information on an aggregate basis as permitted by Item 6.B.

If you are filing compensatory plans, contracts or arrangements, only file copies of the plans and not copies of each individual's personal agreement under the plans, unless there are particular provisions in a personal agreement that should be filed as an exhibit so investors will understand that individual's compensation under the plan.

5. A list showing the number and a brief identification of each material foreign patent for an invention not covered by a United States patent, but only if we request you to file the list.

6. A statement explaining in reasonable detail how earnings per share information was calculated, unless the computation is clear from material contained in the registration statement or report.

7. A statement explaining in reasonable detail how any ratio of earning to fixed charges, any ratio of earnings to combined fixed charges and preferred stock dividends or any other ratios in the registration statement or report were calculated.

8. A list of all your subsidiaries, their jurisdiction of incorporation and the names under which they do business. You may omit the names of subsidiaries that, in the aggregate, would not be a "significant subsidiary" as defined in rule 1-02(w) of Regulation S-X as of the end of the year covered by the report. You may omit the names of multiple wholly owned subsidiaries carrying on the same line of business, such as chain stores or service stations, if you give the name of the immediate parent company, the line of business and the number of omitted subsidiaries broken down by U.S. and foreign operations.

9. Statement pursuant to the instructions to Item 8.A.4, regarding the financial statements filed in registration statements for initial public offerings of securities.

10. Any notice required by Rule 104 of Regulation BTR (17 CFR 245.104 of this chapter) that you sent during the past fiscal year to directors and executive officers (as defined in 17 CFR 245.100(d) and (h) of this chapter) concerning any equity security subject to a blackout period (as defined in 17 CFR 245.100(c) of this chapter) under Rule 101 of Regulation BTR (17 CFR 245.101 of this chapter). Each notice must have included the information specified in 17 CFR 245.104(b) of this chapter.

11. Any code of ethics, or amendment thereto, that is the subject of the disclosure required by Item 16B of Form 20-F, to the extent that the registrant intends to satisfy the Item 16B requirements through filing of an exhibit.

12. (a) Any additional exhibits you wish to file as part of the registration statement or report, clearly marked to indicate their subject matter, and

    (b) any document or part of a document incorporated by reference in this filing if it is not otherwise required to be filed or is not a Commission filed document incorporated in a Securities Act registration statement.

GLOSSARY

A

accrual bond   The final tranche of a collateralized mortgage obligation.

accrued interest   The interest that has accumulated on a fixed-income security since the last interest payment.

active management strategy   A strategy that uses available information and forecasting techniques to seek better returns than a buy and hold portfolio.

admitted assets   The assets an insurance company can include in its balance sheet.

advance refunding   In municipal finance, it is used when a municipality issues a new security to pay off an outstanding bond prior to its call date or maturity date.

aftermarket   The period after the new security begins trading in the secondary market, during which members of the underwriting syndicate may not sell the security for less than the offering price.

Alternative Investment Market (AIM)   The London Stock Exchange's section for young and fast-growing companies.

American depositary receipts (ADRs)   Certificates representing shares of foreign companies traded in the United States.

American terms   Units of a domestic currency per unit of foreign currency viewed from the perspective of someone in the United States.

annuity   A financial product in which policyholders pay premiums in exchange for a regular income for a specified period of time.

arbitrage   The simultaneous purchase and sale of two closely related securities to take advantage of a disparity in their prices; or alternatively, the purchase and sale of the same security in different markets to earn guaranteed profits.

A-shares   Chinese stocks reserved for Chinese residents.

Asian crisis   The financial crisis that swept through many countries in East and Southeast Asia in 1997.

Asia-Pacific Regional Operations Center   Plan introduced by the Taiwanese government in 1995 to promote Taiwan as a regional financial and business hub.

asset-backed commercial paper (ABCP)   Commercial paper backed by certain assets and issued to raise short-term financing.

asset-backed securities (ABS)   Securities backed by non-mortgage assets such as installment loans, leases, receivables, home equity loans, tax liens, revolving credit, commercial loans, and high-yield bonds.

asset-backed securitization   A program where the originator sells an existing pool of assets, such as existing mortgages or receivables, to the special purpose vehicle, which then issues asset-backed securities.

Association of Southeast Asian Nations (ASEAN)   An association formed by countries in Southeast Asia, including Singapore, Brunei, Malaysia, Thailand, the Philippines, Indonesia, and Vietnam.

automobile insurance   A policy wherein the owner pays a premium, and in exchange, the insurance company promises to pay for specific car-related financial losses during the term of the policy.

B

Baby Bunds   A term used to describe the Pfandbriefe; a very safe debt instrument, second only to German government bonds (Bunds), backed by mortgage loans in Germany.

baht   Official currency of Thailand.

Banco de Mexico   Mexico's central bank.

bank dealing   The selling and buying of government bonds by banks in Japan.

bank holding company   A financial holding company that owns and manages subsidiary banks.

Bank of Japan   Japan's central bank.

bankers' acceptance (BA)   A short-term credit instrument created by a nonfinancial firm for international trade and guaranteed by a bank for future payment.

Barron's Confidence Index (BCI)   The ratio of Barron's average yield on 10 top-grade corporate bonds to the average yield on Dow Jones 40 bonds.

base currency   The currency that foreign exchange traders use as a vehicle when trading several different currencies.

Basel II   *See* New Capital Accord.

basis   The difference between the cash market price and futures price.

basis risk   The risk that basis will widen or narrow affecting the effectiveness of a hedge.

beige book   Reports on regional economic conditions in each of the twelve Federal Reserve districts.

best-efforts underwriting   The underwriters agree only to use their best efforts to sell the new security on the issuer's behalf without any guarantee.

bid-asked spread   The difference between the price at which a dealer buys a security and the price at which the dealer sells it.

bid-to-cover ratio   The ratio of the bids received to the amount awarded in an auction.

Big Bang   Major financial reform plans in Japan, announced by the Japanese Prime Minister Hashimoto in November 1996, to modernize Japan's capital markets. This term is borrowed from the British Big Bang, referring to financial market reforms in the United Kingdom.

bilateral conversion   When converting between an EMU currency and a non-EMU currency, the EMU currency is multiplied by the conversion rate to obtain the amount in the target currency.

Black/Scholes model   A model used to price European options contract. The model specifies that the option value depends on factors such as current market price, strike price, volatility, risk-free rate, and time.

blue book   Fed publication that reviews recent and prospective developments related to interest rates, bank reserves, and money supply.

BMA variance   A unique characteristic where the seller of the mortgage-backed securities can deliver the securities which vary by a certain percentage from the originally agreed-upon amount.

bond   A debt instrument that reflects a promise by the issuer to pay the bondholder a fixed amount of interest (the coupon payment) periodically and to repay the borrowed money at the maturity date.

bondes   Long-term Mexican debt securities issued to finance federal government project.

Bovespa   Brazil's main stock exchange.

Brady bonds   Securities issued by emerging countries under the Brady plan in an attempt to solve the debt crisis that many developing countries faced in the 1980s.

broker   An intermediary acting as an agent for one or both parties in a transaction in return for a fee or commission.

B-shares   Chinese stock shares exclusively for foreign investors.

Buenos Aires Stock Exchange   Major stock market in Argentina.

bundle   The simultaneous sale or purchase of a consecutive series of Eurodollar contracts.

Bunds   German government bonds.

buyout fund   Investment firms that invest in leveraged buyouts (LBOs).

C

call option   Gives the holder the right, but not the obligation, to purchase a security at the strike price before the contract expiry date.

call risk The possibility that the issuer will retire (call) all or a portion of the bond before maturity.

callable bonds Bonds that grant the issuer the right to pay off the debt before maturity.

callable pass-through A callable class of a mortgage pass-through.

CAMELS A numerical rating system based on the examiner's judgment of the bank's capital adequacy, asset quality, management quality, earnings record, liquidity position, and sensitivity to market risk.

capital asset pricing model (CAPM) A model that provides a linkage between the risk of a stock and the required rate of return that investors demand. The model states that there is a positive, linear relationship between a stock's required rate of return and its systematic risk.

carry The difference between the interests earned on the securities held in inventory and the financing costs.

cash-flow CBO A type of asset-backed securities that is based on a pool of assets with predictable future cash flows.

catastrophe (CAT) bond A bond with special provisions that require investors to forgive some or all principal or interest in the event that catastrophic losses exceed the trigger specified in the bond.

catastrophe equity put (CatEPut) Put option that insurers can buy from investors if catastrophic losses exceed the specified trigger.

Cedears Depositary receipts in Argentina, representing a class of shares or other securities of foreign companies.

Cetes Credit certificates that oblige the Mexican federal government to pay the owner the face value at maturity.

chaebol A Korean conglomerate.

cheapest to deliver The least expensive security that meets the qualifications for delivery in a futures contract.

city banks Japanese banks that reside in large cities and have nationwide branch networks.

clearing account A firm's money account and securities account at its clearing bank.

closed-end investment company A type of investment company that issues a fixed number of shares listed on a stock exchange or traded over the counter.

collateral buyer The counterparty that takes in securities and lends out funds in a repo transaction.

collateral seller The party that lends securities in exchange for cash in a repo transaction.

collateralized bond obligations (CBOs) Securities backed by high-yield or junk bonds.

collateralized loan obligations (CLOs) Securities backed by commercial loans.

collateralized mortgage obligations (CMOs) A type of mortgage-backed securities that separates the security into several classes with varying maturities, called tranches.

commercial paper A money market product that is a short-term unsecured promissory note.

commodity warrant A warrant that allows the holder to purchase a commodity from the issuer at a specified price.

competitive bid A bid that specifies both the amount and the price the bidder will pay.

competitive bidding A method of bidding where bidders submit sealed bids.

Comprehensive Plan for Financial Revitalization A Japanese government plan, introduced in July 1998, to revitalize the Japanese financial system and help the banks recover from their bad loans.

contingent surplus notes (CSNs) A debt instrument that grants an insurer the right to issue in the future to investors in exchange for cash.

convergence play Trades made on the bond markets based on the anticipated convergence of yields.

convertible bonds Bonds where the holder has the right to convert the par amount of the bond into a certain number of shares of the issuer's common stock.

core deposit A stable deposit that is not highly rate sensitive.

coupon The interest on a fixed income security.

coupon pass-through   In a repo transaction, coupon interest coming due on the collateral is passed through from the collateral buyer to the collateral seller.

coupon roll   A trade where a dealer purchases an on-the-run, or most recently issued, Treasury security from a customer for next-day settlement and simultaneously sells to that customer the same amount of the recently announced new security for forward settlement.

coupon stripping   Securities dealers strip coupons from a coupon Treasury and treat each component coupon and the principal as separate securities.

coverage ratio   The ratio of the total amount of bids submitted to the auction amount.

crawling peg   A system where a central bank keeps an exchange rate within a preset band that allows for small daily slippage against the pegged currency.

credit default swap   A privately negotiated contract with payoffs linked to a credit-related event, such as a default or a credit rating downgrade.

credit derivative   A privately negotiated derivative security with payoffs linked to a credit-related event or benchmark.

credit-linked note   A security in which the coupon or the price of the note links to the performance of a reference asset.

credit rating   A rating agency's opinion of the ability of a security to meet its financial commitments on a timely basis.

credit risk   The possibility of default by counterparties.

credit spread option   Options that focus on the yield differential between credit-sensitive instruments and the reference security.

cross-exchange rate   An exchange rate between a currency pair where neither currency is the U.S. dollar.

currency board   An arrangement where a nation's currency is pegged to another nation's currency and the monetary base is backed by reserves of the foreign currency to which the domestic currency is pegged.

currency option   A contract that gives the buyer of the contract the right to buy or sell a specified amount of one currency for another on or before the expiration date.

currency swap   A financial contract in which two counterparties exchange equal initial principal amounts of two currencies at the spot rate, then exchange a stream of interest payments in the swapped currencies, and finally reexchange the initial principal amounts at maturity.

currency warrant   A warrant that permits the holder to exchange one currency for another at a predetermined rate.

current yield   A bond's annual coupon divided by its market price.

customer repo   Customer-related repos by Fed with dealers on behalf of foreign official accounts.

D

daylight overdraft   The amount a financial institution has overdrawn on the Fedwire during the day.

debt conversion bond   Short-term floating-rate bonds issued without collateral.

default risk   Also known as credit risk; the possibility that the issuer will be unable to meet its financial obligations.

defined contribution plans   Plans where the employee and the employer make regular contributions to the employee's retirement account, and the performance of the investment in the account determines the amount of benefits the employee will receive upon retirement.

deliverable repo   A repo transaction in which the underlying securities are delivered against payment; at maturity, the collateral is returned and the loan plus interest is paid.

delivery month   Also called a futures contract month; identifies the month and year in which a futures contract reaches maturity.

delivery-versus-payment (DVP)   The final transfer of securities happens if and only if the final transfer of funds occurs.

delta   The change in an option or warrant's price for a given change of price of the underlying instrument.

deposit agreement   An agreement between a depositary bank and the issuer of an American Depositary Receipt.

deposit facility   A standing facility within the Eurosystem where financial institutions can make overnight deposits with national central banks.

deposit multiplier   The ratio of the money created by the banking system to the initial injection of reserves.

depositary bank   A bank, upon receiving evidence that shares of the foreign company have been purchased and deposited in a foreign custodian, issues certificates, called American depositary receipts, in the United States representing ownership of those shares.

depositary receipt   A negotiable certificate that represents ownership of shares in a foreign corporation.

derivative security   A contract with its value derived from an asset of an index.

discount bonds   Bonds issued at a discount.

discount brokerage   Firms that only execute trades for independent investors who call on the telephone or use a personal computer to request a trade.

dollarization   A country gives up its own currency and adopts the U.S. dollar as its full legal tender.

Dow Jones Industrial Average (DJIA)   Price-weighted index consisting of 30 large industrial stocks.

duration gap analysis   The analysis of the difference between the duration of assets and that of the liabilities for a bank; it is used to examine how the market value of shareholder equity changes when interest rates change.

Dutch auction   Also known as single-price auction; both competitive and noncompetitive bidders are awarded securities at the price that results from the high yield.

DV01   The change in the price of a bond resulting from a one-basis point change in its yield.

E

effective   When the registration statement has been approved by the SEC and the security can be sold to investors.

efficient market   A market where the market price reflects all relevant information about the security.

electronic communications networks (ECNs)   Computerized trading systems that match buyers and sellers of securities.

emerging market   The securities market of a developing country and the use that country makes of international capital markets.

euro   The official currency of the European Monetary Union.

Euro Interbank Offered Rate (EURIBOR)   The euro interbank term-deposit rate offered by one prime bank to another prime bank in the euro zone.

Euro medium-term notes (Euro MTNs)   Medium-term notes denominated in euros.

Euro straights   Eurobonds that pay a fixed-rate coupon with a stated redemption date.

Eurobonds   Bonds denominated in a currency different from the currency of the country in which they are issued.

Eurocurrency   A currency on deposit outside its country of origin or in international banking facilities in the United States.

euroDR   A negotiable certificate evidencing ownership of ordinary shares in a corporation from a country outside the European Monetary Union.

Euromarket   An offshore money and capital market with trading around the clock in all major financial centers.

European Central Bank (ECB)   It sets and oversees a common monetary policy for the members of the European Monetary Union.

European Economic and Monetary Union (EMU)   A union started in 1999 when participating countries in Europe gave up their national currencies and used the common currency, the euro.

European terms   The domestic currency per unit of foreign currency viewed from the perspective of someone in Europe.

Eurosystem   Refers to the European Central Bank and the national central banks of the member states that have joined the European Monetary Union.

exchange rate   The number of units of one nation's currency that must be rendered to obtain one unit of another nation's currency.

exchangeable bond   Bonds where the bondholders have the option of exchanging the debt for stocks of a second company or several companies, called the convert firm.

Exchange Stabilization Fund   A stock of money kept for foreign exchange market intervention.

exchange-traded fund (ETF)   An index fund or trust listed on an exchange that can be traded like a listed stock during trading hours.

F

facultative reinsurance   An arrangement where transactions with reinsurance occur on an individual basis; the ceding company has the option to offer an individual risk to the reinsurer, and the reinsurer has the right to accept or reject this risk.

fail   A trade fails to settle on the settlement date.

fallen angel   Junk bonds that result from the decline in the credit quality of former investment-grade issues.

federal funds market   The market for bank reserves.

federal funds rate   The overnight interest rate on federal funds.

Federal Open Market Committee (FOMC)   A major component of the Fed; it consists of seven members of the Board and five of the twelve Federal Reserve Bank presidents.

Federal Reserve System   Serves as the U.S. central bank; it consists of the Board of Governors and twelve Federal Reserve Banks (FRBs).

Fedwire   A real-time, gross settlement system used to transfer funds and book-entry securities.

filter trading technique   A technique used to signal trading timing when a security's price moves up by X percent above a previous low; it should be bought and held until the price falls by Y percent below a previous high, at which time the trader should sell the stock.

final prospectus   A formal written document to sell a new security that describes the plan and various aspects for a proposed or an existing business that an investor needs in order to make an informed decision. It includes the issuing price and the underwriting discounts as well.

financial engineering   The design of new financial instruments, such as derivative contracts using sophisticated mathematical and statistical models and computer technology.

financial insurance   Financial guaranty that provides protection against risk of credit downgrade or default.

Financial Times Stock Exchange 100 (FTSE 100)   The value-weighted index of the 100 largest stocks that trade on the London Stock Exchange.

firm commitment underwriting   A situation in which the underwriters guarantee a price for all new shares and resell them to investors.

First Section   A section on the Tokyo Stock Exchange that lists blue chip domestic stocks meeting stringent requirements.

fixed-income security   Debt instrument that pays investors fixed interest income at regular intervals and repays the principal at maturity.

flight to liquidity   A phenomenon where foreign money, flown into the United States as a result of flight to quality, purchases the on-the-run Treasury securities because these securities have higher liquidity.

flight to quality   The purchase of U.S. Treasury securities by foreigners whenever there is a financial or political crisis overseas.

floating-rate notes (FRNs)   Eurobonds with a floating-rate coupon.

floating risk   Consists of waiting risk, pricing risk, and marketing risk.

floor broker   An independent member of an exchange who acts as a broker for other members.

foreign currency bond   A debt security issued in a currency other than the issuer's national currency.

foreign ordinaries   Stocks of foreign companies that do not trade on U.S. markets.

forward contract   An agreement to buy or sell an asset on a certain future date at a certain price.

forward rate   Expected future interest rate calculated from the spot rates.

forward rate agreement (FRA) A forward contract between two parties to exchange an interest rate on a Eurodollar deposit at a given future date.

forward swap A swap when the near and far dates are within one month from the deal date.

front loaded interest reduction bonds Medium-term step-up bonds that pay below-market interest rates for the initial five to seven years, and then pay a floating rate until maturity.

front running An illegal practice in which a broker trades on her own account based on an impending customer order or trade.

full-service firm A brokerage firm that provides full services in brokerage, investment banking, and asset management services to its clients.

fully-modified pass-through Mortgage securities where the federal-sponsored agency guarantees the timely payment of both interest and principal.

fundamental analysis A type of securities analyses that looks at the fundamentals of a company to determine its value.

fundamental analyst Individuals that examine financial statements and economic fundamentals to determine the value of a security and its growth prospects.

future cash-flow securitization A securitization where the originator sells assets (which will produce cash flows in the future) to the special purpose vehicle before the assets have come into existence.

futures contract An exchange-traded contract that has standardized terms such as quantity, quality of the asset, and delivery month.

FX swap A financial contract in which two counterparties agree to exchange two currencies at a particular rate on one date, called the near date, and to reverse payments on a specified subsequent date, called the far date.

G

gap analysis The simplest way of representing the interest rate risk component of market risk. It examines the difference between assets and liabilities in the same maturity range.

general obligation bonds (GOs) Municipal securities with the full faith and credit of the issuer backing the scheduled payments of principal and interest.

GKO (Gosudarstvenniye Kratkosrochiniye Obligatsii) Short-term zero-coupon bond of the sovereign ruble bond market.

Glass-Steagall Act One of the key banking legislation to ensure the soundness and safety of the financial services industry by segregating banks, securities firms, and insurers.

global bonds Debt securities tailored to appeal to investors internationally.

global depositary receipts (GDRs) Depositary receipts that issue through a global offering in two or more markets at the same time.

Gramm-Leach-Bliley Act (GLB) Removed restrictions that had been imposed on the financial services industry during the Great Depression of the 1930s (The Glass-Steagall Act). This act permits a bank holding company to engage in securities underwriting, dealing, or market-making activities through its subsidiaries (called securities subsidiaries). The act also allows the convergence of banking, insurance, investment banking, and asset management.

grantor trust A structure in auto loan securitization that requires principal distributions on the underlying securities to be made on a pro rata basis.

green book Fed publication that contains two parts: (1) summary of recent developments in the U.S. economy and in international markets, and (2) detailed, sector-by-sector coverage of these developments, including a review of trade statistics, international financial transactions, and foreign exchange markets.

green shoe option A provision in underwriting agreement that enables the underwriters to purchase additional shares at an agreed-on price if there is strong demand for the new issue.

growth investor Individuals that care less about value and more about the growth rate of earnings.

guaranteed investment contract (GIC) An investment product issued by an insurance company that provides investors with guaranteed returns.

H

haircut   A percentage of the collateral value in excess of the loan.

Hang Seng Index   A widely followed index of Hong Kong's stock market.

hedge fund   A private investment pool that engages in various trading strategies to pursue better performance. There is very little regulation in hedge fund operations, but investors must meet qualification requirements. There are typically two types of fees: management and incentive fees.

hedge ratio   The number of contracts needed to hedge a position in the spot market.

hedging   The reduction of risk by way of taking the opposite position in the futures market from the trader's cash market position.

hedging risk   The possibility that the hedge is not as effective as anticipated.

Herstatt risk   Also known as settlement risk; a risk that arises because the two legs of a foreign exchange transaction often settle in two different time zones, with different business hours.

hidden reserves   Unrealized gains on equity holdings.

high-water mark   If a hedge fund loses money in a given performance fee period, investors will not be charged in later periods until the losses are made up.

high yield   Also known as the stop yield; it is the highest yield accepted at a Treasury securities auction.

Home Broker   A term introduced by the Bovespa, which refers to trading through the Internet.

Hong Kong Monetary Authority (HKMA) Hong Kong's quasicentral bank.

I

impact cost   The cost of buying liquidity.

implied repo rate   The rate that a seller of a futures contract can earn by buying a security and then delivering it at the settlement date.

implied volatility   The variability in an options contract implied by the current option premium.

incurred loss   Losses that take place during the particular period under consideration.

indexing   When a fund buys securities to replicate the performance of the overall market or an index; also known as passive management.

information trader   Individuals who attempt to profit by trading on information that the market does not know about.

initial margin   Cash or eligible securities that an investor has to deposit before engaging in margin transactions.

inside market   The interdealer market.

insurance   An economic device whereby an individual or a business transfers the risk of uncertain financial losses by payment of a premium.

interdealer broker   Firms that provide brokering services to dealer community.

interest arrears capitalization bonds   Bonds created when commercial banks rescheduled interest arrears on Brazilian, Argentine, and Ecuadorian debt; the interest was used to create new short-term floating rate bonds.

interest only (IO)   A class of mortgage-backed securities where the IO holders receive only the interest payments from the underlying mortgages.

interest rate parity   The condition where exchange rates are interdependent with identical yields across currencies.

interest rate risk   The exposure to adverse changes in rates that affect revenues such as net interest income, securities gains/losses, and other rate-sensitive income/expense items.

interest rate swap   An agreement in which a fixed interest rate is exchanged for a floating interest rate.

international banking facility   A U.S. banking status similar to an offshore banking unit that permits a bank to operate offshore transactions.

Internet banking   Banking service over the Internet where a customer can conduct banking business 24 hours a day.

intrinsic value   The amount by which the strike price is more advantageous than the spot rate to the option holder.

Investment Advisers Act (IAA)   Regulates the activities of investment advisers, including advisers to investment companies and private money managers.

Investment Company Act (ICA)   The act regulates investment companies; under this act, a mutual fund's investment in each security is generally limited to an amount not greater than 5 percent of the fund's assets and not more than 10 percent of the outstanding voting securities of such issuer.

invoice price   The quoted price plus the accrued interest of a coupon security.

issuer safe harbor   A safe harbor that addresses offers and sales by issuers, their affiliates, and securities professionals involved in the initial offerings of securities.

J

Japanese government bonds (JGBs)   Securities issued by the Japanese government.

Japan's Big Bang   Financial reforms in Japan that focused on the deregulation of financial products, promotion of free competition, removal of trading restrictions, and establishment of a reliable framework and rules for fair and transparent transactions.

junk bonds   Also called high yield bonds; these are bonds with credit ratings of BB or lower.

K

keiretsu   A conglomerate of Japanese businesses that cooperate to achieve common goals.

Korea Stock Exchange (KSE)   Korea's main stock exchange.

L

legal risk   The risk that a firm will fail to comply with applicable legal and regulatory requirements and the risk that counterparty's obligations may be unenforceable.

Lehman 5-4-3-2-1   A formula for calculating merger and acquisition advisory fees. Under this formula, 5 percent is paid on the first $1 million of the sale price, 4 percent on the next $1 million, 3 percent on the next $1 million, 2 percent on the next $1 million, and 1 percent on the amount in excess of $4 million.

Level-I ADRs   The most basic ADR; it is the easiest and least expensive way for a foreign company to gauge interest in its securities and to begin building a presence in the United States.

Level-II ADRs   ADRs listed on one of the national exchanges and must comply with the SEC's full registration and reporting requirements.

Level-III ADRs   Similar to Level-II ADRs except that the issuer is allowed to make a public offering.

limit order   An order that instructs a broker to buy or sell at a certain price.

liquidity risk   The chance that an instrument cannot be sold at a reasonable price within a reasonable time frame or a bank will not have sufficient funds to meet its payout obligations.

lockup period   Minimum duration that hedge funds require investments remain in the fund; the common lockup period is one year.

London Club   Private creditors of Soviet era debt.

London Interbank Offered Rate (LIBOR)   A short-term rate quoted in the interbank market in London.

M

Maastricht Treaty   A plan signed in February of 1992 that laid out several requirements for admission to the EMU.

Macaulay duration   The time-weighted average of the discounted future cash flows.

maintenance margin   A requirement by the individual exchange and the brokerage firm that the investor maintain a certain equity level in the margin account.

managed care   A plan where the insurer makes arrangements with a selected network of health-care providers to treat policyholders, who receive an offering of significant financial incentives to use the providers in the network.

margin   A cash deposit a trader must post with a broker in order to trade stocks, bonds, or futures contracts.

marginal lending facility   A standing facility within the Eurosystem where participants gain overnight liquidity from national central banks against eligible assets.

market maker   A party that acts as a buyer for those who wish to sell, and a seller for those who want to buy.

market order   An order that instructs a broker to buy or sell at the best available price in the market.

market risk   The risk that a change in the level of market prices, rates, indices, volatility, correlation, or liquidity, will result in losses for a specified position or portfolio.

market risk rule   A rule that sets minimum capital requirements for market risk exposure.

market value CBO   An investment vehicle used to capitalize on the arbitrage opportunities that exist between high-yield bonds and the lower-cost funds of highly rated debt.

master trust   A structure in which the seller can sell multiple securities from the same trust, all of which share the credit risks as well as the cash flows from one large pool of receivables.

matched book   A repo book in which a repo and a reverse in the same security have the same terms to maturity.

matched sale-purchase   The Fed sells collateral and drains funds from the financial system with the objective of raising interest rates. The Fed later buys back these securities.

medium-term note (MTN)   A corporate debt instrument with a maturity ranging from nine months to thirty years.

merchant banking funds   Funds that invest in corporate and real estate assets by committing capital to long-term equity investment opportunities.

Mercosul   A free trade association established by Brazil, Argentina, Paraguay, and Uruguay through the Treaty of Assuncion on March 26, 1991.

Mexican Stock Exchange   The stock exchange in Mexico.

MinFin bonds   U.S. dollar denominated bonds that carry a 3 percent coupon issued by the Ministry of Finance in 1992 to compensate holders of funds held in the foreign currency account of

Vnescheconombank, the State Bank for Foreign Economic Affairs of the Soviet Union.

modified duration   The Macaulay duration adjusted by yield.

modified pass-throughs   Mortgage securities where, in addition to the timely payment of interest, the Fed agency guarantees that the scheduled principal repayment will be made as collected but no later than a specified date.

mortgage-backed securities (MBS)   Debt instruments backed by residential or commercial mortgages.

mortgage pass-throughs   Mortgage securities where the monthly mortgage payments, net of servicing and insurance fees, are passed along to investors.

Mothers (Market for High Growth and Emerging Stocks)   Market for promising start-ups, established by the Tokyo Stock Exchange.

moving average (MA)   The arithmetic average price of a security or an index over the past predetermined number of days.

municipal notes   Short-term municipal debt instruments with maturities ranging from about 60 days to one year.

municipal securities   Securities that municipalities issue to fund projects for public good.

mutual fund   An investment management company that pools money from a number of investors who share similar investment objectives.

N

Nasdaq Composite   Value-weighted index of stocks that trade in the OTC market.

negotiated deal   A type of underwriting municipal securities in which the issuer and the selected underwriters negotiate the terms of the issue without competitive open bidding.

net asset value (NAV)   The share value of an open-end mutual fund. The value is equal to the value of the fund's assets, less its liabilities, divided by the number of outstanding shares.

net revenues   Total revenues minus interest expenses.

New Capital Accord (also known as Basel II)
The new international banking regulation that Bank for International Settlements has proposed. It is scheduled to take effect in 2006. Basel II introduces a more comprehensive approach to addressing risk, and places more emphasis on banks' internal risk methodologies, supervisory review, and market discipline.

noncompetitive bids Bids in which the investor indicates the amount he or she wants to purchase without specifying a purchase price.

note issuance facility (NIF) A standby credit agreement with a bank that permits a borrower to obtain financing on specific terms if the borrower does not succeed in selling its short-term paper to investors.

notional principal The face amount of derivatives contracts that market participants use to calculate interest and other payments.

O

official dealing rate The repo rate set by Bank of England.

official statement A document that provides detailed financial information about the terms of the proposed municipal security, the issuer's financial status, and its operating data.

OFZ (Obligatsii Federalnogo Zaima) Medium-term floating-rate bonds of the sovereign ruble bond market.

open market operations Trading activities that the Fed conduct to meet its monetary policy objective.

operation risk The possibility that employee error or system failure will occur.

opportunity costs The costs of not executing a trade.

option A financial contract that gives the holder the right, but not the obligation, to buy an asset, in the case of a call option, or sell an asset in the case of a put option, at a specified price during a specific time period.

original issue discount (OID) The difference between the issue price and the par amount in a tax-exempt municipal bond.

outright forward A single purchase or sale of one currency for another.

overnight repos One-day repo transactions.

over-the-counter (OTC) A market where traders execute transactions through a computerized telecommunications network.

owner trust A structure in auto loan securitization in which the deal documents specify the cash flow allocation.

P

pack A simultaneous purchase or sale of an equally weighted consecutive series of Eurodollar futures.

paid losses Losses paid during a particular period regardless of the time when the loss occurred.

par bonds Debt instruments issued at par.

pay-as-you-go A system where pensions to current retirees are paid from current payroll taxes.

pay-to-play The practice of cozying up to government officials to win bond contracts.

Pecto program A stabilization and reform program introduced in Mexico under which wage bargaining and price setting were coordinated to support the overall macroeconomic strategy.

pfandbriefe German mortgage-backed securities.

preliminary prospectus The main document a syndicate uses to sell a new security. The document contains material information about the issuer that investors need to make informed decisions. The document does not include the final issuing price.

prepayment rate The rate at which homeowners pay off their outstanding mortgage balances before maturity date.

prepayment speed assumption (PSA) It assumes that the prepayment rate for new mortgage loans begins at 0.2 percent per annum in the first month and increases by 0.2 percent each month as the mortgages age, eventually reaching a constant rate of 6.00 percent at 30 months.

price risk The risk that the price might decrease.

primary dealer   Financial institutions that actively trade government securities and have established business relationships with the Federal Reserve Bank of New York.

primary market   Where companies issue new securities to raise money.

principal only (PO)   A type of mortgage-backed securities where holders receive payments from the principal repayment of the underlying mortgage payments.

private placement   A securities issue that does not go through the SEC's registration process. The security is sold to a group of qualified investors.

property and casualty insurance   Insurance policies designed to indemnify for damage to property and for legal liability.

put option   A financial contract that gives the holder the right, but not the obligation, to sell a security at the exercise price during the specified time period.

puttable bonds   Bonds that contain a put provision, granting investors the right to put the bonds back to the issuer at par.

Q

qualified institutional buyer (QIB)   An institution that owns and invests on a discretionary basis at least $100 million in securities of an unaffiliated entity.

quality spread   The yield differential between bonds with different quality ratings.

R

real   Official currency of Brazil.

real estate investment trust (REIT)   A trust that pools capital from investors to acquire or to provide financing for real estate.

real estate mortgage investment conduit (REMIC)   A pass-through tax entity that can hold mortgages and can issue multiple classes of pass-through certificates to investors.

Red Chip stock   Stocks of Hong Kong companies that derive significant revenues from China.

regional banks   Banks that operate within a certain geographic area.

registration statement   A statement that must be filed with the SEC for any new issue of securities; it discloses various kinds of important information about the company and the security for investors to consider when deciding whether to invest in the company.

Regulation S   Provides two types of safe harbor exemptions for securities offered overseas without registration.

reinsurance   A contract where one insurance company (the reinsurer) charges a premium to indemnify another insurance company against all or part of the losses it may sustain under the issued policies.

reinvestment risk   The risk that the investor will have to reinvest future coupon income at a yield less than the yield at which he purchased the bond.

renminbi   Official currency of China.

repo book   When a dealer acts as a principal on both sides of a repo transaction, borrowing funds from one client and relending the money to another.

repo rate   The interest rate in a repo transaction.

repurchase agreement (repo)   A sale of securities with a commitment to repurchase the same securities at a specified price in a specified time period.

resale safe harbor   A safe harbor that addresses resales by securities professionals such as brokers.

reserve requirements   The percentage of deposits that a bank must hold either as vault cash or on deposit at a Federal Reserve Bank.

reserves   The funds that depository institutions hold in reserve against deposits.

restricted securities   Securities acquired directly or indirectly in a transaction not involving any public offering.

revenue bonds   Municipal securities with payments secured by revenues derived from certain revenue-producing agencies or enterprises.

revolving underwriting facility (RUF)   A facility through which Euro CP can be issued, where members of the tender panel and the placement agents bid for the commercial paper.

right of substitution   The right of the collateral seller to take back the security and substitute with other collateral of equal value and quality.

risk securitization   A capital market solution where insurers package their catastrophe risk as securities that can be sold to investors.

road show   A key marketing event in which representatives from the company's management meet with financial analysts and brokers to explain the company's market position and discuss how the company will execute its business plan.

ruble   Official currency of Russia.

Rule 144A ADRs   An alternative to Level-III programs where foreign companies can access the U.S. capital markets by issuing ADRs under this rule without going through the lengthy registration process.

Rule 415 (shelf registration)   Allows an issuer to file a single registration document indicating that it intends to sell a certain amount of securities at one or more times within the next two years.

S

S&P 500 Index   Value-weighted index of 500 stocks; it consists of 400 industrial companies, 20 transportation companies, 40 utility firms, and 40 financial companies.

samurai bonds   Yen-denominated bonds issued in the Japanese market under domestic regulations.

Second Section   A Tokyo Stock Exchange category of domestic stocks that do not qualify for the First Section.

secondary market   The market for investors to trade securities that have already been issued.

section 20 subsidiaries   Also known as underwriting subsidiaries; these are bank subsidiaries that have a license to underwrite and deal in securities that a member bank itself could not.

Securities Act   The act regulates new issues of securities. It requires that all prospective investors receive a current prospectus describing the security.

Securities Exchange Act   The act mainly regulates trading of outstanding securities. It regulates brokers-dealers, including principal underwriters and others

who sell shares, and requires them to register with the SEC.

securities subsidiaries   Subsidiaries of bank holding companies that engage in securities underwriting, dealing, or market-making activities.

security market line   The graphic representation of the relationship between risk and return identified by the capital asset pricing model.

seigniorage   The difference between the value of the currency and the cost of printing that currency.

semi-strong form efficiency   A market where current market price reflects all public information.

settlement   The transfer of money and securities between the parties to complete the transaction.

settlement price   The price of the futures trading used to calculate the equity value of the account at the end of the trading day.

settlement risk   Also known as Herstatt risk; a risk that arises because the two legs of a foreign exchange transaction often settle in two different time zones, with different business hours.

shelf registration   A rule that allows certain issuers to file a single registration document indicating the intent to sell a specified amount of a given class of securities within the next two years.

short-dated swap   A swap when both the near and far dates are within one month from the deal date.

short interest   Total number of shares that have been shorted but not yet covered; that is, short sellers have not yet bought back the securities they sold short.

short sale   A trade in which an investor sells a stock that he or she does not own, hoping that the price will fall, and then repurchases the stock at a lower price, thereby earning a profit.

short squeeze   A market phenomenon when an auction participant, or a group of participants, gains control of a majority of a certain security and withholds the supply from the cash or repurchase agreement markets. Thus, short sellers cannot borrow the security to make delivery.

side-by-side program   An approach in American depositary receipt market that allows a foreign issuer to combine the benefits of a publicly traded program with the efficiency of a private offering as a capital-raising tool.

Singapore Exchange (SGX)   Singapore's main stock exchange.

single-price auction   Also known as Dutch auction; both competitive and noncompetitive bidders are awarded securities at the price that results from the high yield.

slippage   A price change between the placement and execution of a trade.

special   Collateral that commands a lower repo rate.

special purpose vehicle (SPV)   An intermediary between the originator and investors. It acquires the assets or receivables from the originator and then issues securities backed by these assets.

specialists   Individuals responsible for maintaining a fair and orderly market on an exchange.

specific risk   The risk that arises from factors specific to the issuer of a security.

speculators   Individuals who attempt to earn profits by speculating on the direction of the market movements.

sponsored ADR   An ADR program supported by the foreign company.

spot rate   The interest rate on zero-coupon security.

spot transaction   A trade in the spot or cash market.

stand-alone trust   A trust buys a single pool of receivables, which it uses as collateral to issue a single security.

standing facilities   European Central Bank offers two types of facilities, including deposit and lending facilities.

statutory accounting system   An accounting system different from the generally accepted accounting principle to which insurance companies are subject to.

stop loss order   An order to sell a stock if the price drops below a given level.

stop order   An order that instructs the broker to buy or sell a security after its price reaches a certain level.

stop yield   The highest yield the Department of Treasury accepts at a Treasury auction.

straight date   The standard contract periods of one, two, three, six, and twelve months.

strategic asset allocation   A value-oriented technique that seeks to increase exposure to the market when recent market performance is poor, and to reduce exposure when recent market performance is good.

streaker bonds   Zero-coupon Eurobonds.

stripped mortgage-backed security   A type of mortgage pass-through securities that divides the cash flow from the underlying collateral on a pro rata basis across security holders.

strong-form efficiency   A market where the market price reflects all information, public and private.

survivorship universal life insurance   An insurance policy that covers two people with one policy where the death benefit is paid to the beneficiary upon the second death.

system repo   Repo transactions by the Fed.

systematic risk   A measure of a stock's risk relative to the overall market.

T

tail   The difference between the average yield of all accepted bids and the high yield in a Treasury auction.

TARGET (Trans-European Automated Real-time Gross settlement Express Transfer system)   The settlement system of cross-border payments in EMU.

tech MARK   A section on the London Stock Exchange that lists innovative technology companies.

technical analysis   It assumes that prices tend to move in trends that persist for certain periods and that these trends can be detected by charts. Technical analysts use information on past prices and trading volumes to predict future prices.

tequila effect   The spillover effect that spread through the Latin markets after Mexico's currency collapse in 1994–95.

term life insurance   An insurance policy that is in effect for a specific period of time where if the insured dies within that timeframe, the beneficiary receives the death payment.

term repos   Repo transactions with maturities longer than one day.

terms currency   The currency that is adjusted as the exchange rate changes in a foreign exchange transaction.

Tesobonos   Short-term Mexican treasury paper denominated in U.S. dollars.

tier 1 capital   Bank's core capital.

tier 1 leverage ratio   The ratio of tier 1 capital to total average assets.

tier 2 capital   Part of bank's capital used to calculate the capital requirements that the Basel Committee on Banking Supervision requires.

timing cost   The costs incurred when an entire order is too large to be presented to the market for a single transaction.

total return swap   A contract that allows an investor to receive the total economic return of an asset without actually owning the asset.

traditional indemnity insurance   An insurance policy where the policyholder pays a certain amount of medical expenses up front, and afterward the insurance company pays the majority of the bill.

Treasury bills   Short-term Treasury securities with a maturity period of up to one year. These bills do not pay coupon. Investors pay a discount price and receive the par amount at maturity.

Treasury bonds   Long-term Treasury securities with a maturity period of more than ten years.

Treasury Inflation-Protection Security (TIPS)   Inflation-indexed notes and bonds; the interest rate is fixed but the principal adjusts for inflation.

Treasury notes   Medium-term Treasury securities that have a maturity of more than one-year but not more than ten years.

treaty reinsurance   A reinsurance arrangement where the transaction encompasses a block of the ceding company's book of business, and the reinsurer must accept all business included within the terms of the reinsurance contract.

triangular arbitrage   The process of trading out of the U.S. dollar into a second currency, then trading it for a third currency, which is in turn traded for the U.S. dollar to earn a profit.

triangular conversion   During 1999–2001, converting between two currencies within the eurozone requires two steps. The initial amount of a currency is first converted to the euro, which is then converted into the target national currency.

triparty repo   A repo where the two counterparties have accounts at the same custodial bank so that the transfer of funds and that of securities occur within the bank.

true sale   A sale where the originator does not retain interest in the assets and must transfer the full title.

trust banks   Banks licensed to engage in banking and trust activities.

U

Udibonos   Bonds linked to inflation and backed by the Mexican federal government.

underwriting discount   The difference between the issuing price and the price the issuer receives from its underwriters.

underwriting subsidiaries   Also known as Section 20 subsidiaries; these are bank subsidiaries that have received permission from the Fed to underwrite and deal in securities that a member bank itself could not do.

underwriting syndicate   A group of securities firms that purchase the entire block of a new security and redistributes the shares to investors.

unit investment trust (UIT)   An investment company that purchases and holds a relatively fixed portfolio of securities. The trust returns money to investors when the securities mature.

universal life insurance   An insurance policy that allows the policy owner to vary, with limitations, the amount and timing of premium payments and the death benefit.

unsponsored ADR   A program banks often initiate in response to investor demand that is not supported by the foreign company.

V

value–at–risk (VaR)   The potential loss in value of a firm's portfolio due to adverse movements in markets over a defined horizon with a specified confidence interval.

value investors   Individuals seeking out companies that they believe the market has incorrectly undervalued.

value traders   Individuals who trade because they believe there is a discrepancy between the market price and the equilibrium value.

variable life insurance   An investment–oriented whole life policy that provides a return based on an underlying portfolio of mutual funds including common stock funds, bond funds, and money market funds.

variable universal life insurance   Combines the flexibility of universal life insurance with the investment account features of variable life insurance.

variation margin   The amount that one must add to bring an equity account back to the initial margin level.

VC angels   Venture funds that provide first-round financing for risky investments.

vehicle currency   When trading a pair of currencies, traders often buy or sell each of these two currencies against a common third currency such as the U.S. dollar as a vehicle currency.

venture capital (VC)   Make equity investments in entrepreneurial companies.

W

weak–form efficiency   A market where prices fully reflect all past market information.

when–issued (WI)   Trading after the Treasury announcement of a new security auction and lasts until the settlement date when the new security is issued and payment is made.

whole life insurance   An insurance policy that has guaranteed premiums and death benefits and a minimum interest rate that will be credited to the funds accumulated in the policy.

Wilshire 5000   Value-weighted index of stocks that trade in the NYSE and the AMEX-Nasdaq.

won   Official currency of South Korea.

World Trade Organization (WTO)   An international organization that administers world trade agreements, fosters trade relations among nations, and solves trade disputes among member countries.

Y

yield burning   When underwriters mark up the bond price in advance refunding, they "burn down" the yield, since bond prices and yields move in opposite directions.

yield curve   Plots of the yield to maturity against the term to maturity for Treasury securities.

yield to maturity   The rate that discounts all future periodic coupons and principal at maturity to the current asked price.

Z

zone examination system   In auditing foreign insurance companies, each state accepts the examination that another state has conducted.

INDEX